Lecture Notes in Economics and Mathematical Systems

For information about Vols. 1–183, please contact your bookseller or Springer-Verlag

Vol. 184: R. E. Burkard and U. Derigs, Assignment and Matching Problems: Solution Methods with FORTRAN-Programs. VIII, 148 pages. 1980.

Vol. 185: C. C. von Weizsäcker, Barriers to Entry. VI, 220 pages. 1980.

Vol. 186: Ch.-L. Hwang and K. Yoon, Multiple Attribute Decision Making – Methods and Applications. A State-of-the-Art-Survey. XI, 259 pages. 1981.

Vol. 187: W. Hock, K. Schittkowski, Test Examples for Nonlinear Programming Codes. V. 178 pages. 1981.

Vol. 188: D. Bös, Economic Theory of Public Enterprise. VII, 142 pages. 1981.

Vol. 189: A. P. Lüthi, Messung wirtschaftlicher Ungleichheit. IX, 287 pages. 1981.

Vol. 190: J. N. Morse, Organizations: Multiple Agents with Multiple Criteria. Proceedings, 1980. VI, 509 pages. 1981.

Vol. 191: H. R. Sneessens, Theory and Estimation of Macroeconomic Rationing Models. VII, 138 pages. 1981.

Vol. 192: H. J. Bierens: Robust Methods and Asymptotic Theory in Nonlinear Econometrics. IX, 198 pages. 1981.

Vol. 193: J. K. Sengupta, Optimal Decisions under Uncertainty. VII, 156 pages. 1981.

Vol. 194: R. W. Shephard, Cost and Production Functions. XI, 104 pages. 1981.

Vol. 195: H. W. Ursprung, Die elementare Katastrophentheorie. Eine Darstellung aus der Sicht der Ökonomie. VII, 332 pages. 1982.

Vol. 196: M. Nermuth, Information Structures in Economics. VIII, 236 pages. 1982.

Vol. 197: Integer Programming and Related Areas. A Classified Bibliography. 1978 – 1981. Edited by R. von Randow. XIV, 338 pages. 1982.

Vol. 198: P. Zweifel, Ein ökonomisches Modell des Arztverhaltens. XIX, 392 Seiten. 1982.

Vol. 199: Evaluating Mathematical Programming Techniques. Proceedings, 1981. Edited by J.M. Mulvey. XI, 379 pages. 1982.

Vol. 200: The Resource Sector in an Open Economy. Edited by H. Siebert. IX, 161 pages. 1984.

Vol. 201: P. M. C. de Boer, Price Effects in Input-Output-Relations: A Theoretical and Empirical Study for the Netherlands 1949–1967. X, 140 pages. 1982.

Vol. 202: U. Witt, J. Perske, SMS – A Program Package for Simulation and Gaming of Stochastic Market Processes and Learning Behavior. VII, 266 pages. 1982.

Vol. 203: Compilation of Input-Output Tables. Proceedings, 1981. Edited by J. V. Skolka. VII, 307 pages. 1982.

Vol. 204: K. C. Mosler, Entscheidungsregeln bei Risiko: Multivariate stochastische Dominanz. VII, 172 Seiten. 1982.

Vol. 205: R. Ramanathan, Introduction to the Theory of Economic Growth. IX, 347 pages. 1982.

Vol. 206: M. H. Karwan, V. Lotfi, J. Telgen, and S. Zionts, Redundancy in Mathematical Programming. VII, 286 pages. 1983.

Vol. 207: Y. Fujimori, Modern Analysis of Value Theory. X, 165 pages. 1982.

Vol. 208: Econometric Decision Models. Proceedings, 1981. Edited by J. Gruber. VI, 364 pages. 1983.

Vol. 209: Essays and Surveys on Multiple Criteria Decision Making. Proceedings, 1982. Edited by P. Hansen. VII, 441 pages. 1983.

Vol. 210: Technology, Organization and Economic Structure. Edited by R. Sato and M.J. Beckmann. VIII, 195 pages. 1983.

Vol. 211: P. van den Heuvel, The Stability of a Macroeconomic System with Quantity Constraints. VII, 169 pages. 1983.

Vol. 212: R. Sato and T. Nôno, Invariance Principles and the Structure of Technology. V, 94 pages. 1983.

Vol. 213: Aspiration Levels in Bargaining and Economic Decision Making. Proceedings, 1982. Edited by R. Tietz. VIII, 406 pages. 1983.

Vol. 214: M. Faber, H. Niemes und G. Stephan, Entropie, Umweltschutz und Rohstoffverbrauch. IX, 181 Seiten. 1983.

Vol. 215: Semi-Infinite Programming and Applications. Proceedings, 1981. Edited by A. V. Fiacco and K. O. Kortanek. XI, 322 pages. 1983.

Vol. 216: H. H. Müller, Fiscal Policies in a General Equilibrium Model with Persistent Unemployment. VI, 92 pages. 1983.

Vol. 217: Ch. Grootaert, The Relation Between Final Demand and Income Distribution. XIV, 105 pages. 1983.

Vol. 218: P. van Loon, A Dynamic Theory of the Firm: Production, Finance and Investment. VII, 191 pages. 1983.

Vol. 219: E. van Damme, Refinements of the Nash Equilibrium Concept. VI, 151 pages. 1983.

Vol. 220: M. Aoki, Notes on Economic Time Series Analysis: System Theoretic Perspectives. IX, 249 pages. 1983.

Vol. 221: S. Nakamura, An Inter-Industry Translog Model of Prices and Technical Change for the West German Economy. XIV, 290 pages. 1984.

Vol. 222: P. Meier, Energy Systems Analysis for Developing Countries. VI, 344 pages. 1984.

Vol. 223: W. Trockel, Market Demand. VIII, 205 pages. 1984.

Vol. 224: M. Kiy, Ein disaggregiertes Prognosesystem für die Bundesrepublik Deutschland. XVIII, 276 Seiten. 1984.

Vol. 225: T. R. von Ungern-Sternberg, Zur Analyse von Märkten mit unvollständiger Nachfragerinformation. IX, 125 Seiten. 1984

Vol. 226: Selected Topics in Operations Research and Mathematical Economics. Proceedings, 1983. Edited by G. Hammer and D. Pallaschke. IX, 478 pages. 1984.

Vol. 227: Risk and Capital. Proceedings, 1983. Edited by G. Bamberg and K. Spremann. VII, 306 pages. 1984.

Vol. 228: Nonlinear Models of Fluctuating Growth. Proceedings, 1983. Edited by R. M. Goodwin, M. Krüger and A. Vercelli. XVII, 277 pages. 1984.

Vol. 229: Interactive Decision Analysis. Proceedings, 1983. Edited by M. Grauer and A. P. Wierzbicki. VIII, 269 pages. 1984.

Vol. 230: Macro-Economic Planning with Conflicting Goals. Proceedings, 1982. Edited by M. Despontin, P. Nijkamp and J. Spronk. VI, 297 pages. 1984.

Vol. 231: G. F. Newell, The M/M/∞ Service System with Ranked Servers in Heavy Traffic. XI, 126 pages. 1984.

Vol. 232: L. Bauwens, Bayesian Full Information Analysis of Simultaneous Equation Models Using Integration by Monte Carlo. VI, 114 pages. 1984.

Vol. 233: G. Wagenhals, The World Copper Market. XI, 190 pages. 1984.

Vol. 234: B. C. Eaves, A Course in Triangulations for Solving Equations with Deformations. III, 302 pages. 1984.

Vol. 235: Stochastic Models in Reliability Theory. Proceedings, 1984. Edited by S. Osaki and Y. Hatoyama. VII, 212 pages. 1984.

continuation on page 405

Lecture Notes
in Economics and
Mathematical Systems

Managing Editors: M. Beckmann and W. Krelle

331

A. Lewandowski A.P. Wierzbicki (Eds.)

Aspiration Based Decision Support Systems

Theory, Software and Applications

Springer-Verlag
Berlin Heidelberg GmbH

Managing Editors

Prof. Dr. M. Beckmann
Brown University
Providence, RI 02912, USA

Prof. Dr. W. Krelle
Institut für Gesellschafts- und Wirtschaftswissenschaften
der Universität Bonn
Adenauerallee 24–42, D-5300 Bonn, FRG

Editors

Dr. Andrzej Lewandowski
Project Leader
Methodology of Decision Analysis Project
System and Decision Sciences Program
International Institute for Applied Systems Analysis
A-2361 Laxenburg, Austria

Prof. Dr. Andrzej Piotr Wierzbicki
Institute of Automatic Control
Warsaw University of Technology
Warsaw, Poland

ISBN 978-3-540-51213-4 ISBN 978-3-662-21637-8 (eBook)
DOI 10.1007/978-3-662-21637-8

2847/3140-543210

Introduction

It is not easy to summarize - even in a volume - the results of a scientific study conducted by circa 30 researchers, in four different research institutions, though cooperating between them and jointly with the *International Institute for Applied Systems Analysis*, but working part-time, sponsored not only by IIASA's national currency funds, but also by several other research grants in Poland. The aims of this cooperative study were defined broadly by its title *Theory, Software and Testing Examples for Decision Support Systems*. The focusing theme was the methodology of decision analysis and support related to the principle of reference point optimization (developed by the editors of this volume and called also variously: aspiration-led decision support, quasi-satisfying framework of rationality, DIDAS methodology etc.). This focusing theme motivated extensive theoretical research - from basic methodological issues of decision analysis, through various results in mathematical programming (in the fields of large scale and stochastic optimization, nondifferentiable optimization, cooperative game theory) motivated and needed because of this theme, through methodological issues related to software development to issues resulting from testing and applications. We could not include in this volume all papers - theoretical, methodological, applied, software manuals and documentation - written during this cooperative study. The selection principle applied for this volume was to concentrate on advances of theory and methodology, related to the focusing theme, to supplement them by experiences and methodological advances gained through wide applications and tests in one particular application area - the programming of development of industrial structures in chemical industry, and finally to give a very short description of various software products developed in the contracted study agreement. The material of this volume is thus divided correspondingly into three unequal parts (it must be noted, however, that the last and shortest part corresponds to the most extensive research effort).

PART 1 is composed of 15 theoretical and methodological papers. It starts with two more general papers, the first explaining the focusing theme of this volume and the second describing the methodology of decision analysis in decision support systems (DSS) of the DIDAS family. The following five papers are devoted to various aspects of linear programming: three represent innovative approaches to large-scale programming problems and new mathematical and algorithmic results in this field, including a new idea of decomposition of augmented Lagrangian functions for large–scale problem – motivated and related to the work on DSS, next addresses basic problems of multiobjective dynamic trajectory optimization, a further one presents a more detailed methodological guide to a multiobjective mathematical programming package HYBRID. We present such a mixture of results on purpose, to show the broad scope of the study, its components of mathematical theory, components of methodological value and an example of methodological background for a software package. A further four papers combine two themes: the use of two reference levels for multiobjective analysis and optimization and the issues of nonlinear optimization in decision-support (starting with differentiable approximations and issues of symbolic differentiation of models and combining with advances in nondifferentiable optimization). The next three papers are related to various methodological aspects of multiobjective decision support for the case of a large number of discrete alternatives and for the case of mixed linear-integer programming models of the class of transshipment problems with facility location. The final paper of this part reports on theoretical advances in interactive decision support for bargaining and negotiations.

PART 2 contains six papers related to experiences in developing and using decision support methodology for a special but rather broad task of programming the development of a processing industry - to be specific, a chosen branch of chemical industry. The team of authors coming from *Joint System Research Department of the Institute of Automatic Control, Academy of Mining and Metallurgy*, Krakow and of the *Industrial Chemical Research Institute*, Warsaw, has worked on various projects for Polish governmental agencies, for international development agencies coordinated by UNIDO and in cooperation with various IIASA projects and programs. They developed a dedicated decision support system MIDA for the complicated task of multiobjective programming of the development of an industrial structure, used this system with various decision makers and for various tasks within chemical industry development, in countries such as China, Algeria, various central African countries - beside Poland. The papers summarize their experiences in these studies and applications. They start with an overview paper that surveys the applications, experiences and the main features of the DSS MIDA, then continue with a paper on the basic model of an industrial structure used in this system, with three papers discussing the methodology of interactive decision analysis in this application area - namely, the problems of multiobjective evaluation of an industrial structure, of hierarchical aspects of this evaluation related to various goals and dynamic development, of spatial allocation and investment scheduling aspects. The final paper of this part describes in more detail the architecture and functions of the DSS MIDA and contains a kind of short manual for this system. Although we tried to exclude software manuals from this volume, since it is devoted mostly to theoretical and methodological issues together with lessons from applications, an exception seems to be justified in the case of the system MIDA, because of the wide range of actual applications of this system: giving a shortened manual illustrates best the inside working aspects of this important and widely tested system.

PART 3 contains short descriptions of software. Following the principles of composition of this volume, we do not include any other manuals, but only short executive summaries and very general descriptions of eight software systems. They comprise four prototype DSS:

- IAC–DIDAS–L – for multiobjective linear and linear dynamic models,
- IAC–DIDAS–N – for nonlinear models, with symbolic model differentiation,
- DISCRET – for the case of a large number of discrete alternatives,

- DINAS – for multiobjective mixed programming models of the type of transshipment problems with facility location;

and three multiobjective mathematical programming systems that can be used when building dedicated DSS:

- HYBRID – for dynamic linear and linear-quadratic models, with a non–simplex solver of augmented Lagrangian type,
- PLP and POSTAN – described together because both are extensions of the MINOS system from Stanford Optimization Laboratory: one towards handling multiobjective problems via reference point optimization, second towards various aspects of post-optimal analysis in this widely used optimization system,
- MCBARG – for supporting bargaining and negotiation.

Neither of these software systems is as widely tested and applied as the DSS MIDA described in Part 2, but all of them contain testing and demonstrative examples as well as some methodological and software developments that might make them interesting for other researchers working in this field.

Table of Contents

Part 1
Theory and Methodology

Decision Support Systems Using Reference Point Optimization

Andrzej Lewandowski, Andrzej P. Wierzbicki

Institute of Automatic Control, Warsaw University of Technology.

Abstract

This paper presents a review of various approaches to decision support, distinguishes a methodological approach based on reference point optimization and reviews advances in this field done in Poland under the contracted study agreement "Theory, Software and Testing Examples for Decision Support Systems" with the International Institute for Applied Systems Analysis.

1 Introduction

The concept of a decision support system – though widely used and developed both in research and in practical applications through more than last ten years — is not yet quite precisely defined. On the other hand, it is possible to give a broad definition of this concept by enumerating possible classes of decision support systems, describing the concept of a decision making process that is fundamental to all decision support systems, defining what a decision support system should and what it should not do, discussing possible approaches to and types of decision support. After attempting such a broad definition, we review in this paper in more detail a specific class of decision support systems — those that use the principle of reference point optimization for generating and evaluating decision alternatives, mostly with help of a computerized analytical model describing the essential features of a decision situation. Many of such systems have been developed during four years of a contracted study agreement between the Polish Academy of Sciences (including, as subcontractors, the Institute of Automatic Control of Warsaw University of Technology, the Institute of Systems Research of Polish Academy of Sciences, the Institute of Automatic Control of the Academy of Mining and Metallurgy of Krakow and the Institute of Informatics of the University of Warsaw) and the International Institute for Applied Systems Analysis, Laxenburg near Vienna, Austria. These developments and implementations are also reviewed in the paper.

2 Concepts and definitions of decision support systems

There are many proposed definition of a decision support systems in the current literature — see, e.g., Keen and Scott-Morton (1978), Sage (1981), Parker and Al-Utabi (1986), Gray (1986), Jarke (1986) and others. However, most of them do not take into account the fact that three main classes of decision support systems have been practically developed in applications and research. These are (see Lewandowski and Wierzbicki, 1987, also next paper):

A) *Simple tools for managerial decision support* (that might be used as building blocks of more sophisticated decision support systems) such as modern data bases, electronic spreadsheet systems, etc. as well as more complex but pragmatically designed systems composed of such tools;

B) *Decision support systems based on logical models and logical inference* whose main function are to help in recognizing a logical pattern in a decision situation; these systems typically involve the use of logical programming languages, expert systems style programming, knowledge bases, other tools of artificial intelligence;

C) *Decision support systems based on analytical models, multiobjective optimization and choice*, whose main functions concentrate on the process of choice among various decision alternatives either specified a priori or generated with help of the system. Such systems typically include a computerized model of a decision situation formulated in analytical terms and elements of multiobjective optimization and evaluation of alternatives.

All these three classes can be further subdivided according to various methodological principles. For example, the systems of the class C can be subdivided in various ways: systems that serve a strategic evaluation of novel decision situations versus systems that support repetitive, tactical decisions; systems that handle a number of discrete alternatives versus those that support the generation and choice among alternatives from a set of continuum power; between the latter, systems that use static linear, dynamic linear, static nonlinear or dynamic nonlinear analytical models that describe a given decision situation; systems in which the methodology of multiobjective alternative evaluation follows a definite (typically, culturally determined) framework of rationality versus systems that try to accommodate intercultural perceptions of rationality, see next paper; etc.

However, there are certain features that are common to all decision support systems. Observe that the systems of classes B and C contain explicitly models of the decision situation, although of different types. The same can be said, in fact, about the systems of the class A: when preparing a simple decision support tool, such as a date base or a spreadsheet, to support a definite decision process, one must assume, even if implicitly, a kind of a model of the decision situation. Thus, we can state that all decision support systems contain such models.

All decision support systems can be subdivided into two large classes: those that are designed to serve essentially *one user* or *decision maker* versus those that are explicitly designed to serve *many users* or *multiple decision makers*. The latter class can be further subdivided into two essentially different subclasses: those that serve *cooperative group decision making* versus those that are designed to help in truly game-like situations that might involve conflict escalation through noncooperative decisions and thus serve *bargaining and negotiations* (through they might and should try to help reaching cooperative decisions, such systems do not take cooperative behaviour of users for granted, see Wierzbicki, 1983a,b). In the latter case, another universal feature of decision support systems becomes apparent: *all decision support systems should be designed* not to serve reaching a single decision, but *to help in organizing a decision process.*

This essential feature of decision support systems was noted by many authors — see, e.g., Parker and Al-Utabi (1986). An early characterization of a decisions process was given by Simon (1958). According to this definition, a decision process consists of the following three steps: *intelligence* — searching the environment for opportunities calling for a decision, *design* — defining the decision situation, inventing, developing and analysing possible courses of action, finally *choice* — selecting a particular course of action from those available. However, the experience in analysing decision processes and constructing decision support systems since this time indicates that a decision process might be much more complicated and contains more essential elements. Cooke and Slack (1984) combine the decision making with problem solving process and define its phases as observation, a formal recognition of a problem, interpretation and diagnosis, the definition of a decision problem, the determination of options or alternatives, an evaluation of options, and selection, implementation and monitoring. When including implementation and monitoring phases in a decision process, a much more sophisticated treatment of various types of uncertainty becomes possible — Wierzbicki (1983a).

The results of Dreyfus (1984) indicate that an essential distinction should be made between *familiar* (even complex) *decision situations* and *novel decision situations* as well as between various levels of expertize of the decision maker in a given field. A master expert in a decision field is able to treat most of the decision situations as familiar ones, recognize them immediately and select and implement a decision instantly with great efficiency. The quality of his decisions might exceed considerably the quality of decisions achieved by any computerized system; we still do not have adequate models and interpretations of the parallel processing of information performed in human mind. However, even master expert recognises (through certain feeling of uneasiness) situations that are novel and deliberates about them. Again, the process of such deliberation is not understood by us fully and is certainly not as ordered and linear as the models of decision processes described above; it ends in a sudden recognition of a decision pattern or in a deeper understanding of the decision problem. An expert of a lower level or a novice in a decision field treats more decision situations as novel and thus needs more logical or analytical decision support.

When seen from this perspective, every decision process is a part of a longer process of learning in order to become a master expert. Thus, a decision process in all novel situations is not necessarily linearly ordered, can have many recourses to earlier stages, while as a decision situation becomes more familiar for a given decision maker, the decision process becomes shorter and finally looses its distinctive phases. This is similar to an adaptive treatment of uncertainty, to the old concept of Feldbaum (1962) of the dual role of control — this of control and that of learning. This also indicates several concepts of dynamics in a decision process. One is related to the fact that decisions are concerned with future events and have dynamic consequences — even if we do use sometimes static models of their consequences in more simple cases. The second reflects the fact that even reaching a single decision is a process, possibly with many phases and recourses and with a role of learning during this process. The third reflects the fact that separate decision processes are embedded in a longer learning process of the decision maker to become a master expert, with its much more complicated dynamics. We can conclude also that the requirement of consistency of a decision maker, essential to many classical approaches to decision analysis, has a fundamental drawback: a learning decision maker can often gain by being inconsistent.

All this indicates that decision support systems can have multiple functions in a decision process. Most important are two general functions: *helping the decisions maker to learn* about the decision situation (to familiarise it by playing with the proxy of reality provided by the decision support system) and *filling in details to the outlines of decision suggested by decision maker* (even a master expert might need this function in more complex decision situation and a learning decision maker needs it the more, while striving to become a master expert). This suggests that the emphasis on the phase of decision choice, typical for more classical approaches to decision processes and decision support, is actually misplaced: if adequately supported, humans can make (until now, and probably for a long time to come) much better decision than most advanced computerized systems — and the problem is not how to replace, but how to support human decision making. There certainly are decision problems of repetitive type that might and should be automated — because of the necessary speed of decisions, because of their tediousness for humans, because of the reliability of automata that do not grow tired and do not have the human right to change their minds — but this becomes then the field of automatic control, not of decision analysis and support.

Even as a tool for learning and filling in details, however, decision support systems can perform many functions in various phases of a decision process. In the first phase of intelligence and observation, main support can come from information processing systems that, when considered alone, need not be decision support systems because they do not necessarily contain a model of the decision situation. When interpreting this information, however, in the phases of formal problem recognition, interpretation and diagnosis, many tentative decision situation models might be tried. Thus *the first function of a decision support system is to help in model formalization, edition, simulation, parametric analysis* etc. Naturally, models used in decision support can be of various types — very simple or more complex, of logical or analytical nature, etc. — and contemporary decision support systems cannot work with all possible classes of models, are necessarily specialized. Nevertheless, good decision support system should contain a *model edition and simulation interface and a directory of models together with a data base of the results of experiments* with these models.

The phase of problem definition typically results in an (explicit or implicit) selection of one of possible models of the decision situation, or at least — of a class of such models. *Decision means* and *ends* are also typically determined in this phase, while the distinction between then is not necessarily sharp: resources allocated to a given problem can be considered both decision outcomes (ends) and decision variables (means). Therefore, it is useful to distinguish more precisely between decision variables in the sense of input variables to a model and decision outcomes in the sense of the output variables, although in some simplistic models this distinction is not sharp either and it is better to speak about decision alternatives (options) and attributes (outcomes). Some of the output variables might be chosen as objectives (or attributes, or criteria) of the decision. In fact, a given model of a decision situation allows typically for various definitions of a decision problem, since various variables of the model can be selected either as decision variables or as decision outcomes. In this sense, a good decision support system should have a *directory of problems* (related to given models) and a *data base of experimental analysis results for given problems.*

The latter feature is necessary in the phase of generating and reviewing or evaluating options and alternatives. If the decision situation is modelled as one with a discrete, exogenously given number of options or alternatives, the generation of alternatives must be done outside of a decision support system. However, in most cases the options or alternatives are not exogenously given — even if discrete — and only limited by certain *constraints* that must be represented in the model. In such a case, or in a case when the number of exogenously given options is very large, the issue of selecting on option for analysis is equivalent to alternative generation. If the decision variables have continuous character (the number of alternatives is of continuum power), there is no difference at all between alternative generation and selecting a decision option for analysis. Such selected alternatives together with results of their analysis or evaluation need a data base.

The phase of selection or choice of a decision can be variously represented in decision support systems. If we insist on the sovereignty of a human decision maker and consider the system as supporting mostly learning and filling in details, then each decision choice proposed by the system must be only tentative and the user must have convenient means of influencing this choice. In such a case, there is no need to make an essential distinction between the phase of alternative generation, analysis and evaluation and the phase of choice: in both of them, the decision support system should use some methodological device for selecting and evaluating an alternative or option while being guided by the general wishes of the user. Various methods of multiobjective decision analysis can be used for this purpose, if the model has analytical form; for models of logical type, the issue of appropriate methodological device for such a purpose is yet open.

It must be stressed here that the insistence on the user's sovereignty is a relatively new feature of decision support systems developed in the last decade together with "high tech — high touch" trend in modern societies (see Naisbit, 1984). Older approach to decision support systems, while stressing that such a system should only help decision makers in reaching decisions, was not quite consistent with this assumption in the phase of decision choice. Typically, such systems (based either on utility maximization or another — often logical — "inference engine") communicate the following message to the user in the phase of choice: "if your answers to my questions have been consistent, your best decision is as follows". This often helps the user, but not sufficiently: he

For example, the studies of human behaviour in situation of social traps or games with paradoxical outcomes — see Rappoport (1984) — and of evolutionary development of behavioural rules that resolve such social traps — see Axelrod (1985) — indicate that evolutionary experience forces humans to accept certain rules of ethical character that stop maximizing behaviour. Any intelligent man after some quarrels with his wife learns that maximization is not always the best norm of behaviour; children learn from conflicts among themselves that cooperative behaviour is also individually advantageous for a longer perspective. All these observations and studies might motivate in the future the development of a new framework of *evolutionary rationality*, but certainly reinforce the conclusions of the satisficing framework that there are rational reasons for stopping maximization in complex situations.

A very important contribution of the satisficing framework is the observation that decision makers often use *aspiration levels* for various outcomes of decisions; in classical interpretations of the satisficing framework, these aspiration levels indicate when to stop optimizing. While more modern interpretations might prefer other rules for stopping optimization, the concept of aspiration levels is extremely useful for aggregating the results of learning by the decision maker: *aspiration levels* represent values of decision outcomes that can be accepted as reasonable or satisfactory by the decision maker and thus are aggregated, adaptable parameters that *are sufficient for a simple representation of his accumulated experience*.

There might be also other frameworks of rationality, such as the *framework of goal- and program oriented planning*, see Glushkov (1972), Pospelov and Irikov (1976), Wierzbicki (1985), that corresponds to the *culture of planning organizations*. This framework has some similarities, but also some differences to the utility maximization framework, the satisficing framework and to the *principle of reference point optimization* developed by Wierzbicki (1980) in multiobjective optimization and decision support.

In order first to include the principle of reference point optimization into the framework of satisficing decisions and then to develop a broader framework that would be useful for decision support for decision makers representing various perspectives of rationality, Wierzbicki (1982, 1984b, 1985, 1986) proposed the following *principles of quasisatisficing decision making* — a quasisatisficing decision situation consists of (one or several) decision makers or *users* that might represent any perspective of rationality and have the right of changing their minds due to learning and of stopping optimization for any reason (for example, in order to avoid social traps) as well as of a decision support system that might be either fully computerized or include also human experts, analysts, advisors. It is assumed that:

- The user evaluates possible decisions on the basis of a set (or vector) of attributes or objective outcomes. These factors can be expressed in numerical scale (quantitatively) or in verbal scale (qualitatively), like "bad", "good" or "excellent". Each factor can be additionally constrained by specifying special requirements on it that must be satisfied. Beside this, objective outcomes can be characterized by their type: maximized, minimized, stabilized — that is, kept close to a given level (which corresponds to foregoing optimization), or floating — that is, included for the purpose of additional information or for specifying constraints. The user has the control over the specification of objective outcomes together with their types and of possible aggregation of such factors.

- One of the basic means of communication of the user with the decision support system is his specification of aspiration levels for each objective outcome; these aspiration levels are interpreted as reasonable values of objective outcomes. In more complex situations, the user can specify two levels for each objective outcome — an aspiration level interpreted as above and a reservation level interpreted as the lowest acceptable level for the given objective outcome.

- Given the information specified by the user — i.e., the specification of objective outcomes and their types, together with aspiration and possibly reservation levels — the decision support system following the quasisatisficing principle should use this guiding information, together with other information contained in the system, in order to propose to the user one or several alternative decisions that are best attuned to this guiding information. When preparing (generating or selecting) such alternative decisions, the decision support system should not impose on the user the optimizing or the satisficing or any other behaviour, but should follow the behaviour that is indicated by the types of objective outcomes. This means that the decision support system should optimize when at least one objective outcome is specified as minimized or maximized and should satisfice (stop optimizing upon reaching aspiration levels) when all objective outcomes are specified as stabilized. The later case corresponds actually to the technique of *goal programming*, see e.g. Ignizio (1978), hence the quasisatisficing decision support can be also considered as a generalization of this technique. By using aspiration or reservation levels for some objective outcomes as constraints, also the goal- and program oriented behaviour can be supported by a quasisatisficing decision support system.

In order to illustrate possible responses of a quasisatisficing decision support system to the guiding information given by the user, let us assume that all specified objective outcomes are supposed to be maximized and have specified aspiration levels or reference points. In this original formulation of the principle of reference point optimization we can distinguish the following cases:

Case 1: the user has overestimated the possibilities implied by admissible decisions (since their constraints express available resources) and there is no admissible decision such that the values of all objective outcomes are exactly equal to their aspiration levels. In this case, however, it is possible to propose a decision for which the values of objective outcomes are as close as possible (while using some uniform scaling, for example implied by the aspiration and reservation levels) to their aspiration levels; the decision support system should tentatively propose at least one or several of such decisions to the user.

Case 2: the user underestimated the possibilities implied by admissible decisions and there exist a decision which results in the values of objective outcomes exactly equal to the specified aspiration levels. In this case, it is possible to propose a decision which improves all objective outcomes uniformly as much as possible. The decision support system should inform the user about this case and tentatively propose at least one or several of such decisions.

Case 3: the user, by a chance or as a result of a learning process, has specified aspiration levels there are uniquely attainable by an admissible decision. The decision support system should inform the user about this case and specify the details of the decision that results in the attainment of aspiration levels

In the process of quasisatisficing decision support, all aspiration levels and the corresponding decisions proposed by the system have tentative character. If a decision proposed by the system is not satisfactory to the user, he can modify the aspiration levels and obtain new proposed decisions, or even modify the specification of objective outcomes or constraints; the process is repeated until the user learns enough to make the actual decision himself or to accept a decision proposed by the system.

The process of quasisatisficing decision making can be formalized mathematically — see, e.g., Wierzbicki (1986) — and the mathematical formalization can be interpreted in various ways; let us consider an interpretation that corresponds to the framework of utility maximization. We assume that the user has a nonstationary utility function that changes in time due to his learning about a given decision situation. At each time instant, however, he can intuitively and tentatively (possibly with errors concerning various aspects of the decision situation) maximize his utility; let this tentative maximization determine his aspiration levels.

When he communicates these aspiration levels to the decision support system, the system should use this information, together with the specification of the decision situation, in order to construct an approximation of his utility function that is relatively simple and easily adaptable to the changes of aspiration levels, treated as parameters of this approximation. By maximizing such an approximative utility function while using more precise information about the attainability of alternative decisions and other aspects of the decision situation — for example, expressed by a model of the decision situation incorporated by expert advice into the decision support system — a tentative decision can be proposed to the user.

Such a tentative approximation of the user's utility function, constructed in the decision support system only in order to propose a tentative decision to the learning decision maker, is called here *order-consistent achievement function* or simply *achievement function*. It should be stressed that the concept of achievement function has been also used in the context of goal programming, but without the requirement of order consistency (achievement functions in goal programming are equivalent to norms and thus satisfy the requirements of Cases 1 and 3 listed above but fail to satisfy the requirements of Case 2).

There are many other interpretations of an order-consistent achievement function (see Wierzbicki, 1986): penalty function related to aspirations treated as soft constrains, a utility function not of the decision maker, but of the decision support system interpreted as an ideal staff trying to follow instructions given by it's boss, a device for automatically switching from norm minimization to maximization in generalized goal programming upon crossing the boundary of attainable outcomes, a mathematical tool for closely approximating the positive cone D in the space of outcomes, an extension of the concept of membership function in a fuzzy set approach to multiobjective optimization, etc.

The general idea of reference point optimization has been independently developed or further used and extended by many researchers — Steuer and Cho (1983), Nakayama and Savaragi (1985), Korhonen and Laakso (1986). The more specific use of order-consistent achievement functions has been developed in many papers of IIASA — see next paper and, specifically, in the contracted study agreement "Theory, Software and Testing Examples for Decision Support Systems" between IIASA and the Polish Academy of Sciences.

4 Recent research on decision support systems in Poland

Under the contracted study agreement, various theoretical issues, special tools for decision support systems mostly based on the quasisatisficing framework and reference point optimization, decision support system prototypes for given classes of substantive models of decision situation (that is, outlines for decision support systems that can be further customized for a specific decision situation with a model of a given class), as well as examples of decision support systems and their applications have been studied and developed.

Between the theoretical issues studied, the following advances have been made:

- special types of simplex and non-simplex algorithms for large scale linear programming problems of dynamic and stochastic type encountered when analysing multiobjective linear programming type models for decision support, by A. Ruszczynski and J. Gondzio, this also includes a new way of decomposing augmented Lagrangian functions for such problems;

- a study of theoretical issues related to a non-simplex algorithm based on augmented Lagrangian regularization for multiobjective optimization of dynamic linear and quadratic programming type models in decision support, by J. Sosnowski and M. Makowski;

- a study of methodological issues related to multiobjective trajectory optimization, particularly for models of dynamic multiobjective linear programming type , by T. Rogowski;

- a study of uncertainty issues in multiobjective optimization through a special interval approach developed by H. Gorecki and A. Skulimowski;

- a study of methodological issues, achievement function forms and robust nonlinear programming algorithms for decision support systems using models of nonlinear programming type, by T. Kreglewski, together with issues of using symbolic differentiation for such models, by J. Paczynski;

- a study of nondifferentiable optimization techniques for applications in multiobjective optimization of nonlinear models, by K. Kiwiel and A. Stachurski;

- a study of mixed-integer multiobjective transhipment and facility location problems using the quasisatisficing framework, by W. Ogryczak, K. Studzinski and K. Zorychta;

- methodological and game-theoretical research for the development of multi-person decision support systems for bargaining and negotiations with multiple objectives, by J. Bronisz, L. Krus and A. P. Wierzbicki.

The decision support tools and decision support system prototypes developed under this research agreement include:

- a multiobjective mathematical programming system — based on reference point optimization — HYBRID, using the mentioned above algorithms by J. Sosnowski and M. Makowski; this system can be used as a core for a more customized decision support systems;

- a decision support system prototype IAC-DIDAS-L (in two variants) for problems with linear programming type models, by T. Rogowski, J. Sobczyk and A. P. Wierzbicki;

- a nonlinear model edition, generation and symbolic differentiation package as a tool for supporting first phases of the decision process with nonlinear models, by J. Paczynski and T. Kreglewski (only some methodological background aspects of this package are described in this volume);

- a decision support system prototype IAC-DIDAS-N for problems with nonlinear programming type models, by T. Kreglewski, J. Paczynski and A. P. Wierzbicki;

- a decision support system prototype DINAS for multiobjective transportation and facility location problems with models of mixed-integer programming type, by W. Ogryczak, K. Studzinski and K. Zorychta;

- a pilot version of a decision support system prototype DISCRET for multiobjective problems with a large number of explicitly given discrete alternatives, by J. Majchrzak;

- a pilot version of a nondifferentiable nonlinear optimization package NOA-1 with possible applications in multiobjective decision support, by K. Kiwiel and A. Stachurski (only methodological background of this package is described in this volume);

- a pilot version of a multi-person decision support system prototype for multiobjective bargaining and negotiations, by J. Bronisz, L. Krus and B. Lopuch;

- a postoptimal analysis package POSTAN and a parametric programming package PLP compatible with the optimization system MINOS and adapted for multiobjective optimization, by G. Dobrowolski, A. Golebiowski, K. Hajduk, A. Korytowski and T. Rys.

Most of the software packages and system prototypes are developed to the level of documented and tested, scientific transferable software; packages and system prototypes include testing and demonstrative examples for their applications. The documentation of these packages and system prototypes will be available from IIASA in autumn 1988.

A separate group concentrated on a range of applications of decision support systems using reference point optimization – in programming the development of industrial structures in chemical industry. A specialized decision support system MIDA has been developed for these purposes by J. Kopytowski, M. Zebrowski, G. Dobrowolski and T. Rys, then widely tested in many applications in Poland and abroad as well as extended to handle hierarchical, spatial, dynamic and scheduling issues by its original authors and M. Skocz, W. Ziembla. The experiences from this field of applications give a strong testing ground for the general development of decision support methodology.

It is necessary to point out that this short review focuses mostly on activities within the contracted study agreement between IIASA and Polish scientific institutions. This research constitutes, however, only a part of research done within the System and Decision Sciences Program regarding problems of theory, implementation and applications of Decision Support Systems. We will not discuss all these activities — they are presented in the recent issues of OPTIONS (1987). It is necessary to mention, however, such important contributions of scientists cooperating with SDS and SDS staff members like multiple criteria optimization aspects of uncertain dynamic systems (Kurzhanski, 1986), several theoretical aspects of multiple criteria optimization (Nakayama, 1986, Tanino, 1986, Sawaragi at all., 1985, Valyi, 1986, 1987) problems of voting and utility theory (Saari, 1987), stochastic programming aspects of DSS (Michalevich, 1986) fuzzy set approach in DSS (Sakawa and Yano, 1987, Seo and Sakawa, 1987), DSS for scheduling (Katoh, 1987) as well as new approaches in development of DSS (Larichev, 1987). Another activity not mentioned in this volume is the development of multi-user cooperative decision support system (SCDAS) implemented in distributed computing environment (Lewandowski and Wierzbicki, 1987, Lewandowski 1988). Finally, several scientific activities coordinated by SDS are also contributing to further advancement of theory and methodology of Decision Support Systems — such as the International Comparative Study in DSS (Anthonisse at all., 1987). Without this stimulating scientific atmosphere and without scientific environment created in SDS it would be definitely not possible to achieve the results presented in this volume.

5 References

Anthonisse, J.M., K.M. van Hee and J.K. Lenstra (1987). Resource constrained project scheduling: an international exercise in DSS development. Centre for Mathematics and Computer Science, Department of Operations research and System Theory, Note OS-N9701, Amsterdam, The Netherlands.

Axelrod, R. (1985). The Evolution of Cooperation. Basic Books, New York.

Bonczek, R. H., Holsapple, C. W. and Whinston, A. B. (1981). Foundations of Decision Support Systems. Academic Press, New York.

Cooke, S. and Slack, N. (1984). Making Management Decision. Prentice-Hall, Englewood Cliffs.

Dinkelbach, W. (1982). Entscheidungsmodelle, Walter de Gruyter, Berlin, New York.

Dreyfus, R. E. (1984). Beyond rationality. In: Grauer, M., Thompson, M., Wierzbicki, A. P. Eds: Plural Rationality and Interactive Decision Processes. Proceedings, Sopron, Hungary, 1984. Lecture Notes in Economics and Mathematical Systems, Vol. 248. Springer-Verlag, Berlin.

Erlandson, F. E. (1981). The satisficing process: A new look. *IEEE Trans. on Systems, Man and Cybernetics,* Vol. SMC-11, No. 11, November 1981.

Feldbaum, A. A. (1962). Foundations of the theory of optimal control systems (in Russian: Osnovy teorii optimalnych avtomaticheskikh sistem). Nauka, Moscow.

Fisher, W. F. (1979). Utility models for multiple objective decisions: Do they accurately represent human preferences? *Decision Sciences,* Vol. 10, pp. 451-477.

Ginzberg M. J. and Stohr E. A. (1982). Decision Support Systems: Issues and Perspectives. In: Ginzberg, M. J., Reitman, W. R. and Stohr, E. A. Eds.: Decision Support Systems, Proceedings of the NYU Symposium on Decision Support Systems, New York, 21-22 May, 1981. North-Holland Publ. Co.

Glushkov, V. M. (1972). Basic principles of automation in organizational management systems (in Russian). *Upravlayushcheye Sistemy i Mashiny,* 1.

Grauer, M., Lewandowski, A., and Wierzbicki, A. P. (1984). DIDAS — theory, implementation and experiences. In: Grauer, M. and Wierzbicki, A. P. Eds: Interactive Decision Analysis, Proceedings, Laxenburg, Austria, 1983. *Lecture Notes in Economics and Mathematical Systems,* Vol. 229. Springer Verlag, Berlin.

Gray, P. (1986). Group Decision Support Systems. In: McLean E. and Sol, H. G. Eds: Decision Support Systems: A Decade in Perspective, Proceedings of the IFIP WG 8.3 Working Conference on Decision Support Systems, Noordwijkerhout, The Netherlands.

Horsky, D. (1984). Estimation of attribute weights from preference comparisons. *Management Science*, Vol. 30, No. 7, July 1984.

Ignizio, J. P. (1978). Goal programming — a tool for multiobjective analysis. *Journal for Operational Research*, 29, pp. 1109-1119.

Jacquet-Lagreze, E. and Shakun, M. F. (1984). Decision Support Systems for Semi-Structured Buying Decisions. *European Journal of Operational Research*, Vol. 16, pp. 48-58.

Jarke, M. (1986). Group Decision Support through Office Systems: Developments in Distributed DSS Technology. In: McLean, E. and Sol, H. G. Eds: Decision Support Systems: A Decade in Perspective, Proceedings of the IFIP WG 8.3 Working Conference on Decision Support Systems, Noordwijkerhout, The Netherlands.

Katoh, N. (1987). An efficient algorithm for bicriteria minimum-cost circulation problem. Working Paper WP-87-98, International Institute for Applied Systems Analysis, Laxenburg, Austria.

Katoh, N. (1987). An efficient algorithm for a bicriteria single-machine scheduling problem. Working Paper WP-87-100, International Institute for Applied Systems Analysis, Laxenburg, Austria.

Keen, P. G. W and Scott Morton, M. S. (1978). Decision Support Systems — An Organizational Perspective. Addison-Wesley Series on Decision Support.

Keeney, R. L. and Raiffa, H. (1976). Decisions with Multiple Objectives: Preferences and Value Tradeoffs, Willey, New York, 1976.

Korhonen, P., and Laakso, J. (1986). Solving a generalized goal programming problem using a visual interactive approach. *European Journal of Operational Research*, 26, pp. 355-363.

Kurzhanski, A. (1986). Inverse problems in multiobjective dynamic optimization. In: Toward Interactive and Intelligent Decision Support Systems, Proceedings, Kyoto, Japan, 1986, Y. Sawaragi, K. Inoue and H. Nakayama, Eds. Lecture Notes in Economics and Mathematical Systems, Vol. 286, Springer-Verlag.

Larichev, O. (1987). New directions in multicriteria decision making research. Working Paper WP-87-67, International Institute for Applied Systems Analysis, Laxenburg, Austria.

Lewandowski, A., Rogowski, T. and Kreglewski T. (1985). A trajectory-oriented extension of DIDAS and its application. In: Grauer, M., Thompson, M., Wierzbicki, A. P. Eds: Plural Rationality and Interactive Decision Processes. Proceedings, Sopron, Hungary, 1984. *Lecture Notes in Economics and Mathematical Systems*, Vol. 248. Springer-Verlag, Berlin.

Lewandowski, A., Johnson, S. and Wierzbicki, A. P. (1986). A prototype selection committee decision analysis and support system, SCDAS: theoretical background and computer implementation. Working Paper WP-86-27, International Institute for Applied Systems Analysis, Laxenburg, Austria.

Lewandowski, A. and A.P. Wierzbicki (1987). Interactive decision support systems — the case of discrete alternatives for committee decision making. Working Paper WP-87-38, International Institute for Applied Systems Analysis, Laxenburg, Austria.

Lewandowski, A. (1988). SCDAS — decision support system for group decision making: information processing issues. Working Paper WP-88-48, International Institute for Applied Systems Analysis, Laxenburg, Austria.

Michalevich, M. V. (1986). Stochastic approaches to interactive multicriteria optimization problems. Working Paper WP-86-10, International Institute for Applied Systems Analysis, Laxenburg, Austria.

Naisbit, J. (1984). Megatrends. H. Mifflin, New York.

Nakayama, H. and Sawaragi, Y. (1983). Satisficing trade-off method for multiobjective programming. In: Grauer, M. and Wierzbicki, A. P. Eds: Interactive Decision Analysis, Springer-Verlag, Berlin-Heidelberg.

Nakayama, H. (1986). Geometrical approach to Iserman duality in linear vector optimization. Collaborative Paper CP-86-02, International Institute for Applied Systems Analysis, Laxenburg, Austria.

OPTIONS (1987). Decision Support Systems, No. 3-4, 1987. International Institute for Applied Systems Analysis, Laxenburg, Austria.

Parker, B. J. and Al-Utabi, G. A. (1986). Decision support systems: The reality that seems to be hard to accept? *OMEGA Int. Journal of Management Science*, Vol. 14, No. 2, 1986.

Pospelov, G. S. and Irikov, V. A. (1976). Program- and Goal Oriented Planning and Management (in Russian). *Sovietskoye Radio*, Moscow.

Rappoport, A. (1984). The uses of experimental games. In: Grauer, M., Thompson, M., Wierzbicki, A. P. Eds: Plural Rationality and Interactive Decision Processes. Proceedings, Sopron, Hungary, 1984. *Lecture Notes in Economics and Mathematical Systems*, Vol. 248. Springer-Verlag, Berlin.

Roy, B. (1971). Problems and methods with multiple objective functions, *Math. Programming*, Vol. 1, pp. 233-236.

Saari, D. (1982). Inconsistencies of weighted Voting Systems. *Math. of Operations Res.*, Vol. 7.

Saari, D. (1987). Symmetry and extensions of Arrow's theorem. Working Paper WP-87-109, International Institute for Applied Systems Analysis, Laxenburg, Austria.

Saaty, T. L. (1982). Decision Making for Leaders: The Analytical Hierarchy Process for Decisions in a Complex World, Lifetime Learning Publ., Belmont.

Sage, A. P. (1981). Behavioural and organizational considerations in the design of information systems and processes for planning and decision support. *IEEE Trans. Systems and Cybernetics*, Vol. SMC-11, No. 9, September 1981.

Sakawa, M. and H. Yano (1987). An interactive fuzzy satisficing method using augmented minimax problems and its application to environmental systems. Research Report RR-87-14, International Institute for Applied Systems Analysis, Laxenburg, Austria.

Sawaragi, Y., H. Nakayama and T. Tanino (1985). Theory of Multiobjective Optimization. Academic Press.

Seo, F. and M. Sakawa (1987). Fuzzy multiattribute utility analysis for collective choice. Research Report RR-87-13, International Institute for Applied Systems Analysis, Laxenburg, Austria.

Simon, H. (1958). Administrative Behaviour, McMillan, New York.

Sprague, R. H. and Carlson, C. Eds. (1982). Building Effective Decision Support Systems. Prentice Hall, Inc.

Stabel C. B. (1986). Decision Support Systems: Alternative Perspectives and Schools. In: McLean, E. and Sol, H. G. Eds: Decision Support Systems: A Decade in Perspective, Proceedings of the IFIP WG 8.3 Working Conference on Decision Support Systems, Noordwijkerhout, The Netherlands.

Steuer, R., and Cho., E. V. (1983). An interactive weighted Chebyshev procedure for multiple objective programming. *Mathematical Programming* 26, pp. 326-344.

Tanino, T. (1986). Sensitivity analysis in multiobjective optimization. Working Paper WP-86-05, International Institute for Applied Systems Analysis, Laxenburg, Austria.

Tanino, T. (1986). Stability and sensitivity analysis in convex vector optimization. Working Paper WP-86-15, International Institute for Applied Systems Analysis, Laxenburg, Austria.

Tversky, A., Kaheman, D. and Slovic, P. (1983). Judgement Under Uncertainty: Heuristic and Biases, Cambridge University Press.

Valyi, I. (1986). On approximate vector optimization. Working Paper WP-86-07, International Institute for Applied Systems Analysis, Laxenburg, Austria.

Valyi, I. (1987). Epsilon solution and duality in vector optimization. Working Paper WP-87-43, International Institute for Applied Systems Analysis, Laxenburg, Austria.

Vlacic, Lj., Matic, B. and Wierzbicki, A. P. (1986). Aggregation Procedures for Hierarchically Grouped Decision Attributes with Application to Control System Performance Evaluation. International Conference on Vector Optimization, Darmstadt, 1986.

Wierzbicki, A. P. (1980). The use of reference objectives in multiobjective optimization. In: Fandel, G. and Gal, T. Eds: Multiple Criteria Decision Making, Theory and Applications. Springer Verlag, Heidelberg.

Wierzbicki, A. P. (1982). A mathematical basis for satisfying decision making. *Math. Modelling*, Vol. 3, pp. 391-405.

Wierzbicki, A. P. (1983a). Negotiation and mediation in conflicts: The role of mathematical approaches and methods. In: Chestnut, H. et al., Eds: Supplemental Ways to Increase International Stability. Pergamon Press, Oxford, 1983.

Wierzbicki, A. P. (1983b). Critical essay on the methodology of multiobjective analysis. *Regional Science and Urban Economics*, Vol. 13, pp. 5-29.

Wierzbicki, A. P. (1984a). Models and Sensitivity of Control Systems. Elsevier, Amsterdam, 1984.

Wierzbicki, A. P. (1984b). Interactive decision analysis and interpretative computer intelligence. In: Grauer, M. and Wierzbicki, A. P. Eds: Interactive Decision Analysis, Proceedings, Laxenburg, Austria, 1983. *Lecture Notes in Economics and Mathematical Systems*, Vol. 229. Springer Verlag, Berlin.

Wierzbicki, A. P. (1985). Negotiation and mediation in conflicts: Plural rationality and interactive decision processes. In: Grauer, M., Thompson M. and Wierzbicki A. P., Eds: Plural Rationality and Interactive Decision Processes, Proceedings, Sopron, 1984. *Lecture Notes in Economics and Mathematical Systems*, Vol. 248. Springer Verlag, Berlin.

Wierzbicki, A. P. (1986). On the completeness and constructiveness of parametric characterizations to vector optimization problems. *OR-Spektrum*, Vol. 8, pp. 73-87.

Wynne, B. (1982). Decision support systems — a new plateau of opportunity or more emperor's clothing? *INTERFACES*, Vol. 12, No. 1, February 1982.

Decision Support Systems of DIDAS Family (Dynamic Interactive Decision Analysis & Support)

Andrzej Lewandowski, Tomasz Kreglewski, Tadeusz Rogowski,

Andrzej P. Wierzbicki

Institute of Automatic Control, Warsaw University of Technology.

Abstract

This paper presents a review of methodological principles, mathematical theory, variants of implementation and various applications of decision support systems of DIDAS family, developed by the authors and many other cooperating researchers during the years 1980–1986 in cooperation with the Systems and Decision Sciences Program of the International Institute for Applied Systems Analysis. The purpose of such systems is to support generation and evaluation of alternative decisions in interaction with a decision maker that might change his preferences due to learning, while examining a substantive model of a decision situation prepared by experts and analysts. The systems of DIDAS family are based on the principle of reference point optimization and the quasisatisficing framework of rational choice.

Introduction

The results reported in this paper are an outcome of a long cooperation between the System and Decision Sciences Program of the International Institute for Applied Systems Analysis (IIASA) and the Institute of Automatic Control, Warsaw University of Technology as well as many other institutions in Poland and in other countries. This cooperation concentrated on applications of mathematical optimization techniques in multiobjective decision analysis and on the development of decision support systems. Although many articles in scientific journals and papers at international conferences described specific results obtained during this cooperation (in fact, four international workshops and several working meetings were organized during this cooperation), one of the main results—the family of Dynamic Interactive Decision Analysis and Support systems—has not been until now comprehensively described. Such a description is the purpose of this paper.

1 Concepts of decision support and frameworks for rational decisions

1.1 Concepts of decision support systems

The concept of a decision support system, though quite widely used and developed in contemporary research, is by no means well defined. Without attempting to give a restrictive definition (since such definition in an early stage of development might limit it too strongly), we can review main functions and various types of decision support.

The main function of such systems is to support decisions made by humans, in contrast to decision automation systems that replace humans in repetitive decisions because these are either too tedious or require very fast reaction time or very high precision. In this sense, every information processing system has some functions of decision support. However, modern decision support systems concentrate on and stress the functions of helping human decision makers in achieving better decisions, following the high tech—high touch trend in the development of modern societies (Naisbitt, 1982). We can list several types of systems that serve such purposes:

- *simple managerial support systems*, such as modern data bases, electronic spreadsheet systems, etc;
- *expert and knowledge base systems* whose main functions relate to the help in recognizing a pattern of decision situation; more advanced systems of this type might involve considerable use of artificial intelligence techniques;
- *alternative generation and evaluation systems* whose main functions concentrate on the processes of choice among various decision alternatives either specified a priori or generated with help of the system, including issues of planning, of collective decision processes and issues of negotiations between many decision makers; more advanced systems of this type might involve a considerable use of mathematical programming techniques, such as optimization, game theory, decision theory, dynamic systems theory etc.

Some authors (Van Hee, 1986) restrict the definition of decision support systems only to the third group while requiring that a decision support system should contain a model of decision support. Although the systems described in this paper belong precisely to this category, we would like to draw the attention of the reader that it is a narrow sense of interpreting decision support systems. With this reservation, we will concentrate on decision support systems in the narrow sense. These can be further subdivided along various attributes into many classes:

- systems that support *operational planning* of repetitive type versus systems that support *strategic planning*, confronting essentially novel decision situations;
- systems that concentrate on the choice between a number of *discrete alternatives* versus systems that admit a *continuum of alternatives* and help to generate interesting or favorable alternatives among this continuum;

- systems that are essentially designed to be used by a *single decision maker ("the user")* versus systems that are designed to help *many decision makers* simultaneously;
- *specialized systems* designed to help in a very specific decision situation versus adaptable *system shells* that can be adapted to specific cases in a broader class of decision situations;
- systems that use versus such that do not use explicitly mathematical programming techniques, such as optimization, in the generation or review of alternatives;
- systems that assume (explicitly or implicitly) a specific *framework of rationality* of decisions followed by the user versus systems that try to accommodate a broader class of perceptions of rationality (Wierzbicki, 1984a).

This last distinction was an important issue in the development of decision support systems described in this paper.

1.2 Frameworks for rational decisions

When trying to support a human decision maker by a computerized decision support system, we must try to understand first how human decisions are made and how to help in making rational decisions. However, the rationality concept followed by the designer of the system might not be followed by the user; good decision support systems must be thus flexible, should not impose too stringent definitions of rationality and must allow for many possible perceptions of rationality by the user.

The first distinction we should make is between the *calculative* or *analytical rationality* and the *deliberative* or *holistic rationality*, the *"hard"* approach and the *"soft"* approach. The most consistent argument for the "soft" or holistic approach was given by Dreyfus (1984). He argues—and supports this argument by experimental evidence—that a decision maker is a learning individual whose way of making decisions depends on the level of expertise attained through learning. A novice needs calculative rationality; an experienced decision maker uses calculative rationality in the background, while concentrating his attention on novel aspects of a decision situation. An expert does not need calculative rationality: in a known decision situation, he arrives at best decisions immediately, by absorbing and intuitively processing all pertinent information (presumably in a parallel processing scheme, but in a way that is unknown until now). A master expert, while subconsciously making best decisions, continuously searches for *"new angles"*—for new aspects or perspectives, motivated by the disturbing feeling that not everything is understood, the feeling that culminates and ends in the *"aha"* or *heureka effect* of perceiving a new perspective. Thus, the holistic approach can be understood as *the rationality of the culture of experts*.

However, even a master expert needs calculative decision support, either in order to simulate and learn about novel decision situations, or to fill in details of the decision in a repetitive situation; novice decision makers might need calculative decision support in order to learn and become experts. These needs must be taken into account when constructing decision support systems that incorporate many elements of calculative rationality.

There are several frameworks for calculative or analytical rationality; most of these, after deeper analysis, turn out to be culturally dependent (Wierzbicki, 1984a). The *utility maximization framework* has been long considered as expressing an universal rationality, as the basis of decision analysis; every other framework would be termed "not quite rational". The abstractive aspects of this framework are the most developed—see, e.g., (Fishburn, 1964, Keeney and Raiffa, 1976)—and a monograph of several volumes would be needed to summarize them. Without attempting to do so, three points should be stressed here. Firstly, utility maximization framework is not universal, is culturally dependent; it can be shown to express the *rationality of a small entrepreneur or consumer facing an infinite market* (Wierzbicki, 1984a). Secondly, its descriptive powers are rather limited; it is a good descriptive tool for representing mass economic behaviour and a very poor tool for representing individual behaviour. Thirdly, it is difficult to account for various levels of expertise and to support learning within this framework.

Many types of decision support systems attempt to approximate the utility function of the user and then to suggest a decision alternative that maximizes this utility function. Most users find such decision support systems not convenient: it takes many experiments and questions to the decision maker to approximate his utility and, when the user finally learns some new information from the support system, his utility might change and the entire process must be repeated. Moreover, many users resent too detailed questions about their utility or just refuse to think in terms of utility maximization. However, a good decision support system should also support users that think in terms of utility maximization. For this purpose, the following *principle of interactive reference point maximization and learning* can be applied.

Suppose the user is an expert that can intuitively, holistically maximize his unstated utility function; assume, however, that he has not full information about the available decision alternatives, their constraints and consequences, only some approximate mental model of them. By maximizing holistically his utility on this mental model, he can specify desirable consequences of the decision; we shall call these desirable consequences a *reference point* in the outcome or objective space. The function of a good decision support system should be then not to outguess the user about his utility function, but to take the reference point as a guideline and to use more detailed information about the decision alternatives, their constraints and consequences in order to provide the user with proposals of alternatives that came close to or are even better than the reference point.

This more detailed information must be included in the decision support system in the form of a *substantive model* of the decision situation, prepared beforehand by a group of analysts (in a sense, such a model constitutes a knowledge base for the system). Upon analysing the proposals generated in the system, the utility function of the user might remain constant or change due to learning, but he certainly will know more about available decision alternatives and their consequences. Thus, he is able to specify a new reference point and to continue interaction with the system. Once he has learned enough about available alternatives and their consequences, the interactive process stops at the maximum of his unstated utility function. If the user is not a master expert and might have difficulties with holistic optimization, the system should support him first in learning about decision alternatives, then in the optimization of his utility; but the latter is a secondary function of the system and can be performed also without explicit models of utility function while using the concept of reference points.

The concept of reference point optimization has been proposed by Wierzbicki (1975, 1977, 1980); following this concept, the principle of interactive reference point optimization and learning was first applied by Kallio, Lewandowski and Orchard-Hays (1980) and then lead to the development of an entire family of decision support systems called DIDAS. However, before describing these systems in more detail, we must discuss shortly other frameworks of calculative rationality.

A concept similar or practically equivalent to the reference point is that of *aspiration levels* proposed over twenty years ago in the *satisficing rationality* framework by Simon (1957, 1958) and by many others that followed the behavioural criticism of the normative decision theory based on utility maximization. This framework started with the empirical observation that people do form adaptive aspiration levels by learning and use these aspirations to guide their decisions; very often, they cease to optimize upon reaching outcomes consistent with aspirations and thus make *satisficing decisions*. However, when building a rationale for such observed behaviour, this framework postulated that people cannot maximize because of three reasons: the cost of computing optimal solutions in complex situations; the uncertainty of decision outcomes that makes most complex optimization too difficult; and the complexity of decision situations in large industrial and administrative organizations that induces the decision makers to follow some well established *decision rules* that can be behaviourally observed and often coincide with satisficing decision making. This discussion whether and in what circumstances people could optimize substantiated the term *bounded rationality* (which implies misleadingly that this is somewhat less than full rationality) applied to the satisficing behaviour and drown attention away from the essential points of learning and forming aspiration levels.

Meanwhile, two of the reasons for not optimizing quoted above have lost their relevance. The development of computers and computational methods of optimization, including stochastic optimization techniques, has considerably decreased the cost and increased the possibilities of calculative optimization; moreover, the empirical research on holistic rationality indicates that expert decision makers can easily determine best solutions in very complex situations even if they do not use calculative optimization. The third reason, supported by empirical observations, remains valid: the *satisficing rationality is typical for the culture of big industrial and administrative organizations* (see also Galbraith, 1967). However, it can today be differently interpreted: the appropriate question seems to be *not whether people could, but whether they should maximize.*

Any intelligent man, after some quarrels with his wife, learns that maximization is not always the best norm of behaviour; children learn best from conflicts among themselves that cooperative behaviour is socially desirable and that they must restrict natural tendencies to maximization in certain situations. In any non-trivial game with the number of participants less than infinity, a cooperative outcome is typically much better for all participants than an outcome resulting from individual maximization. This situation is called a *social trap* and motivated much research that recently gave results of paradigm-shifting importance (Rappoport, 1985, Axelrod, 1985): we can speak about a perspective of ***evolutionary rationality***, where people develop—through social evolution—rules of cooperative behaviour that involve foregoing short-term maximization of gains.

When trying to incorporate the lessons from the perspective of evolutionary rationality into decision support systems, another question must be raised: in which situations should we stop maximizing upon reaching aspiration levels? We should stop maximizing for good additional reasons, such as avoiding social traps or conflict escalation, but if these reasons are not incorporated into the substantive model of the decision situation, the question about foregoing maximization should be answered by the decision maker, not by the decision support system. This constitutes a drawback of many decision support systems based on goal programming techniques (Charnes and Cooper, 1975, Ignizio, 1978) that impose on the user the unmodified satisficing rationality and stop optimization upon reaching given aspirations, called goals in this case.

When trying to modify goal programming techniques and strictly satisficing rationality to account for above considerations, the ***principle of ideal organization*** (Wierzbicki, 1982) can be applied in construction of decision support systems. This principle states that a good decision support system should be similar to an ideal organization consisting of a boss (the user of the system) and the staff (the system), where the boss specifies goals (aspirations, reference points) and the staff tries to work out detailed plans how to reach these goals. If the goals are not attainable, the staff should inform the boss about this fact, but also should propose a detailed plan how to approach these goals as close as it is possible. If this goals are just attainable and cannot be improved, the staff should propose a plan how to reach them, without trying to outguess the boss about his utility function and proposing plans that lead to different goals than stated by the boss.

If, however, the goals could be improved, the staff should inform the boss about this fact and propose a plan that leads to some uniform improvement of all goals specified by the boss; if the boss wishes that some goals should not be further improved, he can always instruct the staff accordingly by stating that, for some selected objectives, the goals correspond not to maximized (or minimized) but ***stabilized*** variables, that is, the staff should try to keep close to the goals for stabilized objectives without trying to exceed them. By specifying all objectives as stabilized, the boss imposes strictly satisficing behaviour on the staff; but the responsibility for doing so remains with him, not with the staff.

The above principle of ideal organization can be easily combined with the principle of interactive reference point maximization and learning; jointly, they can be interpreted as a broader framework for rationality, called ***quasisatisficing*** framework (Wierzbicki, 1984a, 1986), that incorporates lessons from the holistic and the evolutionary rationality perspectives and can support decision makers adherence either to utility maximization or satisficing. In fact, the quasisatisficing framework can also support decision makers following other perspectives of rationality, such as the ***program- and goal-oriented planning and management*** framework. This framework, proposed by Glushkov (1972) and Pospelov and Irikov (1976), represents the culture of planning, but has been independently suggested later also by representatives of other cultures (Umpleby, 1983). In this framework, rational action or program are obtained by specifying first primary objectives, called goals, and examining later how to shift constraints on secondary objectives, called means, in order to attain the goals. In distinction to the utility maximization or satisficing frameworks, the stress here is laid on the hierarchical arrangement of objectives; but the quasisatisficing framework can also handle hierarchical objectives.

2 Quasisatisficing and achievement functions

The main concepts of the quasisatisficing framework, beside the principle of interactive reference point optimization and learning and the principle of ideal organization, are the use of reference points (aspiration levels, goals) as parameters by which the user specifies his requirements to the decision support system (controls the generation and selection of alternatives in the system) as well as the maximization of an order-consistent achievement function as the main mechanism by which the decision support system responds to the user requirements. Achievement functions have been used also in goal programming (Ignizio, 1978), however, without the requirement of order-consistency (Wierzbicki, 1986). When following the principle of interactive reference point optimization and learning, an order-consistent achievement function can be interpreted as an ad hoc approximation of the utility function of the user (Lewandowski et al., 1986); if the user can holistically maximize his utility and interactively change reference points, there is no need for any more precise approximation of his utility function. When following the principle of ideal organization, an order-consistent achievement function can be interpreted as a proxy for utility or achievement function of the ideal staff (the decision support system) guided by aspirations specified by the boss (the user); this function is maximized in order to obtain best response to the requirements of the boss.

Based upon above principles and starting with the system described in (Kallio et al., 1980), many decision support systems have been developed with the participation or cooperation of the authors of this paper (Lewandowski and Grauer, 1982, Grauer et al., 1982, Kreglewski and Lewandowski, 1983, Lewandowski et al., 1984a, Lewandowski et al., 1984b, Makowski and Sosnowski, 1984, Kaden and Kreglewski, 1986), either in IIASA, or in several Polish institutions cooperating with IIASA. The name DIDAS (Dynamic Interactive Decision Analysis and Support) has been first used by Grauer, Lewandowski and Wierzbicki (1983). Other systems based upon such principles are now being developed for implementations on professional microcomputers; all these systems we broadly call here "systems of DIDAS family". However, also other researchers adopted or developed parallely some principles of quasisatisficing framework, represented in the works of Nakayama and Sawaragi (1983), Sakawa (1983), Gorecki et al. (1983), Steuer et al. (1983), Strubegger (1985), Messner (1985), Korhonen et al. (1986) and others; decision support systems of such type belong to a broader family using quasisatisficing principles of rationality or aspiration-led decision analysis and support methods.

Since the maximization of an order-consistent achievement function is a specific feature of systems of DIDAS family, we review here shortly the theory of such functions.

We consider first the basic case where the vector of decisions $x \in R^n$, the vector of objectives or outcomes of decisions $q \in R^p$, and the substantive model of decision situation has the form of a set of admissible decisions $X_0 \subset R^n$ —assumed to be compact—together with an outcome mapping, that is, a vector-valued objective function $f : X_0 \rightarrow R^p$ —assumed to be continuous, hence the set of attainable outcomes $Q_0 = f(X_0)$ be also compact; further modifications of this basic case will be considered later. If the decision maker wants to maximize all outcomes, then the partial ordering of the outcome space is implied by the *positive cone* $D = R^p_+$—which means that the inequality $q' \geq q'' \Leftrightarrow q' - q'' \in D$ is understood in the sense of simple inequalities for each component of vectors q', q''.

However, the cone $D = R^p_+$ has nonempty interior; a more general case is when the decision maker would like to maximize only first p' outcomes, minimize next outcomes from $p' + 1$ until p'', while the last outcomes from $p'' + 1$ until p are to be kept close to some given aspiration levels, that is, maximized below these levels and minimized above these levels; such objectives or outcomes are called *(softly) stabilized*. In this case, we redefine the positive cone to the form

$$D = \{q \in R^p : q_i \geq 0, i = 1, \ldots, p'; q_i \leq 0, i = p'+1, \ldots, p''; q_i = 0, i = p''+1, \ldots, p\} \quad (1)$$

This cone D does not have an interior if $p'' < p$. Since the cone D is closed and the set Q_0 is compact, there exist *D-efficient* (D-optimal) elements of Q_0 , see (Wierzbicki, 1982). These are such elements $\hat{q} \in Q_0$ that $Q_0 \cap (\hat{q} + \tilde{D}) = \emptyset$ where $\tilde{D} = D \setminus \{0\}$; if $p' = p$ and $D = R^p_+$, then D-efficient elements are called also Pareto-optimal (in other words—such that no outcome can be improved without deteriorating some other outcome). The corresponding decisions $\hat{x} \in X_0$ such that $\hat{q} = f(\hat{x})$ are called D-efficient or Pareto-optimal as well. Although the decision maker is usually interested both in efficient decisions and outcomes, for theoretical considerations it is sufficient to analyse only the set of all D-efficient outcomes

$$\hat{Q}_0 = \{\hat{q} \in Q_0 : Q_0 \cap (\hat{q} + \tilde{D}) = \emptyset\}, \qquad \tilde{D} = D \setminus \{0\} \quad (2)$$

Several other concepts of efficiency are also important. The *weakly D-efficient* elements belong to the set

$$\hat{Q}_0^w = \{\hat{q} \in Q_0 : Q_0 \cap (\hat{q} + int\, D) = \emptyset\} \quad (3)$$

In other words, these are such elements that cannot be improved in all outcomes jointly. Although important for theoretical considerations, weakly D-efficient elements are not useful in practical decision support, since there might be too many of them: if $p'' < p$ and the interior of D is empty, then all elements of Q_0 are weakly D-efficient. Another concept is that of *properly D-efficient* elements; these are such D-efficient elements that have bounded trade-off coefficients that indicate how much one of the objectives must be deteriorated in order to improve another one by a unit (for various almost equivalent definitions of such elements see Sawaragi et al., 1985). In applications, it is more useful to further restrict the concept of proper efficiency and consider only such outcomes that have trade-off coefficients bounded by some a priori number. This corresponds to the concept of *properly D-efficient elements with (a priori) bound* ϵ or *D_ϵ-efficient elements* that belong to the set

$$\hat{Q}_0^\epsilon = \{\hat{q} \in Q_0 : Q_0 \cap (\hat{q} + \tilde{D}_\epsilon) = \emptyset\}, \quad (4)$$

$$\tilde{D}_\epsilon = \{q \in R^p : dist(q, D) \leq \epsilon \|q\|\} \setminus \{0\}$$

where $\epsilon > 0$ is a given number (Wierzbicki, 1977). D_ϵ-efficient elements have trade-off coefficients bounded approximately by ϵ and $1/\epsilon$. For computational and practical purposes, an efficient outcome with trade-off coefficients very close to zero or to infinity cannot be distinguished from weakly efficient outcomes; hence, we shall concentrate in the sequel on properly efficient elements with bound ϵ.

When trying to characterize mathematically various types of efficiency with help of achievement functions, two basic concepts are needed: this of *monotonicity*, essential for sufficient conditions of efficiency, and that of *separation of sets*, essential for necessary conditions of efficiency. The role of monotonicity in vector optimization is explained by the following basic theorem (Wierzbicki, 1986):

Theorem 1. Let a function $r : Q_0 \to R^1$ be strongly monotone, that is, let $q' > q''$ (equivalent to $q' \in q'' + \tilde{D}$) imply $r(q') > r(q'')$. Then each maximal point of this function is efficient. Let this function be strictly monotone, that is, let $q' \gg q''$ (equivalent to $q' \in q'' + int\, D$) imply $r(q') > r(q'')$. Then each maximal point of this function is weakly efficient. Let this function be ϵ-strongly monotone, that is, let $q' \in q'' + \tilde{D}_\epsilon$ imply $r(q') > r(q'')$. Then each maximal point of this function is properly efficient with bound ϵ.

The second concept, that of separation of sets, is often used when deriving necessary conditions of scalar or vector optimality. We say that a function $r : R^p \to R^1$ *strongly separates two disjoint sets* Q_1 and Q_2 in R^p, if there is such $\beta \in R^1$ that $r(q) \leq \beta$ for all $q \in Q_1$ and $r(q) > \beta$ for all $q \in Q_2$. Since the definition of efficiency (2) requires that the sets Q_0 and $q + \tilde{D}$ are disjoint (similarly for the definitions (3) or (4)), they could be separated by a function. If Q_0 is convex, these sets can be separated by a linear function. If Q_0 is not convex, the sets Q_0 and $\hat{q} + \tilde{D}$ could be still separated at an efficient point $\hat{q}$, but we need for this a nonlinear function with level sets $\{q \in R^p : r(q) \geq \beta\}$ which would closely approximate the cone $\hat{q} + \tilde{D}$. There might be many such functions; their desirable properties are summarized in the definitions of *order-consistent achievement functions* (Wierzbicki, 1986) of two types: *order-representing functions* (which, however, characterize weak efficiency and will not be considered here) and *order-approximating functions*. The latter type is defined as follows:

Let A denote a subset of R^p, containing $\hat{Q}_0$ but not otherwise restricted, and let $\bar{q} \in A$ denote reference points or aspiration levels that might be attainable or not (we assume that the decision maker cannot a priori be certain whether $\bar{q} \in Q_0$ or $\bar{q} \notin Q_0$). Order-approximating achievement functions are such continuous functions $s : Q_0 \times A \to R^1$ that $s(q, \bar{q})$ is strongly monotone (see Theorem 1) as a function of $\bar{q} \in Q_0$ for any $q \in A$ and, moreover, possesses the following property of order approximation:

$$\bar{q} + D_{\bar{\epsilon}} \subset \{q \in R^p : s(q, \bar{q}) \geq 0\} \subset \bar{q} + D_\epsilon \tag{5}$$

with some small $\epsilon \geq \bar{\epsilon} \geq 0$; together with the continuity requirement, the requirement (5) implies that $s(q, \bar{q}) = 0$ for all $q = \bar{q}$.

If $p' = p$ and $D = R^p_+$, then a simple example of an order-approximating function is:

$$s(q,\bar{q}) = \min_{1\le i\le p} \alpha_i(q_i - \bar{q}_i) + \alpha_{p+1}\sum_{i=1}^{p} \alpha_i(q_i - \bar{q}_i) \tag{6}$$

with $A = R^p$, some positive weighting coefficients α_i (typically, we take $\alpha_i = 1/s_i$, where s_i are some scaling units for objectives, either defined by the user or determined automatically in the system, see further comments) and some $\alpha_{p+1} > 0$ that is sufficiently small as compared to ϵ and large as compared to $\bar{\epsilon}$ (typically, we take $\alpha_{p+1} = \epsilon/p$). This function is not only strongly monotone, but also $\bar{\epsilon}$-strongly monotone. For the more complicated form (1) of the positive cone D, function (6) modifies to:

$$s(q,\bar{q}) = \min_{1\le i\le p} z_i(q_i,\bar{q}_i) + \alpha_{p+1}\sum_{i=1}^{p} z_i(q_i,\bar{q}_i) \tag{7}$$

where the functions $z_i(q_i,\bar{q}_i)$ are defined by:

$$z_i(q_i,\bar{q}_i) = \begin{cases} (q_i - \bar{q}_i)/s_i, & \text{if } 1 \le i \le p', \\ (\bar{q}_i - q_i)/s_i, & \text{if } p'+1 \le i \le p'', \\ \min(z_i', z_i''), & \text{if } p''+1 \le i \le p, \end{cases} \tag{8}$$

with

$$z_i' = (q_i - \bar{q}_i)/s_i', \qquad z_i'' = (\bar{q}_i - q_i)/s_i'' \tag{9}$$

The coefficients s_i, s_i', s_i'' are scaling units for all objectives, either defined by the user (in which case $s_i' = s_i''$, the user does not need to define two scaling coefficients for a stabilized objective outcome) or determined automatically in the system; again, we use here $\alpha_{p+1} = \epsilon/p$.

Since the definition of an order-approximating achievement function requires that only its zero-level set should closely approximate the positive cone, many other forms of such functions are possible. For example, in some DIDAS systems the following function has been used:

$$s(q,\bar{q}) = \min\left[\min_{i\le i\le p} z_i(q_i,\bar{q}_i), \frac{1}{\rho p}\sum_{i=1}^{p} z_i(q_i,\bar{q}_i)\right] + \frac{\epsilon}{p}\sum_{i=1}^{p} z_i(q_i,\bar{q}_i) \tag{10}$$

where the functions $z_i(q_i,\bar{q}_i)$ are defined as in (8), (9) and the coefficient $\rho \ge 1$ indicates to what extent the minimal overachievement is substituted by the sum of overachievements in the level sets for positive values of this function.

At any point $\hat{q}$ that is properly efficient with bound ϵ, an order-approximating function with $\bar{q} = \hat{q}$ strictly separates the sets $\hat{q} + \tilde{D}_\epsilon$ and Q_0. This and related properties of order-approximating functions result in the following characterization of D_ϵ-efficiency (Wierzbicki, 1986):

Theorem 2. Let $s(q,\bar{q})$ be an order-approximating function with $\epsilon > \bar{\epsilon} \ge 0$. Then, for any $\bar{q} \in A$, each point that maximizes $s(q,\bar{q})$ over $q \in Q_0$ is efficient; if $\hat{q}$ is properly efficient with bound ϵ (D_ϵ-optimal), then the maximum of $s(q,\bar{q})$ with $\bar{q} = \hat{q}$ over $q \in Q_0$

is attained at $\hat{q}$ and is equal zero. Let, in addition, $s(q, \bar{q})$ be $\bar{\epsilon}$-strongly monotone with respect to q; then each point that maximizes $s(q, \bar{q})$ over $q \in Q_0$ is properly efficient with bound ϵ.

The essential difference between order-consistent achievement functions and other types of achievement functions, used in goal programming and based on norms, is that the aspiration or reference point $\bar{q}$ needs not to be unattainable in order to achieve efficiency; this is because order-consistent achievement functions remain monotone, even if the reference point crosses the efficient boundary of Q_0. Somewhat simplifying, we can say that an order-consistent achievement function switches automatically from norm minimization to maximization when the aspiration point $\bar{q}$ crosses the efficient boundary and becomes attainable. On the other hand, the characterization by Theorem 2 is obtained without any convexity assumptions, because the order-approximating property of achievement functions results in a constructive though nonlinear separation of sets Q_0 and $\hat{q}+\tilde{D}$ even in nonconvex cases. In fact, the set Q_0 needs not to be even connected and the order-consistent achievement functions can be as well used to characterize solutions of multiobjective discrete or mixed programming. Theorem 2 is valid even if the decision outcomes are elements of infinite-dimensional complete normed (Banach) spaces, as in many cases of multiobjective dynamic trajectory optimization—see (Wierzbicki, 1982).

Order-approximating achievement functions have several interpretations. From the point of view of utility maximization, achievement function can be interpreted as an ad hoc approximation of the utility function of the user, based on the information that he conveyed to the decision support system: the partial preordering of the objective space (which objectives are to be maximized, which minimized and which stabilized) and the aspiration levels $\bar{q}$ for all objectives; if more information is already available, this ad hoc approximation can be improved—see further comments. The coefficient ϵ can be then interpreted as the weight that the user attaches to correcting the underachievement in the worst outcome by average overachievements in other outcomes. However, such an ad hoc approximation is not a classical utility function, since it is context-dependent: it explicitly depends on the aspiration levels $\bar{q}$ that summarize the experience of the user and change due to his learning during interaction, thus changing the approximation of the utility function. On the other hand, the achievement function (6) can have cardinal form: if $\alpha_i = 1/s_i$, then function (6) is independent on affine transformations of outcome space; the same applies to function (7).

When following the principle of an ideal organization, an order-approximating achievement function can be interpreted as the utility function of the staff that is aware of aspirations set by the boss; the maximum of the achievement function is then positive, if the staff can propose a solution that exceeds the aspiration levels, it is negative, if the staff cannot propose a solution that satisfies aspiration levels and only comes as closely as possible to them, and it is zero (Theorem 2) if the staff finds an efficient solution that produces outcomes strictly corresponding to the aspiration levels.

From the point of view of strictly satisficing rationality, one should take function (7) and set $p' = p'' = 0$, that is, let all outcomes be softly stabilized; this is actually done in goal programming approaches. From the point of view of program- and goal oriented planning, one should either assume that the primary objectives are constrained to be equal to their corresponding aspiration levels, thereby modifying the set of admissible decisions X_0 (such objectives or outcomes are called *guided* or *strictly stabilized*), or assign much greater weights to primary objectives than to secondary objectives. We see that the quasisatisficing approach can be used by decision makers following either of these three frameworks of rationality.

Further mathematical properties of order-approximating achievement functions have been also investigated; for example, it can be shown that order-approximating functions give the strongest characterization of efficient solutions for cases where the set Q_0 is of an arbitrary, a priori unknown shape, which is a reasonable assumption in most applied cases (Wierzbicki, 1982). Another important property of an order-approximating function of the form (6) or (7) is that its maximal point $\hat{q}$ depends Lipschitz-continuously on the aspiration point $\bar{q}$ in all cases when the maximum of this function is unique and the set $\hat{Q}_0$ is connected; thus, the user of the decision support system can continuously influence his selection of efficient outcomes by suitably modifying the aspiration or reference point.

Computationally, the maximization of an order-approximating achievement function is either simple—if Q_0 is a convex polyhedral set, then the problem of maximizing (6), (7) or (10) can be rewritten as a linear programming problem—or more complicated for nonlinear or nonconvex problems. In such cases, we must either represent (6), (7) or (10) by additional constraints, or apply nondifferentiable optimization techniques, since the definition of order-approximating achievement functions imply their nondifferentiability at $q = \bar{q}$. Often, it is advisable to use smooth order-approximating functions that give weaker necessary conditions of efficiency than in Theorem 2, but are better suited for computational applications—see further comments.

3 Phases of decision support in systems of DIDAS family

A typical procedure of working with a system of DIDAS family consists of several phases:

A. The definition and edition of a substantive model of analysed process and decision situation by analyst(s);

B. The definition of the multiobjective decision problem using the substantive model, by the final user (the decision maker) together with analyst(s);

C. The initial analysis of the multiobjective decision problem, resulting in determining bounds on efficient outcomes and, possibly, a neutral efficient solution and outcome, by the user helped by the system;

D. The main phase of interactive, learning review of efficient solutions and outcomes for the multiobjective decision problem, by the user helped by the system;

E. An additional phase of sensitivity analysis (typically, helpful to the user) and/or convergence to the most preferred solution (typically, helpful only to users that adhere to utility maximization framework).

These phases have been implemented differently in various systems of DIDAS family; however, we describe them here comprehensively.

Phase A: Model definition and edition.

There are four basic classes of substantive models that have been used in various systems of DIDAS family: multiobjective linear programming models, multiobjective dynamic linear programming models, multiobjective nonlinear programming models and multiobjective dynamic nonlinear programming models. First DIDAS systems have not used any specific standards for these models; however, our accumulated experience has shown that such standards are useful and that they differ from typical theoretical formulations of such models (although they can be reformulated back to the typical theoretical form, but such reformulation should not bother the user).

A *substantive model of multiobjective linear programming type* consists of the specification of vectors of n decision variables $x \in R^n$ and of m outcome variables $y \in R^m$ together with linear model equations defining the relations between the decision variables and the outcome variables and with model bounds defining the lower and upper bounds for all decision and outcome variables:

$$y = Ax; \qquad x^{lo} \leq x \leq x^{up}; \qquad y^{lo} \leq y \leq y^{up} \tag{11}$$

where A is a $m \times n$ matrix of coefficients (obviously, a more general form $y = Ax + b$ can be also considered; it sometimes useful to admit an implicit, recursive definition of the model, see further comments on nonlinear models). Between outcome variables, some might be chosen as guided outcomes, corresponding to equality constraints; denote these variables by $y^c \in R^{m'} \subset R^m$ and the constraining value for them by b^c to write the additional constraints in the form:

$$y^c = A^c x = b^c; \qquad y^{c,lo} \leq b \leq y^{c,up} \tag{12}$$

where A^c is the corresponding submatrix of A. Some other outcome variables can be chosen as optimized objectives or objective outcomes; actually, this is done in the phase B together with the specification whether they should be maximized, minimized or softly stabilized, but we present them here for the completeness of the model description. Some of the objective variables might be originally not represented as outcomes of the model, but we can always add them by modifying this model; in any case, the corresponding objective equations in linear models have the form:

$$q = Cx \tag{13}$$

where C is another submatrix of A. Thus, the set of attainable objective outcomes is $Q_0 = CX_0$ and the set of admissible decisions X_0 is defined by:

$$X_0 = \{x \in R^n : \; x^{lo} \leq x \leq x^{up}; \; y^{lo} \leq Ax \leq y^{up}; \; A^c x = b^c\} \tag{14}$$

By introducing proxy variables and constraints, the problem of maximizing functions (7) or (10) over outcomes (13) and admissible decisions (14) can be equivalently rewritten to a parametric linear programming problem, with the leading parameter $\bar{q}$;

thus, in phases C, D, E, a linear programming algorithm called solver is applied. In initial versions of DIDAS systems for linear programming models, the typical MPS format for such models has been used when editing them in the computer; recent versions of DIDAS systems include also a user-friendly format of a spreadsheet.

A useful standard of defining a *substantive model of multiobjective linear dynamic programming type* is as follows. The model is defined on $T+1$ discrete time periods t, $0 \le t \le T$. The decision variable x, called in this case *control trajectory*, is an entire sequence of decisions:

$$x = \{x[0], \ldots, x[t], \ldots, x[T-1]\} \in R^{nT}, \qquad x[t] \in R^n \tag{15a}$$

and a special type of outcome variables, called *state variables* $w[t] \in R^{m'}$ is also considered. The entire sequence of *state variables or state trajectory*:

$$w = \{w[0], \ldots, w[t], \ldots, w[T-1], w[T]\} \in R^{m(T+1)} \tag{15b}$$

is actually one time period longer than x; the initial state $w[0]$ must be specified as given data. The fundamental equations of a substantive dynamic model have the form of *state equations*:

$$w[t+1] = A[t]w[t] + B[t]x[t]; \qquad t = 0, \ldots, T-1, \qquad w[0] - \textit{given} \tag{16a}$$

The model *outcome equations* have then the form:

$$y[t] = C[t]w[t] + D[t]x[t], \qquad t = 0, \ldots, T-1; \tag{16b}$$

$$y[T] = C[T]w[T] \in R^{m'}$$

and define the sequence of outcome variables or *outcome trajectory*:

$$y = \{y[0], \ldots, y[t], \ldots, y[T-1], y[T]\} \in R^{m'(T+1)} \tag{15c}$$

The decision, state and outcome variables can all have their corresponding lower and upper bounds (each understood as an appropriate sequence of bounds):

$$x^{lo} \le x \le x^{up}, \qquad w^{lo} \le w \le w^{up}, \qquad y^{lo} \le y \le y^{up} \tag{16c}$$

The matrices $A[t]$, $B[t]$, $C[t]$, $D[t]$ of appropriate dimensions can be dependent or independent on time t; in the latter case, the model is called *time-invariant*. This distinction is important in multiobjective analysis of such models only in the sense of model edition: time-invariant models can be defined easier by automatic, repetitive edition of model equations and bounds for subsequent time periods.

Between the outcomes, some might be chosen to be equality constrained or guided along a given trajectory:

$$y^c[t] = e^c[t] \in R^{m''} \subset R^{m'}, \quad t = 0, \ldots, T; \quad e^c = \{e^c[0], \ldots, e^c[t], \ldots, e^c[T]\} \tag{17}$$

The optimized (maximized, minimized or stabilized) objective outcomes of such model can be actually selected in phase B among both state variables and outcome variables (or even decision variables) of this model; in any case, they form an entire *objective trajectory*:

$$q = \{q[0], \ldots, q[t], \ldots, q[T-1], q[T]\} \in R^{p(T+1)}, \qquad q[t] \in R^p \tag{18}$$

If we assume that the first components $q_i[t]$ for $1 \leq i \leq p'$ are to be maximized, next for $p' + 1 \leq i \leq p''$ are to be minimized, last for $p'' + 1 \leq i \leq p$ are to be stabilized (actually, the user in the phase B does not need to follow this order—he simply defines what to do with subsequent objectives), then the achievement function $s(q, \bar{q})$—for example, originally given by (10)—in such a case takes the form:

$$s(q,\bar{q}) = \min\left[\min_{0 \leq t \leq T} \min_{0 \leq i \leq p} z[t], \ \frac{1}{\rho(T+1)p}\sum_{t=0}^{T}\sum_{i=1}^{p} z_i[t]\right] + \frac{\epsilon}{(T+1)p}\sum_{t=0}^{T}\sum_{i=1}^{p} z_i[t] \tag{19}$$

where the functions $z[t] = z(q[t], \bar{q}[t])$ are defined by:

$$z_i[t] = \begin{cases} (q_i[t] - \bar{q}_i[t])/s_i[t], & \text{if } \ 1 \leq i \leq p', \\ (\bar{q}_i[t] - q_i[t])/s_i[t], & \text{if } \ p' + 1 \leq i \leq p'', \\ \min(z_i'[t], z_i''[t]), & \text{if } \ p + 1 \leq i \leq p \end{cases} \tag{20}$$

where

$$z_i'[t] = (q_i[t] - \bar{q}_i[t])/s_i'[t], \qquad z_i''[t] = (\bar{q}_i[t] - q_i[t])/s_i''[t], \tag{21}$$

The user does not need to define time-varying scaling units $s_i[t]$ nor two different scaling units $s_i'[t], s_i''[t]$ for a stabilized objective: the time-dependence of scaling units and separate definitions of $s_i'[t], s_i''[t]$ are needed only in the case of automatic scaling in further phases.

A useful standard for a *substantive model of multiobjective nonlinear programming type* consists of the specification of vectors of n decision variables $x \in R^n$ and of m outcome variables $y \in R^m$ together with nonlinear model equations defining the relations between the decision variables and the outcome variables and with model bounds defining the lower and upper bounds for all decision and outcome variables:

$$y = g(x); \qquad x^{lo} \leq x \leq x^{up}; \qquad y^{lo} \leq y \leq y^{up} \tag{22}$$

where $g : R^n \rightarrow R^m$ is a (differentiable) function. In fact, the user or the analyst does not have to define the function g explicitly; he can also define it recursively, that is, determine some further components of this vector-valued function as functions of formerly defined components. Between outcome variables, some might be chosen as guided outcomes corresponding to equality constraints; denote these variables by $y^c \in R^{m'} \subset R^m$ and the constraining value for them by b^c to write the additional constraints in the form:

$$y^c = g^c(x) = b^c; \qquad y^{c,lo} \leq b^c \leq y^{c,up} \tag{23}$$

where g^c is a function composed of corresponding components of g. In phase B, some other outcome variables can be also chosen as optimized objectives or objective outcomes. The corresponding objective equations have the form:

$$q = f(x) \tag{24}$$

where f is also composed of corresponding components of g. Thus, the set of attainable objective outcomes is $Q_0 = f(X_0)$ where the set of admissible decisions X_0 is defined by:

$$X_0 = \{x \in R^n : \ x^{lo} \leq x \leq x^{up}; \ \ y^{lo} \leq g(x) \leq y^{up}; \ \ g^c(x) = b^c\} \tag{25}$$

In further phases of working with nonlinear models, an order-approximating achievement function must be maximized; for this purpose, a specially developed nonlinear optimization algorithm called *solver* is used. Since this maximization is performed repetitively, at least once for each interaction with the user that changes the parameter $\bar{q}$, there are special requirements for the solver that distinguish this algorithm from typical nonlinear optimization algorithms: it should be robust, adaptable and efficient, that is, it should compute reasonably fast an optimal solution for optimization problems of a broad class (for various differentiable functions $g(x)$ and $f(x)$) without requiring from the user that he adjusts special parameters of the algorithm in order to obtain a solution. The experience in applying nonlinear optimization algorithms in decision support systems (Kreglewski and Lewandowski, 1983, Kaden and Kreglewski, 1986) has led to the choice of an algorithm based on penalty shifting technique and projected conjugate gradient method. Since a penalty shifting technique anyway approximates nonlinear constraints by penalty terms, an appropriate form of an achievement function that differentiably approximates function (7) has been also developed and is actually used. This *smooth order-approximating achievement function* has the form:

$$s(q,\bar{q}) = 1 - \left\{ \frac{1}{p} \left[\sum_{i=1}^{p''} (w_i)^\alpha + \sum_{i=p''}^{p+1} \max((w_i', w_i''))^\alpha \right] \right\}^{1/\alpha} \tag{26}$$

where w_i, w_i', w_i'' are functions of q_i, $\bar{q}_i$:

$$w_i(q_i,\bar{q}_i) = \begin{cases} (q_{i,max} - q_i)/s_i, & \text{if } \ 1 \leq i \leq p' \\ (q_i - q_{i,min})/s_i, & \text{if } \ p' + 1 \leq i \leq p'' \end{cases} \tag{27a}$$

$$\left. \begin{array}{l} w_i'(q_i,\bar{q}_i) = (q_{i,max} - q_i)/s_i' \\ w_i''(q_i,\bar{q}_i) = (q_i - q_{i,min})/s_i'' \end{array} \right\}, \quad \text{if } \ p'' + 1 \leq i \leq p, \tag{27b}$$

and the dependence on $\bar{q}_i$ results from a special definition of the scaling units that are determined by:

$$s_i = \begin{cases} (q_{i,max} - \bar{q}_i), & \text{if } \ 1 \leq i \leq p', \\ (\bar{q}_i - q_{i,min}), & \text{if } \ p' + 1 \leq i \leq p'', \end{cases} \tag{28a}$$

$$\left. \begin{array}{l} s_i' = (q_{i,max} - \bar{q}_i) \\ s_i'' = (\bar{q}_i - q_{i,min}) \end{array} \right\}, \quad \text{if } \ p'' + 1 \leq i \leq p \tag{28b}$$

In the initial analysis phase, the values $q_{i,max}$ and $q_{i,min}$ are set to the upper and lower bounds specified by the user for the corresponding outcome variables; later, they are modified, see further comments. The parameter $\alpha \geq 2$ is responsible for the approximation of the function (7) by the function (26): if $\alpha \to \infty$ and $\epsilon \to 0$, then these functions converge to each other (while taking into account the specific definition of scaling coefficients in (26–28)). However, the use of too large parameters results in badly conditioned problems when maximizing function (26), hence $\alpha = 4, \ldots, 8$ are suggested to be used.

The function (26) must be maximized with $q = f(x)$ over $x \in X_0$, while X_0 is determined by simple bounds $x^{lo} \leq x \leq x^{up}$ as well as by inequality constraints $y^{lo} \leq g(x) \leq y^{up}$ and equality constraints $g^c(x) = b^c$. In the shifted penalty technique, the following function is minimized instead:

$$P(x, \xi', \xi'', \xi, u', u'', v) = -s(f(x), \bar{q}) + \frac{1}{2}\sum_{i=1}^{p'} \xi_i'(\max(0, g_i(x) - y_i^{up} + u_i'))^2 +$$

$$+\frac{1}{2}\sum_{i=p'}^{p''+1} \xi_i''(\max(0, y_i^{lo} - g_i(x) + u_i''))^2 + \frac{1}{2}\sum_{i=p''}^{p+1} \xi(g_i^c(x) - b_i^c + v_i))^2 \quad (29)$$

where ξ', ξ'', ξ are penalty coefficients and u', u'', v are penalty shifts. This function is minimized over x such that $x^{lo} \leq x \leq x^{up}$ while applying conjugate gradient directions, projected on these simple bounds if one of the bounds becomes active. When a minimum of this penalty function with given penalty coefficients and given penalty shifts (the latter are initially equal zero) is found, the violations of all outcome constraints are computed, the penalty shifts and coefficients are modified according to the shifted-increased penalty technique (Wierzbicki, 1984b) and the penalty function is minimized again until the violations of outcome constraints are admissibly small. The results are then equivalent to the outcomes obtained by maximizing the achievement function (26) under all constraints. This technique is according to our experience one of the most robust nonlinear optimization methods.

We omit here the description of the useful standard for defining *substantive models of dynamic nonlinear programming type* that can be obtained by combining the previous cases.

Phase B. The definition of the multiobjective decision analysis problem.

For a given substantive model, the user can define various problems of multiobjective analysis by suitably choosing maximized, minimized, stabilized and guided outcomes. In this phase, he can also define which outcomes and decisions should be displayed to him additionally during interaction with the system (such additional variables are called *floating outcomes*). Since the substantive model is typically prepared by an analyst(s) in the phase A and further phases starting with the phase B must be performed by the final user, an essential aspect of all systems of DIDAS family is the user-friendliness of phase B and further phases; this issue has been variously resolved in consequent variants of DIDAS systems. In all these variants, however, the formulation of the achievement function and its optimization is prepared automatically by the system once phase B is completed.

Before the initial analysis phase, the user should also define some reasonable lower and upper bounds for each optimized (maximized, minimized or stabilized) variable, which results in an automatic definition of reasonable scaling units s_i for these variables.

In further phases of analysis, these scaling units s_i can be further adjusted; this, however, requires an approximation of bounds on efficient solutions.

Phase C. Initial analysis of the multiobjective problem.

Once the multiobjective problem is defined, bounds on efficient solutions can be approximated either automatically or on request of the user.

The 'upper' bound for efficient solutions could be theoretically obtained through maximizing each objective separately (or minimizing, in case of minimized objectives; in the case of stabilized objectives, the user should know their entire attainable range, hence they should be both maximized and minimized). Jointly, the results of such optimization form a point that approximates from 'above' the set of efficient outcomes $\hat{Q}$, but this point almost never (except in degenerate cases) is in itself an attainable outcome; therefore, it is called the *utopia point* $\hat{q}^{uto}$.

However, this way of computing the 'upper' bound for efficient outcomes is not always practical; many systems of DIDAS family use a different way of estimating the utopia point. This way consists in subsequent maximizations of the achievement function $s(q, \bar{q})$ with suitably selected reference points $\bar{q}$. If an objective should be maximized and its maximal value must be estimated, then the corresponding component of the reference point should be very high, while the components of this point for all other maximized objectives should be very low (for minimized objectives, they should be very high; stabilized objectives must be considered as floating in this case, that is, should not enter the achievement function). If an objective should be minimized and its minimal value must be estimated, the corresponding component of the reference point should be very low, while other components of this point are treated as in the previous case. If an objective should be stabilized and both its maximal and minimal values must be estimated, then the achievement function should be maximized twice, first time as if for a maximized objective and the second time as if for a minimized one (while the obtained maximal and minimal values will be denoted by $\hat{q}_i^{uto}$ and $\hat{q}_i^{nad}$, respectively, although it is difficult to say which of them corresponds to the concept of utopia point). Thus, the entire number of optimization runs in utopia point computations is $p'' + 2(p - p'')$. This is especially important in dynamic cases, see further comments. It can be shown that this procedure gives a very good approximation of the utopia point $\hat{q}^{uto}$ in static cases, whereas the precise meaning of very high reference component should be interpreted as the upper bound for the objective minus, say, 0.1% of the distance between the lower and the upper bound, while the meaning of very low is the lower bound plus 0.1% of the distance between the upper and the lower bound.

During all these computations, the 'lower' bound for efficient outcomes can be also estimated, just by recording the lowest efficient outcomes that occur in subsequent optimizations for maximized objectives and the highest ones for minimized objectives (there is no need to record them for stabilized objectives, where the entire attainable range is anyway estimated). However, such a procedure results in the accurate, tight 'lower' bound for efficient outcomes—called *nadir point* $\hat{q}^{nad}$—only if $p'' = 2$; for larger numbers of maximized and minimized objectives, this procedure can give misleading results, while an accurate computation of the nadir point becomes a very cumbersome computational task (see Isermann and Steuer, 1987).

Therefore, some systems of DIDAS family accept user-supplied estimates of "lower" bounds for objectives and, at the same time, offer an option of improving the estimation of the nadir point in such cases. This option consists in additional p'' maximization runs for achievement function $s(q, \bar{q})$ with reference points $\bar{q}$ that are very low, if the objective in question should be maximized, very high for other maximized objectives and very low for other minimized objectives, while stabilized objectives should be considered as floating; if the objective in question should be minimized, the corresponding reference component should be very high, while other reference components should be treated as in the previous case. By recording the lowest efficient outcomes that occur in subsequent optimizations for maximized objectives (and are lower than the previous estimation of nadir component) and the highest ones for minimized objectives (higher that the previous estimation of nadir component), a better estimation $\hat{q}^{nad}$ of the nadir point is obtained.

For dynamic models, the number of objectives becomes formally very high which would imply a very large number of optimization runs—$(p'' + 2(p - p''))(T + 1)$—when estimating the utopia point; however, the user is confronted anyway with p objective trajectories which he can evaluate by 'Gestalt'. Therefore, it is important to obtain approximate bounds on entire trajectories. This can be obtained by $p'' + 2(p - p'')$ optimization runs organized as in the static case, with correspondingly 'very high' and 'very low' reference or aspiration trajectories.

Once the approximate bounds $\hat{q}^{uto}$ and $\hat{q}^{nad}$ are computed and known to the user, they can be utilized in various ways. One way consists in computing a neutral efficient solution, with outcomes situated approximately 'in the middle' of the efficient set. For this purpose, the reference point $\bar{q}$ is situated at the utopia point $\hat{q}^{uto}$ (only for maximized or minimized outcomes; for stabilized outcomes, the reference component $\bar{q}_i$ must be set in the middle of their range estimated earlier) and the scaling units are determined by:

$$s_i = \left| \hat{q}_i^{uto} - \hat{q}_i^{nad} \right|, \qquad 1 \leq i \leq p \tag{30}$$

for all outcomes, including stabilized ones, while the components of the utopia and the nadir points are interpreted respectively as the maximal and the minimal value of such an objective. By maximizing the achievement function $s(q, \bar{q})$ with such data, the neutral efficient solution is obtained and can be utilized by the user as a starting point for further interactive analysis of efficient solutions.

Once the utopia and nadir point are estimated and, optionally, a neutral solution computed and communicated to the user, he has enough information about the ranges of outcomes in the problem to start the main interactive analysis phase.

Phase D. Interactive review of efficient solutions and outcomes.

In this phase, the user controls—by changing reference or aspiration points—the efficient solutions and outcomes computed for him in the system. It is assumed that the user is interested only in efficient solutions and outcomes; if he wants to analyse outcomes that are not efficient for the given definition of the problem, he must change this definition—for example, by putting more objectives in the stabilized or guided category—which, however, necessitates a repetition of phases B, C.

In the interactive analysis phase, an important consideration is that the user should be able to easily influence the selection of the efficient outcomes $\hat{q}$ by changing the reference point $\bar{q}$ in the maximized achievement function $s(q, \bar{q})$. It can be shown (Wierzbicki, 1986) that best suited for the purpose is the choice of scaling units determined by the difference between the slightly displaced utopia point and the current reference point:

$$s_i = \begin{cases} (\hat{q}_i^{uto} - \bar{q}_i + 0.01(\hat{q}_i^{uto} - \hat{q}_i^{nad})), & \text{if} \quad 1 \le i \le p' \\ (\bar{q}_i - \hat{q}_i^{uto} + 0.01(\hat{q}_i^{uto} - \hat{q}_i^{nad})), & \text{if} \quad p' + 1 \le i \le p'' \end{cases} \tag{31a}$$

for maximized or minimized outcomes. For stabilized outcomes, the scaling units are determined then:

$$\left.\begin{aligned} s_i' &= (\hat{q}_i^{uto} - \bar{q}_i + 0.01(\hat{q}_i^{uto} - \hat{q}_i^{nad})) \\ s_i'' &= (\bar{q}_i - \hat{q}_i^{nad} + 0.01(\hat{q}_i^{uto} - \hat{q}_i^{nad})) \end{aligned}\right\}, \quad \text{if} \quad p'' + 1 \le i \le p \tag{31b}$$

It is assumed now that the user selects the reference components in the range $\hat{q}_i^{nad} \le \bar{q}_i \le \hat{q}_i^{uto}$ for maximized and stabilized outcomes or $\hat{q}_i^{uto} \le \bar{q}_i \le \hat{q}_i^{nad}$ for minimized outcomes (if he does not, the system automatically projects the reference component on these ranges). In some DIDAS systems, there is also an option of user-defined weighting coefficients, but the automatic definition of scaling units is sufficient for influencing the selection of efficient outcomes. The interpretation of the above way of setting scaling units is that the user attaches implicitly more importance to reaching a reference component $\bar{q}_i$ if he places it close to the known utopia component; in such a case, the corresponding scaling unit becomes smaller and the corresponding objective component is weighted stronger in the achievement function $s(q, \bar{q})$. Thus, this way of *scaling relative to utopia-reference difference* is taking into account the implicit information given by the user in the relative position of the reference point. This way of scaling, used also in (Nakayama and Sawaragi, 1983, Steuer and Choo, 1983), is implemented only in recent versions of systems of DIDAS family, especially in versions for nonlinear models.

When the relative scaling is applied, the user can easily obtain—by suitably moving reference points—efficient outcomes that are either situated close to the neutral solution, in the middle of efficient outcome set $\hat{Q}_0$, or in some remote parts of the set $\hat{Q}_0$, say, close to various extreme solutions. Typically, several experiments of computing such efficient outcomes give enough information for the user to select an actual decision—either some efficient decision suggested by the system, or even a different one, since even the best substantive model cannot encompass all aspects of a decision situation. However, there might be some cases in which the user would like to receive further support—either in analysing the sensitivity of a selected efficient outcome, or in converging to some best preferred solution and outcome.

Phase E. Sensitivity analysis and convergence.

For analysing the sensitivity of an efficient solution to changes in the proportions of outcomes, a *multidimensional scan* of efficient solutions is implemented in some systems of DIDAS family. This operation consists in selecting an efficient outcome, accepting it as a base $\bar{q}^{bas}$ for reference points, and performing p'' additional optimization runs with the reference points determined by:

$$\bar{q}_j = \bar{q}_j^{bas} + \beta(\hat{q}_j^{uto} - \hat{q}_j^{nad}), \tag{32}$$

$$\bar{q}_i = \bar{q}_i^{bas}, \qquad i \neq j, \qquad 1 \leq j \leq p'',$$

where β is a coefficient determined by the user, $-1 \leq \beta \leq 1$; if the relative scaling is used and the reference components determined by (32) are outside the range $\hat{q}_j^{nad}$, $\hat{q}_j^{uto}$, they are projected automatically on this range. The reference components for stabilized outcomes are not perturbed in this operation (if the user wishes to perturb them, he might include them, say, in the maximized category). The efficient outcomes resulting from the maximization of the achievement function $s(q, \bar{q})$ with such perturbed reference points are typically also perturbed mostly along their subsequent components, although other their components might also change.

For analysing the sensitivity of an efficient solution when moving along a direction in the outcome space—and also as a help in converging to a most preferred solution—a *directional scan* of efficient outcomes can be implemented in systems of DIDAS family. This operation consists again in selecting an efficient outcome, accepting it as a base $\bar{q}^{bas}$ for reference points, selecting another reference point $\bar{q}$, and performing a user-specified number K of additional optimizations with reference points determined by:

$$\bar{q}(k) = \bar{q}^{bas} + \frac{k}{K}(\bar{q} - \bar{q}^{bas}), \qquad 1 \leq k \leq K \tag{33}$$

The efficient solutions $\hat{q}(k)$ obtained through maximizing the achievement function $s(q, \bar{q}(k))$ with such reference points constitute a cut through the efficient set $\hat{Q}_0$ when moving approximately in the direction $\bar{q} - \bar{q}^{bas}$. If the user selects one of these efficient solutions, accepts as a new $\bar{q}^{bas}$ and performs next directional scans along some new directions of improvement, he can converge eventually to his most preferred solution—see (Korhonen and Laakso, 1986). Even if he does not wish the help in such convergence, directional scans can give him valuable information.

Another possible way of helping in convergence to the most preferred solution is choosing reference points as in (33) but using a harmonically decreasing sequence of coefficients (such as $1/j$, where j is the iteration number) instead of user-selected coefficients k/K. This results in convergence even if the user makes stochastic errors in determining next directions of improvement of reference points, or even if he is not sure about his preferences and learns about them during this analysis, see (Michalevich, 1986). Such a convergence is rather slow and, after initial experiments, has not been yet implemented in systems of DIDAS family. Yet another approach for selecting successive reference points which ensures convergence and is relevant to decision maker's behaviour has been recently proposed by Bogetoft at all. (1988).

4 Review of various implementations of systems of DIDAS family

There exist a number of various implementations of systems of DIDAS family. An early, prototype linear version was developed by Kalio, Lewandowski and Orchard-Hays (1980). This version utilized professional LP package SESAME available only on the IBM–370 mainframe computers, therefore it was not transferable. The user interface was rather poor and the usage of the system was limited to its authors and their collaborators.

The second, also linear, version of DIDAS family systems was developed by Lewandowski (1982). It was designed as pre- and postprocessor programs to a commercial LP package with standard MPSX input and output. Due to such design, it was easily transferable and many practical problems were solved using it on various computers. The main drawback of this system was that the interface between pre- and postprocessor and a the LP solver was based on reading and writing disk files, which was very time consuming for larger problems. An interaction with the user was very simple but inconvenient because of long time responses of the system transferring large amount of data.

The design goal of the next version of DIDAS was to eliminate, if possible, disk transfers and changes of data structures inside the system. It was done by Kreglewski and Lewandowski (1983) as a interactive multicriteria extension of MINOS linear programming system (Murtagh and Saunders, 1977); the reference point concepts were implemented accessing MINOS internal data structures. The user interface was redesigned and many new options added. However, the portability problems arose again: MINOS is not easily transferable.

The reference point approach was explored also by many others collaborating authors. A DIDAS/N system developed by Grauer and Kaden (1984) was the first published nonlinear version of such a system. It was based on MINOS/Augmented (Murtagh and Saunders, 1980) nonlinear programming system, an extended version of linear MINOS. Unfortunately, this solver is not robust and efficient enough for realistic nonlinear programming problems. Moreover, the user interface in the DIDAS/N system was rather complicated, hence applications of this system were rather limited. Later, Kaden and Kreglewski (1986) developed another version of nonlinear DIDAS system. Earlier versions of DIDAS were also adapted for special purposes by Strubegger and Messner (Strubegger, 1985, Messner, 1985).

Lewandowski and Kreglewski (1985) developed another, general purpose nonlinear version of DIDAS system. It was based on a solver from Modular System for Nonlinear Programming (Kreglewski et al., 1984) and written completely in FORTRAN, hence easily transferable to arbitrary computer. The user interface was reasonably simple, but preparation of data for the system was not quite straightforward.

The experiences of these developments led in 1985 to two new linear versions: DIDAS-MM and DIDAS-MZ. DIDAS-MM was a further development of the version with MINOS solver, with extended interactive features, special editor for dynamic linear models and graphic features. DIDAS-MZ is based on a linear programming solver from IMSL library which is widely accessible; therefore, DIDAS-MZ is much easier transferable.

In 1986, a new generation of DIDAS family systems was initiated, designed for work on IBM-PC-XT and compatible computers. These are: IAC-DIDAS-L1 and -L2 as well as IAC-DIDAS-N, described in other papers of this volume.

5 Applications of systems of DIDAS family

The first implementation (Kallio et al., 1980) of systems of DIDAS family was devoted to the application in forecasting and planning of the development of Finish forestry and forest industry sectors, based on a substantive model of linear dynamic type. Later, another version of DIDAS systems was applied (Grauer et al., 1982) to planning of energy supply strategies, which led to other applications in the analysis of future energy-economy relations in Austria (Strubegger, 1985) and of future gas trade in Europe (Messner, 1985).

Parallely, applications to forecasting and planning agricultural production in Poland (Makowski and Sosnowski, 1984), to regional investment allocation in Hungary (Majchrzak, 1982), to chemical industry planning (Gorecki et al., 1983) have been initiated. A special version of linear dynamic DIDAS was adapted to flood control problems (Lewandowski et al., 1984b). A nonlinear version of DIDAS was first applied to issues of macroeconomic planning (Grauer and Zalai, 1982); later applications of other nonlinear versions include problems of environmental protection of ground water quality (Kaden and Kreglewski, 1986).

Further applications of DIDAS family systems are reported in other papers in this volume.

6 References

Axelrod, R. (1985). The Evolution of Cooperation. Basic Books, New York, 1985.

Bogetoft, P., A. Hallefjord and M. Kok (1988). On the convergence of reference point methods in multiobjective programming. *European Journal of Operational Research*, Vol. 34, pp. 56–58.

Charnes and Cooper (1975). Goal programming and multiple objective optimization, J. Oper. Res. Soc. 1, pp. 39–54, 1975.

Dreyfus, S.E. (1984). Beyond rationality. In M. Grauer, M. Thompson, A.P. Wierzbicki, editors: Plural Rationality and Interactive Decision Processes, Proceedings, Sopron 1984, Springer Verlag, Berlin.

Fishburn, P.C. (1964). Decision and Value Theory. Wiley, New York, 1964.

Galbraith, J.K. (1967). The New Industrial State, Houghton-Mifflin, Boston, 1967.

Glushkov, V.M. (1972). Basic principles of automation in organizational management systems (in Russian), *Upravlayushcheye Sistemy i Mashiny*, 1, 1972.

Gorecki, H., J. Kopytowski, T. Rys and M. Zebrowski (1983). A multiobjective procedure for project formulation—design of a chemical installation. In M. Grauer and A.P. Wierzbicki, editors: Interactive Decision Analysis, Springer Verlag, Berlin, 1983.

Grauer, M. and S. Kaden (1984). A Nonlinear Dynamic Interactive Decision Analysis and Support System (DIDAS/N) Users Guide, WP-84-23, International Institute for Applied Systems Analysis, Laxenburg, Austria, 1984.

Grauer, M., A. Lewandowski and L. Schrattenholzer (1982). Use of the reference level approach for the generation of efficient energy supply strategies. WP-82-19, International Institute for Applied Systems Analysis, Laxenburg, Austria, 1982.

Grauer, M., A. Lewandowski and A.P. Wierzbicki (1983). DIDAS—theory, implementation and experience. In M. Grauer and A.P. Wierzbicki, editors: Interactive Decision Analysis, Springer Verlag, Berlin, 1983.

Grauer, M. and E. Zalai (1982). A Reference Point Approach to Nonlinear Macroeconomic Planning, WP-82-134, International Institute for Applied Systems Analysis, Laxenburg, Austria, 1982.

Ignizio, J.P. (1978). Goal programming—a tool for multiobjective analysis. *Journal for Operational Research*, 29, pp. 1109–1119, 1978.

Isermann, H. and R. E. Steuer (1987). Computational experience concerning payoff tables and minimum criterion values over the efficient set. *European Journal of Operational Research*, Vol. 33, pp. 91–97.

Kaden, S. and T. Kreglewski (1986). Decision support system MINE—problem solver for nonlinear multi-criteria analysis. CP-86-5, International Institute for Applied Systems Analysis, Laxenburg, Austria, 1986.

Kallio, M., A. Lewandowski and W. Orchard-Hays (1980). An implementation of the reference point approach for multiobjective optimization. WP-80-35, International Institute for Applied Systems Analysis, Laxenburg, Austria, 1980.

Keeney, R.L. and H. Raiffa (1976). Decisions with Multiple Objectives: Preferences and Value Trade-offs. Wiley, New York, 1976.

Korhonen, P. and J. Laakso (1986). Solving a generalized goal programming approaches using a visual interactive approach. *European Journal of Operational Research*, 26, pp. 355–363, 1986.

Kreglewski, T. and A. Lewandowski (1983). MM-MINOS—an integrated interactive decision support system. CP-83-63, International Institute for Applied Systems Analysis, Laxenburg, Austria, 1983.

Kreglewski, T., T. Rogowski, A. Ruszczynski, J. Szymanowski (1984). Optimization methods in FORTRAN, PWN, Warsaw, 1984 (in Polish).

Lewandowski, A. (1982). A Program Package for Linear Multiple Criteria Reference Point Optimization—Short User Manual, WP-82-80, International Institute for Applied Systems Analysis, Laxenburg, Austria, 1982.

Lewandowski, A. and M. Grauer (1982). The reference point approach—methods of efficient implementation. WP-82-26, International Institute for Applied Systems Analysis, Laxenburg, Austria, 1982.

Lewandowski, A., S. Johnson and A.P. Wierzbicki (1986). A Selection Committee Decision Support System: Implementation, Tutorial Example and Users Manual. International Institute for Applied Systems Analysis, Laxenburg, Austria, 1986; presented also at the MCDM Conference in Kyoto, Japan, August 1986.

Lewandowski, A. and T. Kreglewski (1985). A nonlinear version of DIDAS system, Collaborative volume: Theory, Software and Test Examples for Decision Support Systems, International Institute for Applied Systems Analysis, Laxenburg, Austria, 1985.

Lewandowski, A., T. Rogowski and T. Kreglewski (1984a). A trajectory-oriented extension of DIDAS and its applications. In M. Grauer, M. Thompson, A.P. Wierzbicki, editors: Plural Rationality and Interactive Decision Processes, Proceedings, Sopron 1984, Springer Verlag, Berlin.

Lewandowski, A., T. Rogowski and T. Kreglewski (1984b). Application of DIDAS methodology to flood control problems—numerical experiments. In M. Grauer, M. Thompson, A.P. Wierzbicki, editors: Plural Rationality and Interactive Decision Processes, Proceedings, Sopron 1984, Springer Verlag, Berlin.

Majchrzak, J. (1982). The implementation of the multicriteria reference point optimization approach to the Hungarian regional investment allocation model, WP-81-154, International Institute for Applied Systems Analysis, Laxenburg, Austria, 1982.

Makowski, M. and J. Sosnowski (1984). A decision support system for planning and controlling agricultural production with a decentralized management structure. In M. Grauer, M. Thompson, A.P. Wierzbicki, editors: Plural Rationality and Interactive Decision Processes, Proceedings, Sopron 1984, Springer Verlag, Berlin.

Messner, S. (1985). Natural gas trade in Europe and interactive decision analysis, In G. Fandel, M. Grauer, A. Kurzanski and A.P. Wierzbicki, eds., Large-Scale Modelling and Interactive Decision Analysis, Proceedings Eisenach, Springer Verlag, Berlin, 1985.

Michalevich, M.V. (1986). Stochastic approaches to interactive multicriteria optimization problems, WP-86-10, International Institute for Applied Systems Analysis, Laxenburg, Austria, 1986.

Murtagh, B.A. and M.A. Saunders (1977). MINOS User's Guide, Technical Report, SOL-77-9, Systems Optimization Laboratory, Stanford University, 1977.

Murtagh, B.A. and M.A. Saunders (1980). MINOS/Augmented, Technical Report, SOl-80-14, Systems Optimization Laboratory, Stanford University, 1980.

Naisbitt, J. (1982). Megatrends: Ten New Directions Transforming our Lives. Warner Books, New York, 1982.

Nakayama, H. and Y. Sawaragi (1983). Satisficing trade-off method for multiobjective programming. In M. Grauer and A.P. Wierzbicki, editors: Interactive Decision Analysis, Springer Verlag, Berlin, 1983.

Pospelov, G.S. and V.A. Irikov (1976). Program- and Goal-Oriented Planning and Management (in Russian), *Sovietskoye Radio*, Moscow, 1976.

Rappoport, A. (1985). Uses of experimental games. In M. Grauer, M. Thompson and A.P. Wierzbicki, editors: Plural Rationality and Interactive Decision Analysis, Springer Verlag, Berlin, 1985.

Sakawa, M. (1983). Interactive fuzzy decision making for multiobjective nonlinear programming problems. In M. Grauer and A.P. Wierzbicki, editors: Interactive Decision Analysis, Springer Verlag, Berlin, 1983.

Sawaragi, Y., H. Nakayama and T. Tanino (1985). Theory of Multiobjective Optimization, Academic Press, New York, 1985.

Simon, H.A. (1957). Models of Man. Macmillan, New York, 1957.

Simon, H.A. (1958). Administrative Behaviour. MacMillan, New York, 1958.

Steuer, R. and E.V. Choo (1983). An interactive weighted Chebyshev procedure for multiple objective programming. *Mathematical Programming*, 26, pp. 326–344, 1983.

Strubegger, M. (1985). An approach for integrated energy-economy decision analysis: the case of Austria. In G. Fandel, M. Grauer, A. Kurzanski and A.P. Wierzbicki, eds., Large-Scale Modelling and Interactive Decision Analysis, Proceedings Eisenach, Springer Verlag, Berlin, 1985.

Umpleby, S.A. (1983). A group process approach to organizational change. In H. Wedde, ed., Adequate Modelling of Systems, Springer Verlag, Berlin, 1983.

Van Hee, K. (1986). Operations research and artificial intelligence approaches to decision support systems. International Seminar: New Advances in Decision Support Systems, International Institute for Applied Systems Analysis, Laxenburg, Austria, 1986.

Wierzbicki, A.P. (1975). Penalty methods in solving optimization problems with vector performance criteria. VI Congress of IFAC, Boston 1975.

Wierzbicki, A.P. (1977). Basic properties of scalarizing functionals for multiobjective optimization. *Mathematische Operationsforschung und Statistik*, Ser. Optimization 8, Nr 1, 1977.

Wierzbicki, A.P. (1980). The use of reference objectives in multiobjective optimization. In G. Fandel and T. Gal, eds., Multiple Criteria Decision Making, Theory and Applications, Springer Verlag, Heidelberg 1980.

Wierzbicki, A.P. (1982). A mathematical basis for satisficing decision making. *Mathematical Modelling*, 3, pp. 391–405, 1982.

Wierzbicki, A.P. (1984a). Negotiation and mediation in conflicts, II: Plural rationality and interactive decision processes. In M. Grauer, M. Thompson, A.P. Wierzbicki, editors: Plural Rationality and Interactive Decision Processes, Proceedings, Sopron 1984, Springer Verlag, Berlin.

Wierzbicki, A.P. (1984b). Models and Sensitivity of Control Systems, Elsevier, Amsterdam, 1984.

Wierzbicki, A.P. (1986). On the completeness and constructiveness of parametric characterizations to vector optimization problems. *OR-Spektrum*, 8, pp. 73–87, 1986.

Modern Techniques for Linear Dynamic and Stochastic Programs

Andrzej Ruszczynski

Institute of Automatic Control, Warsaw University of Technology.

Abstract

We discuss methods for specializing general linear programming techniques to dynamic and stochastic problems: data structures, basis management and pricing strategies. Next we present two nonstandard techniques: regularized decomposition and feasible direction methods.

1 Introduction

In the last three decades, the theory and computational methods of linear programming developed into a powerful tool for analysing linear models of economic planning and control. Modern linear programming packages (see, e.g., Marsten, 1981, Murtagh and Saunders, 1984) are capable of solving problems with thousands of variables and constraints. Still, linear programming as the area of research is far from being closed. On the one hand, the practice poses new large and complex problems which result from the tendency to describe more and more complex objects of decision making by mathematical models. On the other hand, the trends in modern computer and information technology create a demand for user-friendly decision support systems with an intimate interaction between the decision maker and the computer. The computer is often just a personal computer and this implies very specific requirements from the optimization software involved in such systems: it should be capable of solving large models, fast, use computer resources in an economic way, and it should allow for easy changes in the model.

A detailed discussion of all these issues goes far beyond the scope of this paper. We shall focus our attention here on two main sources of large scale linear models arising in decision making: dynamic structure and stochasticity. We shall discuss the ways in which general linear programming techniques can be specialized for these models to meet some of the computational goals pointed out above. Next, we shall present two nonstandard techniques which appear to be particularly useful for the problems in question.

2 Dynamic structure and stochasticity as sources of large linear models

It is well known that every linear optimization problem can be equivalently expressed in the following form

$$\begin{aligned}&\textit{minimize}\quad c^T x\\&\textit{subject to}\\&Ax = b, \qquad x^{min} \le x \le x^{max},\end{aligned} \tag{1}$$

where x is the vector of activities (including slack/surplus variables), c is a vector of cost coefficients associated with these activities, A is a technology matrix, and b is a vector of resources or demands, which impose conditions on the admissible activities x. In real-life large scale models, the dimension of x (the number of columns of A) and the dimension of b (the number of rows of A) may go into thousands. On the other hand, it is typical that each resource or demand condition (a row of $Ax = b$) involves only few activities and each activity appears in only a relatively small number of conditions. As a result, the constraint matrix A in (1) is usually sparse: most of its entries are zeros. In fact, all modern linear programming codes make use of this feature and contain very sophisticated techniques for storing and factorizing sparse matrices, solving equations with them, and updating the factorization when the data change (see Forrest and Tomlin, 1972, Reid, 1982).

However, there exist important classes of problems in which sparsity alone is not the only feature of the constraint matrix. One of these classes are *linear dynamic-structured problems*, in other words—*linear control problems*. In the simplest formulation of such a problem the variables (activities) are related to time stages $t = 0, 1, 2, \ldots, T$. At each stage t, we deal with two groups of variables: *state variables* s_t and *control variables* u_t. The variables from the neighboring periods are related through the *state equation*

$$s_{t+1} = Gs_t + Ku_t + b_t, \qquad t = 0, 1, 2, \ldots, T-1, \tag{2}$$

where G and K are some matrices of appropriate dimensions and b_t are some known vectors. Let the initial state s_0 be fixed and let the objective function be defined by

$$f(u, s) = \sum_{t=0}^{T-1} (q_t^T u_t + c_{t+1}^T s_{t+1}). \tag{3}$$

Assuming that the only additional constraints on the state and control variables are simple lower and upper bounds

$$s_t^{min} \le s_t \le s_t^{max}, \qquad t = 1, 2, \ldots, T, \tag{4}$$

$$u_t^{min} \le u_t \le u_t^{max}, \qquad t = 1, 2, \ldots, T-1, \tag{5}$$

we can easily write our problem in form (1) with

$$\begin{aligned}x &= (u_0, s_1, u_1, s_2, \ldots, u_{T-1}, s_T),\\c &= (q_0, c_1, q_1, c_2, \ldots, q_{T-1}, c_T),\\b &= (b_0, b_1, \ldots, b_{T-1}),\end{aligned} \tag{6}$$

and

$$A = \begin{bmatrix} -K & I & & & & & & & \\ & -G & -K & I & & & & & \\ & & & -G & -K & I & & & \\ & & & & & & \cdots & & \\ & & & & & & -G & -K & I \end{bmatrix} \tag{7}$$

We see that the numbers of rows and columns of A increase proportionally to the number of periods T, and even for relatively small dimensions of the activities related to a single period the whole problem may have a remarkable size. On the other hand, the matrix (7) is not only sparse, but has a very regular *staircase* structure with multiple occurrence of the same (usually also sparse) matrices G, K and I. We have to take advantage of this if we aim at solving dynamic problems of realistic dimensions.

Let us now pass on to the second class of problems which are of special interest for us. Let us assume that some of the entries of the technology matrix A and the right-hand side b in the linear model (1) are uncertain and that this uncertainty is crucial for the decision making. One of possible modelling approaches to such a situation (see, e.g., Kall et al., 1979) is to assume that A and b are random and may attain one of finite many realizations with some known probabilities:

$$\begin{array}{lll} (A_1, b_1) & \textit{with probability} & p_1 > 0, \\ (A_2, b_2) & \textit{with probability} & p_2 > 0, \\ \dots & & \\ (A_L, b_L) & \textit{with probability} & p_L > 0, \end{array} \tag{8}$$

where $\sum_{l=1}^{L} p_l = 1$. Under these circumstances, however, it is in general no longer possible that the decision x satisfies the constraints $A_l x = b_l$ for all realizations $l = 1, 2, \dots, L$. Therefore, we have to extend our model by introducing some corrective activities y_l associated with the realizations $l = 1, 2, \dots, L$, which compensate the discrepancy $b_l - A_l x$. If we describe our capabilities of correction by a matrix W and assign to y_l the cost vector q and the bounds y^{min} and y^{max}, the correction problem will take the form

$$\begin{array}{l} \textit{minimize} \quad q^T y \\ \textit{subject to} \\ W y_l = b_l - A_l x, \qquad y^{min} \le y \le y^{max}. \end{array} \tag{9}$$

Our aim is now to find such a decision x that makes the correction always possible and minimizes the sum of the direct cost $c^T x$ and the expected future correction cost $\sum_{l=1}^{L} p_l q^T y_l$. The whole problem can be again written as a large scale linear model:

$$\textit{minimize} \quad c^T x \ + p_1 q^T y_1 \ + p_2 q^T y_2 \ + \ \cdots \ + p_L q^T y_L$$

subject to

$$\begin{array}{llllll} A_1x & +Wy_1 & & & & = b_1 \\ A_2x & & +Wy_2 & & & = b_2 \\ \cdots & \cdots & \cdots & \cdots & \cdots & \cdots \\ A_Lx & & & & +Wy_L & = b_L \end{array} \tag{10}$$

$$x^{min} \leq x \leq x^{max}$$
$$y^{min} \leq y_l \leq y^{max}, \qquad l = 1, 2, \ldots, L$$

The constraint matrix of (10),

$$A = \begin{bmatrix} A_1 & W & & & \\ A_2 & & W & & \\ \cdots & \cdots & \cdots & \cdots & \cdots \\ A_L & & & & W \end{bmatrix} \tag{11}$$

has the size proportional to the number L of realizations taken into account, which leads to very large problems already for underlying deterministic models of medium size. Still, similarly to the dynamic case, A is not only sparse but has a very regular (so-called *dual angular*) structure, with multiple occurrence of the correction matrix W and some similarities of the realizations $A_1, A_2, \ldots, A_L$. It is intuitively clear that we have to take advantage of this feature in a method for solving such problems.

3 Specialized versions of the simplex method

When dealing with special classes of problems for which general efficient techniques already exist, it is a natural direction of research to investigate the possibility of exploiting the features of these special problems within the general approach. So, we shall discuss here some most promising specializations of the acknowledged method of linear programming, the *primal simplex method*, for the two classes in question: dynamic and stochastic problems.

In the primal simplex method the constraint matrix A in (1) is split into a square nonsingular *basis matrix* B and a matrix N containing all the remaining columns of A, not included into B. This implies division of the activities x into *basic variables* x_B and *nonbasic variables* x_N. At each iteration of the method the nonbasic variables are fixed on their lower or upper bounds, and the values of the basic variables are given by

$$x_B = B^{-1}(b - Nx_N). \tag{12}$$

We always choose basis matrices B so that

$$x_B^{min} \leq x_B \leq x_B^{max}, \tag{13}$$

where x_B^{min} and x_B^{max} are subvectors of x^{min} and x^{max} implied by the splitting of x into x_B and x_N. Such an x is called a *basic feasible solution*, and at each iteration we try to find a better basic feasible solution by performing the following steps.

Step 1. Find the price vector π by solving

$$\pi^T B = c_B^T, \tag{14}$$

where c_B is the subvector of c associated with x_B .

Step 2. Price out the nonbasic columns a_j of A (i.e. columns of N) by calculating

$$z_j = c_j - \pi^T a_j \tag{15}$$

until a column a_s is found for which $z_s < 0$ and $x_s = x_s^{min}$, or $z_s > 0$ and $x_s = x_s^{max}$.

Step 3. Find the direction of changes of basic variables d_B by solving

$$Bd_B = a_s. \tag{16}$$

Step 4. Determine from $x_B^{min}, x_B^{max}, x_B$ and d_B the basic variable x_{B_r} which first achieves its bound when x_s changes. If x_s hits its opposite bound earlier, change x_s and go to Step 2.

Step 5. Replace the r-th column of B with a_s and x_{B_r} by x_s and calculate values of the new basic variables from (12).

This general strategy can be deeply specialized to account for the features of problems under consideration. These improvements can be divided into three groups:

a) representation of the problem data, i.e. the way in which the matrix A is stored and its columns a_j recovered for the purpose of Step 2;

b) techniques for solving equations (12), (14) and (16), which includes special methods for factorizing the basis matrix B and updating this factorization;

c) pricing strategies, i.e. methods for selecting nonbasic columns a_j at Step 2 to be priced out for testing whether they could be included into B at the current iteration.

Let us discuss these issues in more detail.

Problem data structures

The repeated occurrence of the matrices G, K and I in the constraint matrix (7) of the dynamic model suggests a generalization of the concept of *supersparsity* employed in large linear programming systems (Bisschop and Meeraus, 1980). It is sufficient to store the matrices G and K as files of packed columns (G and K may be sparse themselves). Any time a specific column a_j of A is needed, we can easily calculate from its number j and from the dimensions of activities related to a single period which column of $-K$ or of $\begin{bmatrix} I \\ -G \end{bmatrix}$ and on which position will appear in a_j. Thus the problem data can be compressed in this case to the size of one period and easily stored in the operating memory of the computer, even for very large problems. In a nonstationary problem, where some of the entries of K and G depend on t, we can still store in this way all the stationary data, and keep an additional file of time-dependent entries. The recovery of a column of A would then be slightly more complicated, with a correction to account for the nonstationary entries, but still relatively easy to accomplish. Storage savings would be still significant, because we have grounds to expect that only some entries of A change in time.

The same argument applies to the constraint matrix (11) of the stochastic problem. It is sufficient to store the realizations $A_1, A_2, \ldots, A_L$ and W to reconstruct columns of A, if necessary. But we can go here a little deeper, noting that in practical problems it is unlikely that all the entries of the technology matrix are random. If only some of them are stochastic, many entries of $A_1, A_2, \ldots, A_L$ will have identical values and our problem data structure will still suffer from a considerable redundancy. Thus, we can further compress the structure, as it was done in (Ruszczynski, 1985): we represent each A as

$$A_l = A^0 + \Delta_l$$

where A^0 contains as nonzeros only the deterministic entries of A_l , and Δ_l contains as only nonzeros the l-th realization of the random entries. Therefore it is sufficient to store the nonzeros of A^0 together with its sparsity pattern, the sparsity pattern of the random entries (which is common for all Δ_l), and the nonzeros of Δ_l, $l = 1, 2, \ldots, L$. This structure will only slightly exceed the storage requirements of the underlying deterministic model.

Representation of the basis inverse

It is clear that for constraint matrices of form (7) or (11) the basis matrices B inherit their structure. Although general techniques for factorizing sparse matrices (see, e.g., Forrest and Tomlin, 1972, Reid, 1982, Toczylowski, 1984) are in principle able to cope with such bases, there is still room to exploit their structure within the factorization and updating algorithms.

Let us at first discuss this matter on the simple control problem with the constraint matrix (7). Assuming that all the state vectors $s_1, s_2, \ldots, s_T$ are basic, we obtain the following form of the basis matrix

$$B_0 = \begin{bmatrix} I & & & & & \\ -G & I & & & & \\ & -G & I & & & \\ \cdots & \cdots & \cdots & \cdots & \cdots & \cdots \\ & & & & I & \\ & & & & -G & I \end{bmatrix} \tag{17}$$

B_0 is lower triangular and the equations involving B_0 or B_0^T can be simply solved by substitution. To solve $B_0 d = a$, we partition d into $(d_1, d_2, \ldots, d_T)$ and a into $(a_0, a_1, \ldots, a_{T-1})$ according to the periods, and solve the state equations

$$d_{t+1} = G d_t + a_t, \qquad t = 0, 1, \ldots, T-1 \tag{18}$$

with $d_0 = 0$. Noting that in (15) we have $a_t = 0$ for $t < \tau$ we can start simulation in (18) from τ. To solve $\pi^T B_0 = c$ we need only to back-substitute in the *adjoint equations*

$$\pi_t = G^T \pi_{t+1} + c_t, \qquad t = T, T-1, \ldots, 1 \tag{19}$$

with $\pi_{T+1} = 0$. Again, noting that c_B in (14) changes only on one position from iteration to iteration, we can start the simulation in (19) from the position at which the change occurred.

In general, the basis matrix is not so simple as (17) and some controls are basic, while some state variables are nonbasic. The basis matrix is still staircase, but the blocks on the diagonal (which in (17) are all I) are not necessarily square and invertible:

$$B_0 = \begin{bmatrix} -K_1 & J_1 & & & & & & \\ & -G_1 & -K_2 & J_2 & & & & \\ & & & -G_2 & & & & \\ \cdots & \cdots & \cdots & \cdots & \cdots & \cdots & \cdots & \cdots \\ & & & & & -G_{T-1} & -K_T & J_T \end{bmatrix} \tag{20}$$

where $J_1, J_2, \ldots, J_T$ are some submatrices of I; $K_1, K_2, \ldots, K_T$ are submatrices of K and $G_1, G_2, \ldots, G_{T-1}$ are submatrices of G. A factorization of B is necessary to represent it in a form suitable for solving equations with B and B^T and for corrections when a column of B is exchanged.

We can of course specialize the elimination procedures of (Forrest and Tomlin, 1972) or (Reid, 1982), because we exactly know where to look for nonzeros in particular rows and columns of B. This idea of blockwise elimination has been analysed in (Kallio and Porteus, 1977, Propoi and Krivonozhko, 1978, Wets, 1986). There is, however, a more promising global approach which aims at exploiting features similar to those that led from (17) to equations (18) and (19). Namely, we would like to transform somehow B to a staircase matrix

$$\tilde{B} = \begin{bmatrix} \tilde{B}_{11} & & & & & \\ \tilde{B}_{21} & \tilde{B}_{22} & & & & \\ & \tilde{B}_{32} & \tilde{B}_{33} & & & \\ \cdots & \cdots & \cdots & \cdots & \cdots & \cdots \\ & & & & \tilde{B}_{T-1,T} & \tilde{B}_{T,T} \end{bmatrix} \tag{21}$$

having the diagonal blocks $\tilde{B}_{tt}$ square and nonsingular. Solving equations with $\tilde{B}$ would be almost as simple as with B_0 and would require only inversion of $\tilde{B}_{tt}$, $t = 1, 2, \ldots, T$.

In (Perold and Dantzig, 1979) the pass from B to $\tilde{B}$ is achieved by representing

$$B = \tilde{B}F \tag{22}$$

with F chosen in such a way that $\tilde{B}$ inherits as many columns of B as possible. In particular, all the state columns of B will appear in $\tilde{B}$, so that the diagonal blocks $\tilde{B}_{tt}$ will have large parts common with the identity and will be easy to invert. Moreover, F has also a very special structure

$$F = \begin{bmatrix} D & \\ E & I \end{bmatrix} \tag{23}$$

with D square, invertible, and of relatively low size. Solving the equations with B or B^T resolves now itself to the factorization of $\tilde{B}_{tt}$ (which is easy) and factorization of D (see Perold and Dantzig, 1979). Updating the factors is rather involved, unfortunately.

Another approach has been suggested in (Bisschop and Meeraus, 1980). Since B_0 is particularly easy to invert, we aim at using B_0 as $\tilde{B}$. We do not construct factors as in (22) but rather add new rows and columns to B_0 and work with a larger matrix

$$\hat{B} = \begin{bmatrix} B_0 & U \\ V & \end{bmatrix} \tag{24}$$

Here U contains columns which are in B but not in B_0, and V contains units in columns which are in B_0 but not in B, to explicitly nullify the variables corresponding to these columns. The solution to

$$B \begin{bmatrix} s_B \\ u_B \end{bmatrix} = a \tag{25}$$

can be now computed by

$$u_B = (VB_0^{-1}U)^{-1}VB_0^{-1}a, \tag{26}$$

$$s = B_0^{-1}(a - Uu_B). \tag{27}$$

Thus we need only to solve equations with B_0, which is particularly simple, and to factorize the matrix $VB_0^{-1}U$, which is of much smaller size than B. Similar formulae can be derived for the backward transformation (14). Application of this approach to dynamic and stochastic programs is discussed in detail in (Gondzio and Ruszczynski, 1988).

Let us now pass to the stochastic problem (10). Supposing that the basis contains only the correction activities, its form is particularly simple

$$B_0 = \begin{bmatrix} W_1 & & & \\ & W_2 & & \\ & & \cdots & \\ & & & W_L \end{bmatrix} \tag{28}$$

where W_l, $l = 1, 2, \ldots, L$ are square nonsingular submatrices of W. The inversion of B_0 resolves now itself to the inversion of $W_1, W_2, \ldots, W_L$, which can be done independently. We can also exploit here some similarities between the W's (common columns) to further simplify their inversion (see the bunching procedure discussed for other purposes in Wets, 1986).

In general, however, the basis matrix will be of the form

$$B = \begin{bmatrix} \tilde{A}_1 & \tilde{W}_1 & & & \\ \tilde{A}_2 & & \tilde{W}_2 & & \\ \cdots & \cdots & \cdots & \cdots & \cdots \\ \tilde{A}_L & & & & \tilde{W}_L \end{bmatrix} \tag{29}$$

with the blocks $\tilde{W}_l$, $l = 1, 2, \ldots, L$, not necessarily square and nonsingular. Again, we would like to transform B into a form more suitable for inversion. At the first sight, since B is lower block triangular, both approaches discussed for the dynamic problem are applicable here. We can aim at obtaining factors as in (22) with a $\tilde{B}$ of dual angular structure having invertible diagonal blocks. We can also apply a method based on the formulae (26)–(27) and work with a matrix of form (24).

The relation with the dynamic model, however, follows from rather superficial algebraic similarity of the problem matrices (lower block triangular structure). In fact, in the dynamic model we deal with a phenomenon that evolves in time, whereas the stochastic model describes a phenomenon spread in space. Thus, while we had grounds to assume that many state variables will be basic in the dynamic model (which implied the choice of B_0), we cannot claim the same with respect to the correction activities in the stochastic model and specify in advance some of them to be included into W. Therefore, the approach of (Bisschop and Meeraus, 1980) must be slightly modified here. Instead of working with B, we would prefer to operate on a larger matrix

$$\hat{B} = \begin{bmatrix} W & & & & \tilde{A}_1 \\ J_1 & & & & \\ & W & & & \tilde{A}_2 \\ & J_2 & & & \\ \cdots & \cdots & \cdots & \cdots & \cdots \\ & & & W & \tilde{A}_L \\ & & & J_L & \\ V_1 & & & & \\ & V_2 & & & \\ \cdots & \cdots & \cdots & \cdots & \cdots \\ & & & V_L & \end{bmatrix} \tag{30}$$

in which some of the rows of the matrix V, which are used to nullify the nonbasic correction activities, are added to W to make the diagonal blocks $\begin{bmatrix} W \\ J_l \end{bmatrix}$ square and invertible. Under these circumstances, however, the block diagonal part of $\hat{B}$ is no longer constant, contrary to the matrix B_0 in the form (24) for dynamic problems. The representation (30) and the resulting updating schemes were analysed in the dual (transposed) form in (Kall, 1979), and (Strazicky, 1980). The resulting formulae, however, are so involved and far from the essence of the underlying problem, that it is not clear whether this particular direction can bring a significant progress.

The approach (22) might be more prospective here, but we should be aware of the fact that it is natural to expect that many first stage activities x will be basic, because corrections are usually more expensive. Hence, the blocks $\tilde{W}_l$ in (29) will be far from square and adding to them columns to achieve the block diagonal $\tilde{B}$ will inevitably increase D in (23).

Summing up this part of our discussion, we can conclude that implementations of the simplex method for large dynamic and stochastic problems lead to very detailed linear algebraic techniques that try to exploit the structure of basis matrices to develop improved inversion methods. Although there is still a lot to be done in this direction, one can hardly expect a qualitative progress here.

Pricing strategies

Let us now pass to the problem of selecting nonbasic columns to be priced out at a given iteration for testing whether they could be brought into the basis. Since the selection of a variable to enter the basis largely determines the variable to leave, pricing strategies have a considerable influence on iteration paths of the simplex method and this influence grows with the size of the problem. There are two acknowledged techniques for general large scale linear programs (cf., e.g., Murtagh, 1981):

a) *partial pricing*, where at each iteration a certain subset of nonbasic columns are priced out to select the one to enter;

b) *multiple pricing*, where a list of prospective candidates is stored, and they are priced out again at the next iteration.

These general ideas can be further specialized for the two classes of problems in question. The lower block triangular structure of A in (7) and (11) suggests a natural division of the set of columns into subsets treated together by partial pricing strategies. These subsets correspond to periods in (7) and to the first stage decision x and the realizations in (11). This idea was thoroughly investigated experimentally in (Fourer, 1983) and the conclusions can be summarized as follows:

- rank the blocks (periods, realizations) equally and use them in a cyclic fashion;

- within each block (if it is still large enough) rank the columns equally and also use them in a cyclic fashion.

Again, pure linear algebraic concepts seem to be insufficient to fully specialize the pricing strategies. We should somehow exploit our knowledge of the essence of the underlying model to gain further improvements.

Noting that the dynamic model describes a phenomenon that evolves in time, we have grounds to expect that similar sets of activities will appear in the basis in the neighboring periods. This suggests a simple modification of the partial pricing strategy described above: if a prospective column has been found in period k, price out the corresponding columns from the next periods and bring them to the basis, as long as possible. The initial experiments reported in (Gondzio and Ruszczynski, 1986) indicate that this simple modification may improve the performance significantly (by 20–30% on problems of size 1000 by 2000 on IBM PC/XT).

In the stochastic case the situation is only slightly more complicated. If a correction variable is basic for the realization (A_l, b_l), we have grounds to expect that the corresponding variables will be basic for some neighboring realizations (A_j, b_j). However, contrary to the dynamic model, the notion of 'neighboring realizations' is not so clear and is difficult to implement. Nevertheless, this possibility should at least be investigated experimentally.

4 Feasible direction methods

The main disadvantage of the simplex method when applied to dynamic or stochastic models is that it changes only one nonbasic activity at a time. We have already observed that periods in the dynamic model and realizations in the stochastic model exhibit close similarities. This results in very long iteration paths of the simplex method with some subsequences of iterations used to realize similar changes for many periods or realizations. It would be much more convenient to perform these changes simultaneously.

The *feasible direction methods* (see Gabasov and Kirillova, 1977, Murty and Fathi, 1984) may help us to implement this idea (the simplex method is a feasible direction method, too, but with particularly simple directions). The main difference between these methods and the simplex method is that we change many nonbasic variables at a time and allow x_N to have values between their bounds at intermediate steps. We still preserve the division of x into x_B and x_N and still keep the conditions (12) and (13). However, steps 2, 3 and 4 of the simplex method are modified as follows.

Step 2a. Price out nonbasic columns a_j of A by calculating

$$z_j = c_j - \pi^T a_j \tag{31}$$

and select a subset S of columns a_j such that $z_j < 0$ for $x_j = x_j^{min}$, $z_j > 0$ for $x_j = x_j^{max}$, $z_j \neq 0$ for $x_j^{min} < x_j < x_j^{max}$, (a subset of prospective candidates).

Step 3a. Determine a direction d_N of change of the nonbasic variables x_N such that

$$d_j z_j < 0 \qquad \text{for} \quad j \in S, \tag{32}$$

$$d_j = 0 \qquad \text{for} \quad j \notin S, \tag{33}$$

(in the simplex method d_N has only one nonzero component). Determine the direction of change of the basic variables by solving

$$Bd_B = Nd_N = A_s d_s, \tag{34}$$

where A_s is a submatrix of N formed from the columns selected in *Step 2a*, and d_s is the nonzero subvector of d_N.

Step 4a. Determine from x_B^{min}, x_B^{max}, x_B , d_B and x_s^{min}, x_s^{max}, x_s and d_s the variable which as first achieves its bound, when x_s moves in the direction d_s.

At first we note that when one of the variables which change their values (a basic from x_B or a nonbasic from x_s) will hit its bound, some nonbasic variables will be out of their bounds. So, we should either accept the fact that nonbasics can have arbitrary values in the course of calculation, or construct a basic solution from the current one without increasing the objective value. The second idea has been analysed in (Murty and Fathi, 1984), where a detailed auxiliary algorithm has been described to pass to such a basic solution. This, however, involves many additional steps which may considerably diminish the advantages of changing many nonbasics in a major step. The radical solution of (Gabasov and Kirillova, 1977) seems to be more promising: we allow nonbasics to have values between their bounds. Under this assumption the division of x into basics and nonbasics is no longer determined uniquely by the algorithm. If the previous basics are still between their bounds, we can maintain the division to save on updating. When one of the basics hits its bound we can choose among x_s the variable to replace it. In general, as discussed in (Gabasov and Kirillova, 1977), we should aim at constructing such a basis that allows for an efficient next iteration. This may e.g. be accomplished by selecting a nonbasic which is possibly far away from its bounds. However, there is a need for a more theoretically grounded approach, which could perhaps be based on the analysis of the dual problem.

Since the algebra of the feasible direction method is close to that of the simplex method, we can of course use here all the tricks developed for compact inversion of basis matrices discussed in the previous section.

Leaving aside these technical points, let us now focus our attention on the specialization of the strategy of the feasible direction method to problems having dynamic or stochastic structure. The crucial question here is the choice of the direction of change of nonbasic variables. Although in theory the only limitations are the conditions (32), (33), in practice we have to use more restrictive conditions to limit the number of columns of N to be priced out. Again, as it was in the case of the primal simplex method, we can take advantage of the structure of the constraint matrix and of the similarities of the blocks. Thus, we can try to select to x_s at a given iteration similar activities from different periods/realizations and then make one major step of the method. The only difference is that previously we performed sequences of similar steps bringing to the basis corresponding activities from different blocks, while here we at first select a group of related candidates and then change them simultaneously.

An important feature of the feasible direction approach is the freedom for specifying the starting point. Indeed, once we abandoned the requirement that all nonbasic variables are on their bounds, we are free to start the calculation from a solution which need not be basic. This may help solving practical problems, where reasonable nonbasic solutions can be specified by the user.

Summing up, the feasible direction approach appears to be a promising idea for large scale problems having a dynamic or stochastic structure. It retains the algebraic advantages of the simplex method and provides more freedom for exploiting the structure to shorten iteration paths. The potential of this approach is far from being exploited.

5 The regularized decomposition method

The idea of applying decomposition methods to linear programs of dynamic or stochastic structure has been known since 25 years (Dantzig, 1963), but it is still attractive and provides a framework for new ideas. We shall focus our attention here on the stochastic problem (10), whose structure directly suggests the application of decomposition, and we shall discuss the application of the new *regularized decomposition method* suggested in (Ruszczynski, 1986). As for dynamic problems, the approaches suggested in the literature so far are entirely different and still of rather theoretical importance (see, e.g., Forrest and Tomlin, 1972, Fourer, 1982, Ho and Loute, 1981, Ho and Manne, 1974).

By formulating the dual to (10) we obtain a problem of primal angular structure, to which the Dantzig-Wolfe decomposition method can be applied (Dantzig and Madansky, 1961). Since applying the Dantzig-Wolfe method to the dual is equivalent to applying *the Benders decomposition* to the primal (Lasdon, 1970), we shall discuss our basic ideas in primal terms. See (Ruszczynski, 1988) for the analysis of the regularized decomposition method in dual form.

It can be readily seen that if x is fixed in (10) the minimization with respect to $y_1, y_2, \ldots, y_L$ can be carried out separately by solving for $l = 1, 2, \ldots, L$ *the second-stage subproblems*

$$\textit{minimize} \quad q^T y$$

$$\textit{subject to}$$

$$Wy = b_l - A_l x, \qquad y^{min} \leq y \leq y^{max}. \tag{35}$$

Let us denote the optimal value of (35) by $f_l(x)$, and take the convention that $f_l(x) = +\infty$, if (35) is unsolvable. Then our problem (10) can be equivalently formulated as follows:

$$\textit{minimize} \quad F(x) \equiv c^T x + \textstyle\sum_{l=1}^{L} p_l f_l(x) \tag{36}$$

$$\textit{subject to}$$

$$x^{min} \leq x \leq x^{max}, \tag{37}$$

$$x \in X_l, \qquad l = 1, 2, \ldots, L, \tag{38}$$

where

$$X_l = \{\, x : f_l(x) < +\infty \,\}. \tag{39}$$

We introduce condition (38) to the problem formulation, because we are going to use separate approximations for f_l and for their domains X_l.

Much is known about the functions f_l and the sets X_l (see, e.g., Wets, 1983). In particular, each X_l is a convex closed polyhedron and each f_l is convex and piecewise linear on X_l. Although the pieces of f_l and the facets of f_l are not given explicitly, for each x we can determine a piece of f_l active at $\tilde{x}$, or a linear constraint defining X_l, which is violated at $\tilde{x}$.

Indeed, let (35) be solvable at $x = \tilde{x}$ and let π denote the vector of simplex multipliers associated with the solution. Then it follows from the duality relations in linear programming that for every x

$$f_l(x) \geq f_l(\tilde{x}) - \pi^T A_l (x - \tilde{x}), \tag{40}$$

and the equality holds for $x = \tilde{x}$. If (35) is not solvable for $x = \tilde{x}$, then phase I of the simplex method or the dual simplex method will stop at a certain iteration, at which it will not be possible to move a basic variable y_{Br} towards its feasibility interval $[y_{Br}^{min}, y_{Br}^{max}]$. If π is the r-th row of the basis inverse (if the dual method is used and $y_{Br} > y_{Br}^{max}$), then

$$X_l \subseteq \{\, x : y_{Br} - \pi^T A_l (x - \tilde{x}) \leq y_{Br}^{max} \,\}. \tag{41}$$

Similar formulae hold for the case of $y_{Br} < y_{Br}^{min}$ and for the phase I of the primal simplex method.

We shall call the linear inequalities following from (40) *objective cuts*, and the inequalities following from (41) *feasibility cuts*. Each objective cut can be written as

$$\alpha_l + g_l^T x \le f_l(x) \tag{42}$$

with $g_l = -A_l^T \pi$. Each feasibility cut can be expressed in a similar fashion:

$$\bar{\alpha}_l + \bar{g}_l^T x \le 0 \tag{43}$$

with $\bar{g}_l = -A_l^T \pi$ and an appropriately defined $\bar{\alpha}_l$. Functions f_l and sets X_l are polyhedral and there can be only finite many (although usually quite a few) such cuts.

Next, if we have objective cuts (42) for all $l = 1, 2, \ldots, L$ we can construct an *aggregate cut*

$$\sum_{l=1}^{L} p_l f_l(x) \ge \alpha + g^T x, \tag{44}$$

where (α, g) is computed from (α_l, g_l) by means of averaging

$$\alpha = \sum_{l=1}^{L} p_l \alpha_l, \tag{45}$$

$$g = \sum_{l=1}^{L} p_l g_l. \tag{46}$$

We can now describe the version of the Benders decomposition method for stochastic programs, known as *L-shaped algorithm* (Van Slyke and Wets, 1969).

Let (α^j, g^j), $j \in J$, be the set of aggregate cuts (43) known so far, and let $(\bar{\alpha}^j, \bar{g}^j)$, $j \in \bar{J}$, be the set of feasibility cuts generated previously. At each iteration of the method we perform the following operations.

Step 1. Solve the master problem:

$$\textit{minimize} \quad \tilde{F}(x) \equiv c^T x + v \tag{47}$$

subject to

$$\alpha^j + (g^j)^T x \le v, \qquad j \in J, \tag{48}$$

$$\bar{\alpha}^j + (\bar{g}^j)^T x \le 0, \qquad j \in \bar{J}, \tag{49}$$

$$x^{min} \le x \le x^{max}. \tag{50}$$

Let $\tilde{x}$ be the solution to (47)–(50).

Step 2. Solve for $l = 1, 2, \ldots, L$ the subproblems (35) at $x = \tilde{x}$. If any of them is infeasible, generate the corresponding feasibility cut (43), append it to (49) and go to Step 1. If all subproblems are feasible, check whether $\sum_{l=1}^{L} p_l f_l(\tilde{x}) = v$. If this condition is satisfied, then stop; otherwise generate objective cuts (42), the aggregate cut (43), append it to (48) and go to Step 1.

It is not difficult to observe that this method exactly corresponds to the Dantzig-Wolfe method applied to the dual of (10): the cuts passed to the master (47)–(49) are the proposals passed to the master in the Dantzig-Wolfe method.

The attractiveness of this approach follows from the fact that the solution procedure closely reflects the structure of the original problem. It also allows for some parallelism in subproblem solution. It has, however, inherent drawbacks common for all purely linear cutting plane methods (cf., e.g., Topkis, 1982), and for the Dantzig-Wolfe method (which is in fact their dual counterpart):

- the number of cuts (48), (49) increases in the course of calculation;
- the master problem is unstable: new cuts may imply rapid changes of $\tilde{x}$;
- convergence is slow.

These drawbacks led to the idea of the regularized decomposition method (Ruszczynski, 1986), which combines the Benders decomposition with modern stable techniques of nonsmooth optimization (Kiwiel, 1985). The main idea of the method is to change the master program, which generates successive points x^k at which the subproblems are solved. We aim at constructing such a master which would be able to use the information gained in the past not only in the form of cuts, but also in the form of the best point x found so far.

The method uses objective and feasibility cuts (42) and (43) as before. It does not, however, average them to form aggregate cuts (43), but rather maintains separate sets of cuts for each component f_l:

$$a_l^j + (g_l^j)^T x \le f_l(x), \qquad j \in J_l, \qquad l = 1, 2, \dots, L.$$

Next, the master problem, although quite similar to (47)–(50), is augmented with a quadratic penalty term for the distance of $\tilde{x}$ to the best point x^k found so far:

$$\text{minimize} \quad \tilde{F}^k(x) \equiv \tfrac{1}{2}\|x - x^k\|^2 + c^T x + \textstyle\sum_{l=1}^{L} p_l v_l \tag{51}$$

subject to

$$\alpha_l^j + (g_l^j)^T x \le v_l, \qquad j \in J_l, \qquad l = 1, 2, \dots, L, \tag{52}$$

$$\bar{\alpha}^j + (\bar{g}^j)^T x \le 0, \qquad j \in \bar{J}, \tag{53}$$

$$x^{min} \le x \le x^{max}. \tag{54}$$

The existence of this quadratic term stabilizes the master problem, i.e. makes it less sensitive to the changes in the set of cuts (52)–(53). It also allows for skipping outdated cuts and keeping the total size of the master limited.

The logic of the regularized decomposition method can be summarized as follows.

Step 1. Solve the regularized master (51)–(54), getting a trial point $\tilde{x}$ and objective estimates v_l, $l = 1, 2, \dots, L$.

Step 2. Solve for $l = 1, 2, \dots, L$ the subproblems (35) at $x = \tilde{x}$.

a) If (35) is infeasible, then append the feasibility cut (43) to (53).

b) If (35) is feasible, but $f_l(x) > v_l$, then append the objective cut (42) to the set of cuts J_l in (52).

Step 3. Change the regularizing point x^k according to the following rules.

a) If there were infeasible subproblems (35), set $x^{k+1} = x^k$.

b) If $F(\tilde{x}) = c^T\tilde{x} + \sum_{l=1}^{L} p_l v_l$, then set $x^{k+1} = \tilde{x}$.

c) If $F(\tilde{x}) \leq \gamma F(x^k) + (1-\gamma)(c^T\tilde{x} + \sum_{l=1}^{L} p_l v_l)$ and exactly $n + L$ constraints were active in (51)–(54), then also set $x^{k+1} = \tilde{x}$; otherwise set $x^{k+1} = x^k$.

Step 4. Delete from the cuts (52)–(53) some of those which were not active at the last solution $\tilde{x}$ to the master, and go to Step 1.

It is easy to observe that the number of active cuts (i.e. linearly independent constraints with positive Lagrange multipliers) never exceeds $n+L$, where n is the dimension of x and L is the number of blocks (realizations). Since at Step 2 at most L new cuts may enter (either a feasibility cut or an objective cut for each l), the total number of cuts need not exceed $n + 2L$. In fact, it is usually much smaller, if many bounds (54) are active.

It has been proved in (Ruszczynski, 1986) (for the general case of minimization of a sum of polyhedral functions) that the rules for changing the regularizing point x^k at Step 3 guarantee that the sequence x^k is convergent in finitely many iterations to the solution of our problem. This result obviously applies also to the particular problem we are interested in.

It is easy to observe that the use of the quadratic term in (51) implies that the regularizing point x^k has a great influence on the solution of the master problem. In particular, the starting point x^0 influences considerably the whole iteration path, which is obviously not true for the linear decomposition method. This may significantly reduce the effort required for solving practical problems, where a good starting point is available.

These important theoretical features have been obtained at the expense of replacing a purely linear master problem (47)–(50) by the quadratic problem (51)–(54). To make the regularized decomposition method really competitive, we need an efficient computational technique for solving the regularized master.

Such a technique can be based on the *active set strategy*. It consists in selecting a subset of the constraints (52)–(54) to be satisfied as equalities, solving the resulting equality constrained subproblem, changing the active set, solving the new subproblem, etc. The active set is increased, when a cut not included in it is violated, and it is decreased, when a cut in the active set has a negative Lagrange multiplier in the subproblem.

The equality constraints defined by an active set can be compactly written in the form

$$a + G^T x - E^T v = 0, \tag{55}$$

where a is composed of the constant terms $\alpha^j, \bar{\alpha}^j$ corresponding to the active cuts, G has columns $g^j, \bar{g}^j$, and E is a zero-one matrix whose j-th column is the unit vector e^l if the

j-th cut is an objective cut for f_l, and is a zero column otherwise. Active bounds (54) can also be put into (55) with particularly simple columns of G (unit vectors). Thus each equality constrained subproblem has the form: minimize (51) subject to (55). Denoting by λ the vector of Lagrange multipliers corresponding to the active cuts (55), we can formulate the following necessary and sufficient conditions of optimality:

$$E\lambda = p, \tag{56}$$

$$E^T v + G^T G\lambda = G^T(x^k - c) + a, \tag{57}$$

where $p = (p_1, p_2, \ldots, p_L)$ is the vector of probabilities. The primal solution is defined by

$$x = x^k - c - G^T\lambda. \tag{58}$$

The number of active cuts does not exceed $n + L$ and so does the size of the system (56)–(57). However, the specific structure of E (unit or zero columns and full row rank) makes it possible to further reduce the dimension by representing

$$E = (I, N),$$

$$G = (G_B, G_N),$$

$$a = (a_B, a_N),$$

$$\lambda = (\lambda_B, \lambda_N).$$

After eliminating analytically v and λ_B from (56)–(57) we obtain the equivalent system

$$\hat{G}_N^T \hat{G}_N \lambda = \hat{G}_N^T (x - c - \bar{g}_N) + \hat{a}_N, \tag{59}$$

where

$$\hat{G}_N = G_N - G_B N,$$

$$\hat{a}_N = a_N - N^T a_B,$$

$$\bar{g}_N = G_B p.$$

The system (59) has dimension not exceeding the dimension of x, independently of the number of blocks L, and can be solved by stable numerical techniques for least-squares problems (see Daniel et al., 1976, Ruszczynski, 1986). In the implementation (Ruszczynski, 1985) additional advantages have been drawn from the activity of simple bounds, which further reduces the dimension of (59).

Summing up, not only the regularized master (51)–(54) has a smaller number of cuts than (47)–(50), but the effort for solving it is comparable with the effort for solving linear problems of the same size. These observations have been confirmed by the initial experiments with the regularized decomposition method for large scale stochastic programs, which we report in an extended form elsewhere (Ruszczynski, 1987). They indicate that the method solves medium-size problems (200 by 500) much faster than purely linear techniques, is capable of solving very large problems and the growth of costs is sublinear when the number of realizations L increases.

Conclusions

We discussed some modern computational approaches to large scale linear programs arising from dynamic and stochastic models. In our opinion, two directions deserve more attention as promising tools for decision support systems:

- *feasible direction methods* with special compact inverse techniques borrowed from implementations of the simplex method and with specialized direction-finding procedures;
- *the regularized decomposition method* with decentralized or parallel subproblem solution.

The common feature of these methods is the freedom in specifying the starting point and its strong influence on the cost of calculations, which is crucial for decision support systems, where we usually solve repeatedly similar models. The methods are also more flexible than simplex-based approaches and provide a potential for an interactive control of calculations and for some parallelism. On the other hand, they both can use computer resources at least so economically as the simplex methods and are capable of solving large models.

References

Bisschop, J. and A. Meeraus (1980). Matrix augmentation and structure preservation in linearly constrained control problems. *Mathematical Programming*, 18(1980), pp. 7–15.

Daniel, J.W. et al. (1976). Reorthogonalization and stable algorithms for updating the Gram-Schmidt QR factorization. *Mathematics of Computation*, 30(1976), pp. 772–795.

Dantzig, G. (1963). Linear Programming and Extensions, Princeton.

Dantzig, G. and A. Madansky (1961). On the solution of two-stage linear programs under uncertainty. In: Proceedings of the 4th Berkeley Symposium on Mathematical Statistics and Probability, Vol. 1, University of California Press, Berkeley 1961, pp. 165–176.

Forrest, J.J.H. and J.A. Tomlin (1972). Updated triangular factors of the basis to maintain sparsity in the product form simplex method. *Mathematical Programming*, 2(1972), pp. 263–278.

Fourer, R. (1982). Solving staircase linear programs by the simplex method, 1: inversion. *Mathematical Programming*, 23(1982), pp. 274–313.

Fourer, R. (1983). Solving staircase linear programs by the simplex method, 2: pricing. *Mathematical Programming*, 25(1983), pp. 251–292.

Gabasov, R. and F.M. Kirillova (1977). Linear Programming Methods, Isdatelstvo BGU, Minsk. (in Russian)

Gondzio, J. and A. Ruszczynski (1986). A package for solving dynamic linear programs, Institute of Automatic Control, Warsaw University of Technology.

Gondzio, J. and A. Ruszczynski (1988). A sensitivity method for solving linear stochastic control problems, this volume.

Ho, J. and E. Loute (1981). A set of staircase linear programming test problems. *Mathematical Programming*, 20(1981), pp. 245–250.

Ho, J. and A. Manne (1974). Nested decomposition for dynamic models. *Mathematical Programming*, 6(1974), pp. 121–140.

Kall, P. (1979). Computational methods for solving two-stage stochastic linear programming problems. *ZAMT*, 30(1979), pp. 261–271.

Kall, P., K. Frauendorfer and A. Ruszczynski (1986). Approximation techniques in stochastic programming. In Y. Ermoliev and R. Wets (eds): Numerical Methods in Stochastic Programming, Springer Verlag, Berlin (to appear).

Kallio, M. and E. Porteus (1977). Triangular factorization and generalized upper bounding techniques. *Operations Research*, 25(1977), pp. 89–99.

Kiwiel, K.C. (1985). Methods of Descent for Nondifferentiable Optimization, Springer Verlag.

Lasdon, L.S. (1970). Optimization Theory for Large Systems, Macmillan, New York.

Marsten, R. (1981). The design of the XMP linear programming library. *ACM Transactions of Mathematical Software*, 7(1981), pp. 481–497.

Murtagh, B. (1981). Advanced Linear Programming, McGraw–Hill.

Murtagh, B. and M. Saunders (1984). MINOS 5.0. User's guide. System Optimization Laboratory, Stanford University.

Murty, K.G. and Y. Fathi (1984). A feasible direction method for linear programming. *Operations Research Letters*, 3(1984), pp. 121–127.

Perold, A. and G. Dantzig (1979). A basis factorization method for block triangular linear programs. In I. Duff and G. Stewart (eds): Sparse Matrix Proceedings, SIAM, Philadelphia, pp. 283–313.

Propoi, A. and V. Krivonozhko (1978). The simplex method for dynamic linear programs, RR-78-14, IIASA.

Reid, J. (1982). A sparsity-exploiting variant of the Bartels-Golub decomposition for linear programming bases. *Mathematical Programming*, 24(1982), pp. 55–69.

Ruszczynski, A. (1985). QDECOM: The regularized decomposition method. User's manual. Institute of Operations Research, University Zurich.

Ruszczynski, A. (1986). A regularized decomposition method for minimizing a sum of polyhedral functions. *Mathematical Programming*, 35(1986), pp. 309–333.

Ruszczynski, A. (1987). Regularized decomposition of stochastic programs: algorithmic techniques and numerical results, technical report, Institute of Automatic Control, Warsaw University of Technology.

Ruszczynski, A. (1988). Regularized decomposition and augmented Lagrangian decomposition for angular linear programming problems, this volume.

Strazicky, B. (1980). Some results concerning an algorithm for the discrete recourse problem. In M. Dempster (ed.): Stochastic Programming, Academic Press, London, pp. 263–274.

Toczylowski, E. (1984). A hierarchical representation of the inverse of sparse matrices. *SIAM J. Alg. Disc. Math.* 5(1984), pp. 43–56.

Topkis, J.M. (1982). A cutting plane algorithm with linear and geometric rates of convergence. *JOTA*, 36(1982), pp. 1–22.

Van Slyke, R. and R.J.-B. Wets (1969). L-shaped linear programs with applications to optimal control and stochastic programming. *SIAM J. on Applied Mathematics*, 17(1969), pp. 638–663.

Wets, R.J.-B. (1983). Stochastic programming: solution techniques and approximation schemes. In A. Bachem et al. (eds): Mathematical Programming: The State of the Art, Springer Verlag, Berlin, pp. 507–603.

Wets, R.J.-B. (1986). Large scale linear programming techniques in stochastic programming. In Y. Ermoliev and R. Wets (eds): Numerical Methods in Stochastic Programming, Springer Verlag, Berlin, (to appear).

A Sensitivity Method for Solving Multistage Stochastic Linear Programming Problems

Jacek Gondzio

Systems Research Institute, Polish Academy of Sciences, Warsaw,

Andrzej Ruszczynski

Institute of Automatic Control, Warsaw University of Technology.

Abstract

A version of the simplex method for solving stochastic linear control problems is presented. The method takes advantage of the structure of the problem to achieve utmost memory economy in both data representation and basis inverse management.

1 Introduction

The main purpose of this paper is to present a highly specialized version of the simplex method for solving linear stochastic control problems defined as follows.

Let Ω be a finite probability space, and let

$$x_\omega(t) = Gx_\omega(t-1) + Ku_\omega(t) + z_\omega(t) \ , \qquad t = 1,2,\dots,T \tag{1}$$

be the state equation describing the evolution of a linear dynamic system with state variables $x_\omega(t)$, control variables $u_\omega(t)$ and disturbances $z_\omega(t)$. The problem is to find such a policy $u_\omega(t)$, $t = 1,2,\dots,T$, $\omega \in \Omega$, that the following conditions are satisfied:

a) for each t the random variable $u(t)$ is measurable with respect to $\{ z(1), \dots , z(t) \}$ *(nonanticipativity)*,

b) $\underline{u}(t) \le u_\omega(t) \le \bar{u}(t)$, $t = 1,2,\dots,T$, $\omega \in \Omega$, (2)

c) $\underline{x}(t) \le x_\omega(t) \le \bar{x}(t)$, $t = 1,2,\dots,T$, $\omega \in \Omega$, (3)

d) the linear functional

$$\sum_{\omega \in \Omega} p_\omega \sum_{t=1}^{T} \left[q_x^T(t)\, x_\omega(t) + q_u^T(t)\, u_\omega(t) \right] \tag{4}$$

is minimized.

Although in principle (1)–(4) is a linear programming problem, its size may be too large for standard LP approaches (see, e.g., Murtagh, 1981; Murtagh and Saunders, 1984; Reid, 1982). For this reason a variety of specialized methods have been suggested for some important special cases of (1)–(4) (cf. Fourer, 1982; Fourer, 1983; Perold and Dantzig, 1979; Wets, 1986 and the references therein).

Our aim is to go a step further in this direction to exploit all special features of (1)–(4) within the classical simplex method to achieve utmost memory economy allowing for solution of very large problems on microcomputers.

When considering the simplex method for (1)–(4) three groups of problems arise:

a) representation of the problem constraint matrix;

b) representation of the inverse of the basis matrix and its updating;

c) pricing strategies.

Clearly, crucial for the memory requirements are issues a) and b), so we shall focus on them our attention. We can mention here that pricing strategies were discussed in detail in Fourer (1983), Gondzio and Ruszczynski (1986), Gondzio (1988b) and in the previous paper.

2 The tree formulation

It is convenient to reformulate multistage stochastic programs in a tree–like form (Rockafellar and Wets, 1987). With the set of disturbance realizations (*scenarios*) $z_\omega(t)$, $t = 1, 2, \ldots, T$ we can associate a tree $\mathcal{T}$ with node set J defined as follows. There is one root node i_0 at level 0. At level 1 there are as many nodes $i \in J_1$, as many different realizations of $z_\omega(1)$ may occur. They all have i_0 as their father (predecessor). Generally, each node $i \in J_t$ at level t corresponds to a different realization of $\{ z(1), z(2), \ldots, z(t) \}$. Nodes $j \in J_{t+1}$ are joined with $i \in J_t$ if the realization corresponding to j is a continuation of the realization associated with i.

Each node at level t corresponds to the information available at time t. The requirement of nonanticipativity of controls (which implies nonanticipativity of state trajectories) makes it possible to associate decisions with nodes and reformulate our problem as follows:

find $u(i)$ *and* $x(i)$, $i \in J$, *so as to minimize*

$$\sum_{i \in J} \left[q_x^T(i) x(i) + q_u^T(i) u(i) \right] \tag{5}$$

subject to the constraints

$$x(i) = Gx(f(i)) + Ku(i) + z(i) , \quad i \in J , \tag{6}$$

$$\underline{x}(i) \le x(i) \le \bar{x}(i) , \quad i \in J , \tag{7}$$

$$\underline{u}(i) \le u(i) \le \bar{u}(i) , \quad i \in J . \tag{8}$$

Here $f(i)$ denotes the father of node i, $x(i_0) = 0$, and $\underline{x}(i)$, $\bar{x}(i)$, $\underline{u}(i)$, $\bar{u}(i)$, $q_x(i)$, $q_u(i)$ follow directly from (2)–(4).

Thus the problem is fully defined by the structure of $\mathcal{T}$, vectors $z(i)$, $\underline{x}(i)$, $\bar{x}(i)$, $\underline{u}(i)$, $\bar{u}(i)$, $q_x(i)$, $q_u(i)$ associated with nodes of $\mathcal{T}$, and two matrices: G and K. The storage requirements necessary to represent the problem in this form are very modest.

From the theoretical point of view, we can consider (5)–(8) as a linear programming problem in standard form

$$\textit{minimize} \qquad c_x^T x + c_u^T u , \tag{9}$$

$$\textit{subject to} \qquad B_0 x + N_0 u = b , \tag{10}$$

$$\underline{x} \le x \le \bar{x} , \tag{11}$$

$$\underline{u} \le u \le \bar{u} , \tag{12}$$

where $x = x(J)$, $u = u(J)$, $B_0 x = x(J) - Gx(f(J))$, $N_0 u = Ku(J)$, $b = z(J)$, $\underline{x} = \underline{x}(J)$, $\bar{x} = \bar{x}(J)$, $\underline{u} = \underline{u}(J)$, $\bar{u} = \bar{u}(J)$.

The constraint matrix of (10),

$$A = \begin{bmatrix} B_0 & N_0 \end{bmatrix} \tag{13}$$

may be of enormous size, but has a very special structure, with multiple occurrence of matrices G, K and I. It is clear that any column of A can be easily reconstructed from (5)–(8) and a very efficient technique of double addressing to columns of G and K can be used to avoid excessive storage requirements.

3 The fundamental basis

Inverting the basis matrix is the crucial computational problem in any implementation of the simplex method. The matrix (13) is very sparse, so each basis is very sparse, too, and a good factorization technique (cf., e.g., Murtagh and Saunders, 1984; Reid, 1982) can handle stochastic dynamic problems of remarkable size. However, there is one important feature which is not used by general basis management packages: the block tree structure and the multiple occurrence of columns of G, K and I in the basis. We have to take advantage of that if we want to go beyond the size admitted by standard factorization methods.

There exists a special basis in (9)–(12) for which inversion is trivial: the matrix B_0. Indeed, suppose that all state variables $x(i)$, $i \in J$, are basic variables and the controls $u(i)$, $i \in J$ are nonbasic variables. Then it is trivial to observe that the equation

$$B_0 \, d = a , \tag{14}$$

can be solved by direct simulation of the state equations (6) starting at the root and ending at leaves:

$$d(i) = Gd(\,f(i)\,) + a(i)\ ,\quad i \in J\ , \tag{15}$$

where $d(i_0) = 0$.

Similarly, the transpose system

$$\pi^T B_0 = c_x^T\ , \tag{16}$$

can be solved by simulating in the opposite direction (from the leaves to the root) the *adjoint equations*

$$\pi^T(i) = \sum_{j\in N(i)} \pi^T(j)\, G + c_x^T(i)\ ,\qquad i \in J\ , \tag{17}$$

where $N(i)$ is the set of *sons* of node i,

$$N(i) = \{\, j\ :\ i = f(j)\,\}\ . \tag{18}$$

To see the latter formula, let us consider the scalar product $\pi^T B_0\, d$ for any d. Setting $a = B_0\, d$, from (15) we get

$$\begin{aligned}
\pi^T B_0\, d &= \sum_{i\in J} \pi^T(i)a(i) = \\
&= \sum_{i\in J} \pi^T(i)\big[\, d(i) - Gd(\,f(i)\,)\big] = \\
&= \sum_{i\in J} \pi^T(i)d(i) - \sum_{i\in J} \pi^T(i)\, Gd(\,f(i)\,) = \\
&= \sum_{i\in J} \pi^T(i)d(i) - \sum_{i\in J}\ \sum_{j\in N(i)} \pi^T(j)Gd(i) = \\
&= \sum_{j\in J} \Big[\pi^T(i) - \sum_{j\in N(i)} \pi^T(j)\, G\Big]\, d(i).
\end{aligned}$$

Since d was arbitrary, the above scalar product is equal to $c_x^T d$ if and only if (17) is satisfied.

4 Modified bases

In the previous section we saw that for a basis B_0 containing only state variables, equations with B_0 and B_0^T can be solved by substitution. In general, however, we shall have to deal with bases having columns corresponding to both types of variables, states and controls. Each such basis matrix can be expressed in the form

$$B = \begin{bmatrix} B_{01} & U \end{bmatrix} \tag{19}$$

where B_{01} is a certain submatrix of B_0, and U is a submatrix of N_0. The equation

$$Bd = a\ , \tag{20}$$

can be rewritten as

$$B_{01}\, d_{x1} + U d_{uB} = a \ , \tag{21}$$

with $d = (\, d_{x1} \, , \, d_{uB} \,)$. Setting $d_x = (\, d_{x1} \, , \, d_{x2} \,)$ we can reformulate (21) as follows:

$$\begin{aligned} &\textit{find } d_{uB} \textit{ such that the solution } d_x \textit{ to} \\ &B_0\, d_x = a - U d_{uB} \ , \\ &\textit{has } d_{x2} = 0 \ . \end{aligned} \tag{22}$$

Defining a 0–1 matrix V such that $d_{x2} = V d_x$, we see that

$$d_{x2} = V B_0^{-1} (\, a - U d_{uB} \,) \ ,$$

so

$$d_{uB} = S^{-1} V B_0^{-1} a$$

with

$$S = V B_0^{-1} U \ . \tag{23}$$

This gives us the following sequence of equations producing the solution to (21):

$$B_0 \tilde{d}_x = a \ , \tag{24}$$

$$S d_{uB} = V \tilde{d}_x \ , \tag{25}$$

$$B_0\, d_x = a - U d_{uB} \ , \tag{26}$$

Thus, we have to solve two equations with B_0 , which can be carried out by simulation, and one equation with the *sensitivity matrix* S, whose dimension is equal to the number of new columns in B.

Let us now pass on to the dual equation

$$\pi^T B = c^T \ , \tag{27}$$

Let $c = (\, c_{x1} \, , \, c_{uB} \,)$. Then

$$\pi^T B_{01} = c_{x1}^T \ , \tag{28}$$

$$\pi^T U = c_{uB}^T \ , \tag{29}$$

Define

$$v^T = \pi^T B_{02} - c_{x2}^T \ .$$

Then the system (28)–(29) can be reformulated as follows:

$$\begin{aligned} &\textit{find } v \textit{ such that the solution } \pi \textit{ to} \\ &\pi^T B_0 = c_x^T + v^T V \\ &\textit{satisfies } (29). \end{aligned} \tag{30}$$

Simple calculations lead to the following sequence of equations producing the solution to (21):

$$\tilde{\pi}^T B_0 = c_x^T \ , \tag{31}$$

$$v^T S = c_{uB}^T - \tilde{\pi}^T U \ , \tag{32}$$

$$\pi^T B_0 = c_x^T + v^T V \ . \tag{33}$$

Consequently, (27) has been replaced by two equations with B_0^T and an equation with the sensitivity matrix (23). In fact (31) does not depend on B at all and need be solved only once.

Summing up, equations with modified bases and their transposes can be solved by solving equations with the fundamental basis and with the sensitivity matrix S. Equations with the fundamental basis resolve themselves to simple substitution, so the main difficulty constitute the equations (25) and (32).

Redefinition of the fundamental basis is needed to preserve S from growing to a large dimension. Problem's structure implies that every basis can be transformed by row and column permutations to a nearly triangular form with a small number of spikes (see: Gondzio, 1988a for more detail). After replacing the spikes by the appropriate unit columns we obtain new fundamental basis.

5 The sensitivity matrix

Let us look closer at the matrix S defined by (23) and used in (25) and (32). It's elements are of form

$$s_{ij} = v_i^T B_0^{-1} u_j \ , \tag{34}$$

where $v_i = (0, \dots, 0, 1, 0, \dots 0)$ is the i–th row of the matrix V and u_j is the j–th column of U, i.e. a certain column of N_0 appearing in the basis. The vector v_i has a one at the p–th position if the p–th column of B_0 does not appear in B. Consequently, s_{ik} is the sensitivity of the state variable corresponding to the p–th column of B_0 with respect to the control variable corresponding to the j–th column of U. Thus, S is a square nonsingular submatrix of the full sensitivity matrix

$$Q = B_0^{-1} N_0 \ , \tag{35}$$

but we assume that the size of S is much smaller than the size of Q (which is enormous) and we shall rather compute elements of S only when necessary, instead of calculating Q in advance. That S is nonsingular follows directly from the nonsingularity of the corresponding basis B. Indeed, each solution to (24)–(26) satisfies (20). With a singular S we would have a non–unique d_{uB} from (25), so (20) would have many solutions, a contradiction.

We can easily find the general form of entries of S using the tree model (6) and their interpretation as sensitivities. Let the i–th row of S correspond to $x_k(n)$ and the j–th column of S correspond to $u_l(m)$, where n and m are some nodes of $\mathcal{T}$. If m is on the path from n to the root, then

$$s_{ij} = (G^\tau K)_{kl} \ , \tag{36}$$

where r is the number of stages between n and m. If the path from n to the root does not include m, we have $s_{ij} = 0$.

Another important feature of our approach are specific transformations of S in successive iterations of the simplex method. The following cases may occur.

Case 1: a column a_j from N_0 replaces in B the column a_i from B_0.

We have

$$U' = \begin{bmatrix} U & a_j \end{bmatrix},$$

$$V' = \begin{bmatrix} V \\ e_i^T \end{bmatrix},$$

$$S' = \begin{bmatrix} S & s \\ r^T & \sigma \end{bmatrix}, \tag{37}$$

with

$$s = VB_0^{-1}a_j ,$$
$$r^T = e_i^T B_0^{-1} U ,$$
$$\sigma = e_i^T B_0^{-1} a_j .$$

The vector $B_0^{-1}a_j$ has already been computed to determine the leaving column (see (24)) so the main cost of this update is the pricing $\pi^T U$ with $\pi^T = e_i^T B_0^{-1}$ to find r.

Case 2: a column a_j from N_0 replaces in B the column a_i from N_0.

Assume that a_i was on the p–th position in U. We then have

$$U' = U + (a_j - a_i)\, e_p^T ,$$

$$V' = V ,$$

$$S' = S + de_p^T , \tag{38}$$

where $d = VB_0^{-1}(a_j - a_i)$, i.e. the p–th column of S is changed to

$$s = VB_0^{-1}a_j .$$

Case 3: a column a_j of B_0 replaces in B the column a_i from B_0.

Similarly to Case 2 we have

$$U' = U ,$$

$$V' = V + e_p(e_i - e_j)^T ,$$

$$S' = S + e_p r^T , \tag{39}$$

where p is the index of the row corresponding to a_i, and

$$r^T = (e_i - e_j)^T B_0^{-1} U ,$$

i.e. a row of S is exchanged.

Case 4: a column a_j of B_0 replaces in B a column a_i from N_0.

Let p be the row number in V corresponding to a_j and let q be the column index in U corresponding to a_i. It is easy to observe that V' is then equal to V with the p–th row deleted, U' equals U without the q–th column, and S' can be obtained by deleting the p–th row and the q–th column of S.

6 LU factorization of the sensitivity matrix

The necessity to solve equations (25) and (32) at each iteration of the simplex method creates a need for a factorization of the sensitivity matrix S. There are two issues that should be taken into account in this respect: numerical stability and the possibility of updating the factors when S is modified.

We suggest to use a dense LU factorization

$$S = PLRQ \ , \tag{40}$$

where P and Q are row and column permutations, L is lower triangular with ones on the diagonal and R is upper triangular. That L and R should be treated as dense matrices is obvious: S is a computed matrix with upper block triangular structure. However, the fact that S is a computed matrix with potential ill–conditioning suggests rather the use of the highly stable QR factorization approach (see, e.g., Daniel et al., 1976). This particular choice is suggested in Bisschop and Meeraus (1977). LU factorization is clearly more economical, but we need here carefully designed updating procedures to avoid excessive propagation of round–off errors. Two efficient methods of LU factorization of Bartels and Golub (1969) and of Fletcher and Matthews (1984) are proved to be stable enough for practical applications, although counter examples for their good behaviour are given in Powell (1987). Their highly specialized implementations (see: Reid, 1982 and Fletcher and Matthews, 1984, respectively) do not offer the possibility of updating the factorization in all four cases analysed in section 5. Such possibility exists in a method described in Gill et al. (1987), where sparse LU decomposition is analysed. However, for the reason stated before we need dense LU factorization.

Let us discuss in more detail the method of updating the factors of (40) for the second modification considered in section 5.

Exchange of a column in U implies exchange of a column in S, as in (38). From (40) we see that

$$\hat{S} = PL\tilde{R}Q \ , \tag{41}$$

where $\tilde{R}$ differs from R by one column

$$c = L^{-1}P^{T}d \ . \tag{42}$$

By changing Q in such a way that c is moved in $\tilde{R}$ to the position equal to its length q, we can make $\tilde{R}$ upper Hessenberg with subdiagonal appearing in columns $p, p+1, \ldots, q$. Our aim is to annihilate them. Generally, this can be done by certain permutations $\tilde{P}$ and $\tilde{Q}$ and a nonsingular operator $\tilde{M}$ such that

$$\hat{L} = \tilde{P}L\tilde{M}^{-1} \tag{43}$$

is lower triangular with 1's on the diagonal, and

$$\hat{R} = \tilde{M}\tilde{R}\tilde{Q} \tag{44}$$

is upper triangular. Indeed, from (41), (43) and (44) we then get

$$\hat{S} = P\tilde{P}^T\hat{L}\tilde{M}\tilde{M}^{-1}\hat{R}\tilde{Q}^T Q = \hat{P}\hat{L}\hat{R}\hat{Q}$$

with $\hat{P} = P\tilde{P}^T$ and $\hat{Q} = \tilde{Q}^T Q$.

There are many operators satisfying (43) and (44). To save on calculations and make the modifications easier to implement we suggest to compose $\tilde{P}$, $\tilde{Q}$ and $\tilde{M}$ from sequences of elementary transformations $\tilde{P}_i$, $\tilde{Q}_i$ and $\tilde{M}_i$ annihilating successive subdiagonals of $\tilde{R}$. It is then sufficient to consider for each i 2×2 submatrices of L and $\tilde{R}$ formed from elements having row and column indices equal i and $i+1$:

$$L_i = \begin{bmatrix} 1 & \\ z & 1 \end{bmatrix},$$

$$\tilde{R}_i = \begin{bmatrix} a & c \\ b & d \end{bmatrix}.$$

Our aim is now to choose P, Q and M such that

$$\tilde{P}_i L_i \tilde{M}_i^{-1} = \begin{bmatrix} 1 & \\ z' & 1 \end{bmatrix}, \tag{45}$$

$$\tilde{M}_i \tilde{R}_i \tilde{Q}_i = \begin{bmatrix} a' & c' \\ & d' \end{bmatrix}. \tag{46}$$

Let us at first consider the case with $i+1 \le q$. Then there is a subdiagonal element in the $(i+1)$–st column of $\tilde{R}$ (below d), so we must have $\tilde{Q}_i = I$. Two possibilities remain now, depending on the use of row permutation. In the simplest case $\tilde{P}_i = I$ we obtain from (45)–(46)

$$\tilde{M}_i = \begin{bmatrix} 1 & \\ -b/a & 1 \end{bmatrix}, \tag{47}$$

$$\tilde{M}_i^{-1} = \begin{bmatrix} 1 & \\ b/a & 1 \end{bmatrix}. \tag{48}$$

The second possibility arises for

$$\tilde{P}_i = \begin{bmatrix} 0 & 1 \\ 1 & 0 \end{bmatrix}, \tag{49}$$

which implies an additional exchange of rows of L. From (45)–(46) we then obtain

$$\tilde{M}_i = \begin{bmatrix} z & 1 \\ b/\mu & -a/\mu \end{bmatrix}, \tag{50}$$

$$\tilde{M}_i^{-1} = \begin{bmatrix} a/\mu & 1 \\ b/\mu & -z \end{bmatrix}, \tag{51}$$

with $\mu = az + b$.

So, we have two possibilities to choose among: the simple elimination operators (47)–(48) and the more sophisticated (49)–(51). We choose the one for which the condition index of $\tilde{M}_i$, defined as the ratio of the eigenvalues of $\tilde{M}_i^T \tilde{M}_i$, is minimum: a simple test can be developed to determine the smaller index without calculating it. We can mention here that this particular update of dense LU factors was analysed for different purposes by Fletcher and Matthews (1984) with a simple rule of choosing the operator having smaller entries.

When $i = q$ we have four possibilities, because the exchange of the columns of R becomes admissible. Again, it is a matter of simple transformations to determine the form of $\tilde{M}_i$ in each case and to choose the one that has the minimum condition index.

The remaining cases discussed in section 5 can be analysed similarly (see: Gondzio, 1988a). Case 1 is trivial: a new row is added to L and a new column is added to R. Case 3 is almost symmetric to Case 2 analysed above and Case 4 is a combination of Cases 2 and 3.

7 Conclusions

We have presented here main ideas of a new linear programming method that is a specialization of the simplex method for multistage stochastic problems. The method requires storage only for the LU factorization of the sensitivity matrix because the fundamental basis which is a submatrix of the constraint matrix need no additional memory (only pointers to the appropriate columns have to be stored). This gives substantial savings in comparison with any classical or specialized versions of the simplex method (see: Reid, 1982; Gill et al., 1987; Fourer, 1982; Bisschop and Meeraus, 1980). The method is then especially attractive for implementing it on a small memory computer.

A numerically stable procedure of updating LU decomposition of the sensitivity matrix assures good accuracy of the whole method.

8 References

Bartels, R. H. and Golub, G. H. (1969). The simplex method of linear programming using LU decomposition. *Communication on ACM* 12, pp. 266–268.

Bisschop, J. and Meeraus, A. (1977). Matrix augmentation and the partitioning in the updating of the basis inverse. *Mathematical Programming* 13, pp. 241–254.

Bisschop, J. and Meeraus, A. (1980). Matrix augmentation and structure preservation in linearly constrained control problems. *Mathematical Programming* 18, pp. 7–15.

Daniel, J. W., Gragg, W. B., Kaufman, L. and Stewart, G. W. (1976). Reorthogonalization and stable algorithms for updating the Gram–Schmidt QR factorization. *Mathematics of Computation* 30, pp. 772–795.

Fletcher, R. and Matthews, F. P. J. (1984). Stable modification of explicit LU factors for simplex updates. *Mathematical Programming* 30, pp. 267–284.

Fourer, R. (1982). Solving staircase linear programs by the simplex method, 1: inversion. *Mathematical Programming* 23, pp. 274–313.

Fourer, R. (1983). Solving staircase linear programs by the simplex method, 2: pricing. *Mathematical Programming* 25, pp. 251–292.

Gill, P. E., Murray, W., Saunders, M. A. and Wright, M. H. (1987). Maintaining LU factors of a general sparse matrix. *Linear Algebra and its Applications* 88/89, pp. 239–270.

Gondzio, J. (1988a). Stable variant of the simplex method for solving supersparse linear programs. 3rd International Symposium on Systems Analysis and Simulation, Berlin 1988.

Gondzio, J. (1988b). Simplex modifications exploiting special features of dynamic and stochastic dynamic linear programming problems. *Control and Cybernetics*, 1988 (to appear).

Gondzio, J. and Ruszczynski, A. (1986). A package for solving dynamic linear programs. Institute of Automatic Control, Warsaw University of Technology, 1986 (in Polish).

Murtagh, B. (1981). Advanced Linear Programming. McGraw–Hill, 1981.

Murtagh, B. and Saunders, M. (1983). MINOS 5.0. User's guide. System Optimization Laboratory, Stanford University, 1983.

Powell, M. J. D. (1987). An error growth in the Bartels–Golub and Fletcher–Matthews algorithms for updating matrix factorizations. *Linear Algebra and its Applications* 88/89, pp. 597–621.

Perold, A. F. and Dantzig, G. B. (1979). A basis factorization method for block triangular linear programs. in: Duff, I. S. and Stewart G. W. eds., Sparse Matrix Proceedings 1978, SIAM, Philadelphia, pp. 283–312.

Reid, J. (1982). A sparsity–exploiting variant of the Bartels–Golub decomposition for linear programming bases. *Mathematical Programming* 24, pp. 55–69.

Rockafellar, R. T. and Wets, R. J.–B. (1987). Scenarios and policy aggregation in optimization under uncertainty. WP–87–119, IIASA, Laxenburg 1987.

Wets, R. J.-B. (1986). Large scale linear programming techniques in stochastic programming. in: Ermoliev, Y. and Wets R. J.-B. (eds), Numerical Methods in Stochastic Programming, Springer-Verlag, Berlin 1986.

Regularized Decomposition and Augmented Lagrangian Decomposition for Angular Linear Programming Problems

Andrzej Ruszczynski

Institute of Automatic Control, Warsaw University of Technology.

Abstract

We present two new decomposition methods for large linear programming problems of angular structure. The first one is a special version of the regularized decomposition method and the second one is a decomposable version of the augmented Lagrangian method. For both methods we prove finite termination theorems and establish their duality.

1 Introduction

The main purpose of this paper is to present and compare two decomposition methods for the problem

$$
\begin{array}{llllll}
\textit{minimize} & c_1^T x_1 + & c_2^T x_2 + & \ldots + & c_n^T x_n & \\
\textit{subjectto} & & & & & \\
& A_1 x_1 + & A_2 x_2 & \ldots + & A_n x_n & = b\,, \\
& D_1 x_1 & & & & = d_1\,, \\
& & D_2 x_2 & & & = d_2\,, \\
& & & \ldots & & \\
& & & & D_n x_n & = d_n\,, \\
& x_1 \geq 0, & x_2 \geq 0, & \ldots, & x_n \geq 0\,. &
\end{array}
\tag{1}
$$

First of them is a special version of the regularized decomposition method of Ruszczynski (1986) applied to the dual of (1). Its main feature, as compared with the decomposition principle of (Dantzig and Wolfe, 1960) is that it uses quadratic regularizing terms in the master problem. This stabilizes the master and eliminates difficulties with starting the method while retaining the finite convergence property of the purely linear approach.

In section 3 we present a new decomposable version of the augmented Lagrange function method. While it is well known that the augmented Lagrangian method is finitely convergent for linear problems (cf. Bertsekas, 1982; Poljak and Trietiakov, 1972), its application to decomposable problems of form (1) encountered difficulties due to the existence of non-separable quadratic terms in the augmented Lagrange function (cf. Stoilow, 1977; Tatjewski, 1986; Watanabe et al. 1978). We overcome these difficulties for (1), develop a fully decomposable method based on augmented Lagrangians and prove its finite convergence.

In section 4 we compare both methods and establish their duality. This result is closely related to the connections between augmented Lagrange function methods and proximal point methods discovered by Rockafellar (1976). The duality suggests new modifications and improvements in both methods.

2 Regularized decomposition of the dual problem

Let us formulate the dual of (1):

$$\begin{array}{llllll} \textit{maximize} & b^T u & +d_1^T \pi_1 & +d_2^T \pi_2 & +\ldots & +d_n^T \pi_n \\ \textit{subject to} & & & & & \\ & A_1^T u & +D_1^T \pi_1 & & & \le c_1 , \\ & A_2^T u & & +D_2^T \pi_2 & & \le c_2 , \\ & & & \ldots & & \\ & A_n^T u & & & +D_n^T \pi_n & \le c_n . \end{array} \tag{2}$$

Defining the functions

$$\begin{aligned} f_i(u) &= \max\{\, d_i^T \pi_i \mid D_i^T \pi_i \le c_i - A_i^T u \,\} = \\ &= \min\left\{ (c - A_i^T u)^T x_i \mid D_i x_i = d_i \,,\ x_i \ge 0 \right\} \end{aligned} \tag{3}$$

we can rewrite (2) as

$$\textit{maximize} \qquad F(u) \equiv b^T u + \sum_{i=1}^{n} f_i(u) \,. \tag{4}$$

Since $f_i(u)$ are concave and piecewise linear, (4) is a problem of maximizing a sum of polyhedral functions, the form to which the regularized decomposition method of Ruszczynski (1986) can be applied directly. To simplify our considerations we shall assume throughout this paper that the sets

$$X_i = \{\, x_i : D_i x_i = d_i \,,\ x_i \ge 0 \,\} \,, \quad i = 1,\, 2,\, \ldots,\, n \,. \tag{5}$$

are nonempty and bounded, which implies that $f_i(u)$ are finite for all u.

The main idea of the regularized decomposition method is to solve at each iteration the *regularized master problem*

$$\text{maximize} \qquad -\frac{1}{2}\| u - \bar{u}^k \|^2 + b^T u + \sum_{i=1}^{n} v_i \tag{6}$$

subject to

$$v_i \le \alpha_{ij} - g_{ij}^T u \ , \quad j \in J_i \ , \quad i = 1, 2, \ldots, n \ . \tag{7}$$

Here $\bar{u}^k$ is a certain regularizing point, and $(\alpha_{ij}\, ,\ g_{ij})$ describe so–called *objective cuts* for $f_i(u)$:

$$f_i(u) \le \alpha_{ij} - g_{ij}^T u \quad \text{for all } u \ .$$

These cuts are collected at some previous trial points u^j, $j < k$, so that

$$-g_{ij} \in \partial f_i(u^j)\, , \quad \alpha_{ij} = f_i(u^j) + g_{ij}^T u_j \ . \tag{8}$$

It is not difficult to see that for f_i defined by (3) relations (8) are satisfied by

$$g_{ij} = A_i x_{ij} \ , \tag{9}$$

$$\alpha_{ij} = c_i^T x_{ij} \ , \tag{10}$$

where x_{ij} is the solution of the linear programming problem in (3) at u^j.

The logic of the regularized decomposition method for (2) can be now summarized as follows.

Algorithm 1.

1. Solve the master (6)–(7) at $\bar{u}^k$ getting a trial point u^k and objective estimates v_i^k, $i = 1, 2, \ldots, n$, and calculate $\hat{F}^k = b^T u^k + \sum_{i=1}^{n} v_i^k$. If $\hat{F}^k = F(\bar{u}^k)$ then stop (optimal solution found); otherwise continue.

2. Delete from (7) some cuts inactive at $(u^k,\ v^k)$ so that no more than $n + m$ members remain.

3. For $i = 1, 2, \ldots, n$ calculate $f_i(u^k)$ finding a vertex x_{ik} of X_i which solves the problem in (3). If $f_i(u^k) < v_i^k$ then append the cut defined by (9)–(10) to (7).

4. If $F(u^k) = \hat{F}^k$ or $F(u^k) \ge \gamma \hat{F}^k + (1-\gamma) F(\bar{u}^k)$ and exactly $m + n$ cuts were active at $(u^k,\ v^k)$ then set $\bar{u}^{k+1} = u^k$ (*serious step*); otherwise set $\bar{u}^{k+1} = \bar{u}^k$ (*null step*).

5. Increase k by one and go to **1**.

By active cuts we mean here linearly independent cuts having positive Lagrange multipliers at the solution to (6)–(7).

The method can be started from any $\bar{u}^0$ with the cuts (7) defined by (9)–(10) at the solutions x_{i0} to (3) with $u = \bar{u}^0$. This is a significant difference from the Dantzig–Wolfe method, where finding the first multiplier vector may be difficult, and is due to the fact that the regularized decomposition method goes through nonbasic points, in general. Nevertheless, the method is still finitely convergent.

Theorem 1. *Assume that the sets X_i, $i = 1,2,\ldots,n$, are nonempty and bounded and that (1) has a feasible solution. Then Algorithm 1 after finitely many iterations stops at a point $u^k = \bar{u}^k$ which solves (2). The corresponding optimal solution x^k to (1) is then defined by*

$$x_i^k = \sum_{j \in J_i} \lambda_{ij}^k x_{ij} \ , \quad i = 1,2,\ldots,n \ , \tag{11}$$

where λ_{ij}^k, $j \in J_i$, are the values of Lagrange multipliers at the solution to (6)–(7), and x_{ij}, $j \in J_i$, are the vertices of X_i defining the final active cuts. The optimal objective value satisfies the relation

$$\sum_{i=1}^{n} c_i^T x_i^k = b^T u^k + \sum_{i=1}^{n} v_i^k \ . \tag{12}$$

Proof. Since all the sets X_i given by (5) are nonempty and bounded and the constraints of (1) are consistent, both problems (1) and (2) have optimal solutions. Then (4) is bounded from above and finite convergence of the regularized decomposition method follows directly from the theory of Ruszczynski (1986). It remains to prove (11). Let $J_i^+ = \{ j \in J_i \ : \ \lambda_{ij}^k > 0 \}$. Since $u^k = \bar{u}^k$, from the optimality conditions for (6)–(7) we get

$$b - \sum_{i=1}^{n} \sum_{j \in J_i^+} \lambda_{ij}^k g_{ij} = 0 \ , \tag{13}$$

$$\sum_{j \in J_i^+} \lambda_{ij}^k = 1 \ , \quad i = 1,2,\ldots,n \ , \tag{14}$$

$$\lambda_{ij}^k \geq 0 \ , \quad j \in J_i^+ \ , \quad i = 1,2,\ldots,n \ , \tag{15}$$

and

$$f_i(u^k) = v_i^k = \alpha_{ij} - g_{ij}^T u^k \ , \quad j \in J_i^+ \ . \tag{16}$$

Using (9), (10) and (11) we can rewrite (13) as

$$\sum_{i=1}^{n} A_i x_i^k = b \ . \tag{17}$$

By (14)–(15), $x_i^k \in X_i$. This combined with (17) implies that $x^k = (x_1^k, x_2^k, \ldots, x_n^k)$ satisfies all constraints of (1).

Next, from (9), (10) and (16) we get

$$f_i(u^k) = c_i^T x_{ij} - (u^k)^T A_i x_{ij} \ , \quad j \in J_i^+ \ , \quad i = 1,2,\ldots,n \ .$$

Using (11) and (17) we obtain the following expression for the optimal value of the dual problem

$$\begin{aligned} F(u^k) &= b^T u^k + \sum_{i=1}^{n} f_i(u^k) \\ &= b^T u^k + \sum_{i=1}^{n} \sum_{j \in J_i^+} \lambda_{ij}^k \left(c_i^T x_{ij} - (u^k)^T A_i x_{ij} \right) \\ &= b^T u^k + \sum_{i=1}^{n} \left(c_i^T - (u^k)^T A_i \right) x_i^k = \sum_{i=1}^{n} c_i^T x_i^k . \end{aligned}$$

Consequently, the objective value in (1) at x^k is equal to the optimal value of the dual problem, which combined with the feasibility of x^k implies its optimality. The proof is complete.

3 The augmented Lagrangian decomposition

Let us now return to (1) and consider for it the augmented Lagrange function

$$L_\alpha(x, u) = \sum_{i=1}^{n} c_i^T x_i + u^T (b - \sum_{i=1}^{n} A_i x_i) + \frac{1}{2} \| b - \sum_{i=1}^{n} A_i x_i \|^2 . \tag{18}$$

The augmented Lagrangian method (cf. e.g. Bertsekas, 1982) applied to (1) can be now stated as follows.

Algorithm 2.

1. For fixed multipliers $\bar{u}^k$ solve the problem

$$\textit{minimize} \qquad L_\alpha(x, \bar{u}^k) \tag{19}$$

subject to

$$x_i \in X_i = \{ x_i \, : \, D_i x_i = d_i \, , \; x_i \geq 0 \}, \quad i = 1, 2, \ldots, n . \tag{20}$$

Let $x^k = (x_1^k, x_2^k, \ldots, x_n^k)$ be the solution to (19)-(20).

2. If

$$\sum_{i=1}^{n} A_i x_i^k = b \tag{21}$$

then stop (optimal solution found); otherwise set

$$\bar{u}^{k+1} = \bar{u}^k + b - \sum_{i=1}^{n} A_i x_i^k , \tag{22}$$

increase k by one and go to **1**.

It is well known that the above method is finitely convergent in our case, because (1) is a linear program (see Bertsekas, 1982; Poljak and Trietiakov, 1972). On the other hand, it is sometimes asserted that the augmented Lagrangian method is not suitable for decomposable problems of form (1), because (18) is not separable and thus (19)–(20) cannot be split into independent problems. Various attempts have been made to approximate (18) by a separable function and update the approximation in the course of calculation, but the resulting algorithms are rather involved and no longer finitely convergent for linear problems (cf. e.g. Stoilow, 1977; Tatjewski, 1986; Watanabe et al. 1978; Rockafellar and Wets, 1987). We shall show that these difficulties can be overcome in the linear case and a finitely convergent decomposition method *can* be developed on the basis of Algorithm 2. The key to this result is that we are going *to decompose the method, not the function.*

Since X_i is a bounded convex polyhedron, proceeding as in the development of the Dantzig–Wolfe method (Dantzig and Wolfe, 1960) we can express each $x_i \in X_i$ as

$$x_i = \sum_{j \in J_i^*} \lambda_{ij} x_{ij} \;, \quad i = 1, 2, \ldots, n \tag{23}$$

with

$$\sum_{j \in J_i^*} \lambda_{ij} = 1 \;, \quad i = 1, 2, \ldots, n, \tag{24}$$

$$\lambda_{ij} \geq 0 \;, \quad j \in J_i^* \;, \quad i = 1, 2, \ldots, n, \tag{25}$$

where x_{ij} , $j \in J_i^*$, are all vertices of X_i . With this notation one can rewrite (18) as

$$L_\alpha(\lambda, u) = \sum_{i=1}^{n} \sum_{j \in J_i^*} \alpha_{ij} \lambda_{ij} + u^T \Big(b - \sum_{i=1}^{n} \sum_{j \in J_i^*} \lambda_{ij} g_{ij} \Big) +$$

$$+ \frac{1}{2} \Big\| b - \sum_{i=1}^{n} \sum_{j \in J_i^*} \lambda_{ij} g_{ij} \Big\|^2 \;, \tag{26}$$

where

$$\alpha_{ij} = c_i^T x_{ij} \;, \tag{27}$$

$$g_{ij} = A_i x_{ij} \;. \tag{28}$$

Problem (19)–(20) can be now equivalently stated as follows

$$\begin{aligned} &\textit{minimize} \quad L_\alpha(\lambda, \bar{u}^k) \\ &\textit{subject to} \quad (24) - (25). \end{aligned} \tag{29}$$

One could also obtain (29) by applying the augmented Lagrange function method to the full master problem in the Dantzig–Wolfe method, resulting from substituting (23) in (1).

The crucial observation concerning (29) is the following.

Lemma 1. *Problem (29) has a solution λ^k with at most $n + m$ positive components.*

Proof. Problem (29) has always a solution $\hat{\lambda}$, since (24)–(25) define a compact set. Let

$$\hat{b} = \sum_{i=1}^{n} \sum_{j \in J_i^*} \hat{\lambda}_{ij} g_{ij} .$$

Consider the linear program

$$minimize \quad \sum_{i=1}^{n} \sum_{j \in J_i^*} \alpha_{ij} \lambda_{ij} \tag{30}$$

subject to

$$\sum_{i=1}^{n} \sum_{j \in J_i^*} \lambda_{ij} g_{ij} = \hat{b} . \tag{31}$$

$$\sum_{j \in J_i^*} \lambda_{ij} = 1 , \quad \lambda_{ij} \geq 0 , \quad j \in J_i^* , \quad i = 1, 2, \dots, n . \tag{32}$$

Since (31) implies that the second and the third term in (26) are constant, each solution to (30)–(32) solves (29). Problem (30)–(32) is linear and thus has an optimal basic solution λ^k, which may have no more than $n + m$ positive components. The proof is complete.

Corollary. *With no loss of generality we can assume that the columns* $\binom{g_{ij}}{e_i}$ *corresponding to* $\lambda_{ij}^k > 0$, *where* e_i *is the* i*-th unit vector in* R^n, *are linearly independent.*

Lemma 1 suggests replacing (29) by a *restricted master*

$$minimize \quad \sum_{i=1}^{n} \sum_{j \in J_i} \alpha_{ij} \lambda_{ij} + u^T \left(b - \sum_{i=1}^{n} \sum_{j \in J_i} \lambda_{ij} g_{ij} \right) +$$

$$+ \frac{1}{2} \| b - \sum_{i=1}^{n} \sum_{j \in J_i} \lambda_{ij} g_{ij} \|^2 , \tag{33}$$

subject to

$$\sum_{j \in J_i} \lambda_{ij} = 1 , \quad i = 1, 2, \dots, n , \tag{34}$$

$$\lambda_{ij} \geq 0 , \quad j \in J_i , \quad i = 1, 2, \dots, n , \tag{35}$$

for some subsets $J_i \subseteq J_i^*$, $i = 1, 2, \dots, n$.

The relation between (29) and (33)–(35) is as follows.

Lemma 2. *A solution* λ^k *of the restricted master is a solution of (29) if for*

$$u^k = \bar{u}^k + b - \sum_{i=1}^{n} \sum_{j \in J_i} \lambda_{ij}^k g_{ij} \tag{36}$$

and

$$f_i(u^k) = \min\left\{ (c - A_i^T u^k)^T x_i \mid D_i x_i = d_i \ , \ \ x_i \geq 0 \right\} \tag{37}$$

one has

$$f_i(u^k) \geq v_i^k \ , \ \ i = 1,2,\ldots,n \ , \tag{38}$$

where v_i^k , $i = 1,2,\ldots,n$, *are Lagrange multipliers corresponding to (34).*

Proof. The necessary and sufficient conditions of optimality for (29) are of the form: *there exist Lagrange multipliers* v_i , $i = 1,2,\ldots,n$, *such that*

$$\alpha_{ij} - (\bar{u}^k + b - \sum_{i=1}^{n} \sum_{j \in J_i} \lambda_{ij}^k g_{ij})^T g_{ij} \geq v_i \quad \text{for all } j \in J_i^* \ , \tag{39}$$

$$\alpha_{ij} - (\bar{u}^k + b - \sum_{i=1}^{n} \sum_{j \in J_i} \lambda_{ij}^k g_{ij})^T g_{ij} = v_i \quad \text{if } \lambda_{ij} > 0 \ , \tag{40}$$

and (24)–(25) hold.

We shall prove that λ^k and v^k satisfy these conditions. Since $\lambda_{ij}^k = 0$ for $j \notin J_i$ by (34)–(35), condition (40) follows from optimality conditions for (33)–(35). Next, with a view to (36), (39) is equivalent to

$$\min_{j \in J_i^*}\{ \alpha_{ij} - g_{ij}^T u^k \} \geq v_i \ , \ \ i = 1,2,\ldots,n \, ,$$

and the left side of the above inequality, owing to (27)–(28), can be expressed in form (37). The proof is complete.

The next question that should be clarified is the way of updating the sets J_i , if we fail to satisfy (38). With a view to Lemmas 1 and 2, we can suggest the following rules:

(i) delete from J_i all indices j for which $\lambda_{ij}^k = 0$;

(ii) add to the restricted master the columns

$$\alpha_{ik} = c_i^T x_{ik} \ , \tag{41}$$

$$g_{ik} = A_i x_{ik} \ , \tag{42}$$

for these i, for which (38) is violated, i.e. for which

$$(c_i - A_i^T u^k)^T x_{ik} < v_i^k \ .$$

Lemma 3. *If the sets* J_i *in (33)–(35) are updated according to the rules (i) and (ii), then after finitely many iterations we shall find an optimal solution to (29).*

Proof. The minimum value of (33)–(35) does not change, when columns corresponding to $\lambda_{ij}^k = 0$ are deleted. If the algorithm does not stop, then for at least one i, a new column is added by rule (ii). We shall show that the minimum value of (33)–(35) must decrease in this case. Indeed, denoting by $J_i^+ = \{ j \in J_i \, : \, \lambda_{ij}^k > 0 \}$ we have

$$\frac{\partial}{\partial \lambda_{ij}} L_\alpha (\lambda^k, \bar{u}^k) = \alpha_{ij} - g_{ij}^T u^k = v_i \, , \quad j \in J_i^+ \, ,$$

$$\frac{\partial}{\partial \lambda_{ik}} L_\alpha (\lambda^k, \bar{u}^k) = \alpha_{ik} - g_{ik}^T u^k < v_i \, .$$

Let us consider the direction d_i with components $d_{ij} = -\lambda_{ij}^k$, $j \in J_i^+$, $d_{ik} = 1$. It is a feasible direction by (34) and the definition of J_i^+. The directional derivative of L_α in d_i is negative, which proves the possibility of decreasing the value of (33) below the previous minimum. Since the number of possible sets $J_i \subseteq J_i^*$ is finite and the optimal value of the restricted master decreases, only finitely many exchanges in J_i are possible, which proves the result.

Using these ideas at Step 1 of Algorithm 2 we finally obtain the following decomposition method based on augmented Lagrangians.

Algorithm 3.

1. Solve the restricted master (33)–(35) at $\bar{u}^k$, getting a solution λ^k with at most $n + m$ positive components and Lagrange multipliers v^k corresponding to (34). Calculate u^k by (36).

2. Delete from J_i indices corresponding to $\lambda_{ij}^k = 0$.

3. For $i = 1, 2, \ldots, n$ solve (37) finding a vertex x_{ik} of X_i. If $f_i(u^k) < v_i^k$, then append the column defined by (41)–(42) to (33)–(35).

4. If $f_i(u^k) \geq v_i^k$ for $i = 1, 2, \ldots, n$ (minimum of (29) found) and $u^k = \bar{u}^k$ then stop; else if $f_i(u^k) \geq v_i^k$ for $i = 1, 2, \ldots, n$ but $u^k \neq \bar{u}^k$ then set $\bar{u}^{k+1} = u^k$ (*serious step*); otherwise set $\bar{u}^{k+1} = \bar{u}^k$ (*null step*).

5. Increase k by one and go to **1**.

Our earlier observations can be summarized as follows.

Theorem 2. *After finitely many iterations Algorithm 2 stops at Step 4 at λ^k, v^k and u^k such that the convex combinations*

$$x_i^k = \sum_{j \in J_i} \lambda_{ij}^k x_{ij} \, , \quad i = 1, 2, \ldots, n$$

form an optimal solution to (1), u^k is a vector of Lagrange multipliers corresponding to the linking constraint in (1), and

$$\sum_{i=1}^{n} c_i^T x_i^k = b^T u^k + \sum_{i=1}^{n} v_i^k \, .$$

Proof. Every sequence of null steps is finite by Lemma 3. Any time a serious step is executed, λ^k solves (29), i.e. x_{ik} solve (19)–(20). Since each serious step is identical with (22), the sequence of serious steps is identical with the sequence generated by Algorithm 2 and finite, owing to the finite convergence property of the augmented Lagrangian method for linear problems (cf. Bertsekas, 1982; Poljak and Trietiakov, 1972). The proof is complete.

4 Relation of the two methods

Let us now compare Algorithms 1 and 3. The crucial question here is the relation of the master problems (6)–(7) and (33)–(34).

Lemma 4. *Problems (6)–(7) and (33)–(35) are dual to each other.*

Proof. Let us derive the dual to (6)–(7). Denoting by λ_{ij} multipliers corresponding to (7) we obtain the following form of the dual problem

$$minimize_{\lambda \geq 0} L^*(\lambda, \bar{u}^k),$$

where

$$L^*(\lambda, \bar{u}^k) = \max_{(u,v)} \Big\{ -\frac{1}{2}\|u - u^k\|^2 + b^T u + \sum_{i=1}^{n} v_i + $$
$$+ \sum_{i=1}^{n} \sum_{j \in J_i} \lambda_{ij} \left(\alpha_{ij} - g_{ij}^T u - v_i \right) \Big\} .$$

By noting that $L^*(\lambda, \bar{u}^k) < \infty$ if and only if $\sum_{j\in J_i} \lambda_{ij} = 1$, after elementary transformations we arrive to (33)–(35).

With the two master problems equivalent there is no difficulty in coming to the following conclusion.

Theorem 3. *Algorithm 1 with $\gamma = 0$ and Algorithm 3 are equivalent in the sense that if they are started from the same point $\bar{u}^0$ and the same sets J_i, $i = 1, 2, \ldots, n$, and use the same subalgorithm for solving master problems (6)–(7) and (33)–(35), then they generate identical sequences $\{\bar{u}^k\}$, $\{u^k\}$, $\{v^k\}$ and $\{\lambda^k\}$.*

This result provides a new insight into both methods and suggests some obvious modifications and improvements.

First, the regularized decomposition with $0 < \gamma < 1$ provides new rules for changing multipliers $\bar{u}^k$ in the augmented Lagrangian method. Namely, we could change $\bar{u}^k$ at Step 4 of Algorithm 3 also when

$$\begin{aligned} F(u^k) &= b^T u^k + \sum_{i=1}^{n} f_i(u^k) \\ &\geq \gamma \Big(b^T u^k + \sum_{i=1}^{n} v_i^k \Big) + (1 - \gamma) F(\bar{u}^k) \end{aligned}$$

where

$$F(\bar{u}^k) = b^T\bar{u}^k + \sum_{i=1}^{n} f_i(\bar{u}^k) .$$

In fact, a more simple test $F(u^k) > F(\bar{u}^k)$ would do as well (see Ruszczynski, 1986). Next, we can also observe that for each k

$$\hat{F}^k = b^T u^k + \sum_{i=1}^{n} v_i^k \geq F(\bar{u}^k)$$

and equality occurs if and only if $\bar{u}^k$ is optimal (cf. Step 1 of Algorithm 1). Including these rules into Algorithm 3 shows that Step 1 of the prototype Algorithm 2 can be replaced by a rather special approximate minimization. As a result, we obtain a finitely convergent version of the augmented Lagrangian method with approximate minimization of the Lagrange function. We believe that this observation may be interesting in its own right, apart from the decomposability properties.

Finally, the relation that we discovered here may provide a new insight into non-smooth optimization methods (see Kiwiel, 1985) which motivated the development of the regularized decomposition method. Namely, we can regard them as dual to the augmented Lagrange function method applied to problems with infinitely many constraints.

5 References

Bertsekas, D. P. (1982). Constrained Optimization and Lagrange Multiplier Methods. Academic Press, New York, 1982.

Dantzig, G. B. and Wolfe, P. (1960). Decomposition principle for linear programs. *Operations Research*, no. 8, 1960, pp. 101–111.

Kiwiel, K. C. (1985). Methods of Descent for Nondifferentiable Optimization. Springer-Verlag, 1985.

Poljak, B. T. and Tretiakov, N. V. (1972). An iterative method for linear programming and its economic interpretation. *Matecon*, no. 10, 1974, pp. 81–100, (*Ekonomika i Matematicheskije Metody*, no. VII, 1972, pp. 740–751).

Rockafellar, R. T. (1976). Augmented Lagrangians and applications of the proximal algorithm in convex programming. *Mathematics of Operations Research*, no 1, 1976, pp. 97–116.

Rockafellar, R. T. and Wets, R. J. B. (1987). Scenarios and policy aggregation in optimization under uncertainty. WP–87–119, IIASA, Laxenburg, 1987.

Ruszczynski, A. (1986). A regularized decomposition method for minimizing a sum of polyhedral functions. *Mathematical Programming*, no. 35, 1986, pp. 309–333.

Stoilow, E. (1977). The augmented Lagrangian method in two–level static optimization. *Archiwum Automatyki i Telemechaniki*, no. 22, 1977, pp. 219–237.

Tatjewski, P. (1986). New dual decomposition algorithms for nonconvex separable optimization problems. Preprints of the 4th IFAC Symposium "Large Scale Systems — Theory and Applications", Zurich 1986, pp. 296–303.

Watanabe, N., Nishimura Y. and Matsubara, M. (1978). Decomposition in large system optimization using the method of multipliers. *Journal of Optimization Theory and Applications*, no. 22, 1978, pp. 135–194.

Dynamic Aspects of Multiobjective Trajectory Optimization in Decision Support Systems

Tadeusz Rogowski

Institute of Automatic Control, Warsaw University of Technology.

Abstract

This paper presents some remarks about dynamic aspects of multiobjective trajectory optimization in decision support systems. It starts with a short theoretical reminder of general principles of decision support systems based on reference point optimization and the quasisatisficing framework of rational choice, for the case of linear models as it is implemented in decision support systems IAC–DIDAS–L1 and –L2. It proceeds then to the basic discrete–time dynamic extension of this case and to various continuous–time extensions of multiobjective dynamic optimization. The importance of the concept of multiobjective trajectory optimization is stressed in the paper.

1 Linear multiobjective decision analysis problem - A standard case

The standard form of a multiobjective linear programming problem is defined as follows:

$$maximize\,(q = Cx)\ ;\ X = \{\, x \in R^n \ :\ Ax = b\ , x \geq 0 \,\} \tag{1}$$

where $x \in R^n$, $b \in R^p$, A is a $m \times n$ matrix, C is a $p \times n$ matrix and the maximization of the vector q of p objectives is understood in the Pareto sense: $\hat{x}$, $\hat{q}$ are solutions of (1) if $\hat{q} = C\hat{x}$, $\hat{x} \in X$ and there are no such x, q, with $q = Cx$, $x \in X$ that $q \geq \hat{q}$, $q \neq \hat{q}$. Such solutions, $\hat{x}$ and $\hat{q}$, of (1) are called an *efficient decision* $\hat{x}$ and the corresponding *efficient outcome* $\hat{q}$, respectively. If, in the above definition, it were only required that there would be no x and q, with $q = Cx$, $x \in X$, such that $q > \hat{q}$, then the solutions x, q would be called *weakly efficient*. Equivalently, if the set of all attainable outcomes is denoted by

$$Q = \{\, q \in R^p \ :\ q = Cx\,, x \in X \,\} \tag{2}$$

and so called *positive cones* $D = R^p_+$, $\tilde{D} = R^p_+ \setminus \{O\}$ and $\tilde{\tilde{D}} = int\ R^p_+$ are introduced (thus, $q \geq \hat{q}$ can be written as $q - \hat{q} \in D$, $q \geq \hat{q}$, $q \neq \hat{q}$ as $q - \hat{q} \in \tilde{D}$, and $q > \hat{q}$ as

$q - \hat{q} \in \tilde{\tilde{D}}$), then the sets of efficient outcomes $\hat{Q}$ and of weakly efficient outcomes $\hat{Q}^w$ can be written as:

$$\hat{Q} = \{q \in Q : (\hat{q} + \tilde{D}) \cap Q = \emptyset\} \tag{3}$$

$$\hat{Q}^w = \{\hat{q} \in Q : (\hat{q} + \tilde{\tilde{D}}) \cap Q = \emptyset\} \tag{4}$$

The set of weakly efficient outcomes is larger and contains the set of efficient outcomes; in many practical applications, however, the set of weakly efficient outcomes is decisively too large. For multiobjective linear programming problems, the efficient outcomes are always *properly efficient*, that is, they have bounded *tradeoff coefficients* that indicate how much an objective outcome should be deteriorated in order to improve another objective outcome by a unit.

The *abstract problem of multiobjective linear programming* consists in determining the entire sets $\hat{Q}$ or $\hat{Q}^w$, or at least all vertices or basic solutions of the linear programming problem that corresponds to efficient decisions and outcomes.

The *practical problem of multiobjective decision support*, using linear programming models, is different and consists in computing and displaying for the decision maker (or, generally, for the user of the decision support system) some selected efficient decisions and outcomes. This selection of efficient decisions and outcomes should be easily controlled by the user and should result in any efficient outcome in the set Q he might wish to attain, in particular, also in efficient outcomes that are not necessarily basic solutions of the original linear programming problem; moreover, weakly efficient outcomes are not of practical interest for the user.

Before turning to some theoretical problems resulting from these practical requirements, observe first that the standard formulation of multiobjective linear programming is not the most convenient for the user. Although many other formulations can be rewritten to the standard form by introducing proxy variables, such reformulations should not bother the user and should be automatically performed in the decision support system. Therefore, we present here another basic formulation of the multiobjective linear programming problem, more convenient for typical applications.

A *substantive model* of multiobjective linear programming type consists of the specification of vectors of n decision variables $x \in R^n$ and of m outcome variables $y \in R^m$, together with linear *model equations* defining the relations between the decision variables and the outcome variables and with *model bounds* defining the lower and upper bounds for all decision and outcome variables:

$$y = Ax\,; \qquad x^{\mathrm{lo}} \leq x \leq x^{\mathrm{up}}\,; \qquad y^{\mathrm{lo}} \leq y \leq y^{\mathrm{up}} \tag{5}$$

where A is a $m \times n$ matrix of coefficients. Among the outcome variables, some might be chosen as corresponding to *equality constraints*; let us denote these variables by $y^c \in R^{m'} \subset R^m$ and the constraining value for them — by b^c and let us write the additional constraints in the form:

$$y^c = A^c x = b^c\,; \qquad y^{c,\mathrm{lo}} \leq b^c \leq y^{c,\mathrm{up}} \tag{6}$$

where A^c is the corresponding submatrix of A. The outcome variables corresponding to equality constraints will be called *guided outcomes* here. Some other outcome variables can be also chosen as optimized objectives or *objective outcomes*. Denote the vector ofp objective outcomes by $q \in R^p \subset R^m$ (some of the objective variables might be originally not represented as outcomes of the model, but we can always add them by modifying this model) to write the corresponding objective equations in the form:

$$q = Cx \tag{7}$$

where C is another submatrix of A. Thus, the set of attainable objective outcomes is again $Q = CX$, but the set of admissible decisions X is defined by:

$$X = \{x \in R^n : x^{\text{lo}} \le x \le x^{\text{up}};\ \ y^{\text{lo}} \le Ax \le y^{\text{up}};\ \ A^c x = b^c\} \tag{8}$$

Moreover, the objective outcomes are not necessarily minimized; some of them might be minimized, some maximized, some stabilized or kept close to given *aspiration levels* (that is, minimized if their value is above aspiration level and maximized if their value is below aspiration level). All these possibilities can be summarized by introducing a different definition of the positive cone D:

$$\begin{aligned} D = \{q \in R^p :\ & q_i \ge 0, && i = 1, \ldots, p'; \\ & q_i \le 0, && i = p' + 1, \ldots, p''; \\ & q_i = 0, && i = p'' + 1, \ldots, p\} \end{aligned} \tag{9}$$

where the first p' objectives are to be maximized, the next, from $p' + 1$ to p'', are to be minimized, and the last, from $p'' + 1$ to p, are to be stabilized. Actually, the user needs only to define what to do with subsequent objectives; the concept of the positive cone D is used here only in order to define comprehensively what are efficient outcomes for the multiobjective problem. Given some aspiration levels for stabilized objectives and the requirement that these objectives should be minimized above and maximized below aspiration levels, the set of efficient outcomes can be defined only relative to the aspiration levels.

However, since the user can define aspiration levels arbitrarily, of interest here is the union of such relative sets of efficient outcomes. Let $\tilde{D} = D \setminus \{\emptyset\}$; then the outcomes that might be efficient for arbitrary aspiration levels for stabilized objectives can be defined, as before, by the relation (3). The weakly efficient outcomes are of no practical interest in this case, since the cone D, typically, has empty interior which implies that weakly efficient outcomes coincide with all attainable outcomes.

The stabilized outcomes in the above definition of efficiency are, in a sense, similar to the guided outcomes; however, there is an important distinction between these two concepts. Equality constraints must be satisfied; if not, then there are no admissible solutions for the model. Stabilized objective outcomes should be kept close to aspiration levels, but they can differ from those levels if, through this difference, other objectives can be improved. The user of a decision support system should keep this distinction in mind and can modify the definition of the multiobjective analysis problem by taking, for example, some outcomes out of the guided outcome category and putting them into the stabilized objective category.

By adding a number of proxy variables and changing the interpretation of matrix A, the substantive model formulation (5), (6), (7), (8) together with its positive cone (9) and the related concept of efficiency could be equivalently rewritten to the standard form of multiobjective linear programming (1); this, however, does not concern the user. More important is the way of user–controlled selection of an efficient decision and outcome from the set (3). For stabilized objective outcomes, the user can change the related aspiration levels in order to influence this selection; *it is assumed here that he will use, for all objective outcomes, the corresponding aspiration levels in order to influence the selection of efficient decisions*. The aspiration levels are denoted here $\bar{q}_i$ or, as a vector, $\bar{q}$ and called also, equivalently, *reference points*.

A special way of parametric scalarization of the multiobjective analysis problem is utilized for the purpose of influencing the selection of efficient outcomes by changing reference points. This parametric scalarization is obtained through maximizing the following *order–approximating achievement function* (see Lewandowski et al. 1983; Wierzbicki, 1986):

$$s(q, \bar{q}) = \min\left[\min_{1\le i\le p} z_i(q_i, \bar{q}_i),\quad \left(\frac{1}{\rho p}\right)\sum_{i=1}^{p} z_i(q_i, \bar{q}_i)\right] + \left(\frac{\varepsilon}{p}\right)\sum_{i=1}^{p} z_i(q_i, \bar{q}_i) \tag{10}$$

where the parameter ε should be positive, even if very small; if this parameter would be equal to zero, then the above function would not be order–approximating any more, but *order–representing*, and its maximal points could correspond to weakly efficient outcomes. The parameter ρ should be $\rho \geq 1$; the interpretation of both these parameters is given later.

The functions $z_i(q_i, \bar{q}_i)$ are defined as follows:

$$z_i(q_i, \bar{q}_i) = \begin{cases} (q_i - \bar{q}_i)/s_i, & \text{if} \quad 1 \le i \le p', \\ (\bar{q}_i - q_i)/s_i, & \text{if} \quad p'+1 \le i \le p'', \\ \min(z_i', z_i''), & \text{if} \quad p''+1 \le i \le p, \end{cases} \tag{11}$$

where

$$z_i' = (q_i - \bar{q}_i)/s_i', \qquad z_i'' = (\bar{q}_i - q_i)/s_i'' \tag{12}$$

The coefficients s_i, s_i' and s_i'' are scaling units for all objectives, either defined by the user (in which case $s_i' = s_i''$, the user does not need to define two scaling coefficients for a stabilized objective outcome) or determined automatically in the system (see further comments).

The achievement function $s(q, \bar{q})$ is maximized with $q = Cx$ over $x \in X$; its maximization in the system is converted automatically to an equivalent linear programming problem, different than the original one, and having more basic solutions that depend on the parameter $\bar{q}$. If the coefficient $\varepsilon > 0$, then the achievement function has the following properties (see Wierzbicki, 1986):

a) For an arbitrary aspiration level or reference point $\bar{q}$, not necessarily restricted to be attainable or not attainable, each maximal point $\hat{q}$ of the achievement function $s(q, \bar{q})$ with $q = Cx$ over $x \in X$ is a D_ε–efficient solution, that is, a properly efficient solution with tradeoff coefficients bounded approximately by ε and $1/\varepsilon$.

b) For any properly efficient outcome $\hat{q}$ with trade–off coefficients bounded by ε and $1/\varepsilon$, there exist such reference points $\bar{q}$ that the maximum of the achievement function $s(q, \bar{q})$ is attained at the properly efficient outcome $\hat{q}$. In particular, if the user (either by chance or as a result of a learning process) specifies a reference point $\bar{q}$ that in itself is such properly efficient outcome, $\bar{q} = \hat{q}$, then the maximum of the achievement function $s(q, \bar{q})$, equal zero, is attained precisely at this point.

c) If the reference point $\bar{q}$ is 'too high' (for maximized outcomes; 'too low ' for minimized outcomes), then the maximum of the achievement function, smaller than zero, is attained at an efficient outcome that approximates the reference point uniformly best, in the sense of scaling units s_i. If the reference point $\bar{q}$ is 'too low ' (for maximized outcomes; 'too high' for minimized outcomes and it can happen only if there are no stabilized outcomes), then the maximum of the achievement function, larger than zero, is attained at an efficient outcome that is uniformly 'higher' than the reference point, in the sense of scaling units s_i.

d) By changing his reference point $\bar{q}$, the user can continuously influence the selection of the corresponding efficient outcomes $\hat{q}$ that maximize the achievement function.

The parameter ε in the achievement function sets bounds on trade–off coefficients: if an efficient solution has trade–off coefficients that are too large or too small (say, lower than 10^{-6} or higher than 10^{6}) then it does not differ, for the decision maker, from weakly efficient outcomes — some of its components could be improved without practically deteriorating other components. Another interpretation of this parameter is that it indicates how much an average overachievement (or underachievement) of aspiration levels should correct the minimal overachievement (or maximal underachievement) in the function (10).

The parameter $\rho \geq 1$ can influence the shape of this achievement function only if $\rho > 1$. If $\rho = 1$, then the middle term of this function can be omitted since it is never active in this case. If $\rho > 1$, then this term becomes active only if the achievement function is positive (that is, if the reference point $\bar{q}$ is 'too low ' for maximized outcomes, 'too high' for minimized outcomes and there are nostabilized outcomes). In such a case, the piece–wise linear achievement function (10) has a piece on its positive level–sets that corresponds to the sum of overachievements $(q_i - \bar{q}_i)/s_i$ and not to the minimal overachievement (for maximized outcomes, with corresponding changes for minimized outcomes). This modification becomes stronger for larger ρ, but always occurs only for positive values of the achievement function; it is useful when the user wants to select efficient outcomes that maximize the sum of positive overachievements.

The maximization of the achievement function is a convenient way of organizing interaction between the model and the user. Before the interactive–analysis phase, however, the user must firstly define the substantive model, then define the multiobjective analysis problem by specifying outcome variables that should be maximized, minimized, stabilized, guided or *floating* (that is, displayed for the users' information only, but not included as optimized or guided objectives; various decision variables of interest to the user can be also included into one of these categories). Before the initial analysis phase, the user should also define some reasonable lower and upper bounds for each optimized (maximized, minimized or stabilized) variable, and some reasonable scaling units s_i for these variables. In further phases of analysis, a special automatic way of setting scaling units s_i can be also applied; this, however, requires an approximation of bounds on efficient solutions. Such an approximation is performed in the initial analysis phase.

The 'upper' bound for efficient solutions could be theoretically obtained through maximizing each objective separately (or minimizing, in case of minimized objectives; in the case of stabilized objectives, the user should know their entire attainable range, hence they should be both maximized and minimized). Jointly, the results of such optimization form a point that approximates from 'above' the set of efficient outcomes $\hat{Q}$, but this point almost never (except in degenerate cases) is in itself an attainable outcome; therefore, it is called the ***utopia point***.

However, this way of computing the 'upper' bound for efficient outcomes is not always practical, particularly for problems of dynamic structure (see further comments); thus, IAC-DIDAS-L1 and -L2 use a different way of estimating the utopia point (see Rogowski et al., 1987). This way consists in subsequent maximizations of the achievement function $s(q, \bar{q})$ with suitably selected reference points. If an objective should be maximized and its maximal value must be estimated, then the corresponding component of the reference point should be very high, while the components of this point for all other maximized objectives should be very low (for minimized objectives — very high; stabilized objectives must be considered as floating in this case that is, should not enter the achievement function). If an objective should be minimized and its minimal value must be estimated, then the corresponding component of the reference point should be very low, while other components of this point are treated as in the previous case. If an objective should be stabilized and both its maximal and minimal values must be estimated, then the achievement function should be maximized twice, first time as if for a maximized objective and the second time as if for minimized one. Thus the entire number of optimization runs in utopia point computations is $p'' + 2(p - p'')$. It can be shown that, for problems with static structure (no trajectory objectives), this procedure gives a very good approximation of the utopia point $\hat{q}^{\text{uto}}$, whereas the precise meaning of 'very high' reference should be interpreted as the upper bound for the objective plus, say, twice the distance between the lower and the upper bound, while the meaning of 'very low' is the lower bound minus twice the distance between the upper and the lower bound.

During all these computations, the lower bound for efficient outcomes can be also estimated, just by recording the lowest efficient outcomes that occur in subsequent optimizations for maximized objectives and the highest efficient outcomes for minimized objectives (there is no need to record them for stabilized objectives, where the entire attainable range is estimated anyway). However, such a procedure results in the accurate, tight 'lower' bound for efficient outcomes — called *nadir point* $\hat{q}^{\text{nad}}$ — only if $p'' = 2$; for larger numbers of maximized and minimized objectives, this procedure can give misleading results, while an accurate computation of the nadir point becomes a very cumbersome computational task.

2 Discrete–time dynamic extension of multiobjective linear problems

There are many examples of decision problems that can be analysed by means of substantive model of multiobjective linear programming type; however, many of them have actually a dynamic structure. DIDAS — type systems with multiobjective, dynamic linear programming models have been used in planning energy policies (see Strubegger, 1985; Messner, 1985), agricultural policies (see Makowski and Sosnowski, 1984) as well as in analysing various environmental or technological problems (see Kaden, 1985; Gorecki et al., 1983), another example might be a dynamic multiobjective linear programming model for flood control, where the decision are time sequences trajectories – of outflows of reservoirs and the outcomes are trajectories of flows in various points on the river (Lewandowski et al., 1984a, 1984b).

Discrete multiobjective dynamic programming problem given by state equations (linear model):

$$x(t+1) = A(t)x(t) + B(t)u(t), \qquad t = 0,1,\ldots,T-1, \qquad x(0) \ - \text{ given}, \tag{13}$$

outcome equations:

$$y(t) = C(t)x(t) + D(t)u(t), \qquad t = 0,1,\ldots,T-1, \tag{14}$$

and corresponding bounds, where:

t — is the discrete time variable,

$u(t) \in R^n$ — control trajectory or decision trajectory,

$x(t) \in R^m$ — state trajectory,

$q(t) = y(t) \in R^p$ — outcome trajectory, objective trajectory.

In this case, it is possible to use the following *order–approximating achievement function*:

$$s(q, \bar{q}, \alpha) = \min_{1<i<T} \min_{1<i<p} \alpha_i(t)\Big(q_i(t) - \bar{q}_i(t)\Big) + \alpha_{p+1}\sum_{t=0}^{T}\sum_{i=1}^{p}\alpha_i(t)\Big(q_i(t) - \bar{q}_i(t)\Big) \tag{15}$$

DIDAS methodology can be successfully applied for this purpose.

A computation of an *utopia trajectory* and an approximation of a *nadir trajectory* as in static problem would require in this case $p\star(T+1)$ scalar optimization. However, precise upper bound and lower bound trajectories are not needed in most cases of decision support — their approximate values often suffice.

A convenient way: optimize p times with p different reference trajectories:

$$\bar{q}^{(j)} = \left\{\bar{q}^{(j)}(0), \bar{q}^{(j)}(1), \ldots, \bar{q}^{(j)}(T)\right\}, \qquad j = 1,2,\ldots,p, \tag{16}$$

where the components $\bar{q}_i^{(j)}(t)$ are chosen to be very high if $i = j$ and very low if $i \neq j$ (see e.g.. Lewandowski et al., 1984; Lewandowski and Wierzbicki, 1988).

Approximate upper bound trajectories:

$$\hat{q}_{i,\max}(t) = q_i^{(j)}(t) , \qquad t = 0,1,\ldots,T, \qquad i = 1,2,\ldots,p ;$$

and lower bound for trajectories:

$$\hat{q}^{(j)}_{i,\min}(t) = \min_{1<j<p} q_i^{(j)}(t) , \qquad t = 0,1,\ldots,T, \qquad i = 1,2,\ldots,p ; \tag{17}$$

are obtained this way; later on, we assume that such bounds are determinated and used for determining scaling coefficients.

In similar way, other order–approximating achievement functions or even smooth order–approximating functions, can be rewritten for the case of multiobjective trajectory optimization.

From theoretical and numerical point of view, the solution of a problem of dynamic structure is difficult even in its classical formulation (with single objective function). These problems are discussed in literature elsewhere and there exist many computational methods for solving dynamic optimization problems. However, if we add the problem of analysing trajectories as decision outcomes, beside theoretical and numerical problems, arising from this complication, we face the difficulty that the decision–maker (user) might be baffled in the interpretation of objectives when their number grows. It is a known psychological fact that the human decision–maker cannot compare or evaluate in this mind more than five to ten objects, depending on their complexity; however, this does not mean that these objects should be characterized by only scalar attributes. If the outcomes of decision are represented by a solution of dynamical model, there is a natural way of aggregating them into trajectories: we combine the values of the same outcome for consecutive instants of time, and the number of these instants can grow rather large, but we still deal with same kind trajectory. Once the meaning of a trajectory of outcomes is well understood the specification and/or interpretation of a related reference, aspiration or reservation trajectory becomes easy. Thus, the conclusion that no more than five to ten scalar attributes should be compared is over-simplified: in decision support systems based on substantive models, we can as well compare five to ten trajectories containing a large amount of information (see Lewandowski and Wierzbicki, 1988).

3 General forms of multiobjective dynamic problems

Now, a special question in multiobjective decision analysis and support arises: how general is the class of substantive models of discrete–time dynamic linear nature? Linearity is here an obvious restriction. However, in decision problems of dynamic structure we can distinguish at least the following types of models:

A. continuous–time models given by differential equation (linear or nonlinear, partial or ordinary) and their trajectories interpreted as decision outcomes, that is, with infinite — dimensional outcome spaces;

B. continuous–time models given as above, but with a finite — dimensional outcome space, while outcomes or objectives are defined by a given number of objective functionals;

C. discrete–time models (given a'priori) or discrete–time approximations of continuous–time models which reduces the outcome space to finite dimensions, as discussed in the previous paragraph; however, in the case analogous to A these dimensions will be very large, hence it is useful to distinguish, as above, the case of trajectory optimization, versus traditional multiobjective optimization.

Dynamic models with continuous time can have rather diverse mathematical character, we shall consider here only a relatively simple but widely applied class of such models, described by ordinary differential or difference equations. We shall consider first examples of the case B or its analog within the case C.

EXAMPLE 1. Let us now consider a multiobjective continuous control problem, with finite–dimensional outcomes space, as described by Szidarovszky et al., 1987a,b. The model consist of a state equations:

$$\dot{x}(t) = f\Big(t\,,\, x(t)\,,\, u(t)\Big)\,, \qquad x(t_0) = x_0 \tag{18}$$

and of a multiobjective functional:

$$q_i = \int_{t_0}^{t_1} g_i\Big(t\,,\, x(t)\,,\, u(t)\Big)\; dt \qquad (i = 1, 2, \ldots, n)\,, \tag{19}$$

that should be maximized in each component. Introduce the following notation:

$$\begin{aligned} \bar{q}_i &= \int_{t_0}^{t_1} \Phi_i^\star(t)\, dt\,, \\ D_i &= \int_{t_0}^{t_1} \Big[\Phi_i^\star(\tau) - g_i\Big(\tau\,,\, x(\tau)\,,\, u(\tau)\Big)\Big]\, d\tau\,, \qquad i = 1, 2, \ldots, n. \end{aligned} \tag{20}$$

Observe that:

$$D_i(t_1) = \Phi_i^\star(t) - g_i\Big(t\,,\, x(t)\,,\, u(t)\Big)\,, \qquad D_i(t_0) = 0\,, \tag{21}$$

and $D_i(t_1) \le \bar{q}_i - \underline{q}_i$, where $\underline{q}_i \le \int_{t_0}^{t_1} g_i\Big(t\,,\, x(t)\,,\, u(t)\Big)\, dt\,,\ \ i = 1, 2, \ldots, n.$

A scalarizing function for these objectives can be chosen in various way, for example in way similar to this described in the preceding paragraphs, or more generally see Lewandowski et al., 1988. However, Szidarovszky et al., 1987a, use the weighted l_p norm and show that this problem is equivalent to optimizing the function:

$$\begin{aligned} s(q\,,\, \bar{q}\,,\, \alpha) &= \sum_{i=1}^{n} \alpha_i v_i\Big(D_i(t_1)\Big) = \\ &= \sum_{i=1}^{n} \alpha_i \int_{t_0}^{t_1} v_i'\Big(D_i(t)\Big)\,\Big[\Phi_i^\star - g_i(t\,,\, x\,,\, u)\Big]\; dt = \\ &= \int_{t_0}^{t_1} \sum_{i=1}^{n} \alpha_i v_i'\Big(D_i(t)\Big)\,\Big[\Phi_i^\star - g_i(t\,,\, x\,,\, u)\Big]\; dt\,, \end{aligned} \tag{22}$$

where v_i — is a differentiable monotonous function, e.g. $v_i(t) = t^4$.
Introducing the function:

$$G\Big(t\,,\, x(t)\,,\, D_1(t)\,,\,\ldots\,,\, D_n(t)\,,\, u(t)\Big) = \sum_{i=1}^{n} \alpha_i v_i'\Big(D_i(t)\Big)\Big[\Phi_i^\star(t) - g_i\Big(t\,,\, x(t)\,,\, u(t)\Big)\Big]$$

we have a continuous control problem described by the state equations:

$$\begin{aligned} \dot{x}(t) &= f\Big(t\,,\, x(t)\,,\, u(t)\Big)\,, & x(t_0) &= x_0\,, & \\ \dot{D}(t) &= \Phi_i^\star(t) - g_i\Big(t\,,\, x(t)\,,\, u(t)\Big)\,, & D_i(t_0) &= 0\,, & i = 1,2,\ldots,n \end{aligned} \qquad (23)$$

with final constraints:

$$D_i(t_1) \le \bar{g}_i - \underline{g}_i\,, \qquad i = 1,2,\ldots,n \qquad (24)$$

and a goal function to be minimized:

$$\int_{t_0}^{t_1} G\Big(t\,,\, x(t)\,,\, u(t)\,,\, D_1(t)\,,\,\ldots\,,\, D_n(t)\,,\, u(t)\Big)\, dt\,, \qquad (25)$$

where:

$u(t)$ — control trajectory functions (decision functions),

$x(t), D_1(t),\ldots, D_n(t)$ — state trajectory functions,

$\bar{q}$ — reference point (vector).

Thus — by increasing the dimensionality of the state space — the multiobjective continuous control problem (18)—(19) of the class B is reformulated as a classical dynamic problem with single objective function (23)—(25) (Szidarovszky et al., 1987a).

EXAMPLE 2. Consider a discrete multiobjective dynamic programming problem having the general form:

$$x_j = f_j(\, x_{j-1}\,,\, u_j\,)\,, \qquad x_0 \;-\; \text{given}, \qquad j = 1,2,\ldots,m\,, \qquad (26)$$

$$\sum_{j=1}^{m} g_{ji}(\, x_j\,,\, u_j\,) \;\Rightarrow\; \text{maximize}, \qquad i = 1,2,\ldots,n\,. \qquad (27)$$

As above, define the discrete functions D_{ji}, $\Phi_{ji}^\star$, G_j, then new state transitions functions and constraints are:

$$x_j = f_j(\, x_{j-1}\,,\, u_j\,)\,, \qquad x_0 \;-\; \text{given}\,, \qquad j = 1,2,\ldots,m\,, \qquad (28)$$

$$\begin{aligned} D_{ji} &= D_{j-1,i} + \Phi_{ji}^\star - g_{ji}\Big(f_j(\, x_{j-1}\,,\, u_j\,)\Big)\,, \quad D_{0i} = 0\,, & i = 1,2,\ldots,n, \\ D_{ji} &\le \bar{q}_i - \underline{q}_i\,, & i = 1,2,\ldots,n\,; \end{aligned} \qquad (29)$$

and a goal function to be minimized:

$$F = \sum_{j=1}^{m} G_j \ . \tag{30}$$

More detailed examples were discussed by Szidarovszky et al., 1987a,b, in applications first to regional natural resources management. Second example is a multiobjective optimization model for wine production. In both examples, the model is given by differential or difference equations (continuous–time in the first, discrete–time in the second example) and objective functions are defined by functionals, as is multiobjective optimization of static type. In wine production — two objective functions are defined: the net profit (which is maximized) and maximal manpower demand during growing season (which is minimized). In the scalarizing function, weighting coefficient are utilized for the purpose of influencing the selection of efficient outcomes. Possible, this way of influencing that the selection is not good as by changing aspiration levels in an order–consistent achievement function, but this is not the main point of these examples. The main point is that the dynamic aspects of the models in these examples are of secondary importance: they contribute to the complexity of the model, but do not much influence the complexity of decision problem. If the model in the second example was linear, we could as will rewrite the corresponding decision problem in the standard static way presented in the first paragraph. Truly dynamic aspects of multiobjective choice arise in case A or its analog in case C, when the objectives form dynamic trajectories.

EXAMPLE 3. Consider the question of approximating a continuous–time dynamic linear model, described by ordinary differential equations and with selected trajectories as decision outcomes, by a discrete–time model of the standard form described in the second paragraph of this paper.

Continuous–time dynamic linear problem is given by the following linear state equations:

$$\dot{x}(t) = Ax(t) + Bu(t)\,, \qquad t \in [t_0, t_1], \quad x(t_0) - given, \tag{31}$$

some outcome equations, which are assumed here in a very simplified form just for illustration purposes as:

$$q(t) = x(t), \tag{32}$$

and by some constraints, which shall not be considered in this simplified example.

Here we use the following notation:

$u(t)$ – control trajectory or decision trajectory, a vector function of time;

$x(t)$ – state trajectory, a vector function of time;

$q(t)$ – outcome trajectory, also a vector function of time;

A, B – matrices of suitable dimensions, in this example for simplicity assumed to be constant.

Introduce the following approximation function:

$$x_i = \sum_{j=1}^{m} \varsigma_j^i \beta_j(t), \qquad i = 1, \ldots, n, \tag{33}$$

where $\beta_j(t)$ are basis function from a spline space (the spaces S^1, S^2 and S^3 of piecewise linear, 2–nd or 3–rd order polynomial functions with appropriate smoothness conditions are useful for approximating the state trajectories; the control trajectories could be approximated in the space S^0 of piecewise constant functions, but we omit here the discussion of know aspects of approximating control system equations by a spline function system). The ς_j^i are approximating coefficients and n is the state dimension.

If we consider now outcome trajectories as infinitely dimensional objectives, we have to define consequently reference trajectories as functions of approximating coefficient $\bar{\varsigma}_j^i$:

$$\bar{q}_i(t) = \sum_{j=1}^{m} \bar{\varsigma}_j^i \beta_j(t). \tag{34}$$

An achievement scalarizing function $z_i(q_i, \bar{q}_i)$ given by form (11), depends on term $q_i - \bar{q}_i$ or $(\bar{q}_i - q_i)$. A natural way of generalizing this function to this specific case is based the following observation:

$$q_i - \bar{q}_i = \int_{t_0}^{t_1} (q_i(t) - \bar{q}_i(t))dt = \int_{t_0}^{t_1} \sum_{j=1}^{m} (\beta_j(t)(\varsigma_j^i - \bar{\varsigma}_j^i)dt =$$

$$= \sum_{j=1}^{m} (\varsigma_j^i - \bar{\varsigma}_j^i) \int_{t_0}^{t_1} \beta_j(t)dt = \sum_{j=1}^{m} \beta_j(\varsigma_j^i - \bar{\varsigma}_j^i) \tag{35}$$

where: $\beta_j = \int_{t_0}^{t_1} \beta_j(t)dt$ it is known value.

In this case is a possible to use the achievement function (10) while interpreting $s(q, \bar{q})$ as $s(\varsigma, \bar{\varsigma})$. However, there might be many other approaches to interpreting a reference trajectory in a spline approximation. Generally, the following problem arises: the user of decision system might be not accustomed to spline approximations, and might therefore interpret the coefficients ς_j^i not quite easily. In such a case, a special reference trajectory interface is required: the user might define the reference trajectory by numerical or graphical means, say, using a mouse, and the interface should convert it into a spline approximation. Once the meaning of the function $s(\varsigma, \bar{\varsigma})$ is defined, we can minimize this function, obtain an approximating coefficient ς_j^i, $\; j = 1, \ldots, m; \;\; i = 1, \ldots, n$, and next define the control from the state equation, say, by the simple transformation (assuming that B is convertible in this simplified example):

$$u(t) = B^{-1}(\sum_{j=1} \varsigma_j(\dot{\beta}_j(t) - A\beta_j(t)) \tag{36}$$

or by more advanced approximation methods in the more general case. This very simplified example suggests a number of further questions: how to choose the space depending on particular properties of the model, how to deal with nonlinear models, etc.

4 Technical and implementation issues in multiobjective trajectory optimization

We have seen that various technical problems arise in the manipulation of the reference trajectories. The same applies to other trajectory–type data, such as bounds etc. Other problems arise in the necessary elements of a decision support system that are an user friendly–interface and a data base for results.

The user–friendly interface in the case of trajectory optimization should perform the following functions:

create trajectories,

select trajectories,

modify trajectories (e.g. references) and other data (e.g. scaling factors),

delete trajectories,

display trajectories using graphics terminals.

Another special feature of user–computer interface of a trajectory–oriented extension of DIDAS are special trajectory definition and trajectory interpretation modules (see Lewandowski et al., 1984a,b). The data base for results, in the case of trajectory optimization has functions similar to the static case, with the obvious difference that it should record trajectories.

5 References

Gorecki, H., Kopytowski, J., Rys, T. and Zebrowski M. (1983). A multiobjective procedure for project formulation — design of chemical installation. In Grauer, M. and Wierzbicki, A. P. eds.: Interactive Decision Analysis. Springer Verlag, Berlin.

Kaden, S. (1985). Decision support system for long–term water management in open–pit lignite mining areas. In Fandel, G., Grauer, M., Kurzanski A. and Wierzbicki, A. P. eds.: Large–Scale Modelling and Interactive Decision Analysis. Proceedings Eisenach, Springer Verlag, Berlin.

Lewandowski, A., Grauer, M., Wierzbicki A. P. (1983). DIDAS — theory, implementation and experiences. In Grauer, M., Wierzbicki, A. P. eds.: Interactive Decision Analysis. Proceedings Laxenburg. Springer Verlag, Berlin.

Lewandowski, A., Rogowski, T. and Kreglewski, T. (1984a). A trajectory–oriented extension of DIDAS and its application. In Grauer, M., Thompson, M., Wierzbicki, A. P. eds.: Plural Rationality and Interactive Decision Processes. Proceedings, Sopron. Springer Verlag, Berlin.

Lewandowski, A., Rogowski, T. and Kreglewski, T. (1984b). Application of DIDAS methodology to flood control problems — numerical experiments. In Grauer, M., Thompson, M., Wierzbicki, A. P. eds.: Plural Rationality and Interactive Decision Processes. Proceedings, Sopron. Springer Verlag, Berlin.

Lewandowski, A., Wierzbicki, A. P. (1988a). Aspiration Based Decision Analysis and Support. Part I: Theoretical and Methodological Backgrounds. WP-88-03, IIASA, Laxenburg.

Lewandowski, A., Kreglewski, T., Rogowski, T., Wierzbicki, A. P. (1988b). Decision Support Systems of DIDAS Family. Second paper of this volume.

Makowski, M., Sosnowski, J. (1984). A decision support system for planning and controlling agricultural production with a decentralized management structure. In Grauer, M., Thompson, M., Wierzbicki, A. P. eds.: Plural Rationality and Interactive Decision Processes. Proceedings, Sopron. Springer Verlag, Berlin.

Messner, S. (1985). Natural gas trade in Europe and interactive decision analysis. In Fandel, G., Grauer, M., Kurzanski, A. and Wierzbicki, A.P. eds.: Large-Scale Modelling and Interactive Decision Analysis. Proceedings, Eisenach. Springer Verlag, Berlin.

Rogowski, T., Sobczyk, J., Wierzbicki A. P. (1987). IAC-DIDAS-L, A Dynamic Interactive Decision Analysis and Support System for Multicriteria Analysis of Linear and Dynamic Linear Models on Professional Microcomputers. In Lewandowski, A., Wierzbicki, A. P. eds.: Theory, Software and Testing Examples for Decision Support Systems. WP-87-26, IIASA, Laxenburg.

Steuer, R. (1986). Multiple Criteria Optimization: Theory, Computation and Application. John Wiley & Sons, New York.

Strubegger, M. (1985). An approach for integrated energy-economy decision analysis: the case of Austria. In Fandel, G., Grauer, M., Kurzanski, A. and Wierzbicki, A. P. eds.: Large-Scale Modelling and Interactive Decision Analysis. Proceedings, Eisenach. Springer Verlag, Berlin.

Szidarovszky, F., Gershon, M. Bardossy, A. (1987a). Application of Multiobjective Dynamic Programming to Regional Natural Resource Management. *Applied Mathematics and Computation*, 24:281-301.

Szidarovszky, F., Szenteleki, K. (1987b). A Multiobjective Optimization Model for Wine Production. *Applied Mathematics and Computation*, 22:255-275.

Wierzbicki, A. P. (1980). Multiobjective trajectory optimization and model semiregularization. WP-80-181, IIASA, Laxenburg.

Wierzbicki, A. P. (1986). On the completeness and constructiveness of parametric characterizations to vector optimization problems. *OR Spektrum* 8, 73-87.

Mathematical Programming Package HYBRID

Marek Makowski

*IIASA, Laxenburg, Austria.**

Janusz S. Sosnowski

Systems Research Institute, Polish Academy of Sciences, Warsaw.

Abstract

HYBRID is a mathematical programming package which includes all the functions necessary for the solution of multicriteria LP problems and single-criteria linear-quadratic problems. HYBRID is specially useful for dynamic problems since the applied algorithm exploits the structure of a dynamic problem and the user has the advantage of handling a problem as a dynamic one which results in an easy way of formulation of criteria and of interpretation of results. HYBRID is oriented towards an interactive mode of operation in which a sequence of problems is to be solved under varying conditions (e.g., different objective functions, reference points, values of constraints or bounds). Criteria for multiobjective problems may be easily defined and updated with the help of the package. Besides that HYBRID offers many options useful for diagnostic and verification of a problem being solved. HYBRID is available in two versions: one for VAX 6210 (running under Ultrix-32) and one for a PC compatible with PC IBM/AT/XT.

1 Introduction

The purpose of this report is to provide a sufficient understanding of mathematical, methodological and theoretical foundations of the HYBRID package. Section 1 contains executive summary, short program description and general remarks on solution techniques and package implementation. Section 2 contains mathematical formulation of various types of problems that can be solved by HYBRID. Section 3 presents methodological problems related to solution techniques. Section 4 presents foundations of the chosen solution technique and documents the computational algorithm. Section 5 contains short discussion of testing examples. Last two sections contain conclusions and references.

*on leave from the Systems Research Institute of the Polish Academy of Sciences, Warsaw.

This paper does not include information necessary for using the package. A reader who is interested in usage of the package should consult a User Guide to HYBRID (Makowski and Sosnowski, 1988b). In the User Guide the following topics are discussed:

- the way of choosing various options provided by the package.
- guidelines for formulation and modification of a problem which is to be solved or at least processed by HYBRID.
- the way in which HYBRID provides diagnostics and results.
- a short tutorial example.
- the specification of the MPS standard for input data and an example of the MPS format input file.

1.1 Executive summary

HYBRID is a mathematical programming package which includes all the functions necessary for the solution of linear programming problems. The current version of HYBRID, called HYBRID 3.1, may be used for solving both static and dynamic LP problems (in fact also for problems with a more general structure then the classical formulation of dynamic linear problems). HYBRID 3.1 may be used for both single- and multi-criteria LP problems as well as for single-criteria linear-quadratic problems. Since HYBRID is designed for real-life problems, it offers many options useful for diagnostic and verification of a problem being solved.

HYBRID is a member of the DIDAS family decision analysis and support systems since it is designed to support usage of multicriteria reference point optimization. HYBRID can be used by an analyst or by a team composed of a decision maker and an analyst or—on last stage of application—by a decision maker alone. In any case, we will speak further on about a user of HYBRID package.

HYBRID can serve as a tool which helps to choose a decision in a complex situation in which many options may and should be examined. Such problems occur in many situations, such as problems of economic planning and analysis, many technological or engineering design problems, problems of environmental control. To illustrate possible range of applications, let us list problems for which the proposed approach either has been or may be applied: planning of agriculture production policy in a decentralized economy (both for governmental agency and for production units, Makowski and Sosnowski, 1985a), flood control in a watershed (Kreglewski et al., 1985), planning formation and utilization of water resources in an agricultural region, scheduling irrigation, planning and design of purification plant system for water or air pollution.

To avoid a possible misleading conclusion that the usage of HYBRID may replace a real decision maker, we should stress that HYBRID is designed to help the decision maker to concentrate on his actual decision tasks while HYBRID takes care on cumbersome computations and provides information that serves for analysis of consequences of different options or alternatives. A user is expected to define various alternatives or scenarios, changing his preferences and priorities when learning about consequences of possible decisions.

HYBRID could be used for that purpose as a "stand alone" package, however—after a possible modification of a problem in an interactive way—one can also output the MPS-format file from HYBRID to be used in other packages. The later approach can be used also for a transformation of a multicriteria problem to an equivalent single-criteria LP. HYBRID includes also some diagnostic functions that are not performed by many other linear programming packages, e.g., by MINOS (it is interesting to note that the authors of MINOS actually advise the user to debug and verify the problem with another package before using MINOS).

HYBRID can be used for solving any linear programming problem but it is specially useful for dynamic problems; this covers a wide area of applications of operation researches. Many optimization problems in economic planning over time, production scheduling, inventory, transportation, control dynamic systems can be formulated as linear dynamic problems (Propoi, 1976). Such problems are also called multistage or staircase linear programming problems (Fourer, 1982, Ho and Hanne, 1974). A dynamic problem can be formulated as an equivalent large static LP and any commercial LP code may be used for solving it, if the problem corresponds to single objective optimization. For multicriteria problems, a preprocessor may be used for transformation of that problem to an equivalent LP one. One of the first versions of the system DIDAS was a package composed of a preprocessor and a postprocessor for handling transformation of multicriteria problem and processing results respectively (Lewandowski and Grauer, 1982). Those pre- and postprocesors were linked with an LP package. HYBRID 3.1 has generally a similar structure. The main difference is that—instead of an LP package—another non-simplex algorithm is applied, which exploits the dynamics of a problem and that HYBRID is integrated package with user–friendly interface. Similarly as some other systems of DIDAS family, HYBRID has the advantage of handling a problem as a dynamic one which results in an easy way of formulation of criteria and of interpretation of results, since one may refer to one variable trajectory contrary to a "static" formulation of dynamic problems which involves separate variables for each time period.

HYBRID has been designed more for real-world problems that require scenario analysis than for academic (e.g., randomly generated) problems. Thus HYBRID is oriented towards an interactive mode of operation in which a sequence of problems is to be solved under varying conditions (e.g., different objective functions, reference points, values of constraints or bounds). Criteria for multiobjective problems may be easily defined and updated with the help of the package.

The binary files with HYBRID 3.1 are available from IIASA in two versions: one for VAX 6210 (running under Ultrix-32 ver. 3.0) and one for a PC compatible with IBM/AT/XT.

1.2 Short program description

1.2.1 Preparation of a problem formulation

A problem to be solved should be defined as a mathematical programming model. Formulation of a mathematical programming model is a complex task and this paper is not devoted to discuss this question in detail. Therefore this section is aimed at providing only a short summary of a recommended approach.

Firstly, a set of variables that sufficiently describe the problem—for the sake of the desired analysis—should be selected. It is desired—however not necessary—to define the model in such a way as to possibly exploit the problem structure (further on referred to as a dynamic problem). Secondly, a set of constraints which defines a set of admissible (i.e. acceptable or recognized as feasible by a decision maker) solutions should be defined. Finally a set of criteria which could serve for a selection of a solution should be defined.

The formal definition of criteria can be performed in HYBRID in an easy way. However, it should be stressed that any definition of a complex model usually requires cooperation of a specialist—who knows the nature and background of the problem to be solved—with a system analyst who can advise on a suitable way of formal definition. It should be clearly pointed out that a proper definition can substantially improve the use of any computational technique. For small problems used for illustration of the method, it is fairly easy to define a model. But for real life problems, this stage requires a close cooperation between a decision maker and a team of analysts as well as a substantial amount of time and resources.

For real life problems, the following steps are recommended:

1. Mathematical formulation of the problem being solved should be defined.

2. A data base for the problem should be created. This may be done on PC with a help of a suitable commercial product (such as Framework, dBase, Paradox, Oracle or Symphony). Original data should be placed in this data base. A user need not worry about possible range of quantities (which usually has an impact on computational problems) because HYBRID provides automatic scaling of the model.

3. Verification of the data base and of the model formal definition should be performed.

4. The corresponding MPS standard file should be created. This may be done by a specialized model generator (easily written by a system analyst), or an universal generator such as GEMINI (developed at IIASA), or GAMMA (part of FMPS package on UNIVAC), or LPL (cf Hurlimann, 1988), or by any appropriate utility program of data base software. We strongly discourage the user from creating the MPS file with help of a standard text editor.

1.2.2 Model verification

This stage serves for the verification of model definition which is crucial for real application of any mathematical programming approach.

First stage consists of preprocessing the MPS file by HYBRID, which offers many options helpful for that task. HYBRID points to possible sources of inconsistency in model definition. Since this information is self-explaining, details are not discussed here. It is also advisable to examine the model printout by rows and by columns, which helps to verify model specification and may help in tracing possible errors in MPS file generation.

Second stage consist of solving optimization problems for selected criteria which helps in the analysis of consistency of solutions. For larger problems, the design and application of a problem oriented report writer is recommended. HYBRID generates a "user_file" for that purpose which contains all information necessary for the analysis of a solution.

After an analysis of a solution, a user may change any of the following parameters: values of coefficients, values of constraints and also any parameters discussed in next section. This may be done with help of the interactive procedure which instead of MPS file uses "communication region" that contains problem formulation processed by HYBRID. Therefore, a user needs no longer to care about original MPS file which has the backup function only.

1.2.3 Multiobjective problem analysis

For a given model, the user can define various multiobjective problems to be analyzed. Problem analysis consist of consecutive stages:

- analysis of obtained solution
- modification of the problem
- solution of modified problem.

Analysis of a solution consists of following steps (some of which are optional):

1. The user should examine of values of selected criteria. Since the solution obtained in HYBRID is Pareto optimal, the user should not expect improvement in any criteria without worsening some other criteria. But values of each criterion can be mutually compared. It is also possible to compute the best solutions for each criterion separately. A point (in criteria space) composed of best solutions is called the "utopia" point (since usually it is not attainable). HYBRID provides also a point composed of worst values for each criterion. This point is called "nadir" point. Such information help to define a reference point (desired values of criteria) because it is reasonable to expect values of each criterion to lie between utopia and nadir point.

2. The user may also make at this stage modifications to the original problem without involving the MPS file.

3. For dynamic problems, HYBRID allows also for easy examination of trajectories (referred to by so called generic name of a variable).

Modification of the problem may be done in two ways:

1. At this stage, the user can modify the formulation of the original model. But main activity in this stage is expected after the model is well defined and verified and no longer requires changes in parameters that define the set of admissible (acceptable) solutions. It should be stressed, that each change of this set usually results in change of the set of Pareto-optimal solutions and both utopia and nadir points should be computed again.

2. If the values of all constraints and coefficients that define the admissible set of solutions are accepted, the user should start with computations of utopia point. This can be easily done in an interactive way. After utopia and corresponding nadir points are obtained (which requires n solutions of the problem, where n is the number of criteria defined) the user can also interactively change any number of the following parameters that define the selection of an efficient solution to the multicriteria problem:

   - Reference point (i.e. desired values for each criterion) might be changed. This point may be attainable or non-attainable (cf sect. 2.4).
   - Weights attached to each criterion can be modified.
   - Reference trajectories in dynamic case can be changed as reference points.
   - Regularization parameters in selection function can be adjusted.

3. Additionally, the user can temporarily remove a criterion (or a number of criteria) from analysis. This option results in the computation of a Pareto optimal point in respect to remaining "active" criteria, but values of criteria that are not active are also available for review.

Solution of a problem. The multiobjective analysis problem defined by a user (after possible modification) is transformed by HYBRID to an equivalent LP problem which is solved without interaction of a user (an experienced user may however have an access to the information that characterizes the optimization run).

1.2.4 Remarks relevant to dynamic problems

HYBRID allows for solving both static and dynamic LP models. Static models can be interpreted as models for which a specific structure is not recognized nor exploited. But many real life problems have specific structure which—if exploited—can result not only in much faster execution of optimization runs but also remarkably help in problem definition and interpretation of results.

Numerous problems have dynamic nature and it is natural to take advantage of its proper definition. HYBRID offers many options for dynamic models, such as:

1. In many situations, the user may deal with generic names of variables. A generic name consists of 6 first characters of a name while 2 last characters corresponds to the period of time. Therefore, the user may for example refer to the entire trajectory (by generic name) or to value of a variable for a specific time period (by full name). Such approach corresponds to a widely used practice of generating trajectories for dynamic models.

2. The user may select any of 4 types of criteria that correspond to practical applications. Those can be defined for each time period (together with additional "global" conditions), but this requires rather large effort. Therefore, for dynamic problems, criteria are specified just by the type of criterion and the generic name of the corresponding variable. Types of criteria are discussed in detail later.

3. A model can be declared as a dynamic one by the definition of periods of time. For a dynamic model, additional rules must be observed. These rules correspond to the way in which the MPS file has to be sorted and to the way in which names for rows and columns are selected. These rules follow a widely accepted standard of generation of dynamic models. The formulation of a dynamic model, which is accepted by HYBRID, is actually an extension of the classical formulation of a dynamic model (cf Section 2.2.). In our formulation, a model may contain also a group of constraints that do not follow the standard of state equations.

1.2.5 General description of the software package and data structure

The package is constructed in modules to provide a reasonably high level of flexibility and efficiency. This is crucial for a rational use of computer resources and for planned extensions of the package and possible modification of the algorithm.

The package consists of five subpackages:

- Two preprocessors that serve to process data, enable a modification of the model, perform diagnostics and may supply information useful for the verification of a model. The first preprocessor is used for processing of initial formulation and diagnostics of the model. It also transforms a multicriteria problem to a parametric single criteria optimization problem. The second preprocessor allows for analysis of a solution and for the interactive change of various parameters that may correspond to choice of some option, change of parameters in definition of multicriteria problem, change of matrix coefficients, right hand sides of constraints etc.

- Optimization package called solver of a relevant optimization problem (either static or dynamic).

- Postprocessor that provides results in the standard MPS format and generates the "user file" which contains all information needed for the analysis of a solution; the later option makes it easier to link HYBRID to a specialized report-writer or a graphic package.

- Driver, which eases the usage of all subpackages. The PC version of driver provides a context sensitive help which helps an inexperienced user in efficient usage of the package.

All five subpackages use a binary file that contains all data defining the problem being solved. A second binary file contains a solution obtained by last run of the solver. From the user point of view, HYBRID 3.1 is still one package that may be easily used for different purposes chosen via specification file.

The chosen method of allocating storage in the memory takes maximal advantage of the available computer memory and of the features of typical real-world problems. In general, the matrix of constraints is large and sparse, while the number of all non-zero coefficients that take different numerical values is much smaller than the number of all non-zero coefficients. A super-sparse-matrix technique is therefore applied to store the data that define the problem to be solved. This involves the construction of a table of coefficients which take different numerical values. The memory management is handled by a flexible way. HYBRID is coded partly in C and partly in an extension of Fortran (the latter part is processed by a preprocessor to generate a code which conforms to Fortran 77 standard). Such approach results in a faster (much faster for PC version running under DOS) execution and in a decrease of memory requirements.

Special commands of HYBRID support model verification and problem modification. This is necessary to facilitate scenario analysis and to reduce the problems caused by inappropriate scaling (cf sect. 4.7).

The data format for the input of MPS file and the output of LP results follows standards adopted by most commercial mathematical programming systems (cf e.g. Murtagh, 1981, Makowski and Sosnowski, 1988b).

1.2.6 Outline of the solution technique

HYBRID uses a non-simplex algorithm — a particular implementation of the augmented Lagrangian (or Lagrange multiplier) method — for solving linear programming problems. General linear constraints are included within an augmented Lagrangian function. The LP problem is solved by minimizing a sequence of quadratic functions subject to simple constraints (lower and upper bounds). This minimization is achieved by the use of a method which combines the conjugate gradient method and an active constraints strategy.

In recent years many methods oriented for solving dynamic linear problems (DLP) have been developed. Most of those methods consists of adaptation of the simplex method for problems with a special structure of constraints. In HYBRID, a different approach is applied. A DLP, which should be defined together with a state equation, is solved through the use of adjoint equations and by reduction of gradients to control subspaces (more exactly, to a subspace of independent variables). The method exploits the sparseness of the matrix structure. The simple constraints (lower and upper bounds for non-slack variables) for control variables are not violated during optimization and the resulting sequence of multipliers is feasible for the dual problem. The global constraints (i.e. constraints other then those defined as simple constraints) may be violated, however, and therefore the algorithm can be started from any point that satisfies the simple constraints.

The solution technique can be also used to solve single-criteria quadratic problems with virtually no changes in the algorithm. However, a routine to input and handle the relevant data and a corresponding standard for data input have yet to be designed and implemented. So far only single criteria linear-quadratic problems in the form discussed in Section 2.5 may be solved. The solution method for multi-criteria quadratic problems requires modification of the algorithm. However the necessary modifications will be based on HYBRID 3.1.

1.2.7 General description of options provided by the package

In order to provide general information about capabilities of HYBRID, the main options are listed below. HYBRID offers the following features:

- Input of data and the formulation of an LP problem follow the MPS standard. Additional rules (that concern only sequencing of some rows and columns) should be observed in order to take advantage of the structure of a dynamic problem. An experienced user may speed up computations by setting certain options and/or parameters (cf the HYBRID User Manual).
- The problem can be modified at any stage of its solution (i.e., by changing the matrix of coefficients, introducing or altering right-hand sides, ranges or bounds).
- The multicriteria problem is formulated and solved as a sequence of parametric optimization problems modified in interactive way upon analysis of previous results.
- The solution technique can be chosen. First choice is done by definition of a static or a dynamic problem. Some specialized techniques may be used for badly conditioned problems that usually cause numerical problems. This includes one of two regularization techniques (see Section 4.5) and/or possibility of using preconditioned conjugate gradient method (cf Section 4.6). For a badly scaled problem, an implementation of scaling algorithm is available (as described by Makowski and Sosnowski (1981) and briefly discussed in Section 4.7).
- Comprehensive diagnostics is implemented, including the checking of parallel rows, the detection of columns and rows which are empty or contain only one entry, the splitting of columns, the recognition of inconsistencies in right-hand sides, ranges and bounds, and various other features that are useful in debugging the problem formulation. The package supports a display of a matrix by rows (printing the nonzero elements and names of the corresponding columns, right-hand sides and ranges), as well as a display of a matrix by columns (analogous to displaying by rows). A check of the feasibility of a problem prior to its optimization is optionally performed. More detailed information for an infeasible or unbounded problem is optionally provided by the package.
- All data that correspond to the formulation of the problem being solved are stored in a binary file. An other binary file contains all other information corresponding to a current run. The latter file is stored on disk in certain situations to allow continuation of computations from failed (or interrupted) runs or to run a modified problem while using previously obtained information. Therefore the MPS input file is read and processed only by first preprocessor, which serves for initial formulation of the problem. Such approach allows also for efficient storing of many solutions that may be later used for more detailed analysis, comparisons and modifications.

- Any solution is available in the standard MPS format and in a binary file which contains all data that might be useful for postoptimal analysis and reports.

1.3 Remarks on implementation

HYBRID 3.1 is an extended version of HYBRID 3.03 documented in (Makowski and Sosnowski, 1988a, 1988b). Therefore there are only small changes in the methodological guide in comparison to the methodology presented in (Makowski and Sosnowski, 1988a), because the solution techniques are basically the same. However, there are some important methodological innovations. The main differences are the following:

- The code has been modified as to allow for solution of single criteria linear-quadratic problems.
- The preconditioned conjugate gradient technique for minimizing augmented Lagrangian has been implemented.
- The second regularization option which allows for finding the optimal solution with minimum distance from a given reference point has been made operational.
- The optimization algorithm has been improved by an automatic evaluation of some parameters, a different technical implementation of scaling, some changes in control flow, which results in its faster execution.
- The user interface (for PC version of the code) has been improved. A new approach to usage of the package and to data handling provides for easier use of the package.
- Diagnostics have been improved and several observed bugs have been removed.
- Part of the code has been rewritten in C language. This allows for more efficient memory management and usage. Change in the way of internal data handling resulted in remarkable improvement of execution speed.

2 Statement of optimization problems

2.1 Formulation of an LP problem

We will consider a linear programming problem (P) in the following standard form (see, e.g., Murtagh and Sanders, 1977):

$$\min cx \tag{1}$$

$$b - r \leq Ax \leq b \tag{2}$$

$$l \leq x \leq u \tag{3}$$

where $x, c, l, u \in R^n$, $b, r \in R^m$ and A is an $m \times n$ matrix.

The constraints are divided into two groups: general constraints (2) and simple constraints (3). In the input data file (MPS file) the vectors b is called RHS and the vector r —RANGES. The vector l and u are called LOWER and UPPER BOUNDS, respectively. Obviously, some of bounds and/or ranges may have an infinite value. Therefore HYBRID may be used for solving any LP problem formulated in the way accepted by most of commercial packages.

2.2 Classical formulation of a dynamic LP problem (CDLP)

Before discussing a formulation of a dynamic problem that can be solved by HYBRID 3.1, let us first consider a classical formulation of a dynamic linear programming problem (CDLP) (cf Propoi, 1976) in the following form:

Find a control trajectory

$$u = (u_1, \dots, u_T)$$

and a state trajectory

$$x = (x_1, \dots, x_T)$$

satisfying the state equations with initial condition x_0

$$x_t = A_{t-1}x_{t-1} + B_t u_t - c_t \tag{4}$$

and constraints

$$d_{t-1} - r_{t-1} \leq F_{t-1}x_{t-1} + D_t u_t \leq d_{t-1} \qquad t = 1, \dots, T \tag{5}$$

$$e_t \leq u_t \leq f_t \qquad t = 1, \dots, T \tag{6}$$

$$F_T x_T \leq d_T \tag{7}$$

which minimize the performance index

$$\sum_{t=1}^{T}(a_t x_t + b_t u_t) \tag{8}$$

where:

- $t = 1, \dots, T$ denote periods of time
- state variables x_t, control variables u_t, both for each period, are elements of Euclidian spaces of appropriate dimensions;
- matrices A_t, B_t, D_t, F_t are assumed to be given,
- RHS vectors c_t and d_t, as well as range vector r_t and bounds for control variables e_t and f_t are given,
- initial condition x_0 is given.

The above given formulation has been chosen for the purpose of simplification of presentation only. Actually, the following modifications are accepted:

1. Instead of inequality (5), equality constraints can be used;

2. Since no constraints of bounds type (6) are allowed for state variables x, such constraints may be specified in columns section of MPS file, thus formally are handled as inequality constraints of type (5);

3. Performance index (goal function) can either be specified as single objective or will be replaced by a dummy goal function that is defined by the transformation of a multicriteria problem to a parametric LP problem;

The structure of an CDLP problem (formulated above as in Propoi, 1976) may be illustrated by the following diagram (example for $T = 3$, $u_1, u_2, u_3, x_0, x_1, x_2, x_3$ are vectors, slack variables are not shown):

u_1	u_2	u_3	x_0	x_1	x_2	x_3	rhs	var.
B_1	0	0	A_0	$-I$	0	0	c_1	state eq.
0	B_2	0	0	A_1	$-I$	0	c_2	state eq.
0	0	B_3	0	0	A_2	$-I$	c_3	state eq.
D_1	0	0	F_0	0	0	0	d_0	constr.
0	D_2	0	0	F_1	0	0	d_1	constr.
0	0	D_3	0	0	F_2	0	d_2	constr.
0	0	0	0	0	0	F_3	d_3	final state
b_1	b_2	b_3	0	a_1	a_2	a_3	—	goal

where I is identity matrix and 0 is a matrix composed of zero elements.

2.3 Formulation of a dynamic problem (DLP)

The formulation of CDLP has been chosen for the purpose of simplification of presentation only. Actually HYBRID 3.1 is capable to solve problems of more general class, which will be referred to as Dynamic Linear Programming problems (DLP). Namely, the matrices $B = diag(B_i)$, $D = diag(D_i)$, $F = diag(F_i)$ need no longer be block diagonal matrices. Also matrices below identity matrices need no longer have any specific structure. Therefore the CDLP is a specific example of DLP. One of main generalizations—from a practical point of view—is that a problem with delays for control variables (which is not CDLP-class problem) may be solved by HYBRID. In fact, HYBRID accepts also problems with delays for both state and control variables, provided that state variables for periods "before" initial state do not enter state equations. A choice of criteria for CDLP-class problem is also limited in comparison with that for DLP (cf sect. 4.3).

All variables are divided into two groups: decision variables u and state variables x_t, the latter are specified for each period of time.

A single criteria DLP problem may be formulated as follows:

Find a trajectory x_t and decision variables u such that both:

state equations:

$$-H_t x_t + \sum_{i=0}^{t-1} A_{t-1,i} x_i + B_t u = c_t, \qquad t = 1, \ldots, T \tag{9}$$

with given initial condition x_0
and constraints:

$$d - r \leq \sum_{t=0}^{T} F_t x_t + Du \leq d \tag{10}$$

$$e \leq u \leq f \tag{11}$$

are satisfied and the following function is minimized:

$$\sum_{t=1}^{T} a_t x_t + bu \tag{12}$$

Components of vector u are called decision variables for historical reasons. Actually a vector u may be composed of any variables, some of them may be specified for each time period and enter criteria defined for a dynamic case. But some components of vector u may not be specified for any time period (cf sect. 7.3.1). An example of such variable is "..dummy.", a variable generated by HYBRID for a multicriteria problem. A user may also specify variables independent of time. For the sake of keeping the formulation of the problem as simple as possible we have not introduced a separate name for such variables.

The following two symbols can be used in the specification file for definition of DLP:

NT – number of periods (stands for T in the above formulation)

NSTV – number of state variables in each period (the dimension of vectors x_t)

The user can define state inequalities instead of state equations (9). The slack variables for such inequalities are generated by HYBRID. Therefore, for the sake of the presentation simplicity, only the state equation will be considered further on.

The structure of an DLP problem may be illustrated by the following diagram: (corresponding to an example analogous to the above example for CDLP)

u	x_0	x_1	x_2	x_3	rhs	var.
B_1	A_{00}	$-H_1$	0	0	c_1	state eq.
B_2	A_{10}	A_{11}	$-H_2$	0	c_2	state eq.
B_3	A_{20}	A_{21}	A_{22}	$-H_3$	c_3	state eq.
D	F_0	F_1	F_2	F_3	d	constr.
b	0	a_1	a_2	a_3	—	goal

where H_t is diagonal matrix and 0 is a matrix composed of zero elements.

2.4 Multicriteria optimization

2.4.1 General remarks

The specification of a single-objective function, which adequately reflects preferences of a model user is perhaps the major unresolved difficulty in solving many practical problems as a relevant optimization problem. This issue is even more difficult in the case of collective decision making. Multiobjective optimization approaches make this problem less difficult, particularly if they allow for an interactive redefinition of the problem.

The method adopted in HYBRID 3.1 is the reference point approach introduced by Wierzbicki (1980). Since the method has been described in a series of papers and reports and has been applied to DIDAS (cf Kallio et al., 1980, Lewandowski and Grauer, 1982), we give only general outline of the approach applied. This approach may be summarized in form of following stages:

1. The user of the model (referred to further as the decision maker—DM) specifies a number of criteria (objectives). For static LP problem a criterion is a linear combination of variables. For DLP problems one may also use other types of criteria (cf sect. 2.4.2). The definition of criteria in HYBRID can be performed in an easy way described in the User Manual.

2. The DM specifies an aspiration level $\bar{q} = \{\bar{q}_1, \dots, \bar{q}_{NC}\}$, where $\bar{q}_i$ are desired values for each criterion and NC is a number of criteria. Aspiration level is called also a reference point.

3. The problem is transformed into an auxiliary parametric LP (or DLP) problem. Its solution gives a Pareto-optimal point. If specified aspiration level $\bar{q}$ is not attainable, then the Pareto-optimal point is the nearest (in the sense of a Chebyshev weighted norm) to the aspiration level. If the aspiration level is attainable, then the Pareto-optimal point is uniformly better then $\bar{q}$. Properties of the Pareto-optimal point depend on the localization of the reference point (aspiration level) and on weights associated with criteria.

4. The DM explores various Pareto-optimal points by changing either the aspiration level $\bar{q}$ or/and weights attached to criteria or/and other parameters related to the definition of the multicriteria problem.

5. The procedure described in points 3 and 4 is repeated until satisfactory solution is found.

To give more formal presentation, let us introduce following notation:

NC is the number of criteria

q_i is the i-th criterion

$\bar{q}_i$ is the aspiration level for i-th criterion

w_i is a weight associated with i-th criterion (whereas the user specifies its absolute value which is internally changed to negative depending on the type of criteria—cf sect. 2.4.3).

ε_m is a given non-negative parameter.

A Pareto-optimal solution can be found by the minimization of the achievement scalarizing function in the form

$$\max_{i=1,\ldots,NC}(w_i(q_i - \bar{q}_i)) + \varepsilon_m \sum_{i=1}^{NC} w_i q_i \rightarrow \min$$

This form of achievement function is a slight modification of a form suggested by A. Lewandowski (1982) and by A. Wierzbicki (1978). Note that for $\varepsilon_m = 0$ only weakly Pareto-optimal points can be guaranteed as minimal points of this function. Therefore, the use of a very small ε_m results (except of situations in which reference point has some specific properties) in properly Pareto-optimal solution with trade-off coefficients bounded approximately by $\varepsilon_m NC$ and $1/\varepsilon_m NC$. If ε_m is very small, these properly efficient solutions might practically not differ from weakly efficient (Pareto optimal). On the other hand, too big values of ε_m could drastically change properties associated with the first part of the scalarizing function.

2.4.2 Types of criteria

A user may define any number of criteria. To facilitate the definition 6 types of criteria are available and a user is requested to declare chosen types of criteria before their actual definition. Two types of criteria are simple linear combination of variables and those criteria may be used for both static and dynamic problems. Four other types of criteria correspond to various possible performance indices often used for dynamic problems. Since the latter criteria implicitly relate to the dynamic nature of the problem, they may be used only for variables that are defined for each time period. The only exception is the type DER of criteria, which may be defined by state variables only.

For the sake of simplicity, only the variables of the type x_i (which otherwise is used in this paper to distinguish a state variable in DLP) are used in the following formulae. Note that $x_i = \{x_{it}\}$, $t = 1, \ldots, T$.

An k-th criterion q_k is defined in one of following ways, for static and dynamic LP:

Type MIN

$$q_k = \sum_{t=1}^{T} \sum_{i=1}^{n} a_{it} x_{it} \rightarrow \min$$

where n is number of (state and control) variables, T is number of periods; $T = 1$ is assumed for static LP.

Type MAX

$$q_k = \sum_{t=1}^{T} \sum_{i=1}^{n} a_{it} x_{it} \rightarrow max$$

The following four criteria types are exclusively for dynamic LP:
Type SUP

$$q_k = \max_{t=1,\ldots,T}(x_{it} - \bar{x}_{it}) \rightarrow \min$$

where x_i is a selected state or control variable, $\bar{x}_i$ —its reference trajectory

Type INF

$$q_k = \min_{t=1,\ldots,T}(x_{it} - \bar{x}_{it}) \rightarrow \max$$

Type FOL

$$q_k = \max_{t=1,\ldots,T}(abs(x_{it} - \bar{x}_{it})) \rightarrow \min$$

Type DER (which applies only to state variables)

$$q_k = \max_{t=1,\ldots,T}(abs(x_{it} - x_{it-1})) \rightarrow \min$$

2.4.3 Transformation of multicriteria problem to an auxiliary LP

The transformation is done by HYBRID 3.1, therefore its description here has only informative purpose. This description may be useful in case of using the MPS file (optionally created after modifications and transformation of a problem) as input for another LP package.

Following notation is used throughout this subsection:

- v – name of the auxiliary variable v
- w_i – optional weight coefficient for i-th criterion (default value equal to 1.),
- cn_i – name of i-th criterion,
- ch_t – string (2-characters) which identifies t-th period of time,
- $\bar{q}_i$ – reference point (aspiration level) for i-th criterion,
- q_i – linear combination of variables that defines a criterion of the type MAX or MIN,
- ' ' – delimiters of a string,
- T – number of time periods,
- $x_j = \{x_{jt}\}$, $t = 1, \ldots, T$ is a variable that enters a criterion of a type SUP, INF, FOL or DER.

Transformation will be discussed for each type of criteria:

Type : MIN
additional row (with name which is concatenation of following three strings: '<', cn_i, '···') is generated in form:

$$-v + w_i q_i \leq w_i \bar{q}_i$$

Type : MAX
is transformed in the way similar to type MIN, with additional (internal, for computations only) change of the signs of w_i to negative.

Type : SUP

additional T rows (with names which are concatenations of strings '$<$', cn_i, '.' ch_t, where $t = 1, \dots, T$) are generated in forms:

$$-v + w_i x_{jt} \leq w_i \bar{x}_{jt} + w_i \bar{q}_i$$

Type : INF

is transformed in the way similar to type SUP, with additional (internal, for computations only) change of the signs of w_i to negative.

Type : FOL

- additional T columns (with names which are concatenations of strings '$+$', cn_i, '.', ch_t, where $t = 1, \dots, T$) are generated; in the following formulae this name is replaced by c^+_{it}
- additional T columns (with names which are concatenations of strings '$-$', cn_i, '.', ch_t, where $t = 1, \dots, T$) are generated; in the following formulae this name is replaced by c^-_{it}
- additional T rows (with names which are concatenation of strings '$=$', cn_i, '.', ch_t, where $t = 1, \dots, T$) are generated in form :

$$c^+_{it} - c^-_{it} - x_{jt} = -\bar{x}_{jt}$$

- additional T rows (with names which are concatenations of strings '$<$', cn_i, '.', ch_t, where $t = 1, \dots, T$) are generated in the form:

$$-v + w_i(c^+_{it} + c^-_{it}) \leq w_i \bar{q}_i$$

Type : DER

- additional $2 \times T$ columns are generated in the same way as described for a criterion of the type FOL;
- additional T rows (with names with are concatenations of strings '$=$', cn_i, '.', ch_t, where $t = 1, \dots, T$) are generated in form :

$$c^+_{it} - c^-_{it} - x_{j,t} + x_{j,t-1} = 0.$$

- additional T rows (with names which are concatenations of strings '$<$', cn_i, '.', ch_t) are generated in form :

$$-v + w_i(c^+_{it} + c^-_{it}) \leq w_i \bar{q}_i$$

Auxiliary goal function, which is to be minimized, is generated in the following form:

$$v + \varepsilon_m \Big(\sum_i w_i q_i + \sum_t \Big(\sum_j w_j x_{jt} + \sum_k w_k (c^+_{kt} + c^-_{kt})\Big)\Big)$$

where summation is done over corresponding sets of respective criteria, i.e. indices i, j, k correspond to criteria of type: MIN or MAX, SUP or INF and FOL or DER, respectively; ε_m is given parameter.

The name of auxiliary variable v is '..dummy.', whereas the name of auxiliary goal function is '.dummy..'.

Value of ε_m may be changed by the command MEPS in a routine for modification of multicriteria parameters.

2.5 Formulation of single criteria linear-quadratic problems

HYBRID 3.1 allows for solution of a single-criterion linear-quadratic problem with a simple quadratic term. For a problem which does not have recognized structure (as discussed in sect. 2.3) the formulation takes the following form:

$$\min cx + (\gamma/2)\|x - \bar{x}\|^2$$

subject (2) and (3), where $\bar{x}$ is a given point in the solution space and $\gamma > 0$ is a given parameter.

Similarly, for a dynamic problem one may formulate the problem in the following way:

$$\min \sum_{t=1}^{T} a_t x_t + bu + (\gamma/2)\|u - \bar{u}\|^2$$

subject (9) and (11), where $\bar{u}$ is a given point in the space of independent variables.

3 Theoretical foundations and problems

3.1 General remarks

The most popular methods for solving linear programming problems are based on the simplex algorithm. However, a number of other iterative non-simplex approaches have recently been developed (Mangasarian, 1981, Polyak and Tretiyakov, 1972, Sosnowski, 1981). HYBRID belongs to this group of non-simplex methods. The solution technique is based on the minimization of an augmented Lagrangian penalty function using a modification of the conjugate gradient method. The Lagrange multipliers are updated using a modified version of the multiplier method (Bertsekas, 1976) (see Sections 4.2 and 4.4).

This method is useful not only for linear programming problems but also for other purposes, as described in Section 1.2. In addition, the method may be used to solve problems with non-unique solutions (as a result of regularization—see Section 4.5).

The following notation will be used:

- a_i – denotes the i-th row of matrix A
- x_j – denotes the j-th component of vector x
- $\|x\|$ – denotes the Euclidian norm of vector x
- $(u)_+$ – denotes the vector composed of the non-negative elements of vector u (where negative elements are replaced by zeros)
- A^T – denotes the transposition of matrix A.

3.2 The multiplier method

We shall first explain how the multiplier method may be applied directly to LP problems.

Consider the problem (PO), which is equivalent to the problem (P) defined in Section 2.1:

$$\min cx$$

$$Bx \le d \tag{PO}$$

where $d \in R^p$, B is a $p \times n$ matrix, and $m \le p \le 2(m+n)$. To apply the multiplier method to this problem we proceed as follows:

Select initial multipliers y^0 (e.g., $y^0 = 0$) and $\rho \in R$, $\rho > 0$. Then for $k = 0, 1, \ldots$ determine successive values of x^{k+1}, y^{k+1} where

$$x^{k+1} = \operatorname*{argmin}_x L(x, y^k)$$

and

$$y^{k+1} = (y^k + \rho(Bx_{k+1} - d))_+ \tag{13}$$

where

$$L(x, y^k) = cx + \left(\|(y^k + \rho(Bx - d))_+\|^2 - \|y^k\|^2\right) / (2\rho) \tag{14}$$

until a stopping criterion is satisfied.

The method has the following basic properties:

1. A piecewise quadratic differentiable convex function is minimized at each iteration.
2. The algorithm terminates in a finite number of iterations for any positive ρ.
3. There exists a constant $\bar{\rho}$ such that for any $\rho \ge \bar{\rho}$ the algorithm terminates in the second iteration.

Note that it is assumed above that the function $L(\cdot, y^k)$ is minimized exactly and that the value of the penalty parameter ρ is fixed. Less accurate minimization may be performed provided that certain conditions are fulfilled (see, e.g., Sosnowski, 1981, Bertsekas, 1976). For numerical reasons, a non-decreasing sequence of penalty parameters $\{\rho^k\}$ is generally used instead of a fixed ρ.

3.3 The conjugate gradient method for the minimization of an augmented Lagrangian penalty function

The augmented Lagrangian function for a given vector of multipliers y will be called the augmented Lagrangian penalty function (Flecher, 1981). For minimization of that function the conjugate gradient method has been modified to take advantage of the formulation of the problem. The method may be understood as an modification of the techniques developed by Polyak (1969), O'Leary (1980) and Hestenes (1980) for minimization of a quadratic function on an interval using the conjugate gradient method.

The problem (P) may be reformulated as follows:

$$\min cx$$

$$Ax + z = b$$

$$l \leq x \leq u \qquad \text{(PS)}$$
$$0 \leq z \leq r$$

where $z \in R^m$ are slack variables.

Formulation (PS) has a number of advantages over the initial formulation (PO):

1. The dimension of matrix A in (PS) is usually much smaller than that of matrix B in (PO).
2. The augmented Lagrangian problem is one of minimization of a quadratic function in (PS), and of minimization of a piecewise quadratic in (PO).
3. Some computations only have to be performed for subsets of variables. Note that slack variables are introduced only for ease of interpretation and do not have to be computed.

In (PS) the augmented Lagrangian is defined by

$$L(x, z, y) = cx + \left(\|y + \rho(Ax + z - b)\|^2 - \|y\|^2\right) / (2\rho). \tag{15}$$

We shall first discuss the problem of minimizing $L(x, z, y)$ for given $y, \rho > 0$, subject to lower and upper bounds for x and z. Let us consider the following augmented Lagrangian penalty function

$$F(x, z) = (c/\rho)x + (\|y/\rho + Ax - b + z\|^2 - \|y/\rho\|^2) / 2. \tag{16}$$

The gradient of F is defined by

$$\frac{\partial F}{\partial x} = c/\rho + A^T(z - g)$$
$$\frac{\partial F}{\partial z} = z - g$$

where

$$g = -y/\rho - Ax + b.$$

From the Kuhn-Tucker optimality condition, the following relations hold for the minimum point (x^*, z^*):

$$\frac{\partial F^*}{\partial x_j} \geq 0 \quad \text{if} \quad x_j^* = l_j, \qquad \frac{\partial F^*}{\partial x_j} \leq 0 \quad \text{if} \quad x_j^* = u_j,$$
$$\frac{\partial F^*}{\partial z_i} \geq 0 \quad \text{if} \quad z_i^* = 0, \qquad \frac{\partial F^*}{\partial z_i} \leq 0 \quad \text{if} \quad z_i^* = r_i,$$

and

$$\frac{\partial F^*}{\partial x_j} = 0 \quad \text{if} \quad l_j < x_j^* < u_j$$
$$\frac{\partial F^*}{\partial z_i} = 0 \quad \text{if} \quad 0 < z_i^* < r_i.$$

For any given point such that $l \le x \le u$ it is possible to determine slack variables $0 \le z \le r$ in such a way that the optimality conditions with respect to z are obeyed. Variables z are defined by

$$z_i = \begin{cases} 0 & \text{if} \quad g_i \le 0 \qquad (\partial F/\partial z_i > 0) \\ r_i & \text{if} \quad g_i \ge r_i \qquad (\partial F/\partial z_i < 0) \\ g_i & \text{if} \quad r_i > g_i > 0 \ \ (\partial F/\partial z_i = 0). \end{cases} \tag{17}$$

We shall use the following notation and definitions. The vector of variables x with indices that belong to a set J will be denoted by x^J, and analogous notation will be used for variables g. Let q denote minus the gradient of the Lagrangian penalty function reduced to x-space ($q = -(\partial F/\partial x)$). The following sets of indices are defined for a given point x:
The set of indices I of violated constraints, i.e.,

$$I = \{\, i : g_i \ge r_i \,\} \cup \{\, i : g_i \le 0 \,\}.$$

$\bar{I}$ is the complement of I, i.e.,

$$\bar{I} = \{1, 2, \ldots, m\} \setminus I.$$

The set of indices I can be also interpreted as a set of active simple constraints for z. The set of indices J of variables that should be equal to either the upper or the lower bound, i.e.,

$$J = \{\, j : x_j = l_j \ \text{ and } \ q_j \le 0 \,\} \cup \{\, j : x_j = u_j \ \text{ and } \ q_j \ge 0 \,\}.$$

$\bar{J}$ is the complement of J, i.e.,

$$\bar{J} = \{1, 2, \ldots, n\} \setminus J.$$

For the sake of illustration the matrix A may be schematically split up in the following three ways (see the Figure below): first according to active rows, second according to basic columns and third with illustrate the part of the matrix A for which augmented Lagrangian penalty function is computed. The contents of the matrix A^I_J (for which the augmented Lagrangian penalty function is computed) changes along with computations.

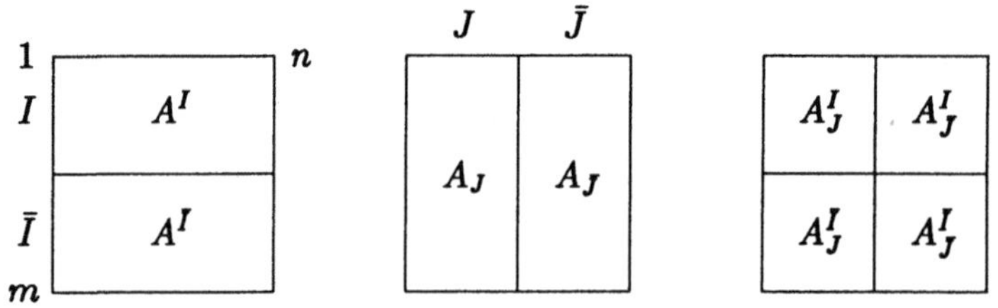

In essence, the augmented Lagrangian penalty function is minimized using the conjugate gradient method with the following modifications:

1. During the minimization process x and z satisfy simple constraints and z enters the augmented Lagrangian in the form defined by (17).

2. The conjugate gradient routine is run until no new constraint becomes active, i.e., neither set I nor set J increases in size. If this occurs, the computed step length is shortened to reach the next constraint, the corresponding set (I or J) is enlarged and the conjugate gradient routine is re-entered with the direction set equal to minus the gradient.

3. Sets J and I are defined before entering the procedure discussed in point 2 and may be only enlarged before the minimum is found. When the minimum with respect to the variables with indices in sets $\bar{J}$ and I has been found, sets J and I are redefined.

4. Minimization is performed subject only to those components of variables x whose indices belong to set $\bar{J}$, i.e., variables that are not currently equal to a bound value.

5. Minimization is performed subject only to those components of variables z whose indices do not belong to set I, i.e., slack variables that correspond to non-active simple constraints for z. Note that, formally, this requires only the use of different formulae for z. In actual fact it is sufficient to know only the set I, which defines the minimized quadratic function.

4 Solution technique

4.1 Algorithm for minimization of augmented Lagrangian

We may now present the algorithm for minimization of the augmented Lagrangian penalty function in a more formal way. The algorithm consists of the following steps:

1. For given y and $\rho > 0$ choose a point x such that $l \leq x \leq u$

2. Compute $g = -y/\rho - Ax + b$

3. Determine sets I and $\bar{I}$

$$I = \{ i : g_i > r_i \} \cup \{ i : g_i < 0 \},$$
$$\bar{I} = \{1, \dots, m\} \setminus I$$

4. Define $\bar{g}$ as follows:

$$\bar{g}_i = \begin{cases} g_i - r_i & \text{if } g_i - r_i > 0 \\ g_i & \text{otherwise} \end{cases}$$

5. Compute the minus gradient:

$$q = -c/\rho + (A^I)^T \bar{g}^I$$

6. Determine sets J and $\bar{J}$

$$J = \{j : x_j = l_j \text{ and } q_j \leq 0\} \cup \{j : x_j = u_j \text{ and } q_j \geq 0\}$$
$$\bar{J} = \{1, \ldots, n\} \setminus J$$

7. If $q_j = 0$ for all $j \in \bar{J}$ then x is a minimum point of the augmented Lagrangian penalty function

8. Set $p^{J} = q^{J}$

9. Compute

$$s = A_J p^J$$
$$h = \|q^J\|^2$$
$$d = \|s^I\|^2$$
$$\alpha(1) = h/d$$

Note that $\alpha(1)$ is the conjugate gradient step length in direction p^J

10. Find the step length that would violate the nearest non-active constraint, i.e., for $i \in \bar{I}$,

$$\alpha(2) = \min_{i \in K} \{g_i/s_i\}, \qquad K = \{i : i \in \bar{I}, s_i > 0\}$$
$$\alpha(3) = \min_{i \in K} \{(g_i - r_i)/s_i\}, \qquad K = \{i : i \in \bar{I}, s_i < 0\}$$

11. Find the step length that would enable a variable to reach a bound, i.e.,

$$\alpha(4) = \min_{j \in K} (l_j - x_j)/p_j, \qquad K = \{j : j \in \bar{J}, p_j < 0\}$$
$$\alpha(5) = \min_{j \in K} (u_j - x_j)/p_j, \qquad K = \{j : j \in \bar{J}, p_j > 0\}$$

12. Determine step length $\alpha = \min_{i=1,\ldots,5}(\alpha(i))$. If $\alpha = \min(\alpha(2), \alpha(3))$ add the row index for which this condition holds to set I and remove that index from set $\bar{I}$. If $\alpha = \min(\alpha(4), \alpha(5))$ add the column index for which this condition holds to set J and remove that index from set $\bar{J}$.

13. Compute the new point $x^J := x^J + \alpha p^J$ and the minus gradient at that point:

$$g_i := g_i - \alpha s_i$$
$$q^J = (A^I_J)^T \bar{g}^I - c^J/\rho$$

14. If $q^J = 0$. go to step 2

15. If $\alpha = \alpha(1)$ continue with the conjugate gradient step, i.e.

$$\beta = \|q^J\|^2/h$$
$$p^J := q^J + \beta p^J$$

and go to step 9

16. Go to step 8

Note that the condition $q^J = 0$ is in practice replaced by $\|q^J\| \leq \varepsilon$, where ε is a gradient tolerance.

4.2 Steps of the multiplier method

Let the violation of i-th constraint in a point x^k be defined in the following way:

$$v_i^k = \max\{\, a_i x^k - b_i, -a_i x^k + b_i - r_i, 0\}$$

and $\|v^k\|_\infty$ denotes the l_∞ norm of violated constraints. The multiplier method will be presented in algorithmic form.

1. Compute an initial vector of multipliers on the basis of the particular option chosen (i.e., either $y^0 = 0$ or y^0 corresponding to the constraints violated at starting point x)

2. Find x^{k+1} which minimizes the augmented Lagrangian penalty function (see Section 3.3) with accuracy ε^k. It is assumed that

   $$\varepsilon^k := \min\left(\varepsilon^k, \|v^k\|_\infty \varepsilon^k\right)$$

   where the sequence $\varepsilon^k \to 0$. In addition, $\varepsilon_{mi} \geq \varepsilon^k \geq \varepsilon_{mx}$, where ε_{mi}, ε_{mx} is the assumed minimum and maximum accuracy, respectively.

3. Compute new multipliers

   $$y_i^{k+1} := \begin{cases} y_i^k + \rho^k(a_i x^{k+1} - b_i) & \text{if } \; y^k + \rho^k(a_i x^{k+1} - b_i) \geq 0 \\ y_i^k + \rho^k(a_i x^{k+1} - b_i + r_i) & \text{if } \; y^k + \rho^k(a_i x^{k+1} - b_i + r_i) \leq 0 \\ 0 & \text{otherwise} \end{cases}$$

4. If $\|y^{k+1} - y^k\| > \varepsilon_d$ then set $\rho^{k+1} = \min\left(\rho^k \rho_s, \rho_{mx}\right)$, $\rho_s > 1.$, ρ_{mx} is a given maximal value of the penalty parameter.

   Set $\varepsilon^{k+1} = \varepsilon^k \varepsilon_s$, where $\varepsilon_s < 1.$ is an assumed parameter,

   Set $k := k + 1$ and go to step 2

5. Set $k := k + 1$ and find x^{k+1} which minimizes the augmented Lagrangian. If x^{k+1} is feasible ($\|v^k\| \leq FEAS$) then assume it as a solution and stop.

   Otherwise set $\rho^{k+1} = \min\left(\rho^k \rho_s, \rho_{mx}\right)$, and $\varepsilon^{k+1} = \varepsilon^k \varepsilon_s$ and go to step 2.

4.3 Solution technique for DLP

We will not repeat reasoning given in the first part of sect. 2.3. Instead, let us point out basic differences between the algorithms for static LP and DLP:

1. Minimization is reduced to a subspace of decision variables. Gradient of Lagrangian penalty function is computed for variables that belong to a subspace of decision variables. This (together with arguments already presented in sect. 3.3) shows advantages due to the use of dynamic structure of DLP problem in comparison with presentation of such a problem as a large LP.

2. The structure of matrices $B_1, \ldots, B_T$ and $F_0, \ldots, F_T$ has no impact for the algorithm nor affects the technique of storage of data, because super-sparse technique is applied (cf sect. 1.4). It should be also pointed out that the method of transforming a multicriteria problem to a parametric LP one introduces constraints (cf sect. 2.4.3) that—for the proposed (cf sect. 2.4.2) types of criteria—do not fit to the staircase structure of CDLP (cf Propoi, 1976). Therefore, any technique that would exploit the staircase structure of DLP would also imply a reduction of a number of criteria types. The alternative is then to treat a problem as a large LP static one or to apply a technique that does not exploit the classical DLP structure.

3. State equations are solved (for given decision variables u) by forward substitution. Therefore any single constraints for state variables have to be treated as general constraints and included into the matrix. Gradient need not to be computed for those variables, but state equation is solved twice (for state variables and variations).

4. A conjugate trajectory Ψ is computed from conjugate equation by backward substitution and has an interpretation of dual variables for state equations. No other variables associated with those rows (defined in sect. 3.3, i.e. Lagrange multipliers, shifted constraints g) are computed for state equations rows.

5. The general structure of the algorithm for DLP is similar to that presented in sect. 3.4. To sum up basic differences one may observe that:

   - we consider a problem that is equivalent to a static LP but reduced to the subspace of decision variables and is solved in the way similar to that described in sect. 3.3 and 3.4,
   - state equations are solved for control variables and for variations,
   - a conjugate trajectory Ψ is computed.

4.4 Algorithm for minimization of augmented Lagrangian for DLP

Now we may present the algorithm for minimization of the augmented Lagrangian function for DLP in a more formal way. Iń each iteration of multiplier method, the following optimization problem is solved: minimize the augmented Lagrangian penalty function

$$F(x,u,z) = \sum_{t=1}^{T}(a_t/\rho)x_t + (b/\rho)u +$$
$$+ \left(\left\|y/\rho + \sum_{t=0}^{T} F_t x_t + Du - d + z\right\|^2 - \left\|y/\rho\right\|^2\right) / 2.$$

subject to

$$-H_t x_t + \sum_{i=0}^{t-1} A_{t-1,i} x_i + B_t u = c_t \qquad t = 1,\dots,T$$

with a given initial condition x_0 and

$$e \leq u \leq f$$
$$0 \leq z \leq r$$

where z is a vector of slack variables, which—as discussed in sect. 3.3—are not used in the algorithm. The algorithm consists of the following steps:

1. For given y and ρ choose a point u such that $e \leq u \leq f$

2. Solve the state equation

$$H_t x_t = \sum_{i=0}^{t-1} A_{t-1,i} x_i + B_t u - c_t \qquad t = 1,\dots,T$$

with given initial condition x_0

3. Compute shifted constraints for constraints (10)

$$g = -y/\rho - \sum_{t=0}^{T} F_t x_t - Du + d$$

and determine sets I, $\bar{I}$

$$I = \{\, i : g_i > r_i \,\} \cup \{\, i : g_i < 0 \,\}$$

while $\bar{I}$ is the complement of I.

4. Define $\bar{g}$ as follows :

$$\bar{g}_i = \begin{cases} g_i - r_i & \text{if } g_i > r_i \\ g_i & \text{otherwise} \end{cases}$$

5. Find the conjugate trajectory by solving backwards the conjugate equations

$$H_t^T \Psi_t = \sum_{i=t}^{T-1} A_{i,t}^T \Psi_{t+1} + (F_t^I)^T \bar{g}^I - a_t/\rho, \qquad t = T-1,\dots,1$$

with boundary condition

$$\Psi_T = (F_T^I)^T \bar{g}^I - a_T/\rho$$

6. Compute the minus gradient reduced to subspace of decision variables

$$q = -b/\rho + (D^I)^T \bar{g}^I + \sum_{t=1}^{T} B_t^T \Psi_t$$

7. Determine sets J and $\bar{J}$

$$J = \{\, j : u_j = e_j \text{ and } q_j \leq 0 \,\} \cup \{\, j : u_j = f_j \text{ and } q_j \geq 0 \,\}$$

while $\bar{J}$ is the complement of J

8. If $q_j = 0$ for all $j \in \bar{J}$ then u is a minimum point of the augmented Lagrangian penalty function

9. Set $p^J = q^J$

10. Solve state equation in variations

$$H_t \sigma_t = \sum_{i=0}^{t-1} A_{t-1,i} \sigma_i + B_t^J p^J \qquad t = 1, \ldots, T$$

with boundary condition $\sigma_0 = 0$

11. Compute

$$s = D^J p^J + \sum_{t=0}^{T} F_t \sigma_t$$

$$h = \|q^J\|^2$$

$$v = \|s^I\|^2$$

$$\alpha(1) = h/v$$

Note that $\alpha(1)$ is the conjugate gradient step length in direction p^J

12. Find the step length that would violate the nearest non-violated constraint, i.e.,

$$\alpha(2) = \min_{i \in K} \{g_i/s_i\}, \qquad K = \{\, i : i \in \bar{I} \text{ and } s_i > 0 \,\}$$

$$\alpha(3) = \min_{i \in K} \{(g_i - r_i)/s_i\}, \qquad K = \{\, i : i \in \bar{I} \text{ and } s_i < 0 \,\}$$

13. Find the step length that would enable a variable to reach a bound, i.e.,

$$\alpha(4) = \min_{j \in K} \{(e_j - u_j)/p_j\}, \qquad K = \{\, j : j \in \bar{J} \text{ and } p_j < 0 \,\}$$

$$\alpha(5) = \min_{j \in K} \{(f_j - u_j)/p_j\}, \qquad K = \{\, j : j \in \bar{J} \text{ and } p_j > 0 \,\}$$

14. Determine step length

$$\alpha = \min_{i=1,\dots,5} (\alpha(i))$$

If $\alpha = \min(\alpha(2), \alpha(3))$ add the row index for which this condition holds to set I and remove that index from set $\bar{I}$. If $\alpha = \min(\alpha(4), \alpha(5))$ add the column index for which this condition holds to set J and remove that index from set $\bar{J}$.

15. Compute :

$$u^J := u^J + \alpha p^J$$

$$x_t := x_t + \alpha \sigma_t$$

$$g_i := g_i - \alpha s_i$$

16. For the new g^I solve the conjugate equation (as in step 5)

17. Compute the minus gradient :

$$q^J = -b^J/\rho + (D^I_J)^T g^I + \sum_{t=1}^{T} (B_t)^T_J \Psi_t$$

18. If $q^J = 0$, then go to 2

19. If $\alpha = \alpha(1)$ continue with the conjugate gradient step, i.e.

$$\beta = \|q^J\|^2/h$$

$$p^J = q^J + \beta p^J$$

and go to step 10

20. Go to step 9

Note that the condition $q^J = 0$ is in practice replaced by $\|q^J\| \leq \varepsilon$. The value of ε may be quite large in the first few iterations; it then decreases as the number of iterations increases.

4.5 Regularization

It is possible that a linear programming problem may have nonunique optimal solutions. Although this is theoretically rare, in practice many problems actually have a large set of widely varying basic solutions for which the objective values differ very little (Sosnowski, 1981). In some cases, the simplex algorithm will stop when a basic solution is recognized as optimal for a given set of tolerances. For problems with a nonunique optimum, the first optimal solution found is accepted, so that one may not even be aware of the non-uniqueness of the solution reported as optimal.

Thus we are faced with the problem of choosing an optimal (or, in most cases, to be more accurate, a suboptimal) solution that possesses certain additional properties required by the user. This problem may be overcome by applying an approach called *regularization*. Regularization (Tikhonov's type) is a way of finding the optimal solution with either minimum Euclidian norm or minimum distance from a given reference point. The first of these options may be activated by a REGZERO statement in the specification file. The second may be chosen by REGREF statement. For the latter case the non-zero values of $\bar{x}$ (see the following formulae) are defined in additional section (called *reference*) in the MPS input file.

The minimum norm solution is obtained by carrying out a sequence of minimizations of regularized augmented Lagrangians rather than one minimization of an "ordinary" augmented Lagrangian (Sosnowski, 1978). Thus minimization of $L(\cdot, y^k)$ in problem (PO) is replaced by

$$x^{k+1} = \operatorname*{argmin}_x L(x, y^k) + \|x - \bar{x}\|^2/(2\eta^k)$$

where $\bar{x}$ is given and

$$\eta^k \to \infty, \qquad \sum_{i=1}^{\infty}(\rho^k/\eta^k))^{1/2} < \infty,$$

In the computer implementation of the algorithm the following rule is assumed for η^{k+1}:

$$\eta^{k+1} = \min(\eta^k \eta_s, \eta_m)$$

η^0, η_s and η_m are given parameters.

4.6 Preconditioned conjugate gradient for minimization of augmented Lagrangian

The algorithm for minimization of the augmented Lagrangian (cf sect. 4.1) theoretically guarantees that the exact solution of a problem will be found after finite number of iterations. However, during the actual computations the rounding errors often cause numerical problems. For accelerating the convergence, the augmented Lagrangian can be minimized by using the preconditioned conjugate gradient method. This method is discussed in details for linear problems in (Golub and Van Loan, 1983) and for least squares problems in (Heath, 1984). Therefore we present only brief summary of the applied approach.

Let us consider again the algorithm for minimization of the augmented Lagrangian penalty function. Assume that the steps 8 – 15 of the algorithm are executed for fixed sets of indices $I, \bar{J}$. In other words, the conjugate gradient algorithm is used for minimization of a quadratic function which has the following Hessian matrix:

$$H = (A^I_J)^T(A^I_J)$$

A matrix M which approximates the Hessian matrix H and for which it is easy to solve the the linear system:

$$Mp^J = q^J$$

will be referred to as the *preconditioning (or scaling) matrix.*

For a given preconditioning matrix M and under assumption that the sets of indices $I, \bar{J}$ do not change, we can use the following modification of the steps 8 – 15 of the algorithm 4.1. This modified algorithm will be called preconditioned conjugate gradient algorithm for minimization of the augmented Lagrangian penalty function. Note that steps 10., 11., 12. are void since the sets of indices $I, \bar{J}$ do not change.

8. Set $p^J = M^{-1}q^J$

9. Compute

$$s = A_J p^J$$
$$h = (q^J)^T M^{-1} q^J$$
$$d = \|s^I\|^2$$
$$\alpha = h/d$$

13. Compute the new point $x^J := x^J + \alpha p^J$ and the minus gradient at that point:

$$g_i := g_i - \alpha s_i$$

$$q^J = (A^I_J)^T \bar{g}^I - c^J/\rho$$

14. If $q^J = 0.$ then STOP

15. Continue with the preconditioned conjugate gradient steps:

$$\beta = (q^J)^T M^{-1} q^J / h$$

$$p^J := M^{-1} q^J + \beta p^J$$

go to step 9.

There is no general rule for a choice of a scaling matrix. Therefore we will discuss briefly possible preconditioned matrix selection options for general formulation of LP problems and for dynamic LP problems.

4.6.1 Scaling matrix for LP problems

For LP problems that do not have a special structure of the matrix A, a scaling matrix M should be an approximation of $H = (A^I_J)^T(A^I_J)$.

Diagonal scaling : A very simple method of scaling which requires only n elements to be stored results in a matrix M which is the diagonal of H.

Let the matrix M be equal to a matrix W^I_J which is defined (for given sets of indices $I, \bar{J}$) as follows:

$$W^I_J = diag(w_j) \qquad j \in \bar{J}$$

where $w_j = \sum_{i \in I} a^2_{ij}$. The matrix W^I_J can be easily updated if the indices sets $I, \bar{J}$ are changed. If a new index k is added to the set I then the respective element should be updated in the following way: $w_j := w_j + a^2_{kj}$. If an index is removed from the set $\bar{J}$ a column and a row should be discarded from the matrix W^I_J.

Cholesky factorization of the scaling matrix : Let n_J be dimension of a subspace in which we minimize the quadratic function, and n_d be an integer number. Assume that after $n_J + n_d$ steps of the ordinary or diagonal scaling conjugate gradient algorithm a minimum is not found. In such a case we can use as the scaling matrix the Hessian:

$$M = (A_J^I)^T (A_J^I)$$

and apply Cholesky factorization for obtaining an inverse of the scaling matrix ($M = R^T R$, where R is upper triangular matrix). Application of such scaling matrix usually results in minimimization of the function in one step of the algorithm.

4.6.2 Scaling matrix for dynamic LP problems

The main advantage of the conjugate gradient algorithm for dynamic LP problems is due to the reduction of a dimension of working space to a dimension of a subspace of independent variables. Therefore an implementation of the preconditioned conjugate algorithm should use as a scaling matrix a matrix which approximates the reduced Hessian. For a general structure of the dynamic problem, the form of the reduced Hessian is rather complicated, thus we suggest a different method for selection of a scaling matrix.

Let us consider the algorithm for minimization of the augmented Lagrangian penalty function – section 4.4. with the assumption that the steps 9 – 20 of the algorithm are executed for fixed sets of indices $I, \bar{J}$.

Matrix scaling : Let $p_k^J, k = 1, \ldots, n_J$ be conjugate directions obtained during n_J steps of the ordinary conjugate gradient algorithm, where n_J is also dimension of the working space. Then an inverse of the reduced Hessian matrix Q may be calculated as:

$$Q = \sum_{k=1}^{n_J} p_k^J (p_k^J)^T / d_k$$

where $d_k = \|s_k^I\|^2$. The preconditioned conjugate gradient algorithm can be used with $M^{-1} = Q$. The matrix M^{-1} may be obtained in the following way:

$$Q_0 = 0$$

$$Q_k = Q_{k-1} + p_k^J (p_k^J)^T / d_k \qquad k = 1, \ldots, n_J$$

$$M^{-1} = Q_{n_J}$$

Diagonal scaling : Instead of using the matrix Q defined above one can use only its diagonal. In such a case if after n_J steps of the conjugate gradient algorithm a minimum is not found, the preconditioned conjugate gradient algorithm is initiated with the scaling matrix $M^{-1} = diag(Q)$.

4.7 Scaling

It is generally agreed that the choice of an appropriate scaling of a problem being solved can be a critical issue for numerical stability. There are obviously two approaches to deal with that problem. First, suggested by Tomlin (1972), assume that an experienced model builder, who uses sensible units may avoid unnecessarily large or small matrix elements. This is true, but requires a lot of time consuming preparations, which are reliable source of frustrating bugs. Therefore, we have followed the second approach, suggested by Curtis and Reid (1972) for solving the scaling problem.

Our approach is discussed in details in (Makowski and Sosnowski, 1981), therefore only short description follows. For the sake of simplicity we consider a problem of scaling on an example of a problem in a form:

$$Ax = b \tag{18}$$

$$d \leq x \leq q$$

where $A \in R^{m \times n}$.

According to Curtis and Reid (1972) matrix A is considered as well-scaled if

$$\sum_{i=1}^{m} \sum_{j \in J_i} \left(\log(abs(a_{ij})) \right)^2 \leq v$$

for some acceptable v. J_i are sets of indices of columns with non-zero elements in i-th row.

Therefore, instead of solving the original problem (18), one can solve an equivalent problem in form

$$(RAC)y = Rb$$

$$C^{-1}d \leq y \leq C^{-1}q$$

$$x = Cy$$

Here $R = diag(r_1, \ldots, r_m)$ and $C = diag(c_1, \ldots, c_n)$ are two diagonal matrices with positive components. In other words, an equivalent problem is formed by multiplying i-th row by r_i and j-th column by c_j.

The problem of scaling boils down to finding coefficients r_i and c_j such that

$$\sum_{i=1}^{m} \sum_{j \in J_i} \left(\log(r_i c_j abs(a_{ij})) \right)^2 \rightarrow \min$$

It is easy to observe that the above stated problem has no unique solution (although the optimally scaled matrix may be unique). Therefore we minimize the following performance index:

$$\sum_{i=1}^{m} \sum_{j \in J_i} \left(\log(r_i c_j abs(a_{ij})) \right)^2 + \beta \sum_{i \in K} \left(\log(abs(r_i rhs_i)) \right)^2 +$$

$$\gamma \sum_{i \in L} \left(\log(abs(c_j bnd_i)) \right)^2 \rightarrow \min$$

where *rhs* and *bnd* are non-zero elements of RHS and bounds, respectively, sets of indices K and L contain indices of rows with non-zero *rhs* and columns with non-zero bounds, respectively.

For numerical reasons the base of logarithms is 2 and obtained coefficients are rounded to nearest integer number.

For this formulation of the scaling problem, it was possible to design a specialized algorithm based on conjugate gradient method. Since an excessive accuracy is not required, the scaling algorithm is very efficient (usually it takes less then 10 iterations regardless of dimension of a problem). Therefore, the scaling option (which is the default) should not be suppressed except if special requirements apply. The values of performance indices (3.7) and (3.8) are displayed both before and (if active) after scaling.

Usually there is no need to change default parameters. Should a change of parameters be desired, it may be done by entering respective values in specification file (SBETA stands for β and SETA stands for γ). Two stopping criteria are used, which may be controlled by parameters SEPS and SEP1. Let v^k be a value of the performance index (3.8). The scaling routine is ended, if $v^k/v^{k-1} \geq$ SEPS or if the norm of gradient is less then SEP1. In addition the number of scaling iterations in constrained by ITSCAL (cf the User Manual).

Scaling coefficients are displayed as additional column in MPS-type output of results. This has only informative purpose, since all results are rescaled internally.

5 Testing examples

HYBRID has been tested on number of examples. For the sake of illustration of the package capabilities several known examples that cover different types of problems have been selected.

5.1 Economic growth model (Manne)

This model is a linear multicriteria version of Manne's model described in (Murtagh and Sanders, 1982).

The variables have the following meaning:

t – time period, $t = 1, 2, \ldots, T$

c_t – consumption

i_t – investment,

k_t – capital in time period t.

The following criteria have been selected for illustration of multicriteria optimization:

$$\max \sum_{t=1}^{T} \beta_t c_t \qquad \text{(of the type MAX)}$$

$$\max k_T \qquad \text{(of the type MAX)}$$

$$\min \max_{t=1,2,\ldots,T} |c_t - \bar{c}_t| \qquad \text{(of the type FOL)}$$

The state equations have the following form:

$$k_t = k_{t-1} + i_t, \qquad t = 1, 2, \ldots, T$$

with k_0 given.

Linear constraints are defined for $t = 1, 2, \ldots, T$

$$c_t + i_t \leq \alpha_{t-1} k_{t-1}$$

$$k_t \geq k_0 + i_0$$

Bounds are given for both control variables (for each variable a constraint is specified for each time period $t = 1, 2, \ldots, T$):

$$c_t \geq c_0$$

$$i_t \leq (1.04)^t i_0$$

The following parameters (where $\alpha = (c_0 + i_0)/k_0$) have been assumed:

$$\beta_t = 0.95^t, \quad b = 0.25, \quad g = 0.03, \quad c_0 = 0.65,$$

$$i_0 = 0.16, \quad k_0 = 3.0, \quad \alpha_t = \alpha(1+g)^{(1-b)t}$$

In the following table the test examples which refers to the modified Manne problem are denoted by ManneT, where T corresponds to a number of periods.

5.2 Flood control problem

The problem is a model (cf Kreglewski et al., 1985) of the water system which consists of three general purpose reservoirs supplying water to the main river reach. The goal of the system dispatcher is to operate the reservoirs in such a way that the flood peak on the main river do not coincide. It is assumed that inflow forecast for each reservoir is known.

The model consists of water balance equations for selected points and for each time period. The capacities of reservoirs are also constraint. Various types of criteria are examined:

FOL – corresponds to following given trajectories of water flow in selected points,

DER – corresponds to minimization water flow changes (in consecutive time periods) in selected points,

MAX – corresponds to minimization of maximal (over time) flow in selected points.

In the following table the test examples which refers to the multicriteria flood control problems are denoted by FloodT, where T corresponds to a number of periods.

5.3 Full dense LP problem

This problem is a modification of the Mangasarian example (Mangasarian, 1981) and has been generated for verification of the package for fully dense LP problems. Computations are performed for one criterion and elements of matrix are equal to 1.0 with exception of diagonal elements for which values of $a_{ii} = i$ are selected.

In the following table the test examples which refers to the modified Mangasarian example are denoted by MangT, where T corresponds to a dimension of LP matrix.

5.4 Linear programming test problems

Four examples from a widely used set of test problems (cf e.g. Gay 1986), namely: Afiro, Adlittle, Share2b and Israel have been also used as testing examples. The last three problems result in badly conditioned Hessian matrices of the augmented Lagrangian.

5.5 Discussion of test results

Testing problems have been solved on a PC compatible with IBM/AT (running at 8 MHz) with 80287 coprocessor (running effectively at 5.3 MHz). The algorithm was implemented with double precision arithmetic (the machine precision about 2.22e-16). The default values of all parameters (this includes initial multipliers equal to zero) were assumed in all runs.

The results of some tests are summarized in the following table. Numbers of rows and columns correspond to a single criterion LP problem, which were obtained by transformation of relevant multicriteria problems. The numbers of gradient iterations correspond to execution of step 8 of the algorithm (cf sect. 4.1).

Problem	Number of crit.	Rows	Cols	Dens. [%]	Time (min.)	Mult. iter.	Grad iter.
Manne05	3	29	27	12	0.08	2	21
Manne10	3	54	52	7	0.18	2	45
Manne20	2	103	102	3	0.25	2	51
Manne30	2	153	152	2	0.52	2	159
Flood03	3	37	37	6	0.37	2	13
Flood05	3	59	59	4	1.50	3	63
Mang20	1	20	20	100	0.33	2	8
Mang30	1	30	30	100	0.98	2	8
Afiro	1	28	32	10	0.17	2	68
Adlittle	1	57	97	8	17.75	10	476
Share2b	1	97	79	10	37.51	24	807
Israel	1	175	142	10	128.63	5	974

Due to super sparse matrix technique applied for storing data, rather long computation time is required for fully dense matrix problems. For dynamic sparse problems better performance of the algorithm was observed. HYBRID is usually slower in comparison to packages which are based on the simplex method but requires less computer memory. On the other hand HYBRID performs detailed diagnostic of a problem being solved and offers a possibility of definition and modification of a multicriteria problem, its conversion to an equivalent single criterion problem, as well as the possibility of effectively solving badly conditioned problems that might be difficult for other systems.

As an illustration of HYBRID performance on a mainframe computer, a modification of the Manne problem (for the sake of creating a larger problem we have introduced 10 sectors instead of one given in formulation in sect. 5.1) for 20 time periods has been solved by both MINOS ver. 5.0 (Murtagh and Saunders, 1983) and HYBRID ver. 3.1. The test has been performed on VAX 780/11 under Berkeley UNIX 4.2. A multicriteria problem with criteria presented in sect. 5.1 has been generated and has been converted by HYBRID to a corresponding single criteria problem and the MPS format input file for MINOS has been generated. The resulting problem has 464 rows, 471 columns and 1463 elements (density 0.7%). MINOS has used 2.9 min. (the sum of user and system time) to solve the above mentioned problem. HYBRID has used 2.28 min. for processing and diagnostic of the problem (which includes interactive definition of initial reference trajectory, conversion of multicriteria problem to the equivalent single criterion problem and generation of MPS format file for the latter problem) and 2.35 min. for solving the problem. On the other hand HYBRID has used less then half of computer memory required by MINOS to solve the problem.

6 Conclusions

First version of HYBRID was made operational on VAX 780/11 and is documented in (Makowski and Sosnowski, 1984). Then we had improved and extended the package for dynamic linear programming models (DLP) and for multicriteria problems (both static and dynamic). The later version is documented in (Makowski and Sosnowski, 1985b). The next version, HYBRID 3.03 (described in Makowski and Sosnowski, 1988b) allowed for more general formulation of problems with recognized structure. The code of HYBRID 3.03 has been improved with taking into account robustness of its usage. Last major revision of the algorithm and code which resulted in HYBRID version 3.1 is summarized in Section 1.3.

HYBRID 3.1 is still a prototype software that requires more testing. It is true that for some problems HYBRID 3.1 performs worse than the commercial packages FMPS and MINOS. If HYBRID is used not only for one run but for scenario analysis (solving the problem with change of multicriteria parameters, matrix elements, RHS etc.) its performance is much better. This is not only due to the fact that MPS file is processed only once in a first run but mainly because in consecutive runs only updates of affected coefficients are made (the problem is generated only for the first run) and because a solution is usually obtained much faster then for the first run. On the other hand HYBRID offers the possibility of formulation, solution and analysis of a linear programming multicriteria problems and of single criteria linear-quadratic problems.

HYBRID provides very useful diagnostics for any LP model and therefore is also useful for a model verification. It could be used for that purpose as "stand alone" package, and—also after possible modification of a problem in interactive way—one may output MPS-format file to be used by other packages. The same approach may be used for transformation of multicriteria problem to equivalent single-criteria LP.

The further development of HYBRID will proceed in following directions:

1. Further modification of the way in which the user communicates with the package. The modification will exploit capabilities of PC and will ease the use of the package.
2. Extensions of capabilities of HYBRID by introduction of new options for definition and handling of multicriteria problem (new types and more flexible definition of criteria, introduction of both aspiration and reservation levels, data base for previous runs etc). Another new option will allow for easy formulation of piece-wise linear goal function for an LP problem.
3. Further improvement of the algorithm and its computer code (automatic evaluation of some parameters, experiments with possible modification of the algorithm) that will result in a faster execution.

We hope that, despite the reservations outlined above, HYBRID 3.1 will eventually be a useful tool with many practical applications. We would be grateful for any criticisms and comments that would help us to improve the package.

7 References

Bertsekas, D.P. (1976). Multiplier methods: a survey. *Automatica*, 12: 133–145.

Curtis, A.R. and J.K. Reid (1972). On the automatic scaling of matrices for Gaussian elimination. *Journal of Mathematics and its applications*, No. 10, pp. 118–124.

Flecher, R. (1981). Practical methods of optimization, vol II, Constrained optimization, Wiley, New York.

Fourer, R. (1982). Solving staircase linear programs by the simplex method. *Mathematical Programming*, 23(1982) 274–313, 25(1983) 251–292.

Gay, D.M. (1986). Electronic Mail Distribution of Linear Programming Test Problems. *Numerical Analysis Manuscript*, 86-0(1986), AT&T Laboratories, Murray Hill, New Jersey.

Golub, G.H. and C.F. Van Loan (1983). Matrix Computations, Johns Hopkins University Press, Baltimore, Maryland.

Heath, M.T. (1984). Numerical Methods for Large Sparse Linear Least Squares Problems. *SIAM J. Sci. Stat. Comput.*, Vol. 5, No. 3, 1984.

Hestenes, M.R. (1980). Conjugate Gradient Methods in Optimization. Springer Verlag, Berlin.

Hurlimann, T. (1988). Reference manual for the LPL Modeling Language. Research Report, University of Fribourg, Fribourg, Switzerland.

Ho, J.K. and A.S. Hanne (1974). Nested decomposition for dynamic models. *Mathematical Programming* , 6(1974) 121–140

Kallio, M., A. Lewandowski and W. Orchard-Hays (1980). An implementation of the reference point approach for multiobjective optimization. WP-80-35, International Institute for Applied Systems Analysis, Laxenburg, Austria.

Kreglewski, T., Lewandowski, A. and T. Rogowski (1985). Dynamic Extension of the DIDAS system and its Application in Flood Control. In M. Grauer, M. Thompson, A.P. Wierzbicki, editors: Plural Rationality and Interactive Decision Processes, Springer Verlag.

Lewandowski, A. and M. Grauer (1982). The reference point optimization approach—methods of efficient implementation. CP-8-S12, IIASA Collaborative Proceedings Series: Multiobjective and Stochastic Optimization Proceedings of an IIASA Task Force Meeting.

Makowski, M. and J. Sosnowski (1981). Implementation of an algorithm for scaling matrices and other programs useful in linear programming, CP-81-37, International Institute for Applied Systems Analysis, Laxenburg, Austria.

Makowski, M. and J. Sosnowski (1984). Hybrid: A mathematical programming package, IIASA, CP-84-9.

Makowski, M. and J. Sosnowski (1985a). A decision support system for planning and controlling agricultural production with a decentralized management structure. In M. Grauer, M. Thompson, A.P. Wierzbicki, editors: Plural Rationality and Interactive Decision Processes, Springer Verlag.

Makowski, M. and J. Sosnowski (1985b). HYBRID 2.1: A mathematical programming package for multicriteria dynamic problems. In A. Lewandowski, A. Wierzbicki, editors: Theory Software and Testing Examples for Decision Support Systems, IIASA, Laxenburg, September 1985.

Makowski, M. and J. Sosnowski (1987). Methodological Guide to HYBRID 3.01: a mathematical programming package for multicriteria dynamic problems. In A. Lewandowski, A. Wierzbicki, editors: Theory Software and Testing Examples for Decision Support Systems, WP-87-26, IIASA, Laxenburg, April 1987.

Makowski, M. and J. Sosnowski (1988a). A Mathematical Programming Package for Multicriteria Dynamic Linear Problems HYBRID. Methodological and User Guide to Version 3.03, WP-88-002, IIASA, Laxenburg, January 1988.

Makowski, M. and J. Sosnowski (1988b). User Guide to a Mathematical Programming Package for Multicriteria Dynamic Linear Problems HYBRID Version 3.1, WP-88-111, IIASA, Laxenburg, December 1988.

Mangasarian, O.L. (1981). Iterative solution of linear programs. *SIAM Journal for Numerical Analysis*, 18(4): 606–614.

Murtagh, B.A. (1981). Advanced Linear Programming: Computation and Practice, Mc Graw–Hill, New York.

Murtagh, B.A. and M.A. Sanders (1977). MINOS – A large-scale nonlinear programming system (for problems with linear constraints). User guide. Technical Report, Systems Optimization Laboratory, Stanford University.

Murtagh, B.A. and M.A. Sanders (1982). A projected Lagrangian algorithm and its implementation for sparse nonlinear constraints. *Mathematical Programming Study*, 16(1982), 84–117.

Murtagh, B.A. and M.A. Saunders (1983). MINOS 5.0 User's Guide, Technical Report SOL 83-20, Systems Optimization Laboratory, Department of Operations Research, Stanford University, Stanford, December 1983.

O'Leary, D.P. (1980). A generalized conjugate gradient algorithm for solving a class of quadratic problems. *Linear Algebra and its Applications*, 34: 371–399.

Polyak, B.T. (1969). The conjugate gradient method in extremal problems. *Computational Mathematics and Mathematical Physics*, 9: 94–112.

Polyak, B.T. and N.V. Tretiyakov (1972). An iterative method for linear programming and its economic interpretation. *Economic and Mathematical Methods*, 8: 740–751, (in Russian).

Propoi, A. (1976). Problems of Dynamic Linear Programming, IIASA, RM-76-78.

Sosnowski, J.S. (1978). Dynamic optimization of multisectorial linear production model. Systems Research Institute, Warsaw, Ph.D. Thesis, (in Polish).

Sosnowski, J.S. (1981). Linear programming via augmented Lagrangian and conjugate gradient methods. In S. Walukiewicz and A.P. Wierzbicki, editors: *Methods of Mathematical Programming*, Proceedings of a 1977 Conference in Zakopane. Polish Scientific Publishers, Warsaw.

Tomlin, J.A. (1972). On scaling linear programming problems. *Mathematical Programming Study 4*, North Holland Publishing Company, Amsterdam.

Wierzbicki, A. (1978). On the use of penalty functions in multiobjective optimization, Institute of Automatics, Technical University of Warsaw.

Wierzbicki, A.P. (1979). A methodological guide to multiobjective decision making, WP-79-122, IIASA.

Wierzbicki, A. (1980). A mathematical basis for satisficing decision making. WP-80-90, IIASA.

Safety Principle in Multiobjective Decision Support in the Decision Space Defined by Availability of Resources

Henryk Gorecki, Andrzej M.J. Skulimowski
Institute of Automatic Control
Academy of Mining and Metallurgy, Cracow.

Abstract

We consider the situation where a decision-maker in a multicriteria optimization problem must follow additional constraints in the criteria space defined by availability of resources. The set defined by such constraints - called demanded set - is assumed to be uncertain as a result of a priori experts estimations. The analysis of numerous real-life situations showed that a method of looking for a non-dominated solution on the so-called skeleton allows to find a solution maximally safe with respect to the random perturbations of the demanded set. We formulate a maximal safety principle as a requirement that the expected value of distance from the solution chosen to the boundary of the demanded set were maximal. Then we prove that the search executed on the skeleton curve satisfies this principle for a class of demanded sets defined by aspiration levels.

1 Introduction

The choice of a compromise solution fulfilling additional conditions with regard to its location in the criteria space is essential in numerous real-life multiple criteria optimization problems. For instance, the choice of a technological process from many variants proposed by experts, taking into account the total cost of investment and the minimal necessary time to start the production, is often based on the analysis of upper and lower bounds for values of the above criteria, (Gorecki, 1981). Such bounds are usually not strict; they are called aspiration levels and are assumed to be imposed independently by experts or the decision-maker after the formulation of the problem, therefore serving as an additional information for selecting the compromise solution.

The nature of aspiration levels is often uncertain and the arising set of demanded values of criteria may be represented as random or fuzzy set. When selecting a compromise solution, the decision-maker is obliged to take into account the possibility of unexpected change of aspiration levels using an uncertainty handling technique. For the case where the demanded set is defined by two aspiration levels such a method has been proposed by Gorecki (1981). In his approach the search for a non-dominated solution has been executed on a line which joins the aspiration levels, and lies inside of so-called skeleton of the demanded set. An outline of the skeleton method may be found in Gorecki (1981) and Wiecek (1984). The numerical implementation of this method has then been developed by Gorecki et al. (1982, 1985). Here, we will present some of its theoretical foundations.

Throughout this paper we will assume that the set defined by the lower and upper aspiration levels, called demanded set, and the attainable set of the criteria values have a non-empty intersection. Then we will analyse the problem of selecting a non-dominated compromise solution from this intersection which is - in some sense - most reliable to the changes of the demanded set. Namely, we look for a problem solution on a specific class of lines called the ordinal skeleton curves of the demanded set. The solution thus obtained will possess the property that the expected value of the distance from the boundary of the demanded set is maximal, or equivalently, that the probability of remaining within the demanded set – whose boundary changes according to some random rules – is maximal.

In this paper we will concentrate our attention on the particular case of the criteria space constraints, namely on the sets defined by aspiration levels of the form

$$Q \;:=\; (q_1 - \Theta) \cap (q_2 + \Theta) \tag{1}$$

where: q_1 and q_2 are the aspiration levels for criteria, denoting the minimal admissible, and the most desired values of the criteria, respectively, and Θ is the positive cone of the partial order in the criteria space. Usually $\Theta = R_+^N$, and

$$Q \;=\; \prod_{i=1}^{N} [q_{1i}; q_{2i}] \tag{2}$$

where $q_1 = (q_{11}, ..., q_{1N})$ and $q_2 = (q_{21}, ..., q_{2N})$, $q_{1i} \geq q_{2i}$ for $1 \leq i \leq N$ and the product of intervals is understood in the Cartesian sense.

2 Problem formulation

Let us consider multicriteria minimization problem /MMP/

$$(F : U \to R^N) \to \min(\Theta) \tag{3}$$

where $F = (F_1, F_2, ..., F_N)$ is the vector objective continuous function, U is a closed subset of the decision space, and Θ is a closed, convex and pointed cone defining the partial order $\leq_\Theta$ in the criteria space R^N. We assume that the set U and the function F are convex, therefore the attainable set $F(U)$ is also convex.

The solution u to the problem will be called *non-dominated* if

$$(F(u) - \Theta) \;\cap\; F(U) = \{F(u)\} \tag{4}$$

The set of non-dominated decisions $P(U, F, \Theta)$ will be called the Pareto set while the corresponding set of non-dominated valuations

$$FP(U, \Theta) := F(P(U, F, \Theta)) \tag{5}$$

will be called the *compromise set*. We will also use the notation $P(V,\Theta) := P(V, id_E, \Theta)$ whenever $V \subset E$.

Moreover, we assume that in the criteria space two points are distinguished, $q_1 := (q_{11}, ..., q_{1N})$ and $q_2 := (q_{21}, q_{22}, ..., q_{2N})$ such that $q_2 \leq_\Theta q_1$. The points q_1 and q_2 will be called the upper, and the lower aspiration levels for the problem (3), respectively.

The aspiration levels are set up by experts independently from the base problem formulation and define so-called demanded set Q for the values of the criteria (cf. formula (1)). We will assume that q_1 is attainable and that

$$P((q_1 - \Theta) \cap F(U), \Theta) = (q_1 - \Theta) \cap FP(U, \Theta) \tag{6}$$

On the contrary, q_2 is assumed to be unattainable strictly dominating point for the attainable set $F(U)$, i.e.

$$FP(U, \Theta) \cap (q_2 + \Theta) \neq \emptyset \tag{7}$$

and

$$P(q_1 - \Theta) \cap F(U), \Theta) = (q_1 - \Theta) \cap FP(U, \Theta) \tag{8}$$

(cf. Skulimowski (1986a)).

Another additional assumption which will be used at this stage of problem solution is that there exist reasonable estimates of the scale coefficients for each scalar criteria $F_1, ..., F_N$. This will enable us to measure the distance of the criteria inside the demanded set basing on locally comparable units of the coordinates of the criterion function. A method of deriving locally comparable units has been proposed by Gorecki (1981) who used the differences between the coordinates of the barycenter of Q and q_1 as the relative units of criteria.

Since this kind of information imposes certain knowledge of the trade-offs between criteria which in our model are uncertain, in the real-life applications we will repeat the execution of the algorithm described in the following section interactively, with the slightly varying values of the scale coefficients.

The demanded set Q plays the role of additional constraints imposed on the solution to the MMP. At this stage we will assume that every non-dominated solution found inside Q is admissible for the decision maker. However, the estimates of q_1 and q_2 are usually uncertain and the satisfactory solution to the problem is the one which lies inside of the actual demanded set Q_η perturbed by a random factor η. To maximize the probability of $u_{opt} \in Q_\eta$ we will define a special class of algorithms of the line-search for a non-dominated solution to MMP inside of Q.

3 The search for a non-dominated solution on a curve

The idea of the algorithm of finding a compromise non-dominated solution presented below consists in replacing the original MMP (3) by a search for a non-dominated solution belonging to a curve g which lies inside the demanded set Q. If Q is defined by (1), g begins at an attainable reference point q_1 and ends at an unattainable dominating one, q_2 i.e. $g(0) = q_1$ and $g(1) = q_2$. The solution thus found belongs to the intersection of $FP(U,\Theta)$ and $g^\star := g([0;1])$, and is non-dominated provided that the set $FP(U,\Theta)$ divides the demanded set into two parts. The latter condition is fulfilled e.g. when $F(U)$ is convex and (6) is satisfied.

The algorithm of the search

The choice of the curve g is based on the analysis of the specific properties of elements of $g^\star$. Consequently we will consider the curves which satisfy the maximal safety principle, i.e. those for which the probability that the compromise solution chosen will remain within the randomly perturbed demanded set is maximal.

This may be achieved by selecting the curve maximizing the mean value of distance from the boundary of the demanded set. Considering moreover the fact that some criteria may turn out to be redundant leads us to choosing the so-called ordinal skeleton curve (Gorecki (1981), Wiecek (1984)) as the curve the search should be expected on.

The general algorithm of the search on a curve g may be sketched as follows:

Step 0 : selection of g, the choice of the algorithm A of detection of a non-dominated point p on $g^\star$,

$$f_o := q_2, \quad i := 1, \quad r_o := 1$$

Step 1 :

$$f_i = A(f_{i-1}, r_{i-1}),$$

Step 2 : check whether f_i is attainable; set $r_i := 1$ if f_i is attainable, *otherwise* $r_i := 0$,

Step 3 :

$$e_i \ := \ \| f_i - f_{i-1} \|$$

if $r_i \leq r_{i-1}$ and $e_i < e_0$

then

$$p := \frac{f_i + f_{i-1}}{2}$$

stop

else $i := i + 1$, *go to* 1.

The result of an execution of the algorithm is a non-dominated solution p. The Pareto-optimality of p is an immediate consequence of the assumption that q_1 and q_2 are separated by the non-dominated surface $FP(U,\Theta)$. The uniqueness is assured if g is a linearly ordered subset of Q which will be assumed further on. The maximal safety of p will be discussed in the following section.

In selecting a curve g so that safety principle is satisfied, a crucial role is played by the norm in the criteria space since it determines the value of the distance of the solution chosen from the exterior (or, equivalently, boundary) of Q. On the other hand, choice of distance influences the properties of the probability distribution of finding a non-dominated point along a curve. The justification of the choice of the norms l_1 or l_∞ in the criteria space is contained in the following subsection.

The algorithm is assumed to possess the following properties

a) $A(f,r) \in g^\star$ whenever $f \in g^\star$

b) $\| f_{i+1} - f_i \| \;<\; \|f_i - f_{i-1}\| \;\; for\ i > 1$

c) the assumed number of iterations of A depends only on the value of $||q_1 - q_2||$, not on the shape of $g^\star$.

To check whether a point F_i belonging to $g^\star$ is attainable one should examine the existence of solutions to the equation

$$f_i = F(u)$$

In convex cases this may be done as proposed by Wiecek (1984).

The value of e_0 must be sufficiently small to assure the accuracy of the method. The recommended value which proved to be adequate in numerical experiments is

$$e_0 := 10^{-4} min\{\rho_i(Q);\; 1 \le i \le N\}$$

where $\rho_i(Q)$ is the diameter of the projection of Q on the i-th axis in the criteria space.

The choice of a distance in the criteria space

We will start this section from the following definition:
Definition 1 : A curve $g : [0,1] \to E$ is linearly ordered iff

$$for\ each\ t_1, t_2 \in [0,1] :\; t_1 \le t_2 \;\Rightarrow\; g(t_1) \le_\Theta g(t_2) \tag{9}$$

where $\le_\Theta$ is the partial order in E. The set of all linearly ordered curves linking the points x and y will be denoted by $L(x,y)$.

Further on we will require that the following property of the line-search for a non-dominated solution, imposed by the choice of the class searching algorithms, is satisfied.
Assumption 1 . Let x and y be two elements of the demanded set Q such that $x \le_\Theta y$. Then the probability of finding a non-dominated point on a linearly ordered curve connecting x and y is constant and does not depend on the choice of this curve.

On the other hand we may require that the search on a curve gives better results when the curve is longer which can be formalized as
Assumption 2. The probability of detecting a non-dominated point on a curve linking two points is proportional to the length of this curve.

Consequently, the Assumptions 1 and 2 imply that all linearly ordered curves linking two fixed points in the criteria space should have the same length. The above requirements imply the limitations in the choice of the distance and the derived differential form (element of distance) which defines the length of the curve.

It is easy to see that the following statement is true.
Proposition 1 : The Assumptions 1 and 2 are fulfilled by the length of the curve generated by the l_1 or l_∞ norm, i.e. by

$$\lambda_1(g) := \int_g dx(l_1) = \int_{[0,1]} (\sum_{i=1}^{n} |g_i(t)|) dt \tag{10}$$

where $g = (g_1, ..., g_N)$ is the curve considered, and $x(l_1)$ is the element of length associated to the L_1 norm. The length of g for l_∞ norm is defined similarly to (10).

Proof of the Proposition 1 is given in Gorecki and Skulimowski (1986b), i.e. we prove that

$$\textit{for each } x, y \in Q, \ a, b \in L(x,y): \ \lambda_1(a) = \lambda_1(b) \tag{11}$$

Observe that only certain distances in R^N satisfy the above requirement (11), e.g. it is not fulfilled by the Euclidean distance.

The Assumptions 1 and 2, and the subsequent distance in the criteria space are in compliance with the assumption about the class of algorithms applied for looking for a non-dominated point on a curve, namely we will assume that these algorithms satisfy:
Assumption 3 . The a priori imposed maximal number of steps of an algorithm of detecting a non-dominated point on a curve g connecting the elements x and y of the criteria space does not depend on the choice of g but on the differences between coordinates of x and y. In particular, it may be defined as

$$max\left\{Ent(\frac{y_i - x_i}{s_i}) : 1 \leq i \leq N\right\},$$

where $Ent(r)$, $r \in R$, is the smallest integer exceeding r, and s_i, $1 \leq i \leq N$, are desired steps of quantification of criteria.

4 The safety principle

We will start this section with some basic definitions and properties. Let us recall that the *demanded set* Q is a closed and connected subset of the criteria space such that

$$FP(U,\Theta) \cap Q \neq \emptyset \tag{12}$$

Remark 1 : When (12) is not satisfied but Q contains some dominating points for the attainable set then Q may be regarded as a target set and a distance scalarization technique may be applied (Skulimowski, 1985a).

Further on we will restrict our consideration to the case where the demanded set appears as a result of upper and lower estimates for the values of the criteria.
Definition 2 . The *interval demanded set* for the problem (3) is given by the formula

$$Q_I := (q_1 - \Theta) \cap (q_2 + \Theta)$$

where:

$$q_1 \leq q_2, \quad q_1 \notin F(U), \quad q_2 \in F(U)$$

Interval demanded set in the case $\Theta := R^N_+$ may be represented as

$$Q_I = \prod_{i=1}^{N} [q_1^i; q_2^i]$$

where q_1^i, q_2^i are lower and upper estimates of the i-th criterion demanded values respectively.

Definition 3 . The subset S_I of the interval demanded set Q_I defined by the formula

$$S_I := \{x \in Q_I : \exists G_i, G_j,\ i \neq j\ \text{– facets of } Q_I, \text{ such that} \tag{13}$$

$$d(x, \partial Q_I) = d(x, G_i) = d(x, G_j)\}$$

where ∂Q_I – the boundary of Q_I – will be called the *skeleton* of Q_I.

Now, let $C(Q)$ be the subset of Q consisting of points maximally distant from the boundary of Q, i.e.

$$C(Q) := \{x \in Q : \forall\, y \in Q, d(y, \partial Q \leq d(x, \partial Q)\} \tag{14}$$

and let q_1 and q_2 be two distinct elements of ∂Q such that $q_2 \leq_\Theta q_1$. If Q is convex then for each element q of the boundary of Q there exist a unique half-line $v(q)$ starting in q and such that the function $d(\bullet, \partial Q)$ grows fastest on $v(q)$ in a neighborhood of each point belonging to $v(q)$. It is easy to see that $v(q)$ links q and $C(Q)$ and it is linearly ordered. Thus we may formulate the following

Definition 4 . The *ordinal skeleton* of Q is the set

$$S_0 := v(q_1) \cup v(q_2) \cup C(Q)$$

It is evident that if $Q = Q_I$ then $S_0 \subset S_I$.

Observe that the narrower are the experts' estimations concerning a criterion F_i the smaller scope of decision is left to the decision-maker. Consequently, in some extreme cases certain criteria can be regarded rather as the constraint functions. Moreover, when the estimates are relatively narrow, one may expect that they are also more accurate than those which allow the decision maker for the broad range of decision.

Thus in some cases the decision-maker can neglect the uncertainty in the estimations concerning one or more coordinates of the objective functions. In such a situation the consideration of the original demanded set Q should be replaced by taking into account the set Q'

$$Q' := pr(i_1, ..., i_k)Q$$

where $pr(i_1, ..., i_k)$ denotes the projection from R^N to R^{N-k} parallel to the axes $i_1, ..., i_k$ of the criteria space.

However, taking an arbitrary linearly ordered curve g contained in $S_0 \subset R^N$ its projection $pr(i_1, ..., i_k)(g)$ may not necessarily be contained in a lower–dimensional $S_0' \subset R^{N-k}$. To ensure that the skeleton curve in R^N is also a skeleton curve in each lower dimensional space we will define the skeleton curve in the following manner.

Definition 5 . The linearly ordered broken line joining q_1 and q_2 defined by the construction below and contained in S_0 will be called the skeleton curve of Q_I and denoted by S.

Construction of the skeleton curve S is as follows:

1. Define

$$d_i = \frac{u_i^0 - l_i^0}{2}; \quad 1 \leq i \leq k;$$

2. Reorder the set d_i so that a new index j increases along with increasing values of d_j : $1 \leq j \leq k$;

3. Compute new pairs of opposite breaking points of S_D according to the formulae:

$$\left.\begin{aligned} l_i^{j+1} &= l_i^j + d_{j+1} \\ u_i^{j+1} &= l_i^j - d_{j+1} \end{aligned}\right\} \quad \textit{for} \quad i < j;\ 0 \leq j \leq k-2$$

$$\left.\begin{aligned} l_i^{j+1} &= l_i^j \\ u_i^{j+1} &= u_i^j \end{aligned}\right\} \quad \textit{for} \quad i > j;$$

We now can to the issue of safety principle.

Proposition 2 (a maximal safety principle). Let $L(q_1, q_2)$ be the set of all curves joining q_1 and q_2 inside Q_I and being linearly ordered. Then for every $g \in L(q_1, q_2)$ and every c such that $c^* \subset S_0$

$$\int_g d(x, \partial Q_I)dP \leq \int_c d(x, \partial Q_I)dP \tag{15}$$

where P is a uniform probability distribution on g or c, and d is the l_1 or l_∞ distance in the criteria space. In particular, (15) holds for the skeleton curve S. Proof of the Proposition 2 has been presented in Gorecki and Skulimowski (1986b).

Corollary 1. In the situation where there is no information about the location of the Pareto set, the search along the skeleton curve S results in finding a non-dominated solution maximally distant to the boundaries of Q_I.

Remark 2: The property (15) of the curve S can serve as a definition of the ordinal skeleton curve in the case when the demanded set is different from Q_I. The proved property (15) of the skeleton curve is closely related to another definition of the safety of the solution admitted.

Definition 6. A non-dominated y solution to the problem (3) will be called *maximally safe* with respect to the change of bounds of Q if for each $x \in FP(U, \Theta)$

$$P(x \in Q_\eta) \leq P(y \in Q_\eta) \tag{16}$$

where η is a probability distribution in the space of closed and convex subsets of the criteria space.

Now let us observe that Proposition 3 implies the following result concerning the safety of the solution to MMP chosen on the skeleton curve S.

Theorem 1. Let X be an arbitrary subset of Q_I. The probability distribution η defining the changes of ∂Q is assumed uniform. Then the maximally safe element of X with respect to the changes of Q belongs to S whenever $S \cap X \neq 0$.

Corollary 2 : A maximal safe non-dominated point belongs to S or is closest to S in $F(U) \cap Q$.

5 An application to a design problem

Let us consider the problem of designing a construction lift taking into account the set of parameters which decide about the commercial success of the product. These criteria include the time of evaluation of the project F_1, the lifting capacity F_2, the maximal range of the arm F_3. We assume that may exist other criteria such as reliability coefficient F_4 or the production price per unit F_5 which should be simply optimized, without paying attention to the constraints in the criteria space and are not included in the model of preferences here presented. The total cost of design and investment may be regarded as a constraint, together with the employment, materials and technology limitations. We assume that all constraints form a set U of admissible design strategies. The annual net income anticipated I may serve as an aggregated utility function which, however, depends on the above listed criteria in an unknown way. We can only assume that I is monotonically depending on the measure of fulfillment of the market's expectations which are expressed by the set Q.

According to the preference model presented in the preceding subsections U is defined by upper and lower limitations for the values of criteria. These parameters can have the following practical interpretation:

F_1l the minimal time necessary to distribute an announcement about the new product to the potential customers, also - if all or a prevailing part of lifts is to be sold to one company - the minimal supply time required by this company;

F_1u estimated upper limit of period warranting a sufficient market's demand, or the maximal supply time required by the commissioning company, or the estimated time a similar lift will be designed and offered by other producers;

F_2l minimal lifting capacity admissible for lifts of this type;

F_2u maximal reasonable lifting capacity estimated basing on the knowledge of potential scope of applications of lifts;

F_3l , F_3u similarly as above - the minimal admissible, and maximal reasonable values of the range of arm.

Each criterion should be optimized inside of the bounds F_{il}, F_{iu}, $1 \leq i \leq 3$, whereas F_1 should be minimized, the other criteria - maximized. To treat the functions F_i in an uniform way we will instead maximize the function $(-F_1)$.

The demanded set Q can be expressed in the form

$$Q = \prod_{i=1}^{3} [F_{il}, F_{iu}]$$

The bounds of Q are uncertain as the values of F_{il} and F_{iu}, $1 \leq i \leq 3$ are only estimates of the real user's needs. By Theorem 1 the strategy chosen on the skeleton set S ensures that the probability of remaining within a perturbed set Q_η maximal, η being a random perturbation coefficient of Q. Roughly speaking, the better the solution chosen fits into the set Q_η, the higher is the income I, on the other hand I should be monotonic with respect to the criteria $F_1, F_2, ..., F_N$. Thus we can conclude that I should be monotonically proportional to the utility function defined by the formula

$$G(u) = d(\tilde{F}(u), \partial Q) I_1(\tilde{F}(u)) + I_2(\hat{F}(u)) \tag{17}$$

where $d(\bullet, \partial Q)$ is the distance to the boundary of Q, $\tilde{F} = (F_1, F_2, F_3)$, $\hat{F} = (F_4, F_5)$ and I_1 and I_2 are certain order representing functions defined so that the maximum of G were non-dominated and situated within $Q \times R^2$ (cf. also formula in the final subsection). Let us note that the values of I_1 and I_2 are entirely independent if the values of $\tilde{F}$ and $\hat{F}$ are not depending on each other.

Hence it follows that the maximal safety with respect to $\tilde{F}$ of a compromise solution chosen is not conflicting with the goal of optimizing F in $Q \times R^2$. According to the results of the preceding subsection such a compromise value of F should be found on the skeleton curve S.

Since we do not impose any decision choice rule for the remaining criteria F_4 and F_5 we might consider two subcases:

1. $\tilde{F}$ and $\hat{F}$ are independent - then we get a family of solutions of form

$$(\tilde{F}_c, \hat{f})_{\hat{f} \in \hat{F}P(U,\Theta)}$$

where $\tilde{F}_c$ is the compromise value of $\tilde{F}$ found on the skeleton curve S.

2. the values of $\hat{F}$ are uniquely determined by $\tilde{F}$ - then we get a unique solution

$$(\tilde{F}_c, \hat{F}(\tilde{F}_c)).$$

A simple numerical example is presented below.

A numerical example

In the above described decision model suppose that :

$$\begin{array}{lcrl} F_{1l} & = & 2 & \text{months}, \\ F_{1u} & = & 12 & \text{months}, \\ F_{2l} & = & 5000 & \text{kilograms}, \\ F_{2u} & = & 25000 & \text{kilograms}, \\ F_{3l} & = & 10 & \text{meters}, \\ F_{3u} & = & 50 & \text{meters}. \end{array}$$

Then we get

$$Q = \prod_{i=1}^{3} [F_{il}, F_{iu}],$$

$$q_1 := (2; 5000; 10), \quad q_2 := (12; 25000; 50).$$

The decision space is defined as the intersection of Q and

$$\tilde{F}(u) := \{(x_1, x_2, x_3) \in R^3_+ : x_1 - 0.002x_2 + 3x_3 \leq 100,\ x_1^2 + 3(0.001x_2)^2 + 0.5x_3^2 \leq 1600\},$$

where U is the set of available design strategies connected with the employment, investment of financial strategies which are not considered here.

The distance in R^3 which serves to define the safety coefficients inside Q is given by

$$d(x,y) = |x_1 - y_1| + \frac{|x_2 - y_2|}{1000} + |x_3 - y_3|.$$

Since F_1 is the only minimized objective function, the criteria F_2 and F_3 can be equivalently taken into account in the minimization problem

$$(F_1', F_2', F_3') \mapsto min \tag{26}$$

after the following transformation:

$$F_i' := -F_i \;,\; F_{il}' := -F_{iu} \;,\; F_{iu}' := -F_{i1} \;,\; i = 2,3 \tag{27}$$

Simultaneously,

$$F_1' := F_1,$$

$$Q' := \prod_{i=1}^{3} [F_{il}', F_{iu}'],$$

and

$$q_1' := (2; -25000; -50), \quad q_2' := (12; -5000; -10).$$

Having found the skeleton curve S and the compromise solution f_c for the transformed problem (26)-(27), one should perform the transformation reverse to (27) to obtain the numerical values interpretable for the decision-maker.

There exist 4 breaking points in the skeleton curve S which can be found according to the construction algorithm given in Def.5 and amount to :

$$q_1 = (7,10,15); \quad q_2 = (7,15,20); \quad q_3 = (7,15,40); \quad q_4 = (7,20,45);$$

The core $C(Q)$ is the rectangle

$$C(Q) = \{(f_1, f_2, f_3) \in R^3 \;:\; f_1 = 7,\; 10 \le f_2 \le 20 \;,\; 15 \le f_3 \le 45\}.$$

The compromise solution $\tilde{f}_c$ can be found on the interval $[q_3, q_4]$ and amounts to *(7; 15.58; 40.58)*. One can observe that in the above case $\tilde{f}_c \in C(Q)$.

6 Final remarks

The algorithm of solving the MMP basing on the search on the skeleton curve has been implemented in FORTRAN and applied to solve real-life problems. The reader is referred to Gorecki et al. (1982, 1985) for a detailed study of decision making in the development analysis in the chemical industry.

The applications presented there show the adequacy of the decisions made via the skeleton method. Some properties of the MMP solution choice algorithm based on applying the skeleton curve have also been discussed by Wiecek (1984). The main idea of this algorithm is the same as in the general algorithm with the curve g replaced by the skeleton curve S. This algorithm can be repeated interactively, with the modified scale coefficients and the lower, and upper experts' estimations, q_2 and q_1, respectively.

The method turned out to be useful as well in case where the existence of the intersection of S and the set of non-dominated points could not been taken for granted basing on the assumptions concerning the objective F and the feasible set U. In particular, a heuristic version of the method could be applied to select a compromise solution in the case of non-convex attainable set $F(U)$ provided the decision-maker is modifying the upper and lower estimates q_1 and q_2 in accordance with the initial information about the location of $FP(U, \Theta)$ he is assumed to posses. The theoretical analysis of such a class of methods, applying the search on the skeleton curve as a single step of the procedure, with the demanded set systematically modified during and interactive decision-making process challenges the perspectives of the further development of the method.

Another possibility of investigating the theoretical fundamentals of the method consists in interpreting the search for a non-dominated solution on S as maximizing certain utility function φ which admits its local maxima on S. In this approach φ can be taken as the membership function of certain fuzzy set which describes the uncertainty of the demanded set Q. This function can have the form

$$\varphi_Q(x) := \frac{d(x, q_1)}{d(q_1, q_2)} \frac{d(x, \partial Q)}{max(y, \partial Q) : y \leq_\Theta x}$$

It follows immediately from the above formula that φ_Q has the desired property mentioned above, i.e.

$$0 \leq \varphi_Q(x) \leq 1$$

$$\varphi_Q(x) = 1 \Leftrightarrow x = q_2,$$

$$argmax\{\varphi_Q(x) : x \leq_\Theta q_1\} \in S$$

and, moreover, φ_Q is order representing (Wierzbicki, 1980).

These properties could provide for a combination of fuzzy set theory and the skeleton method.

References

Gorecki, H., (1981). Problem of choice of an optimal solution in a multicriteria space. *Proceedings of the 8th IFAC World Congress.* Kyoto 1981; Pergamon Press, London, Vol. 10, pp 106-110.

Gorecki, H., A.M. Skulimowski (1986a). A joint consideration of multiple reference points in multicriteria decision-making. *Found. Contr. Engrg. 11; No. 2.*

Gorecki, H., A.M. Skulimowski (1986b). Group decision-making maximally safe with respectto the change of aspiration levels. (to appear).

Gorecki, H., G. Dobrowolski, J. Kopytowski, M. Zebrowski (1982). The quest for a concordance between technologies and resources as a multiobjective decision process. M. Grauer, A. Lewandowski, and A.P. Wierzbicki Eds. *Multiobjective and Stochastic Optimization*, IIASA Collaborative Paper CP-82-S12, Laxenburg, Austria, pp 463-476.

Gorecki, H., G. Dobrowolski, T. Ryś, M. Wiecek, M. Zebrowski (1985). Decision support system based on the skeleton method - the HG package. *Interactive Decision Making, Proc. Sopron 1984* , pp 269-280.

Skulimowski, A.M. (1985a). Solving vector optimization problems via multilevel analysis of foreseen consequences. *Found. of Control Engrg., 10; No. 1.*

Skulimowski, A.M. (1985b). Generalized distance scalarization in Banach spaces, *Rev. Belge de Stat., Inf. Rech. Operationelle, 25, No.1* , pp 3-14.

Skulimowski, A.M. (1986). A sufficient condition for Θ-optimality of distance scalarizing procedures. *Proc. of the Int. Conference on Vector Optimization* J.Jahn, W.Krabs (Eds.), Darmstadt, 5-8 August 1986.

Wierzbicki, A.P. (1980). On the use of reference objectives in multicriteria optimization. G.Fandel, T.Gal (Eds.) *Multiple Criteria Decision Making - Theory and Application.*

Wiecek, M. (1984). The skeleton method in multicriteria problems. *Found. Contr. Engrg., 9, No.4*, pp 193-200.

Nonlinear Optimization Techniques in Decision Support Systems

Tomasz Kreglewski

Institute of Automatic Control, Warsaw University of Technology.

Abstract

Various aspects of the use of nonlinear models and nonlinear optimization algorithms in model-based decision support systems are discussed. Differences between linear and nonlinear cases are examined. A standard formulation for some class of nonlinear models is proposed. Special forms for the scalar-valued achievement functions especially developed for nonlinear optimization are proposed for scalarizing multiple criteria nonlinear optimization problems in the case of two reference (reservation and aspiration) levels specified by the user. A method of an automatic creation of derivatives for model equations together with a way of speeding-up their calculations is presented. Most of the concepts presented in this paper are implemented in the IAC-DIDAS-N system (see Kreglewski et al., 1988) developed by the author and his collaborators during their cooperative research with the System and Decision Sciences Program of the International Institute for Applied Systems Analysis.

1 Introduction

The decision analysis and support systems of DIDAS family (Dynamic Interactive Decision Analysis and Support — see second paper of this volume) are designed to support interactive work with a model of the decision problem, formalized mathematically and computerized. The work with such models is supported by multicriteria optimization tools used for a selection of data presented to the user. The learning aspects of the work with the model are also taken into account. Often there are two kinds of users of such decision support systems: analysts and decision makers. The former prepare the model and formalize the multicriteria decision problem, whereas the latter use the system either as a tool for on-line decision making or as a training and case-study tool.

A model-based decision support system, regardless of the type of models and problems considered, consists of some standard parts: the model itself, the *solver* (optimization code for selecting optimal decisions in the sense of current problem formulation) and the interfaces between the model, the solver and the user of the system. The degree of complexity of these interfaces depends on the type of a model (linear or nonlinear, static or dynamic etc.), on the type of a decision situation (single or multiple criteria, deterministic or with some uncertainty etc.) and on the requirements for the level of *user-friendliness* of the system. The interface between the user (mostly the analyst) and the model is called model generator. It is a tool for preparing the model, for its edition and simulation as well as verification of the model when learning about the model behaviour.

2 The model definition

We propose here a specific format for the definition of a nonlinear model; this format has been proved to be useful for multicriteria analysis of such models. The definition of a nonlinear model includes the specification of vectors representing *input variables* $x \in R^n$, *parameters* $z \in R^l$ and *outcome variables* $y \in R^m$, nonlinear *model equations* defining the relations between inputs, parameters and outputs of the model and *model bounds* defining lower and upper bounds for inputs and outputs:

$$y = f(x, z, y), \qquad x^{\rm lo} \leq x \leq x^{\rm up}, \qquad y^{\rm lo} \leq y \leq y^{\rm up} \tag{1}$$

where function $f : R^n \times R^l \times R^m \longrightarrow R^m$, $f = [f_i]$, $i = 1, \ldots, m$, should define the outcomes y in an explicit way. If some outcomes y_i depend on some other outcomes y_j, then it influences only the necessary order of calculations of functions f_i, f_j for given inputs x and parameters z. However, this dependence should be explicitly recursive, without loops and thus without need for internal iterative calculations.

The edition of the model described by (1) is the edition of numbers — elements of vectors $x^{\rm lo}$, $x^{\rm up}$, $y^{\rm lo}$, $y^{\rm up}$, z and initial values of x, and the edition of formulae $f_i(x, z, y)$. The edition of numbers is a standard operation in all number-crunching software and can be easily performed using e.g. standard or specialized spreadsheet. The formulae edition should be performed in a way as close as possible to the standard mathematical notation. A full-screen or window editor with some special options for formula validation can be used for this purpose. The necessity of formulae edition makes the preparation of nonlinear models different from a preparation of linear ones.

Another difference appears when the edition of a model is finished. A linear model is then ready, whereas a nonlinear model requires validation by many simulation runs, often resulting in updates of its formulation. In many cases standard mathematical notation is not sufficient and some additional logical structures like *if..then..else..* must be used to avoid illegal mathematical computations like square root of negative argument etc. Moreover, formulae editor should be equipped with some debugging tools to help the user looking for the formula (and the exact place in the formula) with such illegal operations. Sometimes other tools like step-by-step calculations are necessary.

During interactive analysis of optimal model characteristics nonlinear programming algorithms are used. Experience shows that gradient-type algorithms are more robust and efficient than non-gradient ones (see e.g. Kreglewski at al., 1984); thus, all gradients of model equations must be calculated. Numerical estimation of gradients is not accurate enough and is very time consuming, therefore it should not be used in decision support systems. Although analytical formulae for derivatives could be supplied by the user, this approach is not recommended for at least two reasons. Firstly, the creation of such formulae is a very cumbersome and time consuming task. Secondly, mistakes in user–supplied formulae for derivatives are found to be the main reason of unsuccessful applications of nonlinear optimization tools.

Thus, formulae for derivatives of model equations should be processed symbolically inside the model preparation part of a decision support system. This function of the system could be even invisible to the user except the cases when some numerical errors occur in calculation of derivatives during simulations of the model. It implies some additional functions of formulae editor.

The class of models (1) for decision support systems with efficient optimization included is therefore restricted to models with differentiable model equations. Moreover, logical structures used in formulae should be used with great care, in order not to include nondifferentiabilities or even discontinuities. Implementation of automatic verification algorithms to check differentiability is very difficult and may eliminate even some admissible types of functions.

3 Formalization of a decision problem

The model outcomes y_i, $i = 1, \ldots, m$, may be of different types. Some of them may be only intermediate, internal in their essence, results inside the model. Others may form various kinds of model constraints. Finally, some of outcomes are quality measures of the model behaviour or *objective outcomes*. In particular decision situations objective outcomes have to be minimized, maximized or stabilized (i.e. kept close to a given level). In a multicriteria decision problem separate outcomes can be each of a different type.

In optimization–based decision support systems it is assumed that the user is interested only in efficient solutions (that is, such that no objective can be improved without deteriorating some other objective). If, at some stage of the work, the user finds that this assumption is no longer valid, he can redefine the decision problem formalization by adding new objectives.

An important part of a definition of a decision problem based on the nonlinear model is a classification of constraints into three classes. The first class contains linear constraints; these are all bounds on variables x and bounds on outcomes that depend linearly on variables x. Linear constraints are always satisfied during any optimization process. The two other classes contain nonlinear constraints formed by bounds on outcomes that depend on variables x in a nonlinear way. In the second class there are so called 'hard' constraints (e.g. technological balances). These constraints should be satisfied exactly (within given accuracy), at least at each calculated optimal point, because other model outcomes can have meaningless values if this constraints are not satisfied. The existence of such constraints is the main difficulty for optimization algorithms and may lead to its inefficiency. The last class of constraints is a class of so called 'soft' constraints, mostly of some economical nature. The reason for distinguishing this class is that there are some measurable costs of violation of these constraints. Thus in many cases these constraint outcomes can be treated as additional objective outcomes with some trade–offs between other objective values and violations of these 'soft' constraints.

4 Initial analysis of a decision situation

Before an interactive analysis of the decision problem, the user should first learn about ranges of changes of efficient objective outcomes. The most important information concerns the best attainable values of particular objectives calculated independently. These values are practically never attainable jointly, hence the name *utopia point* is given for the point in the objective space composed of them. The point in the objective space composed of the worst efficient values is called *nadir point*, however its exact calculation is a very difficult computational task — for nonlinear models there is even no constructive method for such calculation. A rough estimation of the nadir point can be obtained just by recording the worst values received during calculations of utopia point components.

The ranges of efficient values of objectives are used as scaling factors for objectives while constructing the scalar–valued achievement function that is next used for calculating efficient solutions (other than utopia point components). This function will be discussed in detail in the next section.

Additionally, another efficient point may be calculated. So called *neutral solution* is an efficient solution situated 'in the middle' of the range of efficient outcomes. It is obtained by minimization of the distance to the utopia point, using differences between utopia and nadir components as scaling factors. The important feature of such scaling method is that relative achievement of each objective (the ratio of the distance from the solution to the utopia point and the distance from the nadir point to the utopia point) is exactly the same (except some non–convex and rather degenerate problems with discontinuous set of efficient solutions). The relative achievement factor can have a value in the range from zero (if the neutral solution is at the utopia point) to one (if the neutral solution is at the nadir point). Both extreme values represent degenerate, ill–defined multiple criteria problems. The interpretation of the values inside the range depends on dimensionality of the decision problem (the number of objectives), however, using a simple transformation one can calculate so called *conflict coefficient*:

$$c = \frac{r}{n-1}\left[(n^2-2)-(n^2-2n)r\right] \tag{2}$$

where n is the number of objectives and r is the relative achievement factor. The conflict coefficient is equal to zero if the neutral solution is just at the utopia point. It means that there are no conflicts among objectives. On the other hand, the conflict coefficient is equal to two if the neutral solution is just at the nadir point. It means that objectives are totally in conflict, however, such situation cannot exactly occur in the case of continuous models.

The essential feature of the conflict coefficient defined by (2) is that it is equal to one if there is an exact linear substitution between objectives. Moreover, all values above one represent non–convex problems.

The conflict coefficient is a very useful way of an initial classification of the decision problem. If it is rather close to zero, then the selection process of efficient solutions can be expected to be fast, but if it is greater than one, then the selection process may be difficult and time–consuming.

5 Parametric scalarization of a multiobjective problem

The parametric scalarization is achieved by a scalar–valued achievement function. However, before the presentation of this function, a formal mathematical notation of the decision problem must be introduced. In further analysis it is assumed that parameters z have known, fixed values z_0. To simplify the notation, an explicit input–output relation is used:

$$y = F(x) = f(x, z_0, y) \tag{3}$$

According to the model definition (1), the set of admissible decisions X is defined by:

$$X = \{ x \in R^n : x^{lo} \leq x \leq x^{up} ; \quad y^{lo} \leq F(x) \leq y^{up} \} \tag{4}$$

There are p objectives that form the objective space R^p being the subspace of the outcome space R^m. Some of objective outcomes can be minimized, some maximized and some stabilized (that is, minimized if their values are above ***stabilization levels*** and maximized if their values are below stabilization levels). All these possibilities can be summarized by defining the order in the objective space by introducing a positive cone D:

$$\begin{aligned} D = \{ q \in R^p : \ & q_i \geq 0 , && 1 \leq i \leq p' ; \\ & q_i \leq 0 , && p' + 1 \leq i \leq p'' ; \\ & q_i = 0 , && p'' + 1 \leq i \leq p \} \end{aligned} \tag{5}$$

where the first p' objectives, are to be maximized, the next from $p' + 1$ until p'' — minimized, and the last from $p'' + 1$ until p — stabilized. Let $q = F_q(x)$ be the vector of all objectives selected among all outcomes defined by (3) and $Q = F_q(X)$ be the set of attainable objective outcomes. F_q is composed of corresponding components of F. The multiobjective nonlinear programming problem is to maximize q_i, $i = 1, \ldots, p'$, minimize q_i, $i = p'+1, \ldots, p''$, and stabilize q_i, $i = p''+1, \ldots, p$ over the set of admissible decisions (4). Thus $\hat{q} \in Q$ is an efficient solution (Pareto optimal) iff there is no such $q \in Q$ that $q - \hat{q} \in \tilde{D}$, where $\tilde{D} = D \setminus \{\emptyset\}$. The set of all efficient outcomes (the Pareto set) can be written as:

$$\hat{Q} = \left\{ \hat{q} \in Q : (\hat{q} + \tilde{D}) \cap Q = \emptyset \right\} \tag{6}$$

If in the above definitions the set $\tilde{D}$ is replaced by the set $\tilde{\tilde{D}} = int\ D$, then such solutions will be only ***weakly efficient***. However as there are stabilized objectives (i.e. $p'' < p$), then the set $\tilde{\tilde{D}}$ is empty and thus all attainable objectives are weakly efficient. Therefore, weakly efficient solutions are of no practical interest to the user. Moreover, some efficient solutions for multiobjective nonlinear programming problems may have unbounded trade–off coefficients that indicate how much an objective should be deteriorated in order to improve another objective by a unit; therefore it is important to distinguish also a subset $\hat{Q}^p \subset \hat{Q}$ called the set of *properly efficient* solutions, such that the corresponding trade–off coefficients are bounded. A properly efficient solution with trade–off coefficients that are very high or very low does not practically differ from a weakly efficient solution. Thus, some a priori bound on trade–off coefficients should be defined and properly efficient solutions that do not satisfy this bound should be excluded. This can be done by defining a slightly broader cone:

$$D_\epsilon = \left\{ q \in R^p \ : \ \text{dist}\,(q\,,\,D) \le \epsilon\,\|q\| \right\} \tag{7}$$

where any norm in R^p is used, also to define the distance between q and D. The corresponding modified definition of the set of all D_ϵ–efficient solutions has the form:

$$\hat{Q}^{pe} = \left\{ \hat{q} \in Q \ : \ (\hat{q} + \tilde{D}_\epsilon) \cap Q = \emptyset \right\} ; \qquad \tilde{D}_\epsilon = D_\epsilon \setminus \{\emptyset\} \tag{8}$$

Solutions belonging to the set $\hat{Q}^{pe}$ are properly efficient with trade–off coefficients a priori bounded by approximately ε and $1/\varepsilon$; such solutions are also called *properly efficient with* (a priori) *bound*.

The selection of properly efficient solutions with bound and the corresponding decisions (values of variables x) should be easily controlled by the user and should result in any objective values in the set $\hat{Q}^{pe}$ he may wish to attain. The way of user–controlled selection of a properly efficient solution is based on the *reference point* concept (see Wierzbicki, 1982; Lewandowski and Wierzbicki, 1988). The selection method proposed here uses two user–selectable reference levels. This method can be used also in decision support systems with linear models, however, in the case of nonlinear models with possible nonconvexities, the use of this two reference levels approach is especially recommended.

For minimized and maximized objectives the user can specify two kinds of reference levels: *aspiration levels* denoted here $\bar{q}_i$ or $\bar{q}$ as a vector called *aspiration point* and *reservation levels* denoted $\bar{\bar{q}}_i$ or $\bar{\bar{q}}$ as a vector called *reservation point*. The aspiration levels represent the levels that the user would like to attain (although the aspiration point as whole is not attainable in most cases), whereas the reservation levels could be interpreted as 'soft' lower limits for objectives (for maximized objectives; upper limits for minimized objectives). Reservation levels $\bar{\bar{q}}_i$ for maximized objectives should be 'below' the aspiration levels $\bar{q}_i$ $(\bar{\bar{q}}_i < \bar{q}_i\ ,\ i = 1,\ldots,p')$, whereas reservation levels $\bar{\bar{q}}_i$ for minimized objectives should be 'above' the aspiration levels $\bar{q}_i$ $(\bar{\bar{q}}_i > \bar{q}_i\ ,\ i = p'+1,\ldots,p'')$.

For each stabilized objective q_i the user can specify the *lower reservation level* denoted $\bar{\bar{q}}_i^l$ and the *upper reservation level* denoted $\bar{\bar{q}}_i^u$. It is assumed that the stabilization level q_i^s is given implicitly as a mean value of two reservation levels $q_i^s = (\bar{\bar{q}}_i^l + \bar{\bar{q}}_i^u)/2$, thus the user defines the *reservation range* around the stabilization level. Moreover the *lower aspiration level* $\bar{q}_i^l = q_i^s - \delta(\bar{\bar{q}}_i^u - \bar{\bar{q}}_i^l)/2$ and the *upper aspiration level* $\bar{q}_i^u = q_i^s + \delta(\bar{\bar{q}}_i^u - \bar{\bar{q}}_i^l)/2$ are additionally defined, thus the *aspiration range* is δ times narrower than the reservation range with q_i^s being the center of both ranges. The coefficient δ can have some default value, but it can be changed by the user.

The aspiration and reservation points, called jointly *reference points*, are both user–selectable parameters (for minimized and maximized objectives; for stabilized objectives two reservation levels are user–selectable). A special way of parametric scalarization of the multiobjective analysis problem is utilized for the purpose of influencing the selection of efficient solutions by changing reference points. This parametric scalarization is obtained through maximizing an *order–approximating achievement function* (see Wierzbicki, 1983, 1986). There are several forms of such functions; properly efficient outcomes with approximate bound ε, $1/\varepsilon$ are obtained when maximizing a function of the following form:

$$s(q, \bar{q}, \bar{\bar{q}}) = \min\Big(\min_{1\le i\le p''} z_i(q_i, \bar{q}_i, \bar{\bar{q}}_i), \min_{p''+1\le i\le p} z_i(q_i, \bar{\bar{q}}_i^{\,l}, \bar{\bar{q}}_i^{\,u}) \Big) +$$

$$+\varepsilon\Big(\sum_{i=1}^{p''} z_i(q_i, \bar{q}_i, \bar{\bar{q}}_i) + \sum_{i=p''+1}^{p} z_i(q_i, \bar{\bar{q}}_i^{\,l}, \bar{\bar{q}}_i^{\,u})\Big) \tag{9}$$

where the parameter ε should be positive, even if very small; if this parameter is equal to zero, then the above function will not be order–approximating any more, but *order–representing*, and its maximal points can correspond to weakly efficient outcomes.

The functions $z_i(q_i, \bar{q}_i, \bar{\bar{q}}_i)$ for maximized objectives $(i = 1, \ldots, p')$ are defined by:

$$z_i(q_i, \bar{q}_i, \bar{\bar{q}}_i) = \min\Big((q_i - \bar{\bar{q}}_i)/s_i', \; 1 + (q_i - \bar{q}_i)/s_i'' \Big) \tag{10}$$

and the functions $z_i(q_i, \bar{q}_i, \bar{\bar{q}}_i)$ for minimized objectives $(i = p'+1, \ldots, p'')$ are defined by:

$$z_i(q_i, \bar{q}_i, \bar{\bar{q}}_i) = \min\Big((\bar{\bar{q}}_i - q_i)/s_i', \; 1 + (\bar{q}_i - q_i)/s_i'' \Big) \tag{11}$$

while the functions $z_i(q_i, \bar{\bar{q}}_i^{\,l}, \bar{\bar{q}}_i^{\,u})$ for stabilized objectives $(i = p''+1, \ldots, p)$ are defined by:

$$\begin{aligned} z_i(q_i, \bar{\bar{q}}_i^{\,l}, \bar{\bar{q}}_i^{\,u}) &= \min(z_i^l, z_i^u) \\ z_i^l &= \min\Big((q_i - \bar{\bar{q}}_i^{\,l})/s_i', \; 1 + (q_i - \bar{q}_i^{\,l})/s_i'' \Big) \\ z_i^u &= \min\Big((\bar{\bar{q}}_i^{\,u} - q_i)/s_i', \; 1 + (\bar{q}_i^{\,u} - q_i)/s_i'' \Big) \end{aligned} \tag{12}$$

where

$$\begin{aligned} \bar{q}_i^{\,l} &= q_i^s - \delta(q_i^s - \bar{\bar{q}}_i^{\,l}), \\ \bar{q}_i^{\,u} &= q_i^s + \delta(\bar{\bar{q}}_i^{\,u} - q_i^s), \\ q_i^s &= (\bar{\bar{q}}_i^{\,u} - \bar{\bar{q}}_i^{\,l})/2 . \end{aligned} \tag{13}$$

The coefficients $s_i' > 0$, $s_i'' > 0$ in (10), (11) and (12) are scaling units for all objectives and are determined automatically to obtain the following common *absolute achievement measure* for all *individual criterion achievement functions* $z_i(q_i, \cdot, \cdot)$:

$$z_i = \begin{cases} 1+\eta & \text{if } q_i = q_i^{uto} \quad (q_i^s \text{ for stabilized objectives}) \\ 1 & \text{if } q_i = \bar{q}_i \quad (\bar{q}_i^{\,l} \text{ or } \bar{q}_i^{\,u} \text{ for stabilized objectives}) \\ 0 & \text{if } q_i = \bar{\bar{q}}_i \quad (\bar{\bar{q}}_i^{\,l} \text{ or } \bar{\bar{q}}_i^{\,u} \text{ for stabilized objectives}) \end{cases} \tag{14}$$

where q_i^{uto} is the utopia point component for objective q_i , $i = 1, \ldots, p''$, and $\eta > 0$ is an arbitrary coefficient.

For minimized or maximized objectives ($i = 1, \ldots, p''$), scaling coefficients s_i' and s_i'' depend on relations between aspiration level $\bar{q}_i$, reservation level $\bar{\bar{q}}_i$ and limit q_i^{uto} of all attainable efficient values of objective q_i :

$$s_i' = \bar{q}_i - \bar{\bar{q}}_i \,, \quad s_i'' = (\, q_i^{uto} - \bar{q}_i \,)/\eta \,, \quad \text{if} \qquad 1 \le i \le p' \,, \\ s_i' = \bar{\bar{q}}_i - \bar{q}_i \,, \quad s_i'' = (\, \bar{q}_i - q_i^{uto} \,)/\eta \,, \quad \text{if} \quad p' + 1 \le i \le p'' \,. \tag{15}$$

For stabilized objectives ($i = p'' + 1, \ldots, p$), scaling coefficients s_i' and s_i'' depend on the distance between $\bar{\bar{q}}_i^{\,l}$ and $\bar{\bar{q}}_i^{\,u}$ (i.e. reservation range) and on the user defined coefficient δ (i.e. on relations between aspiration and reservation ranges):

$$\left.\begin{aligned} s_i' &= (1-\delta)(\,\bar{\bar{q}}_i^{\,u} - \bar{\bar{q}}_i^{\,l}\,)/2 \\ s_i'' &= \delta\,(\,\bar{\bar{q}}_i^{\,u} - \bar{\bar{q}}_i^{\,l}\,)/(\,2\eta\,) \end{aligned}\right\} \quad \text{if } p'' + 1 \le i \le p \,. \tag{16}$$

Parameter η in (15) and (16) is selected according to current relations between $\bar{q}_i$, $\bar{\bar{q}}_i$, q_i^{uto}, and the value of coefficient δ :

$$\eta = \min\left(\min_{1 \le i \le p'} \frac{q_i^{uto} - \bar{q}_i}{\bar{q}_i - \bar{\bar{q}}_i} \,, \min_{p'+1 \le i \le p''} \frac{\bar{q}_i - q_i^{uto}}{\bar{\bar{q}}_i - \bar{q}_i} \,, \frac{\delta}{1-\delta} \right) \tag{17}$$

Three sets of conditions must hold for this selection of s_i' and s_i'' :

$$\begin{aligned} &\bar{\bar{q}}_i < \bar{q}_i < q_i^{uto} \,, && \text{if} \qquad 1 \le i \le p' \,, \\ &q_i^{uto} < \bar{q}_i < \bar{\bar{q}}_i \,, && \text{if} \quad p' + 1 \le i \le p'' \,, \\ &\bar{\bar{q}}_i^{\,l} < \bar{\bar{q}}_i^{\,u} \,, && \text{if} \quad p'' + 1 \le i \le p \,. \end{aligned} \tag{18}$$

The achievement function $s(\,q\,,\bar{q}\,,\bar{\bar{q}}\,)$ can be maximized with $q = F_q(x)$ over $x \in X$; however, the function (9) is nondifferentiable (for example, if $q = \bar{q}$). On the other hand, if the function $F(x)$ (and thus also $F_q(x)$) is differentiable, then the maximization of function (9) can be converted automatically to an equivalent differentiable nonlinear programming problem by introducing proxy variables and substituting the min operation in (9) by a number of additional inequalities. If the coefficient $\varepsilon > 0$, then the achievement function has the following properties (see Wierzbicki, 1986):

a) For any arbitrary aspiration and reservation points satisfying conditions (18), but not necessarily restricted to be attainable ($\bar{q} \in Q$, $\bar{\bar{q}} \in Q$) or not attainable ($\bar{q} \notin Q$, $\bar{\bar{q}} \notin Q$), each maximal point $\hat{q}$ of the achievement function $s(\,q\,,\bar{q}\,,\bar{\bar{q}}\,)$ with $q = F_q(x)$ over $x \in X$ is a D_ε–efficient solution, that is, a properly efficient solution with trade–off coefficients bounded approximately by ε and $1/\varepsilon$.

b) For any properly efficient outcome $\hat{q}$ with trade–off coefficients bounded by ε and $1/\varepsilon$, there exist such aspiration $\bar{q}$ and reservation $\bar{\bar{q}}$ points that the maximum of the achievement function $s(q, \bar{q}, \bar{\bar{q}})$ is attained at the properly efficient outcome $\hat{q}$. In particular, if the user (either by chance or as a result of a learning process) specifies some attainable but not efficient reservation point $\bar{\bar{q}}$ and an aspiration point $\bar{q}$ that in itself is such properly efficient outcome, $\bar{q} = \hat{q}$, and if conditions (18) are satisfied, then the maximum of the achievement function $s(q, \bar{q}, \bar{\bar{q}})$, equal to one, is attained precisely at this point.

c) If the aspiration point $\bar{q}$ is 'too high' (for maximized outcomes; 'too low' for minimized outcomes), then the maximum of the achievement function, smaller than one, is attained at an efficient outcome $\hat{q}$ that best approximates uniformly, in the sense of scaling units s'_i, the aspiration point. If the aspiration point $\bar{q}$ is 'too low' (for maximized outcomes; 'too high' for minimized outcomes), then the maximum of the achievement function, larger than one, is attained at an efficient outcome $\hat{q}$ that is uniformly, in the sense of scaling units s''_i, 'higher' than the aspiration point.

d) By changing his aspiration $\bar{q}$ and reservation $\bar{\bar{q}}$ points, the user can continuously influence the selection of the corresponding efficient outcomes $\hat{q}$ that maximize the achievement function.

The parameter ε in the achievement function determines bounds on trade–off coefficients: if an efficient solution has trade–off coefficients that are too large or too small (say, lower than 10^{-6} or higher than 10^{6}), then it does not differ for the decision maker from weakly efficient solutions — some of its components can be improved practically without deteriorating other components. Another interpretation of this parameter is that it indicates how much an average overachievement (or underachievement) of aspiration levels can correct the minimal overachievement (or maximal underachievement) in the function (9).

The achievement function (9) can be transformed to an equivalent form if taking into account the scaling coefficients determined by (15) and (16) and assuming that the parameter $\varepsilon = 0$:

$$s(q, \bar{q}, \bar{\bar{q}}) = 1 + \eta - \max\left(\max_{1 \le i \le p''} \tilde{z}_i(q_i, \bar{q}_i, \bar{\bar{q}}_i) , \max_{p''+1 \le i \le p} \tilde{z}_i(q_i, \bar{\bar{q}}_i^{\,l}, \bar{\bar{q}}_i^{\,u}) \right) \qquad (19)$$

with

$$\begin{aligned} \tilde{z}_i(q_i, \bar{q}_i, \bar{\bar{q}}_i) &= \max(w'_i, w''_i), & 1 \le i \le p'', \\ \tilde{z}_i(q_i, \bar{\bar{q}}_i^{\,l}, \bar{\bar{q}}_i^{\,u}) &= \max(w_i^{-'}, w_i^{-''}, w_i^{+''}, w_i^{+'}), & p''+1 \le i \le p, \end{aligned} \qquad (20)$$

where

$$w'_i = \begin{cases} \eta + \dfrac{\bar{q}_i - q_i}{\bar{q}_i - \bar{\bar{q}}_i}, & \text{if} \quad 1 \le i \le p', \\ \eta + \dfrac{q_i - \bar{q}_i}{\bar{\bar{q}}_i - \bar{q}_i}, & \text{if} \quad p'+1 \le i \le p'', \end{cases} \qquad (21)$$

$$w_i'' = \begin{cases} \eta \dfrac{q_i^{\text{uto}} - q_i}{q_i^{\text{uto}} - \bar{q}_i}\,, & \text{if} \qquad 1 \le i \le p'\,, \\ \eta \dfrac{q_i - q_i^{\text{uto}}}{\bar{\bar{q}}_i - q_i^{\text{uto}}}\,, & \text{if} \qquad p'+1 \le i \le p''\,, \end{cases} \tag{22}$$

$$\left.\begin{aligned} w_i^{-\prime} &= \eta + \frac{\bar{q}_i{}^l - q_i}{\bar{q}_i{}^l - \bar{\bar{q}}_i{}^l} \\ w_i^{-\prime\prime} &= 2\eta \frac{q_i^s - q_i}{\bar{q}_i{}^u - \bar{q}_i{}^l} \\ w_i^{+\prime\prime} &= 2\eta \frac{q_i - q_i^s}{\bar{q}_i{}^u - \bar{q}_i{}^l} \\ w_i^{+\prime} &= \eta + \frac{q_i - \bar{q}_i{}^u}{\bar{\bar{q}}_i{}^u - \bar{q}_i{}^u} \end{aligned}\right\} \text{if } p''+1 \le i \le p\,, \tag{23}$$

with q_i^s , $\bar{q}_i{}^l$ and $\bar{q}_i{}^u$ given by (13).

The maximization of an achievement function is performed by a nonlinear optimization algorithm. Since this maximization is performed repetitively, at least once for each interaction with the user that changes the parameters $\bar{q}$ or $\bar{\bar{q}}$, this optimization algorithm must be very robust and efficient; therefore, according to our experience, only gradient type algorithms should be used to perform this task. However, the functions (9) or (19) are nondifferentiable and cannot be used as scalarizing functions if gradient optimization algorithms are used. Therefore an appropriate form of an achievement function that differentiably approximates function (9) has been developed. This *smooth order–approximating achievement function* has the form:

$$\begin{aligned} s(q, \bar{q}, \bar{\bar{q}}) = 1 + \eta - \Bigg\{ \sum_{i=1}^{p''} \Big[\big(\max(0, w_i')\big)^\alpha + \big(w_i''\big)^\alpha \Big] + \\ + \sum_{i=p''+1}^{p} \Big[\big(\max(0, w_i^{-\prime})\big)^\alpha + \big(\max(w_i^{-\prime\prime}, w_i^{+\prime\prime})\big)^\alpha + \big(\max(0, w_i^{+\prime})\big)^\alpha \Big] \Bigg\}^{1/\alpha} \end{aligned} \tag{24}$$

where w_i' , w_i'' , $w_i^{-\prime}$, $w_i^{-\prime\prime}$, $w_i^{+\prime\prime}$ and $w_i^{+\prime}$ are given by (21), (22) and (23).

The parameter $\alpha \ge 2$ is responsible for the approximation of the function (9) or (19) by the function (24): if $\alpha \to \infty$ and $\varepsilon \to 0$, then these functions converge to each other (if taking into account the specific definition of scaling coefficients in (9)). However, the use of too large parameters α results in badly conditioned problems when maximizing function (24), hence $\alpha = 4 \div 10$ is suggested to be used. During numerical computations a slightly simpler *scalarizing function* may be used and minimized:

$$\begin{aligned} \tilde{s}(q, \bar{q}, \bar{\bar{q}}) = \sum_{i=1}^{p''} \Big[\big(\max(0, w_i')\big)^\alpha + \big(w_i''\big)^\alpha \Big] + \\ + \sum_{i=p''+1}^{p} \Big[\big(\max(0, w_i^{-\prime})\big)^\alpha + \big(\max(w_i^{-\prime\prime}, w_i^{+\prime\prime})\big)^\alpha + \big(\max(0, w_i^{+\prime})\big)^\alpha \Big] \end{aligned} \tag{25}$$

The function (25) must be minimized with $q = F_q(x)$ over $x \in X$, while X is determined by simple bounds $x^{\text{lo}} \le x \le x^{\text{up}}$ as well as by constraints $y^{\text{lo}} \le F(x) \le y^{\text{up}}$.

6 Creation and calculation of derivatives

Model equations are functions of general, even very complicated, form with addition, subtraction, multiplication, division and power operators, subexpressions in parentheses and standard mathematical functions (like *sin* or *arctan*). Moreover *if..then..else..* logical structures can be used as case selectors for alternate parts of expressions. Values of these functions and values of their derivatives are required during simulation and optimization processes.

Values of partial or total derivatives are useful as sensitivity indices during simulation of a model at user–supplied points. If the simulation point is the end–point of an optimization process, then values of derivatives can be used for post–optimal analysis. Values of derivatives are necessary during the optimization process, since practically only gradient–type nonlinear programming algorithms are efficient and robust enough to be applied in interactive decision support systems.

For accuracy and efficiency reasons, derivatives should be calculated analytically rather than numerically using more or less advanced concepts of finite difference intervals. A user–friendly decision support system designed to work with nonlinear models must be therefore equipped with a symbolic differentiation tool for an automatic creation of derivatives.

Symbolic transformations are much more time–consuming than numerical calculations. Although the generation of derivatives must be done only once after each change of the formula, a full symbolic transformation from a source formula of functions to source formulae of its derivatives is a time–consuming task even for mainframe computers. On the other hand, calculations of functions and derivative values are repeated many times during optimization process, thus code used for their calculation should be compact and efficient.

Any method calculating automatically all derivatives (like table method proposed and exploited by Kalaba, 1983) is not acceptable. The Jacobian matrix of model equations is often sparse, therefore adequate structural analysis should be performed for a selection of derivatives to be created and calculated. Integrated formulae compiler should then be used to generate a code for calculating values of functions and values of all necessary non-constant derivatives.

Such a compiler may consist of the one–pass but recursive top–down parser which converts the source formula into a sequence of commands of a stack machine (Wirth, 1976). These commands can be then either interpreted by a hypothetical stack machine or executed as a binary code using hardware stack. The latter method can be applied for example on IBM PC type microcomputer with a numerical coprocessor using a hardware register stack of the coprocessor.

The top–down parsing must be performed several times for each formula; once in order to create code (or commands) for calculating a function value and next some number of times (according to results of the structural analysis) in order to create codes for calculating derivative values. However, parsing and extracting subsequent syntactical items from a source formula is found to be much more time–consuming task than the generation of a code. Hence, it is reasonable to implement a two–pass compiler for this purpose.

In the first pass, performed only once jointly for function and derivatives, an intermediate code is created as a result of parsing of source formula with encoding subsequent syntactical elements. All semantical and syntactical errors in formula are detected in this pass. Moreover, structural analysis can be done and graph of logical dependences can be created. This graph is used later for organising calculations of the whole model. Functions must be calculated in the proper order because some outcomes may depend on others. Furthermore, total derivatives are calculated numerically combining partial derivatives in the appropriate order.

The second compilation pass is performed independently for a function and all derivatives required, according to the results of structural analysis. The intermediate code is processed now and either binary codes or sequences of commands are created. This action can be done very fast because it is based on binary data and doesn't need error checking (it is only done following successful termination of the first pass, therefore, intermediate code is always correct).

The comparison of formulae for a function and its derivatives leads to the observation that very often they have many similar subexpressions. Thus, substantial speed–up of calculations is possible due to appropriate arrangement of computations avoiding multiple calculations of these common subexpressions. Basic theoretical results of the structural analysis of model equations and its derivatives can be found in Wierzbicki (1977, 1985). In the computer implementation, some partial results obtained during calculations of the function value are stored in a buffer and then used during calculations of derivative values. Although it is conceptually simple, the computer implementation was rather difficult.

These general ideas will be explained here using a very simple example. If outcome y_1 depends on variable x_1 as a product of two nonlinear functions:

$$y_1(x_1) = a(x_1) * b(x_1) \; ,$$

then its derivative is:

$$\frac{\partial \, y_1(x_1)}{\partial \, x_1} = a(x_1) * \frac{\partial \, b(x_1)}{\partial \, x_1} + \frac{\partial \, a(x_1)}{\partial \, x_1} * b(x_1)$$

Values of $a(x_1)$ and $b(x_1)$ are obtained and stored in the buffer during calculations of $y_1(x_1)$.

Thus, for the calculation of the derivative $\frac{\partial y_1(x_1)}{\partial x_1}$ only partial derivatives $\frac{\partial a(x_1)}{\partial x_1}$ and $\frac{\partial b(x_1)}{\partial x_1}$ are calculated but values of $a(x_1)$ and $b(x_1)$ are taken from the buffer.

Similar procedures can be used for division and power operations as well as for calculations of standard function derivatives. If, additionally, logical structures *if..then..else..* are used in a formula, then values of logical expressions following *if* are calculated only once during calculation of the function value. The boolean values (transferred through adequate buffer) are then consistently used during calculations of derivative values.

Another important way of speeding–up computations of derivatives consists in an appropriate simplification of derivatives. This can be done again as a result of structural analysis. Very often, not all parts of a complicated function depend on all variables. If in the above example outcome y_1 depends on two variables x_1 and x_2 again as a product of two nonlinear functions but with different arguments:

$$y_1(x_1, x_2) = a(x_1) * b(x_2) ,$$

then its derivative is:

$$\frac{\partial y_1(x_1, x_2)}{\partial x_1} = \frac{\partial a(x_1)}{\partial x_1} * b(x_2) ,$$

therefore, only $\frac{\partial a(x_1)}{\partial x_1}$ must be calculated.

During implementation of both methods of speeding–up the calculations of derivatives some trade–off must be taken into account. Detailed structural analysis and perfect simplification may be much more time consuming than many calculations of only partially simplified derivatives. However, the transfer of some partial results and even a rough simplification of derivatives give substantial decrease of calculation time, especially in the case of a large number of variables.

The proposed method of creation of a code for derivative calculations is not exactly a method of symbolic calculations. Only binary codes are generated instead of a source text of derivative formulae. It may be an important disadvantage while the model is developed and tested, especially if numerical difficulties occur during derivative calculations. However, the generation of a source derivative formula from the binary code for visualisation and debugging purposes is a very cumbersome task. Moreover, partial results and boolean value transfers make rather difficult the presentation of these formulae in a reasonable way.

Some other possibilities of an automatic generation of derivatives in decision support systems with nonlinear models are discussed by Lewandowski (1986).

7 References

Kalaba, R., Rasakhoo, N. and Tishler, R. (1983). Nonlinear Least Squares via Automatic Derivative Evaluation. *Applied Mathematics and Computation*, 12, pp. 119–137.

Kreglewski, T., Rogowski, T., Ruszczynski, A. and Szymanowski, J. (1984). Optimization Methods in FORTRAN (in Polish), PWN, Warsaw.

Kreglewski, T., Paczynski, J., Granat, J. and Wierzbicki A. P. (1988). IAC-DIDAS-N A Dynamic Interactive Decision Analysis and Support System for Multicriteria Analysis of Nonlinear Models with Nonlinear Model Generator supporting model analysis. WP-88-112, International Institute for Applied Systems Analysis, Laxenburg, Austria.

Lewandowski, A. (1986). Problem Interface for Nonlinear DIDAS. WP-86-50, International Institute for Applied Systems Analysis, Laxenburg, Austria.

Lewandowski, A., Wierzbicki A. P. (1988). Aspiration Based Decision Analysis and Support, Part I: Theoretical and Methodological Backgrounds. WP-88-3, International Institute for Applied Systems Analysis, Laxenburg, Austria.

Wierzbicki, A. P. (1977). Models and Sensitivity of Control Systems (in Polish), WNT, Warsaw (English edition — Elsevier, Amsterdam 1985).

Wierzbicki, A. P. (1982). A Mathematical Basis for Satisficing Decision Making. *Mathematical Modelling* 3, pp. 391–405.

Wierzbicki, A. P. (1986). On the Completeness and Constructiveness of Parametric Characterizations to Vector Optimization Problems. *OR Spektrum* 8, pp. 73–87.

Wirth, N. (1976). Algorithms + Data Structures = Programs. Prentice Hall, Englewood Cliffs.

Nonlinear Computer Models — Issues of Generation and Differentiation

Jerzy Paczynski

Institute of Automatic Control, Warsaw University of Technology.

Abstract

This paper presents remarks on the methodology of generation of computer models for nonlinear problems. The automatic differentiation of the model is discussed and implementation hints are given. The presentation is based on the experience gained during implementations of a nonlinear model generator, the IAC-DIDAS-N system and observations of other software produced under the contracted study agreement with IIASA.

1 From abstract model formulation to the generation of a computerized model

A fairly abstract formulation of the equation of a model (or process bounds) has the form

$$P(x, u, z, a) = O \in \overline{B}_x$$

where $x \in B_x$ denotes internal variables, $u \in B_u$ denotes control variables, $z \in B_z$ denotes disturbances and $a \in B_a$ denotes parameters. $P : B_x \times B_u \times B_z \times B_a \rightarrow \overline{B}_x$ is a nonlinear mapping of bounds. $\overline{B}_x$ is the space of bounds, usually isomorphic to B_x. The above equation is accompanied by the output equation in an explicit form

$$y = V(x, u, z, a)$$

where $V : B_x \times B_u \times B_z \times B_a \rightarrow B_y$ is the output mapping. A wide spectrum of models — including dynamic, distributed, etc. formulations — can be described in this general form by suitable choice of spaces and operators.

It is difficult to draw more detailed conclusions from the general form of the equation of bounds. Therefore the concept of a resolving mapping R is introduced; it is an operator which determines x while given u, z, a. In most cases the resolving operator is realized in a feedback system, so the notation

$$x = R(P(x, u, z, a))$$

will be used. The existence and properties of this operator usually are investigated by using the contraction mapping theorem. Details depend very strongly on the spaces assumed, often it can be a numerical iterative process. In special but very important for applications cases the bounds equation has an explicit form

$$x = Q(u, z, a).$$

Structural properties of the model can be visualized in the form of a generalized directed graph (Wierzbicki, 1984). The nodes of this graph can be of three sorts:

i) a node denoted by a circle corresponds to a variable,

ii) a node denoted by a double circle corresponds to the ordered n-tuple of variables and is labelled with it,

iii) a node denoted by a square corresponds to a value which is stabilized.

The arcs of the graph are labelled with operators; to improve readability the identity operators I can be omitted.

Typical examples are presented in Fig. 1 for the equations: a) $P(x,u) = 0$ b) $x = R(x,u)$

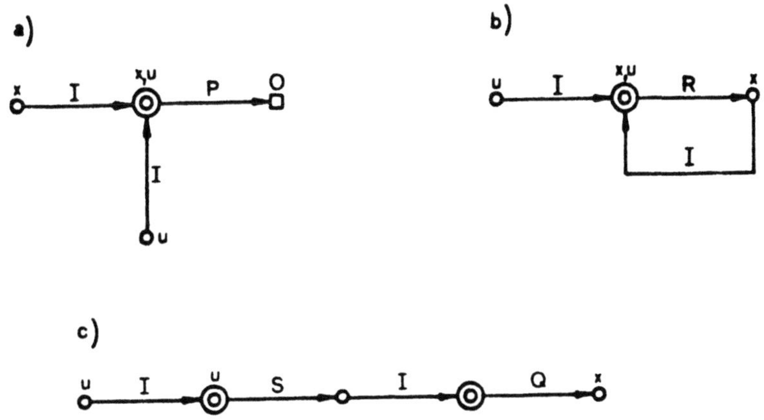

Figure 1.

The arc labelled with a non-identity operator must start from a node of the "double circle" sort. Thus in case of a composite operator an additional node must be inserted. E.g. the equation

$$x = Q(S(u))$$

corresponds to the graph presented in Fig. 1c.

From the implementation point of view a computer model can have one of the following forms:

- a program in a simulation language,
- a procedure (or a collection of them) in an universal programming language,
- a program in a declarative language,
- a set of entries in a spreadsheet.

This list is by no means exhaustive, it is rather the indication of the wide spectrum of possible solutions. However, to build a computer model on the base of a "bare" language or programming system requires specialized knowledge of the relevant aspects of the computer science and techniques, in addition to the specific science determined by the modeled problem. Proficiency in this specific science is not necessarily accompanied by the proficiency in using software tools. Therefore the whole process can be time-consuming and frustrating the user.

Therefore, a modern software must be equipped with a user-friendly interface, which will hide most technical details from the user. In the described context it should support the following three main functions:

i) Edition. It should be done in terms of the corresponding problem science only,

ii) Verification. A safe environment for model verification (performing partial or complete calculations, simulations etc.) should be provided,

iii) Modification. Easy transfer between two previous phases is necessary for efficient construction of a model.

Many examples of the need and development of such interfaces can be found in this book (see e.g. DIDAS, DINAS, HYBRID, DISCRET). More detailed references to papers on interfaces for nonlinear models are given in (Paczynski and Kreglewski, 1987).

2 The user interface

The general class of nonlinear models ("a nonlinear model is a model, which is not linear") cannot be effectively handled and in any programming system the scope of interest must be sufficiently limited, e.g. DIDAS-N handles static models expressed by explicit formulae. The goal of an editor is to allow the user to formulate his problem as close as possible to "natural mathematical notation". Details of the implementation of the editor will differ strongly depending on the particular class of input problems and the form of desired output; however in every case it is desirable to protect the user from direct contact with the language in which the implementation is written.

The means by which the user expresses himself form another language — the input language of the editor. Users do not need to be aware of that fact, but the implementers can use the theory of formal languages and compiler design. In the process of designing of an editor most problems arise from the lack of precise meaning of: "natural mathematical notation". The problem is whether the implementer and a user have similar understanding of that phrase. Intuitively it means "near to one's notational habits".

These habits are created by mathematical education and by experience in programming languages. However, a closer look revels that those sources are completely inconsistent. Typical problems will be illustrated below on the example of expressions, which are an indispensable part of any input language.

Expressions are composed of constants, names (e.g. variables), parenthesis, some set of standard functions and operators (e.g. denoted by the characters +, -, *, /, ^). The operator properties are usually described by their precedence and associativity. It seems however that school mathematics establishes accepted conventions only for binary operators (excluding the power operator). Further patterns can be sought in popular programming languages and tools. Such review depicts only the total lack of approved conventions. The most exotic rules are used in APL. All operators have the same precedence level and are right-associative, e.g. 2*3+4 evaluates to 14. This contradicts even the "school" rules. Similar properties have the operators (messages) in Smalltalk-80, they have the same precedence but are left-associative, e.g. 2+3*4 evaluates to 20. Leaving these cases out of considerations, most problems arise from the treatment of unary minus. Aho and Ullman (1977) give a dramatic warning: "Beware the treatment of unary minus!". Three different syntaxes can be considered as eligible candidates for the input language. They will be presented below using the notation of Modified Backus-Naur Form. The meaning of meta-symbols is as follows:

=	—	denotes the definition,
|	—	separates alternative options within the clause,
"..."	—	terminal symbols are quoted,
(...)	—	exactly one of the enclosed alternatives must be selected,
[...]	—	denotes zero or one occurrence of the enclosed subclause,
{...}	—	denotes zero or any number of occurrence of the enclosed subclause.

Syntax S1

```
expression = ["+"] simple_expression { ("+" | "-") simple_expression }
simple_expression = term { ("*" | "/") term }
term = signed_factor { "^" signed_factor }
signed_factor = ["-"] factor
```

Syntax S2

```
expression = ["+"] simple_expression { ("+" | "-") simple_expression }
simple_expression = signed_term { ("*" | "/") signed_term }
signed_term = ["-"] term
term = factor { "^" factor }
```

Syntax S3

```
expression = ["+" | "-"] simple_expression
             { ("+" | "-") simple_expression }
simple_expression = term { ("*" | "/") term }
term = factor { "^" factor }
```

The S1 syntax is used e.g. in ALGOL 68 and SNOBOL. It has the following operator precedences:

$$\text{- (unary)} \quad > \quad \hat{} \quad > \quad *\,,\,/ \quad > \quad +\,,\,\text{- (binary)}.$$

The S2 syntax is used e.g. in FORTRAN, BASIC, PL/I, Lotus 1–2–3 by Lotus (1983), MUSIMP (the implementation language for MUMATH symbolic computation system by Microsoft (1983)). It has the following precedences:

$$\hat{} \quad > \quad \text{- (unary)} \quad > \quad *\,,\,/ \quad > \quad +\,,\,\text{- (binary)}.$$

The S3 syntax is that of PASCAL extended with the power operator. Its precedences are:

$$\hat{} \quad > \quad *\,,\,/ \quad > \quad +\,,\,\text{- (unary and binary)}.$$

Each syntax has its peculiarities, e.g.

in S1:	$-2\hat{}2 = 4$, but $4 - 2\hat{}2 = 0$;
in S2, S3:	$-2\hat{}2 = -4$.

The syntax rules must be supplemented by associativity rules. In our context they are essential only for the power operator. The problem is whether it is right-associative, i.e. `a^b^c` evaluates as `a^(b^c)`, or left-associative: `(a^b)^c`, as typically tacitly assumed in elementary schools. Both cases lead to completely different values, e.g. `2^(2^3)=256` while `(2^2)^3=64`. Thus the semantics of a formula depends on the chosen rule. Associativity affects not only the process of formula evaluation, but even the process of computation of derivatives. For the right-associative power operator

```
d(e^x^2)/dx = 2xe^x^2,
```

(e denotes here the base of natural logarithms), while for the left-associative one

```
d(e^x^2)/dx = 2e^(2x).
```

It seems that courses in differential calculus do not explicitly declare associativity but tacitly use the first variant, see e.g. examples in the classical russian textbook (Fichtenholz, 1966), vol. I, par. 99. MUMATH assumes right associativity (under normal setting, properties of all operators can be freely modified by the user). Similarly does MACSYMA, perhaps the world's largest computer algebra system.

Associativity rules used in programming languages are not unique. Aho and Ullman (1977) state on p. 47: "ALGOL evaluates all binary operators left-associatively. FORTRAN lets the compiler designer choose the associativity, and PL/I evaluates all binary operators left-associatively, except for exponentiation, which is right-associative". In the implementations of BASIC used by the author the power operator was left-associative, and in implementations of FORTRAN — right-associative. In hand calculators it is left-associative, perhaps due to hardware and software limitations.

The examples above do not form a complete syntax of expressions, the remaining part is not free of problems too although they are less drastic. Of course any syntax convention will do *as long a user is aware of its properties*; the simplicity of expressions is especially deceiving.

The presence of an editor forces the user to master another 'language'. This effort must be justified by benefits. An interactive, problem-oriented support must be assured during edition and the language must be sufficiently simple.

Properties of all but 'academic' nonlinear models can contain many 'mysteries'. One cannot hope that the first variant of the model will allow for the solution of the problem. Most likely the 'solver' (e.g. an optimization algorithm) will encounter numerical problems. Creation of a safe environment (i.e. own error handling, perhaps with the indication of suspected place and suggestions of improvement) for model verification is equally important as an easy edition. Creation of a model may need many iterations of both phases. Easy and fast transfer between them is necessary for general efficiency of the system.

3 Automatic differentiation of the model – General concepts and implementation hints

Differentiation of a model arises in several contexts, e.g.

- series expansion,
- solution of implicit equations based on the implicit function theorem,
- sensitivity analysis,
- optimization.

In any specific formulation of the abstract model class described above, it is necessary to check the existence and properties of the derivatives (Gateaux or Frechet) of the model. In the implementation practice the classical differential calculus is often used, but nevertheless a manual differentiation presents considerable problems in the case of large and complicated models. This process is very prone to analytical errors which can make the model inconsistent. The existence of such errors is, as a rule, very hard to detect. Awareness of this situation leads often to the practical abandonment of theoretically promising methods, e.g. using sensitivity models in simulation languages or calculating Hessians matrices in optimization. Implementation of the automatic differentiation plays therefore an important role in various problems of system analysis.

It will be assumed in the following that all necessary conditions of differentiability and of the applicability of the implicit function theorem etc. are fulfilled. The rules of differentiation of a model can be easily formulated in terms of its graph representation (Wierzbicki, 1984):

i) the graph of the total derivative retains the structure of the model,

ii) all non-identity arc labels are advanced one arc backwards and are replaced by the operators of appropriate derivatives,

iii) vacant labels are filled with the identity operators.

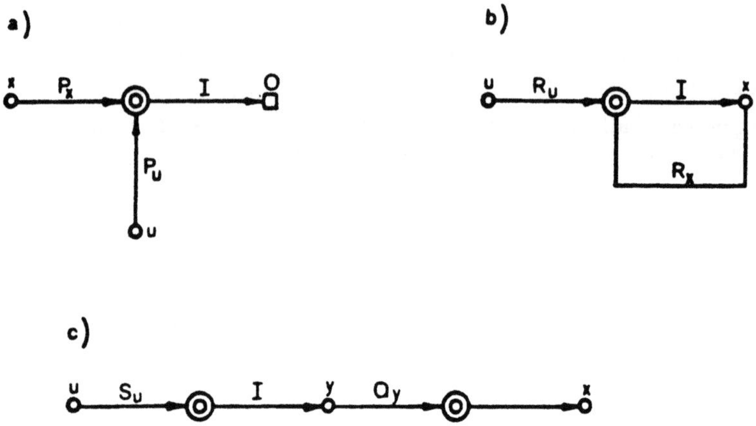

Figure 2.

Total derivatives of the graphs presented in Fig. 1 are presented in Fig. 2.

In every finite graph, it is possible to distinguish a finite number of closed feedback loops corresponding to implicit operations and a finite number of feedforward connections corresponding to composite operations. Thus the subsequent applications of the above rules gives the desired result.

It should be stressed that in some cases the graph may be rather a conceptual device than an element of implementation. In the creation of a sensitivity model it may be used explicitly, while in other cases it may be used implicitly by the application of recursive procedures.

Many problems of automatic differentiation (in more narrow context) have been discussed by Rall (1981) but computer implementations presented there are rather obsolete. From the computational point of view the differentiation of the model strongly resembles the process of compilation. General information about compilers can be found e.g. in (Aho and Ullman, 1977). The model equations must be described in a form suitable for computer analysis. Thus the first step is the creation of the input language (the problem language). This language must assure an easy interface with the user and an easy interface with the differentiating program. In practice some iterations are often needed until a mature form of the language is obtained.

The process of the automatic differentiation usually can be divided into some phases. The first one is the lexical analysis, i.e. the division of characters of the input language into groups that logically belong together — into symbols as e.g. identifiers of variables, symbols of operators. The output of the lexical analyzer is a stream of symbols, which is passed to the next phase, to the syntax analyzer (parser). The parser checks whether the symbols appearing at its input form a legal sequence of the input language (defined by its syntax rules) and produces an intermediate code. This code can be of very diverse nature, according both to the details of the problems and to the details of the particular implementation. A graph, a tree or a stack structure are typical examples. This intermediate form of the model is actually differentiated and thus another structure in the intermediate form, representing the derivative, is produced.

Usually the derivative must be simplified to an acceptable form. This phase is one of the hardest to implement due to its internal complication and nonexistence of the "simplest" canonical forms. The goal of simplification depends heavily on details of the particular problem. In the case of a simulation program it can be the number and the interconnection pattern of the modeling blocks, in the case of the evaluation of values — the computation efficiency measured as time, when the output has the form of symbolic formulae — similarity to the analogous result obtained by a mathematician.

In the final step this code is transferred into the form of the output language. Occasionally it can coincide with the input language, however many different forms are possible e.g. files with a simulation program or with a numerical procedure, a code for the calculations on a virtual computer or just formulae.

Under the contract with IIASA two differentiation packages were implemented for applications in differentiable optimization packages and decision analysis and support system. The first package, used in the IAC-DIDAS-N system, is oriented towards efficient calculation of values of derivatives; the second, used in a nonlinear model generator, is oriented on symbolic presentation of formulae of derivatives.

References

Aho A.V. and D. Ullman (1977). Principles of Compiler Design. Addison Wesley.

Fichtenholz G.M. (1966). Handbook of Differential and Integral Calculus. Nauka. (in russian).

Paczynski J. and T. Kreglewski (1987). Nonlinear Model Generator. In: Theory, Software and Testing Examples for Decision Support Systems. WP-87-26, IIASA, Laxenburg, Austria.

Rall L.B. (1981). Automatic Differentiation: Techniques and Applications. Springer.

Wierzbicki A. (1984). Models and Sensitivity of Control Systems. Elsevier.

Issues of Effectiveness Arising in the Design of a System of Nondifferentiable Optimization Algorithms

Krzysztof C. Kiwiel, Andrzej Stachurski

Systems Research Institute, Polish Academy of Sciences, Warsaw.

Abstract

This paper describes NOA, a package of Fortran subroutines for minimizing a locally Lipschitz continuous function subject to locally Lipschitzian inequality and equality constraints, general linear constraints and simple upper and lower bounds. The package implements several descent methods that accumulate subgradients of the problem functions and use quadratic programming for search direction finding. We discuss some choices made in the implementation and indicate their potential merits and drawbacks.

1 Introduction

NOA is a collection of Fortran subroutines designed to solve nondifferentiable optimization (NDO) problems of the following form

minimize

$$f(x) := \max\{ f_i(x) : i = 1,\dots,m_0 \} , \tag{1a}$$

subject to

$$F_i(x) \le 0 \quad \text{for} \quad i = 1,\dots,m_I , \tag{1b}$$

$$F_i(x) = 0 \quad \text{for} \quad i = m_I + 1,\dots,m_I + m_E , \tag{1c}$$

$$Ax \le b \quad \text{and} \quad x_i^L \le x_i \le x_i^U \quad \text{for} \quad i = 1,\dots,n , \tag{1d}$$

where the vector $x = (x_1, \dots , x_n)^T$ has n components (superscript T denotes transposition), f_i and F_i are locally Lipschitz continuous functions, and where the $m_A \times n$ matrix A, the m_A–vector b and the n–vectors x^L and x^U are constant; vector inequalities apply to all components.

The user has to provide a Fortran subroutine for evaluating the problem functions and their single subgradients (called generalized gradients by Clarke (1983)) at each x

in $S_L = \{ x \in R^n \ : \ Ax \leq b, \ \ x^L \leq x \leq x^U \}$. For instance, if F_i is smooth then its subgradient $g_{F_i}(x)$ equals the gradient $\nabla F_i(x)$, whereas for the max function

$$F_i(x) = \max\left\{ \varphi(x; z) \ : \ z \in Z \right\} \tag{2}$$

with φ smooth and Z compact, $g_{F_i}(x)$ may be computed as the gradient $\nabla_x \varphi(x, z(x))$ (with respect to x), where $z(x)$ is an arbitrary maximizer in (2). (Surveys of subgradient calculus may be found in Clarke (1983) and Kiwiel (1985d).)

The nonlinear functions f_i and F_i should be upper semidifferentiable (see (18)). This property is likely to hold in most applications (see Bihain, 1984; Mifflin, 1977). Thus the potential application area of general purpose NDO methods is vast. We note, however, that particular classes of NDO problems (e.g. minimax problems) can be solved more efficiently by specialized methods (see, e.g. Fletcher, 1981; Kiwiel, 1988c).

For unconstrained problems NOA implements the descent methods of Kiwiel (1985a, 1985d, 1986c), which stem from the works of Lemarechal (1978) and Mifflin (1982). Linearly constrained problems are solved by the methods of Kiwiel (1985b, 1986b, 1987b). Problems with nonlinear constraints are solved by the feasible point methods of Kiwiel (1985d, 1988b) (which follow the approach of Mifflin (1982)), the constraint linearization method of Kiwiel (1987a), or the exact penalty function methods of Kiwiel (1985c, 1988a) (see also Polak, Mayne and Wardi, 1983).

NOA seems to be the first implementation of descent methods for nonlinearly constrained NDO problems. (The system of Lemarechal, which implements an ε – steepest descent method of Lemarechal, Strodiot and Bihain (1981), is restricted to problems with simple bounds.) Thus in developing NOA we have been faced with a number of implementation issues, and some of our choices may not be the best ones. It seems worthwhile, therefore, to discuss their possible merits and drawbacks. This may help both the potential users and the developers of NDO algorithms.

Our exposition will be rather informal, but we shall try to address some questions that are usually ignored in papers that analyse particular methods. Our judgements may seem subjective, and we refrain from supporting them by numerical examples, which would take up too much space and could always be deemed inconclusive.

We refer the reader to Lemarechal (1986) for a recent review of other NDO methods.

NOA may be used for solving multiobjective (vector) minimization problems with $m > 1$ objective functions $\{\varphi_i\}_{i=1}^m$ and a feasible set S (defined, e.g., by the constraints of (1)). To this end, one may choose a "good" point $q^{\min} \in R^m$ in the objective space and a "bad" point $q^{\max} \in R^m$ ($q_i^{\min} < q_i^{\max}$ for all i) that define the scalarizing function

$$s(x; q^{\min}, q^{\max}) = \max_{i \leq i \leq m} \frac{\varphi_i(x) - q_i^{\min}}{q_i^{\max} - q_i^{\min}} + \varepsilon \sum_{i=1}^{m} \frac{\varphi_i(x) - q_i^{\min}}{q_i^{\max} - q_i^{\min}} ,$$

where $\varepsilon \geq 0$ is a parameter. Then the problem

$$\text{minimize} \qquad s(x; q^{\min}, q^{\max}) \qquad \text{over all } \ x \in S$$

is a scalarized version of the vector one, and its (local) solutions are (locally) efficient (taking $\varepsilon > 0$ prevents them from being only weakly efficient; see, e.g. Wierzbicki, 1986).

By choosing $(q^{\min}, q^{\max})$ interactively and minimizing $s(\cdot\,; q^{\min}, q^{\max})$, the user may scan the Pareto set in the search for a satisfying solution. Since the scalarizing function s has the structure of (1a), it can be minimized by NOA whenever all the objectives φ_i are locally Lipschitzian and one can evaluate their subgradients. On the other hand, when all φ_i are twice continuously differentiable, then it may be more efficient to use specialized minimax methods with superlinear or quadratic local convergence rates (see, e.g. Fletcher, 1981). However, even in this case it is not clear whether such specialized methods can provide approximate solutions quickly, and their robust implementations are still unavailable. Anyway, NOA seems quite efficient and robust at reasonable accuracy requirements (see Bronisz and Krus, 1985). Additional motivation for using max–type scalarizing functions can be found in (Wierzbicki, 1986) and other papers in this volume.

The paper is organized as follows. Section 2 reviews some basic concepts, which are discussed in more detail in Section 3 devoted to linearly constrained convex minimization. In sections 4, 5 and 6 we describe, respectively, exact penalty methods, the constraint linearization method and the feasible point method for convex problems. Extensions to nonconvex problems are treated in Section 7. Finally, we have a conclusion section.

We use the following notation. R^n denotes the n–dimensional Euclidean space with the usual inner product $\langle \cdot, \cdot \rangle$ and the associated norm $|\cdot|$. Superscripts are used to denote different vectors, e.g. x^1 and x^2.

Our general reference on nondifferentiable optimization is Clarke (1983). We say that $f : R^n \to R$ is locally Lipschitzian if for any bounded set B in R^n there exists a finite constant L such that $|f(x) - f(y)| \le L|x - y|$ for all $x, y \in B$. The subdifferential of f at x is $\partial f(x) = conv\left\{ \lim \nabla f(y^i) \;:\; y^i \to x \text{ and } f \text{ is differentiable at each } y^i \right\}$, where $conv$ denotes the convex hull and ∇f denotes the gradient of f.

2 General concepts

In this section we review some useful general concepts.

Define the objective, inequality and equality constraint functions

$$f(x) = \max\left\{ f_i(x) \;:\; i = 1, \ldots, m_0 \right\},$$

$$F_I(x) = \max\left\{ F_i(x) \;:\; i = 1, \ldots, m_I \right\},$$

$$F_E(x) = \max\left\{ \max\left[F_i(x), -F_i(x) \right] \;:\; i = m_I + 1, \ldots, m_I + m_E \right\}.$$

Let $S_I = \left\{ x \;:\; F_I(x) \le 0 \right\}$, $S_F = \left\{ x \;:\; F(x) \le 0 \right\}$ and $S = S_L \cap S_F$, where

$$F(x) = \max\left\{ F_I(x), F_E(x) \right\}$$

is the total constraint function. Then we may reformulate (1) as

$$\text{minimize } f(x), \tag{3a}$$

$$\text{subject to } \ F(x) \le 0 \ \text{ and } \ x \in S_L \ . \tag{3b}$$

Define the exact penalty function with a penalty coefficient $c > 0$

$$e(x; c) = f(x) + c \max\Big\{ F(x), 0 \Big\} .$$

Given a fixed $c > 0$, each solution x_c to the problem

$$\text{minimize } \ e(x; c) \ \text{ over all } \ x \in S_L \tag{4}$$

solves (3) if it is feasible $\Big(F(x_c) \le 0\Big)$. This holds if c is sufficiently large, (3) has a solution and its constraints are sufficiently regular (see, e.g. Clarke, 1983).

The solution algorithms of NOA are feasible with respect to the linear constraints, i.e. they generate successive approximations to a solution of (3) in S_L . The user must specify an initial estimate x^0 of the solution, and the orthogonal projection of x^0 on S_L is taken as the algorithm's starting point x^1 .

Two basic techniques are used for nonlinear constraints. In the first one, which solves (4) with a suitably chosen c, the initial x^1 need not lie in S_F and the successive points converge to a solution from outside of S_F . The second one uses a feasible point method which keeps the successive iterates in S_I if $x^1 \in S_I$.

The algorithms of NOA are based on the following concept of descent methods for NDO. Starting from a given point an iterative method of descent generates a sequence of points, which should converge to a solution. The property of descent means that successive points have lower objective (or exact penalty) function values. To find a descent direction from the current iterate, the method replaces the problem functions with their accumulated piecewise linear (polyhedral) approximations. Each linear piece of such an approximation is a linearization of the given function, obtained by evaluating the function and its subgradient at the trial point of an earlier iteration. The polyhedral approximations and quadratic regularization yield a local approximation to the original optimization problem, whose solution (found by quadratic programming) provides the search direction. Next, a line search along this direction produces the next approximation to a solution and the next trial point, detecting the possible gradient discontinuities. The successive polyhedral approximations are formed to ensure convergence to a solution without storing too many linearizations. To this end, subgradient selection (or aggregation) techniques are employed.

3 Linearly constrained convex minimization

The problem of minimizing a convex function $f : R^n \to R$ over S_L may be solved in NOA by the method of Kiwiel (1987b). To avoid repetitions in subsequent sections, most of the basic ideas will be discussed in detail for this method only.

Let $g_f(y)$ denote the subgradient of f at y calculated by the user's subroutine. Thus at each y we can construct the linearization of f

$$\bar{f}(x; y) = f(y) + \langle g_f(y), x - y \rangle \ \text{ for all } \ x , \tag{5}$$

which is a lower approximation to f $\Big(f \ge \bar{f}(\cdot\,; y) \ \text{ by convexity}\Big)$.

Given a starting point $x^1 \in S_L$, the algorithm generates a sequence of points $x^k \in S_L$, $k = 2,3,\ldots$, that converges to a minimizer of f on S_L . At the k–th iteration the method uses the following approximation to f

$$\hat{f}^k(x) = \max\left\{ \bar{f}(x;y^j) \ : \ j \in J_f^k \right\} \tag{6}$$

derived from the linearizations of f at certain trial points y^j of earlier iterations j, where the index set $J_f^k \subset \{1,\ldots,k\}$ typically has $n+2$ elements. Note that $\hat{f}^k$ may be a tight approximation to f around y^j, $j \in J_f^k$, since $f(y^j) = \hat{f}^k(y^j)$.

The best feasible direction of descent for f at x^k is, of course, the solution $\hat{d}^k$ to the problem $\min\{ f(x^k+d) \ : \ x^k + d \in S^L\}$, since $x^k + \hat{d}^k$ minimizes f on S_L . The algorithm finds an approximate descent direction d^k to

$$\text{minimize} \ \ \hat{f}^k(x^k+d) + |d|^2/2 \ \ \text{,subject to} \ \ x^k + d \in S_L \ , \tag{7}$$

where the regularizing penalty term $|d|^2/2$ is intended to keep $x^k + d^k$ in the region where $\hat{f}^k$ should be close to f; without this term (7) need not have a bounded solution.

In practice we need a stopping criterion for detecting that the method may terminate because further significant progress is unlikely. The algorithms of NOA typically exhibit only linear rate of convergence, and we have to content ourselves with solutions with relative accuracy of up to seven digits in the objective value; otherwise the final progress may be painfully slow. The nonpositive quantity

$$v^k = \hat{f}^k(x^k + d^k) - f(x^k)$$

is an optimality measure of x^k , since

$$f(x^k) \le f(x) + |v^k|^{1/2}|x - x^k| - v^k \quad \text{for all} \quad x \in S_L \ . \tag{8}$$

The algorithm terminates if

$$|v^k| \le \varepsilon_s\left(1 + |f(x^k)|\right) \ , \tag{9}$$

where $\varepsilon_s > 0$ is a final accuracy tolerance provided by the user. (The term $|f(x^k)|$ is included to make this test less sensitive to the scaling of f (multiplication of f by a positive constant), but only large scaling factors are accounted for.) Usually in practice for $\varepsilon_s = 10^{-(l+1)}$ and $l = 3,4$ or 5 termination occurs when $|f(x^k) - f(x^*)|$ is about $10^{-l}(1 + |f(x^*)|)$, and $|x - x^*|$ is about $10^{-l/2}(1 + |x^*|)$, where x^* is a minimizer of f on S_L . Of course such estimates may be false for ill–conditioned problems and thus it is rather surprising that the criterion (9) is quite reliable in practice. Some explanation may be deduced from the fact that when the quadratic term is inactive in (7), i.e. $x^k + d^k$ minimizes $\hat{f}^k$ on S_L then $f(x^*) \ge \hat{f}^k(x^*) \ge \hat{f}^k(x^k + d^k) = f(x^k) + v^k$.

On the other hand, when f is polyhedral termination should occur at some iteration with $v^k = 0$ (and optimal x^k). In practice computer rounding errors prevent the vanishing of v^k , but still we may use a rather small ε_s in (9), e.g. $\varepsilon_s = \varepsilon_M^{2/3}$, where ε_M is the relative machine accuracy.

If the algorithm does not terminate, then the negative value of $v^k = \hat{f}^k(y^{k+1}) - f(x^k)$ predicts the descent $f(y^{k+1}) - f(x^k)$ for the move from x^k to the trial point $y^{k+1} = x^k + d^k$. Usually v^k over–estimates the descent because $f \geq \hat{f}^k$ and $\hat{f}^k$ need not agree with f at y^{k+1} if its linearizations do not reflect discontinuities in ∇f around x . The algorithm makes a serious step to $x^{k+1} = y^{k+1}$ if

$$f(y^{k+1}) \leq f(x^k) + m_L v^k \ , \tag{10}$$

where $m_L \in (0\,,\,1)$ is a parameter; otherwise a null step $x^{k+1} = x^k$ provides the new linearization $\bar{f}(\cdot\,;\,y^{k+1})$ for improving the next model $\hat{f}^{k+1}$ of f.

We typically use $m_L = 0.1$ in (10); in practice $m_L > 0.5$ may result in many null steps, whereas $m_L < 0.1$ may produce damped oscillations of $\{x^k\}$ around the solution (little descent is made at each serious step). We note that in theory finite termination for polyhedral problems can be ensured with $m_L = 1$ (see Kiwiel, 1987a), but our experiments indicate that $m_L = 0.1$ is more efficient.

The user may trade off storage and work per iteration for speed of convergence by choosing the maximum number M_g of past linearizations involved in the approximations $\hat{f}^k$. To ensure convergence, the method selects for keeping the linearizations active at the solution to subproblem (7) (their indices enter J_f^{k+1} together with $k+1$), whereas inactive linearizations may be dropped. More linearizations enhance faster convergence by providing more accurate $\hat{f}^k$, but the costs of solving subproblem (7) may become prohibitive. Using M_g greater than its minimal possible value $n+3$, $M_g = 2n$ say, frequently increases the overall efficiency. To save storage, the algorithm may be run with $M_g \geq 3$ by employing subgradient aggregation instead of selection, but this will usually decrease the rate of convergence (sometimes drastically!).

The algorithm described so far is rather sensitive to the objective scaling, mainly due to the presence of the arbitrary quadratic term in subproblem (7). For greater flexibility, the user may choose a positive weight u in the following version of (7)

$$\min\left\{\hat{f}^k(x^k + d) + u\,|d|^2/2 \ : \ x^k + d \in S_L\right\} .$$

If f varies rapidly, increasing u from 1 will decrease $|d^k|$, thus localizing the search for a better point to the neighborhood of x^k. On the other hand, too "large" u will produce many serious, but short steps with very small $|\,x^{k+1} - x^k|$, and convergence will be slow. We intend to implement in NOA the technique of Kiwiel (1988d) for choosing the weight u adaptively. At present we note that suitable line searches (see Section 7) may offset an improper choice of u.

Subproblem (7) is solved in NOA by a special subroutine for quadratic programming (see Kiwiel, 1986a). This subroutine is quite efficient. Still when there are many general linear constraints some work could be saved at direction finding by considering only almost active constraints, i.e. only rows A_i of A such that $A_i x^k \geq b_i - \varepsilon_\alpha^k$ for some activity tolerance $\varepsilon_\alpha^k > 0$. A reasonable choice of ε_α^k which does not impair convergence is $\varepsilon_\alpha^k = -v^{k-1}$ (or $\varepsilon_\alpha^k = \max\{-v^{k-1}, 10^{-6}\}$). However, the gain in effort at direction finding could be outweighted by an increase in the number of iterations required to reach an acceptable solution (cf. Nguyen and Strodiot, 1984). Hence this option is not included in NOA, which is intended for small–scale problems. For the same reason we have refrained from implementing reduced (sub)gradient strategies (cf. Bihain, Nguyen and Strodiot, 1987; Panier, 1987).

4 Exact penalty methods for convex problems

Suppose that problem (3) is convex (i.e. f and F are convex) and satisfies the generalized Slater qualification ($F(x) < 0$ for some $x \in S_L$). Then problems (3) and (4) are equivalent if c is large enough. Moreover, we may easily compute linearizations of $e(\cdot\,; c)$ from those of f and F.

The methods of NOA with a fixed penalty coefficient require the user to specify c. The first one solves (4) by the algorithm of Section 3 (i.e. $e(\cdot\,; c)$ replaces f). The second one exploits the additive structure of $e(\cdot\,; c)$ in its approximation

$$\hat{e}(x\,; c) = \hat{f}^k(x) + c\max\left\{\hat{F}^k(x)\,,\,0\right\} \tag{11}$$

formed from $\hat{f}^k$ (see (5)) and

$$\hat{F}^k(x) = \max\left\{\bar{F}(x\,; y^j) \,:\, j \in J_F^k\right\}\,,$$

$$\bar{F}(x\,; y) = F(y) + \langle g_F(y)\,,\,x-y\rangle \quad \text{with} \quad g_F(y) \in \partial F(y)\,.$$

The second method is usually faster, since its approximations $\hat{e}^k(.\,; c)$ are more accurate (have more linear pieces) (cf. Kiwiel, 1988a). For both methods termination occurs if (cf. (9))

$$|v^k| \le \varepsilon_s\left(1 + |e(x^k\,; \rho)|\right) \quad \text{and} \quad F(x^k) \le \varepsilon_F\,, \tag{12}$$

where ε_s and ε_F are positive accuracy and feasibility tolerances (provided by the user), whereas

$$v^k = \hat{e}^k(x^k + d^k\,; c) - e(x^k\,; c) \tag{13}$$

yields the optimality estimates (cf. (8))

$$e(x^k\,; c) \le e(x\,; c) + |v^k|^{1/2}|x - x^k| - v^k\,, \quad \forall x \in S_L\,, \tag{14}$$

$$f(x^k) \le f(x^k) + |v^k|^{1/2}|x - x^k| - v^k\,, \quad \forall x \in S\,. \tag{15}$$

Both methods may be allowed to choose the penalty coefficient automatically. Then at the k–th iteration we use $c = c^k > 0$ (e.g. in (11)). The initial $c^1 > 0$ may be specified by the user. The penalty coefficient is increased only if x^k is an approximate solution to (4) (i.e. it minimizes $e(.\,; c^k)$ to within some positive tolerance δ_c^k), but it is significantly infeasible (i.e. $F(x^k)$ is "large"). The specific updating rule of Kiwiel (1985c) based on (14) reads

$$\text{if} \quad -v^k > \delta_c^k \quad \text{or} \quad F(x^k) \le -v^k \quad \text{set} \quad c^{k+1} = c^k \quad \text{and} \quad \delta_c^{k+1} = \delta_c^k\,;$$

$$\text{otherwise set} \quad c^{k+1} = \kappa_c c^k \quad \text{and} \quad \delta_c^{k+1} = \kappa_\delta \delta_c^k\,,$$

where $\kappa_c > 1$ and $\kappa_\delta \in (0, 1)$ are parameters (e.g. $\kappa_c = 2$, $\kappa_\delta = 0.1$ for $c^1 = 10$ and $\delta_c^1 = -v^1$). We are currently preferring the alternative "parameter–free" rule of Kiwiel (1988a)

$$\text{if } F(x^k) \leq -c^k v^k \text{ set } c^{k+1} = c^k \text{ , otherwise } c^{k+1} = 2c^k \text{ .}$$

In theory both rules ensure automatic limitation of penalty growth, and they are quite efficient in practice (i.e. they seldom produce a too large c^k, which hinders the minimization of $e(.; c^k)$). However, none of them is entirely satisfactory because they are too sensitive to the constraint scaling.

5 The constraint linearization method

The convex problem of Section 4 may be solved in NOA by the constraint linearization method of Kiwiel (1987a), which is frequently more efficient than the algorithms of Section 4.

At the k–th iteration the algorithm finds d^k to

$$\begin{aligned} &\text{minimize } \hat{f}^k(x^k + d^k) + |d|^2/2 \text{ ,} \\ &\text{subject to } \hat{F}^k(x^k + d) \leq 0 \text{ and } x^k + d \in S_L \text{ .} \end{aligned} \tag{16}$$

The solution d^k is an approximate descent direction for $e(.; c^k)$ at x^k, provided that c^k is greater than the Lagrange multiplier $\tilde{c}^k$ of the first constraint of (16). Hence the algorithm sets $c^{k+1} = c^k$ if $c^k \geq \tilde{c}^k$; otherwise $c^{k+1} = \max\{\tilde{c}^k, \kappa_c c^k\}$, where $\kappa_c > 1$ is a parameter (e.g. $\kappa_c = 2$), and $c^1 = 0$. Again v^k given by (13) and (11) satisfies the optimality estimate (15), which justifies the termination test (12). Naturally, $e(.; c^{k+1})$ replaces f in the improvement test (10).

The additional constraint activity in (16) reduces the number of degrees of freedom, and may lead to faster convergence in comparison with the methods of Section 4. However, when x^1 is very far from a solution, the present method may generate a much larger value of c^k than the former ones, and then it becomes less efficient.

6 Feasible point methods

The convex problem of Section 4 may also be solved in NOA by the feasible point method of Kiwiel (1985d, 1988b). This method uses the approximations $\hat{f}^k$ and $\hat{F}^k$ of f and F in the search direction finding subproblem

$$\text{minimize } \hat{H}^k(x^k + d) + |d|^2/2 \text{ , subject to } x^k + d \in S \text{ ,}$$

where

$$\hat{H}^k(x) = \max\left\{ \hat{f}^k(x) - f(x^k), \hat{F}^k(x) \right\}$$

approximates the improvement function

$$H(x; x^k) = \max\left\{ f(x) - f(x^k), F(x) \right\} .$$

Thus, if $F(x^k) \le 0$, we wish to find a feasible ($\hat{F}^k(x^k + d^k) < 0$) direction of descent ($\hat{f}(x^k + d^k) < f(x^k)$), whereas for $F(x^k) > 0$, d^k should be a descent direction for F ($\hat{F}^k(x^k + d^k) < F(x^k)$), since then we would like to decrease the constraint violation. Naturally, $H(.;x^k)$ replaces f in the improvement test (10) with $v^k = \hat{H}^k(x^k + d^k) - H(x^k, x^k)$, and (9) is used as a stopping criterion. In other words, this is just one iteration of the method of Section 3 applied to the minimization of $H(\cdot;x^k)$ over S_L !

In effect the algorithm runs in two phases. Phase 1 reduces the constraint violation, while phase 2 (if any) keeps x^k feasible and decreases $f(x^k)$.

The algorithm is, in general, more reliable than the exact penalty methods of Sections 4 and 5, because it does not need to choose the penalty coefficient. Also it is more widely applicable, since it need not in fact require the evaluation of f and g_f at infeasible points. Unfortunately, its convergence is usually much slower, because it cannot approach the boundary of the feasible set at a fast rate.

7 Methods for nonconvex problems

Nonconvex minimization problems are solved in NOA by natural extensions of the methods described in Sections 3, 4 and 6, see Kiwiel (1985a, 1985d, 1986b, 1986c, 1988a).

For simplicity, let us consider the problem of minimizing a locally Lipschitzian function f on S_L. In the nonconvex case the subgradient $g_f(y)$ may be used for modelling f around x only when y is close to x (we no longer have $f \ge \bar{f}(\cdot;y)$). The subgradient locality measure

$$\alpha_f(x;y) = \max\left\{ |f(x) - \bar{f}(x;y)|\,,\ \gamma_s|x-y|^2 \right\} \tag{17}$$

with a parameter $\gamma_s > 0$ indicates how much $g_f(y)$ differs from being a subgradient of f at x. At the k–th iteration the algorithm uses the following modification of (6) for finding d^k via (7)

$$\hat{f}^k(x) = f(x^k) + \max\left\{ -\alpha_f(x^k;y^j) + \langle g_f(y^j), x - x^k\rangle \ :\ j \in J_f^k \right\}.$$

In the convex case with $\gamma_s = 0$ this approximation is equivalent to (6) (since $f(x^k) \ge \bar{f}(x^k;y^j)$). For $\gamma_s > 0$ the local subgradients with small weights $\alpha_f(x^k;y^j)$ tend to influence d^k more strongly than the nonlocal ones.

The above definition of α_f is rather arbitrary (cf. Mifflin, 1982), and it is not clear how the value of γ_s should reflect the degree of nonconvexity of f (in theory any $\gamma_s > 0$ will do). Of course, for convex f $\gamma_s = 0$ is best. Larger values of γ_s are essential for concluding that x^k is optimal because $\hat{f}^k$ indicates that f has no feasible descent directions at x^k. On the other hand, a large γ_s may cause that after a serious step all the past subgradients will become inactive at the search direction finding. Then the algorithm will be forced to accumulate local subgradients by performing many null steps.

It is, therefore, reassuring to observe that $\gamma_s = 1$ seems to work quite well in practice (cf. Kiwiel, 1988a). However, it may be necessary to scale the variables so that they are of order 1 at the solution (to justify the Euclidean norm in (17)). Since automatic scaling could be dangerous, it is not implemented in NOA, but we intend to pursue this subject in the future.

Another feature of the nonconvex case is the need for line searches. Two cases are possible when a line search explores how well $\hat{f}^k$ agrees with f between x^k and $x^k + d^k$. Either it is possible to make a serious step by finding a stepsize $t_L^k \in (0, 1]$ such that the next iterate $x^{k+1} = x^k + t_L^k d^k$ has a significantly lower objective value than x^k, or a null step $x^{k+1} = x^k$ ($t_L^k = 0$) which evaluates f and g_f at the new trial point $y^{k+1} = x^k + t_R^k d^k$, with $t_R^k \in (0, 1]$, should improve the next model $\hat{f}^{k+1}$ that will yield a better d^{k+1}.

More specifically, a serious step $t_L^k = t_R^k > 0$ is taken if

$$f(x^{k+1}) \leq f(x^k) + m_L t_L^k v^k ,$$

$$t_L^k \geq \bar{t} \text{ or } \alpha_f(x^k; x^{k+1}) > m_v |v^k| ,$$

whereas a null step occurs with $0 = t_L^k < t_R^k \leq \bar{t}$ and

$$-\alpha_f(x^k; y^{k+1}) + \langle g_f(y^{k+1}), d^k \rangle \geq m_R v^k ,$$

where m_L, m_R, m_v and $\bar{t}$ are positive parameters. A simple procedure for finding t_L^k and t_R^k is given in Kiwiel (1986c) for the case of $m_L + m_v < m_R < 1$ and $\bar{t} \leq 1$. Since the aim of a null step is to detect discontinuities of g_f on the segment $[x^k, x^{k+1}]$, this procedure requires that f and g_f be consistent in the sense that

$$\begin{aligned} &\limsup_{i\to\infty} \langle g_f(x + t^i d), d \rangle \geq \liminf_{i\to\infty} \big[f(x + t^i d) - f(x) \big] / t^i \\ &\text{for all } x, d \in R^n , \quad \{t^i\} \subset R_+ , \quad t^i \downarrow 0 . \end{aligned} \tag{18}$$

In practice we use $m_L = 0.1$, $m_R = 0.5$, $m_v = 0.1$, $\bar{t} = 0.1$ and simple quadratic interpolation for diminishing trial stepsizes (see Remark 3.3.5 in Kiwiel, 1985d). Yet our crude procedure seems to be quite efficient; it requires on average less than two function evaluations (cf. Kiwiel, 1988a). On the other hand, our experience with more sophisticated procedures that insist on directional minimizations (cf. Mifflin, 1984) is quite negative. The resulting increase in the number of f–evaluations is not usually offset by a reduction in the number of iterations. This is not efficient in applications where the cost of one f–evaluation may dominate the effort in auxiliary operations (mainly at quadratic programming) per iteration.

We should add that in practice we employ the locality measures

$$\alpha_{f,j}^k = \max\left\{ |f(x^k) - \bar{f}(x^k; y^j)| , \gamma_s (s_j^k)^2 \right\}$$

that over–estimate $\alpha_f(x^k; y^j)$ by using the upper estimate $s_j^k = |y^j - x^j| + \sum_{i=j}^{k-1} |x^{i+1} - x^i|$ of $|x^k - y^j|$, which can be updated without storing y^j.

The extensions to the nonconvex case of the methods of Sections 4 and 6 follow the lines sketched above. We only add that all the problem functions should satisfy the semidifferentiability condition (18). In fact the convergence analysis of Kiwiel (1988a) requires the equality constraints to be continuously differentiable, but we have managed to solve many problems with nondifferentiable equality constraints.

We may add that each method of NOA has another version that uses subgradient deletion rules instead of subgradient locality measures for localizing the past subgradient information (see, for instance, Kiwiel, 1985a and Kiwiel, 1986c). It is not clear which version is preferable, since their merits are problem-dependent. We intend to clarify this situation in the near future.

8 Conclusions

We have presented an overview of several NDO algorithms that are implemented in the system NOA. The emphasis has been laid on practical difficulties, but they can only be resolved by further theoretical work. We hope, therefore, that this paper will contribute to the development of NDO methods.

9 References

Bihain, A. (1984). Optimization of upper-semidifferentiable functions. *Journal of Optimization Theory and Applications*, 44, pp. 545–568.

Bihain, A., Nguyen, V. H. and Strodiot, J.-J. (1987). A reduced subgradient algorithm. *Mathematical Programming Study*, 30, pp. 127–149.

Bronisz, P. and Krus, L. (1985). Experiments in calculation of game equilibria using nonsmooth optimization. In: Lewandowski, A. and Wierzbicki, A. P. eds., Software, theory and testing examples in decision support systems, pp. 275–286. International Institute for Applied Systems Analysis, Laxenburg, Austria.

Clarke, F. H. (1983). Optimization and nonsmooth analysis. Wiley Interscience, New York.

Fletcher, R. (1981). Practical Methods of Optimization, vol.II, Constrained Optimization. Wiley, New York.

Kiwiel, K. C. (1985a). A linearization algorithm for nonsmooth minimization. *Mathematics of Operations Research*, 10, pp. 185–194.

Kiwiel, K. C. (1985b). An algorithm for linearly constrained convex nondifferentiable minimization problems. *Journal of Mathematical Analysis and Applications*, 105, pp. 452–465.

Kiwiel, K. C. (1985c). An exact penalty function method for nonsmooth constrained convex minimization problems. *IMA Journal of Numerical Analysis*, 5, pp. 111–119.

Kiwiel, K. C. (1985d). Methods of descent for nondifferentiable optimization. *Lecture Notes in Mathematics*, 1133. Springer, Berlin.

Kiwiel, K. C. (1986a). A method for solving certain quadratic programming problems arising in nonsmooth optimization. *IMA Journal of Numerical Analysis*, 6, pp. 137–152.

Kiwiel, K. C. (1986b). A method of linearizations for linearly constrained nonconvex nonsmooth optimization. *Mathematical Programming*, 34, pp. 175–187.

Kiwiel, K. C. (1986c). An aggregate subgradient method for nonsmooth and nonconvex minimization. *Journal of Computational and Applied Mathematics*, 14, pp. 391–400.

Kiwiel, K. C. (1987a). A constraint linearization method for nondifferentiable convex minimization. *Numerische Mathematik*, 51, pp. 395–414.

Kiwiel, K. C. (1987b). A subgradient selection method for minimizing convex functions subject to linear constraints. *Computing*, 39, pp. 293–305.

Kiwiel, K. C. (1988a). An exact penalty function method for nondifferentiable constrained minimization. Prace IBS PAN, 155, Warszawa.

Kiwiel, K. C. (1988b). Computational Methods for Nondifferentiable Optimization. Ossolineum, Wroclaw (in Polish).

Kiwiel, K. C. (1988c). Descent methods for quasidifferentiable minimization. *Applied Mathematics and Optimization*, 18, pp. 163-180.

Kiwiel, K. C. (1988d). Proximity control in bundle methods for convex nondifferentiable minimization. *Mathematical Programming*, (to appear).

Lemarechal, C. (1978). Nonsmooth optimization and descent methods. Report RR-78-4, International Institute for Applied Systems Analysis, Laxenburg, Austria.

Lemarechal, C. (1986). Constructing bundle methods for convex optimization. In: J. B. Hiriart–Urruty, ed., Fermat Days: *Mathematics for Optimization*, pp. 201–240. North–Holland, Amsterdam.

Lemarechal, C., Strodiot, J.-J., and Bihain, A. (1981). On a boundle algorithm for nonsmooth optimization. In: *Nonlinear Programming*, 3 (O. L. Mangasarian, R. R. Meyer and S. M. Robinson, eds.), pp. 245–281. Academic Press, New York.

Mifflin, R. (1977). Semismooth and semiconvex functions in constrained optimization. *SIAM Journal on Control and Optimization*, 15, pp. 959–972.

Mifflin, R. (1982). A modification and an extension of Lemarechal's algorithm for nonsmooth minimization. *Mathematical Programming Study*, 17, pp. 77–90.

Mifflin, R. (1984). Stationarity and superlinear convergence of an algorithm for univariate locally Lipschitz constrained minimization. *Mathematical Programming*, 28, pp. 50–71.

Nguyen, V. H., and Strodiot, J.-J. (1984). A linearly constrained algorithm not requiring derivative continuity. *Engineering Structures*, 6, pp. 7–11.

Panier, E. (1987). An active set method for solving linearly constrained nonsmooth optimization problems. *Mathematical Programming*, 37, pp. 269–292.

Polak, E., Mayne, D. Q., and Wardi, Y. (1983). On the extension of constrained optimization algorithms from differentiable to nondifferentiable problems. *SIAM Journal on Control and Optimization*, 21, pp. 179–203.

Wierzbicki, A. P. (1986). On the completeness and constructiveness of parametric characterizations to vector optimization problems. *OR Spektrum*, 8, pp. 73–87.

A Methodological Guide to the Decision Support System DISCRET for Discrete Alternatives Problems

Janusz Majchrzak

Systems Research Institute, Polish Academy of Sciences, Warsaw.

Abstract

DISCRET is a package created to solve the basic multicriteria decision making problems in which a finite set of feasible alternatives is explicitly given and for each alternative the values of all criteria describing its attributes interesting for the decision maker (DM), were evaluated and listed in a file. The DM is assumed to be rational in the sense that he is looking for an nondominated (Pareto-optimal) alternative as his final solution of the problem.

The implemented approach is based on a fast technique for selecting the nondominated alternatives set and/or representation (subset) of this set. The reference point approach tools are also available for the user are also available for the user for the final selection of his most preferred alternative, together with some interactive display facilities.

1 Introduction

1.1 Scope of the report

This report aims to:

- provide the information necessary to use the DISCRET package and to understand its structure as well as the capabilities of the implemented approach,
- discuss such methodological issues associated with the implemented approach, which might be interesting for the user and which justify the chosen approach,
- attract and encourage the reader to take the advantage of the package utilization,

It is assumed that the reader and the package user possess just the very basic information about multicriteria optimization and discrete choice problems.

1.2 Purpose of the DISCRET package

DISCRET is a package created to solve basic multicriteria choice problems in which a finite set of feasible alternatives (and decisions) is explicitly given and, for each alternative, the values of all criteria describing its attributes interesting to the decision maker (DM) were evaluated and listed. The DM is assumed to be rational in the sense that he is looking for an efficient (Pareto-optimal) solution as his final solution of the problem.

Such a discrete multicriteria optimization problem is rather a problem of choice than optimization, since all the information necessary to make a decision is readily available. Such a problem is rather trivial for any human being as long as the number of alternatives is small (say, less than ten or twenty). However, if the number of alternatives and/or criteria grows, the limits of human information processing capabilities are reached and some decision support facilities have to be utilized to guarantee a proper and efficient decision making.

The purpose of the DISCRET package is to support the DM in his search for final decision in an interactive and user-friendly manner. It is assumed that the DM has only a limited knowledge of the problem he wants to solve at the beginning of the session with DISCRET. Therefore, during the session no difficult questions are asked (for example, about criteria trade-offs, DM' utility function or pairwise comparisons of alternatives). The package-provided information enables the DM to gather the experience related to his problem's specific features as well as his own preferences.

The implemented approach seems to be easy to understand and approve even for a user who is not very familiar with multicriteria optimization techniques.

The DISCRET package has been designed to solve medium-size discrete multicriteria problems with the number of alternatives ranging from few hundreds to few thousands. The number of criteria is in the current version restricted to 20 (mainly due to the limitations of display facilities).

During the session the user controls the decision-making process by choosing suitable options from the displayed "menu". Therefore, he does not have to learn and remember any command pseudo-language. This feature, together with special procedures for handling user's mistakes and with self-explanatory package messages, makes the package user-friendly and allows for an unexperienced user.

1.3 Fields of the package applications

In many real-life problems, decision variables take their values from a discrete set rather than from a continuous interval. Usually, there is a finite number of available facility location sites, the facility size or production capability may be chosen from a discrete set of values, during a design process the components are chosen from a set of typical elements available on the market, etc. Such problems form the "natural" field of applications for the DISCRET package.

Another field of possible applications of the DISCRET package consists of cases in which the original problem is actually continuous (rather than discrete) but the analysis restricted just to a finite number of alternatives appearing in this problem may be interesting and useful for the DM, since it may result in an enlightening and a more precise definition of his preferences, region of interest or aspiration levels.

Situations falling under the latter category may occur for at least two following reasons. Firstly, if a sample of alternatives together with the corresponding criteria values is readily available, the utilization of the DISCRET package may enable the DM to gain an insight into the original multicriteria problem. The analysis of an assembly of runs of a simulation model is an example of this case. Secondly, for the purpose of an initial analysis of a problem in which the decision variables actually take their values from continuous intervals, the DM may take into consideration just a few values for each decision variable or to generate a random sample of alternatives.

An encouraging factor that may attract the DM is the fact that the DISCRET package makes no restrictions on the forms of the criteria. Therefore, attributes as complicated as required may be considered.

2 Background

2.1 The discrete multicriteria optimization problem

Package DISCRET has been created to support—in an interactive manner—multicriteria optimization and decision making for problems with a finite number of discrete alternatives. Such problems are frequently referred to as implicit constraints or explicit alternatives problems.

Let us consider the following discrete multicriteria optimization problem (DMOP). It is assumed that a set X^0 of feasible discrete alternatives is explicitly given and for each of its elements all criteria under consideration have been evaluated. The criteria values for all feasible discrete alternatives form the set Q of feasible outcomes or evaluation.

$$\min_{x \in X^0} f(x)$$

$$X^0 = \{x_1, x_2, \ldots, x_n\} \subset X = R^s$$
$$f(x) = (f^1(x), f^2(x), \ldots, f^m(x))$$
$$f : X^0 \to Q$$
$$Q = \{f_1, f_2, \ldots, f_n\} \subset F = R^m$$
$$f_j = f(x_j), \quad j = 1, 2, \ldots, n$$

Furthermore, it is assumed that a domination cone Λ is defined in the objective space F. As in most applications the positive orthant is considered, $\Lambda = R^m_+$ and $\tilde{\Lambda} = R^m_+ \setminus \{0\}$. The domination cone introduces the partial pre-order relation "$\prec$" into the objective space:

$$\forall f_1, f_2 \in F, \quad f_1 \prec f_2 \iff f_1 \in f_2 - \tilde{\Lambda}$$

The element f_1 dominates f_2 in the sense of the partial pre-order induced by the domination cone Λ.

Element $\bar{f} \in Q$ is nondominated in the set of feasible elements Q, if it is not dominated by any other feasible element. Let $N = N(Q) \subset Q$ denote the set of all nondominated outcomes in the objective space and let $N_X = N(X^0) \subset X^0$ denote the set of the corresponding nondominated alternatives (decisions) in the decision space. To solve the DMOP it means to find the set N of nondominated outcomes and the corresponding set N_X of nondominated decisions.

Notice that DMOP is described by the two sets Q and X^0 defined above (together with m, n and s). Therefore the package input files supplied by the user must contain these two sets.

Observe also that no assumptions were made about the nature of the criteria functions f_i. In fact, the only requirement for them is that they should assign numerical values to the alternatives, indicating their attractiveness with respect to the attribute under consideration. In particular, the criteria functions may be of the qualitative type. The single restriction is that values assigned to alternatives by criteria should be expressed by numbers and that the user is able to indicate whether he wishes to increase or decrease these numbers. In doing so, he defines or changes the domination cone Λ.

Observe also that the above abstract definition of a solution to DMOP is not very practical: the set N of all nondominated outcomes might be very large and difficult to compute, and its full computation might be useless if the user decides to change the domination cone Λ. Therefore, an important issue is to find some representation of the set N, not the entire set.

2.2 Overview of existing approaches

The discrete multicriteria optimization problem (DMOP) is a combinatorial problem involving sorting and one could expect a large number of papers in the bibliography devoted to this subject. However, the problem did not focus much attention of the researchers—except in its utility theoretical variant that actually transforms the problem to a single–criteria one—and the bibliography we are able to point at consists only of (Kung et al., 1975, Polak and Payne, 1976, Stahn and Petersohn, 1978), plus some reports of the earlier research summarized there.

The insignificant interest in methods for solving DMOP could be explained by the fact that the solution of the DMOP, the whole set of nondominated alternatives is not the solution of the multicriteria decision making problem (MCDMP), a selected preferred alternative. However, since the efficiency of methods dealing with MCDMP usually depend on the number of alternatives, it is wise to reject the dominated alternatives.

A rather large number of approaches have been suggested for the solution of the MCDMP involving discrete alternatives. They differ both in the problem formulation and the assumptions about the decision maker (DM). Let us mention here just some most interesting ones. The method suggested in (Keeney and Raiffa, 1976) is based on utility functions constructed first for each criterion and then combined into a global utility function. In (Zionts, 1981) a linear, while in (Kõksalan et al., 1984) a quasiconvex underlying utility function of the DM is assumed and the best alternative according to an approximation of this utility function is found by asking for answers to a number of comparisons between pairs of alternatives. Other methods, e.g. (Roy, 1971) or (Siskos,

1982), are based on outranking relations. In (Rivett, 1977), multidimensional scaling techniques are used to obtain a graph pointing from least to most preferred alternatives.

Other group of approaches (some of them were proposed originally for some different problems) is based on an observation that if the number of the alternatives is small, then the DM is able to make a decision intuitively, without any formalism of expressing his preferences. If the number of alternatives is larger, then one has to reduce it for the DM by selecting a small but representative sample. Several methods for obtaining such a representation were proposed. They utilize cluster analysis (Tõrn, 1980, Morse, 1980), filtering (Steuer and Harris, 1980) or random sampling (Baum et al., 1981).

Approaches from the first of the two above-mentioned groups place the burden on the DM. He is asked to supply the information about his preferences by the evaluation of the alternatives —by pairwise comparisons or rankings for example. These evaluations are substantial for the methods. Each of these methods is based on certain implicit or explicit assumptions about the DM, such that, for example, he has an utility function expressing his preferences. The size of the problems that can be solved is limited by the DM's ability to provide the required amount of information by ranking or comparing pairwise the alternatives.

In the approaches from the second group, the burden is placed rather on the computer. The crucial point here is whether the obtained representation of the nondominated set will be illustrative for the DM. No special assumptions about the DM are made. He is only expected to prefer the nondominated alternatives rather than the dominated ones.

Our approach presented in this report may be classified as one of the second group. It is based on a new efficient method for DMOP, which also can efficiently produce a representation of the nondominated set.

2.3 The method of dominated approximations

The implemented method is of the explicit enumeration type. It is called the method of dominated approximations and is based on the following concept.

Def. 1 Let Q be the set of all feasible alternative outcomes, N the set of corresponding nondominated alternative outcomes and Λ the domination cone. Set A is called a dominated approximation of N iff

$$N \subset A - \Lambda$$

In other words, A is a dominated approximation of N iff for each $f_i \in N$ there exists $f_j \in A$ such, that $f_i \prec f_j$ in the sense of the partial pre-order induced by Λ.

We will say that the approximation A_2 dominates the approximation A_1 of the nondominated set N iff

$$A_1 \subset A_2 + \Lambda$$

Hence, as the worst approximation of N we can consider the entire set Q, while the best approximation is the set N itself. The method of dominated approximations generates a sequence of approximations A_k, $k = 0, 1, 2, \ldots, l$ such that

$$Q = A_0 \supset A_1 \supset A_2 \supset \cdots \supset A_k \supset \cdots \supset A_l = N$$

Thus, given Q and Λ we are supposed to determine $N = N(Q)$. Assume that all criteria are to be minimized.

Step_0 Let $A_0 = Q$, $N_0 = \emptyset$, $k = 0$.

Step_1 If $A_k \setminus N_k = \emptyset$ then STOP with $N_k = N$, else choose any index $i \in I = \{1, 2, \ldots, m\}$ and find $\bar{f} \in Q$ such that the i–th component of it is minimal in $A_k \setminus N_k$:

$$\bar{f}^i = \min_{A_k \setminus N_k} f^i$$

(See Remark 2).
Set $N_{k+1} = N_k \cup \{\bar{f}\}$.

Step_2 Create the new approximation A_{k+1} by rejecting from $A_k \setminus N_{k+1}$ all elements dominated by $\bar{f}$ (see Remark 1)

$$A_{k+1} = \Big(\{A_k \setminus N_{k+1}\} \setminus \{(\bar{f} + \tilde{\Lambda}) \cap (A_k \setminus N_{k+1})\}\Big) \cup N_{k+1}$$

Set $k = k + 1$ and go to Step_1.

Remark 1. While rejecting the elements dominated by $\bar{f}$ it is sufficient to compare elements of the set $A_k \setminus N_{k+1}$ with $\bar{f}$ according to all but i-th criterion, since $\bar{f}^i$ is minimal among all f^i in $A_k \setminus N$.

Remark 2. The minimum may happen to be non-unique. Let B be the set of those elements $f_j \in A_k \setminus N_k$ for which f_j^i appear to be minimal in $A_k \setminus N_k$. Actually not all elements of B are nondominated. One has to solve the following problem. Given B and Λ select $N(B)$. The above presented method may be used for this task with $A_0 = B$ and $I = I \setminus \{i\}$. This recurrence is applied until an unique minimum is found in the Step_1 of the algorithm. Then, after the execution of Step_2 one has to return to the lower level of recurrence. On each level *Remark 1* holds.

Note that if the recursion described in *Remark 2* would not be applied, then the set of weakly nondominated alternatives would be determined by the above algorithm.

In order to measure the efficiency of the method, let us consider the number of scalar comparisons $S(m, n, p)$ required by the method to solve the DMOP with m criteria, n feasible alternatives and p nondominated alternatives. From the analysis of the method one can easily obtain

$$S(m, n, p) \leq \frac{mp}{2}(2n - p - 1)$$

As one can see, the method solves easily problems with small p. In practical problems p is usually a small fraction of n; the worst case is for $p = n$, i.e. when all alternatives are nondominated. Note that the performance of the method does not depend on the permutation of the alternatives.

2.4 Selection of a representation of the nondominated set

The biggest advantage of the method of dominated approximations is its ability to select a representation of the nondominated set N instead of the entire set N. Unlike other known approaches which find the entire nondominated set first and then select a representation (differently defined for each of those methods), the presented method selects a representation at once. This fact provides much gain in algorithmic efficiency.

Let t_i, $i = 1, \ldots, m$ be some given tolerance coefficient for the m criteria under consideration, $t_i \geq 0$, and $T_i = (t_1, t_2, \ldots, t_{i-1}, 0, t_{i+1}, \ldots, t_m)$ be a vector in the objective space. For the sake of simplicity let us assume that all criteria are to be minimized. The following modification of the method of dominated approximations suffices to obtain a representation instead of the whole nondominated set. In the Step_2 of the method not only the elements dominated by the nondominated element $\bar{f}$ (found in the Step_1 by minimization over the i-th criterion values) have to be rejected, but also elements dominated by $f = \bar{f} - T_i$. Hence, in Step_2 is modified to:

$$A_{k+1} = \left(\{A_k \setminus N_{k+1}\} \setminus \{(\bar{f} - T_i + \tilde{\Lambda}) \cap (A_k \setminus N_{k+1})\}\right) \cup N_{k+1}$$

Observe that because the representation contains less elements than the nondominated set, it will be obtained with a smaller computational effort. Figure 1 illustrates the role of the tolerance coefficients in the process of selecting a representation.

The author is not aware of the existence of any other methods that could be effectively applied for a problem with few hundreds or few thousands of alternatives.

2.5 Outline of the approach and introduction to DISCRET

To start the session with DISCRET the user has to supply the file containing set Q of the criteria values for all feasible alternatives, the file containing some problem and data specifications and (optionally) the file containing the set X^0 of feasible decisions (the *load* command). These files, called the data, the specification and the additional data file respectively, describe the problem under consideration.

After the problem generation and implementation phase the user may obtain the information about the criteria values ranges and he may put the lower and/or upper bounds on the values of some/all criteria (the *bounds* command).

The bounds setting may be utilized by the user for several purposes. This is the list of some most relevant:

- to eliminate irrelevant alternatives from further considerations,
- to specify his current region of interest in the objective space,
- to redefine his problem as a problem with a fewer criteria as the original one (as in the method of equality/inequality constraints—see Lin, 1976), for example, a bicriteria problem.

In the next step the user may run the DMOP solver (by executing the command *solve*) to eliminate the dominated alternatives by an explicit enumeration technique. The tolerances for criteria values play an important role here. If they are all equal

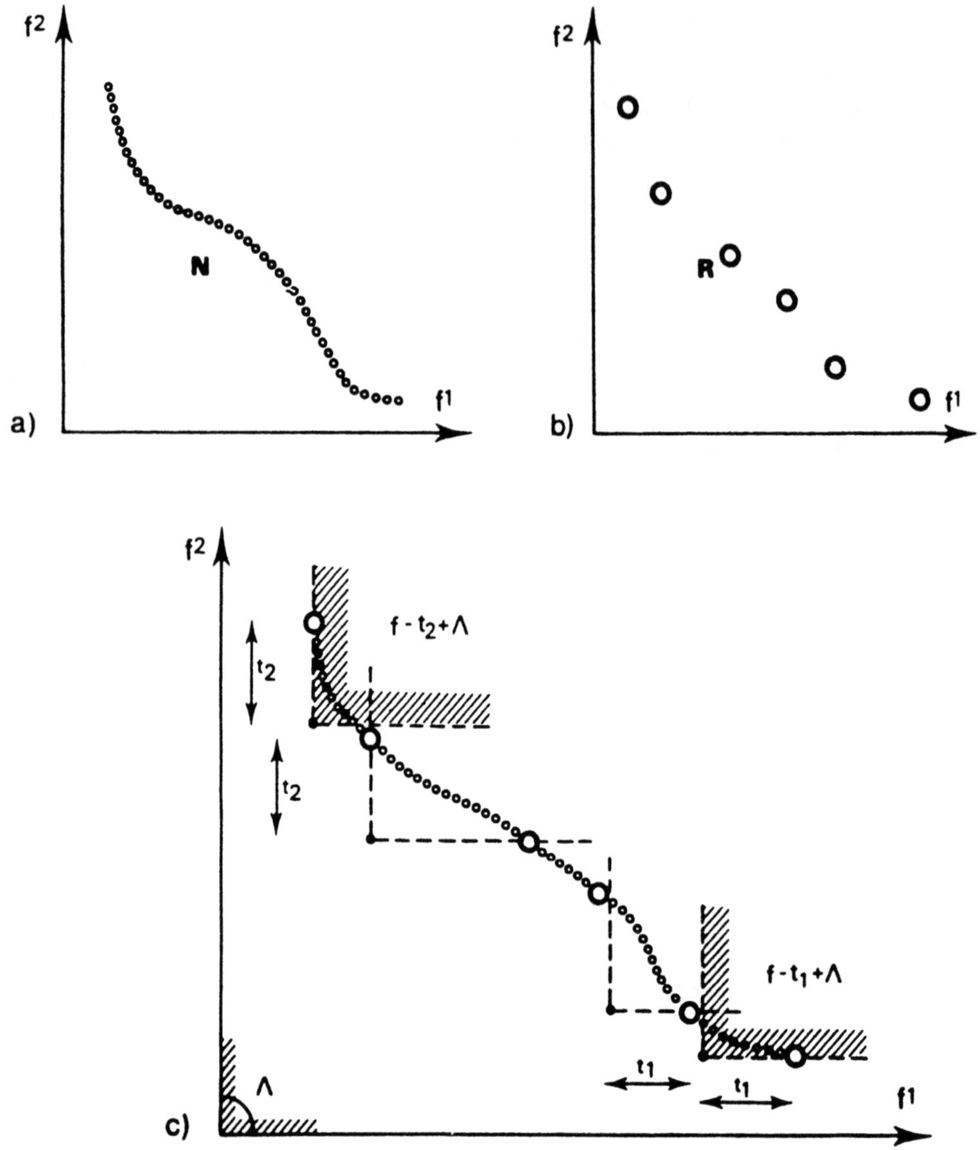

Figure 1: Selection of the representation $R = R(N) = R(Q)$ of the nondominated set $N = N(Q)$. Only nondominated elements are marked for the sake of simplicity of illustration.

a) the nondominated set N.
b) the representation R of the set N.
c) illustration of the tolerance mechanism.

zero or have small positive values that correspond to indifference limits of the DM's for criteria values, the whole set of the nondominated solutions will be obtained. If the values of tolerances are equal to some significant fractions of the corresponding criteria ranges, then a representation of the set of nondominated solutions will be obtained. The representation is a subset of the set of nondominated solutions preserving its shape and containing the smaller number of elements, the larger were chosen tolerance coefficients.

After the nondominated set or its representation has been obtained, the user may proceed in one of the following paths:

- choose a new region of his interest by a proper bounds setting (by using the command *bounds*),
- obtain a more or less dense representation by decreasing or increasing the tolerances (by using the commands *solve*),
- use graphic display to learn more about the problem and utilize the reference point approach (by using the command *analyse*).

It is worth to mention here that—unlike in other known techniques of obtaining a representation of the nondominated set—our approach not only does not require any additional computational effort but even decreases the time of computation with the ratio of $\#R$ to $\#N$, where $\#N$ and $\#R$ are the number of elements in the nondominated set N and its representation R, respectively.

Once any subset of the set N of nondominated solutions has been obtained, one can select the corresponding decisions from the additional data file (the command *pick*).

The DISCRET package provides also some more detailed information about the problem under consideration. A nondominated and a dominated linear approximations of the set of nondominated solutions are calculated (the command *analyse*). These approximations are obtained in the following way. A linear function is defined by the combination of the criteria with coefficients determined by the criteria ranges. This function is then minimized and maximized over the set of nondominated elements to obtain the nondominated and dominated approximation, respectively.

The information contained in the lower and upper bounds for criteria, in criteria ranges and in nondominated and dominated approximations gives a good overview of the shape of nondominated set. To learn more about the variety of available alternatives, the user may use another facility provided by the DISCRET package (in the command *analyse*), namely the graphical display of two-dimensional subproblems on the terminal screen. The user chooses two criteria for the vertical and horizontal axes, while the other criteria are:

- left unbounded—the whole problem is projected on the two-dimensional subspace of the space of objectives, just as if all but the two selected criteria were ignored,
- restrictively bounded—a two-dimensional "slice" is cut out of the original m-dimensional problem.

Enlargements of the chosen display fragments may be obtained simply by specifying new bounds for the criteria on the axes. Another display feature indicates how many elements does each of the 800 display points represent. This feature may be useful to detect and investigate the cluster structure of the problem.

The powerful tool of the reference point approach (Wierzbicki, 1979) is also available for the user (in the command *analyse*). By determining a reference point, he exhibits his aspiration levels for criteria values, confronts them with the obtained solution and modifies them and the reference point. The graphical displays mentioned above could also be useful on this stage of the decision making process.

During a session with DISCRET the user does not have to necessarily follow the entire procedure presented above. Once the problem generation and specification phase has been completed, he may utilize the package facilities in any order, repeat some steps (commands) or their sequences.

The ability of ignoring some of the criteria temporarily (by specifying that they are to be neither minimized nor maximized) opens to the DM a possibility of using a lexicographic or group-lexicographic approach. He may also, besides the actual criteria, introduce in an identical way some additional criterion expressing his utility, goal or preference function or any global criterion and use them on any arbitrary chosen stage of the decision making process. Such additional criteria have to be evaluated for each alternative during the problem generation phase (just as in the case of the original criteria).

The package offers also the possibility of an immediate return to any of the previous stages of the session, provided that the user have saved them into files (the *save* and *load* commands).

3 Structure and features of the package

3.1 General description

The current pilot version of the DISCRET package consists of eight FORTRAN77 programs. In order to run any of them the user has to type an appropriate program name (command) on his terminal. A list of DISCRET programs is presented below.

- *test1* — first test problem generator (the Dyer's Engine Selection Problem), a separate program.
- *test2* — second test problem generator (the location-allocation problem), a separate program.
- *load* — loads the problem from the data and specification ASCII files.
- *bounds* — informs about the criteria values ranges (utopia and nadir points), nondominated and dominated approximations of the set of alternatives and supports setting of new bounds on criteria values.
- *solve* — solves the discrete multicriteria optimization problem with explicit alternatives (implicit constraints), i.e. finds the set of nondominated or weakly nondominated elements or its representation, keeping or rejecting duplicate elements.

- *analyse* — supports the reference point approach and simple graphic displays of the nondominated set.
- *save* — saves the problem into the data and specifications ASCII files.
- *sort* — sorts the alternatives in increasing/decreasing order with respect to the values of a specified criterion, a *save* subcommand.
- *pick* — finds decisions corresponding to the chosen outcomes in criteria space, a *save* subcommand.

During the command execution, the user controls the process by choosing suitable items from the displayed menu (a list of options available at the moment). The menu system has been chosen instead of a pseudo-language of control commands because it does not require from the user to learn and remember a set of commands.

Each menu contains an amount of information sufficient to make the decision which of the displayed options is the most suitable one. If the user is asked to enter some information, everything he types is checked. If he makes a mistake, a message is displayed on the screen. Usually the message not only indicates the error but also shows the correct form of the required input.

In the next chapters the package commands will be briefly presented. We will not go into details of each menu since they are self-explanatory. The user will gather all the necessary experience during an introductory session with DISCRET. The test problems may be created by the commands *test1* and *test2*. The description of the test problems can be found in the user's training manual.

3.2 Problem loading phase

The command *load* loads the problem by reading the data file and the specification file. The user may also utilize it as an "unsave" facility which would allow him to return to any problem previously created and saved during the DISCRET session.

3.3 The bounds setting phase

The command *bounds* reads the input data, evaluates the criteria values ranges and displays them together with the nondominated and dominated approximation of the set of alternatives. If the user is not satisfied with the ranges of criteria values or with the values of approximations he can change them.

Knowing the ranges of criteria values, the DM may decide that some of the values of criteria does not interest him at all or at least temporarily. The command *bounds* makes it possible to change the DM's region of interest. By setting the appropriate lower and/or upper bounds for criteria values, the DM restricts further considerations to a smaller region of the objective space—his current region of interest. Only these alternatives that satisfy the bounds will be contained in the output data file produced by the command *bounds*.

Notice that the command *bounds* can select only a subset of alternatives from the input data. If the DM wants to consider a completely different region of interest, he has to supply the input data file containing that set of alternatives.

To illustrate this point assume, just for the sake of simplicity, that all criteria are to be minimized. Observe that if the decreasing of an upper bound for one criterion results in increase of the lower value for some other criterion, then it indicates that a part of the nondominated set did not satisfy the bounds and was rejected. If this was not the purpose of the user, he should return to less restrictive bounds. This remark may be useful on the initial stage of the problem analysis, when the user should become acquainted with the entire variety of the available alternatives.

3.4 The DMOP solving phase

The command *solve* results in solving the DMOP i.e. it selects the nondominated outcomes out of the set of feasible solutions. If the tolerances for all criteria values are equal to zero or have some small positive values corresponding to the computer arithmetic accuracy (for example, 1.0e–10) or criteria values measurement accuracy, then all nondominated outcomes are found. If the tolerances have larger positive values equal to some significant fractions of the criteria values ranges, then just a subset of the nondominated set, called its representation, is selected.

The command *solve* asks the user also about the type of the solution he is looking for. It has the ability to find either the set of nondominated outcomes or weakly nondominated outcomes. If there are duplicate outcomes (that is, if the same outcome vector corresponds to two different decisions), then they can be treated as distinguished ones (and all preserved) or as identical ones (and all but one rejected). Options more sophisticated than the default option (nondominated outcomes, duplicates rejected) do make sense in the cases when at least for some criteria rough values where initially given and they are supposed to be refined in some next stage of the decision making process, or when some of the criteria are more important then the other.

3.5 The problem saving phase

Once the nondominated set (or its representation or a part of it corresponding to the current region of interest of the user selected by setting of bounds) has been obtained, the user may wish to save it in order to continue the job later or to list its elements and analyse them.

The subcommand *sort* sorts the elements of the input data file according to increasing or decreasing values of criteria chosen by the user. Another option is to sort the alternatives in increasing or decreasing order according to their identifiers. When sorted before being printed, any set of alternatives appears to be more readable and hence more useful for analysis.

The subcommand *pick* selects from the additional input data file any additional information corresponding to the elements contained in the data file. Typically, this additional information describes the decisions leading to the obtained nondominated solutions.

The mechanism provided by the subcommands *sort* and *pick* may be especially useful in the case when the package user is an analyst. Properly sorted data (a nondominated set representation adequate to the current stage of the decision making process) will be more readable for the DM.

3.6 The phase of selecting final solution

The command *analyse* was designed to help the user to define his region of interest in a more precise way or to find his final solution.

At the beginning, the user will be informed about the criteria best and worse values—the utopia and nadir points. In order to provide some more detailed but still aggregated information about the shape of the nondominated set (or its representation or just a part of it) the nondominated and dominated linear approximations are evaluated.

A linear combination of criteria with coefficients proportional to the criteria ranges is minimized and maximized over the nondominated set to obtain its nondominated and dominated approximation respectively. Each of these approximations may be characterized by a single parameter standing for the percentage of the range it cuts off out of each criterion values range, see Figure 2 for illustration. Solutions obtained from the linear approximations are also displayed. This aggregated information seems to provide good aggregate data on the shape of the nondominated set, no matter how many criteria are under considerations.

In order to learn more about the criteria trade-offs, the user may display on the screen of his terminal a simple graphic figure for a two-dimensional subproblem. By setting bounds on all but two criteria he is able to cut a "slice" out of the m-dimensional problem. The entire subset selected in this way will be represented by 800 fields on the screen.

Finally, the user may enter the reference point approach, interactively introduce reference point exhibiting his aspiration levels for criteria values and analyse the obtained solutions. The reference points need not to be attainable and the obtained solution is the nondominated point nearest to the reference point in the sense of the scalarizing function. A scalarizing function based on the Euclidean-norm is used. Let q be the reference point introduced by the user. Then, assuming that all criteria are to be minimized, the following scalarizing function is minimized:

$$S(f-q) = -\|f-q\|^2 + \rho\|(f-q)_+\|^2$$

where $(f-q)_+$ denotes the vector with components $\max(0, f-q)$, $\|\bullet\|$ denotes the Euclidean norm and $\rho > 1$ is a penalty scalarizing coefficient. See (Wierzbicki, 1979), for example, for more information about the reference point approach.

4 Test examples

4.1 The Dyer's "Engine Selection Problem"

For the purpose of testing the package and to be used during introductory sessions with DISCRET, a generator of the Dyer's "Engine Selection Problem" (see Dyer, 1973, or

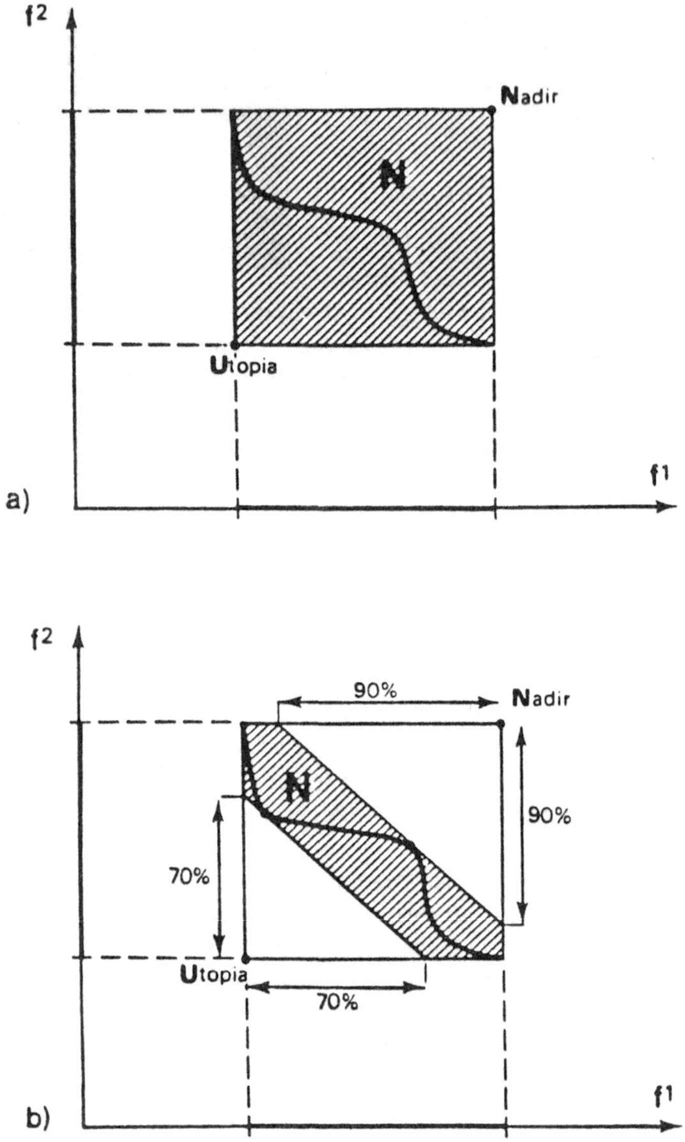

Figure 2: Two types of the aggregated information about the nondominated set N.

a) Information about the nondominated set N offered by the ***utopia*** point and the ***nadir*** point.

b) Information carried by the nondominated (70%) and dominated (90% of criteria range) approximations of the set N.

Törn, 1980) has been implemented. This is a very simple example of a DMOP. However, it is rather well known in the literature devoted to this field of research and therefore it seems that it will suit well as a small illustrative test problem.

Let us consider a DM who designs a new automobile and he has to choose an engine for that car. Suppose that the variety of available engines is described by three parameters (decision variables):

x_1 — compression ratio

x_2 — carburation ratio (in square inches)

x_3 — piston displacement (in cubic inches)

Suppose that the DM's preferences are described by the following three criteria:

f_1 — cost of the engine

f_2 — horsepower

f_3 — mileage per gallon

The following DMOP was proposed by Dyer (1973)—see also (Törn, 1980).

Problem definition:

$$\begin{aligned} \textit{minimize}: \quad f_1(x) &= 133(x_1 - 8) + 10x_2 + x_3 + 2000 \\ \textit{maximize}: \quad f_2(x) &= 20(x_1 - 8) + x_2 + 0.5x_3 \\ \textit{maximize}: \quad f_3(x) &= -1.67(x_1 - 8) - 0.2x_2 - 0.05x_3 + 35 \end{aligned}$$

subject to:

bounds:

$$\begin{aligned} 8 \leq \; & x_1 \leq 11 \\ & x_2 \leq 40 \\ 100 \leq \; & x_3 \leq 200 \end{aligned}$$

constraints:

$$\begin{aligned} 50x_1 - 30x_2 + x_3 &\leq 400 \\ 20x_1 - 3x_2 &\leq 160 \\ x_3/x_2 &\leq 20 \end{aligned}$$

Problem generation:

Dyer and Törn proposed the following scheme to generate uniformly a set of decisions :

$$\begin{aligned} &\text{for } x_1 = l_1 \text{ step } s_1 \text{ until } u_1 \\ &\text{for } x_2 = l_2 \text{ step } s_2 \text{ until } u_2 \\ &\text{for } x_3 = l_3 \text{ step } s_3 \text{ until } u_3 \end{aligned}$$

where l_i, u_i are the lower and upper bounds for x_i, $i = 1,2,3$ while s_i are the corresponding step size. If—following Dyer and Törn—the initial data are:

	l_i	s_i	u_i
$i=1$	8	1	11
$i=2$	10	10	40
$i=3$	100	20	200

then 84 generated points satisfy the problem constraints. Another way to generate a test problem is a random generation of decision vectors x within bounds l and u. This test problem is generated by the DISCRET's command *test1*.

4.2 The location-allocation problem

The second test problem is a facility location-allocation problem. It is based on the problem presented by Lee, Green and Kim (1981).

A firm is evaluating six potential sites of plant location (in four different states) that would serve four customer centers. The problem is where should the plants be opened and what should be the production volume of each of the new opened plants. Let $i = 1,2,\ldots,i_{\max} = 6$ be the locations index and let $j = 1,2,\ldots,j_{\max} = 4$ be the customer center index.

Decision variables:

$y_i = 0/1$ if a plant is not opened / opened at location i,

z_i — production volume (size) of a plant opened at location i.

Model variables and parameters:

p_j — total demand of customer center j,

c_{ij} — unit transportation cost from facility i to the customer center j,

g_i — fixed cost of opening a facility at location i (in \$1000),

l_i — life quality score for location i,

z_i^u — production upper limit for facility at location i (due to the state environment quality standards),

z_i^l — production lower limit,

z_i^s — production increment step size,

k^i — location i production limits due to state environment quality standards,

d_{ij} — demand placed on facility i by the customer center j,

$$d_{ij} = \frac{y_i\, e^{-bc_{ij}}}{\sum_i y_i\, e^{-bc_{ij}}},$$

x_{ij} — quantity of units transported from location i to the customer center j,

$$x_{ij} = \frac{d_{ij}}{\sum_j d_{ij}} \min\Big\{ z_i, \sum_j d_{ij} \Big\},$$

n — number of opened facilities.

Constraints:

1. Fixed cost limitation (in $1000):

$$\sum_i g_i y_i \leq 2000$$

2. Production limitations due to state environment quality standard:

$$z_i \leq k_i, \quad i = 1, \ldots, i_{\max}$$

3. Favored customer center service level :

$$z_1 y_1 + z_2 y_2 \geq 50$$

4. Number of opened facilities :

$$n_{\min} = 1 \leq n \leq 3 = n_{\max}$$

Criteria:

1. Unsatisfied demand level :

$$\min f_1 = \sum_i \sum_j (d_{ij} - x_{ij})$$

2. Favored customer center (no. 1) service level :

$$\max f_2 = \frac{\sum_i y_i x_{i1}}{p_1}$$

3. Total cost :

$$\min f_3 = f_5 + f_6 + f_7$$

4. Average life quality score :

$$\max f_4 = \frac{\sum_i y_i l_i}{\sum_i y_i}$$

5. Fixed cost :

$$\min f_5 = \sum_i y_i g_i$$

6. Transportation cost :

$$\min f_6 = \sum_i \sum_j s_{ij} x_{ij}$$

7. Production cost :

$$\min f_7 = \sum_i z_i e^{-\alpha z_i}$$

8. Unsold production :

$$\min f_8 = \sum_i \max\Big\{ 0, \Big(z_i - \sum_i x_{ij} \Big) \Big\}$$

Alternatives generation scheme:

The set of feasible alternatives is generated by the following three nested loops.
1. Consider opening $n = n_{\min}, \ldots, n_{\max}$ facilities.
2. Generate all n locations subsets of the set of locations (n—elements combinations of $i_{\max}$ elements set).
3. For each facility opened at location i consider its all available sizes z_i ranging from z_i^l to z_i^u with the increment step size z_i^s.

4.3 How to get started

At the very beginning of the session a problem to be solved has to be supplied. For the first session execute the DISCRET command *test1*. When the test problem is already generated, look at three files that were produced: the specification file, the data file and the additional data file.

Whenever you do not remember the names of the files you have created during the session, display the *history.fil* from your current directory. This file contains the history of your session.

In order to learn how to describe the details of your problem for DISCRET, print the specification file produced by the command *test1*. Then execute the specify command and try to create a specification file identical to that obtained from *test1*.

If you already know how to specify your problem, try some other DISCRET commands. For the first time, execute them in the following order: *bounds*, *solve*, *analyse*, *sort*, *pick*, just to learn what they can actually do for you.

Later on try to select your most preferable solution(s). Notice that DISCRET commands can be executed in any order (if only it does make any sense for you). Refer to the *history.fil* to recall the history of your session.

5 Conclusions

The DISCRET package for multicriteria optimization and decision making problems with finite number of discrete alternatives has been briefly presented. It is the author's hope that this report will attract the reader and encourage him to use the package.

DISCRET is an interactive package. The user may execute its commands in any order once the problem generation and specification phase has been completed. The variety of paths the user may follow guarantees flexibility in meeting his demands.

The author will be grateful for any critical remarks and comments concerning both the approach and the package itself. All such suggestions would be very helpful and may result in further package improvements.

6 References

Baum, S., W. Terry and U. Parekh (1981). Random sampling approach to MCDM. In J.N. Morse (ed): Organizations: Multiple Agents with Multiple Criteria, Lecture Notes in Economics and Math. Systems, 190.

Dyer, J.S. (1973). An empirical investigation of a man-machine interactive approach to the solution of a multiple criteria problem. In T.L. Cochrane and M. Zeleny (eds): Multiple Criteria Decision Making, University of South California Press.

Keeney, R.L. and H. Reiffa (1976). Decisions with Multiple Objectives: Preferences and Value Tradeoffs, New York, Wiley.

Kŏksalan, M., M.H. Karwan and S. Zionts (1984). An improved method for solving multiple criteria problems involving discrete alternatives. *IEEE Transactions on Systems, Man and Cybernetics*, Vol. SMC-14, No. 1, pp. 24–34.

Kung, H.T., F. Luccio and F.P. Preparata (1975). On finding the maxima of a set of vectors. *Journal of the Association for Computing Machinery*, Vol. 22, No. 4, pp. 469–476.

Lee, S.M., G.I. Green and C.S. Kim (1981). A multiple criteria model for the location-allocation problem. *Comput. and Ops Res.*, Vol. 8, pp. 1–8.

Lin, J.G. (1976). Three methods for determining Pareto-optimal solutions of multiple-objective problems. In Ho and Mitter (eds.): Directions in Large-Scale Systems. Many-Person Optimization and Decentralized Control, Plenum Press, New York and London.

Majchrzak, J. (1984). Package DISCRET for multicriteria optimization and decision making problems with discrete alternatives. IIASA Conference on Plural Rationality and Interactive Decision Processes, Sopron, Hungary, 16–26 August, 1984.

Morse, J.N. (1980). Reducing the size of the nondominated set: pruning by clustering. *Comput. and Ops Res.*, Vol. 7, No. 1–2, pp. 55–66.

Payne, A.N. and E. Polak (1980). An interactive rectangle elimination method for biobjective decision making. *IEEE Transactions on Automatic Control*, Vol. AC-25, No. 3, pp. 421–432.

Polak, E. and A.N. Payne (1976). On multicriteria optimization. In Ho and Mitter (eds.): Directions in Large-Scale Systems. Many-Person Optimization and Decentralized Control, Plenum Press, New York and London.

Rivett, P. (1977). Multidimension scaling for multiobjective policies. *Omega*, Vol. 5, pp. 367–379.

Roy, B. (1971). Problems and methods with multiple objective functions. *Math. Programming*, Vol. 1, pp. 239–266.

Siskos, J. (1982). A way to deal with fuzzy preferences in multi-criteria decision problems. *Eur. J. Op. Res.*, Vol. 10, pp. 314–324.

Stahn, H. and U. Petersohn (1978). Discrete polyoptimization. *Systems Science*, Vol. 4, No. 2, pp. 101–109.

Steuer, R.E. and F.W. Harris (1980). Intra-set point generation and filtering in decision and criterion space. *Comput. and Ops Res.*, Vol. 7, No. 1–2, pp. 41–53.

Tõrn, A.A. (1980). A sampling-search-clustering approach for exploring the feasible/efficient solutions of MCDM problems. *Comput. and Ops Res.*, Vol. 7, No. 1–2, pp. 67–79.

Wierzbicki, A.P. (1979). A methodological guide to multiobjective decision making, WP-79-122, International Institute for Applied Systems Analysis, Laxenburg, Austria.

Zionts, S. (1981). A multiple criteria method for choosing among discrete alternatives. *Eur. J. Op. Res.*, Vol. 7, pp. 143–147.

A Generalized Reference Point Approach to Multiobjective Transshipment Problem with Facility Location

Wlodzimierz Ogryczak, Krzysztof Studzinski,

Krystian Zorychta

Institute of Informatics, Warsaw University.

Abstract

This paper describes the methodological background of the Dynamic Interactive Network Analysis System (DINAS) which enables the solution of various multiobjective transshipment problems with facility location using IBM-PC XT/AT microcomputers. DINAS utilizes an extension of the classical reference point approach to handling multiple objectives. In this approach the decision-maker forms his requirements in terms of aspiration and reservation levels, i.e., he specifies acceptable and required values for given objectives. A special TRANSLOC solver was developed to provide DINAS with solutions to single-objective problems. It is based on the branch and bound scheme with a pioneering implementation of the simplex special ordered network (SON) algorithm with implicit representation of the simple and variable upper bounds (VUB & SUB). DINAS is prepared as a menu-driven and easy in usage system armed with a special network editor which reduces to minimum effort associated with input a real-life problem.

1 The DINAS System

DINAS is a decision support system designed for solving multiobjective transshipment problems with facility location on IBM-PC XT/AT or compatibles. It requires 640K RAM and a hard disk or at least one floppy disk. DINAS can process problems consisting of:

- up to seven objective functions,
- a transportation network with up to one hundred of nodes and a few hundreds of arcs,
- up to fifteen potential locations.

A mathematical model of the problem is described in Section 2.

DINAS consists of three programs prepared in the C programming language:

1. an interactive procedure for efficient solutions generation,

2. a solver for single-objective problems,

3. a network editor for input data and results examination.

The basic concept of the interactive scheme for efficient solutions generation is as follows:

- the DM works with the system in an interactive way so that he can change his aspiration and reservation levels in any direction;

- after editing the aspiration and reservation levels, the system computes a new efficient solution by solving a corresponding single-objective problem;

- each computed efficient solution is put into a special solution base and presented to the DM as the current solution in the form of tables and bars which allow him to analyze performances of the current solution in comparison with the previous solutions.

Operations available in the DINAS interactive procedure are partitioned into three groups and corresponding three branches of the main menu: PROCESS, SOLUTION and ANALYSIS. The PROCESS branch contains basic operations connected with processing the multiobjective problem and generation of several efficient solutions. There are included operations such as editing and converting the problem, computation of the pay-off matrix, and finally, generation a sequence of efficient solutions depending on the edited aspiration and reservation levels.

The SOLUTION branch contains additional operations connected with the current solution. The DM can examine in details the current solution using the network editor or analyse only short characteristics such as objective values and selected locations. Values of the objective functions are presented in three ways: as a standard table, as bars in the aspiration/reservation scale and as bars in the utopia/nadir scale. The bars show percentage level of each objective value with respect to the corresponding scale. The DM may also print the current solution or save it for using in next runs of the system with the same problem. There is also available a special command to delete the current solution from the solution base if the DM finds it as quite useless.

The ANALYSIS branch collects commands connected with operations on the solution base. The main command COMPARE allows the DM to perform comparison of all the efficient solutions from the solution base or of some subset of them. In the comparison only the short characteristics of the solutions are used, i.e., objective values in the form of tables and bars as well as tables of selected locations. Moreover, some commands which allow the DM to select various efficient solutions from solution base as the current solution are included in this branch. There exists also an opportunity to restore some (saved earlier) efficient solution to the solution base.

A special TRANSLOC solver has been prepared to provide the multiobjective analysis procedure with solutions to single-objective problems. The solver is hidden from the user but it is the most important part of the DINAS system. It is a numerical kernel of the system which generates efficient solutions. Even for a small transshipment problem with facility location the corresponding linear program has a rather large size. For this reason it cannot be solved directly with the standard simplex algorithm. In order to solve the program on IBM-PC XT/AT microcomputers it is necessary to take advantage of its special structure. A general concept of the TRANSLOC solver is presented in Section 4 whereas theoretical backgrounds of some special computational techniques are discussed in Sections 5 and 6.

DINAS is armed with the built-in network editor EDINET. EDINET is a full-screen editor specifically designed for input and edit data of the generalized network model defined in Section 2. The essence of the EDINET concept is a dynamic movement from some current node to its neighbouring nodes, and vice versa, according to the network structure. The input data are inserted by a special mechanism of windows while visiting several nodes. Independently, a list of the nodes in the alphabetic order and a graphic scheme of the network is available at any time. A special window is also used for defining objective functions.

2 The generalized network model

A network model of the problem consists of nodes that are connected by a set of direct flow arcs. The set of nodes is partitioned into two subsets: the set of fixed nodes and the set of potential nodes. The fixed nodes represent "fixed points" of the transportation network, i.e., points which cannot be changed. Each fixed node is characterized by two quantities: supply and demand. The potential nodes are introduced to represent possible locations of new points in the network. Some groups of the potential nodes represent different versions of the same facility to be located (e.g., different sizes of a warehouse). For this reason, potential nodes are organized in the so-called selections, i.e., sets of nodes with the multiple choice requirement. Each selection is defined by the list of included potential nodes as well as by lower and upper numbers of nodes which have to be selected (located). Each potential node is characterized by a capacity which bounds maximal flow through the node. The capacities are also given for all arcs but not for the fixed nodes.

A several linear objective functions are considered in the problem. The objective functions are introduced into the model by given coefficients associated with several arcs and potential nodes. They will be called cost coefficients independently of their real character in the objective functions. The cost coefficients for potential nodes are, however, understood in a different way than for arcs. The cost coefficient connected to an arc is treated as the unit cost of the flow along the arc whereas the cost coefficient connected to a potential node is considered as the fixed cost associated with the use (location) of the node rather than as the unit cost.

In the DINAS system we place two restrictions on the network structure:

- there is no arc which directly connects two potential nodes;

– each potential node belongs to at most two selections.

Both the restrictions are not very strong. The first one does not imply any loss of generality since every two of potential nodes can be separated by introduction of an artificial fixed node if necessary. The second requirement, in general, restricts the class of problems. However, in practical models usually each potential node belongs to exactly one selection or sometimes to two selections in more complex problems.

For simplicity of the model and the solution procedure, we transform the potential nodes into artificial arcs. The transformation is performed by duplication of all potential nodes. After the duplication is done all the nodes can be considered as fixed and each potential node is replaced by an artificial arc which leads from the node to its copy. Due to the transformation we get a network with the fixed structure since all the nodes are fixed. Potentiality of artificial arcs does not imply any complication because each arc in the network represents a potential flow. Moreover, all the bounds on flows (i.e., capacities) are connected to arcs after this transformation. Additional nonstandard discrete constraints on the flow are generated only by the multiple choice requirements associated with the selections. Cost coefficients are connected only to arcs, but the coefficients connected to artificial arcs represent fixed costs.

A mathematical statement of this transformed problem takes the form of the following generalized network model:

minimize

$$\sum_{(i,j)\in A\setminus A_a} f_{ij}^p x_{ij} + \sum_{(i,j)\in A_a} f_{ij}^p y_{ij}, \quad p = 1,2,\dots,n_0 \tag{1}$$

subject to

$$\sum_{(i,j)\in A} x_{ij} - \sum_{(j,i)\in A} x_{ji} = b_i, \quad i \in N \tag{2}$$

$$0 \le x_{ij} \le c_{ij}, \quad (i,j) \in A \setminus A_a \tag{3}$$

$$0 \le x_{ij} \le c_{ij} y_{ij}, \quad (i,j) \in A_a \tag{4}$$

$$g_k \le \sum_{(i,j)\in S_k} y_{ij} \le h_k, \quad k = 1,2,\dots,n_s \tag{5}$$

$$y_{ij} = 0 \text{ or } 1, \quad (i,j) \in A_a \tag{6}$$

where the following notations are used:

n_0 — number of objective functions,

N — set of nodes (including copies of potential nodes),

n_s — number of selections,

A — set of arcs (including artificial arcs),

A_a — set of artificial arcs,

f_{ij}^p — cost coefficient of the p-th objective associated with the arc (i,j),

b_i — supply-demand balance at the node i,

c_{ij} — capacity of the arc (i,j),

g_k — lower number of (artificial) arcs to be selected in the k-th selection,

h_k — upper number of (artificial) arcs to be selected in the k-th selection,

S_k — set of (artificial) arcs that belong to the k-th selection,

x_{ij} — decision variable that represents flow along the arc (i,j),

y_{ij} — decision variable equal 1 for selected arc and 0 otherwise.

The generalized network model of this form includes typical network constraints (2) with simple upper bounds (3) as well as a special discrete structure (5) – (6) connected to the network structure by variable upper bounds (4). While solving the model we have to take advantages of all these features.

3 Interactive procedure for handling multiple objectives

There are many different concepts for handling multiple objectives in mathematical programming. We decided to use the so-called reference point approach which was introduced by Wierzbicki (1982). This concept was further developed in many papers and was used as a basis for construction of the software package DIDAS (Dynamic Interactive Decision Analysis and Support system). The DIDAS package proved to be useful in analysing conflicts and assisting in decision making situations (Grauer et al., 1984).

The basic concept of the reference point approach is as follows:

1. the decision-maker (DM) forms his requirements in terms of aspiration levels, i.e., he specifies acceptable values for given objectives;

2. the DM works with the computer in an interactive way so that he can change his aspiration levels during sessions of the analysis.

In our system, we extend the DIDAS approach. The extension relies on additional use of reservation levels which allow the DM to specify necessary values for given objectives (Wierzbicki, 1986).

Consider the multi-objective program associated with the generalized network model:
minimize q
subject to

$$q = F(x,y)$$

$$(x, y) \in Q$$

where

q represents the vector,

F is the linear objective vector-function defined by (1),

Q denotes the feasible set of the generalized network model, i.e., the set defined by conditions (2) – (6).

The reference point technique works in two stages. In the first stage the DM is provided with some initial information which gives him an overview of the problem. The initial information is generated by minimization of all the objectives separately. More precisely, the following single objective programs are solved:

$$\min\{F^p(x,y) + \frac{r_0}{n_0}\sum_{i=1}^{n_0} F^i(x,y) : (x,y) \in Q\}, \quad p = 1,2,\ldots,n_0 \tag{7}$$

where F^p denotes the p-th objective function and r_0 is an arbitrarily small number. The so-called pay-off matrix

$$R = (q_{pj}), \qquad p = 1,\ldots,n_0; \qquad j = 1,\ldots,n_0$$

which yields information on the range of numerical values of each objective is then constructed. The p-th row of the matrix R corresponds to the vector (x^p, y^p) which solves the p-th program (7). Each quantity q_{pj} represents a value of the j-th objective at this solution (i.e., $q_{pj} = F^j(x^p, y^p)$). The vector with elements q_{pp}, i.e., the diagonal of R, defines the utopia (ideal) point. This point, denoted further by q^u, is usually not attainable but it is presented to the DM as a lower limit to the numerical values of the objectives.

Taking into consideration the j-th column of the matrix R we notice that the minimal value in that column is $q_{pp} = q^u_p$.

Let q^n_j be the maximal value, i.e.,

$$q^n_j = \max_{1 \leq p \leq n_0} \{q_{pj}\}$$

The point q^n is called the nadir point and may be presented to the DM as an upper guideline to the values of the objectives. Thus, for each objective F^p a reasonable but not necessarily tight upper bound q^n and a lower bound q^u are known after the first stage of the analysis.

In the second stage, an interactive selection of efficient solutions is performed. The DM controls the selection by two vector – parameters: his aspiration level q^a and his reservation level q^r, where

$$q^u \leq q^a < q^r \leq q^n$$

The support system searches for the satisfying solution while using an achievement scalarizing function as a criterion in single-objective optimization. Namely, the support system computes the optimal solution to the following problem:

minimize

$$\max_{1 \le p \le n_0} u_p(q, q^a, q^r) + \frac{r_0}{n_0} \sum_{p=1}^{n_0} u_p(q, q^a, q^r) \tag{8}$$

subject to

$$q = F(x, y)$$

$$(x, y) \in Q$$

where r_0 is an arbitrarily small number and u_p is a function which measures the deviation of results from the DM's expectations with respect to the p-th objective, depending on a given aspiration level q^a and reservation level q^r.

The computed solution is an efficient (Pareto–optimal) solution to the original multiobjective model. It is presented to the DM as a current solution. The DM is asked whether he finds this solution satisfactory or not. If the DM does not accept the current solution he has to enter new aspiration and/or reservation levels for some objectives. Depending on this new information supplied by the DM, a new efficient solution is computed and presented as a current solution. The process is repeated as long as the DM needs.

The function $u_p(q, q^a, q^r)$ is a strictly monotone function of the objective vector q with value $u_p = 0$ if $q = q^a$ and $u_p = 1$ if $q = q^r$. In our system, we use (similarly as in Wierzbicki 1986) a piece–wise linear function u_p defined as follows:

$$u_p(q, q^a, q^r) = \begin{cases} a_p(q_p - q_p^a)/(q_p^r - q_p^a), & \text{if} \quad q_p < q_p^a \\ (q_p - q_p^a)/(q_p^r - q_p^a), & \text{if} \quad q_p^a \le q_p \le q_p^r \\ b_p(q_p - q_p^r)/(q_p^r - q_p^a) + 1, & \text{if} \quad q_p^r < q_p \end{cases}$$

where a_p and b_p $(p = 1, 2, \ldots, n_0)$ are given positive parameters. In the DINAS system, the parameters a_p and b_p are defined according to the formulae

$$a_p = \frac{a(q_p^r - q_p^a)}{(q_p^a - q_p^u)}$$

$$b_p = b(q_p^r - q_p^a)$$

where a and b are positive parameters computed as follows

$$a = 0.1 \min_{1 \le j \le n_0} \frac{(q_j^a - q_j^u)}{(q_j^r - q_j^a)^2}$$

$$b = 10 \max_{1 \le j \le n_0} \frac{1}{(q_j^r - q_j^a)}$$

The parameters a_p and b_p satisfy inequalities: $a_p < 1$ and $b_p > 1$, and thereby the achievement functions u_p are convex. Minimization of the function u_p is then equivalent to minimization of a variable u_p defined as follows:

$$u_p = v_p + b_p v_p^- - a_p v_p^+ \tag{9}$$

$$v_p - v_p^+ + v_p^- = (q_p - q_p^a)/(q_p^r - q_p^a) \tag{10}$$

$$0 \le v_p \le 1 \tag{11}$$

$$v_p^+ \ge 0, \quad v_p^- \ge 0 \tag{12}$$

4 General concept of the TRANSLOC solver

The TRANSLOC solver has been prepared to provide the multiobjective analysis procedure with solutions to single–objective problems. According to the interactive procedure described in Section 3 the TRANSLOC solver has to be able to solve two kinds of single–objective problems: the first one associated with calculation of the pay–off matrix (problems (7)) and the second one associated with minimization of the scalarizing achievement function (problems (8)). Both kinds of the problems have, however, the same main constraints which represent the feasible set of the generalized network model. Moreover, the other constraints of both the kinds of problems can be expressed in very similar ways. So, we can formulate a general single–objective problem for the TRANSLOC solver as follows:

$$\text{maximize } s \tag{13}$$

subject to

$$\sum_{(i,j)\in A} x_{ij} - \sum_{(j,i)\in A} x_{ji} = b_i, \quad i \in N \tag{14}$$

$$w_k + \sum_{(i,j)\in S_k} y_{ij} = h_k, \quad k = 1,2,\ldots,n_s \tag{15}$$

$$u_p - v_p + d_p^+ - d_p^- = 0, \quad p = 1,2,\ldots,n_0 \tag{16}$$

$$v_p - \frac{1}{a_p}d_p^+ + \frac{1}{b_p}d_p^- - \sigma_p \left(\sum_{(i,j)\in A\setminus A_a} f_{ij}^p x_{ij} + \sum_{(i,j)\in A_a} f_{ij}^p y_{ij} \right) = \delta_p, \quad p = 1,\ldots,n_0 \tag{17}$$

$$u_0 - \sum_{p=1}^{n_0} u_p = 0 \tag{18}$$

$$s + z + \frac{r_0}{n_0} u_0 = 0 \tag{19}$$

$$0 \le x_{ij} \le c_{ij}, \quad (i,j) \in A \setminus A_a \tag{20}$$

$$0 \le w_k \le h_k - g_k, \quad k = 1,2,\ldots,n_s \tag{21}$$

$$x_{ij} \le c_{ij} y_{ij}, \quad (i,j) \in A_a \tag{22}$$

$$u_p \le z, \quad p = 1,2,\ldots,n_0 \tag{23}$$

$$y_{ij} = 0 \text{ or } 1, \quad (i,j) \in A_a \tag{24}$$

and depending on the kind of optimization:

$$d_p^+ = 0, \quad d_p^- = 0, \quad p = 1,2,\ldots,n_0 \tag{25}$$

for the utopia point calculation or

$$d_p^+ \geq 0, \; d_p^- \geq 0, \; 0 \leq v_p \leq 1, \; p = 1, 2, \ldots, n_0 \tag{26}$$

for the achievement scalarizing function optimization, respectively, where: $\sigma_p = 1$ and $\delta_p = 0$ during utopia point calculation, $\sigma_p = 1/(q_p^r - q_p^a)$ and $\delta_p = -q_p^a/(q_p^r - q_p^a)$ during the minimization of the achievement scalarizing function, whereas all the other quantities are the same as in Sections 2 and 3.

The above single-objective problem is a typical mixed integer linear program, i.e., it is a typical linear program with integrality conditions for some variables (namely y_{ij}). Mixed integer linear programs are usually solved by branch and bound approach with utilization of the simplex method. The TRANSLOC solver also uses this approach. Fortunately, only a very small group of decision variables is required to be integer in our model. Therefore we can use a simple branch and bound scheme in the solver.

Even for a small transshipment problem with facility location, the corresponding linear program (13) – (23) has rather large size. For this reason it cannot be solved directly with the standard simplex algorithm. In order to solve the program on IBM–PC XT/AT microcomputers, it is necessary to take advantages of its special structure.

Note that the inequalities (20) – (21) and (25) or (26) are standard simple upper bounds (SUB) which are usually processed outside of the linear programming matrix (Orchard–Hays, 1968). Similarly, inequalities (22) and (23) can be considered as the so-called variable upper bounds (VUB) and processed outside of the matrix due to a special technique. Basic rules of the technique for SUB & VUB processing are developed in Section 5.

The main group of equality constraints (14) represents typical network relations. Similarly, the equalities (15) and (16) include only variables with unit coefficients. All the rows (14) – (16) can be handled in the simplex method as the so-called special ordered network (SON) structure. Basic rules of the SON technique used in the TRANSLOC solver are developed in Section 6.

Thus only a small number of inequalities (17) – (19) has to be considered as typical rows of linear program. While taking advantage of this fact, the TRANSLOC solver can process transhipment problems of quite large dimensions.

5 Implicit representation of VUB & SUB constraints

The single - objective program (13) – (26) includes many inequalities of special simple forms. They can be partitioned into two groups. The first one consists of the so-called simple upper bounds (SUB), i.e., inequalities of the form $0 \leq x_j \leq c_j$ for some variables x_j and constants c_j, such as conditions (20) – (21), (26) with respect to variables v_p, and continuous form of (24). The second one includes the so-called variable upper bounds (VUB), i.e., inequalities of the form $x_j \leq c_j x_k$ for some variables x_j, x_k and constants c_j, such as conditions (22).

SUB constraints are usually implicitly represented in commercial simplex codes (see e.g. Orchard-Hays, 1968). Schrage (1975) proposed some technique for implicit representation of VUB constraints. The technique was further developed and led to effective implementations (see e.g. Todd, 1982).

The techniques presented in the literature deals, however, only with a simple form of VUB constraints. Namely, it is assumed that $c_j = 1$ in all VUBs and there are no upper bounds on x_k variables. The restriction of consideration to only unit variable upper bounds usually does not imply any loss of generality since it can be attained by a proper scaling of the problem. Unfortunately, in our model such scaling techniques cannot be used without destroying of the special SON structure (see Section 6). Therefore we were forced to extend the VUB techniques in such a way that nonunit variable upper bounds as well as some simple upper bounds on x_k variables were acceptable.

With respect to the VUB & SUB structure the linear program under consideration can be formulated as follows. The numerical data consist of an $m \times n$ matrix A of rank m, a column m-vector b, a row n-vector f and a column n-vector c. In addition, the index set $N = \{1, 2, \ldots, n\}$ is partitioned into $J \cup K$, where J represents the so-called sons, i.e., variables which appear on the left-hand-side of variable upper bounds, and K represents the so-called fathers, i.e., variables which appear on the right-hand-side of variable upper bounds. Any variable that is not involved in any variable upper bound is regarded as a childless father. The set J is further partitioned into the sets $J(k)$, $k \in K$, where $J(k)$ is the set (possible empty) of sons of the father $k \in K$. It is assumed that the son has only one father and that no father has a father. The father connected to a son x_j will be denoted by $k(j)$. The problem is then

$$\max \ fx$$

subject to

$$Ax = b$$

$$x_j \leq c_j x_k \quad \text{for all} \quad k \in K \text{ and } j \in J(k)$$

$$x_k \leq c_k \quad \text{for all} \quad k \in K$$

$$x \geq 0$$

Let s_j be a slack variable for the variable upper bound $x_j \leq c_j x_k$, so that

$$x_j + s_j = c_j x_k, \qquad x_j \geq 0, \qquad s_j \geq 0$$

Consider a basic solution to the problem. The basis consists of the $m + v$ columns corresponding to some sons x_j, some fathers x_k and some slacks s_j (where v denotes the number of VUBs). From each VUB either one slack s_j or one son x_j belongs to the basis. Calculation of the basic slacks is out of our interest and they can be simply dropped from the basis, i.e., the corresponding rows and columns can be dropped. Further, the basic sons which arrive in the other VUBs can be eliminated by submission $x_j = c_j x_k$. So, the whole basic solution can be computed from an $m \times m$ basis consisting of some linear combinations of columns from matrix A.

A basic solution to the problem is characterized as follows. The set of sons is partitioned into the three sets $J = JL \cup JU \cup JB$, where JL denotes the set of nonbasic sons fixed at their lower limits (i.e., $x_j = 0$), JU denotes the set of nonbasic sons fixed at their upper limits (i.e., $x_j = c_j x_k$) and JB denotes the set of basic sons. Similarly, the set of fathers is partitioned into three sets $K = KL \cup KU \cup KB$, where KL denotes the set of nonbasic fathers fixed at their lower limits (i.e., $x_k = 0$), KU denotes the set of nonbasic fathers fixed at their upper limits (i.e., $x_k = c_k$), and KB denotes the set of basic fathers. The basis B consists of the columns corresponding to basic sons $B_j = A_j$ and of the columns corresponding to basic fathers given by the formula

$$B_k = A_k + \sum_{j \in J(k) \cap JU} c_j A_j$$

Consider a basic solution given by a basis B and sets JL, JU, JB, KL, KU, KB. For the determination of a nonbasic variable to be enter the basis in the simplex algorithm it is necessary to compute the so-called reduced costs. Let z_i denote an ordinary reduced cost connected to the column A_i, i.e.,

$$z_i = f_i - f_B B^{-1} A_i, \qquad i \in J \cup K$$

where f_B denotes the basic part of the cost vector f. Due to implicit representation of VUBs the reduced costs associated with several nonbasic variables take then form

$$d_j = z_j \qquad \text{for} \qquad j \in J$$

$$d_k = z_k + \sum_{j \in J(k) \cap JU} c_j z_j, \qquad \text{for} \qquad k \in K$$

Thus, in comparison with pricing in the standard simplex algorithm, the pricing with implicit representation of VUBs needs a calculation of linear combinations of ordinary reduced costs as the only one additional operation.

Due to handling of the SUB structure together with the VUB constraints, a nonbasic variable x_j or x_k is considered as potential incoming variable if one of the following conditions fulfils:

$$d_j < 0 \quad \text{and} \quad j \in JL,$$

$$d_j > 0 \quad \text{and} \quad j \in JU,$$

$$d_k < 0 \quad \text{and} \quad k \in KL,$$

$$d_k > 0 \quad \text{and} \quad k \in KU.$$

Implicit representation of VUBs makes some degenerated simplex iterations so simple that they can be performed on line during pricing. Namely, if x_j is an incoming variable and $k(j) \in KL$, then the corresponding simplex iteration depends only on change sets JL and JU, i.e., x_j is moved from the set JL to the set JU or vice versa. Such an operation can be performed while pricing before the computation of reduced costs for fathers.

Let x_s $(s \in J \ \text{ or } \ s \in K)$ be a variable chosen for enter the basis. Considering changes in the basic solution while the value of x_s is either increased for $s \in JL \cup KL$ or decreased for $s \in JU \cup KU$ by a nonnegative parameter Θ we get six formulae for upper bounds on the parameter Θ and six corresponding formulae for determination of the outgoing variable (for details see Ogryczak et al., 1987). Crossing these formulae with four types of incoming variables we get 19 types (5 criss-crossings are not allowed) of the simplex transformations performed in the algorithm with implicit representation of the VUB & SUB structure. The simplest transformation depends only on moving some variable from one set to another without any change of the basis. Most of the transformations depend on performing one of the following operations:

(a) some basic column multiplied by a scalar is added to another basic column;

(b) some basic column is replaced by a nonbasic column or a linear combination of nonbasic columns.

More complex transformations use both the above operations and the most complex one needs two operations of type (a) and one operation of type (b).

6 The simplex SON algorithm

The simplex special ordered network (SON) procedure was developed by Glover & Klingman (1981, 1985). It is a partitioning method for solving LP problems with embedded network structure. Every problem of this type is characterized by a full row rank matrix A partitioned as follows:

$$A = \begin{pmatrix} ANN & ANL \\ ALN & ALL \end{pmatrix}$$

where $ANN(m \times n)$ denotes the matrix corresponding to a pure network problem and the other submatrices $ANL(m \times p)$, $ALN(q \times n)$, $ALL(q \times p)$ consist of any real elements.

The matrix A of the auxiliary LP problem discussed in Section 3 has obviously this form. The matrix ANN is an incidence matrix corresponding to the transportation network studied in Section 2. Therefore each constraint represented by a row of ANN corresponds to a node of the network and will be referred to as node constraint. Moreover, each variable represented by a column of ANN corresponds to an arc of the network and will be referred to as arc variable. There are two classes of the ANN columns: columns containing exactly two non-zero entries in ANN (one $+1$ and one -1) called ordinary arcs and columns containing exactly one non-zero entry in ANN ($+1$ or -1) called slack arcs. The -1 entry in a column indicates the node where the arc begins and the $+1$ entry in a column indicates the node where the arc ends. If a column has exactly one nonzero element pointing one of the arc endpoints then an artificial node outside the network can be meant as the second arc endpoint.

The SUB and VUB simplex algorithms use a basis B which is composed of $m + q$ linearly independent columns selected from the matrix A. Any basis B may be partitioned as follows:

$$B = \begin{pmatrix} B_{11} & B_{12} \\ B_{21} & B_{22} \end{pmatrix}$$

where B_{11} is a nonsingular submatrix of ANN. It appears to be better for the effectiveness of the algorithm if rank of B_{11} is as large as possible.

Let $x_B = (x_{B_1}, x_{B_2})$ denote the basic part of the decision variable vector x, where x_{B_1}, x_{B_2} correspond to the B_{11} and B_{12} submatrices, respectively. Thus the basic variables x_{B_1} are exclusively arc variables. The basic variables x_{B_2} may also contain arc variables. Similarly, the rows of B_{11} are exclusively node rows but the matrix (B_{21}, B_{22}) may also contain node rows.

The basis inverse B^{-1} may be written as follows

$$B^{-1} = \begin{pmatrix} B_{11}^{-1} + B_{11}^{-1}B_{12}V^{-1}B_{21}B_{11}^{-1} & -B_{11}^{-1}B_{12}V^{-1} \\ -V^{-1}B_{21}B_{11}^{-1} & V^{-1} \end{pmatrix}$$

where $V = B_{22} - B_{21}B_{11}^{-1}B_{12}$.

Define the so called master basis tree (MBT) associated with a given basis. The set of nodes of the tree contains all the nodes of our LP/embedded network problem plus an external node called the master root. Thus MBT always contains $m+1$ nodes

$$N = \{0, 1, \ldots, m\}$$

where 0 is the master root, and m arcs. The nodes of MBT that correspond to rows of B_{21} are called externalized roots (ER's). Each ER is connected to the master root by an externalized arc (EA).

All of the ordinary arcs in B_{11} belong to MBT. There may be two types of slack arcs associated with B_{11}. If a slack arc in B_{11} is a slack arc of ANN then the arc is replaced by an arc between the master root and its unique node. If a slack arc in B_{11} is an ordinary arc in ANN, it is replaced by an arc between its nodes in ANN (one of these endpoints is an ER node).

The arcs in the master basis tree have a natural orientation defined as follows: if an edge (u, v) belongs to MBT and node u is nearer the master root than v, then u is called the predecessor of v, and v is called the immediate successor of u. Thus we will refer to a basis arc as conformable if its ANN direction agrees with its MBT orientation, and refer to the arc as nonconformable otherwise.

The master basis tree is represented by the following node functions.

1. PRED
   The values of the function are defined as follows:
   $PRED[i]$ = the predecessor of node i in MBT .
   For convenience $PRED[0] = -1$.

2. THREAD
   The function defines a connecting link (thread) which passes through each node exactly once. If i is a node on the thread, then $THREAD[i]$ is the next one. The alternation of the nodes on the thread is defined by using the preorder method of tree passage.

3. RETHREAD
   It is a pointer which points in the reverse order of the thread, i.e., if $THREAD[i] = j$ then $RETHREAD[j] = i$.

4. DEPTH
   The value $DEPTH[i]$ specifies the number of arcs in the predecessor path of node i to the master root.

5. LAST
   The value $LAST[i]$ specifies the node in the subtree $T(i)$ that is the last node of this subtree in THREAD order.

6. CONF
   Each node i in MBT represents the predecessor arc of the node. If the arc is conformable then $CONF[i] = +1$, otherwise $CONF[i] = -1$.

Let $P = \begin{pmatrix} P_1 \\ P_2 \end{pmatrix}$ denote the column vector selected to enter the basis matrix (P_1 specifies the part of P associated with B_{11} and P_2 the part associated with B_{21}). Similarly $\alpha = \begin{pmatrix} \alpha_{B1} \\ \alpha_{B2} \end{pmatrix}$ denotes the representation of P in terms of B.

We have $\alpha = B^{-1}P$ and hence using the partitioning formula for B^{-1} we obtain the following system of equations

$$\alpha_{B2} = V^{-1}(-B_{21}B_{11}^{-1}P_1 + P_2)$$

$$\alpha_{B1} = B_{11}^{-1}(P1 - B_{12}\alpha_{B2})$$

Suppose that the matrix $D = V^{-1}$ (i.e., the right down corner part of the matrix B^{-1}) is attained in the explicit form. Thus, the multiplication by the matrix in the former formula may be simply performed. Both the formulas include a multiplication $x = B_{11}^{-1}G$ with some vector G. This multiplication is equivalent to solving an upper triangular system $\tilde{B}_{11}\tilde{x} = \tilde{G}$, where the matrix $\tilde{B}_{11}$ consists of the rows and columns of B_{11} ordered according to the corresponding nodes and arcs on the THREAD line of MBT.

Each column of $\tilde{B}_{11}$ has at most two nonzero elements. One of them is located at the diagonal and corresponds to a node v while the second one (if exist) is located above the diagonal and corresponds to the predecessor of v. Hence, if the THREAD line is passed backward and the node v is came across then the value of the variable represented by v is computed and simultaneously the value of the variable represented by the predecessor of v is modified. Thus a single pass through the master basis tree along the RETHREAD line is sufficient for computing the x solution. The cost of such a procedure is proportional to the number of nodes in MBT.

Let $c_B = (c_{B1}, c_{B2})$ denote the vector of basis cost coefficients. The dual vector $w = (w_1, w_2) = c_B B^{-1}$ is needed at the pricing step of the simplex method and may be computed as follows:

$$w_2 = (c_{B2} - c_{B1}B_{11}^{-1}B_{12})V^{-1}$$

$$w_1 = (c_{B1} - w_2 B_{21})B_{11}^{-1}$$

The multiplication by the matrix V^{-1} may be directly computed since the matrix is assumed to be kept in the explicit form. Further, both the last formulas include multiplications of the form $w = HB_{11}^{-1}$ which can be effectively executed using the master basis tree structure for B_{11}, similarly as while computing the primal solution x.

Consider a single step of the simplex method. When the incoming and outgoing variables are chosen then the whole basis representation has to be changed and adjusted to the new situation. Thus, the problem arises how to change in a single simplex iteration the matrix D and the functions describing the master basis tree.

Let x_s and x_r denote the incoming and outgoing variables, respectively, and let x_t be the so-called transfer variable that belongs to x_{B2} and replaces x_r in x_{B1} , if it is possible.

At each iteration, the variables can alter by the transitions:

- Incoming variable x_s : $x_N \rightarrow x_{B1}$ or x_{B2}
- Outgoing variable x_r : x_{B1} or $x_{B2} \rightarrow x_N$
- Transfer variable x_t : $x_{B2} \rightarrow x_{B1}$, or no change
- Transfer ER nodes : $x_{B1} \rightarrow x_{B2}$ (one ER more),
  or $x_{B2} \rightarrow x_{B1}$ (one ER less), or no change.

If an arc is added to the master basis tree then a loop is closed. In order to have a tree in the next iteration also, the loop must be cut and exactly one arc from the loop must be deleted. It is the fundamental exchange rule for the master basis tree.

At each iteration the matrix D is transformed by elimination using a given pivot row. The following cases appear when the elimination is performed:

- the pivot row is within the rows of D;
- the pivot row is outside of D;
- a row and a column of D are dropped;
- a new row and a new column are added to D;
- a column (row) of D is replaced by another column (row) from outside of D.

Combining the elimination cases with the transition rules for the incoming, outgoing and transfer variables we get seven types of basis exchange steps. When x_{B1} is maximal relative to x_{B2}, exactly one of the seven types of basis exchange steps will occur and their updating prescriptions will maintain x_{B1} maximal.

The main features of the discussed approach are cheap multiplication algorithms with basis inverse, accelerated labelling algorithms for modifying the master basis tree in an efficient manner and a compact form of the basis inverse occupying a small memory space only.

7 Concluding Remarks

Initial experiences with the DINAS system on small testing examples confirm appropriateness of the used methodology for solving multiobjective transshipment problems with facility location. The interactive scheme is very easy to understand and it provides the DM with compressed the most important characteristics of generated efficient solutions. Moreover, the DM controls the system with unsophisticated parameters: aspiration and reservation levels. In effect, one easily reaches a satisfactory solution in a few interactive steps.

On the other hand, we have noticed that introducing of multiple objectives into the transshipment problem with facility location transformed this easy discrete problem into a complex one. Namely, it has been proved that the single-objective problem connected with minimization of the achievement function is far more complex than the original single-objective problems connected with minimization of several objective functions. The original single-objective problem is solved with the branch and bound method after examination only a few number of subproblems while minimization of the achievement function requires to analyse many branches of the tree. Thus for solving large real-life problems, rather a more advanced hardware than the standard IBM-PC XT should be used.

8 References

Glover, F., Klingman, D. (1981). The simplex SON method for LP/embedded network problems. *Mathematical Programming Study* 15, pp. 148-176.

Glover, F., Klingman, D. (1985). Basis exchange characterization for the simplex SON algorithm for LP/embedded networks. *Mathematical Programming Study* 24, pp. 141-157.

Grauer, M., Lewandowski, A., Wierzbicki, A. (1984). DIDAS — theory, implementation and experiences. In M. Grauer, A.P. Wierzbicki (eds), Interactive Decision Analysis. Springer, Berlin 1984.

Ogryczak, W., Studzinski, K., Zorychta, K. (1987). A solver for the transshipment problem with facility location. In A. Lewandowski and A. Wierzbicki (Eds.), Theory, Software and Testing Examples for Decision Support Systems. IIASA, Laxenburg.

Orchard-Hays, W. (1968). Advanced Linear-Programming Techniques. McGraw-Hill, New York.

Schrage, L. (1975). Implicit representation of variable upper bounds in linear programming. *Mathematical Programming Study* 4, pp. 118-132.

Todd, M.J. (1982). An implementation of the simplex method for linear programming problems with variable upper bounds. *Mathematical Programming* 23, pp. 34-49.

Wierzbicki, A.P. (1982). A mathematical basis for satisficing decision making. *Math. Modelling* 3, pp. 391-405.

Wierzbicki, A.P. (1986). On the completeness and constructiveness of parametric characterizations to vector optimization problems. *OR Spektrum* 8, pp. 73-87.

Solving Multiobjective Distribution–Location Problems with the DINAS System

Wlodzimierz Ogryczak, Krzysztof Studzinski,

Krystian Zorychta

Institute of Informatics, Warsaw University.

Abstract

DINAS is a decision support system which enables the solution of various multiobjective transshipment problems with facility location using IBM–PC XT/AT or compatibles. DINAS is prepared as a menu–driven and easy in usage system equipped with a special network editor which reduces to minimum effort associated with input a real–life problem. To illustrate the interactive procedure and the system capabilities we present in this paper using of DINAS to analyse a small testing example. As the test problem we use an artificial part of the real–life model connected with the health service districts reorganization.

1 Introduction

The distribution–location type problems belong to the class of most significant real–life decision problems based on mathematical programming. They are usually formalized as the so–called transshipment problems with facility location. In this paper we show how such multiobjective problems can be solved using our decision support system DINAS (see previous paper).

A network model of the transshipment problem with facility location consists of nodes connected by a set of direct flow arcs. The set of nodes is partitioned into two subsets: the set of fixed nodes and the set of potential nodes. The fixed nodes represent "fixed points" of the transportation network, i.e., points which cannot be changed whereas the potential nodes are introduced to represent possible locations of new points in the network. Some groups of the potential nodes represent different versions of the same facility to be located (e.g., different sizes of a warehouse etc.). For this reason, potential nodes are organized in the so–called selections, i.e., sets of nodes with the multiple choice requirement. Each selection is defined by the list of included potential nodes as well as by a lower and upper number of nodes which have to be selected (located).

A homogeneous good is distributed along the arcs among the nodes. Each fixed node is characterized by two quantities: supply and demand on the good, but for mathematical statement of the problem only the difference supply–demand (the so-called balance) is used. Each potential node is characterized by a capacity which bounds maximal flow of the good through the node. The capacities are also given for all the arcs but not for the fixed nodes.

A few linear objective functions are considered in the problem. The objective functions are introduced into the model by given coefficients associated with several arcs and potential nodes. They will be called cost coefficients independently of their real character. The cost coefficients for potential nodes are, however, understood in a different way than for arcs. The cost coefficient connected to an arc is treated as the unit cost of the flow along the arc whereas the cost coefficient connected to a potential node is considered as the fixed cost associated with activity (locating) of the node rather than as the unit cost.

Summarizing, the following groups of input data define the transshipment problem under consideration:

- objectives,
- fixed nodes with their balances,
- potential nodes with their capacities and (fixed) cost coefficients,
- selections with their lower and upper limits on number of active potential nodes,
- arcs with their capacities and cost coefficients.

In the DINAS system we placed two restrictions on the network structure:

- there is no arc which directly connects two potential nodes;
- each potential node belongs to at most two selections.

The first restriction does not imply any loss of generality since each of two potential nodes can be separated by an artificial fixed node, if necessary. The second requirement is not very strong since in practical models usually there are no potential nodes belonging to more than two selections.

The problem is to determine the number and locations of active potential nodes and to find the good flows (along arcs) so as to satisfy the balance and capacity restrictions and, simultaneously, optimize the given objective functions. A mathematical model of the problem is described in details in the previous paper of this volume.

DINAS enables a solution to the above problems using an IBM–PC XT/AT or compatibles. It requires 640K RAM and a hard disk or at least one floppy disk. DINAS can process problems consisted of:

- up to seven objective functions,
- a transportation network with up to one hundred of nodes and a few hundreds of arcs,

- up to fifteen potential locations.

DINAS consists of three programs prepared in the C programming language:

- an interactive procedure for efficient solutions generation,
- a solver for single–objective problems,
- a network editor for input data and results examination.

For handling multiple objectives Dinas utilizes an extension of the reference point approach proposed by Wierzbicki (1982). The basic concept of the interactive scheme is as follows:

- the DM works with the system in an interactive way so that he can change his aspiration and reservation levels in any direction;
- after editing the aspiration and reservation levels, the system computes a new efficient solution by solving a corresponding single–objective problem;
- each computed efficient solution is put into a special solution base and presented to the DM as the current solution in the form of tables and bars which allow him to analyse performances of the current solution in comparison with the previous solutions.

A special TRANSLOC solver has been prepared to provide the multiobjective analysis procedure with solutions to single–objective problems. The solver is hidden from the user but it is the most important part of the DINAS system. It is a numerical kernel of the system which generates efficient solutions. The concept of TRANSLOC is based on the branch and bound scheme with a pioneering implementation of the simplex special ordered network (SON) algorithm proposed by Glover and Klingman (1981) with implicit representation of the simple and variable upper bounds (VUB & SUB) suggested by Schrage (1975). The mathematical background of the TRANSLOC solver was given in details by Ogryczak et al. (1987).

DINAS is equipped with the built–in network editor EDINET. It is a full–screen editor specifically designed for input and edit data of the network model of the transshipment problems with facility location . The essence of the EDINET concept is a dynamic movement from some current node to its neighbouring nodes, and vice versa, according to the network structure. The input data are inserted by a special mechanism of windows while visiting several nodes. The principles of using the editor are presented in Section 4.

In this paper an example of problem of health service districts reorganization is considered. Such problems connected with reorganization of the primary health service in a district of Warsaw were successfully solved with the MPSX/370 package by Ogryczak and Malczewski (1988). Now such an analysis connected with location of new hospitals in Warsaw macroregion using the DINAS system on an IBM–PC AT microcomputer is prepared. To illustrate the interactive procedure and the system capabilities we present in details using of DINAS to analyse a test problem constructed as a small artificial part of this real–life model.

2 The problem

The problem of health service districts reorganization connected with location of new health–care centers can be formulated as follows. The region under consideration is assumed to consist of some number of geographically defined subareas or census blocks with known distribution of the population. A number of health–care centers is available in the region but their capabilities to offering health services is not sufficient. Therefore some new facilities are located. The problem depends on determination of the locations and capacities of some new centers as well as on assignment of individuals to the centers (new and old). The proposed solution should be optimal with respect to a few objective functions and simultaneously it must be accepted by the competent decision maker.

To set the stage, we consider as a region a part of city as it is shown in Fig. 1. The five major highways divide the region into 12 subareas. For each of these areas the demand on health–care services is identified in thousands of visits per year. These quantities are included in Table 1.

Area	*Demand*
Ribes	24.5
Larix	25.0
Robur	21.0
Arnika	20.5
Rumex	19.0
Pinus	20.0
Acer	16.0
Bobrek	22.0
Picea	15.0
Litwor	20.5
Betula	13.0
Erica	23.5

Table 1: Demands on health services

Within the region there are two health–care centers offering services: Pond and Hill. They can offer 100 and 90 thousands of visits per year, respectively. Thus the total supply of services amounts 190 while the total demand on services in the region is 240. Therefore some new health–care centers should be located within the region.

There are considered four potential locations for the new centers: Ice, Fiord, Bush and Oasis. The locations are divided into two subsets associated with the corresponding two subregions:

$$North = \{Ice, Fiord\},$$

$$South = \{Bush, Oasis\}.$$

The distance between two potential locations in the same subregion are relatively small whereas each of them can meet the demands on health services. Therefore the locations belonging to the same subregion are considered as exclusive alternatives, i.e., no more than one location from the subregion can be used. Moreover, different designed capac-

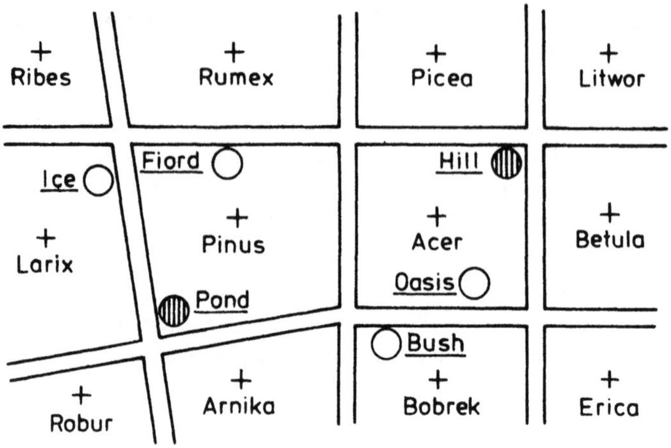

Figure 1: The region under consideration

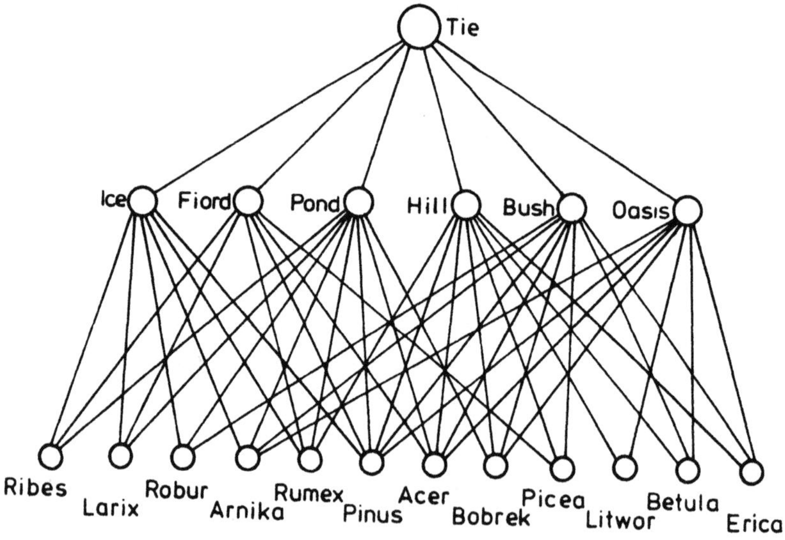

Figure 2: A scheme of the network

ities of health centers are associated with several locations. Table 2 lists capacities of the designed potential health–care centers.

Location	*Capacity*	*Subregion*
Ice	50	North
Fiord	60	North
Bush	50	South
Oasis	60	South

Table 2: Potential health–care centers

One must decide which potential health–care centers have to be built so as to meet the total demand on health services. The decision should be optimal with respect to the following criteria:

- minimization of the average distance per visit;
- maximization of the overall proximity to centers;
- minimization of the investment cost;
- maximization of the population satisfaction.

The first two criteria are connected with distances between health–care centers and areas assigned to them. Taking into account the urban morphology and the transportation network, it was accepted that the city–block metric was the best approximation to real distances. Therefore we define the distance between an individual and the health center as the rectangular distance between the centre of the corresponding area and the location of the health–care center. Certain connections between the areas and the health centers are eliminated as unacceptable due to too long distances or other troubles with transport. The distances between several areas and all the health centers are given in Table 3. The unacceptable connections are denoted by putting asterisks ($\star$) as a distance.

The overall proximity to the health care services is defined as a sum of all the individual proximity coefficients. The individual proximity is assumed to be inversely proportional to square of the distance to the health–care center. More precisely, the individual proximity coefficients are defined according to the following formula (compare Abernathy and Hershey, 1972):

$$p_{ac} = 1/(d_{ac} + \epsilon)^2$$

where d_{ac} denotes the distance between the corresponding area a and the health–care center c, and ϵ is an arbitrarily small positive number. The proximity coefficients for the whole region under consideration are given in Table 4.

The investment cost and the population satisfaction level are assumed to be a sum of fixed costs and a sum of fixed satisfaction levels connected with several possible locations, respectively. In our example the fixed coefficients take values given in Table 5.

	Pond	*Hill*	*Ice*	*Fiord*	*Bush*	*Oasis*
Ribes	4.14	⋆⋆⋆	2.34	3.03	⋆⋆⋆	⋆⋆⋆
Larix	2.61	⋆⋆⋆	1.35	3.63	⋆⋆⋆	⋆⋆⋆
Robur	2.19	⋆⋆⋆	3.96	⋆⋆⋆	4.38	⋆⋆⋆
Arnika	1.74	⋆⋆⋆	4.08	⋆⋆⋆	2.70	3.51
Rumex	4.53	4.32	2.85	1.35	⋆⋆⋆	⋆⋆⋆
Pinus	2.28	4.14	1.80	0.81	2.94	4.14
Acer	4.02	1.95	⋆⋆⋆	3.27	1.77	1.56
Bobrek	3.84	4.17	⋆⋆⋆	⋆⋆⋆	1.35	1.65
Picea	⋆⋆⋆	2.01	⋆⋆⋆	3.30	4.71	⋆⋆⋆
Litwor	⋆⋆⋆	2.22	⋆⋆⋆	⋆⋆⋆	⋆⋆⋆	4.65
Betula	⋆⋆⋆	1.95	⋆⋆⋆	⋆⋆⋆	4.02	3.06
Erica	⋆⋆⋆	3.72	⋆⋆⋆	⋆⋆⋆	3.42	2.46

Table 3: Distance coefficients

	Pond	*Hill*	*Ice*	*Fiord*	*Bush*	*Oasis*
Ribes	5.83	⋆⋆⋆	18.26	10.89	⋆⋆⋆	⋆⋆⋆
Larix	14.68	⋆⋆⋆	54.87	7.59	⋆⋆⋆	⋆⋆⋆
Robur	20.85	⋆⋆⋆	6.38	⋆⋆⋆	5.21	⋆⋆⋆
Arnika	33.03	⋆⋆⋆	6.01	⋆⋆⋆	13.72	8.12
Rumex	4.87	5.36	12.31	54.87	⋆⋆⋆	⋆⋆⋆
Pinus	19.24	5.83	30.86	152.42	11.57	5.83
Acer	6.19	26.30	⋆⋆⋆	9.35	31.92	41.09
Bobrek	6.78	5.75	⋆⋆⋆	⋆⋆⋆	54.87	36.73
Picea	⋆⋆⋆	24.75	⋆⋆⋆	9.18	4.51	⋆⋆⋆
Litwor	⋆⋆⋆	20.29	⋆⋆⋆	⋆⋆⋆	⋆⋆⋆	4.62
Betula	⋆⋆⋆	26.30	⋆⋆⋆	⋆⋆⋆	6.19	10.68
Erica	⋆⋆⋆	7.23	⋆⋆⋆	⋆⋆⋆	8.55	16.52

Table 4: Proximity coefficients

In the next section we show how the above problem can be formulated as a multiobjective transshipment problem with facility location, i.e., in the form which can be processed by the DINAS system.

3 The network model

The problem of health service districts reorganization connected with location of new health–care centers stated in the previous section can be easy formulated as a multiobjective transshipment problem with facility location. The areas and existing health–care centers are, certainly, fixed nodes of the network under consideration. Similarly, all the potential locations of new health centers are treated as potential nodes. Arcs represent all the possible assignments of patients to the health–care centers, i.e., arcs are associated with all the nonempty cells in Table 3 or 4. A flow along the arc from a center c to an area a expresses a number of visits in the area a serviced by the center c. In order to

	Ice	*Fiord*	*Bush*	*Oasis*
Investment	200	212	186	201
Satisfaction	176	87	100	192

Table 5: Investment and satisfaction coefficients

balance the problem in terms of supply and demand an artificial node Tie with supply equal to the overall demand is introduced. There are also defined additional arcs from the artificial node to each health-care center (existing or potential). Capacity of the existing health-care centers (Pond and Hill) are then represented as capacities of the arcs from Tie to the corresponding fixed nodes. A scheme of the network is presented in Fig. 2.

Now we can define several groups of data of the multiobjective transshipment problem with facility location. As we have mentioned in Section 1 the fixed node is characterized only by the balance, i.e., difference between the corresponding supply and demand. Table 6 lists supplies, demands and balances for all the fixed nodes in our model. Note that the sum of supplies is equal to the sum of demands and thereby the sum of balances is equal to zero.

Node	*Supply*	*Demand*	*Balance*
Ribes	0	24.5	-24.5
Larix	0	25.0	-25.0
Robur	0	21.0	-21.0
Arnika	0	20.5	-20.5
Rumex	0	19.0	-19.0
Pinus	0	20.0	-20.0
Acer	0	16.0	-16.0
Bobrek	0	22.0	-22.0
Picea	0	15.0	-15.0
Litwor	0	20.5	-20.5
Betula	0	13.0	-13.0
Erica	0	23.5	-23.5
Pond	0	0	0
Hill	0	0	0
Tie	240	0	240

Table 6: Fixed nodes

In the transshipment problem with facility location objective functions are considered as sums of linear functions of flows along several arcs and fixed costs connected with the used locations. In our model objective functions can be divided into two groups. Functions Investment (cost) and Satisfaction (level) are independent of the assignment decisions and thereby they have not coefficients connected with flows along arcs (i.e., these coefficients are equal to 0). On the other hand, functions (average) Distance and (overall) Proximity depend only on assignment decisions and they have not contain fixed terms connected with locational decisions. Fixed coefficients of the functions Investment and Satisfaction can be directly taken from Table 5. Similarly, the linear coefficients of the function Proximity are given in Table 4. The linear coefficients of the function Distance are defined as quotients of the corresponding distances by the sum of demands, i.e., as $d_{ac}/240$.

There are four potential nodes which represent the potential locations of the health-care centers, i.e., Ice, Fiord, Bush, Oasis. The data connected with the potential nodes are listed in Table 7. Here and thereafter the objective functions are denoted by abbreviations of the corresponding names.

Node	*Capacity*	*Fixed costs*			
		invest	*satisf*	*dist*	*prox*
Ice	50	200	176	0	0
Fiord	60	212	87	0	0
Bush	50	186	100	0	0
Oasis	60	201	192	0	0

Table 7: Potential nodes

As we have already mentioned the locations belonging to the same subregion are considered as exclusive alternatives, i.e., no more than one location from the subregion can be used. Therefore we introduce into the network model selections which represent such a type of requirements. In our model there are two selections associated with to subregions: North and South. Both the selections have the lower numbers equal to 0 and the upper numbers equal to 1. It guarantees that at most one potential node in each selection is active. The complete data connected with selections are given in Table 8.

Selection	*Alternative nodes*	*Lower number*	*Upper number*
North	Ice, Fiord	0	1
South	Bush, Oasis	0	1

Table 8: Selections

The last group of data is connected with the arcs. The arcs are characterized by their capacities and objective functions coefficients. The cost coefficients have been already discussed while consideration of the objective functions. Capacities of the arcs from the artificial node Tie to the nodes representing health–care centers (Pond, Hill, Ice, Fiord, Bush, Oasis) express capacities of the corresponding centers. The arcs connecting the nodes representing health–care centers with the nodes representing the areas have essentially unlimited capacities. However, in practice, flows along these arcs are also bounded by capacities of the corresponding health–care centers and we use them as arcs capacities. All the data connected with arcs are listed in Table 9.

From	*To*	*Capacity*	*invest*	*satisf*	*dist*	*prox*
Tie	Pond	100	0	0	0	0.
Tie	Hill	90	0	0	0	0.
Tie	Ice	50	0	0	0	0.
Tie	Fiord	60	0	0	0	0.
Tie	Bush	50	0	0	0	0.
Tie	Oasis	60	0	0	0	0.
Pond	Ribes	100	0	0	.01725	5.83
Pond	Larix	100	0	0	.010875	14.68
Pond	Robur	100	0	0	.009125	20.85
Pond	Arnika	100	0	0	.00725	33.03
Pond	Rumex	100	0	0	.018875	4.87
Pond	Pinus	100	0	0	.0095	19.24
Pond	Acer	100	0	0	.01675	6.19
Pond	Bobrek	100	0	0	.016	6.78
Hill	Rumex	90	0	0	.018	5.36
Hill	Pinus	90	0	0	.01725	5.83
Hill	Acer	90	0	0	.008125	26.30
Hill	Bobrek	90	0	0	.017375	5.75
Hill	Picea	90	0	0	.008375	24.75
Hill	Litwor	90	0	0	.00925	20.29
Hill	Betula	90	0	0	.008125	26.30
Hill	Erica	90	0	0	.0155	7.23
Ice	Ribes	50	0	0	.00975	18.26
Ice	Larix	50	0	0	.005625	54.87
Ice	Robur	50	0	0	.0165	6.38
Ice	Arnika	50	0	0	.017	6.01
Ice	Rumex	50	0	0	.011875	12.31
Ice	Pinus	50	0	0	.0075	30.86
Fiord	Ribes	60	0	0	.012625	10.89
Fiord	Larix	60	0	0	.015125	7.59
Fiord	Rumex	60	0	0	.005625	54.87
Fiord	Pinus	60	0	0	.003375	152.42
Fiord	Acer	60	0	0	.013625	9.35
Fiord	Picea	60	0	0	.013750	9.18
Bush	Robur	50	0	0	.01825	5.21
Bush	Arnika	50	0	0	.01125	13.72
Bush	Pinus	50	0	0	.01225	11.57
Bush	Acer	50	0	0	.007375	31.92
Bush	Bobrek	50	0	0	.005625	54.87
Bush	Picea	50	0	0	.019625	4.51
Bush	Betula	50	0	0	.01675	6.19
Bush	Erica	50	0	0	.01425	8.55
Oasis	Arnika	60	0	0	.014625	8.12
Oasis	Pinus	60	0	0	.01725	5.83
Oasis	Acer	60	0	0	.0065	41.09
Oasis	Bobrek	60	0	0	.006875	36.73
Oasis	Litwor	60	0	0	.019375	4.62
Oasis	Betula	60	0	0	.01275	10.68
Oasis	Erica	60	0	0	.01025	16.52

Table 9: Arcs

4 Input of the problem

As we have already mentioned DINAS is armed with the built–in network editor EDINET. EDINET is a full–screen editor specifically designed for input and edit the data of the problem to be analysed. The DINAS interactive procedure works with a special file containing whole information defining the problem and the EDINET editor enables to prepare this file. The main data of the problem can be divided into two groups:

- logical data defining the structure of a transportation network (e.g., nodes, arcs, selections);
- numerical data describing the nodes and arcs of the network (e.g., balances, capacities, coefficients of the objective functions).

The general concept of EDINET is to edit the data while defining the logical structure of the network. More precisely, the essence of the EDINET concept is a dynamic movement from some current node to its neighbouring nodes, and vice versa, according to the network structure. The input data are inserted by a special mechanism of windows, while visiting several nodes. At any time only one of the windows representing different kinds of the data is active. The corresponding part of the data can be then inserted. While working with the editor the DM activates several windows.

The editor is menu–driven and its main menu branches into the three available groups of operations: FILE, PRINT NETWORK, EDIT NETWORK. EDIT NETWORK is the main branch of the menu. It contains such operations as LIST NODES, NETWORK, SELECTIONS and OBJECTIVES.

The problem editing usually starts by using the LIST NODES command. The corresponding window consists of all the nodes in the alphabetic order, that have been inserted so far. While starting with a new problem the list is, obviously, empty. The DM can move the pointer along the list to select a node, or simply type a name of a new node. Then the main screen of the editing process appears. The screen contains the following windows: CURRENT NODE, NODE FROM and NODE TO. The node selected from the list (or typed) is presented as the current node and the corresponding CURRENT NODE window is active. The screen connected to our health service problem is shown in Fig. 3. The potential node Bush is there used as the current node. The CURRENT NODE window contains the data describing the node such as the capacity, the corresponding selection and the objective coefficients.

The DM can edit, correct or examine the data connected with the current node, or activate the NODE FROM or NODE TO window. The NODE FROM window contains names of the nodes that precede the current node in the network and names of the corresponding arcs. Similarly, the NODE TO window contains names of the nodes and arcs which directly succeed the current node in the network. If the NODE FROM or NODE TO window is activated then the DM can select one of the nodes contained in the window or type a new node name.

Now, similarly as in the case of the current node, the window corresponding to the selected (or typed) node appears and the DM can edit, correct or examine the data connected to the node.

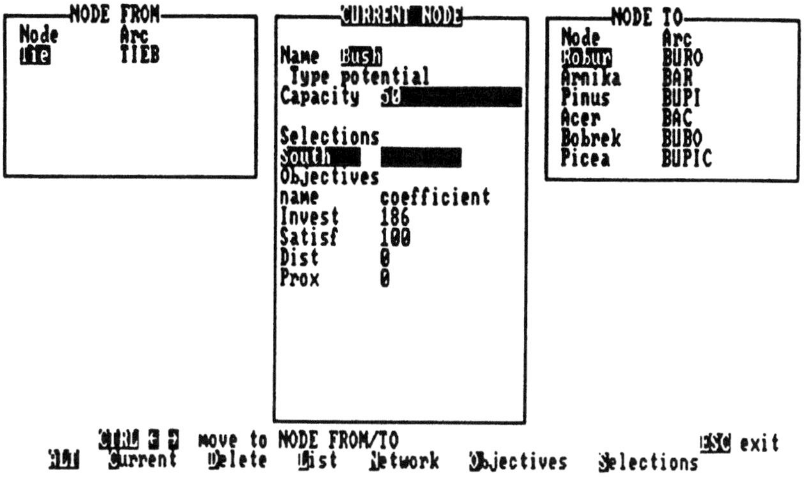

Figure 3: CURRENT NODE, NODE FROM and NODE TO windows

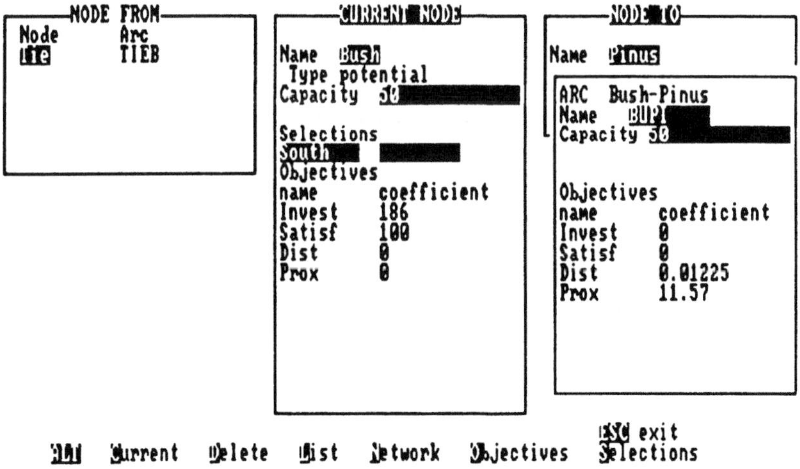

Figure 4: ARC window

After the node definition or examination the DM can activate the ARC window associated with this node. Then the data of the arc which connects the selected node to the current node, can be also edited, corrected or examined. The arc definition is illustrated in Fig. 4. The Pinus node is there selected in the NODE TO window. Hence, the ARC window contains the information connected to the arc called BUPI which starts at Bush and ends at Pinus.

Each of the nodes contained in the NODE FROM or NODE TO window can be changed into the current node. After such an operation the selected node is put into the CURRENT NODE window. The NODE FROM and NODE TO windows are then modified according to the network structure.

Independently of the list of nodes, a graphic scheme of the network is available at any time. For instance, a part of the scheme for our health service problem is presented in Fig. 5. One can examine the network while moving along the scheme. Each visited node can be selected as the current node to restart the editing process.

Some special windows are associated with selections and objectives. The SELECTION window lists the nodes belonging to several selection. The SELECTION window in Fig. 6 contains two selections: North and South, defined in our test problem. The additional BOUNDS window enables editing of the lower and upper bounds on a number of potential nodes which can be used in the selection.

Similarly, the OBJECTIVES window allows us to define objective functions by putting their names and types of optimization (min or max). If an objective is defined then the information connected with this objective is automatically inserted into all the potential node and arc windows.

The other branches of the menu contain some technical operations on the network file. There are available commands which enable to save the edited network (SAVE), to restore a previously edited network for further modifications (LOAD), or to print a compressed description of the network (PRINT NETWORK).

5 Introductory multiobjective analysis

The interactive analysis of the multiobjective problem can be performed with DINAS by the DM who is not familiar with neither computer techniques nor mathematical programming. DINAS is a menu-driven system with very simple commands. Operations available in the DINAS interactive procedure are partitioned into three groups and corresponding three branches of the main menu (see Table 10): PROCESS, SOLUTION and ANALYSIS.

The PROCESS branch contains basic operations connected with processing the multiobjective problem and generation of several efficient solutions. There are included problem definition operations such as calling the EDINET editor for input or modification of the problem (PROBLEM) and converting of the edited problem with error checking (CONVERT). Further, in this branch the basic optimization operations are available: computation of the pay-off matrix with the utopia and nadir vectors (PAY-OFF) and generation of efficient solutions depending on the edited aspiration and reservation levels (EFFICIENT). As the last command in this branch is placed the QUIT

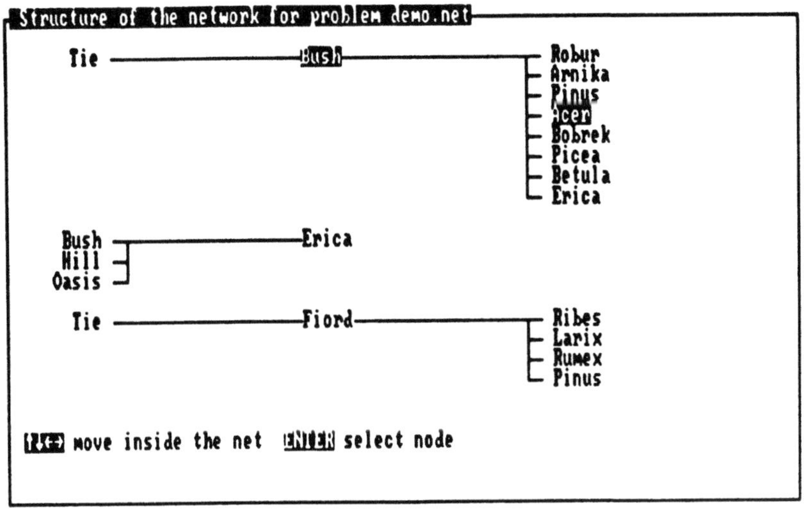

Figure 5: NETWORK window

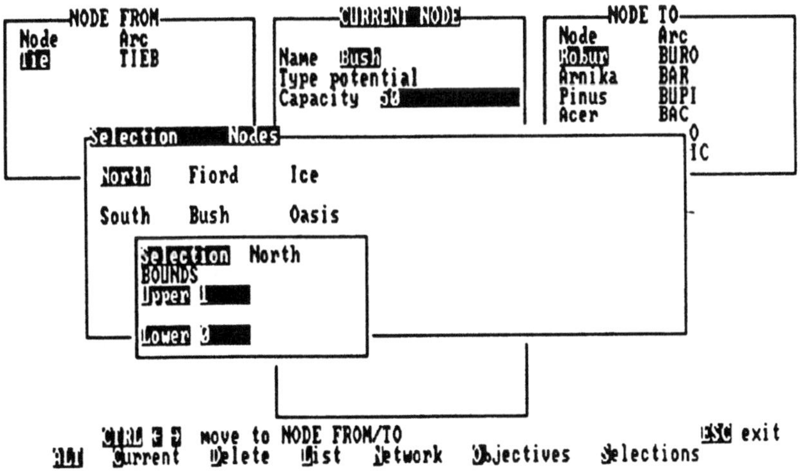

Figure 6: SELECTION window

Process	*Solution*	*Analysis*
Problem	Summary	Compare
Convert	Browse	Previous
Pay–Off	Save	Next
Efficient	Delete	Last
Quit		Restore

Table 10: The DINAS main menu

operation which allows the DM to finish work with the system.

The SOLUTION branch contains additional operations connected with the current solution. The DM can examine in details the current solution using the network editor (BROWSE) or analyse only short characteristics such as objective values and selected locations (SUMMARY). Values of the objective functions are presented in three ways: as a standard table, as bars in the aspiration/reservation scale and as bars in the utopia/nadir scale. The bars show percentage level of each objective value with respect to the corresponding scale. The DM may also print the current solution (BROWSE) or save it for using in next runs of the system with the same problem (SAVE). There is also available a special command to delete the current solution from the solution base if the DM finds it as quite useless (DELETE).

The ANALYSIS branch collects commands connected with operations on the solution base. The main command COMPARE allows the DM to perform comparison of all the efficient solutions from the solution base or of some subset of them. In the comparison only the short characteristics of the solutions are used, i.e., objective values in the form of tables and bars as well as tables of selected locations. Moreover, some commands which allow the DM to select various efficient solutions from solution base as the current solution are included in this branch (PREVIOUS, NEXT and LAST). There exist also an opportunity to restore some (saved earlier) efficient solution to the solution base (RESTORE).

In this and next sections we present an outline of the basic multiobjective analysis performed on our test problem. We do not discuss all the capabilities of the system which can be used in such an analysis. More details of this analysis were described by Ogryczak et al. (1988a).

Having defined and converted the problem as the first step of the multiobjective analysis one must perform the PAY–OFF command. It executes optimization of each objective function separately. In effect, we get the so–called pay–off matrix presented in Table 11. The pay–off matrix is a well–known device in multiobjective programming. It gives values of all the objective functions (columns) obtained while solving several single–objective problems (rows) and thereby it helps to understand the conflicts between different objectives.

Execution of the PAY–OFF command provides also us with two reference vectors: the utopia vector and the nadir vector (see Table 12). The utopia vector represents the best values of each objective considered separately, and the nadir vector express the worst values of each objective noticed during optimization of another objective function.

Optimized function	*Objective values*			
	invest	*satisf*	*dist*	*prox*
invest	186	100	2.61	4976
satisf	401	368	2.17	6385
dist	413	279	2.03	8782
prox	398	187	2.12	8854

Table 11: Pay–off matrix

The utopia vector is, obviously, not attainable, i.e., there are no feasible solutions with such objective values.

	Objective values			
	invest	*satisf*	*dist*	*prox*
utopia	186	368	2.03	8854
nadir	413	100	2.61	4976

Table 12: Utopia and nadir vectors

While analysing Tables 11 and 12 we find out that the objective values vary significantly depending on selected optimization. Only for the average distance we notice the relative variation less than 30% whereas for the other objectives it even overstep 100%. Moreover, we recognize a strong conflict between the investment cost and all the other objectives. While minimizing the investment cost we get the worst values for all the other objectives. On the other hand, while optimizing another objective function we get doubled investment cost in comparison with its minimal value.

Coefficients of the nadir vector cannot be considered as the worst values of the objectives over the whole efficient (Pareto–optimal) set. They usually estimate these values but they express only the worst values of each objective noticed during optimization of another objective function. In further analysis we will show that these estimations can be sometimes overstep.

Due to the special regularization technique used while computation of the pay–off matrix (see Ogryczak et al., 1988) each generated single–objective optimal solution is also an efficient solution to the multiobjective problem. So, we have already available in the solution base four efficient solutions connected with several rows of the pay–off matrix. Using different commands of DINAS we can examine in details these solutions. In particular, we can recognize locations structure for several solutions. The first solution which minimizes the investment cost is based on only one new health–care center located at Bush. Each other solution use two new centers what explains their significantly higher investment costs. They are based on the following locations: Ice and Oasis, Fiord and Oasis, Bush and Fiord.

6 Interactive analysis

Having computed the utopia vector we can start the interactive search for a satisfying efficient solution. As we have already mentioned DINAS utilizes aspiration and reservation levels to control the interactive analysis. More precisely, the DM specifies acceptable values for several objectives as the aspiration levels and necessary values as the reservation levels. All the operations connected with editing the aspiration and reservation levels as well as with computation of a new efficient solution are included in the EFFICIENT command.

At the beginning of the interactive analysis we compute the so–called neutral solution. For this purpose we accept the utopia vector as the aspiration levels and the nadir vector as the reservation levels. In effect, we get the fifth efficient solution based on location two new health–care centers at Bush and at Ice. The investment cost of this solution is rather high (invest=386) whereas the other objectives get middling values (satisf=276, dist=2.26, prox=6457).

Apart from the solution connected with minimization of the investment cost all the other solution are based on location of two new health–care centers what implies a high investment cost. Therefore we try to find an efficient solution with small investment cost (one new center) and relatively good values of the other objectives. For this purpose we define the aspiration and reservation levels as it is given in Table 13.

	invest	*satisf*	*dist*	*prox*
aspiration	186	300	2.08	8500
reservation	250	200	2.50	7000

Table 13: Aspiration/reservation levels for Solution No. 6

In effect, we get the sixth efficient solution based on location of one new health–care center at Oasis. The investment cost is small (invest=201), the satisfaction level has middling value (satisf=192) while the average distance is very large (dist=2.58) and the overall proximity is even less than the corresponding coefficient of the nadir vector (prox=4933). The system automatically correct the nadir vector by putting the new worst value as the proper coefficient.

To avoid too small values of the overall proximity in the next solution we modify the reservation level for this objective putting 8000 as the new value. After repeating the computation we get the seventh efficient solution based on the sole new health–care center located at Ice. Due to the very convenient form of solution presentation in DINAS we can easy examine performances (in terms of objective values) of the new solution in comparison with the previous one. The overall proximity, the average distance and the investment cost are slightly better (prox=5287, dist=2.53 and invest=200) while the overall satisfaction level is a few percent worse (satisf=176).

After analysis of two last efficient solutions we make a supposition that it is necessary to relax requirements on the satisfaction level for making possibility to find an efficient solution with good values of the average distance and the overall proximity under small the investment cost. So, we change the reservation level associated with the function satisf on 100. The system confirms our supposition. We get the eighth efficient solution based on the sole new health–care center located at Fiord. The solution guarantees quite large overall proximity (prox=7691) and relatively small average distance (dist=2.38) under small investment cost (invest=212). On the other hand, the satisfaction level has a value even less than the corresponding coefficient of the nadir vector (satisf=87). Despite of the latter the solutions seems to be very interesting among the other efficient solutions based on location of a sole health–care center.

Further search for a satisfying efficient solution based on only one new health–care center have finished without success. Namely, for different values of the aspiration and reservation levels the same efficient solutions have been generated. So, to complete the analysis we try to examine another efficient solutions. For this purpose we relax requirements on the investment cost. Among others, while using the aspiration and reservation levels given in Table 14 we get the ninth efficient solution. It is based on the same location of new centers as the third solution (Fiord and Oasis) and thereby it gives the same investment cost (invest=413) and satisfaction level (satisf=279). However, the average distance and the overall proximity differs slightly (dist=2.04 and prox=8791).

	invest	*satisf*	*dist*	*prox*
aspiration	200	300	2.10	8800
reservation	400	200	2.50	8400

Table 14: Aspiration/reservation levels for Solution No. 9

Finally, we examine all the generated efficient solutions using special comparison tools available in DINAS. The solutions are listed in Tables 15 and 16. A careful analysis of these solutions leads us to the following conclusion. The investment cost cannot be regarded as a typical objective function since its values depend rather on the number of new health–care centers than on their locations. It only partitions all the efficient solutions into two groups: solutions based on a sole new health–care center and solutions based on location of two new centers. Therefore it is necessary to look for a good solution based on a sole new center which can be expanded to a better solution by adding the second new center. In our opinion, the first new health–care center should be located at Fiord (Solution 8). It is the only one efficient solution (based on a sole new center) which gives acceptable values of the average distance and the overall proximity (see Fig. 7). This solution gives also the worst value of the satisfaction level. However, further development of this solution by adding the new health–care center at Oasis (Solution 9) leads to a quite high value of the satisfaction level and makes further significant improvements with respect to the average distance and the overall proximity (see Fig. 8). Both the proposed solutions have the highest investment costs in the corresponding groups of solutions but variation of this objective among solutions of the same group is so small that it cannot be considered as a serious weakness.

Due to offering by DINAS easy way for modification the problem we can perform an additional analysis while changing some objective functions. While repeating the multiobjective analysis with omitted objective function invest we get the ninth solution

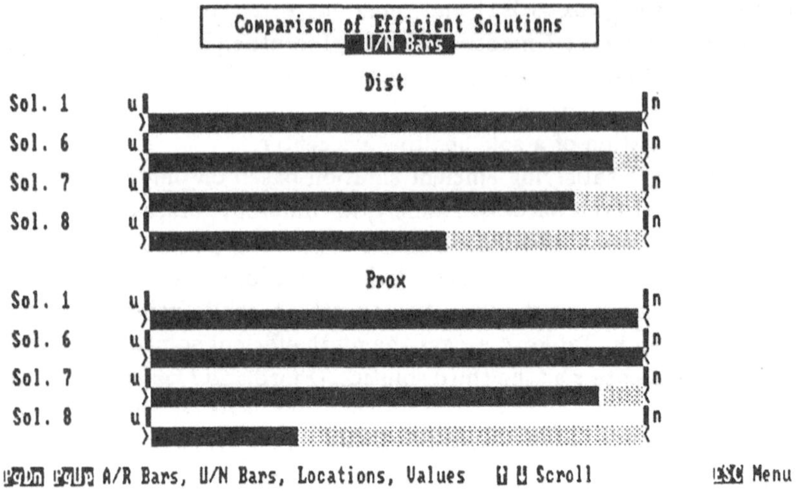

Figure 7: Utopia/nadir bars for selected solutions

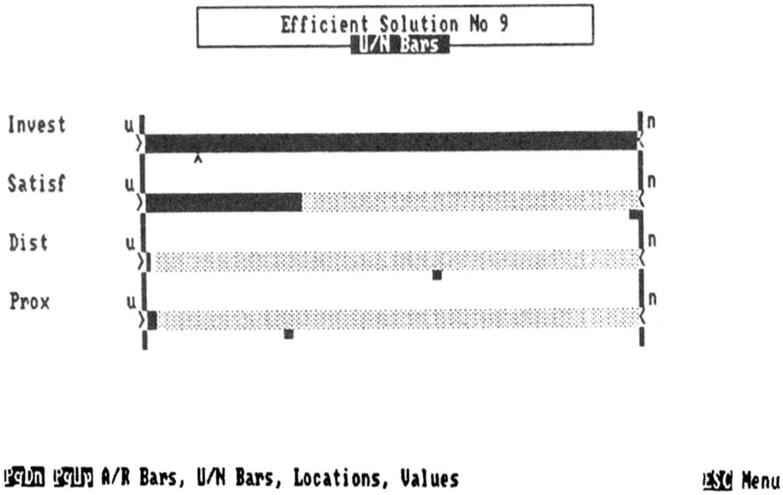

Figure 8: Utopia/nadir bars for the current solution

	invest	*satisf*	*dist*	*prox*
Solution 1	186	100	2.61	4976
Solution 2	401	368	2.17	6385
Solution 3	413	279	2.03	8782
Solution 4	398	187	2.12	8854
Solution 5	386	276	2.26	6457
Solution 6	201	192	2.58	4933
Solution 7	200	176	2.53	5287
Solution 8	212	87	2.38	7691
Solution 9	413	279	2.04	8791

Table 15: Efficient solutions — objective values

	Bush	*Fiord*	*Ice*	*Oasis*
Solution 1	yes	no	no	no
Solution 2	no	no	yes	yes
Solution 3	no	yes	no	yes
Solution 4	yes	yes	no	no
Solution 5	yes	no	yes	no
Solution 6	no	no	no	yes
Solution 7	no	no	yes	no
Solution 8	no	yes	no	no
Solution 9	no	yes	no	yes

Table 16: Efficient solutions — locations

as the neutral solution what confirms optimality of this solution with respect to good values of all the three objectives.

Using the BROWSE command we can examine in details the selected solutions with the EDINET editor. It turns out that in the eighth efficient solution the health–care center Hill is assigned to areas: Acer, Picea, Litwor, Betula and Erica. The health–care center Pond services areas: Bobrek, Arnika, Robur, Larix and a small part of Ribes. The new health–care center Fiord services only areas Pinus, Rumex and the main part of Ribes. Capacity of the new center Fiord is completely used whereas in the old centers we have noticed some small free capacities. It suggests that the old health–care centers have nonoptimal location with respect to the considered objective functions. The ninth efficient solution confirms this observation. The additional new health–care center at Oasis takes the area Acer and the main part of Erica from the region of Hill and the area Bobrek from the region of Pond. So, in this solution both the new health–care centers use the whole their capacities whereas the old centers use only 50–70% of their capacities. In effect, all the health–care centers have well balanced charges.

7 Concluding remarks

Initial experiences with the DINAS system on small and medium testing examples confirm appropriateness of the used methodology for solving multiobjective transshipment problems with facility location. The interactive scheme is very easy and supported by many analysis tools. So, a satisfactory solution can be usually reached in a few interactive steps.

As it has been showed in this paper application of DINAS is not limited to typical transshipment problems. DINAS can be successfully used to solve different distribution–location problems. The problem of health service reorganization connected with location of new health–care centers presented in the paper is only an example among many others real–life decision problems which can be solved with DINAS.

While solving with DINAS real–life problems on IBM–PC XT/AT microcomputers, the single–objective computations take, obviously, much more time than while using some standard optimization tools (like the MPSX/370 package) on a mainframe. However, our experiences with both these approaches allow us to suppose that DINAS, in general, will take much less time for performing of the whole multiobjective analysis.

8 References

Abernathy, W. J., Hershey, J. C. (1972). A spatial–allocation model for regional health–services planning. *Oper. Res.* 20, pp. 629–642.

Glover, F., Klingman, D. (1981). The simplex SON method for LP/embedded network problems. *Mathematical Programming Study* 15, pp. 148–176.

Ogryczak, W., Malczewski J. (1988). Health care districts planning by multiobjective analysis with the MPSX/370 package. *Archiwum Automatyki i Telemechaniki*, 32, pp.369–381.

Ogryczak, W., Studzinski, K., Zorychta, K. (1987). A solver for the transshipment problem with facility location. In A. Lewandowski and A. Wierzbicki (Eds.), Theory, Software and Testing Examples for Decision Support Systems. IIASA, Laxenburg.

Ogryczak, W., Studzinski, K., Zorychta, K. (1988a). Dynamic Interactive Network Analysis System DINAS: User Training Manual. Technical Report.

Schrage, L. (1975). Implicit representation of variable upper bounds in linear programming.*Mathematical Programming Study* 4, pp. 118–132.

Wierzbicki, A. P. (1982). A mathematical basis for satisficing decision making. *Math. Modelling* 3, pp. 391–405.

Towards Interactive Solutions in a Bargaining Problem

Piotr Bronisz, Lech Krus

Systems Research Institute, Polish Academy of Sciences, Warsaw,

Andrzej P. Wierzbicki

Institute of Automatic Control, Warsaw University of Technology.

Abstract

The paper deals with interactive arbitration processes in a bargaining problem. Principles of constructing such processes are discussed, and several solution concepts are considered, first in unicriterial and then in multicriterial case. The analysis is preceded by a review of the axiomatic basis of Nash and Raiffa solution concepts.

1 Introduction: The need of interactive bargaining procedures

The bargaining problem has a long and distinguished history of research. Most of attention, however, was given to normative axiomatic characterizations of cooperative solutions for the bargaining problem, under the assumption that players, even if they have multiple objectives, can be characterized by corresponding utility functions. There are several reasons for trying to relax these assumptions and for designing interactive bargaining procedures. These reasons include:

- The development of interactive decision support systems on modern computers that might be also used for bargaining and negotiation support;

- The wide use of gaming—as opposed to game theory—in support of learning about conflict situations that indicates the need of combining properly extended and relaxed game theoretical principles with practical gaming processes;

- Known reservations to the practical applicability of utility theory and, in particular, recently raised reservations to the universal validity of this theory as a basis for decision making in cross-cultural situations (see, for example, Grauer, Thompson and Wierzbicki, 1985) that imply the importance of interactive processes in decision support;

- Recent research results in deliberative, holistic decision making (see, for example, Dreyfus, 1985) that indicate the need of considering calculative, analytic means of decision analysis mainly as a support in *learning to make decisions* and thus again imply the importance of interactive processes of learning;

- Recent research results in evolutionary rationality (see, for example, Axelrod, 1985) that indicate the importance of an evolutionary development of cooperative strategies in most repetitive non-zero sum games and thus again imply the need for broadening normative approaches.

Thus, there is a need of developing interactive processes of bargaining, in particular for the case of multiple criteria of interest to each player. With all these reservations about and aims to broaden the scope of the normative, single-criteria bargaining theory, we start this paper precisely from the normative, axiomatic foundations and try to broaden them while attempting to preserve the abstract power of an axiomatic approach, by introducing other postulates or axioms that might be more adequate when constructing interactive processes of bargaining.

While there has been many attempts to construct interactive bargaining processes, we would like to express our debt to Howard Raiffa, whose concepts dominate in this paper, and to Gunther Fandel whose ideas (see Fandel, 1979) and direct cooperation (Fandel and Wierzbicki, 1985) motivated much of this paper.

2 The bargaining problem in terms of utility theory: problem formulation

We consider a finite set of players, $N = \{1, 2, \ldots, n\}$, where each player has preferences over the feasible outcomes which are represented by a cardinal (von Neumann and Morgenstern) utility function. A particular outcome of the game can be represented as a vector in n-dimensional Euclidean space, $\Re^n$, where the i-th component is the utility of the i-th player. A bargaining game is described by a pair (S, d), where $S \subset \Re^n$ is a set of all feasible outcomes (the outcome set, sometimes called the agreement set), and $d \in S$ is an outcome of the game already experienced by all players, called a status quo point or a disagreement point. Any outcome from S can be the result of the bargaining game, if it is specified by unanimous agreement of all the players. In the event that no unanimous agreement is reached, it is assumed that the disagreement point d is the result of the game. Following Nash (1950, 1953), Roth (1979b), we confine ourselves in Section 2-5 to bargaining games (S, d) satisfying the following conditions: S is a compact, convex subset of $\Re^n$, and there is at least one point x in S such that $x > d$ (i.e. $x_i > d_i$ for all $i \in N$). Let B denote the class of all such bargaining games.

A solution for the bargaining problem is a function $f : B \to \Re^n$ which assigns to each bargaining game (S, d) in B a point of S, denoted $f(S, d)$. When no confusion will result, the outcome $f(S, d)$ will sometimes be referred to as the solution of the bargaining game (S, d).

Some models presented in the literature assume that the utilities of all players are disposable, and enlarge the set of feasible outcomes S to the set

$$S^\star = \{ x \in \Re^n : y \le x \le z \text{ for some } y, z \in S \}$$

(see Nash, 1953, p.131 for justification of such an approach). Let $B^\star$ denote the class of all bargaining games $(S, d) \in B$ with disposable utility, i.e. satisfying $S = S^\star$. If a solution for the bargaining problem is defined on $B^\star$ and is strongly Pareto optimal (see Property 4 in further text) then it may be extended to the class B because strongly Pareto optimal points are unaffected by the transition from S to $S^\star$.

3 Nash and Raiffa axiomatic models of bargaining

In this section, we present two most important axiomatic models of bargaining known in the literature. These axiomatic models do not describe real bargaining situations which can occur during a particular game, they describe only some normative properties of the set of possible agreements for the class B of bargaining games. The axiomatic solutions for the bargaining problem are derived axiomatically, by specifying first desirable axiomatic properties and then the corresponding solution. For a more detailed description of axiomatic models of bargaining, see (Roth, 1979b) and (Roth and Malouf, 1979).

J.F. Nash (1950, 1953) proposed that a solution should possess the following four axiomatic properties, and has then shown that the properties define a unique solution to the bargaining problem.

Property 1. *Invariance Under Positive Affine Transformation of Utility.* For any bargaining game $(S, d) \in B$, if T is an arbitrary affine transformation such that $Tx = (a_1 x_1 + b_1, \ldots, a_n x_n + b_n)$, $a_i > 0$ for $i \in N$, then $Tf(S, d) = f(TS, Td)$.

Property 2. *Symmetry.* Suppose that $(S, d) \in B$ is a symmetric game, that is $d_1 = d_2 = \cdots = d_n$ and if x is contained in S, then for every permutation π on N, $\pi^\star x$ is also contained in S. Then $f_1(S, d) = f_2(S, d) = \cdots = f_n(S, d)$.

Property 3. *Independence of Irrelevant Alternatives other then Disagreement Point.* For bargaining games (S, d) and (T, d) in B, if $S \subset T$ and $f(T, d) \in S$ then $f(S, d) = f(T, d)$.

Property 4. *Strong Pareto Optimality.* For any bargaining game $(S, d) \in B$, there is no $x \in S$ such that $x \ge f(S, d)$, $x \ne f(S, d)$.

Property 1 is imposed because a cardinal utility function is unique up to an order preserving affine transformation, i.e. the origin and scale chosen for a cardinal utility function are arbitrary. Property 2 reflects a "fairness" principle, all the players have "equal ability of bargaining", and the solution depends only on information in (S, d). In the case when we have some additional information about bargaining abilities of the players, Harsanyi and Selten (1972) show that there is a unique solution possessing Properties 1, 3, and 4. Property 3 is the most difficult to substantiate (see Luce and Raiffa, 1957), it requires that the solution selects an outcome using a rule which depend only on the disagreement point and on the selected outcome itself, and not on any other outcomes in the feasible set. Property 4 says that the players are "collectively rational".

Theorem 1. (Nash, 1950) There exists a unique solution of the bargaining problem on B that possesses Properties 1–4. This unique solution (called here Nash solution) is defined by:

$$f(S,d) = F(S,d) = \arg\max_{x \in S_d} \prod_{i \in N} (x_i - d_i)$$

where $S_d = \{ x \in S : x \geq d \}$.

H. Raiffa (1953) proposed another solution for a two person bargaining problem, which was axiomatically characterized by Kalai and Smorodinsky (1975), and generalized to the n-person case by Thomson (1980). Let $I(S,d)$ denote the ideal point of the game (S,d), i.e.

$$I_i(S,d) = \max \{ x_i : x \in S,\, x \geq d \} \quad \text{for} \quad i \in N.$$

Property 5. *Weak Pareto Optimality.* For any bargaining game $(S,d) \in B$, there is no such $x \in S$ that $x > f(S,d)$.

Property 6. *Individual Monotonicity.* If (S,d) and (T,d) are bargaining games such that $S \subset T$ and that for some $i \in N$ and all $j \in N,\ j \neq i,\ I_j(S,d) = I_j(T,d)$ hold then $f_i(S,d) \leq f_i(T,d)$.

Property 5 is a weaker version of collective rationality, Property 6 states that if the set S is enlarged to a set T in such a way, that the expansion occurs only in the direction of the i-th player, then the i-th player payoff in the enlarged game (T,d) should be at least as large as his payoff in the original game (S,d).

Theorem 2.

a. (Thomson, 1980) There exists a unique solution of the bargaining problem on B^* that possesses Properties 1, 2, 5, and 6. This unique solution (called Raiffa one-shot solution) is defined by:

$$f(S,d) = G(S,d) = d + h(S,d)[I(S,d) - d]$$

where $h(S,d) = \max \{ h \in \Re : d + h[I(S,d) - d] \in S \}$. This means that $G(S,d)$ is the unique intersection point of the segment connecting $I(S,d)$ to d with the boundary of S.

b. (Kalai and Smorodinsky, 1975) In the two person case there exists a unique solution on B possessing Properties 1, 2, 4, and 6; this solution is the function $f = G$ defined as above.

c. (Roth, 1979b) In the n-person case, $n \geq 3$, no solution exists on B possessing Properties 1, 2, 5, and 6.

d. (Roth, 1979a) In the n-person case, $n \geq 3$, no solution exists on B^* possessing Properties 1, 2, 4, and 6.

It is easy to show that the Raiffa one-shot solution (as well as the Nash solution) satisfies the following property:

Property 7. *Independence of Irrelevant Alternatives other than Disagreement Point and Ideal Point.* For bargaining games (S,d) and (T,d) in B, if $I(S,d) = I(T,d),\ S \subset T$, and $f(T,d) \in S$ then $f(S,d) = f(T,d)$.

4 A model of negotiations

We are interested here in a model of negotiations for the bargaining problem, which describes not only the set of possible final agreements for the class B of bargaining games (i.e. a solution $f : B \rightarrow \Re^n$), but which also gives a constructive procedure describing the process of reaching $f(S,d)$ for any game $(S,d) \in B$.

In our model, a bargaining game $(S,d) \in B$ is played in several rounds $1,2,\ldots,T$ (it may be finite or infinite process, hence $T \leq \infty$). In each round t, each player $i \in N$ announce a "demand" d_i^t; if these demands jointly are admissible, i.e.

$$d^t \in S^\star = \{ x \in S : y \leq x \leq z \text{ for some } y, z \in S \},$$

and acceptable to all players, then they are taken as the result of this round of negotiations (otherwise, this round is unsuccessful and the process begins again from d^{t-1}). The final admissible and acceptable demands d^T of all players are supposed to constitute a solution for the game (S,d). We assume that the model satisfies the following postulates:

P1. $d^0 = d, \quad d^t \in S^\star \quad \text{for} \quad t = 1,2,\ldots,T$,

P2. $d^t \geq d^{t-1} \quad \text{for} \quad t = 1,2,\ldots,T$,

P3. $d^T \;\; (= \lim_{t\to\infty} d^t \text{ if } T = \infty)$ is a strongly Pareto optimal point in S.

The above postulates have the following intuitive interpretations. We assume that the process starts at the disagreement point (no player will agree to get less than his disagreement payoff). Moreover, the process is monotonically progressive (no player will accept an improvement of demands of another player at the cost of his concession, a diminishing of his demands). Finally, the process leads to a strongly Pareto optimal outcome in S.

Following Fandel and Wierzbicki (1985), at each round of the process we assume additionally that the demands of all players are limited by a principle of α-limited confidence. Let $I(d^{t-1}) \in \Re^n$ be such that $I_i(d^{t-1}) = \max\{ x_i : x \in S, \, x \geq d^{t-1} \}$, i.e. $I(d^{t-1})$ is the ideal point of the set S restricted to the outcomes not worse than d^{t-1}.

P4. *Principle of α-limited confidence.* Let $0 < \alpha_i^t \leq 1$ be a given confidence coefficient of the i-th player at round t. Then acceptable demands are limited by:

$$d^t - d^{t-1} \leq \alpha_{\min}^t [I(d^{t-1}) - d^{t-1}]$$

for $t = 1,\ldots,T$, where $\alpha_{\min}^t$ is a joint confidence coefficient at round t, $\alpha_{\min}^t = \min\{\alpha_1^t,\ldots,\alpha_n^t\}$.

Intuitively, the postulate P4 states that a single-round gain in the process should not exceed $\alpha_{\min}^t$ part of the maximal cooperative gain for each player at round t. We assume here that when the players agree on an outcome d^{t-1}, then the outcomes $S \setminus \{ x \in S : x \geq d^{t-1} \}$ play no further role in the future part of the process. The principle of α-limited confidence follows from the fact that, in many practical applications the players have limited confidence in their ability to describe and predict precisely all consequences and possible outcomes, hence each player attempts to prevent any other player from receiving disproportionally large gains.

There are interesting relations between a confidence coefficient and the conflict coefficient concept proposed by Wierzbicki (1987). For each $x \in S$ and each t define the following coefficient, called cooperative conflict coefficient relative to status quo point d^{t-1} :

$$D(d^{t-1}, x) = \max_{i \in N} \{(I_i(d^{t-1}) - x_i) \; / \; (I_i(d^{t-1}) - d_i^{t-1})\}$$

It has many interesting properties (see Wierzbicki, 1987). The minimal conflict coefficient defined by : $D_{\min}(d^{t-1}) = \min_{x \in S} D(d^{t-1}, x)$ is equal to zero if and only if the ideal point of the set S restricted to the outcomes not worse than d^{t-1} belongs to S, i.e. if there is no conflict in the bargaining problem. It is equal to $(1 - (1/n))$ if the set S is the smallest convex set containing d^{t-1} such that $I(d^{t-1})$ is its ideal point. In each round t a value of confidence coefficient α_i^t of the i-th player can be limited on the base of a minimal conflict coefficient. It should be such that $0 < \alpha_i^t \leq (1 - D_{\min}(d^{t-1}))$, if $\alpha_i^t = (1 - D_{\min}(d^{t-1}))$ for all $i \in N$ than the players might get maximal improvement of payoffs. Moreover, the ratio $\alpha_i^t \; / \; (1 - D_{\min}(d^{t-1}))$ characterizes percentage of maximal improvement assumed by the i-th player.

Remark. The drawback of the conflict coefficient $D(d^{t-1}, x)$ is that it depends on the dimension n. To correct for this dependence, it is reasonable, following suggestion of Kreglewski (1984), to use the following transformation:

$$TD(d^{t-1}, x) = 2D(d^{t-1}, x) + (n(n-2)/(n-1))D(d^{t-1}, x)(D(d^{t-1}, x) - 1)$$

where the transformed conflict coefficient $TD(d^{t-1}, x)$ has the property that $TD(d^{t-1}, I(d^{t-1})) = 0$, $TD(d^{t-1}, d^{t-1}) = 2$, and $TD(d^{t-1}, (d^{t-1} + I(d^{t-1})) \; / \; n) = 1$, which corresponds to a good intuitive interpretation of measuring the conflict by 1 if the players accept the simplest compromise between objectives.

In order to further characterize the behaviour of players during the negotiation process, we introduce the following principle of recursive rationality.

P5. *Principle of recursive rationality.* Given d^t, at each round t, there is no such outcome $x \in S^*$, $x \geq d^t$, $x \neq d^t$ that x satisfies P4.

This can be interpreted that, at each round t, every player is a rational individual: he tries to maximize his demand according to the principle of α-limited confidence, knowing that larger demands will be not accepted by other players.

We can prove the following theorem (see Appendix).

Theorem 3. For any n-person bargaining game $(S, d) \in B$ and any confidence coefficients $\alpha_{\min}^t$, $t = 1, \ldots, T$ such that $0 < \epsilon \leq \alpha_{\min}^t \leq 1/n$ there is a unique process d^t, $t = 0, 1, \ldots, T$ satisfying the postulates P1–P5. The process is described in the iterative way:

$$d^0 = d$$
$$d^t = d^{t-1} + \alpha_{\min}^t [I(d^{t-1}) - d^{t-1}]$$

where T is the smallest t with $d^t = d^{t+1}$ or $T = \infty$.

Because S was assumed to be convex, we can observe that the process is infinite for $\alpha_{\min}^t < 1/n$. We can also notice that for $0 < \alpha_{\min}^t \leq 1/n$ the postulates P1–P5 involve the following postulate:

P6. *Principle of proportional gains.* For each round t, $t = 1,\dots,T$, there is a number $\beta > 0$ such that

$$d^t - d^{t-1} = \beta[I(d^{t-1}) - d^{t-1}].$$

On the basis of the postulate P6, we can generalize the result for any confidence coefficients $\alpha^t_{\min}$ such that $0 < \alpha^t_{\min} \leq 1$.

Theorem 4. For any bargaining game $(S,d) \in B$ and any confidence coefficients $\alpha^t_{\min}$ such that $0 < \epsilon \leq \alpha^t_{\min} \leq 1$, $t = 1,2,\dots,T$ there is a unique process d^t, $t = 0,1,\dots,T$ satisfying the postulates P1–P6. The process is described in the iterative way:

$$d^0 = d$$
$$d^t = d^{t-1} + \beta^t_{\min}[I(d^{t-1}) - d^{t-1}] \qquad \text{for} \quad t = 1,\dots,T$$

where $\beta^t_{\min} = \alpha^t_{\min}$ if d^t belongs to $S^\star$, elsewhere $\beta^t_{\min}$ is the maximal number such that $\beta^t_{\min} < \alpha^t_{\min}$ and d^t belongs to $S^\star$; T is the smallest t with $d^t = d^{t+1}$ or $T = \infty$.

The proof of Theorem 4 is a simple modification of the proof of Theorem 3. From convexity and disposability of payoffs in S it follows that if improvement in directions along coordinates of some players is possible, an improvement in any direction being their combination is also possible.

Figure 1 shows an example of the process for the confidence coefficient $\alpha^t_{\min} = 1/2$ in a two person bargaining game (S,d).

Now, we show that the assumption in the postulate P1 that d^t belongs to $S^\star$ rather to S is important. Let us consider an example of three-person game $(S,d) \in B$ such that $d = (0,0,0)$ and S is the convex hull of d and the points $(0,1,1)$ and $(1,0,1)$. It is easy to verify that if we set $d^t \in S$ in P1 then the process satisfying the postulates P1–P5 is not unique, hence Theorem 3 does not hold. Moreover, the postulate P6 does not follow from P1–P5, and there is no process satisfying P1, P3, and P6, hence Theorem 4 is not true.

Let $\alpha = (\alpha_1, \alpha_2, \dots)$ denote infinite sequence of real numbers such that $0 < \epsilon \leq \alpha_t \leq 1$ for $t = 1,2,\dots$. Let $G^\alpha : B \to \Re^n$ be a solution defined by: for each bargaining game $(S,d) \in B$, $G^\alpha(S,d)$ is equal to the final demands d^T of the players in the process with the joint confidence coefficients $\alpha^t_{\min} = \alpha_t$ for $t = 1,2,\dots$

We can shown the following properties of the solution G^α (Bronisz, Krus, Wierzbicki, 1987):

- Feasibility. $G^\alpha(S,d)$ belongs to S.
- Strong individual rationality. $G^\alpha(S,d) > d$.
- Strong Pareto optimality. (see Property 4)
- Symmetry. (see Property 2)
- Invariance under positive affine transformations of utility. (see Property 1)
- Continuity. Let $(S_j,d) \in B$ be a sequence of bargaining games defined for a sequence of sets S_j such that $\lim_{j\to\infty}(S_j,d) = (S,d)$ (in the Hausdorff topology) and $(S,d) \in B$. Then $\lim_{j\to\infty} G^\alpha(S_j,d) = G^\alpha(S,d)$.

Let $G^0 : B \to \Re^n$ be the solution (called here Raiffa continuous solution) defined by:

$$G^0(S,d) = \lim_{\alpha \to (0,0,\ldots)} G^\alpha(S,d).$$

It can be shown (Bronisz and Krus, 1986a) that the limit exists and $G^0(S,d)$ is the final demands of the players in the continuous process of negotiation described by the following initial-value problem

$$\begin{aligned} dx_i/dt &= f_i(x) - x_i \qquad \text{for} \quad i = 1,\ldots,n \\ x(0) &= d, \end{aligned}$$

where $f_i(x) = \max\{y_i : y \in S,\ y \geq x\}$. It has been also shown (Bronisz and Krus, 1986b) that the solution $G^0(S,d)$ has all the properties presented above.

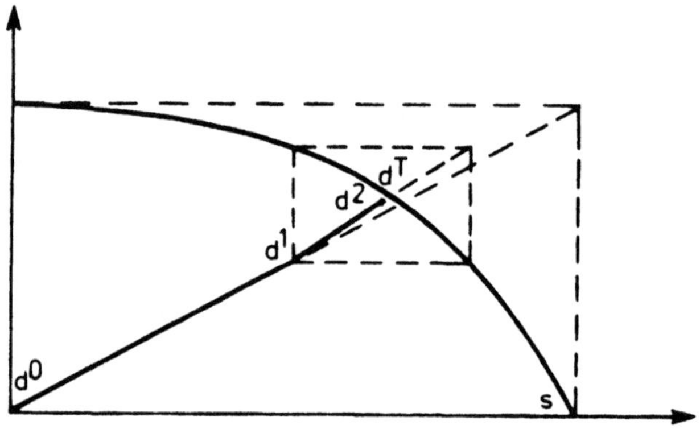

Figure 1.

5 Comparison of the Nash and the Raiffa solutions to the proposed solutions

It is easy to verify that in the two-person case we obtain $G^{(1,1,\ldots)} = G$, that is the solution following from the negotiation process with the confidence coefficients $\alpha = (1,1,\ldots)$ is equivalent to the Raiffa one-shot solution. Moreover, for $n \geq 3$ and any game $(S,d) \in B$ if the Raiffa one-shot solution gives strongly Pareto optimal outcome $G(S,d)$ then $G^{(1,1,\ldots)}(S,d) = G(S,d)$. However, $G^{(1,1,\ldots)}$ does not coincide with the generalization of the Raiffa solution proposed by Imai (1983).

For any bargaining game $(S,d) \in B$ let $I^{1/2}(S,d) \in \Re^n$ be such that

$$I_i^{1/2}(S,d) = \max\{x_i : x \in S,\ x \geq (I(S,d) + d)\,/\,2\}.$$

Intuitively $I_i^{1/2}(S,d)$ is the maximal payoff of the i-th player if the other player get at least a half of their maximal payoffs improvements.

In two-person case, let us consider the solution $H : B \to \Re^2$ following from the two-rounds process with the confidence coefficients $\alpha = (1/2, 1, 1, \ldots)$. This solution has the following property.

Property 8. *Independence of Irrelevant Alternatives other than Disagreement Point (d), Ideal Point ($I(S,d)$), and the point* $I^{1/2}(S,d)$. For any bargaining games (S,d) and (T,d) in B if $I(S,d) = I(T,d)$, $I^{1/2}(S,d) = I^{1/2}(T,d)$, $S \subset T$, and $f(T,d) \in S$ then $f(S,d) = f(T,d)$.

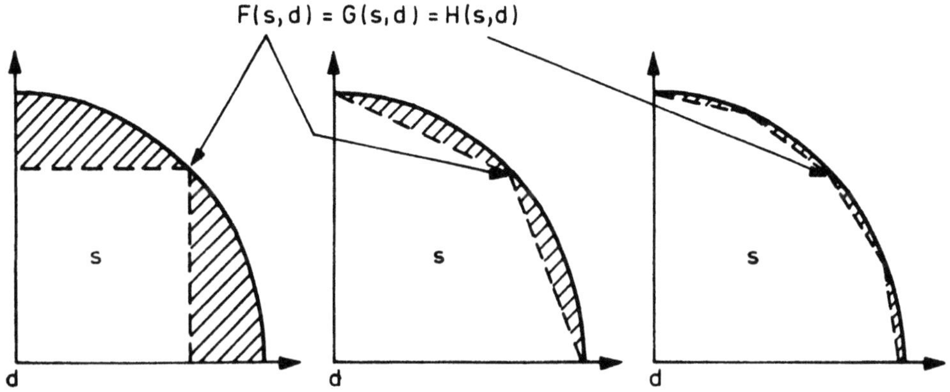

Figure 2 Figure 3 Figure 4

Property 8 is a weaker version of Property 7, which in turn is a weaker version of Property 3. It is easy to verify that the solutions F, G, as well as H satisfy Property 8, the solutions G and H satisfy Property 7, the solution H satisfies Property 8. We will show now an example that a weakening of the property of independence of irrelevant alternatives properties (P3 to P7 and P7 to P8) can improve monotonicity of the solutions (in the sense of a better utilization of information about a bargaining game). Consider a two-person game $(S,d) \in B^\star$ defined by $d = (0,0)$, $S = \{ (x_1, x_2) \in \Re^2 : x \geq 0,\ x_1^2 + x_2^2 \leq 1 \}$ Because (S,d) is a symmetric game, hence the Nash, the Raiffa one-shot, and the H solutions coincide, $F(S,d) = G(S,d) = H(S,d)$. The game (S,d) is presented in Figures 2, 3, and 4 while the set S is limited by a continuous line. For simplicity, confine our consideration to games $(T,d) \in B^\star$ such that $T \subset S$. From Property 3, it follows that each game $(T,d) \in B^\star$ such that the upper boundary of T lies in the shaded area in Figure 2 has the same Nash solution $F(T,d) = F(S,d)$. Property 7 implies that each game $(T,d) \in B^\star$ such that the upper boundary of T lies in the shaded area in Figure 3 has the same Raiffa one-shot solution $G(T,d) = G(S,d)$. Property 8 implies that each game $(T,d) \in B^\star$ such that the upper boundary of T lies in the shaded area in Figure 4 has the same H solution $H(T,d) = H(S,d)$. Moreover it is easy to notice that only symmetric games (T,d) have the same Raiffa continuous solution as the game (S,d). This shows that a relaxation of the property of independence of irrelevant alternatives decreases the set of bargaining games having the same solution, what makes possible an improvement of monotonicity.

6 A multicriteria bargaining problem: problem formulation and definitions

Let $N = \{1, 2, \ldots, n\}$ be a finite set of players, each player having m objectives. A multicriteria bargaining game is defined as a pair (S, d), where an agreement set S is a subset of $n \star m$-dimensional Euclidean space $\Re^{n*m}$, and a disagreement point d belongs to S. If we assumed that the objectives of each player can be aggregated to an utility function, then the multicriteria game would be converted in a single-criteria one. However, we assume here that for some reasons—such as practical limitations of the utility theory—the aggregation of player's objectives is impossible.

For every point $x = (x_i, \ldots, x_n) \in \Re^{n*m}$, $x_i \in \Re^m$, $x_i = (x_{i1}, \ldots, x_{im})$, let x_{ij} denote the amount of the j-th objective for the i-th player. We assume that each player tries to maximize all his objectives.

A point $x^i \in S$ is defined as *i-nondominated*, $i \in N$, if there is no $y \in S$ such that $y_i \geq x^i_i$, $y_i \neq x^i_i$. A point $u \in \Re^{n*m}$ is defined as a *utopia point relative to aspirations* (RA utopia point) if for each player $i \in N$, there is an i-nondominated point $x^i \in S$ such that $u_i = x^i_i$.

The i-nondominated point is an outcome which could be achieved by a rational player i if he would have full control of the moves of other players. Let us observe that in the unicriterial case there is only one i-nondominated point, in the multicriterial case considered here there is a set of such points. That requires each player i, $i \in N$, to investigate the set of i-nondominated points in S as m-dimensional multicriteria decision problem and then to select one i-nondominated point as his most preferable outcome. The preferable i-nondominated point can be selected by the i-th player using, for example, the achievement function approach proposed by Wierzbicki (1982); in this case, the i-th player specifies his aspirations in his outcome space and a decision support system proposes the i-nondominated point by maximizing an achievement function.

The RA utopia point generated by the selected in this way i-nondominated points, $i \in N$, carries information about the most preferable outcomes for all the players. The RA utopia point significantly differs from the ideal point defined by the maximal values of all objectives in set S.

7 The concept of a solution

In this section, we confine our consideration to the class B^m of all multicriteria bargaining games (S, d) satisfying the following conditions:

(i) S is compact and there is $x \in S$ such that $x > d$,
(ii) S is comprehensive, i.e. for $x \in S$ if $d \leq y \leq x$ then $y \in S$.

Assumption (ii) states that objectives are disposable, i.e. that if the players can reach the outcome x then they can reach any outcome worse than x. Observe that we do not assume convexity of the agreement set.

For technical reasons, it is necessary to confine attention to utopia points $u > d$. Let $U(S,d)$ denote the set of all the RA utopia points u for a bargaining game (S,d) such that $u > d$.

A solution for the multicriteria bargaining problem is a function $f^m : B^m \times \Re^{n*m} \to \Re^{n*m}$ which associates to each $(S,d) \in B^m$ and each RA utopia point $u \in U(S,d)$ a point of S, denoted $f^m(S,d,u)$.

The following G^m function is proposed as the solution of multicriteria bargaining problem:

$$G^m(S,d,u) = d + h(S,d,u)[u-d],$$

where $(S,d) \in B^m$, $u \in U(S,d)$, and $h(S,d,u) = \max\{ h \in \Re : d + h(u-d) \in S \}$.

Intuitively, the outcome $G^m(S,d,u)$ is a unique point of intersection of the line connecting u to d with the boundary of S.

It can be shown (Bronisz and Krus, 1987) that this solution can be characterized by the following axioms.

A1. *Weak Pareto optimality.* There is no such $x \in S$ that $x > f^m(S,d,u)$.

A2. *Invariance under Positive Affine Transformations of Objectives.* Let $Tx = (T_1x_1, \dots, T_nx_n)$ be an arbitrary affine transformation such that $T_ix_i = (a_{ij}x_{ij} + b_{ij})_{j=1,\dots,m}$, where $a_{ij} > 0$, $i \in N$. Then $f^m(TS,Td,Tu) = T\, f^m(S,d,u)$.

For any point $x \in \Re^{n*m}$ and for any permutation π on N, let $\pi^*x = (x_{\pi(1)}, \dots, x_{\pi(n)})$. We say that (S,d) is a symmetric game if $d_1 = d_2 = \cdots = d_n$ and if $x \in S$ then for every permutation π on N, $\pi^*x \in S$.

A3. *Symmetry.* For symmetric bargaining game (S,d), if $u_1 = u_2 = \cdots = u_n$ then $f_1^m(S,d,u) = f_2^m(S,d,u) = \cdots = f_n^m(S,d,u)$.

A4. *Restricted Monotonicity.* If (S,d) and (T,d) are such that a RA utopia point $u \in U(S,d) \cap U(T,d)$ and if $S \subset T$ then $f^m(S,d,u) \le f^m(T,d,u)$.

Theorem 5. (Bronisz and Krus, 1987) There exists a unique solution satisfying the axioms A1–A4. It is the solution $G^m : B^m \times \Re^{n*m} \to \Re^{n*m}$.

It is easy to notice that in the unicriterial case, i.e. when $m = 1$, each bargaining problem (S,d) has a unique RA utopia point which coincide with the ideal point and the solution coincides with the Raiffa solution. The following theorem describes another connection between our concept and the Raiffa solution (Bronisz and Krus, 1987).

For $(S,d) \in B^m$, let $x^i \in S$ be an i-nondominated point defined by the i-th player and $u \in U(S,d)$ be the RA utopia point generated by $x^1, x^2, \dots, x^n$. The points $d, x^1, x^2, \dots, x^n$ generate a convex hull H^n, each point x in H^n can be uniquely presented in the form

$$x = d + (a_1(u_1 - d_1), \dots, a_n(u_n - d_n)),$$

where $0 \le a_i \le 1$ for $i \in N$. Let $S^H = S \cap H^n$ and P be the mapping from H^n to $\Re^n$ defined by :

$$P(d + (a_1(u_1 - d_1), \dots, a_n(u_n - d_n))) = (a_1, \dots, a_n).$$

Theorem 6. (Bronisz, Krus, 1987) If G denotes the n-person Raiffa one-shot solution then $P(G^m(S,d,u)) = G(P(S), P(d))$.

Theorem 6 shows that the n-person Raiffa solution concept can be applied directly to the multicriteria game (S,d) if we confine consideration to the outcomes in S^H, i.e. to intersection of the agreement set S with the convex hull H^n.

8 The concept of an interactive solution

The proposed concept is a generalization of the process in Section 3. We confine our consideration to multicriteria bargaining games (S,d) satisfying the conditions (i), (ii) and, for technical reasons, the following condition.

(iii) For any $x \in S$, let $Q(x) = \{ i : y \geq x,\ y_i > x_i \text{ for some } y \in S \}$. Then for any $x \in S$, there exists $y \in S$ such that $y \geq x$, $y_i > x_i$ for each $i \in Q(x)$.

Intuitively, $Q(x)$ is the set of all coordinates in $\Re^{n*m}$, payoffs of whose members can be increased from x in S. Condition (iii) states that the set of Pareto optimal points in S contains no "holes". We do not assume convexity of S, however, any convex set satisfies Condition (iii).

In our model, a bargaining game (S,d) is played in several rounds $1,2,\ldots,T$, in which the successive outcomes, denoted d^t, are determined.

We generalize the postulates P1–P6 in the following way.

MP1. $d^0 = d,\quad d^t \in S^* \quad \text{for} \quad t = 1,2,\ldots,T,$

MP2. $d^t \geq d^{t-1} \quad \text{for} \quad t = 1,2,\ldots,T,$

MP3. $d^T \ (= \lim_{t\to\infty} d^t \text{ if } T = \infty)$ is a strongly Pareto optimal point in S.

In any round t, let $u(d^{t-1})$ be the RA utopia point of the set $\{ x \in S : x \geq d^{t-1} \}$ reflecting the preferences of the players.

MP4. *Principle of α-limited confidence.* Let $0 < \alpha_i^t \leq 1$ be a given confidence coefficient of the i-th player at round t. Then acceptable demands are limited by:

$$d^t - d^{t-1} \leq \alpha^t_{\min}[u(d^{t-1}) - d^{t-1}]$$

for $t = 1,\ldots,T$, where $\alpha^t_{\min}$ is a joint confidence coefficient at round t, $\alpha^t_{\min} = \min\{\alpha^t_1,\ldots,\alpha^t_n\}$.

The similar relation of the confidence coefficient and conflict coefficient can be observed as in the unicriterial case. For each round t define the conflict coefficient by:

$$D(d^{t-1},u,x) = \max_{\substack{i\in N \\ j\in\{1,\ldots,m\}}} \{(u_{ij}(d^{t-1}) - x_{ij}) \ / \ (u_{ij}(d^{t-1}) - d^{t-1}_{ij})\}.$$

The minimal conflict coefficient defined by $D_{\min}(d^{t-1},u) = \min_{x\in S} D(d^{t-1},u,x)$ limits in the same way a maximal value of confidence coefficients of the players in each round t.

MP5. *Principle of recursive rationality.* Given d^t, at each round t, there is no such outcome $x \in S^*$, $x \geq d^t$, $x \neq d^t$ that x satisfies MP4.

MP6. *Principle of proportional gains.* For each round t, $t = 1,\ldots,T$, there is a number $\beta > 0$ such that

$$d^t - d^{t-1} = \beta[u(d^{t-1}) - d^{t-1}].$$

We can prove the following theorem (Bronisz, Krus and Lopuch, 1987).

Theorem 7. For any multicriteria bargaining game (S,d) satisfying conditions (i) and (iii) and for any confidence coefficients $\alpha^t_{\min}$ such that $0 < \epsilon \leq \alpha^t_{\min} \leq 1$, $t = 1,2,\ldots,T$ there is a unique process d^t, $t = 0,1,\ldots,T$ satisfying the postulates MP1–MP6. The process is described in the interactive way:

$$\begin{aligned} d^0 &= d \\ d^t &= d^{t-1} + \beta^t_{\min}[u(d^{t-1}) - d^{t-1}] \qquad \text{for} \quad t = 1,\ldots,T, \end{aligned}$$

where $\beta^t_{\min} = \alpha^t_{\min}$ if d^t belongs to S^*, elsewhere $\beta^t_{\min}$ is the maximal number such that $\beta^t_{\min} < \alpha^t_{\min}$ and d^t belongs to S^*; T is the smallest t with $d^t = d^{t+1}$ or $T = \infty$.

It is easy to verify that for a multicriteria bargaining game (S,d) such that $G^m(S,d,u)$ is a strongly Pareto optimal point in S, the interactive negotiation process with the confidence coefficient $\alpha^t_{\min} = 1$ for $t = 1$ yields the final outcome $d^T = d^1 = G^m(S,d,u)$.

9 Application of the interactive solution in decision support for simulation games

In a model-based decision support situation we assume that a computerized model of the gaming situation (called here the substantive model of the game) has been developed with some specific interpretation in real life. The model should describe in mathematical relations outcomes of the players as dependent on their decision variables. In case of bargaining game it should allow at least describe bargaining set and disagreement point. Several different prototypes of the model use and decision support in simulation gaming can be used (Wierzbicki, 1987) including: playing the simulated game without decision support, game analysis module, tentative arbitration module, module of interactive decision support systems for individual players, interactive fair mediation module. The structure of a decision support system that would include all of the prototypes (modules) is presented in the Figure 5.

Playing the simulated game without any decision support is widely and almost solely applied prototype. The game analysis module should at least compute current and minimal conflict coefficients.

Assuming that in initial period of the game the status quo outcome is established, the module would inform the players what is the minimal conflict coefficient compared to the status quo. In a further period of gaming, current conflict coefficients could be computed and displayed, together with various graphical images. The tentative arbitration module can calculate besides conflict coefficients, a one shot cooperative solution, for example Raiffa solution, Nash cooperative solution or others. The solution can be proposed to the players as arbitrated one. They would not be obliged to accept the arbitrated solution, but the knowledge of it might have a considerable impact on their behaviour. The interactive decision system can allow particular player for interactive selection of his moves that best serve his multiple objectives (assuming some moves of other players). A further degree of sophistication would allow each player to put himself tentatively

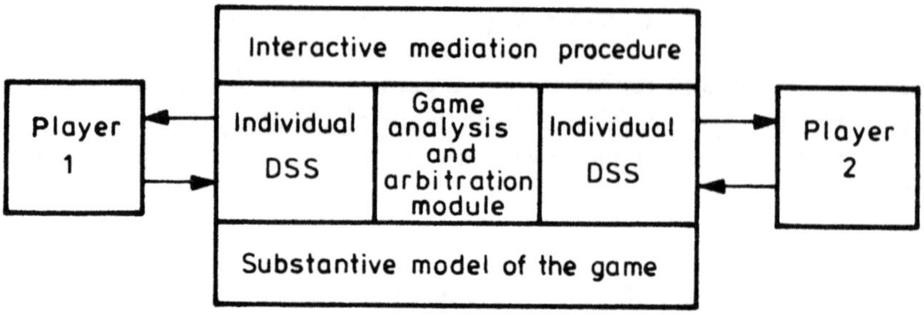

Figure 5: The structure of a decision and mediation support system for simulation games.

in the position of other players, assume their objectives (which would not necessarily be assumed correctly, since each player has the right of privacy of his analysis and, in particular, his objective selection). In this mode, he could analyze cooperative outcomes. The results of the analysis might have a basis for unsupported, verbal negotiations between players.

The interactive mediation module can be based on the principle of limited confidence and a "single text" procedure, see e.g. (Raiffa, 1982). The full procedure of using this prototype might include all previous prototypes to prepare data for the mediation module. The concept of interactive solution can be base for construction of the procedure. In the following, an idea of the procedure based on the concept of the interactive solution is presented. The idea has been implemented in an experimental system supporting multiobjective bargaining (Bronisz, Krus, Lopuch, 1987). The procedure consists of a number of rounds. Each round t starts from the current status quo point d^{t-1} (the first round starts from the status quo of the game). The player having information about conflict coefficient at the point, specifies his current confidence coefficient α_i^t and assuming some moves of other players tests different direction improving his payoffs from the current status quo in space of his objectives. The directions can be specified by use of reference points. For a particular direction (reference point) the system calculates the corresponding solution and conflict coefficient. This information for some number of tests allows the player to specify his aspiration levels for the objectives. This stage of the procedure is performed independently for all the players. The system is informed about objectives of the players, their aspiration levels and their confidence coefficients. The system derives individual utopia components relative to aspirations of the players and maximal confidence coefficient $\alpha_{\max}^t$, establishes resulting confidence coefficient α^t, and calculates result of the round d^t together with corresponding conflict coefficient, according to the following formulas:

$$d^t = d^{t-1} + \alpha^t[u^t - d^{t-1}],$$

where $\alpha^t = \min\{\alpha_1^t, \ldots, \alpha_n^t, \alpha_{\max}^t\}$ and u^t is utopia point relative to aspirations of the players.

The outcomes of particular players resulting from d^t and conflict coefficient are proposed to the players as the mediated ones. The players are asked to state whether they accept the result. If they all do, next round of mediated improvements is computed; if some of them do not, they can revert to any of the previous prototypes.

10 Conclusions

We have presented here a theoretical basis for interactive arbitration schemes in bargaining games. An iterative model of negotiations has been formulated in the case of unicriterial bargaining game under the principle of α-limited confidence of players. According to the model, a process starting from the disagreement point and leading to the Pareto optimal point of the agreement set has been constructed. Uniqueness of such a process has been shown. An interactive process for multicriteria bargaining games has been also considered utilizing a new solution concept being generalization of Raiffa solution and an extension of the principle of α-limited confidence.

Appendix

Proof of Theorem 3.

To simplify notation, let:

$$d^t = d^t(S, d),\ I(d^{t-1}) = I(S, d^{t-1}(S, d)),\ t = 1, 2, \ldots, T.$$

For any $0 < \alpha \leq 1/n$, let us consider the process described by:

$$d^0 = d,\ d^t = d^{t-1} + \alpha[I(d^{t-1}) - d^{t-1}] \text{ for } t = 1, 2, \ldots, T.$$

For any round t, let

$$x = 1/n * (x^1 + x^2 + \cdots + x^n),$$

where $x^i = (x_1^i, \ldots, x_n^i)$, $x_i^i = I_i(d^{t-1})$, $x_j^i = d_j^{t-1}$ for $j \neq i$. The points x^i belong to S^*, hence from convexity of S^*, $x \in S^*$. Because

$$d^t \leq d^{t-1} + 1/n * [I(d^{t-1}) - d^{t-1}] = x,$$

thus $d^t \in S^*$ and the process described above satisfies the postulate P1. It is easy to notice that the process satisfies also the postulates P2, P4, and P5. Now, we show that the process satisfies the postulate P3. If T is the smallest t with $d^t = d^{t+1}$ then $I(d^t) = d^t$, i.e. there is no coordinate of d^t which may be improved, thus d^t is a strongly Pareto optimal point in S^* (also in S, see p.I.1). In other case, let us consider the sequence

$\{d^t\}_{t=0}^{\infty}$. This sequence is monotonically increasing and limited, so it is convergent. Let $d^T = \lim_{t\to\infty} d^t$ and let us assume that d^T is not a strongly Pareto optimal point in $S^\star$. Then for any round t, we have:

$$\|d^t - d^{t-1}\| = \alpha\|I(d^{t-1}) - d^{t-1}\| \geq \alpha\|I(d^T) - d^T\| = \text{const} > 0,$$

thus this sequence is not convergent. Contradiction. This proves that the process described above satisfies the postulates P1–P5.

The uniqueness of the process follows from the fact that for each round t, $t = 1, 2, \dots, T$, there exists one and only one point

$$d^t = d^{t-1} + \alpha[I(d^{t-1}) - d^{t-1}]$$

satisfying the postulates P4 and P5.

References

Axelrod, R. (1985). The Evolution of Cooperation, Basic Books, New York.

Bronisz, P. and L. Krus (1986a). A New Solution of Two-Person Bargaining Games, ZTSW-17-1/86, Report of Systems Research Institute, Polish Academy of Sciences, Warsaw.

Bronisz, P. and L. Krus (1986b). A Dynamic Solution of Two-Person Bargaining Games, ZTSW-17-3/86, Report of Systems Research Institute, Polish Academy of Sciences.

Bronisz, P. and L. Krus (1987). The Raiffa Solution for Multicriterial Bargaining Problems, ZTSW-17-1/87, Report of Systems Research Institute, Polish Academy of Sciences, Warsaw.

Bronisz, P., L. Krus and B. Lopuch (1987). An Experimental System Supporting Multiobjective Bargaining Problem. A Methodological Guide. In A. Lewandowski, A.P. Wierzbicki, editors: Theory, Software and Testing Examples for Decision Support Systems, IIASA, Laxenburg, (forthcoming).

Bronisz, P., L. Krus and A. Wierzbicki, (1987). Towards interactive solutions in Bargaining Problem, RP.I.02.1.4, Report of Institute of Automatic Control, Warsaw University of Technology.

Dreyfus, S. (1985). Beyond Rationality. In M. Grauer, M. Thompson, A.P. Wierzbicki (eds): Plural Rationality and Interactive Decision Processes, Proceedings, Sopron 1984, Springer Verlag, Heidelberg.

Fandel, G. (1979). Optimale Entscheidungen in Organizationen, Springer Verlag, Heidelberg.

Fandel, G. and A.P. Wierzbicki, (1985). A Procedural Selection of Equilibria for Supergames, (private unpublished communication).

Grauer, M., M. Thompson and A.P. Wierzbicki (eds) (1985). Plural Rationality and Interactive Decision Processes, Proceedings, Sopron 1984, Springer Verlag, Heidelberg.

Harsanyi, J.C. and R. Selten (1972). A Generalized Nash Solution for Two-Person Bargaining Games with Incomplete Information. *Management Sciences*, Vol. 18, pp. 80–106.

Imai, H. (1983). Individual Monotonicity and Lexicographical Maxmin Solution. *Econometrica*, Vol. 51, pp. 389–401.

Kalai, E. and M. Smorodinsky (1975). Other Solutions to Nash's Bargaining Problem. *Econometrica*, Vol. 43, pp. 513-518.

Kreglewski, T. (1984). private communication.

Luce, R.D. and H. Raiffa (1957). Games and Decisions: Introduction and Critical Survey, New York: Wiley.

Nash, J.F. (1950). The Bargaining Problem. *Econometrica*, Vol. 18, pp. 155–162.

Nash, J.F. (1953). Two-Person Cooperative Games. *Econometrica*, Vol. 21, pp. 129–140.

Raiffa, H. (1953). Arbitration Schemes for Generalized Two-Person Games. *Annals of Mathematics Studies*, No. 28, pp. 361–387, Princeton.

Roth, A.E. (1979a). An Impossibility Result Concerning n-Person Bargaining Games. *International Journal of Game Theory*, Vol. 8, pp. 129–132.

Roth, A.E. (1979b). Axiomatic Models of Bargaining. *Lecture Notes in Economics and Mathematical Systems*, Vol. 170, Springer Verlag, Berlin.

Roth, A.E. and M.W.K. Malouf (1979). Game-Theoretical Models and the Role of Information in Bargaining. *Psychological Review*, Vol. 86, pp. 1163–1170.

Thomson, W. (1980). Two Characterization of the Raiffa Solution. *Economic Letters*, Vol. 6, pp. 225–231.

Wierzbicki, A.P. (1982). A Mathematical Basis for Satisficing Decision Making. *Mathematical Modelling*, Vol. 3, pp. 391–405.

Wierzbicki, A.P. (1983). Negotiation and Mediation in Conflicts, I: The Role of Mathematical Approaches and Methods, WP-83-106, IIASA, Laxenburg; also in H. Chestnat et al., eds: Supplemental Ways to Increase International Stability, Pergamon Press, Oxford, 1983.

Wierzbicki, A.P. (1985). Negotiation and Mediation in Conflicts, II: Plural Rationality and Interactive Decision Processes. In M. Grauer, M. Thompson, A.P. Wierzbicki, eds: Plural Rationality and Interactive Decision Processes, Proceedings, Sopron 1984, Springer Verlag, Heidelberg.

Wierzbicki, A.P. (1987). Towards Interactive Procedures in Simulation and Gaming: Implications for Multiperson Decision Support. In: Methodology and Software for Interactive Decision Support, Proceedings of International Workshop, Albena (forthcoming).

Part 2
Applications and Experiences

MIDA: Experience in Theory, Software and Application of DSS in the Chemical Industry

Jerzy Kopytowski *
Industrial Chemistry Research Institute
Maciej Zebrowski
Joint Systems Research Department of the Institute for Control and Systems Engineering, Academy of Mining and Metallurgy, Cracow, and the Industrial Chemistry Research Institute, Warsaw.

Abstract

DSS and methodology for programming development of the chemical industry called MIDA or Multiobjective Interactive Decision Aid have been developed and since then are extensively applied.

It was done already in a variety of cases and in diverse decision as well as cultural environments. On the verge of the second decade of this type of activity, an experience in theory, software and application is presented. It is aimed at pointing out important aspects in all spheres of the activities considered. The paper covers perspective and scope of the development programming domain showing how the identification of the field opened way to establishing of a theoretical and methodological framework and to consequent development of the MIDA system, its architecture and software development. The experience goes beyond the particular field of MIDA application and seems to be generally meaningful and therefore useful in development and application of various decision support tools and systems.

1 Introduction

1.1 Origin and motivation

On the verge of the second decade of the research work in the area of Decision Support Systems, concentrated on a methodology for Programming Development of the Chemical Industry, an experience gained so far calls for synthetic review and presentation.

The unremitting search for an efficient development strategy constitutes a vast, fundamental and vital task of management of practically every industry in today's fast changing world. This was the most strongly formulated motivation behind the

*at present with UNIDO, Vienna.

research reported initially in our paper (Gorecki, Kopytowski and Zebrowski, 1978). The motivation not only persisted since then but perhaps became even stronger through all that time. In fact it is very effectively stimulated by a tremendous progress in the DSS development and applications decisively supported by even more rapid and overwhelming developments in computer hardware and software.

The role of this paper is twofold. First, it is an introduction to the whole chapter which summarizes results of research and application in the domain of MIDA DSS for programming development of the chemical industry. Second, which is perhaps more important, it is to provide a synthetic presentation of key issues and experience gathered so far which goes beyond a particular DSS and its applications. Hence the experience seems to be generally applicable in the Decision Support domain.

The whole chapter displays in detail selected problems outlined, in this paper, which is an introductory one not merely to support the viewpoint presented but to provide a wider but also more detailed conceptual and methodological framework that laid a foundation for the results gained..

1.2 The scope of the paper

The paper is organized as follows. First, perspective and scope of the programming development of the chemical industry is presented. It is aimed at presentation of key identification issues which determined development of MIDA system and the methodology. It is followed by a briefly commented list of major and recent applications of MIDA to present decision problems and the scope of services performed. Based on this, a synthetic review of the experience in theory, software and applications is given using regular references to the papers from this chapter since they are included in the bibliography.. Conclusions and prospects for the future research are also provided.

1.3 Organization and implementation of the research

The organization and implementation of the research has been developed from its beginning in 1977 and is still in process since the research is an open-ended one in this problem- and application-oriented task. This is reflected in the origin of Joint System Research Department (JSRD) which is a joint venture of the academic institution, namely Institute for Control and Systems Engineering in the Academy of Mining and Metallurgy (ICSE - AMM) and strictly application-rooted organization, i.e. Industrial Chemistry Research Institute (ICRI). The problem-oriented approach can be opposed to the rather common practice which is based on a setting of a general goal: development of DSS for Multiobjective Decision Problems. The latter situation which may be called a tool-oriented approach as opposed to the problem-oriented one can prove its effectiveness in general research aimed at purely scientific results. It is perhaps less effective when tangible effects of a real application are to be reached.

It should be greatly appreciated that in all phases of the work, especially in the course of the identification and the applications, highly qualified experts have been taking part. These experts represent an experience of high level decision makers combined with a deep technological and economic knowledge. Only this kind of a background combined with the skills of much younger scientists specializing in systems analysis, optimization and control theory as well as computer science could produce a special synergic effect boosting the progress of the work.

1.4 Collaboration with IIASA

Here an important role of collaboration with IIASA must be called into light. It provided a very important platform in MIDA development. The collaboration, due to the type of tasks undertaken by JSRD has been very intensive and involved during last eight years a pretty number of projects and programs which are to be named here. It is to be done not only for the sake of courtesy but to show how wide is the range of problems covered when a DSS such MIDA is to be developed along the way it was assumed to be done.

The most important was the collaboration with SDS or System and Decision Science Program. Especially under chairmanship of A.P. Wierzbicki it provided mutual exchange of approaches and experience. As particularly useful for development of MIDA we evaluate the reference point concept (Wierzbicki 1980) and collaboration at early stages of DIDAS (Lewandowski 1982) development and especially appreciate a close collaboration with A.Lewandowski (Dobrowolski et. al. 1982).

An intensive work was done in parallel for REN or Resources and Environment Area (under J.Kindler) (Dobrowolski et al. 1984). An extensive exchange of scientific contacts was continued through all that time with the Energy Program. Important effects were also gained from the work for Sustainable Development of the Biosphere Program under Bill Clark (Zebrowski and Rejewski, 1987)

These three collaborative links helped to broaden and deepen the identification effort with good effects, especially for the methodological progress. Last but not least an important gain in the software development experience is owing to collaboration with ACA or Advanced Computer Applications program. This also led to valuable applications (Zebrowski et al. 1988).

Concluding, one should emphasize that the variety of approaches and problems tackled in this collaboration played an important role in the progress achieved in seemingly narrow field of development and application of MIDA, and contributed to the results which can be generalized.

2 Scope and perspective of development programming

2.1 Chemical industry and management of change

The world is permanently passing through a chain of great economic, social and technological changes. Recognition of this fact and of the need to control the forces of change has stimulated worldwide interest in the problems of change and methods for coping with them.

Nowhere is the need for management of change more crucial than in the industrial sector, where many factors can affect the growth or decline of individual industries and the resulting industrial structure. The process of change with perhaps the highest impact affects the chemical industry.

Here we concentrate on management of the chemical industry due to the problems it faces as a result of global change, particularly as a result of changing patterns of raw materials and energy use.

The importance of the chemical industry is often greatly underestimated. Not only does it provide soaps, detergents, medicines, but also pesticides, fertilizers, synthetic rubbers, plastics, synthetic fibers... - in fact, our modern technological society could be said to be founded on the chemical industry.

One of the most surprising facts about this industry is that a large proportion of its many products are derived from only a very small number of starting materials, of which hydrocarbons are probably the most important.

As the processing of natural resources with mineral or agricultural origin proceeds, the chains are branching with each processing phase from one generation of intermediates to another. So the developed chemical industry presents in fact ever growing network of interlinked technologies. Final or market goods originating from this network provide only a small share of the total chemical production which does not exceed 25% of the final turnover of the industry.

A practical goal has been to develop a methodology capable of proposing possible restructuring and/or structuring of various sectors of the chemical industry (see e.g. Borek et al., 1978, Gorecki et al.,1978). The approach chosen takes into account a variety of interrelated and alternative production processes (either in use or under development), compares their efficiency, their consumption of different resources etc. and finds the combination of technologies that best meets particular needs while staying within the limits imposed by the availability of resources and environmental constraints.

2.2 Programming development - MIDA approach

From the above essential overview two spheres to be identified emerge. First is the sphere of the present and forecasted performance of the industry which is a result of the identification. It should be described formally in order to represent the changes that transform the industrial structure in time. Second is the sphere of management of the changes where decisions are to be worked out and a decision support is to be developed and naturally embedded into the decision process.

It means that a basic model of industrial structure must be created that reflects the first sphere. It must be based on important assumptions regarding the decision and its corresponding aggregation level as well as boundaries of the industrial structure considered. If the management of change is going to be executed through programming development, then such an activity can be considered as a process of design of an Industrial Development Strategy (IDS).

IDS design is considered as a decision process based on generation of efficient development alternatives expressed in terms of goals, critical or indispensable resources as well as selected array of technologies which are to be utilized. The alternatives are to be generated, selected and ranked along assumed efficiency measures.

The aim of the development programming or IDS design is a selection of the alternative which is to change the industrial structure by means of investment over the time. Due to the dynamic properties of the development process, and specifically the development cycle of technology (Dobrowolski et al. 1985), the time span under consideration is of the range of 10 - 15 years. The straightforward conclusion is that due to the dynamic nature of the development process, IDS design is to be treated and solved as a dynamic problem. It has to be strongly underlined, however, that any attempt to formulate a general multidimensional dynamic problem as a means for generating feasible development alternatives must lead to oversimplification and severe loss of important factors which should not be overlooked. At the same time, any decomposition must assure that through a coherent methodology all the subproblems can be solved as integral parts of the same system. A fundamental premise for the phenomena of development is the fact that as time perspectives become longer (5,10,15... years), the reliability and accuracy of data describing the future decreases.

To meet the challenge of a real application in a complex decision environment, a method better responding to a managerial practice was elaborated. It is based on a decomposition of this in fact dynamic problem along space and time. This will be briefly presented further on after describing substantial results obtained from identification. So before going into discussion of the kind of properties of a decision problem (or problems) that are to be formulated and solved, let us make a step further in the identification of IDS design.

To perform IDS design with focus on generation of development alternatives and their selection, following elements are to be considered:

- Existing industrial structure in terms of consumption coefficients capacities and relevant economic data,

- Potentially available technologies for construction of new plants,

The above two categories form a technological repertoire out of which a new industrial structure is to be devised providing that a harmony between existing elements and the new ones must be sustained. The next category of elements for analysis are:

- resources which are to be utilized in order to implement a new structure, such as investment, manpower, water, energy etc as well as resources which are to be supplied as feedstock to run the new structure.

- some of the resources considered are selected in a special way and called critical resources due to the fact that their availability is a necessary condition to make development alternative feasible.

Critical are those resources which are nominated as such by the decision maker for either being particularly scarce or difficult to obtain; examples may be crude oil, manpower, energy or capital. In practice the set of critical resources is closely related to the set of criteria, since the aim is to find an optimal solution with respect to all critical resources. Technological constraints are quite easily identified and are related to factors such as production capacities and operating conditions. All other elements in the analysis, such as demand for a particular product, the availability of (noncritical) raw materials, fall into the category of complementary or auxiliary information which describes environment to the industrial activities such as terms of trade - specifically prices. On the contrary, a demand for selected significant products as well as availability of selected significant feedstock falls into the category of critical resources.

It is clear that whether a resource is selected as critical or not, it depends on the formulation of the decision problem. In fact, a resource can be nominated to one category or to the other by the decision maker and that in a simple way assures flexibility of predecision analysis since each reassignment to or from the list of critical resources corresponds to a redefinition of a decision problem..

With the above background we can now define the task of IDS design or generating efficient development alternatives as **a quest for concordance between available resources and technologies.**

The state of concordance is to be evaluated along well defined rules and measures for evaluation (and selection) of the efficiency of achieving goals (outputs) from resources supplied to industrial structure (inputs). Such rules and measures form a model of efficiency evaluation which is to be established in order to solve the quest for concordance to yield a feasible development alternatives. This problem area is dealt with in (Zebrowski, 1989).

Technological repertoire, critical resources, constraints and other factors describing the problem (or a particular industrial situation), are to be mapped into second or PDA model of a technological network.

Since it is intuitively obvious that such a process is to be performed through the generation and analysis of multitude of alternatives and their selection, then a mechanism is to be provided that enables to handle the situation. The appropriate models and means for handling the problem of quest for concordance may be organized into a system which is called simply DSS or Decision Support System.

The above philosophy stands behind development of MIDA system and the methodology. In the next step we shall present the assumptions used and a decomposition of the development problem which were applied for practical implementation of the above philosophy.

The effective approach taken in MIDA methodology in the practical implementation of the idea of the quest for concordance can be presented as follows. With respect to the decision level of the programming development, MIDA locates the IDS design on a level which could be named an intermediate economy level (Dobrowolski et al, 1985, Zebrowski 1987). It goes between a macroeconomic level and microeconomic or corporate level. The first one proves to be too aggregated; a single technology cannot be considered in the analysis. Therefore a selection and assessment of appropriate technologies cannot be done at the macroeconomic level. On the other hand, a corporate or enterprise level also proves to be inadequate. This level is too narrow and particular to comprise complex technological and economic relationships which interact in the development process in the chemical industry.

By identifying, defining and choosing the intermediate level, as operational one for programming development, an important original feature has been decided in MIDA development. It comes together with the choice of an entity for setting the feasible scope of the industrial problems which may be regarded as a basic object of the decision analysis. It was called PDA or Production Distribution Area. It helped to respond to the necessity of a formal modeling of industrial structure (IS) of the chemical industry. In fact, this subject is formally described in (Dobrowolski, Zebrowski, 1989).

Due to a possibility of simple aggregation and desaggregation of the elements described in terms of the PDA model, and the PDA level can be split into several levels along so-called problem hierarchy (Gorecki et al. 1983, Dobrowolski et al. 1985). This assures flexibility of the analysis and well corresponds to the industrial practice allowing at the same time to apply MIDA on different levels of aggregation (with data appropriate to the level considered). It makes the concept and application of the PDA model very flexible and rather universal.

From the process of quest as considered so far on the PDA level, a goal structure can be selected representing the assumed state of IS at the end of the horizon covered by the analysis. However, to complete the task of programming, development of a feasible way of transition from the present or actual IS to the selected, final IS is to be optimally selected. The transition is to take into account the following classes of factors:

- technological and market priorities,
- location possibilities,
- construction potential capabilities,
- availability of investment.

In short, to consider these factors, the investment necessary for the transition must be allocated both in space and time.
Therefore three levels emerge and provide a decomposition assumed in MIDA:

- selection of the final or goal IS,
- space allocation of investment,
- time allocation of investment (or investment scheduling).

Appropriate feedback between these levels provides through the space and time allocation a feasibility analysis of the goal structure originally selected.

The three level hierarchy and specifically, the space allocation and investment scheduling levels are discussed both theoretically and practically (through example) in (Skocz, Zebrowski and Ziembla, 1989).

It must be underlined at this point, that the decomposition of the IDS applied in MIDA approach corresponds to the managerial practice. On the other hand, it can be conceptually opposed to more theoretical approaches based on dynamic programming and generally aims at global solution to be obtained from one model (see for e.g. Kendrick 1978, Dobrowolski and Rys, 1981).

The approach applied in MIDA follows from the common decision practice. First the goal "what" must be selected, then questions "where and how" should be answered. The decisive factor here is that the spatial allocation demands more detailed information related to sites and this must be confronted with spatially disaggregated values obtained from global solution in terms of critical resources. Site specific constraints must be also obeyed.

There is also one more methodological disadvantage coming from globally formulated and solved problems - difficulty of interpretation - especially of cause - effect type. Too many factors are involved at once to enable that kind of analysis. It makes a real interaction with decision maker rather illusory.

3 Evaluation of experience in DSS

3.1 Major MIDA applications

Some most important and representative applications for the scope assumed in this presentation of MIDA system and methodology were selected. The list of applications to be discussed is as follows:

1. **Polish Government Energy Program** - MIDA was used to elaborate a strategy for integration of energy and chemical sectors. MIDA study contributed to the fact that a new development, namely energochemical processing of coal, was brought to light and attained its place in the long-term policy.

2. JSRD competed successfully in offering its services to **UNIDO** and performed the following projects [1]esults obtained from these projects as well as from the SADCC study mentioned further on are documented in UNIDO Reports, distribution of which is restricted:

   - Master Plan for Development of the Chemical Industry in Iran,
   - Master Plan for Development of the Chemical Industry in Algeria,
   - Master Plan for Development of the Petrochemical Industry in Algeria.

   Within the framework of the above projects the services covered:

   - delivery and installation of equipment and adjacent software as well as delivery and installation of MIDA Decision Support System,
   - training of the counterpart personnel (using lectures, video tapes, top executive seminars and most of all *learning by doing* methodology),
   - elaboration of the development program in various alternatives,
   - industrial and system analysis consulting.

3. **Shanxi Case Study** - this application was done as a part of ACA project in IIASA for Shanxi Province in People's Republic of China and services performed were similar to those described for UNIDO, but the DSS software was developed as a spatially oriented version of the models incorporated in MIDA. The development program for coal based chemical industry was elaborated for the Shanxi

[1]R

province and technical expertise was also shared with the counterpart (Zebrowski et al.,1988).

4. **SADCC Study** - *Study of the manufacture of industrial chemicals in the member states of SADCC* - this application was done under the contract with a consulting firm. The firm was contracted for a UNIDO project for SADCC countries. SADCC stands for Southern African Development Coordination Conference. Its members are 9 countries: Angola, Botswana, Lesotho, Malawi, Mozambique, Swaziland, Tanzania, Zambia, Zimbabwe. The consulting company contracted JSRD to perform application of MIDA system for the above study.

The above applications can be categorized to show range of problems and areas that can be tackled with a DSS and methodology such as MIDA as well as to provide a useful generalization of experience ained.

First category

A problem area related to the development of industrial sectors such as chemical and energy industries is selected. A research is to be carried out and forecasts provided with various technological and development alternatives. This is kind of predecision analysis which includes both research and application type of activities. The responsibility of JSRD as a contracted party covers all the work and study that may be considered as a kind of long range research programs with step by step results to be produced in form of progress and final reports. Results are used by various governmental agencies as well as other scientific centers.

This kind of application is exemplified by no 1 on the above list.

Here a DSS is used by the team performing the job mainly as a laboratory tool. No clearly defined decision maker is present in the process. In such case a variety of skills and experience, specifically presence of industrial experts in the team is especially decisive for good results to be obtained. In such cases by in parallel promoting a work devoted to the problem and a work done on developing methodology and DSS system proves to be fruitful and effective. Such in fact is organization of work assumed by JSRD.

Second category

A development program is to be elaborated for a foreign partner. Such were the applications that were contracted by JSRD with UNIDO. This covers wide span of services and responsibilities. The period assigned for the job is relatively very short : in the range of 1,5 - 3 month.

The DSS is to be delivered and installed together with computer equipment. Moreover, a user's team must be trained in a variety of skills including not only operation of DSS but first of all methodology of its application. These circumstances impose variety of demands which for the lack of space and the type of paper cannot be discussed in details but must be of deep concern. They can be briefly presented as follows.

The principle of operation of a DSS and methods applied should be as clear as possible and as simple as possible at the same time they must eliminate omitting or loss of any essential factors.

A great attention in DSS architecture, functioning and methodology must be paid to facilitate procedures which may help in validating both : simple source data and resulting development alternatives.

Users' involvement is a key factor, both to assure obtaining valuable and useful alternatives that would be accepted for implementation and to establish self-reliance of the users' team (including a decision maker). This can be done through very extensive educational effort and specifically by working out a "learning by doing" methodology. This must be backed also by very clear and well edited documentation supporting all activities as well as results of the project.

If one would like to compare the two above categories of application it could be formulated as follows.

First category provides more scientific and broad approach but is much less demanding in terms of software development, methodology and reliability of the system. On the other hand the second category provides extremely heavy duty testing of all elements taking part in the project.

This includes also all skills and abilities of people involved. It also provides important insights coming from different cultural and decision environments.

Moreover it provides also very useful cases which are an inspiration for the future developments in all aspects : theoretical, software and methodological.

Third category.

The system and methodology are to be adopted for different environment and are to be embedded in another system. Such is the case of the Shanxi case study a work done for ACA IIASA project contracted with Peoples Republic of China (Zebrowski et al., 1988).

Apart from the previous remarks formulated for the case of UNIDO projects which remain valid, some additional observations can be formulated.

A DSS becomes a module of a larger system. All kinds of problems of interfacing with other types of software arise. The same concerns interfaces with other models.

At the same time in this particular case new elements specific for spatial allocation backed by scheduling of investment were also developed. In general this kind of applications help finding another way to generalization and standardization of architecture and functionality of the DSS not to mention new theoretical and methodological developments which usually also come in dealing with new, original problems.

Fourth category

The last but not least category is the one when there is no direct contact with the field. The interface comes through third party. It provides a very useful kind of verification of system and methodology. It was the case of the fourth application listed above.

The experience gained so far from a single case reported here may be too limited to be generalized but due to difference in approaches and experience represented by the third party which is supposed to be professional in the field of programming development, a new light can be brought on the own approach which has to defend itself in such circumstances. In fact it also helps to test and improve system and methodology with procedures for validation of data and results.

The above remarks summarize briefly experience in the domain of DSS as gained from major, categorized for that purpose applications of MIDA. Generality of categorization as well as of the relevant experience prove to be useful not only for a specific DSS such as MIDA.

Following this line it seems to be worthwhile to further synthesize the experience and knowledge gained both from application and research point of view.

We may continue with general methodological and theoretical aspects of Decision Support after presenting some selected theoretical and software developments of MIDA system and methodology. Then, this will lead to conclusions and prospects for the future.

3.2 Theory and software

The substantial and perhaps decisive effort was devoted to the identification of the chemical industry, and the mechanisms behind its development (Kopytowski et al. 1982). Special emphasis was given to emerging from this concept of an industrial structure and its properties.

This led to development of a basic model and methodology (Dobrowolski et al. 1984). By proposing the concept of locating the programming development activity, as one executing the management of change on the intermediate economy level (Dobrowolski et al. 1986) an indispensable theoretical background for programming development was established.

In parallel, through all that time, MIDA system was developed. The system was born in terms of conceptual framework and its basic functional and architectural structure surprisingly early (Borek et al. 1978). This was possible owing to the very strongly problem oriented research and applications being executed in parallel.

But nevertheless a necessity of formulating a basic theory of the field of a DSS application is to be spell out very strongly. The theory enables then for proper elaboration of the DSS architecture and helps in implementation of the system. The system can then be verified and improved from application to application and consequently from version to version.

The basic model of an IS described in (Dobrowolski, Zebrowski, 1989) in the currently stabilized form is sufficiently general and can be applied (and already was applied) in the variety of specific problems going beyond an immediate scope of development programming. It can be also used in practically any process industry. The methodology for the case specific model adaptation was also developed (see (Dobrowolski, Zebrowski, 1989))

A useful theoretical development described in (Zebrowski, 1989) contributed, through development of the model, to the multiobjective evaluation of industrial structures. It reflects the hierarchy and relation between efficiency and substitution providing a key interface between intermediate economy level of the programming development and the macroeconomic level or the environment of decision making analysis considered. This concept has also wider application potential then original field of MIDA.

The hierarchical decomposition described above, applied to the development programming also may be regarded as a theoretical development which contributed not only to the current state of the MIDA approach and the system. The theoretical developments in spatial allocation and scheduling of investment have the two aspects: they contributed to MIDA development and may be regarded as more generally applicable.

Traditionally from the theoretical point of view, a formal decomposition of the model such as PDA should be considered especially when dimensionality is of concern. Our findings are not in conformity with the traditional approach. We found that practical way leads not through numerical decomposition of large PDA model but through step by step synthesis of smaller models which after being optimized and evaluated are to be integrated into one big model. The following aspects were taken into account. Validation of primary data for PDA model can be efficiently achieved when dealing with smaller models. The same, even to greater extent, considers interpretation of results especially with respect to properties of various technologies, applicability of feedstock, attainability of goals etc.

Therefore it can be summarized that both from theoretical and practical points of view, the real problem is rather on the side of synthesis of large PDA model aimed at generation of efficient development alternatives (alternative developoment programmes) as opposed to mentioned before "traditional" theoretical approach leading through decomposition of primary big model into smaller submodels.

One of important areas of research was, and still remains, the problem of evaluation and selection of development alternatives (development programmes) leading to their ranking and selection. The first step was done based on application of SCDAS concept (Dobrowolski, Zebrowski, 1987). The idea of ranking and selection of development alternatives was experimented with on the case of alternative technologies. It was a test example for the idea of application of the proposed approach to the ranking and selection of development programmes.

All the identification, theoretical and application activities were accompanied by the software development.

The important synthesizing effect is provided by knowledge and *know-how* gained at the border of all the above activities with focus on implementation of DSS and its software. This can be found in the MIDA architecture and is described in (Dobrowolski, Rys, 1988). Again experience gained in this field goes well beyond a particular DSS. The paper also describes software elements which are parts of a DSS MIDA.

Beside the MIDA development, a variety of other software tools was also developed. It is worth to mention just two examples of packages described shortly in the part 3 of this volume. These are POSTAN — postoptimal analysis package (Dobrowolski et al. in print.) and PLP or Parametric Programming Package (Golebiowski in print.). A variety of other software developed could be quoted not only as useful for MIDA but also as generally applicable as every day tools. They provided an important professional upgrade of the team involved.

4 Conclusions and future prospects

When concluding the kind of review of a substantial period of experience in the theory, software and application of a DSS such as MIDA, one should aim at pointing out its general as well as elsewhere applicable aspects.

This can be done from the perspective of the fact that MIDA DSS and MIDA methodology have been developed and applied in the substantial number and variety of cases. More over it was done in a diverse decision as well as cultural environments.

The research program aimed at the development of a DSS for programming development of the chemical industry although was (and is) an open ended one but at the some time was (and is) very strongly problem and application oriented. It was very much supported by the team work organized with participation of high class industrial experts representing both decision making and technical skills. The synergic effect of all the above enumerated elements proved to be decisive for obtaining results reported so far.

Extensive and conceptually wide collaboration with IIASA provided a scientific back up which must not be underestimated.

MIDA does play a double role in the game. It is a permanently improved scientific tool which provides together with already accomplished case studies a unique laboratory for research and application in two related areas: in programming development of the chemical (and process industries) and in development of decision support tools and systems.

MIDA is also a professional DSS package offered as a product on the market. The demand coming from competition exerts a specific kind of pressure on its development and performance.

Now we can naturally involve a problem of learning. In the above mentioned systems role in research as a laboratory tool the aspect of learning should be exposed and considered. This situation is similar to the role of DSS in the process of a decision analysis considered as a process of learning. In MIDA a decision maker is cast in a creative role and interacts with the system in the process of generating efficient alternatives of development. This in fact is a process of learning and a creative thinking. By assuming a creative role of a decision maker we have also assumed a subjective factor to be present in the process, since it represents other side of the creative involvement. Decision maker presides over the process but also must take full responsibility for the effect.

MIDA experience strongly supports profound ideas represented in the book by Stuart and Hubert Dreyfus (1986) with the meaningful title "Mind over machine. The Power of Human Intuition and Expertise in the Era of the Computer".

DSS can only assist a decision maker and experts in their strive to design and select an efficient development alternative. An optimal solution obtained from DSS is to be considered as an important but just a factor in the process.

DSS may also help in training of those who aim at becoming experts. They are bound the climb through the levels proposed by Dreyfuses: from novice, through advanced beginner, competent proficient to the expert.

However when a real application is to be accomplished, the team of experts must represent the highest level of expertise. In some instances, when getting into a new case, an expert may be forced to step down to the level of proficiency, the level of competence may not be acceptable. Then DSS proves to be useful in helping with the quick and efficient upgrade — back to the level of expertise.

The development of MIDA is going to be continued in all respects presented in this paper.

In the field of theory work is foreseen both on mechanisms of development as well as on resource allocation problems, both in space and in time.

Further work in the direction of ranking and selection of development alternatives will, as it is expected, lead to implementation of a new module for MIDA system which would serve as a tool for evaluation of alternatives by a group of experts.

New models are to be developed especially concerning fine chemicals obtained from periodic and batch processing. This would be complementary to MIDA type of DSS covering so called light or fine chemical industry (e.g. colorants, pharmaceuticals) due to its specific technological and marketing properties.

CAD type of approach is envisaged aimed at development of some engineering tools useful both in programming development and design of new technologies.

All these efforts are supposed to be accompanied by methodological developments.

The base and verification for all the activities will be provided by applications.

Acknowledgements

The contribution of industrial experts collaborating in all phases of MIDA development and applications hardly can be overestimated. The gratitude must be expressed to W.Marek, S.Gibinski, J.Wojtania and J.Wilczynski. H.Gorecki contributed substantially in scientific part of development. The collaboration with A.Lewandowski and A.Wierzbicki is to be once again acknowledged.

References

Bellman, R. (1961) Adaptive Control Process — a Guided Tour. Princeton University Press, Princeton, New Jersey.

Borek, A.,G. Dobrowolski, M. Zebrowski, (1979) Applications of System Analysis in Management of Growth and Development of the Chemical Industry. CHEM/SEM.8/R.16 Report of Chemical Industry Committee of the United Nations.

Dobrowolski, G., Rys T. (1981) A Dynamic Model for Development Programming of Production — Distribution Area. Theory and Applications. Materials of School of Economic Systems Simulation, Trzebiatowice (in Polish)

Dobrowolski, G., H. Gorecki, J. Kopytowski, M. Zebrowski (1982) The Quest for a Concordance Between Technologies and Resources as a Multiobjective Decision Process. Multiobjective and Stochastic Optimization, pp. 463-475, IIASA Collaborative Paper CP-82-512, Laxenburg, Austria.

Dobrowolski, G., Kopytowski J., Lewandowski A., Zebrowski M. (1982) Generating Efficient Alternatives for Development of the Chemical Industry. IIASA Collaborative Paper CP-82-54, Laxenburg, Austria.

Dobrowolski, G., J. Kopytowski, J. Wojtania, M. Zebrowski (1984) Alternative Routes from Fossil Resources to Chemical Feedstock. IIASA Research Report RR-84-19, Laxenburg, Austria.

Dobrowolski, G., M. Zebrowski (1985) Decision Support in Substitution Analysis for IDS - Industrial Development Strategy Exemplified by the Fuel and Feedstock Sector of the Chemical Industry. The Application of DIDAS. Theory, Software and Test Examples for Decision Support Systems, A. Lewandowski and A. Wierzbicki eds., IIASA, Laxenburg, Austria.

Dobrowolski, G., J. Kopytowski, T. Rys, M. Zebrowski (1985) MIDA - Multiobjective Interactive Decision Aid in the Development of the Chemical Industry. Theory, Software and Test Examples for Decision Support Systems, A. Lewandowski and A. Wierzbicki eds.,IIASA, Laxenburg, Austria.

Dobrowolski, G., T. Rys, K. Hajduk, A. Korytowski (in print) POSTAN3 - Extended Postoptimal Analysis Package for MINOS. To appear in IIASA Collaborative Series, Laxenburg, Austria.

Dobrowolski, G., M. Zebrowski (1987) Ranking and Selection of Chemical Technologies Application of SCDAS Concept. Theory, Software and Testing Examples for Decision Support Systems, A. Lewandowski and A. Wierzbicki eds., pp. 233-241, WP-87-26, IIASA, Laxenburg, Austria.

Dobrowolski, G., T. Rys (1989), Architecture and Functionality of MIDA , in the same volume.

Dobrowolski, G., M. Zebrowski (1989), Basic Model of an Industrial Structure, in the same volume.

Dobrowolski, G., M. Zebrowski (1989) - Hierarchical Multiobjecive Approach to a Programming problem , in the same volume

Dreyfus, H.L., S.E. Dreyfus (1986) Mind over machine. The Power of Human Intuition and Expertise in the Era of the Computer. Second Ed. Bosil Blachwell Ltd., Oxford UK.

Golebiowski, A. (in print) PLP - A Package for Parametric Programming. To appear in IIASA Collaborative Series, Laxenburg, Austria.

Gorecki, H., J. Kopytowski, T. Rys, M. Zebrowski (1984) Multiobjective Procedure for Project Formulation - Design of a Chemical Installation. In: M. Grauer, A.P. Wierzbicki (Eds.) Interactive Decision Analysis - Proc. of Int. Workshop on Interactive Decision Analysis and Interpretative Computer Intelligence Springer Verlag pp. 248-259.

Kendrick, D. A., A.J. Stoutjestijk (1978) The Planning of Industrial Investment Programs. Vol. 1. A Methodology. Johns Hopkins University Press, Baltimore, M.D., for World Bank Research Publications.

Kopytowski, J., J. Wojtania, M. Zebrowski (1981) Fossil as Key Resources of Hydrocarbons for the Chemical Industry - the Burning Problem of Industrial Development. IIASA Collaborative Paper CP-81-20, Laxenburg, Austria.

Lewandowski, A., S. Johnson, A. Wierzbicki (1986) A Prototype Selection Committee Decision Analysis Support System SCDAS: Theoretical Background and Computer Implementation. IIASA Working Paper WP-86-27, Laxenburg, Austria.

Rejewski, P., M. Zebrowski (1987) ERIS - Energochemical Regional Integrated System. Paper presented in IIASA Workshop on Integrated Energy Systems, Laxenburg, Austria.

Skocz, M., M. Zebrowski (1986) An Extended Resources Allocation Method in Design of Industrial Development Strategy. *Proceedings of IFAC Symposium on Large Scale Systems, Zurich.*

Skocz, M., M. Zebrowski, W. Ziembla (1989), Spatial Allocation and Investment Scheduling in the Development Programming, in the same volume.

Wierzbicki, A.P. (1980). The Use of Reference Objectives in Multicriteria Optimization - Theoretical Implications and Practical Experience. IIASA Working Paper WP-79-66, Laxenburg, Austria.

Zebrowski, M. (1987) Multiobjective Evaluation of Industrial Structures. MIDA Application to the case of the chemical industry. Theory, Software and Testing Examples for Decision Support Systems, A. Lewandowski and A. Wierzbicki eds., WP-87-26, IIASA, Laxenburg, Austria.

Zebrowski, M., P. Rejewski (1987) Technological Innovations for Ecologically Sustainable Development, IIASA Working Paper WP-87-17, Laxenburg, Austria.

Zebrowski, M. (1987) A Guide to the Integrated Development Programming. Joint Systems Research Department Report for UNIDO Project. Vienna, Austria.

Zebrowski, M., G. Dobrowolski, T. Rys, M. Skocz, W. Ziembla (1988) Industrial Structure Optimization: The PDAS Model. Expert Systems for Integrated Development: A Case Study of Shanxi Province The People's Republic of China, Final Report, IIASA, Laxenburg, Austria.

Zebrowski, M. (1989) Multiobjective Evaluation of Industrial Structures, in the same volume.

Basic Model of an Industrial Structure

Grzegorz Dobrowolski, Maciej Zebrowski
Joint System Research Department
of the Institute for Control and Systems Engineering,
Academy of Mining and Metallurgy, Cracow,
and the Industrial Chemistry Research Institute, Warsaw.

Abstract

This is the second paper in the series dealing with the development programming of the chemical industry. The paper introduces a basic model of an industrial structure that is used in many variations in the MIDA system and is a kernel of extended models constructed for special cases in the field. It reflects static behavior of a chosen branch or an area of the chemical industry. The model is called PDA — Production Distribution Area.

1 Introduction

The primary version of the model called PDA — Production Distribution Area was published in 1978 (Borek at al.). Currently presented version — stabilized formally few years ago as a result of its extensive use (see for example Dobrowolski et al. 1984) — constitutes a formal base for the Model Management System of MIDA (see the last paper in the series). Moreover, the PDA was a core in somehow complicated models of the chemical industry e.g. the Spatial PDA (Zebrowski et al. 1988).

Such a role of the PDA model in the whole activity stems from its open character and a way of its formulation. The openness means here that:

- a final shape of an operational PDA depends on a chemical branch modeled (data for the model),
- instead of a criterion or criteria, formulas named below the aggregates are proposed with possibility to combine them and to obtain complete optimization problem,
- there is a freedom in creation of constraints that may be put on the aggregates also,
- to formulate other new aggregated it is possible basing on the lower layer of the model that reflects static behavior of a network representing a strongly connected production structure of the chemical industry.

The model in its type is a quasi-linear programming one because some optimization scenarios are possible using pure linear formulas:

- a single objective case with a choice of criteria,
- a multi objective case,
- a linear-fractional case for a single objective.

As this is the second paper in the series dealing with the development programming of the chemical industry, a reader is expected to refer to the rest of the series and to the bibliography as usual.

2 Verbal description of the model

One of the most interesting facts about the chemical industry is that a large proportion of its products are derived from only a very small number of raw materials. As the processing of natural resources with mineral or agricultural origin is going downstream, the chains that represent ways of processing are branching from one generation of intermediates to another. To complicate this figure some chains are coupled together across few generations making loops. Moreover, there exist alternative routes leading to particular intermediates and there are also alternative routes and technologies that produce various final products. So the developed chemical industry presents in fact ever changing network of interlinked technologies.

A particular branch of the chemical industry can be modeled as a network of production processes aggregated to simple production functions and distribution flows for a group of chemicals specified. The following components are considered in the model:

- chemicals and other resources and their flows in the PDA represented by balance nodes satisfying the mass balance principle,
- chemical transformations represented by processes that process chemicals exchangeable with the environment into other exchangeable chemicals,
- other indispensable resources also in terms of their flows.

A simple transition function is defined for the process elements by yield and consumption coefficients together with a capacity constraint. The network is constructed in the way that processes are connected to each other throughout balance nodes.

Relations between the components of the model are to reflect well-known phenomena existing in the chemical industry:

- a chemical can either go to or be obtained from a number of the transformations,
- a chemical transformation may either produce or consume a number of chemicals,
- one or more chemical processes can run on one chemical installation,
- certain resources are necessary for operation of any installation,

- chemicals and resources can be exchanged via their flows with the environment.

Interaction with the environment is assumed by I/O flows of chemicals and other resources (sources and sinks of the network).

The domain of the model application and also through considering yield or consumption coefficients with respect to capacities allow all formulas of the model to be linear.

All the above is comprised in a lower layer of the model that is a bipartite network with constraints. Moreover, using the described flows, a set of aggregates can be evaluated for the PDA. The aggregates are constructed on the base of cost calculation scheme using prices and of energy equivalent calculation using the lower heating value. Additionally two lists of prices are used with the exchange rate as a parameter. It corresponds to the economy with a non-convertible currency and prices different for domestic and foreign markets.

Below all modeled phenomena will be described in rather brief form. First, a short comment on interpretation will be done and next, equations are presented.

3 Elements of the model

There are five types of elements of the model:

1. Installations - indexed by set I,
2. Processes - indexed by set P,
3. Media - indexed by set J,
4. Markets - indexed by set M.
5. Special resources - indexed by set S.

To reflect the possibility of running a number of different chemical processes on the same hardware the element called installation was introduced. Processes of the particular installation are dependent on a common capacity constraint.
The idea of installation splits I/O flows into two categories called:

media - flows which are interchanged between processes themselves and between processes and environment of the PDA, i.e. raw materials, products and by-products.

special resources - flows which are interchanged between installations and environment (common for all processes running on a particular installation), e.g.. investment, manpower.

To model an interface between the PDA and its environment, markets for media are introduced. The markets introduce characteristics of I/O media in terms of their sellability and availability. There may be up to four markets for a particular medium: domestic sale, domestic purchase, foreign sale (export) and foreign purchase (import). Because the category of special resources is not numerous they are treated separately.

Having in mind that media constitute a majority of flows, nobody ought to be surprised that it is a means for modeling not only particular chemicals, energy carriers but also pollutants in bulk (solid waste, liquid waste, emission) or in groups of toxic substances.

4 Formulas

Let us introduce variables of the model:

z_p, $p \in P$ - a level of production of process p,
y_j^m, $j \in J$, $m \in M$ - an amount of medium j bought or sold on market m.

An auxiliary equation describes amount of a given medium produced or consumed.

$$y_j = \sum_{p \in P_j^+} b_{jp} \, z_p - \sum_{p \in P_j^-} a_{jp} \, z_p \quad , \quad j \in J \tag{1}$$

while the symbols above are defined as follows:
P_j^- - a subset of processes where medium j is consumed,
a_{jp} z_p - quantity of medium j consumed (consumption coefficient),
P_j^+ - a subset of processes where medium j is produced,
b_{jp} z_p - quantity of medium j produced (yield coefficient).

Balance equation for media

$$\sum_{m \in M_j^+} y_j^m - \sum_{m \in M_j^-} y_j^m = y_j \quad , \quad j \in J \tag{2}$$

where:
M_j^+ - a subset of markets where medium j may be sold,
M_j^- - a subset of markets where medium j may be bought,

Balance of special resources

Formulas for a balance of the special resources have the same shape and only interpretation of coefficients is different.

$$Q^s = \sum_{i \in I} \sum_{p \in P^i} q_p^s \, z_p \quad , \quad s \in S \tag{3}$$

where: P^i - the subset of processes running on the installation i.

For each special resource the coefficient q_p^s is estimated as a value related to the capacity of the process p.
The following special resources are defined in the PDA model:

- investment in a portion counted in the convertible currency, that must be paid abroad (the coefficient is a unit investment cost),
- investment in a portion counted in the local currency spent locally (unit investment cost for local expenses),
- labor — unskilled workers (a ratio men to capacity),
- supervision,
- labor — laboratory & control.

The applied above approach means that dependencies of investment and labor with respect to the capacity are linearized. To sustain reliability of the model at this point, a procedure for adjustment is assumed to keep an obtained production level reasonably close to the capacity.

Other special resources can be introduced for any special applications of the model.

Constraints on flows

Market constraints

$$\underline{y}_j^m \le y_j^m \le \bar{y}_j^m \ , \quad m \in M_j^+ \cup M_j^- \ , \quad j \in J \tag{4}$$

Special resources constraints

$$\underline{Q}^s \le Q^s \le \bar{Q}^s \ , \quad s \in S \tag{5}$$

Capacity constraints for processes

$$\sum_{p \in P^i} \frac{1}{\bar{z}_p} z_p \le 1 \ , \quad i \in I \tag{6}$$

where: $\bar{z}_p$ - production capacity of the process p.

When a number of processes are to run on the same installation, the capacity is calculated under an assumption that the particular process occupies the whole installation.

Reconstruction constraints

$$\sum_{p \in P^o} \frac{1}{\bar{z}_p} z_p + \sum_{p \in P^n} \frac{1}{\bar{z}_p} z_p \le 1 \ , \quad o, n \in I \tag{7}$$

Indexes o and n denotes an installation to be reconstructed and an installation after reconstruction, respectively. The constraint is defined for all couples of installation specified. There is a linearization of an exclusion condition that the old and new installations can not run simultaneously. Such a trick is successful when links of the installations in the network are similar.

Aggregates

Production value

$$\sum_{j \in J} \sum_{m \in M_j^+} c_j^m \, y_j^m \tag{8}$$

where: c_j^m - a price of medium j on the market m.

Cost of materials

$$\sum_{j \in J} \sum_{m \in M_j^-} c_j^m \, y_j^m \tag{9}$$

Another aggregate can be obtained as a difference of the production value and the cost of materials that is called the manufacturing value added.

Production cost

$$\sum_{i \in I} \sum_{p \in P^i} \alpha_p \, z_p \; + \sum_{j \in J} \sum_{m \in M_j^-} c_j^m \, y_j^m \tag{10}$$

where: α_p - a unit process cost coefficient for process p. The coefficient includes all cost factors modeled except the cost of materials. There are the cost of special resources and — depending on an assumed scheme of cost calculation — depreciation, taxes, assurance, overheads, etc.

The production cost can be used to get a formulas for profit and in turn for simple rate of return.

Energy equivalent of production

$$\sum_{j \in J} \sum_{m \in M_j^+} e_j^m \, y_j^m \tag{11}$$

where: e_j^m - unit energy equivalent of medium j.

For media that are not an energy carriers the lower heating value is used as the coefficient.

Energy equivalent of materials

$$\sum_{j \in J} \sum_{m \in M_j^-} e_j^m \, y_j^m \tag{12}$$

Using the two above aggregates derivative ones can be obtained: the energy lost and the energy efficiency.

5 Summary

As it was shown the PDA model constitutes the base for various operational models used by the MIDA system and methodology. The final formulation is gained as an effect of the following steps:

1. Selection of a type of the model by fixing a set of aggregates used.
2. Definition of the particular network and its constraints according to data about an area of the chemical industry under consideration.
3. Selection of criterion or criteria and putting limitation to aggregates.

Such an approach to construction of the model is suitable when it may be incorporated into a DSS system.
The steps in a MIDA environment are realized as follows:

1. Selection of a particular computer implementation of the MIDA.
2. Generation of the model automatically done by the computer system according to a contents of data base.
3. Selection or alteration during interactive session with the MIDA.

The PDA model presented proved its applicability in many diverse cases (discussed in the preceding paper). It was also tried in a dynamic version (Dobrowolski and Rys 1981), however this route was not selected in MIDA for implementation.

References

Borek, A., Dobrowolski G., Zebrowski M. (1978) GSOS — Growth Strategy Optimization System for the Chemical Industry. In: Advances in Measurement and Control MECO'78, pp. 1128-1131, vol. 3, Acta Press, Athens.

Dobrowolski, G., Rys T. (1981) Dynamiczny model programowania rozwoju sieci produkcyjno-handlowej. Teoria i aplikacja. In: Symulacja systemow gospodarczych. Szkola Trzebieszowice'81. Suplement, K. Nowak A. Pelech, eds., pp. 1-22, Towarzystwo Naukowe Organizacji i Zarzadzania, Wroclaw, Gliwice.

Dobrowolski, G., Kopytowski J., Wojtania J., Zebrowski M. (1984) Alternative Routes from Fossil Resources to Chemical Feedstock. IIASA Research Report RR-84-19, Laxenburg, Austria.

Zebrowski, M., Dobrowolski G., Rys T., Skocz T., Ziembla W. (1988) Industrial Structure Optimization: The PDAS Model. In: Expert Systems for Integrated Development: A Case Study of Shanxi Province The People's Republic of China, Final Report, Volume I, pp. 87-134. IIASA, Laxenburg, Austria.

Multiobjective Evaluation of Industrial Structures

Maciej Zebrowski
Joint Systems Research Department
of the Institute for Control and Systems Engineering,
Academy of Mining and Metallurgy, Cracow,
and the Industrial Chemistry Research Institute, Warsaw.

Abstract

Problem of multiobjective evaluation of Industrial Structures is presented. It is located in the context of programming development of the chemical industry. The boundaries of the decision space are defined. Efficiency evaluation model is presented based on the concept of Output (O) and Input (I) efficiency relations of an Industrial Structure subject to the programming of its development. Some implications of the model on decision support system DSS and its methodology are highlighted backed with the example of a multiobjective evaluation of a particular industrial structure.

1 Introduction

In order to provide a DSS well fitted to the decision problem of programming development as presented in the introductory paper an appropriate framework for evaluation of industrial structures (IS) in question must be set up.

By the nature of the problem it is a multiobjective one. In this paper such a framework is presented.

It consists of two levels:

- The first level is an efficiency evaluation model. The one that reflects the efficiency relations between resources assigned to the IS and resources that as a result are obtained from it.
- Second or the lower level contains a model of IS which is a subject of multiobjective evaluation.

While this model or a PDA type of model is discussed in the preceding paper in this series here attention is focused on the efficiency evaluation model. However, it should be mentioned that the efficiency evaluation model is of the general type and it can be coupled with various models (and/or their versions) of an IS.

The origin of the model discussed goes back to the substitution phenomena, which by their nature are involved in the development process of any IS and may be considered synonymous with its development.

Then the boundaries of the decision space are discussed and it is shown that they naturally evolve from the properties of the techno-economic systems.

The model for the multiobjective efficiency evaluation is discussed. It is based on prerequisites which in a formal way reflect natural preferences in the decision making practice and are represented by efficiency ratios of consumed (or input) and obtained (or output) resources.

They are in agreement with the properties of the techno-economic system in general and what obviously follows with the properties of IS discussed in particular.

Implications of the model on the DSS and thus the methodology of its application are briefly highlighted opening way to the example of the multiobjective evaluation of the particular IS described by a PDA model of Fuels and Feedstock branch of the chemical industry.

The research reported here was sponsored by the Polish Government Energy Program, but since the sponsor willingly accepted collaboration with IIASA specifically with the Study on Theory, Software and Testing Examples for Decision Support Systems, the concepts originated in the initial project were further developed and as such are presented.

2 Formal framework for the multiobjective evaluation

2.1 Origin and problem statement

Development of on industrial structure (IS) is equivalent to its transformation (in the course of time) by means of investment. The process of transformation involves substitution phenomena.
Three types of substitution can be enumerated:

- substitution of feedstock,
- substitution of final products,
- substitution of technologies.

Physically, it is substitution of technologies - old by new - that enables for the two other types of substitution to take place.

Consequently, in programming development, the key activity is a generation and then assessment of development alternatives. From an alternative to alternative all three types of substitution are involved and have to be clearly assessed.

To asses alternatives considered and substitution involved is the goal of the predecission analysis. The assessment must be done along well established rules for efficiency evaluation.
Two layers or two levels must be identified:

- First represents efficiency evaluation rules. These can be mapped in the model that reflects efficiency relations between resources assigned (consumed) and resources obtained (or resulting). These rules are to be applied to the IS considered.

- Second layer or level represents industrial structure itself. In general it is to be mapped in the model specific for the IS considered, while the first level remains basically intact. In particular a PDA type of model, described in the second paper of the series is involved (Dobrowolski and Zebrowski,1988).

Therefore attention is to be focused on the first level namely on the efficiency evaluation model.

2.2 Boundaries of decision space

Boundaries of a decision space stem from the nature of development of industrial structures and can be considered as generally applicable concept for a techno-economic system. First the concept of efficiency can be introduced.
Two types of efficiency can be considered:

- economic efficiency,
- physical efficiency.

The first can be exemplified by profit or MVA (Manufacturing Value Added). It is natural that only domain of positive values is interesting from the point of view of decision analysis. This is equivalent to values greater than 1 if the efficiency is to be expressed in the terms of ratio and means that one is interested only in a domain in which a gain is assumed as a result of PDA activity.

For the second type of efficiency i.e. physical, due to its nature the corresponding ratio must be smaller than 1 since for the physical properties of any industrial system a loss must accompany any material processing. This in turn can be exemplified by yield or consumption coefficients describing efficiency of conversion process of feedstock into products. The other example would be energy conversion efficiency or ECE.

From the above it can be concluded that decision space is naturally delimited by efficiency domain. Simply by choosing efficiency ratios, decision maker delimits the decision space making it feasible from the point of view of development analysis.

2.3 The model

Without loosing generality we may use PDA model to represent IS model in our considerations.

Let us consider a PDA (or an IS) taking into account only two types of resources - consumed or utilized by the PDA and those that may result from this utilization. They can be respectively denoted as:

$$\begin{array}{lcl} y^I & - & \text{input resources,} \\ y^O & - & \text{output resources.} \end{array}$$

The resources of y^I and y^O type could be chemical raw materials, semi-products and products as well as water, technological energy and investment. The set of solutions of a PDA model designates, a maximum range of substitution dependent on the repertoire of technologies considered in the network. In real life cases, the range of substitution is narrowed by additional restrictions imposed on y^I resources (availability) and y^O resources (salability and/or demand patterns) and the production level (production capacities). Such constraints may either represent actual information (as a result of identification) or also be postulated in order to obtain additional information on the substitution properties of the network.

We specify now some general prerequisites that enable further formalization of the control of substitution process and thus will be useful for efficiency evaluation of a PDA.

Prerequisite 1. Efficient-feasible state.

The states of a PDA that satisfy specific additional constraints are considered as feasible, whereas such feasible states that:

$$y^O \mapsto max$$
$$y^I \mapsto min$$

are regarded as efficient-feasible.

The assumption that we might restrict the analysis to efficient-feasible states limits the substitution range. Therefore at this stage of considerations we restrict the substitution analysis to such cases which are most efficient. As it will be explained below, efficiency can be formally expressed in a number of other ways.

Although this assumption may seem to be intuitively obvious, it is practically difficult to satisfy it if the number of y^I and y^O flows is large. This obstacle may be overcome by following a modified prerequisite instead:

Prerequisite 2. Aggregate efficiency.

Instead of optimizing each component of flow of the resources y^I and y^0 a smaller number of attributes can be defined to characterize the resources y^I and y^O thus enabling for their aggregation. These aggregates will be used for representation of the area resources. The price of a product or a raw material, or their heating values may be regarded as examples of such attributes.

We assume that it is possible to characterize the input resources by n_i aggregate quantitative attributes that will be minimized and the output resources by n_0 attributes that will be maximized:

$$a^I(y^I) \in R^{n_i}$$
$$a^0(y^0) \in R^{n_0}$$

where R^{n_i}, R^{n_0} - the corresponding spaces of real vectors.

Aggregate attributes can be also obtained through subtraction of other attributes provided those attributes have the same physical meaning and formal rules of subtraction are followed. Economic efficiency calculated as a difference between value of the

total sale of PDA and the total cost of production in a particular state of the flows of resources, or the total energy balance of the PDA calculated as the difference between total energy consumed and total energy obtained (in products) may serve as examples of such aggregates.
We shall thus assume that:

- the attributes of resources of both I and O type can be quantified in positive numbers only,
- attributes of I,O resources are classified accordingly as consumed (minimized) and obtained (maximized),
- the difference between two attributes of O-I type can be defined in cases of attributes of the same nature, whereas for $O > I$, the result of subtraction O-I brings gain to the system while for $O < I$ the result of I-O means loss.

Thus, the Prerequisite 1 is modified to the following:

$$a^O \mapsto max$$

$$a^I \mapsto min$$

and correspondingly for attributes that allow for subtraction:

$$a^O - a^I \mapsto max$$

$$a^I - a^O \mapsto min$$

Three remarks can be related to the above principles of aggregation:

1) The number of attributes a^I, a^0 decreases with aggregation, hence satisfying Prerequisite 2 is easier than satisfying Prerequisite 1.

2) The substitution may be limited also by imposing constraints on aggregate attributes.

3) Substitution may take place both on the side of input aggregates and on the side of output aggregates. Should such a substitution occur, each state of the PDA can be characterized by different efficiency of the transition from inputs to outputs. Therefore, the concept of efficiency is fundamental for the model and it will be explained further in detail.

Prerequisite 3. Equivalence and efficiency.

Either the resources or their aggregate attributes are considered as hierarchically equivalent. It results from the fact that following Prerequisites 1 or 2 the optimization applies equivalently to all resource components or individual attributes, which corresponds to multiobjective optimization in Pareto sense.

A hierarchy of resources or attributes can be introduced first when entering the sphere of the formulation of a development thesis (Dobrowolski and Zebrowski, 1985). Such a formulation is discussed in the following paper (Dobrowolski and Zebrowski, 1988).

Within the formal framework of the substitution model one should solve the problem of how to represent the efficiency of substitution. The efficiency rules are to provide a formal interface between substitution and preferences assigned by a decision maker when formulating a development thesis.

Therefore let us analyze again Prerequisite 1. As it was mentioned, it comprises the operations min, max and connects de facto substitution with its efficiency. Observe that in order to consider a substitution of that kind at least two resources of the same type and one of the opposite must be considered, i.e. two output resources and one input resource or vice versa. For instance, raw materials substitution usually means a substitution of a raw material 1 for a raw material 2; obviously the efficiency of such an operation must be related to the product or products obtained.

The problem arises how to express efficiency of obtaining a given product y^0 from raw materials ${y_1}^I$ or ${y_2}^I$. It may be solved by introducing the concept of efficiency ratios where:

$$\frac{y^0}{y_1^I}, \quad \frac{y^0}{y_2^I}, \quad \mapsto \quad max$$

denotes the efficiency of obtaining y^0 from y_1^I or y_2^I, respectively, while

$$\frac{y_1^I}{y^0}, \quad \frac{y_2^I}{y^0}, \quad \mapsto \quad min$$

denotes the efficiency of consuming y_1^I and y_2^I, respectively, to obtain y^0. Therefore, they may be regarded as equivalent inverse intensity ratios. The same applies also for the aggregate attributes:

$$\frac{a^I}{a^O} \quad \mapsto \quad min$$

$$\frac{a^O}{a^I} \quad \mapsto \quad max$$

while, in the above example, the attribute a^I might jointly characterize the case of

resources y_1^I, y_2^I. The above ratios are a natural generalization and provide very practical efficiency indicators. The same applies to ratios built on differential aggregates; a good example of such combined ratio may be:

$$\frac{a_1^O - a_1^I}{a_2^I - a_2^O} \quad \mapsto \quad max$$

where denominator expresses resources consumed (such as net energy balance) while the numerator expresses resources obtained (such as added value).
We can conclude this discussion by following remarks:

- Prerequisites 1, 2 and 3 provide for a simple analysis of substitution of elementary resources (of I,O type) based on a chosen set of intensity ratios.

- The area of substitution is limited by the assumptions of optimization of chosen indicators.

When formulating a development thesis in the multiobjective industrial development analysis for a given PDA, the key issue is that of critical resources. The decision maker may, for the sake of the formulation of the development thesis, assign a status of critical resource to any of the resources of O or I type as well as their aggregates (Dobrowolski et al. 1984) According to MIDA methodology, a critical resource is defined as single resource or an aggregate attribute which obtained this status through the decision maker's choice, as it was considered by him as crucial (critical) for the implementation of the development thesis.

In the context of the efficiency evaluation model considered here, the status of a critical resource could be assigned e.g. to the resource that was chosen in order to find out a possibility and efficiency of its substitution by another resource. Hence a PDA model is then examined to enable the analysis of substitution efficiency as a part of analysis resulting from development thesis.

2.4 Toward decision support for multiobjective evaluation of industrial development strategy–IDS

Before discussing a real life example let us make some additional observations. The intensity ratios built on the input and output aggregates when used as criteria for multiobjective problem, attain their extreme values in vertices of Pareto optimal surface. It was proposed (Dobrowolski and Zebrowski, 1984) to define this area denoted by the efficient vertices in the criteria space as Attainable Performance Area (APA).

It was described in the paper on basic or PDA model (second in the series) that a technological repertoire or a set of technologies is naturally divided into two subsets. The first represents existing technologies while the second - potentially available technologies that require additional investment. Therefore two types of respective industrial structures must be distinguished: the first, that assures the attainability of current production goals by existing technologies and the second that comprises those technologies that can be introduced by means of investment.

The formal framework presented above provides a good point of departure for devising a DSS tool for the evaluation of industrial development strategies in terms of intensity ratios which are practically used and well interpretable by decision makers. This approach became then naturally a part of MIDA methodology (Dobrowolski et al. 1985).

To make this extension applicable, following methodological steps are to be considered. The starting one is the evaluation of APA which is to be represented by selected set of intensity ratios and which is to be agreed with the decision maker as a complete set for a given stage of analysis. All the necessary conditions for the evaluation of the **existing** state in terms of its performance such as production goal as well as a set of other defining conditions (see an example below and also (Dobrowolski and Zebrowski, 1985)) are to be known. Another distinguished structure is the one that may be called an **ultimate** or **goal** structure. This is defined by a similar set of parameters and conditions as those describing the existing structure with the fundamental difference that they correspond to the aspirations of the decision maker.

The above provides a first step in the analysis. Next comes the analysis of Attainable Performance Area (APA). There is no unique way of analyzing this type of Pareto set. It should be adjusted to the particular needs of a decision maker when solving a particular case; however, the necessary information, that is, the efficient vertices must be designated. Then a feasible method for acquiring knowledge about the properties of APA is to be chosen. APA, let us remind, reflects properties of the available repertoire of technologies assembled into alternative industrial structures. These structures represent potential alternatives for industrial development strategy that are Pareto optimal with respect to intensity ratios (criteria) accepted for their evaluation. A practical feasible indication for devising such a method is to define some cross sections of APA, parameterized by a ratio representing a decision variable which is a driving force for the development. This could be represented for example, by intensity ratio built on investment. Obviously such a ratio is indispensable when a set of intensity ratios is being considered by a decision maker.

Next comes, as a natural step, the evaluation of various development trajectories expressed in terms of horizon of implementation of alternative development strategies. This gives to the decision maker an idea about the dynamics of achieving the goal structure as represented by a completion of a chosen industrial development strategy. From that stems a natural mode of parameterizing an implementation horizon by the period of investment return.

Having all the above information, the decision maker can also obtain the resulting values of critical resources which are to be consumed or can be obtained with respective strategies. This knowledge compared with corresponding data from the analysis performed for the existing state is a very practical method of evaluating substitution of critical resources due to the substitution of technologies within respective industrial structures. All the above considerations will be now illustrated by means of a practical industrial example.

3 Example of multiobjective evaluation of IDS

3.1 Energy and chemical feedstock PDA

Based on the formal background presented above, the problem may be referred to a particular PDA. Purposefully an area was chosen that was described before in other works (see for e.g. Dobrowolski and Zebrowski, 1985 and also next paper in this volume), since it may serve as a good example and illustration of MIDA approach. For brief the model considered here will be denoted PDA-EF (Energy and Feedstock).

Let us start from presenting shortly a considered object of the analysis. Its dimensions amount the number of 89 installations (processes) and 65 raw materials, semi-products and products. They were chosen from a given data base (see Dobrowolski et al. 1984) and constitute the model of PDA. Thereby a repertoire of attainable production structures was determined together with indispensable resources of all sorts and this delimits space for alternative development strategies.

The PDA covers the production of motor fuels (gasoline, diesel oil, jet-fuel) basic hydrocarbon chemical raw materials (aromatics, olefines, methanol, etc.) and heating oil from crude oil, coal, lignite and gas.

In principle it is an area connected with crude oil processing. Methanol which is regarded as a potential fuel and raw material for a number of new applications, was added to this area. It is enriched by processing of coal and lignite. Technologies for processing natural gas are also present but with limited representation (mostly for methanol production).

Consequently the PDA includes existing plants (refineries, methanol, aromatics and olefines plants) as well as the future ones based on a range of technologies for processing coal and lignite (gasification, liquefaction, pyrolysis, critical extraction of coal, etc.). New plants for crude oil processing are also included.

Information about the PDA necessary for analysis, may be ordered as follows:

1. Technological repertoire is given (described by respective parameters and production capacities – for existing and new technologies).

2. Substitution of critical resources that are primary energy carriers (a basic feedstock) is to be evaluated. These are:

    - crude oil,
    - hard coal,
    - lignite,
    - natural gas.

3. It is assumed that the range of substitution is limited through demand for the output critical resources imposed by the strategy of higher level (macroeconomic production goals). This comprises following products:

    - ethylene,
    - benzene,
    - methanol,
    - diesel oil,
    - carbonizate from coal,
    - carbonizate from lignite.

    This demand describes a goal production level while existing production levels are also defined.

4. The following values are assumed to be the attributes that enable for aggregation:
   - prices of I, O resources (including technological energy, that is, steam and electric energy),
   - heating values of raw materials and products existing in the PDA.
5. The following aggregates are defined:
   - IE - input energy - technological energy used by PDA and energy contained in raw materials,
   - OE - output energy - energy gained in the products,
   - II - input investment,
   - IV - input value - value of purchase of raw materials and energy,
   - OV - output value - value of sale of the products.

   Additionally a differential aggregate can be defined:

   AV = OV - IV - which is interpreted as the Added Value.
6. Efficiency ratios expressed in terms of the defined aggregates are as follows:
   - OE/IE - Energy Conversion Efficiency
   - OV/IV - Economic Efficiency ratio,
   - AV/II - Efficiency of Investment, which is equivalent to RI - Return on Investment.

Let us consider the multiobjective problem based on the following three efficiency ratios:

$$OE/IE \mapsto \max ;$$

$$OV/IV \mapsto \max ;$$

$$AV/II \mapsto \max ;$$

A set of states of the PDA-EF model defining possible substitution will be a solution to this problem. Observe that:

- Prerequisites 1 and 2 are satisfied for the representation of the assumed attributes;
- The problem is formulated in the Pareto sense (equivalence of criteria) and, therefore, Prerequisite 3 is also satisfied;
- Efficiency of substitution is considered in terms of assumed criteria.

Symbol of experiment	Criterion name	OV / IV	OE / IE	AV / II	II (Input Investment)
V	Economic efficiency (OV / IV)	1.80516	0.72361	0.25237	15576
E	Energy conversion efficiency (OE / IE)	1.51682	0.87435	0.62281	4340
I	Return on Investment (AV / IV)	1.48720	0.77076	2.02212	1130

Table 1: APA - Attainable Performance Area - Vertices

Therefore, the set of solutions comprises only such alternatives of substitution, for which the three efficiency ratios have greater value than the rejected ones. Such set of solutions can be presented as a surface in the criteria space, which will be shown in the next paragraph. In such a way, the substitution area for all input and output resources existing in PDA-EF was obtained. It can be expressed in terms of assumed efficiency ratios and in absolute values of critical resources gained or consumed. These two types of parameters describe industrial structure rather adequately from the point of view of a decision maker since they provide information about the scale or level of operation and its intensity (Skocz, Zebrowski, 1986). At the same time, this information serves best for the comparison of various development alternatives. The completeness of ratios as well as list of critical resources taken into consideration may vary from case to case but the principle remains unchanged.

In the case discussed here the surface representing the set of solutions of the problem of optimal substitution is spanned by three vertices of this Pareto surface. They may be interpreted as follows:

$OE/IE\ (max)$ denotes the state of PDA-EF with the greatest energy efficiency.
$OV/IV\ (max)$ denotes the state of PDA-EF with the greatest economic efficiency.
$AV/II\ (max)$ denotes the state of PDA-EF with the best investment efficiency.

3.2 Experiments with the model

Experiments with a PDA-EF model are summarized in Tables 1-4 and visualized by Figure 1.

APA or Attainable Performance Area of PDA-EF is shown in Table 1. This gives an idea of the substitution flexibility of the technological repertoire as expressed in terms of the three selected ratios. Another important information given in that table it the cost of investment (II) which is to be involved to attain a structure corresponding to respective vertices. The difference in calculated values of II is more than 10 fold, while the corresponding ratios are not so dramatically different however the experienced decision maker knows that even several per cent difference in intensity ratios should not be underestimated. Table 4 - which is a summary table - provides a relation between the existing industrial structure and APA. It shows also the consumption of critical

V, I, E vertices

VE projection of Pareto surface on plane of economic efficiency (OV/IV) and energy conversion efficiency (OE/IE)

VI-1, EI-1 lines corresponding to constant value of return of investment

VI-2,E

VI-3, VE-3

VI-4, VE-4

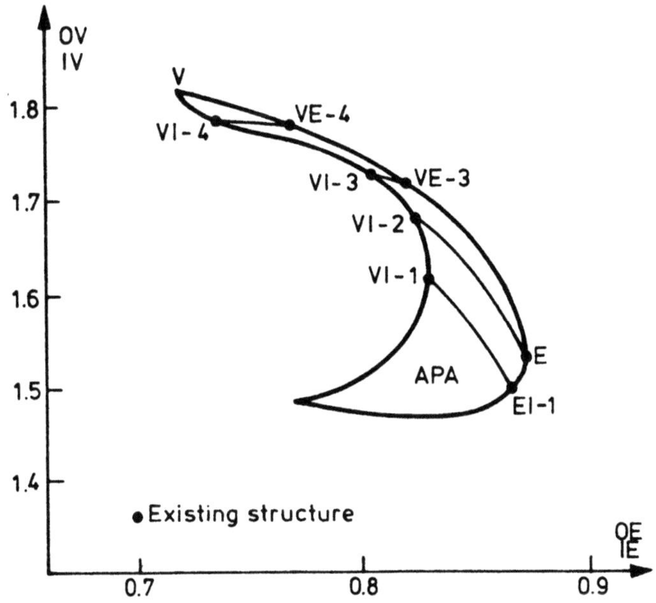

Figure 1: Pareto set for Fuels and Feedstock PDA.

No	Value of AV / II	Symbol of Experiment	OV / IV	OE / IE mln $	II	Symbol of Experiment	OV / IV mln $	OE / IE	II
1	1.00000	VI - 1	1.61349	0.83056	2646	EI - 1	1.48593	0.86807	2573
2	0.62281	VI - 2	1.68658	0.8260	4724	E	1.51682	0.87435	4340
3	0.45372	VI - 3	1.73178	0.79939	7348	VE - 3	1.70738	0.82508	6612
4	0.30815	VI - 4	1.78349	0.7291	12545	VE - 4	1.77041	0.77374	11728

Table 2: APA - Attainable Performance Area - Cross Sections parameterized by value of AV/II

resources for respective industrial structures and their substitution as related to their intensity ratios.

Table 2 contains cross sections of APA as visualized on Figure 1. Cross sections are defined by the fixed value of the rate of return on investment, namely AV/II.

With the above knowledge it is useful to perform the following evaluation of APA (illustrated by Table 3.). This evaluation is done in order to figure out the implementation horizon and the rate of return on investment as parameterized by a return period. This is a better methodological approach than the one based only on a pre-defined return of investment ratio.

The reader is invited to get a closer insight by evaluating the data himself. It may be added that - with such simple calculations - a good feeling of dynamic properties of the evaluated strategies can be achieved by a decision maker. This is meant in the sense of feasibility of a given strategy in time related to the indispensable investment level. Naturally the value of the information on development dynamics lies rather in the comparison of various industrial development strategies than in the calculation of static indices. Without a preliminary comparison of basic indices, however, the choice of alternatives for further investigation cannot be carried out. The dynamic aspects are, in terms of investment schedule, discussed in the separate paper of this series.

Finally, Table 4 provides information which summarizes the results of the analysis.

4 Conclusions

We may conclude that by incorporating in MIDA system and methodology the concepts presented in this paper, it became a practically oriented and advanced DSS. The simple theoretical framework provided a good interface between the system and a decision maker.

In particular the concept of APA utilized in this paper proved to be very useful owing to its practical and clear interpretation. The progress described here demanded, however, a very substantial effort on the side of software implementation, specifically a linear fractional programming solver developed by G. Dobrowolski, which was implemented and embedded in MIDA system. Similarly, an *Optimist* software package implemented by T. Ryś was an important software tool enabling MIDA to be used for the type of analysis described in this paper.

Production Unit	Capacity	Location	Construction	
			Start	Finish
Dibutyl Phthalate	3000	A	2.0	3.5
Dinitrotoluene	22000	B	2.5	3.5
Dioctyl Phthalate	40000	A	2.0	3.5
Ethylbenzene (Benzene Alkylation)	75000	A	2.0	3.5
Ethylene Glycol and Oxide	15000	A	0.5	2.0
Melamine-Formaldehyde Resin	10000	B	0.5	2.0
Phenol-Formaldehyde Resol Syrup	10000	B	0.5	2.0
Phosgene from Chlorine and CO	22000	B	2.5	4.0
Phtalic Anhydride from o-Xylene	27000	A	1.0	2.5
Polyether Polyol for Polyurethanes	38000	B	2.5	4.0
Polyethylene Terephthalate from TA	40000	A	1.5	3.0
Polystyrene General Purpose	30000	A	2.0	4.0
Polystyrene High Impact	10000	A	2.0	4.0
Polyurethane Resin from Polyol and TDI	50000	B	3.5	4.5
Propylene Oxide (Ethylbenzene Process)	27000	A	1.5	3.5
Sodium Alkylbenzene Sulfonate	40000	B	0.5	2.5
Sulfuric Acid from Sulfur	100000	B	0.5	2.0
TDA from Dinitrotoluene	14000	B	2.5	4.0
TDI from TDA	17000	B	2.5	4.5
Terephthalic Acid from p-Xylene	35000	A	1.0	2.5
Unsaturated Polyester Resin	10000	A	1.0	2.5
Urea-Formaldehyde Syrup	15000	B	0.5	2.0

Table 2: Spatial allocation and investment schedule for structure S_1

Production Unit	Capacity	Location	Construction	
			Start	Finish
ABS Resin	10000	A	8.0	9.0
Acetic Acid from Methanol	40000	C	6.5	8.5
Acrilonitrile (Propylene Ammoxidation)	50000	B	6.5	8.5
Bisphenol from Phenol and Aceton	15000	A	8.0	9.5
Butadiene from C_4 Extraction	35000	B	5.0	7.0
Butene-1 (Ethylene Dimerization)	12000	C	7.5	8.5
Caprolactam from Cyclohexane	50000	A	6.5	8.5
Carbon Black from Carbon Black Oil	30000	A	4.5	6.5
Chlorine (electrolysis)	100000	B	7.5	9.0
Cyclohexane from Benzene	50000	A	6.5	8.0
Epoxy Resin	20000	A	8.0	9.5
Ethyl Acetate	5000	C	7.5	8.5
Ethylene Glycol and Oxide	20000	B	5.5	7.0
Ethylene from Ethane	150000	C	5.5	8.0
Ethylene from Naphtha MS Cracking	150000	B	4.0	6.5
Methylmethacrylate Cyanohydrin Proc.	10000	B	7.0	9.0
Nylon 6 (chips)	30000	A	6.5	8.5
Polyethylene High Density	80000	B	4.5	6.5
Polyethylene Linear Low Density	120000	C	6.0	8.0
Polymethylmethacrylate	5000	B	7.5	9.0
Polypropylene (Amoco Technology)	50000	B	5.0	7.0
Polyvinyl Acetate Emulsion	50000	C	8.5	10.0
Polyvinyl Chloride Suspension	50000	B	8.0	10.0
Primary Alcohol Ethoxylate	10000	A	5.5	7.5
Primary Alcohol Ethoxysulfonate	10000	A	5.5	7.5
Primary Alcohol Sulfonate	10000	A	5.5	7.5
Primary Alcohols C_6 – C_{12}	15000	A	5.0	7.0
SAN Resin	5000	A	8.0	9.0
Styrene-Butadiene Rubber	45000	A	4.5	7.0
Unsaturated Polyester Resin	10000	A	8.0	9.5
Vinyl Acetate from Ethylene	50000	C	8.0	9.5
Vinyl Chloride (Oxychlorination)	50000	B	8.0	10.0

Table 3: Spatial allocation and investment schedule for final structure S_2

Acknowledgements

Author feels deeply indebted to his co-workers from JSRD and would like to express his gratitude to G. Dobrowolski who assisted in conceiving the primary version of the model (M. Zebrowski, 1987). W. Ziembla helped significantly in the last stage of completion of the paper when the concept of APA was utilized for IDS evaluation. The above does not take off the responsibility from the author for any faults that may occur in the presented paper.

References

Borek, A.,G. Dobrowolski, M. Zebrowski, (1979) Applications of System Analysis in Management of Growth and Development of the Chemical Industry. CHEM/SEM.8/R.16 Report of Chemical Industry Committee of the United Nations.

Dobrowolski, G., J. Kopytowski, J. Wojtania, M. Zebrowski (1984) Alternative Routes from Fossil Resources to Chemical Feedstock. IIASA Research Report RR-84-19, Laxenburg, Austria.

Dobrowolski, G., M. Zebrowski (1985) Decision Support in Substitution Analysis for IDS - Industrial Development Strategy Exemplified by the Fuel and Feedstock Sector of the Chemical Industry. The Application of DIDAS. Theory, Software and Test Examples for Decision Support Systems, A. Lewandowski and A. Wierzbicki eds., IIASA, Laxenburg, Austria.

Dobrowolski, G., J. Kopytowski, T. Rys, M. Zebrowski (1985) MIDA - Multiobjective Interactive Decision Aid in the Development of the Chemical Industry. Theory, Software and Test Examples for Decision Support Systems, A. Lewandowski and A. Wierzbicki eds.,IIASA, Laxenburg, Austria.

Skocz, M., M. Zebrowski (1986) An Extended Resources Allocation Method in Design of Industrial Development Strategy. *Proceedings of IFAC Symposium on Large Scale Systems, Zurich.*

Zebrowski, M. (1987) Multiobjective Evaluation of Industrial Structures. MIDA Application to the case of the chemical industry. Theory, Software and Testing Examples for Decision Support Systems, A. Lewandowski and A. Wierzbicki eds., WP-87-26, IIASA, Laxenburg, Austria.

Hierarchical Multiobjective Approach to a Programming Problem

Grzegorz Dobrowolski, Maciej Zebrowski
Joint System Research Department
of the Institute for Control and Systems Engineering,
Academy of Mining and Metallurgy, Cracow,
and the Industrial Chemistry Research Institute, Warsaw.

Abstract

This is the forth paper in the series dealing with the development programming of the chemical industry. In the paper it is shown how a development thesis can be formulated and a development alternative generated using a MIDA computer system. A methodological framework of the MIDA utilization is introduced illustrated by an exemplary hierarchical, multiobjective development thesis. To obtain development alternatives for such a thesis the DIDAS approach is used to solve optimization problems on levels of the hierarchy and to assure coordination between some of them. A thesis is equivalent to substitution analysis of critical resources such as crude oil, gas, coal, lignite and investment, energy for a selected branch of the chemical industry. Results of the analysis are presented.

1 Introduction

The research reported here was partly sponsored by IIASA Contracted Study Agreement on Theory, Software and Testing Examples for Decision Support Systems and partly by the Polish Government Energy Program.

This is the forth paper in the series dealing with the development programming of the chemical industry. Therefore just few terms playing an important role for the contents of the paper will be briefly reminded here. A reader is expected to refer to the rest of the series and to the bibliography as usual.

A **development thesis** is a term that represents — expressed mostly qualitatively — aspirations, goals, preferences, limitations of a decision maker. A **development alternative** is equivalent to structured technologically and expressed quantitatively a development program of the particular industrial branch. **PDA** — Production Distribution Area (see the second paper of the series) is a model that can be useful as a basis for transformation of a development thesis into a development alternatives. **MIDA** — Multiobjective Interactive Decision Aid is a computer system to support all activities related to the transformation a development thesis into a development alternative.
The aim of this paper is three-fold :

1. To show how a development thesis can be formulated and a development alternative or alternatives generated using the MIDA.
2. To show an application of the DIDAS (see Kallio et al. 1980, Lewandowski et al. 1981) in the design of development alternatives in the chemical industry.
3. To report results of the substitution analysis for selected critical resources, such as crude oil, natural gas, coal and lignite in the area of relevant chemical industry. The substitution analysis involves also aggregated resources such as energy and investment.

Substitution of resources stems from the very nature of the chemical processing. Usually alternative routes lead from a feedstock to products (through various semi-products) owing to the existence of alternative processing ways of chemicals. To those alternatives correspond a variety of industrial structures which may be selected to perform the above transformations.

The results of our efforts directed towards performing the above task are presented in the following way.

Section 2 serves as a setting of a formal framework for the use of MIDA for generation development alternatives along the course of a development analysis. The development alternatives design is a very broad subject and in our research we have worked on its various aspects (see Borek et al. 1979, Dobrowolski et al. 1980, Dobrowolski et al. 1982, Dobrowolski et al. 1984).

Next comes Section 3 on the substitution analysis of critical resources such as crude oil, gas, coal, lignite (feedstock side) and investment effectiveness, energy (aggregates), etc. The substitution analysis is introduced by a development thesis of the hierarchical multiobjective form. The analysis starts from a short description of the area: PDA dealing with fuel and chemical feedstock production with 89 technologies and 65 products.

Next the results of the analysis are presented to illustrate the effectiveness of the MIDA system. The last section contains conclusions.

2 Generation of development alternatives with PDA model

We shall now discuss basic assumptions and methodological guidelines in the process of generating development alternatives according to the MIDA approach. It will be presented out from the point of view of a decision maker and his experts what does not limit possibility of placing the whole process within any type of an organizational scheme.

To initiate the process of problem formulation, a decision maker has to prepare a development thesis. It is not easy to specify this term since a development thesis means verbalized description of decision maker's vision, expectations, limitations and other aspects regarding development of industry which can be a branch or anything like a

PDA with its boundaries not necessarily precisely defined at this stage. Needless to say that a basic thing at this stage is a sound knowledge about the existing industry.

So at first this verbalized knowledge is to be expressed in terms of production goals, policy measures imposed from outside such as expected interest rates, taxes, availability of resources such as raw materials etc. Also at that stage a decision maker should specify which resources are to be considered as critical. This concerns wide spectrum such as investment, manpower, water, selected raw materials e.g. crude oil or intermediates like ethylene or methanol. Also preferences in terms of expected performance such as maximization of certain yields like fuels, minimization of energy consumption are to be spelled out.

At the same time all the knowledge related to a development thesis is used in order to pre-specify a technological repertoire of an industrial branch or an area of the chemical industry including existing and potentially available technologies and described in terms of the PDA model. The PDA model is precisely described in the second paper of the series, a particular PDA (a model of the particular chemical branch) for which the analysis was carried out is described in Section 3. Here we can simply assume that the PDA model is available and we may consider it as a black box.

Using the PDA model the decision maker plays a specific game in which he tries his image of a real object and its environment against technological conditions and possibilities reflected by the model of PDA. The only rule of the game is that the decision maker ought to be familiar with all features of the model.
Let us gather the features in a methodological order:

1. Given PDA.
   Source information on PDA describing :

   - chemical processes (existing and potential)
   - flows of chemicals
   - other physical flows (like : energy, water, wastes, etc.).

   Bipartite network as the model of PDA reflects :

   - balance of the flows
   - transitions of the flows performed by processes

2. Given physical feasibility conditions

   - capacities of at least existing processes
   - restrictions on I/O flows
     Remarks :

     The above data describe chemical processes and a production structure built from them. They are well defined, quantified and also for the given moment are assumed to be constant (however it may happen that some of them are even erroneous).

     Capacities of new technologies may be assumed as unknown and should result from the analysis.

3. Given marketing information :

    - prices and their relations (known and forecasted)
    - demand for or availability of chemicals
      Remarks :

        The above data however well defined are relatively much more uncertain then data on technology (see also remark above).

        This may affect results of the analysis in the case of error but is not considered to be so critical otherwise.

Based on the above a development thesis can be formulated. It means that following points are to be fulfilled:

1. Critical resources are chosen and named.

2. Possible restrictions imposed on the critical resources are defined.

3. Preferences or possible criteria are selected based on the critical resources.

4. Goals (points 2 and 3) and their hierarchy is defined.

Amounts of media defined as the critical resources characterize a production goal or availability of raw materials. The production goal which may be expressed in terms of ranges of production levels to be attained, represents strong driving force and, in fact, imposes on the PDA a constraint which is practically decisive for alternatives that can be devised. Aggregates selected as the critical resources express at the same time preferences to the performance of the PDA model since it is intuitively obvious that one is expecting to minimize cost of production and purchase as well as cost of investment and energy consumed hoping to maximize sales value.

The better explanation of the nature of a development thesis will be given through an example. This will be done later.

3 Development thesis for Energy & Chemical Feedstock PDA

Let us start from presenting shortly a considered object of the analysis. It is the same Energy & Chemical Feedstock PDA that was used as an object of multiobjective evaluation in the previous paper in the series.

Its dimensions amount the number of 89 installations (processes) and 65 raw materials, semi-products and products. They were chosen from a given data base (see Dobrowolski et al. 1984) and constitute the model of PDA. Thereby a repertoire of attainable production structures was determined together with indispensable resources of all sorts and this delimits space for alternative development strategies.

The PDA covers the production of motor fuels (petrol, oil, jet-fuel) basic hydrocarbon chemical raw materials (aromes, olefines, methanol, etc.) and heating oil from crude oil, coal, lignite and gas.

In principle it is an area connected with crude oil processing. Methanol which is regarded as a potential fuel and raw material for a number of new applications, was added to this area. It is enriched by processing of coal and lignite. Technologies for processing natural gas are also present but with limited representation (mostly for methanol production).

Consequently the PDA includes existing plants (rafineries, methanol, aromes and olefines plants) as well as the future ones based on a range of technologies for processing coal and lignite (gasification, liquidization, pyrolysis, critical extraction of coal, etc.). New plants for crude oil processing are also included.

Let us remind that such a model contains the repertoire of production structures that can be selected with respect to the development thesis expressed by the decision maker. The key problem in the analysis would be substitution of natural hydrocarbons (crude oil, gas) by coal and lignite for assumed array of chemical production.

The existing plants that were included into the model do not cover the possibilities of their reconstruction and modernization as it goes beyond the scope of the paper.

Due to the illustrative character of the development analysis considered here one of the important aspects such as terms of trade is only signaled. In practice much attention is paid to price relations (see Dobrowolski et al. 1984) and they are regarded to be an important factor in the analysis. In the case considered here the prices of basic energy carriers and obtained from them derivatives were assumed on the level of average world prices from early 80-ties.

Having in mind methodological considerations and assumptions described in the previous section we may now formulate the development thesis.

1. It is assumed that all necessary data and information are available and known to the decision maker (as well as to his experts). We shall refer to the above knowledge in the course of analysis whenever it would be necessary.

2. The following critical resources were selected :

    Production of :
        methanol
        benzene
        ethylene
        diesel oil
    Cost of production
    Value of sales
    Investment
    Total energy consumed
    Consumption of :
        crude oil
        natural gas
        coal
        lignite

3. Assignment of restrictions, preferences and tendencies to the critical resources. The process of assignment of restrictions, preferences and tendencies is a decisive task since it results in

Hierarchy of goals :

Level 1. Production of : methanol, benzene, ethylene, diesel oil is to be carried within defined range.

Remarks :

The selected products are of strategic type for other PDA's and industrial sectors. Therefore the assumptions or forecasts on their availability are considered to be of most importance.

The ranges are imposed on the decision maker by environment of the PDA and at the moment he can only trace their impact.

Level 2. Operational efficiency which is expressed by ratio of value of (yearly) sales, by (yearly) cost of production is assumed to be not less than 1.3.

Remarks :

From the efficiency analysis it is known that for the Energy & Chemical Feedstock PDA maximum for this ratio is 1.35.

By setting ratio to be not smaller than 1.3 which is only a slight relaxation from its maximum, the decision maker has made an important choice of his own. Of course, this could be a result of negotiations with the financial authorities based on the analysis of the PDA (carried out with respect to the rate of return ratio).

Level 3. Investment, total energy consumption are to be minimized.

Remark :

It is a property of the industrial hardware especially in the chemical industry that the energy saving plants are capital intensive. Therefore there is a contradiction in such a goal which has to be resolved through learning about possible trade-off's.

Level 4. Consumption of the critical feedstock : crude oil, natural gas, coal and lignite is to be minimized.

Remarks :

All the above critical resources are at the same time primary energy carriers.

On this level a feedstock substitution is to be analyzed and a relation of level 3 and 4 found out.

Special emphasis is on crude oil and gas since they are to be almost totally imported.

From this four-level hierarchy which is to be treated more as exemplification than as a strict rule in the case of the substitution analysis, following conclusions may be drawn.

Level 1 which concerns production goal may as its alternative describe availability of feedstock which would convert the case of the problem how to best achieve production goal into the decision problem how to utilize best the available feedstock. Obviously a third case may occur that is a combination of these two. So the Level 1 imposes a constraint on variety of development alternatives of the PDA.

Level 2 provides a driver in terms of efficiency ratios or ratio, which is to drive a selection of alternatives within constraints imposed on preceding level. Levels 3 and 4 emphasize in the development thesis a substitution which is to be analyzed and selected under assumed conditions. In this case the substitution analysis will be two-level with the higher level expressed in terms of aggregates and the lower level as substitution of selected feedstock.

This can be done by solving two hierarchically coupled Multiobjective Optimization Problems MOP corresponding to the levels 3 and 4 respectively.

Now in order to formulate the solving scheme as the next step in the methodology a particular method (tool) has to be selected. In our case we have selected the DIDAS (see Kallio et al. 1980, Lewandowski et al. 1981). The choice was based on two facts :

1. Our experience in the DIDAS application for generating efficient alternatives for the development in the chemical industry (see Dobrowolski et al. 1982).

2. The property of the reference point approach (see Wierzbicki 1979). The optimal solution in the Pareto sense is obtained as the closest to the point selected by the decision maker in the space of resources. This point is called the reference point.

To build up a methodology for solving the problem such as the one above let us formulate the following observations and remarks.

- All levels operate on the same model of the PDA.

- A solution from a given level may be used as a natural reference point for solving the MOP from the neighboring higher level. The result simply tells the decision maker (not imposing anything on him) what would be the solution on the given level closest from the one comforting him on the lower level.

- Therefore a feasible direction of solving hierarchy of MOPs is from the bottom to the top level.

- It is important that upward direction assures optimality of the higher level. However the optimal solution on a given level will be only suboptimal on the lower level.

- The open question is how to initiate process of finding an acceptable solution on the lowest level.

A methodological approach for solving a hierarchical MOP such as discussed here emerges as a kind of conclusion from the above remarks.

Analysis is to start from the lowest level which in our case would be level 4 on which minimization of consumption of primary energy carriers is assumed. As a result of solving MOP of level 4 we obtain the optimal (in the Pareto sense) amounts of the critical resources it is of crude oil, gas, coal and lignite. The development alternative which assures this actual level of consumption of the critical resources, demands at the same time, a given amounts of the resources which are assumed as objectives for the higher level (here level 3). In the particular case these will be investment and total energy consumption, to which corresponds the development alternative most effective from the point of view of saving the primary energy carriers.

The values of investment and total energy consumption are going to be used as a reference point for solving the problem of the higher (in this case 3) level. Here the meaning of the term reference point has its real value. It shows how a certain development alternative chosen from the point of view of goals of one level (here level 4) from repertoire of the PDA refers to the development alternative which is going to be chosen on the higher level (it is 3).

Therefore it can be seen that the above procedure supports the decision maker giving him the ability to solve hierarchical problem assuring coordination of goals assumed on the particular levels.

4 Numerical results

We may take a look at some results of the substitution analysis described in the previous section.

First the properties of the PDA as seen on the level 3 are shown on Figure 1. It can be seen that as condition on effectiveness set by the effectiveness ratio R_{oe} is relaxed, the attainable range of the optimal substitution of total energy consumption by investment widens. In the case of maximum attainable efficiency $R_{oe} = 1.35$ no substitution is possible as could be expected from the properties of the PDA model. On the other extreme we find the case of unconstrained effectiveness which corresponds to situation where the level 2 would be deleted.

Of course, the term optimal substitution means here Pareto-optimality with respect to total energy consumption and investment.

In the case considered here the constraint on efficiency (level 2) was assumed to be $R_{oe} = 1.3$, and for that value substitution is further investigated. Table 1 shows the substitutional flexibility of the Energy & Chemical Feedstock PDA as expressed in terms of the critical resources. Experiments no. 1–5 illustrate the spectrum of possible substitution (with no. 1 and 5 representing the *corner* solutions). For comparison given is (experiment no. 0) the solution for $R_{oe} = 1.35$, it is the maximum possible efficiency ratio.

One may comment on these results with the following remarks :

- For the assumed effectiveness ratio equal to 1.3 the selected production structures are oriented towards crude oil processing with limited consumption of coal and gas.
- Such a selection is imposed by the constraints from the level 1 where ranges of strategic products are assumed. One of them is diesel oil which with the known technologies can be best obtained from crude oil.

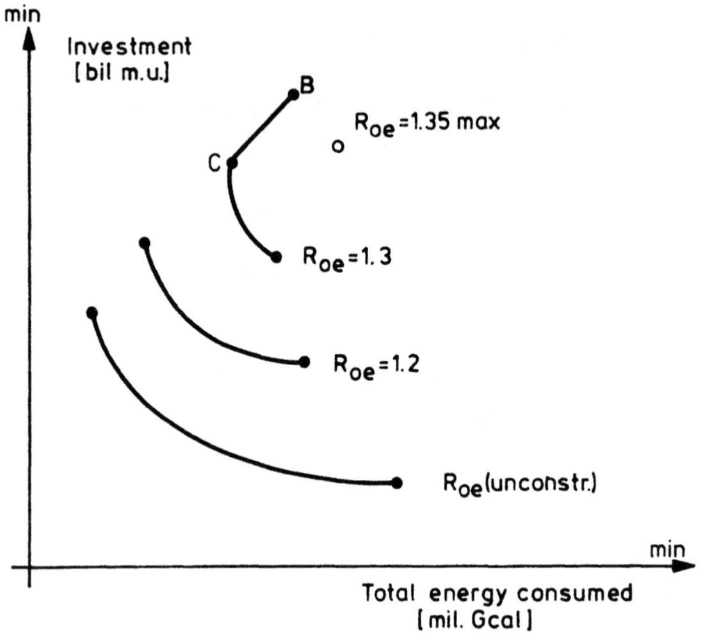

Figure 1: On the level 3

Experiment no.		0	1	2	3	4	5
Operational effectiveness ratio		1.35	1.3	1.3	1.3	1.3	1.3
Investment	*bil.m.u.*	1066.	581.	557.	497.	478.	460.
Total energy consumption	*mil.Gcal*	318.	259.	259.	263.	266.	268.
Crude oil	*mil.tons*	22.2	21.1	21.4	21.8	21.8	21.8
Natural gas	*bil.cub.m*	1.4	0.	0.	0.	0.	0.
Coal	*mil.tons*	0.	0.	0.	0.	0.	0.
Lignite	*mil.tons*	23.8	11.0	10.1	10.3	11.8	12.0
Economic efficiency	*bil.m.u.*	244.	177.	179.	180.	182.	183.

Table 1: Substitutional flexibility of Energy & Chemical Feedstock PDA.

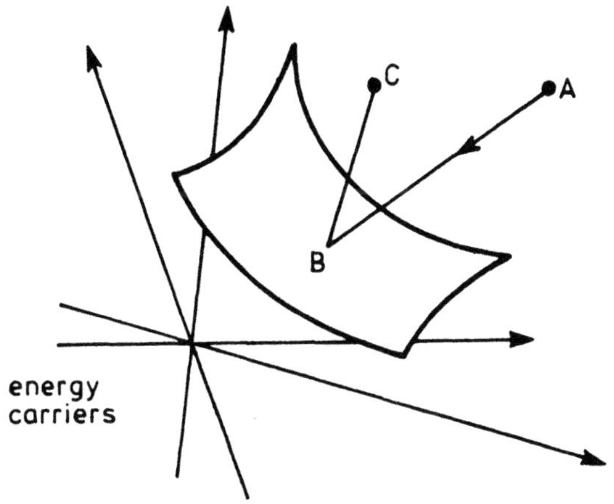

Figure 2: On the level 4

- Constraints of the level 1 have limited very strongly the possibility of substitution among primary energy carrier. Promotion of coal processing and production of diesel oil are contradictive goals and therefore the higher level imposes the result.
- Basic substitution can be seen on the level 3 and it can take place within choice of various technologies of processing crude and lignite.
- The case of the maximum efficiency moves the choice to completely new magnitude of investment (practically double).
- From the point of view of effectiveness analysis another drawback from insisting on maximizing just R_{oe} ratio can be shown. On the other hand return on investment which is calculated as ratio of economic efficiency to investment is much worse in the case of $R_{oe} = 1.35$ than in any other case (experiments no. 1–5, see table 1). At the same time within all range of substitution in the case discussed terms of return of investment turn out to be stable.

However the above consideration go beyond strictly defined substitution analysis it is important to show how the both types of analysis interleave, and feedbacks naturally may arise.

Figure 2 illustrates the process of analysis as seen from the level 4. Point A represents an initial reference point chosen for the level 4. Projected on the surface of Pareto-optimal solutions it produces the point B, which in turn used as a reference for the level 3 leads to the point C which is not optimal any more for the level 4.

In Figure 1 the points B and C visualize the mechanism of a search for acceptable strategy : from reference solution B (transformed result of the level 4) to the final solution C (level 3).

		Ref. lev.4	Sol. lev.4 and Ref. lev.3	Sol. lev.3
Operational effectiveness ratio			1.3	1.3
Investment	*bil.m.u.*		1175.	570.
Total energy consumption	*mil.Gcal*		302.	258.
Crude oil	*mil.tons*	15.	17.6	21.
Natural gas	*bil.cub.m*	1.5	1.4	0.
Coal	*mil.tons*	15.	4.2	0.
Lignite	*mil.tons*	25.	27.6	11.
Economic efficiency	*bil.m.u.*		198.	176.

Table 2: Results of analysis.

Table 2 contains three columns. The first describing the reference point stands for the estimated availability of crude oil, gas, coal and lignite. It represents kind of expectations of the decision maker not the real constraints. The PDA response which is optimal with respect to minimization of the critical resources consumption, is shown in the second column of table 2. Due to the heavy use of lignite and some processing of coal the proposed development alternative would be both capital (investment 1175 billions m.u.) and energy (302 millions Gcal) consuming. This is the production structure of the PDA which is oriented towards minimization of crude through substitution of coal and lignite. By using the values of investment and energy consumption obtained as a reference for the 3rd level we find in column 3 a resulting strategy which is optimal with respect to investment and total energy consumption. From the first sight it can be seen that it practically coincides with experiment no. 1 (table 1). It means that the minimum energy corner has been attained. It can be concluded that due to presence of the level 4 representing strategy based on conservation of primary energy carriers the resulting development alternative obeys it by choosing compromise solution biased by the energy conservation policy.

5 Conclusions

In the paper the methodological framework for use of the MIDA computer system was described.

The basic terms as a development thesis, development alternatives were introduced. They interrelations were formally described and exemplified by the case of substitution analysis for the given area of the chemical industry that is the Energy & Chemical Feedstock PDA.

All activities to carry the analysis out were supported by the MIDA system. The multiobjective hierarchy of goals constituting the development thesis imposes application of the DIDAS as a tool for solving multiobjective optimization problems on levels of the hierarchy and for an especially designed schema of coordination between them.

In our approach we have exposed the role of creativity in the development analysis and therefore a subjective factor which is to be introduced by the decision maker.

The complete results of our investigation are much more detailed since they contain information such as production levels, capacity utilization etc. This kind of information was omitted here as not being directly relevant to the scope of this paper. It will be enclosed in the report prepared for the cosponsor of this project it is the Polish Government Energy Program.

References

Borek, A., Dobrowolski G., Zebrowski M. (1979) Applications of System Analysis in the Management of Growth and Development of the Chemical Industry. CHEM/SEM.8/R.16 Report of the Chemical Industry Committee of the United Nations.

Dobrowolski, G., Kopytowski J., Zebrowski M. (1980) Development Forecast of Production Structure. Proceedings of the XIV Union of Polish Architects Congress, June 1980, Zakopane, Poland, pp. 19–26.

Dobrowolski, G., Kopytowski J., Lewandowski A., Zebrowski M. (1982) Generating Efficient Alternatives for Development of the Chemical Industry. IIASA Collaborative Paper CP-82-54, Laxenburg, Austria.

Dobrowolski, G., Kopytowski J., Wojtania J., Zebrowski M. (1984) Alternative Routes from Fossil Resources to Chemical Feedstock. IIASA Research Report RR-84-19, Laxenburg, Austria.

Kallio, M., Lewandowski A., and Orchard-Hays W. (1980), An Implementation of the Reference Point Approach for Multiobjective Optimization. IIASA Working Paper WP-80-35, Laxenburg, Austria.

Lewandowski, A., and Grauer M. (1982) The reference point optimization approach — methods of efficient implementation. In M. Grauer, A. Lewandowski and A.P. Wierzbicki (Eds.) IIASA Collaborative Paper CP-82-s12, Laxenburg, Austria.

Wierzbicki, A.P. (1979) The Use of Reference Objectives in Multiobjective Optimization — Theoretical Implications and Practical Experience. IIASA Working Paper WP-79-66, Laxenburg, Austria.

Spatial Allocation and Investment Scheduling in the Development Programming

Maciej Skocz, Maciej Zebrowski, Wieslaw Ziembla
Joint Systems Research Department
of the Institute for Control and Systems Engineering,
Academy of Mining and Metallurgy, Cracow,
and the Industrial Chemistry Research Institute, Warsaw.

Abstract

In the paper we describe a decision support system for programming development of process industries. The system offers facilities such as long term analysis and design of the industrial structure development with an emphasis on investment allocation efficiency. Thus, three levels of the system corresponding to relevant decision making tasks are distinguished. First is devoted to a quest for an optimal industrial structure and its development trajectory, second aims at spatial allocation of production units selected on the first level, the third is responsible for the investment scheduling. The method is exemplified by a case of the petrochemical industry.

1 Introduction

From the decision maker (DM) point of view, industrial development can be viewed as a process of changing production structure by means of investment over the course of time. There is no definite method of choice of appropriate time horizon for industrial development programming. Any choice may be disputable and criticized as an arbitrary assumption.

Here MIDA approach and decomposition applied to the problem that were only highlighted in the introductory paper are discussed.

For our considerations two qualitatively distinguishable activities are to be performed in the development programming. First goes a quest for an optimal industrial structure, second is how to determine a strategy that would transform the existing structure into the optimal one by the end of the time horizon. The industrial development strategy design problems are basically two-dimensional, one dimension being time and the second one, space were discussed separately in our papers (Skocz, Zebrowski and Ziembla, 1987, Skocz and Ziembla, 1987). Both types of activity will be discussed in the paper and the natural hierarchy which evolves will play an important role in formulation of the process. This hierarchy opens way for decomposition of the whole problem and thus enables application of specific algorithms for all levels of the hierarchy. Such a practical method corresponds to a real-life management tasks and therefore naturally becomes a core of a specialized Decision Support System (DSS) such as MIDA.

The above approach is presented in the paper along the following lines. First, the problem of programming industrial development is identified. The case of petrochemical industry has been chosen for exemplification of the problem as the most complex and general representation of process industries. Then, three layers of programming development are distinguished. The quest for an optimal industrial structure which is a task solved on the upper layer of the system has been extensively described in other papers (Borek et al. 1987, Dobrowolski G. et al. 1984, Dobrowolski et al. 1985) and in this series. Here emphasis is given to show its impact on initiating the investment planning process. From this naturally evolves a problem of the investment spatial allocation and scheduling devoted to an efficient implementation of the optimal industrial structure.

An important role in such a management system is given to a feedback between the three layers. This feedback varies in time; as an immediate goal the investment spatial allocation and scheduling activity can be applied as a plausibility test of the industrial structure to be attained. The other role of this feedback comes into effect in a preliminary phase of implementation of the planned structure. As the structure development is distributed over a long time-span, the described sequence of steps may be repeated a number of times so as to reflect a knowledge and experience gathered by the management in the course of time.

Basing on the above observations, appropriate procedure has been developed and described in Section 5.

To illustrate the approach and the method, an example based on a real-life case of the petrochemical industry is added. The case illustrates the problem of spreading over the planning period a massive investment which is to be balanced against economic constraints such as e.g. the assumed rate of return. On the other hand, technological constraints are also to be satisfied due to strong interdependence between chemical plants (sources and sinks).

2 Programming development of a process industry

From a very broad and complex area of programming development of a process industry we are extracting here only those elements that are indispensable to show how investment allocation is embedded in this activity. A broader view on the subject can be found in other papers of our group (Dobrowolski et al. 1982, Dobrowolski et al. 1984, Dobrowolski et al. 1985). As has been mentioned, the programming development process is a multilevel, dynamic activity, considered as a permanent task of the management. Its time horizon extends ten, fifteen or more years ahead.

The highest level of the hierarchy was named (Borek et al. 1978, Dobrowolski et al. 1984) a Production-Distribution Area (PDA) level. PDA comprises a selected domain of the process industry composed into a kind of a network. Nodes of the network are technological processes, while arches represent flows of raw materials, intermediates and products. A selection of boundaries of such a system usually poses a problem itself (see e.g. Dobrowolski et al. 1984). For the sake of this paper it is sufficient to assume that PDA is a selected branch that consumes particular resources and supplies particular products. The proposed approach, however, seems to be a sufficiently wide concept concerning any production system with defined inputs, outputs and coefficients of i/o transformation.

From a formal point of view, PDA model is stated in a linear programming convention and as such one it constitutes a core of the DSS. Basing on the model, on a request of the decision maker, a number of multi- or single- objective optimization problems can be generated and solved according to an assumed scenario. The scenario is a formally expressed development thesis representing expectations of a DM based on his up-to -date knowledge. With help of the DSS, a development thesis is transformed into industrial development strategy through a chain of interactive procedures. In general, a scenario comprises information that are characterized below in an aggregated form:

- existing structure of the industry described in the form of a PDA,
- new or potentially available technologies that can be included into the PDA structure by means of investment (the existing and new technologies are a basic repertoire for selecting future production structure),
- availability of resources (so called critical resources) such as raw materials, energy, manpower etc.; a special emphasis will be given to availability of investment capital,
- demand patterns for selected products,
- terms of trade for all other resources, intermediates, products etc,
- objectives to be used for selection of ultimate as well as intermediate structures in terms of consecutive PDAs.

Objectives are formulated in terms of various efficiency relations between critical resources e.g. profit/energy, input energy/output energy, profit/investment capital. It is important to underline here that analysis on this level should lead to selection of PDA structures according to their "intensive properties" such as expressed by the above fractional objectives.

Let us focus now on a dynamic process of generating of industrial structures. Within the time horizon any particular PDA structure represents a cross- section of a development trajectory from the initial to the final state. Intermediate structures (substructures) correspond to conditions imposed by scenarios issued for times T_i, $i \in I$. A number of such cross-sections, indexed by i, is up to DM and usually corresponds to 5-year periods what is independent on economic system.

Anyway, a selection of the times T_i, $i \in I$ should result from interactions of the industry with the surrounding world (forecasted production goals, changing resource availability, macroeconomic forecasts etc). By decomposing the development trajectory into a limited number of subperiods DM can practically simulate scenarios "what-if" separately for any substructure subject to its relations with the environment . This task may be fulfilled by different methods of which dynamic programming method seems to be a straightforward concept. However, taking into account practical applicability of the method, including computational effectiveness on one hand and on the other interactive properties of the DSS, we have decided otherwise.

The method proposed in the paper is based on the following step-wise approach:

1. investigation of the existing structure,
2. selection of the ultimate final structure corresponding to the end of programming horizon,
3. generating intermediate development patterns (substructures) for selected times T_i, $i \in I$.

The above steps are done according to scenarios resulting from development thesis. The presented approach leads to compression of information that is necessary to generate large-scale development programs and enables better perception of the results. The above steps constitute one iteration of the PDA level and provide the DM with a primary version of development program. This program is to be verified on second and third levels described in the next sections.

3 Spatial allocation of production units in investment planning

A next decision task to be solved is the spatial allocation of production units that are already selected as members of a production network to be developed. In other words, this new decision problem is to decompose a production structure S_i into a set of local substructures S_i^l, $l \in L$ subject to conditions specific for particular location (sites).

Obviously, sites should be regarded as places of distinct features, which influence the investment condition and production process later on. A goal of the decomposition is to achieve minimum cost of investment and operation (including manufacturing and transportation costs) of the whole production system while satisfying the production task.

To get a closer view on the problem, let us have a comment on component of the costs. The investment costs can strongly depend on a place, especially if conditions for differently developed countries are being compared, or even between developing countries themselves. For example, in North-African countries, the so-called location factor, which multiply investment cost related to West Europe, can vary from 1.3–1.4 on a see-side to 2.0 and more on interior. Regardless of local conditions, the decomposition of production structure can rise investment costs, since smaller units are relatively more expensive. This can be illustrated by the following formula:

$$inv = inv_{ref} \left(\frac{cap}{cap_{ref}} \right)^{\alpha}$$

where the exponential factor is less than 1.0 when the capacity is bigger than cap_{ref} (the least economically recommended capacity), and bigger than 1.0 otherwise.

Location of production units strongly influence the operation costs as well. Some components of the operation cost can be derived from different investment costs, another components are a consequence of various prices of water and energy, waste management, expenses on manpower, transportation, etc. The above can be also real constraints imposed on production planned in a given site (e.g. limited availability of water, energy or manpower).

A spatial factor to be considered is transportation. This results from:

- various transportation alternatives (means and routes, such as highways, railroads, water, pipes) to be used for the same products,
- spatial dispersion of demand for chemical products or feedstock,
- unbalanced existing industrial structure.

The transportation problem has been widely investigated so now only the aspect related to spatial allocation of investment will be described. It seems to be important to note at this place that for transportation modeling a decomposition of demand for products or feedstock supply is indispensable.

Since local factors create more detailed conditions to be taken into account in programming development, a solution to the spatial problem will verify the preliminary global development program. A result obtained will require, however, a further examination by construction time constraints. This problem will be described in the next section, so now let us to complete the considerations with formulation of the spatial allocation problem (Skocz and Ziembla, 1987, Zebrowski et al. 1988).

Modeling of spatial allocation (of production units) in investment planning

First, the symbols are categorized and defined.

Symbol	*Definition*
SETS AND INDEXES	
$l \in L$	Plant location
$m \in M$	Marketing center
$k \in K$	Production process
$j \in J$	Chemical or medium (feedstock, intermediate, product)
$r \in R$	Route/mean of transport
LM	Redefined set of sites and markets, $LM = L \cup M$
VARIABLES	
z	Process level (production level)

x	Amount of substance transported by route/mean
q	Investment capital need to plant construction

PARAMETERS

a	Production (output) coefficient
b	Consumption (input) coefficient
c	Unit market price
d	Unit transportation price
α	Scaling exponent for plant investment calculation
AV	Market availability of feedstock
DE	Market demand for substance
RC	Transportation capacity

Second, the constraints of the spatial allocation are specified.

PRODUCTION LEVELS BALANCE

$$z_k \leq \sum_{l \in L} z_{kl} , \quad k \in K$$

LOCAL BALANCE ON RAW MATERIALS, INTERMEDIATES AND FINAL PRODUCTS

$$\sum_{k \in K} a_{kj} z_{kl} - \sum_{k \in K} b_{kj} z_{kl} = \sum_{n \in LM} \sum_{r \in R_{nl}} x_{jr} - \sum_{n \in LM} \sum_{r \in R_{ln}} x_{jr} , \quad l \in LM, \ j \in J$$

RAW MATERIALS SUPPLY AVAILABILITY BALANCE

$$\sum_{l \in L} \sum_{r \in R_{ml}} x_{jr} \leq AV_{jm} , \quad m \in M, \ j \in J$$

PRODUCT DEMAND BALANCE

$$DE_{jm} = \sum_{n \in L} \sum_{r \in R_{lm}} x_{jr} , \quad m \in M, \ j \in J$$

TRANSPORTATION CAPACITY BALANCE FOR ROUTE/MEAN

$$\sum_{j \in J} x_{jr} \leq RC_r , \quad r \in R_{ln}, \ l, n \in LM$$

and also:

$$x_{jr} \geq 0 , \ z_{kl} \geq 0 , \quad j \in J, \ k \in K, \ r \in R_{nl}, \ n, l \in LM$$

Next objectives can be formulated as follows:

TRANSPORTATION COST

$$TC = \sum_{j \in J} \sum_{l \in LM} \sum_{n \in LM} \sum_{r \in R_{nl}} d_{jr} x_{jr}$$

INVESTMENT COST

$$IC = \sum_{l \in L} \sum_{k \in K} q_{kl}$$

where:

$$q_{kl} = q_k \left(\frac{z_{kl}}{z_k}\right)_i^{\alpha}$$

MANUFACTURING COST

$$MC = VC + CC$$

where:

- VC (various cost) depends on cost of raw materials in linear relationship and several parameters [1]

$$VC \sim \sum_{j\in J} \sum_{m\in M} \sum_{l\in L} \sum_{r\in R_{ml}} x_{jr}c_{jm} ,$$

- CC (constant cost) depends on investment cost in linear form and several parameters

$$CC \sim \sum_{l\in L} \sum_{k\in K} q_{kl} .$$

4 Investment scheduling problem

The investment scheduling problem consists of sequencing and scheduling of the construction of plants that will finally compose the assumed industrial network. According to any optimal substructure of the network S_i^l ,$i \in I$, $l \in L$ determined for given planning periods, each investment planning problem has its own pattern structure to be completed within a relevant time-horizon T_i, $i \in I$. Given the times of final and partial completion of the network, as well as the corresponding final and intermediate patterns to be achieved under certain conditions, one may formulate the investment scheduling problem.

The goal of investment scheduling is to enhance investment efficiency and capital turnover; as a practical decision rule one may accept here minimizing of completion time subject to limited investment capital (distributed over multiple year intervals) or, in a broader sense, maximizing of overall profit gained in the production network.

Such objectives have certain consequences in the problem formulation. It might be observed for the minimal time objective that since the program has to satisfy precedence relations imposed on substructures and also on particular plants within the substructures, the intermediate completion times might be relaxed in the investment planning problem. To increase investment efficiency, the industrial substructures and the final network will be scheduled as closest to their due dates as possible. The same relaxation we will assume for the second objective of the scheduling problem.

In the case of a solution that violates due dates (both delays and time savings are of concern), what is naturally a most common case, the investment schedule has to be evaluated in terms of higher-level decision objective(s). It means that for any intermediate due date T_i one has to determine a structure s_i^l that really corresponds to T_i . Then, if s_i^l differs from S_i^l , consequences of implementation of s_i^l instead of S_i^l should be evaluated. Following the analysis of the consequences, one will be faced with two following classes of situations:

[1] The exact formula for cost calculation is given in MIDA User's Manual, 1987, and Guide to Development Programming (Zebrowski, 1987).

- the investment schedule for a period i may be maintained,
- the investment schedule for a period i should be changed in order to attain the assumed substructure S_i^l in the due time T_i (obviously by a modification of the originally assumed time distribution of investment capital. One of the most natural approaches towards changing investment schedule in order to achieve a strict completion time of a given substructure, is to identify investment capital bottleneck subject to the required conditions.

Hence, three different scheduling strategies are of concern - first two that aim at minimizing completion time or maximizing the overall profit gained in the production system, and a different one that minimizes investment indispensable for completion of selected substructures in their due times. It should be emphasized that if modification of investment distribution cannot be accepted then new local substructures must be generated on spatially allocation level, or even upper level. Therefore, an investment schedule of spatial by allocated production unit obtained on the lower decision level can be converted into an investment plan through interaction with three levels of DSS.

Because of the space limitation we attach only some mathematical formulation of considered investment scheduling problems, whereas solving algorithms are described in other our papers (Skocz, Zebrowski and Ziembla, 1987, Zebrowski et al. 1988).

Modeling of investment scheduling

The symbols are categorized and defined as follows:.

Symbol	*Definition*
SETS AND INDEXES	
$i \in I$	Planning period (macro - structural level)
$l \in L$	Production site
$k \in K$	Production process
$(j,k) \in RT$	Technological predecessorship relation
$\tau \in (T_{i-1}, T_i]$	Time unit (micro - scheduling level)
VARIABLES	
v	Starting time for plant construction
g	time investment consumption for plant
PARAMETERS	
e	Profit rate for plant corresponding z capacity
T_{i-1}	Starting interval of planning period
T_i	Last interval of planning period
AI	Availability of investment capital (or other resources) on site

RI	Requirement on investment capital (or other resources) for plant in time its construction
p	Plant construction time

Next, constraints are specified.
CONSTRUCTION TIME CONSTRAINTS

$$T_0 < v_{kl} \leq T_i - p_k , \quad k \in K, \ l \in L$$

PREDECESSORSHIP CONSTRAINTS

$$v_{kl} + p_k \leq v_{jl} + p_j , \quad (k,j) \in RT$$

INVESTMENT (RESOURCE) TIME BALANCE

$$\sum_{k \in K} g_{kl}(\tau) \leq AI_{il}(\tau) , \quad l \in L, \tau \in (T_{i-1}, T_i]$$

where:

$$g_{kl} = \begin{cases} 0 & \text{if } \tau < v_{kl} \\ RI_{kl}(\tau) & \text{if } v_{kl} < \tau \leq v_{kl} + p_k \\ 0 & \text{if } \tau > v_{kl} + p_k \end{cases}$$

Objective can be formulated as follows:
MAXIMUM TOTAL PROFIT

$$TP = \sum_{i \in I} \sum_{k \in K} e_{kl} [T_n - v_{kl} + p_k]$$

$$max\ TP \equiv min \sum_{i \in I} \sum_{k \in K} e_{kl} v_{kl}$$

MINIMUM COMPLETION TIME

$$CT = \max_{k \in K} (\tau_{kl} + p_k)$$

MINIMUM "INVESTMENT MODIFICATION"

$$IM = \min_{\tau \in (T_0, T_n)} | AI_i(\tau) - \sum_{k \in K} g_{kl}(\tau) |$$

5 Interaction between decision levels

From the description of investment spatial allocation and scheduling problems, one may derive a clear idea of interaction between various levels of decision analysis (Figure 1).

The upper level that is responsible for creating development of the industrial structure in a long run defines tasks for investment spatial allocation of production unit level as well as one of investment scheduling and supervises their work. In that sense, it should initialize the second level with the initial and final structure of the production network as well as selected substructures (intermediate patterns) that constitute some important checkpoints of the network development S_i , $i \in I$. Each substructure is determined by the set of technologies and their production levels:

$$S_i = \{(k, z), \ k \in K\}$$

On the second level these substructures are decomposed into local subnetworks with respect to investment-, manufacturing-, and transportation costs as the objectives. Obviously, additional data are necessary to solve this problem:

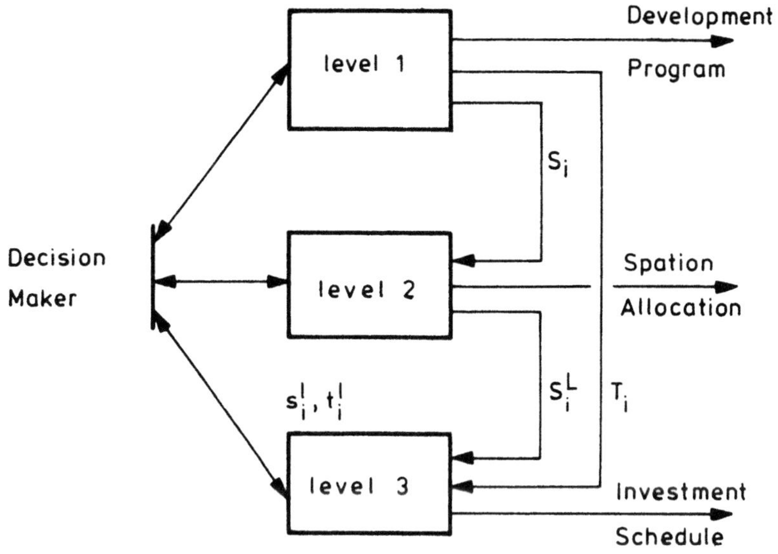

Figure 1: Interactive decision making system

- spatial distribution of feedstock availability (for each marketing center and site)
- spatial dispersion of production demand (for each marketing center)
- availability of transport (means and routes capacity)
- unit cost utilities (water, energy) in sites, prices on markets and unit costs of transport

The resulting Pareto-optimal spatial allocated substructures S_i should be next analyzed towards agreement with predecision prerequisites. If this tasks cannot be done (e.g. too high transportation cost in the case of a strictly limited number of production sites under strongly dispersed high tonnage products demand or resources supply, or too high investment cost in the case of more decentralized production) then a modification of the structure S_i on the upper level should be performed. One can try to search for a technology perhaps less efficient but based on local resources (reduction of transportation cost) or a technology which economic capacity is less then previously selected. Otherwise, when the results of decomposition satisfy the goals expressed by selected criteria, the results obtained is a starting point to the last level of the decision system, i.e. a verification of local structures S_i^l with respect to their completion times. The following input data are given to investment scheduling level:

- local substructures S_i^l, $i \in I$, $l \in L$
- investment capital corresponding local substructures S_i^l

- starting and completion times of the final network as well as completion times T_i ,$i \in I$ of intermediate pattern structures (substructures). The latter due dates are relaxed at this stage of the scheduling problem.
- profit rates e_{kl}, $k \in K$, $l \in L$ of all plants that are to constitute the network (i.e. potential profits to be gained in unit time).

In addition, time distributed investment constraints must be specified: they reflect different factors of local construction engineering, camps, works, transport of machinery as well as investment capital constraints. Next, the investment scheduling problem with profit- or completion time- type objective can be solved.

As an output of the scheduling procedure, the upper level is supplied with the following information:

- structures s_i^l that can be actually completed exactly in the times T_i, $i \in I$,
- actual intermediate and final completion times t_i^l corresponding to the assumed pattern substructures S_i^l, $i \in I$, $l \in L$,
- actual time distribution of investment capital consumption in sites.

Evaluation of the resulting schedule usually leads to reformulation of initial assumptions of the scheduling program. As has been mentioned, new scheduling tasks are derived from those investment schedules where substructures are to be completed in disagreement with the due dates and, moreover, this fact cannot be accepted, i.e.:

$$\max_{l \in L} t_i^l \geq T_i$$

Then, on the requirement of the first level, programs that minimize "modification of investment time distribution" to satisfy due times are worked out.

If this modification can not be accepted, then it is necessary for the second or even first level to review development program that was originally setup. In order to draw assumptions for an improved program trade-offs between intermediate and final structures, their completion times, selection of production sites and investment capital should be investigated. After compromising trade-offs are found, a new program can be drawn and evaluated following the described procedure.

The above is to be performed on three levels according to their functions with the relevant feedback through a necessary number of iterations between the levels. These iterations take place through interaction between a decision maker and DSS. This again proves a creative and subjective role of the decision maker in the design of the industrial development program (Gorecki et al. 1984).

6 An example - A case study in petrochemical industry

As an example we present results of elaboration of a development program of petrochemical industry in a developing country by means of three levels version of MIDA system (structures optimization, spatial allocation and investment scheduling modules).

Production Unit	Capacity	Location
Ethylene from Light Naphtha	130000	site A
Polyethylene LD (Autoclave Reactor)	50000	site A
Benzene from Reformate	80000	site A
p-Xylene and o-Xylene	40000	site A
Vinyl Chloride Via Oxychlorination	50000	site A
PVC Suspension Polymerization	50000	site A
Chlorine (electrolysis)	100000	site A
Methanol from Natural Gas	100000	site B
Formaldehyde	25000	site B
Phenolic Resin	10000	site B

Table 1: Existing industrial structure - S_0.

We assumed a 10 year planning horizon divided into 5-year intervals. Correspondingly, three structures S_0, S_1, S_2 are to be concerned where S_0 denotes an existing one, S_1 an intermediate one and S_2 a final structure.

First, S_0 was analyzed and found as a weakly developed and unbalanced production system. In Table 1 a set of technological units (with yearly capacities) corresponding to S_0 is given. It results from the analysis that S_0 cannot satisfy the demand; on the other hand, some valuable intermediates are expelled to external markets.

Taking into account the need for products and availability of resources, a design of final structure S_2 developed from S_0 was undertaken. To solve this problem, MIDA structure optimization module was used. A list of potential technologies to be selected within S_2 comprised of 135 plants of petrochemical feedstock (naphtha, LPG, NPG, condensate etc.) conversion into plastics, rubbers, fibers, detergents etc. As a result of optimization, the structure S_2 characterized by minimal simple rate of return was determined. A basic description of S_2 is given in Table 2. The investment value for the optimal case is 2.3 bil. \$, net income 359 mil. \$, so pay-back period is 6.3 years.

Subject to assumed limitation of 570 mil. \$ (25% of total amount) to be spent in the first period, i.e. between T_0 and T_1 and up to additional goals:

- utilization of surplus (unbalanced) production of ethylene - 60000 t, benzene - 80000 t, o-xylene - 25000 t, p-xylene - 40000 t and toluene - 10000 t yearly,
- maximum profit over investment as objective,

the intermediate structure S_1 was selected.

This is illustrated also in table 2. After the design of S_1 and S_2 has been done, the task of the first level was accomplished in iteration 1.

For spatial decomposition of the development program three sites were assumed:

A - where existing plants, refinery and crude oil deposits were located

B - densely populated with developed other branches of the industry

Basic Results	Unit	Values for	
		Structure S_1	Structure S_2
Investment Capital	mil. $	572	2280
Net Income	mil. $	101	359
Manufact. Value Added	mil. $	258	833
Import	mil. $	110	205
Export	mil. $	160	372
Domestic Purchase	mil. $	126	310
Domestic Sale	mil. $	345	1194
Pay-back Period	years	5.7	6.3

Table 2: Global results for selected final structure - S_2 and intermediate one - S_1.

C - densely populated, where deposits of NPG were found.

In all sites we assumed existence of marketing centers, and in addition the one foreign trade center. Data about transportation, investment costs, costs of utilities, as well as constraints on water, energy and manpower were identified. The optimization problem was solved in order to minimize total cost of manufacturing and transportation. The result of the decomposition of S_1 and S_2 into substructures located in sites A,B,C is illustrated in Table 3 (for S_1) and Table 4 (for S_2).

To realize the task of the third level, problems of investment scheduling for implementation of the development programs in sites were formulated and solved. As a time interval on this level half-year-intervals were assumed. For each of the intervals, constraints on the investment capital to be spent were imposed. Resulting schedules (starting and completion time for each plant construction) are given also in Table 3 and Table 4.

The latter solution to the development problem terminates the first iteration of the procedure supported by the DSS.

7 Conclusions

A multilevel version of MIDA system, aimed at design of industrial development strategy is described in the paper. Numerical results illustrating the process of deriving optimal industrial structure are presented.

To classify the presented system within the DSS domain devoted to industrial development programming, let us make the following observations.

In general, relatively few systems of this type are described in detail with respect to methodology and practical results. Despite the rather scarce information, it can be concluded that two extreme approaches to the problem have evolved.

The first one is based on large and complex integrated models (e.g. Stoutjesdijk and Kendrik, 1978, Sophos et al. 1980, Palmer et al. 1984). The second extreme approach which recently seems to gain more attention puts less emphasis on formal

Production Unit	Capacity	Location	Construction	
			Start	Finish
Dibutyl Phthalate	3000	A	2.0	3.5
Dinitrotoluene	22000	B	2.5	3.5
Dioctyl Phthalate	40000	A	2.0	3.5
Ethylbenzene (Benzene Alkylation)	75000	A	2.0	3.5
Ethylene Glycol and Oxide	15000	A	0.5	2.0
Melamine-Formaldehyde Resin	10000	B	0.5	2.0
Phenol-Formaldehyde Resol Syrup	10000	B	0.5	2.0
Phosgene from Chlorine and CO	22000	B	2.5	4.0
Phtalic Anhydride from o-Xylene	27000	A	1.0	2.5
Polyether Polyol for Polyurethanes	38000	B	2.5	4.0
Polyethylene Terephthalate from TA	40000	A	1.5	3.0
Polystyrene General Purpose	30000	A	2.0	4.0
Polystyrene High Impact	10000	A	2.0	4.0
Polyurethane Resin from Polyol and TDI	50000	B	3.5	4.5
Propylene Oxide (Ethylbenzene Process)	27000	A	1.5	3.5
Sodium Alkylbenzene Sulfonate	40000	B	0.5	2.5
Sulfuric Acid from Sulfur	100000	B	0.5	2.0
TDA from Dinitrotoluene	14000	B	2.5	4.0
TDI from TDA	17000	B	2.5	4.5
Terephthalic Acid from p-Xylene	35000	A	1.0	2.5
Unsaturated Polyester Resin	10000	A	1.0	2.5
Urea-Formaldehyde Syrup	15000	B	0.5	2.0

Table 3: Spatial allocation and investment schedule for structure S_1

Production Unit	Capacity	Location	Construction	
			Start	Finish
ABS Resin	10000	A	8.0	9.0
Acetic Acid from Methanol	40000	C	6.5	8.5
Acrilonitrile (Propylene Ammoxidation)	50000	B	6.5	8.5
Bisphenol from Phenol and Aceton	15000	A	8.0	9.5
Butadiene from C_4 Extraction	35000	B	5.0	7.0
Butene-1 (Ethylene Dimerization)	12000	C	7.5	8.5
Caprolactam from Cyclohexane	50000	A	6.5	8.5
Carbon Black from Carbon Black Oil	30000	A	4.5	6.5
Chlorine (electrolysis)	100000	B	7.5	9.0
Cyclohexane from Benzene	50000	A	6.5	8.0
Epoxy Resin	20000	A	8.0	9.5
Ethyl Acetate	5000	C	7.5	8.5
Ethylene Glycol and Oxide	20000	B	5.5	7.0
Ethylene from Ethane	150000	C	5.5	8.0
Ethylene from Naphtha MS Cracking	150000	B	4.0	6.5
Methylmethacrylate Cyanohydrin Proc.	10000	B	7.0	9.0
Nylon 6 (chips)	30000	A	6.5	8.5
Polyethylene High Density	80000	B	4.5	6.5
Polyethylene Linear Low Density	120000	C	6.0	8.0
Polymethylmethacrylate	5000	B	7.5	9.0
Polypropylene (Amoco Technology)	50000	B	5.0	7.0
Polyvinyl Acetate Emulsion	50000	C	8.5	10.0
Polyvinyl Chloride Suspension	50000	B	8.0	10.0
Primary Alcohol Ethoxylate	10000	A	5.5	7.5
Primary Alcohol Ethoxysulfonate	10000	A	5.5	7.5
Primary Alcohol Sulfonate	10000	A	5.5	7.5
Primary Alcohols $C_6 - C_{12}$	15000	A	5.0	7.0
SAN Resin	5000	A	8.0	9.0
Styrene-Butadiene Rubber	45000	A	4.5	7.0
Unsaturated Polyester Resin	10000	A	8.0	9.5
Vinyl Acetate from Ethylene	50000	C	8.0	9.5
Vinyl Chloride (Oxychlorination)	50000	B	8.0	10.0

Table 4: Spatial allocation and investment schedule for final structure S_2

models and is practically devolved of optimization algorithms. Instead, it applies a very thorough evaluation of alternatives based on a multiattribute analysis done by experts that includes various "soft" factors (Keeney et al. 1986, Siskos et al. 1986, Lewandowski et al. 1986).

In the case reported a combination of both approaches is used. Optimization models and algorithms are used to support the process of generating alternative solutions being the development options. On the other hand, it is assumed that experts and decision makers will be engaged in evaluation and selection of the alternatives.

Such an approach provided an extension of MIDA methodology and resulted in a version of DSS for development programming. A basic concept of described version of MIDA system is to introduce a modular and hierarchical structure of the models involved. It improves their comprehension and enables interaction of the user (decision maker) in selection of a final solution. It is our hope that the above features coming from the "learning by doing" approach were reflected in the paper.

Acknowledgements

The authors wish to express their gratitude for contribution and close collaboration to St. Gibinski. His outstanding expertize in development programming cannot be overestimated.

The software development which was decisive to implement and apply the concept presented was completed with respect to scheduling by T. Rys. Spatial PDA model and generator were implemented by G. Dobrowolski. Their highly skilled contribution in software development is appreciated.

References

Borek A., G. Dobrowolski, M. Zebrowski (1978) GSOS - Growth Strategy Optimization System for the Chemical Industry. Proc. of MECO-78, Athens.

Dobrowolski G., J. Kopytowski, A. Lewandowski, M. Zebrowski (1982) Generating Efficient Alternatives for Development of the Chemical Industry. IIASA Collaborative Paper CP-82-54, Laxenburg, Austria.

Dobrowolski G., J. Kopytowski, J. Wojtania, M. Zebrowski (1984) Alternative Routes from Fossil Resources to Chemical Feedstock. IIASA Research Report RR-84-19, Laxenburg, Austria.

Dobrowolski G., J. Kopytowski, T. Rys, M. Zebrowski (1985) MIDA (Multiobjective Interactive Decision Aid) in the Development of the Chemical Industry. In: Theory, Software and Test Examples for Decision Support System pp. 219-234. IIASA, Laxenburg, Austria.

Gorecki H., J. Kopytowski, T. Rys, M. Zebrowski (1984) Multiobjective Procedure for Project Formulation - Design of a Chemical Installation. In: M. Grauer, A.P.

Wierzbicki (Eds.) Interactive Decision Analysis - Proc. of Int. Workshop on Interactive Decision Analysis and Interpretative Computer Intelligence Springer Verlag pp. 248-259.

MIDA User's Manual (1987) Joint System Research Department, Cracow, Poland.

Kenney R., J. Lathrop, A. Sicherman (1986) An Analysis of Baltimore Gas and Electric Company's Technology Choice. *Oper. Res. J.*, Vol. 34, No 1.

Lewandowski A., S. Johnson, A. Wierzbicki (1986) A Prototype Selection Committee Decision Analysis and Support System SCDAS : Theoretical Background and Computer Implementation. IIASA Working Paper WP-86-27, Laxenburg, Austria.

Palmer K., N. Boudwin, H. Patton, A. Rowland, J. Sammes, D. Smith (1984) A Model-Management Framework for Mathematical Programming. An Exxon Monograph. John Wiley and Sons, New York.

Siskos J., J. Lombard, A. Qudiz (1986) The Use of Multicriteria Outranking Methods in Comparison of Control Options Against Chemical Pollutant. *J. Op. Res. Soc.*, Vol 37, No 4.

Skocz M., M. Zebrowski, W. Ziembla (1987) A Method for Design of Industry Development Strategy. In: Preprints of X IFAC Congress in Munich 1987.

Skocz M., W. Ziembla (1987) Spatial PDA Modeling for Industrial Development with Respect to Transportation Costs. In: Theory, Software and Testing Examples for Decision Support System pp. 224-236. IIASA Working Paper WP-87-26, Laxenburg, Austria.

Sofos A., E. Rotstein, G. Stephanopolous (1980) Multiobjective Analysis in Modeling the Petrochemical Industry. *Chemical Engineering Science*, Vol 35, No 12.

Stoutjesdijk A., D. Kendrick (1978) The Planning of Industrial Investment Programs. A World Bank Research Publications, John Hopkins Univ. Press, Baltimore and London.

Zebrowski M. (1987) Guide to Development Programming in the Chemical Industry. Joint System Research Department, Cracow, Poland.

Zebrowski M., G. Dobrowolski, T. Rys, M. Skocz, W. Ziembla (1988) Industrial Structure Optimization: The PDAS Model. In: Expert Systems for Integrated Development: A Case Study of Shanxi Province The People's Republic of China, Final Report, Volume I, pp. 87-134. IIASA, Laxenburg, Austria.

Architecture and Functionality of MIDA

Grzegorz Dobrowolski, Tomasz Rys
Joint System Research Department
of the Institute for Control and Systems Engineering,
Academy of Mining and Metallurgy, Cracow,
and the Industrial Chemistry Research Institute, Warsaw.

Abstract

The last paper in the series is devoted to description of features of MIDA — Multiobjective Interactive Decision Aid designed by the authors for programming development of the chemical industry. Because MIDA system was used to carry out the analysis reported in the former papers, the reader can find here details that can supplement his opinion of the whole activities in the application field. The paper attempts to gather most of important assumptions that can be formulated with respect to the architecture and functionality of a DSS and to show how they can be realized in the support system based in its core on the multiobjective optimization problem.

1 Introduction

The last paper in the series contains description of MIDA — Multiobjective Interactive Decision Aid that is not only a DSS but also a name for methodology of programming development of the chemical industry (Dobrowolski et al. 1985).

The paper consists of two parts. The first three sections present the main features of MIDA system on a background of approaches to the construction of decision support systems known from the literature. This gives an opportunity for enumeration of important aspects of architecture and functionality of MIDA system which ought to be taken into account when a new DSS based on an optimization problem is built.

The second part of the paper, it is section 5, contains detailed description of MIDA system. Walking down MIDA menu system all available options are briefly described to illustrate ideas introduced in the first part of the paper as well as to clarify details omitted in previous papers of the series that deal with applications of the system. Especially, the second paper about the PDA model is complementary for understanding the structure of MIDA data base.

Research and applications in the field of computer supported programming development of chemical industry are known among industrial and scientific circles in the world. Especially multinationals are leading experts in this field with EXXON and their monograph (Palmer et al. 1984). Another example might be a group working for the

World Bank who have published a book on programming development of the fertilizers industry (Kendrick and Stoutjestijk 1984). A number of researchers (Sophos at al. 1980) have devoted their work to the problems of the technological background of the development of chemical industry.

2 Some classification aspects

What type of DSS is MIDA ?

Wang and Courtney (1984) found out the following actors involved in activities around DSS:

- a model builder,
- a system administrator who is responsible for selecting and configuring the DSS, coordinating the decision making environment and monitoring the operation of the DSS,
- an information supplier who provides data needed for the decision making task,
- a decision maker who is responsible for defining the decision making task.

In the case of MIDA, the above roles are shared among a group of designers and a user. A main assumption here is that the system, taking into account its delicate area of application, is rather personal. Then the user plays the role not only of decision maker but also of a model builder (to establish those details which are an object of the decision task themselves), information supplier (because of the same reason, especially when uncomparable sources are available) and system administrator (some options have an open character and need completion) as well.
Sprague (1980) differentiates systems designated as DSS into three types:

- *specific DSS* - a hardware and software system that allows a user to deal with a specific set of related problems,
- *DSS generator* - hardware and software that provides capabilities to build a *specific DSS* quickly and easily,
- *DSS tool* - a hardware or software element that facilitates the development of an item from the both above classes.

It is obvious from introduction that our MIDA is of the specific type. Even the second part of Sprague's (1980) definition appears to be sustained as long as the phrase *set of related problems* roughly means some elasticity in a problem formulation.

Data-oriented versus Model-oriented DSS

A particular branch of the chemical industry can be modeled as a network of production processes aggregated to simple production functions and distribution flows for a group of chemicals specified. The model is called PDA — Production Distribution Area (Dobrowolski et al., 1984).

A dichotomy between data-oriented and model-oriented DSS introduced by Alter (1980) cannot be easy resolved for MIDA.

Data availability in MIDA (to provide the user with desired descriptive information) is of equal importance with modeling capability (to provide him with normative information). It is assumed that both types of information play their roles in the process of self-learning, experimenting and approaching towards a decision.

While looking at the model as an effect of identification and structuralization of the development programming problem, MIDA can be regarded as a model-oriented DSS because it imposes a structure and views of the database and supplies a whole model management system.

Model Management Capability

As opposed to those problems that are well structured, the problem of programming development is tried in different ways that are rather of taste of a decision maker a matter. Some agreement is observed with respect to modeling basic properties of the industry (the basic model of PDA) but the choice of attributes that are aggregated or evaluated is individual. In brief, a question arises what criteria ought to be formulated to complete a mathematical model.

Bonczek et al. (1979) proposed the following taxonomy for analyzing the degree of knowledge that is assumed for the user with respect to model utilization:

- the user can procedurally specify a model's algorithm,
- the user is familiar with a collection of pre-specified models available,
- the model, if exists, is hidden and only some consequences can be observed.

The best characteristic of MIDA gives the medial case.

The core of the system is an optimization problem that is constructed of PDA basic model fed by DBMS — Data Base Management System and interactively supplemented with a criterion or criteria. This is done by the user selecting pre-defined aggregates that evaluate PDA basic model. In addition, specific models can be created for various branches of the chemical industry with the possibility of parametric modification.

3 Elements of architecture

Basic architecture

A framework for DSSs proposed by Sprague (1980) decomposes it into:

- a dialogue management system DMS that comprises all user interfaces,

- a database management system DBMS that involves the creation, storage, manipulation and retrieval of data,
- a model management system MMS that performs functions corresponding to those of DBMS but with respect to models.

MIDA implementation has shown that the above structure ought to be supplemented by a fourth subsystem gathering all auxiliary functions that are vital for utilizing DSS as a computer system.

The strongest assumption about *user friendliness* calls for functions such as maintenance of archive, making backups and re-installing of the system that can be done from inside the system. An auxiliary subsystem AS provides the user (esp. unexperienced one) with a comfortable interface to suitable commands of a computer operating system.

Although all software elements of MIDA can be, with some effort, assigned to one of the above subsystems, a natural order of calling system options from the user perspective does not accord with the discussed decomposition.

Two levels of MIDA control

A difficult issue to be resolved is the conflict between an open character of MIDA methodology and MIDA the specific character of implementation which requires definitions of all operating options and their interrelations.

A concept of wide utilization of *macros* is an often suggested remedium from this conflict. DSS generators ought to be equipped with specially designed languages to build the macros for composite reviews of databases, generation of typical models, etc.

The MIDA has to be a complete, compact computer tool that obviously strongly bounds the user's activities but on other hand only in such aspects that may be useful, especially for beginners. Some compromise has been attained by introducing two levels of control of the system. The first level is tailored for an unexperienced user. All options of this level have been previously programmed so that just a choice among them is needed. This corresponds to the macro idea. Much effort has been devoted in order to make these options handy and reliable.
Although the options of level 1 cover the problem area satisfactorily, the implementation offers also a 2nd level which comes deeper into MIDA architecture and opens way for more complicated tasks. Unfortunately, operation on the level 2 needs more practice and knowledge.

Dialogue management system

The best characteristics of DMS is the variety of screens used. MIDA uses three types of screens following a taxonomy proposed by Jarke at al. (1984):

- information display (title screens, help screen, results of the database views),
- data entry/update (access to the database, input values to programs),
- menu choice (fixed and open set of choices).

Although graphic screens built of drawings rather than texts can be put into the information display class, it is worthwhile to emphasize their existence because they create a new interface of quite special features.

The nature of the system is such that output information is mostly of numerical type. A special mode of display is applied to avoid long numerical tables.

The information is grouped in small portions, possibly not exceeding a single screen, that form basic views of the data becoming more detailed from screen to screen. The highest level of such a hierarchy consists of graphic-type screens that present information using simple diagrams (pie- or bar-charts) with names and few numbers that only roughly give values or amounts in relative units. The level is used to evoke a proper impression of basic proportions between values of most importance; meanwhile, the lowest level has to produce the long tables inevitable for printed reports.

A single session with MIDA usually consists of a sequence of calls to chosen options of the system. As the way of utilization ought to follow methodological indicators, the order of calling is pre-defined and ought to be strongly recommended to the user.

The above observation introduces an idea of guiding menu system applied in MIDA. Every time it is possible, menu screens show the next appropriate options for continuing the procedure. Help screens available at each step of the procedure make clear a momentary offer of the system.

On any level of the menu system, so-called hot keys are at the disposal of the users. These hot keys cause:

- return to the parental menu,
- immediate quitting the system,
- temporary escape to the operating system,
- displaying an adequate portion of the help text.

4 Detailed description of MIDA

MIDA computer system has been designed as a *menu-driven, screen oriented* and *user-friendly* Decision Support System. It means that everybody who operates the system is guided with a hierarchically organized collection of menus that contain all functional options that the system offers. Therefore no direct calls to the computer operating system are required and the software incorporated in the system is transparent to the user.

The menus are organized into a tree-like structure that means that the main menu (root menu) branches off to submenus. After the user selects a required option from among those listed in a given menu, the system can either switch him to the corresponding submenu or directly performs a function when a selected option is at a leaf of the menu tree.

The structure of the menu system organizes the functional description of the system. Some obvious options will be only mentioned without any detailed description.
Here is the main menu of the system:

1. PREPARE AND REVIEW DATABASE
2. GENERATE PROBLEM
3. PERFORM EXPERIMENTS
4. SELECT AND DISPLAY RESULTS
5. LOOK-OVER EXPERIMENTS ARCHIVE
6. AUXILIARY FUNCTIONS

PREPARE AND REVIEW DATABASE

By using this option of the main menu, the user gets access to MIDA relational DBMS. DBMS consists of a database, which is an organized collection of information, and a relational management system that enables the user to enter, store, manipulate and retrieve information organized into the database.

DBMS Module is designed according to the philosophy of MIDA and incorporated into DSS system. Because the database aims at feeding the DSS with the input data that are used for generating optimization problems based on PDA model, the database structure has been designed up to the requirements of the whole system. Therefore its functions take into account special requirements and structure of the a system.

All functions of MIDA DBMS were programmed using INFORMIX Relational Data Base System (1987).

Organization of the database

The information contained in the database is organized into several groups, called tables (or database tables). This way of the database organization stems from two main factors: a natural hierarchy of information used by MIDA system and a convenient data retrieval mode. The information is stored in a format that allows the database software to answer questions quickly and cooperate efficiently with other modules of the system.

The database consists of the following tables:

MAIN PARAMETERS table
INSTALLATION table
COMMENTS TO INSTALLATION table
PROCESS table
PROCESS INPUT OR OUTPUT MEDIA table
CHEMICAL OR MEDIUM table
MARKET table
COMMENTS TO MEDIA table

The above tables are mutually connected by links defined throughout the database. These connections create a logical structure of the data stored that allows for efficient cross-table queries and access to different data required by the system.
Here is the submenu that specifies basic functions provided DBMS.

1. ENTER AND UPDATE DATA
2. REVIEW PDA
3. Check PDA Consistency

4. Print Last Review
5. Repeat Last Review

Enter and Update Data

By selecting this option of the system, the user communicates with the DBMS of MIDA. He is guided by a collection of forms that are used as an input vehicle to feed into the system's database parameters of chemical processes, technological and economic data concerning installations as well as information about markets and selected macroeconomic factors (policy measures).

Using the forms the user can browse through records and files to find information based on a search relation. Once a record is displayed, he can delete or modify it and also add new records. Moreover, the DBMS provides extensive options of data checking and protection.

Data manipulation using forms

Functions supported by the DBMS for the data manipulations can be called when a required form is displayed by selecting one of the options contained in the submenu of the ENTER and UPDATE DATA function i.e.

1. Installation/Processes
2. Media
3. Main Parameters

The data manipulation rules are common for all the forms called by the above three options. Once a form is selected, the user is able to add, delete, find and update rows of a table interactively. Actions of the user are supervised by DBMS checking whether entries fall within a specified range, correspond to the types declared or meet other requirements. During data entering and updating, relevant prompts and comments are guiding the user.

The database functions (commands) appear at the top of any screen. The commands can be executed by typing the first character of the command, in either upper or lower case.

A detailed description of more important functions is given below. The most important command is ADD; to perform alteration already entered data, UPDATE and REMOVE can be used proceeded by QUERY command to fix the row of interest. Other commands play auxiliary roles. On the higher level of MIDA control, the user can operate here without knowing details about all the commands of this option.

The ADD command

After the command a is pressed, the screen displays blank columns or default values and is ready for adding a new data. While adding new row, the system is guiding the user with comments and warnings.

The QUERY, NEXT and PREVIOUS Commands

The q QUERY command is used for finding certain rows in the database. After q is typed, one of the columns (fields) should be filled with a search value. When the ESC key is pressed, all the rows with the selected search value will be located and put in a current list. The current list can be examined with the NEXT and PREVIOUS commands. If another query is done, a new current list is created.

In addition to searching for equal values, it is possible to search on the basis of relational operators. Queries can involve more than one column. Each column can contain either a search value or a relational operator followed by a search value. The query function locates all rows that contain the combinations of columns satisfying the search relations and values.

The asterisk and question mark characters have a special effect when performing searches on character columns. They represent an undefined substring or character, respectively, in the searching value.

To specify a range of values as a search criterion, one should place low and high limits for the range into the column, separated by a colon.

The UPDATE command

The UPDATE command u is for changing the contents of the currently displayed row. While changing the contents of the columns, the system can alert the user if the changes are inconsistent with the declared types of data to be introduced. In such cases, the system does not allow the cursor to travel outside the column until there is a correct entry in it.

The REMOVE command

After pressing r the system asks for confirmation that the row is to be deleted. The command is executed if Y or y is pressed.

The MASTER and DETAIL commands

These commands support cross-table queries throughout the database. This more sophisticated query mechanism takes advantage of the hierarchical, tree-like structures of the database (the consecutive levels of the hierarchy comprise INSTALLATION table, PROCESS table and PROCESS I/O MEDIA table that constitute one structure as well as MEDIA and MARKET table in the other one). In general, the MASTER command allows for joining the currently displayed row to a table of a higher hierarchy level that is related to the previous one (master table). For example, if a row of the MARKET table is displayed, pressing MASTER causes switching to the MEDIA table. On the rows of the MEDIA table the user can perform further queries.

As opposed to the MASTER command, the DETAIL command allows for joining the currently displayed row to a table of a lower hierarchy level that is related to the previous one (detail table). For example, if a INSTALLATION table row is displayed, one can switch to the related rows of the PROCESS table by pressing the DETAIL command.

Specification of the input data

While manipulating with the data to be stored or stored already in the database, the user is supported with computer forms that are input and update vehicles of the database. Each data base table has its own form. Each form is displayed on a separate screen, except the CHEMICAL OR MEDIUM form and MARKET form that are displayed together on one screen.

The practical meaning of the input data corresponding to particular forms is discussed below. The forms should be filled in the sequence as they follow in this section. It allows for checking some cross-references during inputing data.

CHEMICAL or MEDIUM form

The form is called by selection of Media option of the submenu. It contains the following columns:

number - is assigned automatically as a consecutive one. It appears after correct filling the whole form. Therefore, the cursor omits this column.

name - name of the medium is to be entered.

code - is not required to be entered. The column can be used for auxiliary information storage.

unit - the name of measure unit or its symbol (it is to be the same as in PROCESS I/O MEDIA table and as relevant to prices introduced.

lower heating value - heating value of a medium is to be entered (in unified units e.g. Gcal) for a unit assumed in the column above. This column is to be filled twice.

date of issue - a time of data validity is to be written (year, month, day).

number of markets - a number of markets is to be written as a digit (1–4). In the case of removing previously entered market or adding another one the user should remember that he has to change this column.

MARKET form

If this form is filled directly after CHEMICAL or MEDIUM form, the information on the market is treated as corresponding to the medium introduced. Therefore the form is displayed together with the MEDIUM form by selecting Media option of the submenu. If the MARKET form is filled later, then each medium is to be searched using the database query command. The MARKET form may be filled only after the medium has been entered to CHEMICAL or MEDIUM form. The following columns are specified in the form:

market type - a letter which defines a type of the market (a comment on symbols used appears in lower part of the screen): **e** - export, **i** - import **p** - domestic purchase, **s** - domestic sale.

price - unit price of a product should be entered while holding consistency with the *unit* column in CHEMICAL OR MEDIUM form. The price is to be expressed in unified currency i.e. in L.C. (local currency) when the *market type* is defined as *p* or *s* and in a convertible currency otherwise.

lower limit - concerns a lower sell ability or availability level of a given medium from a given market.

upper limit - analogous to the above.

COMMENTS TO MEDIUM form

The columns included to the form are reserved for additional descriptive-type information about a given medium.

MAIN PARAMETERS form

This form is displayed after the Main Parameters option of the database submenu is selected. The following items are included into this form:

PDA name - a name of area of interest (chemical branch).

location factor - it is a ratio of the Fixed Capital Investment for local conditions over the standard (Gulf coast) case. Default value is fixed as 1.

exchange rate - the exchange rate of Local Currency to the convertible currency should be entered.

blcc depreciation - the depreciation rate in % is to be entered. The default value is 10%.

offsite depreciation - the depreciation rate in % is to be entered. The default value is 5%.

debt/equity ratio - the share of external loan in the FCI value in % is to be entered.

interest on debt - the interest rate in % is to be entered.

working capital - the relative value in % of the Total Capital Investment is to be entered.

interest on working capital - the interest rate in % is to be entered.

insurance - the relative value in % of the Fixed Capital Investment is to be entered. The default value is 0.5%.

property tax & rent - the relative value in % of the Fixed Capital Investment is to be entered.

labor wages - the average yearly wages of labor in L.C.

supervision wages - the average yearly wages of supervisors in L.C.

laboratory wages - the average yearly wages of laboratory staff in L.C.

laboratory materials - a relative value in % of laboratory wages. The default value is 100%.

operation supply cost - this includes costs of maintenance materials done as a percentage of Fixed Capital Investment. The default value is 0.8%.

direct overhead - a relative value in % of the sum of direct labour, supervision and maintenance costs. The default value is 60%.

maintenance cost - a relative value in % of the Fixed Capital Investment. The default value is 5%.

administration - a relative value of cost in % of the sum of direct labour, supervision and maintenance cost. The default value is 15%.

sale & marketing - a relative value in % of Factory Manufacturing Cost. The default value is 15%.

R & D cost - research and development cost. The default value is 3%.

INSTALLATION form

This form, as well as COMMENTS TO INSTALLATION form, PROCESS form and PROCESS I/O MEDIA forms can be accessed by selecting the Installations/Processes option of the database submenu. The following columns are included into the form:

installation number - is assigned automatically as a consecutive one. It appears after correcting filling in the whole form. The cursor omits the column.

installation name - the name of installation should be entered.

installation code - a column for additional information may not be filled in this moment.

installation type - enter an adequate letter: o - for existing installation, p - for planned installation, r - for installation being under redevelopment.

reconstruction reference - write a number of the installation that is to be redeveloped (only if option *r* is has been used).

battery limits - a value of battery limits (blcc); to be entered twice so as to avoid mistakes. Attention should be paid to units — they have to be the same for the whole base (e.g. millions, thousands etc).

offsite - a proportion of offsite to blcc expressed in % is to be introduced.

labour, supervision, laboratory and control - number of workers employed.

number of processes - a number of processes which run in the installation and will be specified in the PROCESS form, for each installation at least one process must occur.

scaling exponent - a parameter that is commonly used for rescaling the investment cost for the different capacity.

investment domestic - a share of domestic investment in FCI, expressed in %.

date of issue - the date of data validation (year, month, day).

After the form is filled, and the row is added, a number is assigned to all installations (in *installation number* column). The numbers are unique codes of installations in the given base.

COMMENTS TO INSTALLATION form

In this form a space for additional information on the installation is reserved. This information, if needed, can be entered as a character string (text) into the sequence of columns. Basically, the information would comprise recommendations for a technology to be developed and a company that is foreseen to implement the installation.

PROCESS form

This form is selected by pressing the DETAIL command from the level of the INSTALLATION form. The following columns appear in the PROCESS form:

process number - is assigned automatically as consecutive one, it appears after correct filling the whole form. The cursor omits the column.

process name - the name of process should be entered.

process code - a column for additional information; not required to be entered.

capacity - production capacity per year in the assumed measure units. production capacity is usually expressed as an amount of production (more rarely as an input amount) of the medium which is a *capacity reference.*

capacity reference - code of the medium which is a basis for calculation of technological coefficients related to other inputs or outputs of the process.

number of media - a number of raw materials, products and utilities occurring in the process.

installation reference - is not entered, the number is assigned automatically, number of installation appears to which the process is added.

The user can return to the INSTALLATION form level by pressing the MASTER command on the PROCESS form level or quit by pressing the END command.

PROCESS INPUT OR OUTPUT MEDIA form

This form is accessed by pressing the DETAIL command from the level of PROCESS form. The following data are of concern:

process reference - is not entered, it appears automatically if an adequate PROCESS form has been filled before.

medium reference - code of the medium.

input-output - a letter is to be written: `o` - for products, by-products and other process outputs (e.g. steam in an exothermic process), `i`. - for media consumed in the process, also for utilities.

coefficient - consumption or production coefficient of a medium in a given process (recalculated for the unit of main product i.e. capacity reference in PROCESS form). The column is to be filled twice. A coefficient for the medium defined in PROCESS form as a capacity reference is always equal to 1.

The user can return to the PROCESS form by pressing the MASTER command from the PROCESS I/O MEDIA level or quit by pressing the END command.

Review PDA

Taking into account the specific application of MIDA database, a selection of database reviewing options are supported in the system.
Here is a menu of possible reviews to be selected from the REVIEW PDA level:

1. Medium Distribution (by number)
2. Medium Distribution (by name)
3. Purchase Limits
4. Sale Limits
5. ECE - Energy Conversion Efficiency
6. Profitability
7. Manufacturing Value Added
8. Process Inputs and Outputs (by number)
9. Process Inputs and Outputs (by name)
10. Single Plant Evaluation
11. Processes List
12. Media List (with prices)
13. Advanced Reviewing
14. Print Last Review
15. Repeat Last Review

Reviews 1–4, 8, 9 are to display the contents of the database from the MIDA methodology (level 1) point of view. They allow for showing the connections between those data that constitute the technological network as well as for a comprehensive information on some items stored in the database.

The options are very useful for learning, data validation especially when a strategy assumed for data gathering is distributed in the sense that particular information about an installation or a chemical may come from different sources as far as formal requirements are sustained.

Options 5–7, 10 are to calculate and display economic and technological parameters for evaluation of particular chemical processes and also for display of selected information concerning the market. Besides learning and data validation these options play a direct role in the decision process allowing simple evaluation and ordering of technological alternatives.

Below the standard database reviewing options contained in the REVIEW PDA submenu are briefly described.

Medium Distribution (by number)
Medium Distribution (by name)

These options allow for listing the processes in which a given medium occurs. In the first option the medium is defined by its number, in the second one by its name or a name-based search string (for example instead of searching by the full name `ammonia` it is possible to write `ammo*`). After one of the options is selected, all processes connected to the medium are displayed, with an information whether the medium is of input (i) or output (o) type in each process. This information is followed with relevant consumption coefficients of the medium related to main products of the processes.

Sale Limits
Purchase Limits

The two options are to display limits of the sell ability and availability of all media for which such limits are imposed. Both limits concern upper and lower bounds of sell ability (of products) and availability (of raw materials).

ECE — Energy Conversion Efficiency

For any process an energy conversion efficiency is calculated and displayed as a ratio (%) between the output and input energy. In addition, a total energy supplied to the process (both the energy contained in input media and the technological energy) is given. To make the output list more concise, it is assumed that only those processes of the ECE beyond a declared range will be displayed. The default ECE range (as assumed to be acceptable) is 60–90%.

Profitability

For each process its profitability derived from the production value — PV and total manufacturing cost — TMC is calculated and displayed. On the display absolute values of a unit manufacturing cost as well as a ratio of PV vs. TMC expressed in % are given. To make the output list more concise, it is assumed that only those processes of profitability lying beyond a declared range are displayed (the default range is 70–150%). If for any process some data are missing (e.g. some prices are equal to 0), its profitability will be displayed regardless the value.

Manufacturing Value Added

For each product a Manufacturing Value Added is calculated and displayed. This is expressed as an absolute value of unit input (cost of raw materials, supplies, utilities and maintenance materials) and as a relation of MVA over the input value expressed in %. Similarly to the options 5, 6, for the sake of brevity, only those processes of MVA lying beyond a declared range are displayed (the default range is 90-170%).

Process Input/Output (by number)
Process Input/Output (by name)

The functions of the above options are self-explanatory. Besides the inputs and outputs of each process the technological coefficients related to a main product are displayed.

Single Plant Evaluation

For each plant (installation) the selected information either retrieved directly from the data base or preprocessed as complex factors is given. The information comprises the following data [1]:

Capacity,
Fixed Capital Investment — FCI,
Product Value — PV,
Total Manufacturing Cost — TMC,
Profit,
Simple Rate of Return,
Break-Even Point,
Manufacturing Value Added — MVA,
MVA/FCI,
MVA/PV,
PV/FCI,
Energy Consumption.

Processes List

This option provides a list of all processes stored in the database, described by names and capacities.

Media List

This option provides a list of all media stored in the database, described by names and prices corresponding to certain kinds of markets.

Advanced Reviewing

The option falls into those that form the 2nd level of MIDA control. To use this option effectively the user has to know not only the special language but the structure of database with internal names of tables and fields.

The option provides the user with extensive capabilities for data reviewing, updating and deletion with respect to large group of the rows. It is supported with an Structured Query Language SQL which combines power and flexibility with easy use.

After pressing this option of MIDA submenu, the user gets an access to the SQL menu-like interface. Functions offered on the SQL menu allows the user to handle with SQL scripts. He can prepare a new one (NEW or MODIFY commands) using his favorable text editor, perform (CHOOSE, RUN) previously done and store the SQL script (SAVE) for further use.

The SQL script is built from SQL commands defined both in ANSI standard (mainly SELECT, UPDATE, DELETE commands) and in RDS INFORMIX (see INFORMIX 1987) extensions that add many miscellaneous commands comfortable for a data base administrator. Below a basic explanation of most important commands' syntax is given.

[1] Break-even Point — this economic indicator determines a production level expressed as a part of production capacity which assures an equilibrium of cumulative receipts (profit) with cumulative production costs.

It do not exhaust all the language capabilities — in fact the flexibility and power of data retrieval are limited only by imagination of the user.

The SELECT command

The SELECT command is for retrieval of selected contents of the database.
The syntax of the SELECT command is as follows:

```
SELECT clause       FROM clause
                  { WHERE clause          }
                  { GROUP BY clause       }
                  { HAVING clause         }
                  { ORDER BY clause       }
                  { INTO TEMP clause      }
```

Briefly, the SELECT clause names a list of columns of expressions to be retrieved, the FROM clause names a list of tables, the WHERE clause sets conditions on the rows, the GROUP BY clause groups rows together, the HAVING clause sets conditions on the groups, the ORDER BY clause orders the selected rows, and the INTO TEMP clause puts the results into a temporary table.

The UPDATE and DELETE Commands

The UPDATE and DELETE commands permit modification or deletion of database rows in mass. The syntax of the commands is as follows:

```
UPDATE table_name SET    column_name = expr         |
                         column_list = expr_list    |
                         * = expr_list
                       { WHERE clause }

DELETE FROM table_name { WHERE clause }
```

Updating of the data is gained by specification of a table name and a column name (or names) and a new contents of this column done by an arithmetical expression. Rows to be affected may be picked up using WHERE clause. DELETE command may be applied to a whole table indicated by a name or to chosen rows given by WHERE clause.

During the above commands is executed, the affected rows or columns can be displayed, one at a time, and the system prompts to verify that a change or deletion is required.

Print Last Review

It is one of AS (auxiliary subsystem) functions that causes the system to prepare a hard copy of results of the last applied review already shown on the screen.

Repeat Last Review

Results of the last review are saved and can be send to the screen on request. This option is useful when after doing some operations outside the Review PDA option the user wants to recall previous values of a certain review.

Check PDA Consistency

This option provides the user with a possibility of automatic checking of inconsistencies and errors that can occur in the database. The program traces for errors that violate the structure of data corresponding to the structure of PDA basic model.

When an incorrect situation is found, the system displays a list containing information on the error status, number and names of items that are subjects of the error followed by a comment. Basically, two kinds of errors are distinguished: errors `E` and warnings `W`. The first kind makes further calculations impossible (a generated model due to its structure cannot give the optimal solution); the second is not critical for further processing though warnings can indicate on facts that can substantially influence the solution.
Data checking performed bases on:

- information redundancy purposefully introduced into the data base,
- analysis of reference in the data base,
- analysis of constraints put on media distribution.

The following situations cause error `E` messages:

`wrong number of media` - different number of media in a process and a number of corresponding rows in the PROCESS I/O MEDIA table.

`wrong number of markets` - different number of markets declared for a medium and a number of corresponding rows in the MARKET table.

`wrong number of processes` - different number of processes in an installation and a number of corresponding rows in the PROCESS table.

`product out of network` - a medium occurs in the table CHEMICAL OR MEDIUM but it is not specified among the technological data.

`output locked` - a medium is specified as an output of the network but no sale market was defined for this product.

`input locked` - a medium is specified as an input of the network but no purchase market was defined for it.

`wrong price relation` - prices set out for purchase or import as well as for sale or export are in relation that is not realistic from the economic viewpoint. Basically, sale- or export-prices should exceed those of purchase or import. Otherwise, if such data are introduced to the PDA model, it causes circulation of products beyond the production network (as it means that it is beneficial to buy products and then sell them without any processing).

Moreover, the system can display the following warnings:

`output import redundant` - the indicated product is an output of the production network, and moreover, import on the product is assumed.

`input export redundant` - the indicated product is an input of the production network, and moreover, export on the product is assumed.

`mixed limited` - the indicated product is both a process input and a process output. There is a constraint imposed on the flow of this product inside the network.

GENERATE PROBLEM

The option establishes a bridge between DBMS and MMS. The optimization model is generated from the database using DBMS mechanisms; on the other hand selection of different version of PDA basic model is, in fact, a domain of MMS.
Here is a content of the menu displayed on the GENERATE PROBLEM level:

1. Generate Model (capacities constrained)
2. Generate Model (capacities relaxed)
3. Model Adaptation
4. Dictionary Adaptation

The basic function of the module is selection and transformation of data stored in the database into so-called MPS file, DICTIONARY file and CHANGE file.

The MPS file contains information organized according to linear programming standard of IBM called MPS (Mathematical ... 1976) and widely used for such applications.

It is important that the structure of the MPS file reflects an assumed structure of the model selected for simulation experiments.

The DICTIONARY file contains description of selected MPS codes (names) in natural language and report specification for every optimization run. In principle, the file is a cross- reference array that combines MPS codes and real-life names as well as parameters of scale and units introduced for variables that occur in the solution. The latter file determines an order and classification (attribute-oriented cross-cutting groupings) of the reported results due to requirements of the user.

The CHANGE file points at aggregates that are used for objectives definition or media that can be modified during simulation experiments on a given model. The file also defines set of criteria that can be selected for an optimization run, kind of constraints or single parameters.

The first two options of the menu cause MPS file generation either corresponding to a PDA model with incorporated constraints on capacities of processes as determined in the database or without those constraints. The second option is especially useful at the initial stage of the analysis to estimate production levels that meet global conditions as e.g. investment value assumed, production goal etc.

Options 3, 4 come from 2nd level of MIDA control and enable adaptation of the model and intervention into a default contents of the report on optimization, respectively.

PERFORM EXPERIMENTS

By selection of this main menu option, the user activates the MMS. It consists of an integrated optimization package devised for solving linear programming problems of three types:

LP problems with a single objective function, solved using revised simplex method,

FLP problems with single fractional linear objective function,

MLP multicriteria problems solved through the reference point method (Wierzbicki 1979).

Capabilities of the MMS allow for flexible definition of optimization experiments and rough analysis of results. They are as follows:

- the user may choose optimization mode and may change this mode during the work with the package,
- a selected criterion (or criteria) from a pre-defined set can be selected,
- constraints can be changed for selected variables of the model,
- a so-called utopia point is calculated automatically in the case of multiobjective problems,
- a fast review of optimization results is possible,
- clear and understandable reports of results can be created,
- results can be stored on disk files for further analysis,
- a basis solution calculated for an initial problem is maintained, what results in significant acceleration of computations in the case of repeated usage of the package with the same starting base,
- postoptimal analysis can be done with respect to constraints introduced by markets.

The following actions are also possible to support analysis on 2nd level devised mainly for model designers:

- any of the elements of generalized simplex matrix using MPS codes may be changed,
- the results can be stored in MPS output standard (Mathematical... 1976).

Though some of the above functions may seem to be redundant as compared to those contained in other menus of the system, they have been implemented intentionally to run experiments more efficiently when changes of the input data do not violate dimensions of the initial problem.

Below all functions provided by the menus of MMS will be listed. It aims at giving a comprehensive view on the structure of the subsystem only because while using it the user can be always supported with detailed instructions of Help.

The main menu of the module is as follows:

1. Select Optimization Type
2. Input Manager
3. Run Solver
4. Output Manager
5. Exit

In principle, all options 2 – 5 of the main menu can be executed in any order; nevertheless to guide the user while solving the problem, the system highlights the options following a logical order of the solving procedure. The options of the menu comprise key components of the problem formulation, solving, reporting and modification.

Select Optimization Type

This option should be executed as the first one to determine type of the optimization. A selected type can be changed during the session.

When the Select Optimization Type option is executed, the system offers the following submenu:

1. Single Objective
2. Multiobjective
3. Fractional

Regardless which one of the above types is chosen, the system then asks whether the user wants to start from a previously calculated basic solution (`old basis`) and displays names of those bases that have been stored already. To get more information about existing basis files, it is possible to call Help. If no one of the listed bases can be used for the current problem, the user should select the New Basis option displayed as the first one on the list of simplex bases and then will be asked for a name of the `new basis` file. It is important that starting calculations from an old basis (if possible) brings solution of the problem much faster which is crucial for efficient solving large-scale problems.

Input Manager

This option is for a scenario definition of an optimization problem to be solved. When a choice of the starting basis is decided, the system returns to Input Manager option of the main menu. On this level a detailed formulation of the problem can be done following the options of the submenu:

1. Prepare Objectives
2. Bound Items
3. Run MPS-like Modifier
4. Calculate Utopia Point (if applicable)
5. Exit

As opposed to the main menu, the user is free to execute the options in any order.

Prepare Objectives

Activation of this option causes displaying a screen of data entry/update type. The user can choose from a set of pre-defined aggregates those that are to form current criterion or criteria. Simultaneously a direction of optimization is determined. The criteria selection is performed by using the keys for moving through the menus. To choose an optimization direction the user should:

1. move the cursor to the third column of the screen

2. press SPACE BAR until a desired direction will be displayed, i.e.:

   `min` - minimization,

   `max` - maximization,

   `flo` - ignore,

   `den` - a denominator; which is only applicable to the fractional optimization — in this case `min` or `max` indicates a numerator.

When the user has decided to do a single objective optimization, he can define only one objective from the list. If he has declared to perform a multiobjective experiment, he is provided with a similar list containing an additional fourth column reserved for a reference point value. The similar mechanism allows to enter new values for the reference point. Because the list displayed for Prepare Objectives option may exceed the space of one screen (window), it can be scrolled down or up.

Bounds Item

If the user wants to modify constraints on the aggregates or variables that represent market conditions this option is adequate. It can be done in a similar way as assigning new values for the reference point.

To define new lower (upper) bound the user should pick the given item up and move the cursor to the third (fourth) column of the screen and enter new value. It is obvious that a lower bound should be less than or equal to the corresponding upper bound.

The two above options of MMS (level 1) are used to complete or interactively modify the optimization problem.

Run MPS-like Modifier

It is an option from 2nd level of control that allows changing any LP-matrix element. Using this option requires a good knowledge of the model associated with the MPS file structure (Mathematical ... 1976). Because a wrong update of the file can damage the model, this option should be used **with caution**. First, the Section Definition Command should be entered to define the MPS section to be updated. This command can be followed by updating commands corresponding to the Section Definition Command. Each section definition command must be typed without blanks and each updating command must start from a blank and consist of a number of fields (like in the MPS file) separated by at least one blank. The update of a section is terminated by a new section definition command. The section definition command `endata` ends modification and quits the option.

Any time the `@` command can be introduced for looking through the MPS file. In the multiobjective case an original (not preprocessed) file is taken into account.

Calculate Utopia Point

The option runs series of optimization problems and searches for an utopia point corresponding to the defined set of objectives. This option obviously applies to a multiobjective optimization.

Run Solver

The option activates the solving procedure for the currently defined problem (if it is possible).

Analysis of infeasible and unbounded solutions

The cases of infeasible or unbounded solutions can happen quite often while doing simulation experiments. Especially for complex and large-scale models it can be difficult to trace reasons for infeasibility or unboundness.

To support diagnosis of these reasons, the system provides an analysis of such cases, if required. The analysis consists of giving names of variables that have contradictory constraints (infeasible case) or that cause unbounded solution. When the solution tends to violate an upper constraint (bound) of a variable, the comment `TOO HIGH` is written. When the solution tends to violate the lower bound imposed, the comment `TOO LOW` is displayed. It means that in the `TOO HIGH` case, the upper bound of the variable should be increased, and correspondingly, in the `TOO LOW` case, the lower bound should be decreased. Dependent on a kind of a bound violated, five categories of bounds can be signaled together with a name of variable: `import`, `export`, `domestic purchase`, `domestic sale` and `process`. In the second category of infeasibility caused by an unmatched balance equation, the analysis giving a name of balance equation violated while solving a problem is displayed.

If the unbounded solution occurs, the system provides a necessary diagnosis of the case by indicating a variable that caused the situation. In a very rare case of unbounded solution met in the phase 1 of simplex algorithm, the systems warns the user that the analysis could be irrelevant.

Both cases can be analyzed on the basis of MPS-like solution that can be stored on a diskfile by selecting an appropriate option of the Output Manager under a name extended by `.mps`

Output Manager

After an experiment is run successfully, the user can be supported by the Output Manager to review and store results of the optimization. Here is the corresponding submenu:

1. Show Criteria Solution
2. Show Fast Report
3. Show Report
4. Compare with Previous Run
5. Postoptimal Analysis
6. Store Report
7. Store MPS-like Solution
8. Prepare Solution for Storing in Database
9. Store Results
10. Print Last Report
11. Show Utopia Point
12. Exit

Show Criteria Solution - the values and optimization directions of objectives for the current solution will be displayed,

Show Fast Report - the current solution will be quickly displayed in a rough form,

Show Report - the current solution will be displayed in as nicely as possible formatted form. Only non-zero values will be taken into account. It is possible to review this report conveniently,

Compare with Previous Run - a comparison of the current solution with the previous one (if any) will be performed on assumed level of accuracy (i.e.requested by the user).

Postoptimal Analysis - the postoptimal analysis performs ordinary ranging on the bounds. For each lower bound and each upper bound, the subroutine determines the maximum range in which the bound can vary without affecting the optimal basis. The option is a problem oriented implementation of a type of the postoptimal analysis of POSTAN 3 package (see Dobrowolski at al. 1984).

Store Report - the previously prepared report will be stored in a file named by the user,

Print Last Report - either the report generated by the option 3 or postoptimal analysis report can be printed,

Store MPS-like Solution - the solution will be prepared in special (MPS-standard) form which can be useful for model developers. This form is practically unreadable for normal users but can be useful for tracing consecutive steps of the solving procedure (the format of the printout is described in (Murtagh and Saunders 1977). The system will ask for the file name for storing the results,

Prepare Solution for Storing in Database - the solution will be prepared in a format acceptable by data base management system. This solution can be loaded into the database and analyzed by DBMS utilities.

Store Results - the current solution will be stored for future analysis. The following files will be created: report, solution for DBMS, an utopia value (if calculated) and value(s) of criteria,

Show Utopia Point - a value of utopia point will be displayed (if calculated by Input Manager after calling the multiobjective option),

Exit - goes to the upper level menu.

SELECT AND DISPLAY EXPERIMENT

Again the user is armed with DBMS but now the reviews can go not only through input data but results of an experiment as well.

The option is to be selected after an optimization experiment is run. It provides the user with a variety of reports on the solution dependent on several solution-components that might be of interest to him. Some of the reports are standard (level 1 of MIDA control), the other (level 2) can be printed out on request of the user who can design a format and content by himself.

Here the whole menu offered by pressing the option follows:

1. Select Experiment to Display
2. Report on Optimization
3. PDA Evaluation
4. Processes
5. Import
6. Export
7. Domestic Purchase
8. Domestic Sale
9. Domestic Sale form Import
10. Single Plant Evaluation
11. Medium Distribution (by number)
12. Medium Distribution (by name)

13. Process Inputs and Outputs (by number)
14. Process Inputs/Outputs (by name)
15. Advanced Reviewing (via informer)
16. Print Last Review
17. Repeat Last Review

Select Experiment to Display

Since the results of various experiments can be stored in the system during a session with MMS, not only those of the recent one can be reported. To recall results of experiments done already, this option should be pressed before selecting any one listed below.

Scenario

A scenario containing information about assumptions set for the simulation experiment is displayed. The scenario is preceded by a name of an experiment and an optimal criterion value.

PDA Evaluation

Development programs (as expressed by optimal solutions relevant to assumed conditions) are to evaluated by means of the following indicators:

Fixed Capital Investment — FCI,
    Domestic Investment,
PDA Net Income — NI,
    NI/FCI,
    PDA Import,
    PDA Domestic Sale,
Production Profit,
    Simple Rate of Return,
    Production Import,
    Domestic Sale of Production,
Manufacturing Value Added — MVA,
    MVA/FCI,
Gross Production Value — GPV
    MVA/GPV,
Export,
Domestic Purchase,
Energy Consumption,
Direct Labour,
Supervisory Labour,
Laboratory and Control.

As can be observed, the above indicators are classified into three categories that correspond to PDA as a whole and to the production system itself. This is done to explicate evaluation of development programs from two various viewpoints. The indicators are be calculated after the experiment for an assumed scenario is performed, i.e. as a post-optimization analysis of the generated development program. As can be seen, some aggregates give criterion value(s) while the other are performance indicators only.

Processes

The report on processes provides a two-fold information. First, a share of investment cost over process-units is displayed. For the sake of better visualization of the results, the values in % are shown in a bar chart shape. Next, the user can quit the review or request for a more detailed information. Now, production volumes of processes are displayed both in absolute values and as a portion of an assumed level. Those that are omitted in the report have the production equal to zero.

Import

Similarly to the review Processes, the report has two functional sections. The first one gives a share of particular media in total import of the PDA in a bar chart shape. The second section provides information on quantity and value of products imported by the PDA.

Export

This review is analogous to the one about import, and the data are displayed in the same mode.

Domestic Purchase

This report provides information on domestic purchase of media in the PDA. The report is analogous to the one about import and export, and the data are displayed in the same mode.

Domestic Sale

This report provides information on domestic sale of products of the PDA. The report is analogous to the one about import and export, and the data are displayed in the same mode.

Domestic Sale from Import

This report shows complementary imports of market goods that is necessary for meeting domestic demands. Import of a medium is expressed in proportion to the whole volume of its sale in %.

Single Plant Evaluation

This report provides a complex information concerning any single process or installation, relevant to an optimal production level calculated during a simulation experiment. The components of the report are the same as for the Single Plant Evaluation suboption of Review PDA.

Gross Production

This component of the report provides a total production value calculated as a sum of production values over all processes of the PDA.

Medium Distribution (by number)

Similarly to the reports as above, this one gives information divided in two segments — two bar charts located with opposite orientation. The first one shows sources of a given medium in the PDA with relative quantities of the medium gained, the second one contains the outputs. This way the user obtains a graphical image of balance of the medium in the network, corresponding to an optimal solution. As in the option described above a picture is followed (on request) by a table with detailed distribution of the medium.

Medium Distribution (by name)

The function of the report is analogous to the last described option, but it does not provide the graphic part of report.

Process Input/Output (by number)
Process Input/Output (by name)

A specification of all inputs and outputs of a given process is displayed. It contains quantities of inflows and outflows of the process. The process can be selected either by its number or by name.

Advanced Reviewing (via SQL)

Quite similar to the Advanced Reviewing of the database, this option provides a powerful reporting mechanism based on the same Structured Query Language — SQL described already (see INFORMIX ..., 1987).

Therefore, using the same syntax of the commands, the user can select and retrieve information concerning results of optimization experiments as it was done for the source data stored in the database. This is a result of loading the solution to the database.

LOOK-OVER EXPERIMENTS ARCHIVE

This option provides a user with tools for the maintenance of an archive of results stored during the work with the PERFORM EXPERIMENTS option. Here is the menu offered:

1. Scenarios of Stored Experiments
2. Compare Experiments
3. Remove Experiment
4. Print Last Review
5. Repeat Last Review

Display Scenarios of Stored Experiments

This option shows a content of the experiments archive. In the archive those experiments that are meaningful for the user are to be stored. The experiments are represented by their names given by the user during running the PERFORM EXPERIMENTS option and scenarios set for those experiments.

Compare Experiments

This option is run when a comparison of results of various experiments is required. When the option is selected, the user can choose experiments to be compared from among those displayed on the screen. In principle, if the user picks up no more than 3 experiments, the output is produced on the screen and can be printed out as well. Otherwise, only a printout is possible. The system can recapitulate the differences between the results following one of the COMPARISON MODES (up to the user's convenience):

1. Different Elements
2. All Elements
3. Percent Relation

In the All Elements mode, the system displays all components of the solution regardless their values. As opposed to this mode, the modes Different Elements and Percent Relation introduce only different elements of the results to the comparison table. In the first one all the results are quoted in absolute values, the second one sums us differences in a relative manner (in %) with respect to the basic solution. As a basic solution, results of the first selected experiments are taken.

Remove Experiment

To do up the archive file, those experiments that are no longer important should be removed. An experiment that is to be removed can be indicated on the list displayed by using the same mechanism as for all menus (i.e. by highlighting the name of an experiment to be deleted).

AUXILIARY FUNCTIONS

The system provides the user with tools for making backups of the database contents. Here is the relevant menu:

1. Store D.B. on Diskette
2. Restore D.B. from Diskette

3. Store D.B. in ASCII format
4. Restore D.B. from ASCII format
5. Reinstall MIDA System

Store Database on Diskette

This option is to do backups of the database contents. It is recommended to do backups reasonably often, i.e. after each substantial update of the database. Otherwise any failure of the computer or the hard disk can spoil a lot of work invested in the data entering. Before pressing the option 3, a formatted high density diskette should be inserted in a slot. The principle is that one base can be stored on one diskette.

Restore Database from Diskette

This option restores a previous contents of the database stored on a high density diskette. To restore a database contents, a new, empty database should be established e.g. by using of a Reinitialize Database option.

Store Database in Ascii Format

This option produces a dump of a database contents in the form of an character file. It is useful for making a compact backups of databases especially when the same database should be installed on another operating system (e.g. when it is to be moved from DOS to XENIX). In addition, the character dumps are a convenient form of a database reviewing, especially for experienced users.

Restore Database from Ascii Format

This option loads a new, empty database from ascii dumps.

Reinitialize Database

This option establishes a new, empty database in the current directory. The former contents of the database, if such one exists in the directory is **removed.**

5 Summary

MIDA presented in this paper exists in two implementations: for DOS and for UNIX (XENIX, ULTRIX) operating systems. These implementations, regardless slight differences that arise as an effect of implementation in different computer environments, are the same from the user point of view.

Until now, MIDA is extensively used in three different places in the world, supporting several different development problems of the chemical industry on the national level. Moreover, some elements of MIDA methodology and software tools are implemented in the fourth place.

The above fact suggests that some new modification to the system may come soon as a consequence of use by various people and in various places.

Acknowledgements

The section on description of MIDA is based on *MIDA — User's Manual* that was prepared by our friend and collaborator dr Maciej Skocz. We are very obliged him for a possibility of quoting large parts of the text.

References

Alter, S.L. (1980) Decision Support Systems: Current Practice and Computing Challenges. Addison-Wesley Publishing Co., New York.

Bonczek, R.H., C.W. Holsapple and A.B. Winston (1979) Computer based support of organizational decision making. *Decision Science,* Vol. 10, no. 2, pp. 268–291.

Dobrowolski, G., K. Hajduk, A. Korytowski and T. Rys (1984) POSTAN — A Package for Postoptimal Analysis (An Extension of MINOS). IIASA Collaborative Paper CP-84-32, Laxenburg, Austria.

Dobrowolski, G., J. Kopytowski, J. Wojtania and M. Zebrowski (1984) Alternative Routes from Fossil Resources to Chemical Feedstock. IIASA Research Report RR-84-19, Laxenburg, Austria.

Dobrowolski, G., J. Kopytowski, T. Rys and M. Zebrowski (1985) MIDA (Multiobjective Interactive Decision Aid) in the Development of Chemical Industry. In Theory, Software and Testing Examples for Decision Support Systems. A. Lewandowski and A. Wierzbicki (Eds) pp. 235–251, IIASA Collaborative Paper, Laxenburg, Austria.

INFORMIX — Relational Database System. User's Manual. (1987) Relational Database Systems, Inc.

Jarke, M., M.T. Jelassi and E.A. Stohr (1984) A Data-driven User Interface Generator for a Generalized Multiple Criteria Decision Support System. *IEEE Computer Society Reprint,* Silver Spring, USA.

Kendrick, D.A. and Stoutjestijk A.J. (1978) The Planning of Investment Programs. Vol. 1 A Methodology. Johns Hopkins University Press, Baltimore M.D., World Bank Research Publications.

Mathematical Programming System/360 Version 2, Linear and Separable Programming — User's Manual (1976) IBM Document no. H20-0476-2.

Murtagh, B.A. and M.A. Saunders (1977) MINOS — A Large-Scale Linear Programming System. User's Guide. Technical Report SOL 77-9, System Optimization Laboratory, Stanford University, California.

Sophos, A., Rotstein E. and Stephanopoulos G. (1980) Multiobjective analysis in modeling the petrochemical industry. *Chemical Engineering Science* , Vol. 35(12), pp. 2415–2426.

Sprague, R.H. (1980) A framework for the development of decision support systems. *MIS Quarterly* ,vol. 4, no. 4, pp. 1-26.

Palmer, K. (1984) A model management framework for mathematical programming. An EXXON Monograph, Wiley New York.

Wang, M.S. and J.F. Courtney (1984) A Conceptual Architecture for Generalized Decision Support System Software. *IEEE Transaction on System, Man, and Cybernetics,* vol. 14, no. 5, pp. 701–711.

Wierzbicki, A. P. (1979) The Use of Reference Objectives in Multiobjective Optimization — Theoretical Implications and Practical Experience. Working Paper WP-79-66, International Institute for Applied System Analysis, Laxenburg, Austria.

Part 3
Short Software Descriptions

IAC–DIDAS–L
A Dynamic Interactive Decision Analysis and Support System for Multicriteria Analysis of Linear and Dynamic Linear Models on Professional Microcomputers

Tadeusz Rogowski, Jerzy Sobczyk, Andrzej P. Wierzbicki

Institute of Automatic Control, Warsaw University of Technology.

1 Purpose of the packages

IAC–DIDAS–L1 and L2 are two versions of software packages – prototype versions of decision analysis and support systems – for interactive, multiobjective analysis for ***models describing substantive aspects of a decision situation*** that are represented ***in linear programming or dynamic linear programming form***. Such models are often used to represent situations of complex decisions involving economic, environmental and technological aspects. Models of this type must be formulated by teams of analysts specialized in a given field, before they can be helpful to decision makers. Once formulated, however, such models can be used in many ways to learn about decision options and predicted results.

2 Methodological background

IAC–DIDAS–L systems ***can be used either by analysts*** specialized in modelling ***or by decision makers*** experienced in a given field but not necessarily computer specialists. These systems help in organizing work with decision models in a process of interactive, dynamic decision support. First, they help in model edition and initial analysis; then in the formulation of a multiobjective decision analysis problem; then in the initial assessment of bounds of decision outcomes or objectives for a given problem.

A model of multiobjective linear programming type is characterized by its decision variables, its outcome variables defined by linear model equations, and its constraints or bounds on various variables. In multiobjective analysis, ***the user can select objective variables*** (mostly among outcome variables) ***that might be minimized, maximized or stabilized*** close to given values. This constitutes the definition of multiobjective analysis problem. For a given problem, the package can help in computing bounds on efficient (multiobjectively optimal) values of the objective variables and in suggesting a compromise efficient solution. All this is done in IAC–DIDAS systems by special multiobjective optimization methodology and special optimization solvers; but *the user* needs not to be bothered with these specialized details, because he *can influence the choice of an efficient solution* (decisions and outcomes) *by specifying his reference point or aspiration levels* for the objective outcomes he has determined, and asking the system to find the efficient solution that matches his aspirations most closely.

An interactive multiobjective analysis of the problem based on the principle of reference point optimization is performed, while the user (the analyst or the decision maker) indicates the type of solutions that he is interested in by specifying his aspiration levels for objective outcomes (or for their trajectories in the dynamic case) and the decision support system responds to his directions by solving a special optimization problem and answering, whether his aspirations are attainable. If not, the system proposes decisions with outcomes that come uniformly as close as possible to the stated aspiration levels. If the aspiration levels are attainable but cannot be exceeded, the system proposes decisions with outcomes that precisely match the aspiration levels. If the aspiration levels can be exceeded, the system proposes decisions with outcomes that uniformly exceed the aspirations. By changing the aspiration levels, *the user can easily control and select such decision options that are best suited for his preferences*.

Finally, the system can also help in a post-optimal analysis of a selected decision option by examining various options that are close to it. All results of analysis can be illustrated graphically on the monitor screen. The user can also have print-outs of selected results of analysis.

The system helps also the user to keep track of consecutive results of analysis and stores results marked by the user as important in a special *result directory*. Because the user can formulate various multiobjective decision problems for given model of substantive aspects of the decision situation (by maximizing or minimizing multiobjective various model outcomes, etc.), the system keeps also track of various problem formulations. Finally, the system allows also to work with various models of one or more decision situations; thus, the system has also *model and problem directory*.

The system includes two demonstrative models with some problem formulations and illustrative results of their analysis; by watching these demonstrations, the user can easily learn how to work with the system. One of the demonstrative examples used in both versions illustrates *a diet composition problem* and the other example depends on the system version. In the version L1 that includes the possibility of working with dynamic models but uses a more specialized format of model edition, *an example of controlling two reservoirs on a river* illustrates dynamic problems of decision analysis. In the version L2 that is essentially limited to static models but has an easy and user-friendly spreadsheet format of model edition, *an example from agricultural economics* illustrates the possibilities of the system.

3 Short program description

IAC–DIDAS–L1 and L2 are software packages from the class of *prototypes* of interactive multiobjective decision analysis and support systems. When supplemented by a model of the substantive aspects of a decision situation (involving economic, environmental, technological etc. aspects), they can serve both as tools of model analysis used by specialists and as decision support systems used by decision makers that are experienced in a given substantive field (but not necessarily computer specialists) that want to investigate various aspects of many decision options. These packages are developed to the level of *scientific transferable software*, that is, are tested and documented enough to be used widely in research. The IAC–DIDAS–L packages are designed for use with models of multiobjective linear programming and dynamic linear programming type.

IAC–DIDAS–L1 is written in FORTRAN, contains a special linear programming optimization *solver* for multiobjective problems, that results in relative fast execution of optimization runs during interactive analysis but requires the preparation of the model of substantive aspects of decision situation in the MPS format (standard for linear programming specialists but not necessarily easy for an average user); on the other hand, this version allows also for an easy edition and analysis of dynamic models.

IAC–DIDAS–L2 is written in PASCAL, contains another version of linear programming optimization solver adapted for multiobjective problems and supports an interactive definition and edition of the model of substantive aspects of decision situation in a user-friendly format of a spreadsheet.

Both versions have *user interfaces* with helps displaying various commands used depending on the stage of decision analysis process. Both versions have *data bases with directories* of various models, multiobjective analysis problem formulations and various results of analysis. Both versions have *graphic interfaces* helping to illustrate results of analysis.

4 Hardware requirements

Both IAC–DIDAS–L1 and L2 are implemented on professional microcomputers compatible with IBM–PC/XT (with a hard disk, Hercules or color graphics or EGA card and, preferably, a coprocessor) or a similar IBM–PC/AT configuration.

References

Rogowski, T., J. Sobczyk, A. P. Wierzbicki (1988). IAC–DIDAS–L Dynamic Interactive Decision Analysis and Support System, Linear version. WP-88-110, International Institute for Applied Systems Analysis, Laxenburg, Austria.

HYBRID
A Mathematical Programming Package

Marek Makowski

*IIASA, Laxenburg, Austria.**

Janusz S. Sosnowski

Systems Research Institute, Polish Academy of Sciences, Warsaw.

1 Purpose of the package

HYBRID 3.1. is a mathematical programming package which includes all the functions necessary for the solution of linear programming problems, both static and dynamic (in fact also for problems with structure more general then the classical formulation of dynamic linear problems). HYBRID 3.1. may be used for both single- and multi-criteria problems. The package may be also used for solving single-criteria linear-quadratic problems. Since HYBRID is designed for real-life problems, it offers many options useful for diagnostics and verification of a model for a problem being solved.

HYBRID is a member of DIDAS family of decision analysis and support systems which is designed to support multicriteria analysis via reference point optimization. HYBRID can be used by an analyst or by a team composed of a decision maker and an analyst or—on last stage of application—by a decision maker alone. HYBRID is a tool which helps to choose a decision in a complex situation in which many options may and should be examined. Possible applications include problems of economic planning and analysis, management, technological or engineering design problems, problems of environmental control.

2 Methodological and theoretical backgrounds

A multicriteria problem is transformed by HYBRID to an equivalent single criterion problem. Therefore a multicriteria problem is solved as a sequence of parametric optimization problems modified by a user in interactive way upon analysis of previous results.

*on leave from the Systems Research Institute of the Polish Academy of Sciences, Warsaw.

HYBRID uses a non-simplex algorithm - a particular implementation of the Lagrange multiplier method - for solving linear programming problems. General linear constraints are included within an augmented Lagrangian function. The LP problem is solved by minimizing a sequence of quadratic functions subject to simple constraints (lower and upper bounds). This minimization is achieved by the use of a method which combines the conjugate gradient method and an active constraints strategy. The method exploits the sparseness of the matrix structure. A dynamic problem is solved through the use of adjoint equations and by reduction of gradients to control subspaces. The simple constraints (lower and upper bounds for non-slack variables) for control variables are not violated during optimization and the resulting sequence of multipliers is feasible for the dual problem. Constraints other then those defined as simple constraints may be violated, however, and therefore the algorithm can be started from any point that satisfies the simple constraints.

3 Description of implementation

HYBRID is coded partly in C language and partly in an extension of Fortran-77 (functions coded in Fortran, after processing by a preprocessor, conform to the ANSI standard of Fortran-77). The PC version has also a user friendly driver (with context sensitive help) and functions that ease analysis of a solution and modification of parameters of multicriteria problem.

4 Hardware requirements

HYBRID 3.1. may be used on VAX 6210 (running under Ultrix-32) and on IBM–PC XT/AT or compatible (with any graphic card). The PC version for small problems requires 256kB RAM, for larger problems a configuration with more RAM is needed. The coprocessor is strongly recommended but a version of HYBRID is available also for a PC configuration without coprocessor.

5 References

Makowski, M. and J. Sosnowski (1988). User Guide to a Mathematical Programming Package for Multicriteria Dynamic Linear Problems HYBRID Version 3.1, WP-88-111, International Institute for Applied Systems Analysis, Laxenburg, Austria, December 1988.

IAC–DIDAS–N
A Dynamic Interactive Decision Analysis and Support System for Multicriteria Analysis of Nonlinear Models

Tomasz Kreglewski, Jerzy Paczynski, Janusz Granat,

Andrzej P. Wierzbicki

Institute of Automatic Control, Warsaw University of Technology.

1 Purpose of the package

The decision analysis and support systems of DIDAS family—that is, Dynamic Interactive Decision Analysis and Support systems —are specially designed to support interactive work with a substantive model of a decision situation while using multicriteria optimization tools. They stress the learning aspects of such work, such as the right of a decision maker to change his priorities and preferences when learning new facts. DIDAS systems can be used either by analysts who want to analyse their substantive models, or by teams of analysts and decision makers, or even by decision makers working alone with a previously defined substantive model; in any case, we shall speak further about *the user* of the system.

There are several classes of substantive models that all require special technical means of support. The IAC–DIDAS–N version is designed to support models of multiobjective nonlinear programming type. Models of this type include two classes of variables: *input variables* that can be subdivided into *decision variables* (means of multiobjective optimization) and *parametric variables* (model parameters that are kept constant during multiobjective analysis but might be changed during parametric or sensitivity analysis)—and *outcome variables* that can be subdivided into several types, the most important of them being *optimized outcomes* or *objectives* (the ends of multiobjective optimization that can be either maximized or minimized or stabilized, that is, kept close to a desired level). The user might change the classification of outcome variables and select his objectives among various outcome variables when defining an multiobjective analysis problem.

For all input and outcome variables, a reasonably defined nonlinear model should include *lower* and *upper bounds*, that is, reasonable ranges of admissible changes of these variables. Moreover, an essential part of a nonlinear model definition are *model equations*, that is, nonlinear functions that define the dependence of all outcome variables on input variables. To make the model definition easier for the user, it is assumed that outcome variables are defined consecutively and that they can depend not only on input variables, but also on previously defined outcome variables.

The IAC–DIDAS–N system helps in definition, edition, initial analysis and verification, optimization and multiobjective decision analysis of a rather broad class of nonlinear models. An important feature of IAC–DIDAS–N is that it supports also automatic calculations of all derivatives of nonlinear model functions.

2 Methodological background

A typical procedure of working with the IAC–DIDAS–N system consists of several phases.

In the first phase, a user—typically, an analyst—defines the substantive model and edits it on the computer. IAC–DIDAS–N supports the definition and edition of substantive models in an easy but flexible standard format of a spreadsheet, where the input variables correspond to spreadsheet columns and the outcome variables—to spreadsheet rows; special cells are reserved for various additional information. Another new feature of IAC–DIDAS–N is a symbolic differentiation facility that supports automatic calculations of all derivatives required by a nonlinear programming algorithm. The user does not need to laboriously calculate many derivatives and to check whether he did not make any mistakes; he only defines model equations or outcome functions in a form that is acceptable for the symbolic differentiation program—which admits functions from a rather wide class. The spreadsheet format allows also for display of computed values of automatically determined formulae for derivatives in appropriate cells. The user of IAC–DIDAS–N can also have several substantive models recorded in special model directories, use old models to speed up the definition of a new model, etc., while the system supports automatically the recording of all new or modified models in an appropriate directory.

In further phases of work with DIDAS-type systems, the user—here typically an analyst working together with the decision maker—specifies a multiobjective analysis problem related to his substantive model and participates in an initial analysis of this problem. There might be many multiobjective analysis problems related to the same substantive model: the specification of a multiobjective problem consists in designating types of model outcomes, especially objective outcomes that shall be optimized, and specifying bounds on outcomes. For a given definition of the multiobjective analysis problem, the decision and outcomes in the model are subdivided into two categories: those that are *efficient* with respect to the multiobjective problem (that is, such that no objective can be improved without deteriorating some other objective) and those that are inefficient. It is assumed that the user is interested only in efficient decisions and outcomes (this assumption is reasonable provided he has listed all objectives of his concern; if he has not, or if some objectives of his concern are not represented in the model, he can still modify the sense of efficiency by adding new objectives, or changing the types of objectives).

One of main functions of DIDAS-type systems is to compute efficient decisions and outcomes – following interactively various instructions of the user – and to present them to the user for analysis. This is done by using the principle of reference point optimization – that is, solving a special parametric nonlinear programming problem resulting from the specification of the multiobjective analysis problem; for this purpose, IAC–DIDAS–N contains a specialized nonlinear programming algorithm called solver. Following the experiences with previous versions of nonlinear DIDAS systems, a special robust nonlinear programming algorithm was further developed for IAC–DIDAS–N.

The main phase of work with the IAC–DIDAS–N system consists in interactive scanning of efficient outcomes and decisions, guided by the user through specifying two *reference points* called *reservation point* and *aspiration point* in the objective space, i.e. *reservation levels* and *aspiration levels* for each objective; the system admits also the more simple option of specifying either only an aspiration level or only a reservation level for some objectives. The user can get additional information about the range of possible outcomes during so called initial analysis of multiobjective problem and thus he can reasonably specify his reference levels: aspiration level that he would like to attain and reservation level that he would like to satisfy in any case. The system suggests some initial values for both reference points.

IAC–DIDAS–N utilizes the aspiration and the reservation levels as parameters in a special achievement function coded in the system, uses its solver to compute the solution of a nonlinear programming problem equivalent to maximizing this achievement function, and responds to the user with an attainable, efficient solution and outcomes that strictly correspond to the user-specified references (in the sense of being possibly close to the aspirations if they are unattainable, and uniformly better than aspirations if they are attainable).

3 Short program description

The IAC–DIDAS–N system (Institute of Automatic Control, Dynamic Interactive Decision Analysis and Support, Nonlinear version) is a decision support system designed to help in the analysis of decision situations where a mathematical model of substantive aspects of the situation can be formulated in the form of a multiobjective nonlinear programming problem.

The system supports the following general functions:

- definition and edition of a substantive model of the decision situation in a user-friendly format of a spreadsheet.

- specification of a multiobjective decision analysis problem related to the substantive model.

- initial multiobjective analysis of the problem, resulting in estimating bounds on efficient outcomes of decisions and in learning about some extreme and some neutral decisions.

- interactive analysis of the problem with the stress on learning possible efficient decisions and outcomes, organized through system's response to user-specified aspiration and reservation levels for objective outcomes. The system responds with efficient objective outcomes obtained by maximization of an achievement function that is parameterized by the user-specified aspirations and reservations.

4 Hardware requirement

The program can be run on an IBM–PC–XT, AT or a compatible computer with Hercules Graphics Card, Color Graphic Adapter or Enhanced Graphics Adapter and, preferably, with a numeric coprocessor and a hard disk. If a numeric coprocessor is available then the coprocessor version of the system can be used taking advantage of the coprocessor computational capacity, otherwise only the emulation version of the system can be used with less computational capabilities. The system programs are recorded on two diskettes. Each diskette contains compiled code of one version of the system together with some data files with demonstrative examples of nonlinear models.

References

Kreglewski T., J. Paczynski, J. Granat, A. P. Wierzbicki (1988). IAC–DIDAS–N A Dynamic Interactive Decision Analysis and Support System for Multicriteria Analysis of Nonlinear Models with Nonlinear Model Generator supporting model analysis. WP-88-112, International Institute for Applied Systems Analysis, Laxenburg, Austria.

DISCRET
An Interactive Decision Support System for Discrete Alternatives Multicriteria Problems

Janusz Majchrzak

Systems Research Institute, Polish Academy of Sciences, Warsaw.

1 Executive summary

DISCRET is a system created to solve basic multicriteria choice problems in which a finite set of feasible alternatives (and decisions) is explicitly given and for each alternative the value of all criteria describing its attributes interesting to the decision maker (DM) were evaluated and listed. The DM is assumed to be rational in the sense that he is looking for a Pareto-optimal solution as his final solution of the problem.

Such a decision problem is rather trivial for any human being as long as the number of criteria and alternatives is small (say, 3–5 criteria, 7–15 alternatives) However, if the number of alternatives and/or criteria grows, the limits of human information processing capabilities are reached and some decision support facilities have to be utilized to guarantee a proper and efficient decision making.

In many real–life problems the decision variables take their values from a discrete set rather than from a continuous interval. Usually there is a finite number of available facility location sites, the facility size or production capability may be chosen from a discrete set of values, during a design process the components are chosen from a set of typical elements available on the market, etc. Such problems form the "natural" field of applications for the DISCRET system.

Another field of possible applications of the DISCRET system consists of cases in which the original problem is actually continuous (rather than discrete) but the analysis restricted just to a finite number of alternatives appearing in this problem may be interesting and useful for the DM, since it may result in an enlightening and a more precise definition of his preferences, region of interest or aspiration levels.

Situations falling under the latter category may occur for at least two following reasons. Firstly, a sample of alternatives together with the corresponding criteria values may be readily available (from simulation model runs for example). Secondly, for the purpose of an initial analysis the DM may take into considerations just a few values for each decision variable or generate a random sample of alternatives.

The DISCRET system makes no restrictions on the forms of the criteria. Therefore, attributes as complicated as required may be considered.

To start the session with DISCRET the DM has to supply the file containing set of the criteria values for all feasible alternatives, the problem specification file and (optionally) the file containing the set of feasible decisions. These files, called the data, specification and the additional data file respectively, describe the problem under consideration.

After loading the problem the DM may obtain the information about the criteria values ranges and he may put the lower and/or upper bounds on the values of some/all criteria. The bounds setting may be utilized to eliminate irrelevant alternatives from further considerations or to specify the current region of interest in the objective space.

In the next step the DM may eliminate the dominated alternatives by an explicit enumeration technique. The tolerances for criteria values play an important role here. If they are all equal zero or have small positive values that correspond to indifference limits of the DM's for criteria values, the whole set of the nondominated solutions will be obtained. If the values of tolerances are equal to some significant fractions of the corresponding criteria ranges, then a representation of the set of nondominated solutions will be obtained. The representation is a subset of the set of nondominated solutions preserving its shape and containing the smaller number of elements, the larger were chosen tolerance coefficients.

The biggest advantage of the implemented enumeration method is its ability to select a representation of the nondominated set instead of the entire set. Unlike other known approaches which find the entire nondominated set first and then select a representation (differently defined for each of those methods), the presented method selects a representation at once. This fact profits in efficiency. Observe that because the representation contains less elements than the nondominated set, it will be obtained with a smaller computational effort.

The powerful tool of the reference point approach is also available for the DM. By determining a reference point, he exhibits his aspiration levels for criteria values, confronts them with the obtained solution and modifies them and the reference point. To learn more about the problem the graphic display of two–dimensional subproblems on the terminal screen can be utilized. The DM chooses two criteria for the vertical and horizontal axes, while the other criteria are restrictively bounded — a two–dimensional "slice" is cut out of the original m–dimensional problem. The graphical displays are very useful on this stage of the decision making process, since the DM can see clusters (groups) of alternatives.

DISCRET is an interactive system. The DM may execute its commands in any order. The variety of paths the DM may follow guarantees flexibility in meeting his demands. The implemented approach seems to be easy to understand and approve even for a user who is not very familiar with multicriteria optimization techniques.

2 Short program description

The interactive decision support system DISCRET has been designed to solve medium–size discrete multicriteria choice problems with the number of alternatives ranging from few hundreds to few thousands. The number of criteria is in the current version restricted to 20 (mainly due to the limitations of display facilities).

The program is recorded on a diskette(s) and should be installed on an IBM–PC–XT/AT or a compatible computer with a Color Graphic Adapter, Enhanced Graphic Adapter or Hercules Graphic Card and a hard disk. The compiled code is distributed together with a number of files it requires and with two test problems generators providing demonstrative examples.

The system supports the following menu–controlled general functions:

— Loading user's problems in an easy to prepare standard of an ASCII file form.

— Criteria values ranges (utopia and nadir points) display, and new criteria values bounds setting to define the user's current region of interest.

— Solving the discrete multicriteria optimization problem with explicit alternatives (implicit constraints), i.e. finding the set of nondominated or weakly nondominated elements or it's representation, keeping or rejecting duplicate elements, etc.

— The reference point approach, i.e. selection of nondominated alternatives that correspond to user-supplied aspiration levels for criteria.

— Graphic display of the two–dimensional "slices" of the problem showing the user alternatives clusters (groups).

References

Majchrzak J. (1988). DISCRET: An Interactive Decision Support System for Discret Alternatives Multicriteria Problems. WP–88–113, International Institute for Applied Systems Analysis, Laxenburg, Austria.

DINAS
Dynamic Interactive Network Analysis System

Wlodzimierz Ogryczak, Krzysztof Studzinski, Krystian Zorychta

Institute of Informatics, Warsaw University.

1 Purpose of the system

DINAS is a scientific transferable software tool which enables the solution of various multiobjective transshipment problems with facility locations. For a given number of fixed facilities and customers and for a number of potential facilities to be optionally located, DINAS provides the user with a distribution pattern of a homogeneous product under a multicriteria optimality requirement. While working in an interactive mode, the user gets optimal locations of the potential facilities and a system of optimal flows of the product between nodes of the transportation network. With DINAS one can analyse and solve such problems as:

- the transportation problem with new supply and/or demand points location,
- the problem of warehouses location,
- the problem of stores location for the agricultural production,
- the problem of service centers location and districts reorganization,

and many other real-life distribution-location problems.

2 The problem statement

DINAS works with problems formulated as multiobjective transshipment problems with facility location. A network model of such a problem consists of nodes connected by a set of direct flow arcs. The set of nodes is partitioned into two subsets: the set of fixed nodes and the set of potential nodes. The fixed nodes represent "fixed points" of the transportation network, i.e., points which cannot be changed, whereas the potential nodes are introduced to represent possible locations of new points in the network. Some groups of the potential nodes represent different versions of the same facility to be located (e.g., different sizes of a warehouse etc.). For this reason, potential nodes are organized in the so-called selections, i.e., sets of nodes with the multiple choice requirements. A homogeneous good is distributed along the arcs among the nodes. Each fixed node is characterized by two quantities: supply and demand on the good. Each potential node is characterized by a capacity which bounds maximal good flow through the node. The capacities are also given for all the arcs but not for the fixed nodes. A few linear objective functions are considered in the problem. The objective functions are introduced into the model by given coefficients associated with several arcs and potential nodes (the so-called cost coefficients, independently of their real character). The cost coefficient connected to an arc is treated as the unit cost of the flow along the arc. The cost coefficient connected to a potential node is considered as the fixed cost associated with locating of the node (e.g., an investment cost). Summarizing, the following groups of input data define the transshipment problem under consideration:

- objectives,
- fixed nodes with their supply-demand balances,
- potential nodes with their capacities and (fixed) cost coefficients,
- selections with their lower and upper limits on number of active potential nodes,
- arcs with their capacities and cost coefficients.

The problem is to find the best (satisfying) location and flow scheme, i.e., to determine the number and locations of active potential nodes and to find the good flows (along arcs) so as to satisfy the balance and capacity restrictions.

3 Methodological and theoretical backgrounds

DINAS does not solve the multiobjective problem. It rather makes the user selecting the best solution during interactive work with the system. According to some user's requirements DINAS generates various efficient solutions which can be examined in details and compared to each other. The user works with the computer in an interactive way so that he can change his requirements during the sessions. The DINAS interactive procedure utilizes an extension of the reference point optimization. The basic concept of that approach is as follows:

- the user forms his requirements in terms of aspiration and reservation levels, i.e., he specifies acceptable and required values for given objectives;
- the user works with the computer in an interactive way so that he can change his aspiration and reservation levels during the sessions.

DINAS searches for the satisfying solution while using an achievement scalarizing function as a criterion in single-objective optimization.

4 Description of the implementation

DINAS is prepared as a menu-driven and easy in usage system. The system consists of three programs prepared in the C programming language:

- the network screen editor for friendly data input and results examination;
- the solver for single-objective optimization;
- the main interactive procedure for handling multiple objectives.

The basic version of the system is capable of solving problems with seven objective functions, about one hundred of fixed nodes, a few hundreds of arcs, and fifteen potential nodes organized in a few selections.

5 Hardware requirements

DINAS runs under Disk Operating System (DOS version 3.00 or higher) on an IBM-PC XT/AT or compatibles equipped with Hercules, EGA or CGA card and requires 640 K RAM. A hard disk is recommended but not necessary. One double-sided double-density floppy disk drive is sufficient to run DINAS. The system can be installed in two versions: with taking advantages of the Numeric Data Processor chip, or without using the NDP chip. However, for solving large real-life problems the version with the NDP chip is strongly recommended. A printer is useful but not necessary since all the reports can be routed directly to a printer or to a disk file for printing at a later time.

References

Ogryczak, W., K. Studzinski, K. Zorychta (1988). Dynamic Interactive Network Analysis System – DINAS, version 2.1. User's Manual. WP–88–114, International Institute for Applied Systems Analysis, Laxenburg, Austria.

MCBARG
A System Supporting Multicriteria Bargaining

Piotr Bronisz, Lech Krus, Bozena Lopuch

Systems Research Institute, Polish Academy of Sciences, Warsaw.

1 Executive summary

Many aspects of economic, environmental, or technological activity are influenced directly by bargaining between and among individuals, firms, and nations ("players"). In the pure bargaining problem, considered in the MCBARG system, the bargaining conditions are determined entirely by the bounds of discussion, within which the final outcome is determined by the interaction of the players. Even in the case of one individual, firm, and nation, there are many situations of complex decision, the decision maker needs help to learn about possible decision options, decision consequences. The MCBARG system enables learning process of the players, and supports reaching the final outcome in the multicriteria bargaining problem. It is based on the theoretical results presented in Bronisz, Krus, Wierzbicki (this volume).

The multicriteria bargaining problem is a generalization of classical bargaining problem, under assumption that the utility functions of participants are not given explicitly. This generalization follows from the fact that an aggregation of participant's or player's objectives is often impossible, because of various practical limitations of the utility theory. The problem is defined by an agreement set — the set of outcomes that can be reached under unanimous agreement of the players, and by a disagreement (status quo) point which is a result of the problem if there is no such an agreement.

The proposed interactive process consists in generation of sequence of outcomes leading to a nondominated solution. The process is based on limited confidence principle, taken from practical observation, which says that the players have limited confidence in their ability to predict consequences and possible outcomes, hence each player tries to prevent other players from receiving disproportionally large gains. The generated outcomes are consistent with preferences of the players. The process assures also some fairness rules and is resistent to various manipulations of the players .

The algorithm consists of a number of rounds. Each round starts at the current status quo point (the first round starts from the initial status quo point). At each round the player specifies his confidence coefficient (i.e. defines part of the maximal improvement of the outcomes the counter players can obtain in the round). Furthermore assuming some moves of the other players, he tests different improvement directions for his objectives. This phase of the work with MCBARG system consists in an interactive scanning of outcomes guided by each player through specifying reference points in the objective space. The reference points are composed of aspiration levels of each player for his objectives. The players get additional information about the range of possible outcomes for a given confidence coefficient and some assumed actions of the counter players. This information is useful for reasonable specification of the aspiration levels. The system generates also some initial values for the aspiration levels and calculates corresponding outcomes (called neutral outcomes). The scanning of the player outcomes is performed in the system through directional optimization and lexicographic improvement of the week Pareto outcomes. The system responds to the player with an attainable, efficient (under the assumed confidence coefficient) outcomes that strictly correspond to the player–specified aspirations. The results obtained for a number of different reference points can be easily compared through scrolling option in both numerical and graphical form. To finish this phase, the player is required to select, according to his preferences, his reference point indicating his preferable improvement direction. These points selected independently by all the players are basis for calculation of the result of the round. The result,is calculated following the limited confidence principle (the minimal confidence coefficient is used for all players) and trying to improve outcomes for all players in the directions specified by their reference point. Thus, the system acts as a neutral mediator proposing a single-test provisional agreement improving the initial situation and forming a basis for next round of negotiations. The results are presented independently to the players in form of report, and the players can go to the next round assuming the obtained result as a new status quo point. The process terminates when an efficient, strictly Pareto-optimal solution in the agreement set is reached.

The system includes a generator and an editor of the model of the bargaining problem for which the interactive process is organized. The model describes the agreement set in form of a set of inequalities, and the status quo point. The generator and the editor enable introducing linear or nonlinear formulas defining the inequalities using standard operators and functions. An illustrative example has been prepared which relates to the problem of cooperation of two farms. The problem consists in division of products resulting from cooperation between two farms, according to the preference of farm owners.

2 Short program description

The MCBARG system is a decision support system designed to help in analysis of decision situation and mediation in multicriteria bargaining problem in which a mathematical model of the problem can be formulated by a status–quo point and a system of inequalities describing agreement set in objective space of the players.

The program is recorded on one diskette that should be installed on an IBM–PC–XT, AT or compatible computer with Hercules Graphics Card, Color Graphic Adapter (CGA) or Enhanced Graphics Adapter (EGA). A diskette contains compiled code of the program together with some data files for a demonstrative example of the bargaining problem.

The system supports the following general functions:

— The definition and edition of a model of the bargaining problem together with the specification of the multicriteria decision problem.

— Interactive mediation by generation of a sequence of outcomes (depending on player-specified aspirations), leading to a nondominated solution in agreement set.

— Report of the final, efficient solution of the problem.

The second function proceeds in a number of rounds and in each round the system supports:

— Initial multiobjective analysis of the bargaining problem for each player, that results in estimating bounds on efficient outcomes and learning about the extreme and neutral outcomes.

— Unilateral, interactive analysis of the problem with the stress on learning, organized through system response to user specified confidence coefficients and aspiration levels for objective outcomes. The systems responds with efficient (under the assumed confidence coefficient) objective outcomes.

— Calculation of the multilateral, cooperative solution of the round. Reporting the results of the already performed rounds.

References

Bronisz, P., L. Krus, B. Lopuch (1988). MCBARG: A System Supporting Multicriteria Bargaining. WP–88–115, International Institute for Applied Systems Analysis, Laxenburg, Austria.

POSTAN 3 and PLP
Extensions of MINOS for Postoptimal Analysis

Grzegorz Dobrowolski, Tomasz Rys
Joint System Research Department
of the Institute for Control and Systems Engineering,
Academy of Mining and Metallurgy, Cracow,
and of Industrial Chemistry Research Institute, Warsaw.
Adam Golebiowski, Krystyn Hajduk, Adam Korytowski
Institute for Control and Systems Engineering,
Academy of Mining and Metallurgy, Cracow.

1 General information

POSTAN3 (Dobrowolski et al.), an extended version of POSTAN (Dobrowolski et al. 1984) and POSTAN2 (Dobrowolski et al. 1987), is a postoptimal analysis package for linear and linear-fractional programming problems. It may also be used to solve linear-fractional problem by a direct, noninteractive method. The package is composed of a number of FORTRAN routines which are incorporated into MINOS, the well-known linear and non-linear programming code developed by Murtagh and Saunders (1977). The postoptimal analysis is performed after MINOS has found an optimal solution, and is initiated by adding new specifications to the original list of MINOS specifications.

The main objective of POSTAN3 is ranging, i.e., determining the ranges in which certain parameters (or groups of parameters) may be changed without affecting the optimal solution and/or the optimal basis. Sensitivity coefficients which are not included in the output of the unmodified version of MINOS are also determined.

Two new auxiliary modules have been implemented in POSTAN3 to improve its user interface:

- a module for programming a sequence of optimization problems,
- a module for decoding and selective printing of results.

PLP (Golebiowski) is a software package for parametric linear programming. It is also an extension of MINOS and is initiated by adding some specifications to the original list of MINOS specifications. PLP uses MINOS as the solver of optimization problems. It includes sections which create an interactive framework for parametric programming and perform ranging and housekeeping procedures.

Optionally, PLP gives a complete parametric programming analysis for one, or more, of the following vectors: cost, rhs, and bounds. In the same run, several problems of this kind can be solved and for each, the starting point may be the original optimal solution or the final solution obtained in the last problem.

2 Notes on implementations

The available implementations of the packages can be divided into two groups:

1. Main frame implementations that are destined for large scale optimization problems requiring a powerful computer system. An important parameter of the computer system at this point is operational memory available to a process.

2. Personal computer implementations that can run under restriction with respect to dimensionality of the problem. The minimum hardware configuration is 640 kB of operational memory and a mathematical co-processor.

Main frame

POSTAN batch mode version. Software requirements: FORTRAN IV-E compiler.

PLP batch mode version. Software requirements: FORTRAN IV-E compiler.

OPT interactive mode, screen-oriented, menu-driven version. Software requirements: FORTRAN 77, C Language compilers, UNIX or XENIX operating system. There is a special implementation of POSTAN. In place of advanced postoptimal routines the reference point multiobjective optimization method is incorporated.

Personal computer

POSTAN batch mode version. Software requirements: FORTRAN 77 compiler.

OPT interactive mode, screen-oriented, menu-driven version. Software requirements: FORTRAN 77, C Language compilers, DOS or XENIX operating system. There is a special implementation of POSTAN. In place of advanced postoptimal routines the reference point multiobjective optimization method is incorporated.

PCPOST interactive mode, window-oriented, menu-driven version. Software requirements: FORTRAN 77, C Language compilers, DOS operating system. There is a full implementation of POSTAN.

3 Formulation of linear programming problem

The formulation of the linear problem analyzed by POSTAN3 and PLP is the sane as for MINOS. Minimize (or maximize) a linear cost function

$$F(x) = a_0 x \tag{1}$$

subject to m row constraints:

$$d_i \leq a_i x \leq g_i \ , \quad i = 1, ..., m \tag{2}$$

and n constraints on separate variables:

$$d_{m+i} \leq x_i \leq g_{m+i} \ , \quad i = 1, ..., n \quad . \tag{3}$$

Here x is an n-dimensional column vector of decision variables, a_0 is an n-dimensional row vector of cost coefficients (also called the *objective row*), the a_i, $i = 1, ..., m$, are n-dimensional row vectors, the lower bounds d_i, $i = 1, ..., m+n$, are real numbers or $-\infty$, and the upper bounds g_i, $i = 1, ..., m+n$, are real numbers or $+\infty$. Of course, if the bounds take the values $+\infty$ or $-\infty$ the corresponding relation (2) or (3) must be replaced by a strict inequality. If $d_i = g_i$, then the variable x_i is said to be *fixed*. If $d_i = -\infty$ and $g_i = +\infty$ the variable x_i is said to be *free*. Analogous terms are used to describe the rows $a_i x$.

It should be recalled that in MINOS the two-sided inequality constraints (2) are not stated explicitly, but rather specified using *ranges*. More precisely, a one-sided inequality is introduced in the form $a_i x \leq g_i$ (type L) or $a_i x \geq d_i$ (type G), together with a real number r_i called the *range*. In the first case, the difference between the right-hand side g_i and this number yields the lower bound ($d_i = g_i - r_i$); in the second case the sum of the right-hand side d_i and the real number r_i gives the upper bound ($g_i = d_i + r_i$).

As option of POSTAN3 and PLP are expressed in terms of the internal formulation of the linear problem we shall recall this concept. The linear programming problem (1) – (3) is transformed by MINOS into the following internal form: Minimize (or maximize) the variable

$$-\tilde{x}_{n+1+\text{obj}} \tag{4}$$

subject to equality constraints:

$$\tilde{A}\tilde{x} = 0 \tag{5}$$

and inequality constraints:

$$\tilde{l} \leq \tilde{x} \leq \tilde{u} \quad . \tag{6}$$

Here $\tilde{A}$ is an $(m+1) \times (n+m+2)$-matrix:

$$\tilde{A} = \begin{bmatrix} \tilde{a}_1 & \tilde{b}_1 & \\ \cdot & \cdot & \\ \cdot & \ddots & I \\ \cdot & \cdot & \\ \tilde{a}_{m+1} & \tilde{b}_{m+1} & \end{bmatrix} , \tag{7}$$

where I denotes the $(m+1) \times (m+1)$ identity matrix and where

$$\tilde{a}_i = a_i \quad i < \text{obj}\ , \quad \tilde{a}_{obj} = a_0\ , \quad \tilde{a}_i = a_{i-1} \quad i > \text{obj}\ , \tag{8}$$

$$\tilde{b}_i = b_i \quad i < \text{obj}\ , \quad \tilde{b}_{obj} = 0\ , \quad \tilde{b}_i = b_{i-1} \quad i > \text{obj}\ ,$$

where

$$b_i = \begin{cases} 0 & \textit{if } d_i = -\infty \textit{ and } g_i = +\infty \\ d_i & \textit{if } d_i \text{ is finite } \textit{and } g_i = +\infty \\ g_i & \textit{if } g_i \text{ is finite} \end{cases}$$

The first n components of the extended vector of decision variables $\tilde{x} \in R^{n+m+2}$ form a subvector identical to x; these components are described as ***structural***. Element $\tilde{x}_{n+1}$ is called the ***right-hand-side component***; it is fixed at -1. The remaining components of $\tilde{x}$ are called ***slack*** or ***logical components***. The objective variable $\tilde{x}_{n+1+\text{obj}}$ is free. The vector of lower bounds $\tilde{l}$ and the vector of upper bounds $\tilde{u}$ are defined as follows:

$$\tilde{l}_i = d_{m+i} \quad i = 1, ..., n\ , \quad \tilde{l}_{n+1} = -1, \quad \tilde{l}_{n+1+\text{obj}} = -\infty\ , \tag{9}$$

$$\tilde{u}_i = g_{m+i} \quad i = 1, ..., n\ , \quad \tilde{u}_{n+1} = -1, \quad \tilde{u}_{n+1+\text{obj}} = +\infty\ .$$

Now let $i = n + 1 + j$, $j = 1, ..., m$. Then

$$\tilde{l}_i = h_i, \ \tilde{u}_i = k_i \ \textit{for}\ j < \text{obj} \ \textit{and}\ \tilde{l}_i = h_{i-1}, \ \tilde{u}_i = k_{i-1} \ \textit{for}\ j > \text{obj} \tag{10}$$

where

$h_i = k_i = 0$ if the j-th row constraint is fixed (i.e., of type E)

$h_i = 0$, $k_i = +\infty$ if $d_j = -\infty$ and g_j is finite (one-sided constraint of type L)

$h_i = -\infty$, $k_i = 0$ if d_j is finite and $g_j = +\infty$ (one-sided constraint of type G)

$h_i = 0$, $k_i = g_j - d_j$ if d_j and g_j are finite

$h_i = -\infty$, $k_i = +\infty$ if the j-th row constraint is free .

4 Postoptimal analysis for linear problems in POSTAN3

Here we give a list of ranging options of POSTAN3 for linear problems.

Ranging on costs

Ordinary ranging

For each cost component a_0^i, $i = 1, \ldots, n$ the largest range is determined in which a_0^i may vary without affecting the optimal solution. While the range for a_0^i is being determined, all other components a_0^j, $j \neq i$, remain fixed at their original values. Some information on the change of state of variables at the boundaries is also given.

Directional ranging

For a given increment $\Delta a_0 \in R_n$ of the cost vector a_0 , the largest real $t_{\max} \geq 0$ is determined such that for every cost vector of the form $a_0 + t\Delta a_0$, $t \in [0, t_{\max}]$, the optimal solution is the same as at the point, a_0 (i.e., at $t = 0$). The boundary cost components $a_0^i + t_{\max}\Delta a_0^i$, $i = 1, \ldots, n$ and some information on the change of state of variables at the boundary are also given.

Ranging on right-hand sides

Ordinary ranging

For each component $\tilde{b}_i$, $i = 1, \ldots, m+1$ of the rhs vector (except for the objective row, $i \neq obj$), the maximum range is determined in which $\tilde{b}_i$ may vary without affecting the optional basis. While the range for $\tilde{b}_i$ is being determined, all other components $\tilde{b}_j$, $i \neq j$ are fixed at their original values. It should be noted that the rhs vector $\tilde{b}$ is not always the rhs of a constraint system in the original formulation (1) – (3); the user should refer to (5) – (11). Some information on the change of state of variables at the boundaries is given.

Directional ranging

For a given vector of increments $\Delta\tilde{b} \in R^{m+1}$ of the rhs vector $\tilde{b}$, the largest real $t_{\max} \geq 0$ is determined such that for every rhs of the form $\tilde{b} + t\Delta\tilde{b}$, $t \in [0, t_{\max}]$, the optimal basis is the same as at the point $\tilde{b}$ (i.e., at $t = 0$). At the boundary $t = t_{\max}$ either the optimal solution vanishes or one of the basic variables changes its state. Its name and the type of change are given. together with the boundary values of rhs elements.

Ranging on bounds

Ordinary ranging

For each lower bound $\tilde{l}_i$ and each upper bound $\tilde{u}_i$, $i = 1, \ldots, n+m+2$ two ranges are determined: range A which is the maximum range in which the bound may vary without affecting the optimal solution, and range B, which is the maximum range in which the bound may vary without affecting the optimal basis. While these ranges are being determined for $\tilde{l}_i$ (or $\tilde{u}_i$), all other bounds remain fixed at their original values. Some information is given on the change of state of variables at the boundaries. This analysis is not performed for fixed variables.

Directional ranging

For a given vector of increments $\text{col}(\Delta\tilde{l}, \Delta\tilde{u}) \in R^{2(m+n+2)}$ of the vector of bounds $\text{col}(\tilde{l}, \tilde{u})$, two real numbers are determined:

- $t_{\text{maxa}} \geq 0$, the largest real number such that for every bound vector of the form $\text{col}(\tilde{l}, \tilde{u}) + t\,\text{col}(\Delta\tilde{l}, \Delta\tilde{u})$, $t \in [0, t_{\text{maxa}}]$, the optimal solution is the same as for the bound vector $\text{col}(\tilde{l}, \tilde{u})$, i.e., at $t = 0$.

- $t_{\text{maxb}} \geq 0$, the largest real number such that for every bound vector of the form $\text{col}(\tilde{l}, \tilde{u}) + t\ \text{col}(\Delta\tilde{l}, \Delta\tilde{u})$, $t \in [0, t_{\text{maxb}}]$, the optimal basis is the same as for the bound vector $\text{col}(\tilde{l}, \tilde{u})$, i.e., at $t = 0$.

Boundary values of the elements of bound vector and some information on the change of state of variables at the boundaries are also given.

4.0.1 Ordinary ranging on elements of constraint matrix

For selected elements a^i_j, $i = 1, \ldots, n$, $j = 1, \ldots, m$ of the constraint matrix $\text{col}(a_1, a_2, \ldots, a_m)$ (see (2)) the largest range is determined in which a^i_j may vary without affecting the optimal basis or the state of nonbasic variables. The list of the selected elements is given in the data. While the range for a^i_j is being determined, all other elements a^l_k, $k \neq l$ and/or $j \neq l$, are fixed at their original values. The sensitivity of the optimal cost with respect to the elements is also calculated. In addition, some information on the change of state of variables at the boundaries is given.

Directional ranging on constraint rows

For a given increment vector $\Delta a_i \in R_n$ of the constraint vector a_i, $i = 1, \ldots, m$, the largest range $(t_{\text{min}}, t_{\text{max}})$ is determined such that for every i-th constraint vector of the form $a_i + t\Delta a_i$, $t \in (t_{\text{min}}, t_{\text{max}})$, the optimal basis and the state of nonbasic variables are the same as at the point a_i (i.e., at $t = 0$). The sensitivity of the optimal cost with respect to parameter t at $t = 0$ is also calculated. In addition, the boundary values of the constraint row a_i and some information on the change of state of variables at the boundaries are given.

Directional ranging on structural columns of constraint matrix

For a given vector of increments Δa_i of the column a_i, $i = 1, \ldots, n$, the largest range $(t_{\text{min}}, t_{\text{max}})$ is determined such that for every i-th constraint column of the form $a_i + t\Delta a_i$, $t \in (t_{\text{min}}, t_{\text{max}})$, the optimal basis and the state of nonbasic variables are the same as at the point a_i (i.e., at $t = 0$). The sensitivity of the optimal cost with respect to parameter t at $t = 0$ is calculated. addition, the boundary values of the column a_i and some information on the change of state of variables at the boundaries are given.

5 Parametric programming options of PLP

Parametric analysis of cost

The cost vector $a_0 = ({a_0}^1, {a_0}^2, ..., {a_0}^n)$ (see (1)) is changed along a direction given by the user, $\Delta a_0 = (\Delta {a_0}^1, \Delta {a_0}^2, ..., \Delta {a_0}^n)$ according to the formula:

$$a_0(t) = a_0(0) \ + \ t\Delta a_0 \ , \ t \ \geq \ 0 \tag{12}$$

where $a_o(0)$ is the starting value of cost. If the structural variable, say $\tilde{x}_i$, is fixed then $\Delta {a_0}^i$ is automatically set to zero, regardless of the value given in the data.

PLP determines a sequence of values of the parameter denoted by $t_0,\ t_1, ...,\ t_k$, such that $0 = t_0 < t_1 < t_2 < ... < t_k$ and in each of the intervals $[t_i,\ t_{i+1}),\ i = 0, ..., k-1$ the optimal solution is constant and in each case the optimal basis is different. The integer k :

1. may be defined by the user as the maximum number of iterations,
2. may be determined by the condition that the optimal solution is constant for every $t \geq t_k$ and different from that in $[\ t_{k-1},\ t_k)$,
3. may be determined by the condition that there are no optimal solutions for every $t < t_k$.

Parametric analysis of rhs

The right-hand side vector $\tilde{b} =$ col $(\tilde{b}_1, ..., \tilde{b}_{m+1})$ (see (7) and (8)) is changed along a direction given by the user, $\Delta\tilde{b} =$ col$(\Delta\tilde{b}_1, ..., \Delta\tilde{b}_{m+1})$, according to the formula:

$$\tilde{b}(t) = \tilde{b}(0)\ +\ t\Delta\tilde{b}\ \ ,\ t\ \geq\ 0 \tag{13}$$

where $\tilde{b}(0)$ is the starting value of rhs. The component of $\Delta\tilde{b}$ which correspond to the objective row is automatically set to zero, $\Delta\tilde{b}_{obj} = 0$.

PLP determines a sequence of values of the parameter denoted by $t_0,\ t_1, ...,\ t_k$ such that $0 = t_0 < t_1 < t_2 < ... < t_k$ and in each of the intervals $[t_i,\ t_{i+1}),\ i = 0, ..., k-1$ the optimal basis is constant and in each

1. may be defined by the user as the maximum number of iterations,
2. may be determined by the condition that the optimal solution is constant for every $t \geq t_k$ and different from that in $[\ t_{k-1},\ t_k)$,
3. may be determined by the condition that there are no optimal solutions for every $t < t_k$.

Parametric analysis of bounds

The vector of bounds col$(\tilde{l},\ \tilde{u})\ \in\ R^{2(n+m+2)}$ (see (9)) is changed along a direction given by the user, col$(\Delta\tilde{l},\ \Delta\tilde{u})$, according to the formula:

$$\text{col}(\tilde{l}(t),\ \tilde{u}(t))\ \ =\ \ \text{col}(\tilde{l}(0),\ \tilde{u}(0))\ +\ t\ \ \text{col}(\Delta\tilde{l},\ \Delta\tilde{u})\ ,\ t\ \geq\ 0 \tag{14}$$

where col$(\tilde{l}(0),\ \tilde{u}(0))$ is the starting value of bounds. The bound increments $\Delta\tilde{l}_i,\ \Delta\tilde{u}_i$ which corresponds to fixed variables are automatically set to zero regardless of the values given in the data.

If there is no lower and/or upper bound for the i-th variable $\tilde{x}_i$ (see (6)) the corresponding increment $\Delta\tilde{l}_i$ and/or $\Delta\tilde{u}_i$, respectively, is also automatically set to zero.

PLP determines a sequence of values of the parameter denoted by $t_o,\ t_1, ...,\ t_k$ such that $0 = t_0 < t_1 < t_2 < ... < t_k$ and in each of the intervals $[t_i,\ t_{i+1}),\ i = 0, ..., k-1$ the optimal basis is constant and in each case different. The integer k :

1. may be defined by the user as the maximum number of iterations,

2. may be determined by the condition that the optimal solution is constant for every $t \geq t_k$ and different from that in $[\,t_{k-1},\ t_k)$,

3. may be determined by the condition that there are no optimal solutions for every $t < t_k$.

Each interval $[t_i,\ t_{i+1})$ is optionally divided into two subintervals $[t_i,\ t_i{}^a)$, $[t_i{}^a,\ t_{i+1})$. The interval $[t_i, t_i{}^a)$ is the maximum interval where the optimal solution remains constant and not only the optimal basis. It often happens that $t_i = t_i{}^a$.

Dependent and independent work

All three kinds of analysis can be performed in one run. The starting point for the next kind of analysis may be either the original starting optimal solution (The Independent Work) or the last optimal solution obtained in the preceding analysis (The Dependent Work). The continuation is impossible if the optimal solution vanishes.

Controlling output

In each of the three kinds of analysis the following information is available. The user has to specify the frequency of printing the complete current optimal solution in MINOS format. This means that the complete printout is given for the values of parameters t equal to t_{0+}, t_{p+}, $t_{2p+}, \ldots$, and $t_{(k-1)+}$ or t_{k+} depending on whether the optimal solution exists for $t < t_k$. The notation t_{i+} means that we take the right-hand limit of the optimal solution at t_i. The user specifies frequency of printing the so called PLP ITERATION LOG. This is a short message containing most important information about current change of optimal solution (value of the parameter t, change of optimal basis, current value of objective function).

Tolerances

The performance of PLP is strongly affected by the choice of tolerances. Especially important are two tolerances determined in MINOS : the tolerance of optimality (TOLD) and the tolerance of feasibility (TOLX). In the proper procedures of the PLP the following general rule is adopted. All quantities greater than or equal to 1.E+15 are taken as equal to infinity and all quantities whose absolute value is less than 1.E-9 are regarded as equal to zero.

6 Linear-fractional programming in POSTAN3

The LFP part of POSTAN3 deals with linear-fractional programming problems of the form: Minimize

$$F(x) = \frac{cx + \alpha}{dx + \beta} \quad \text{where } x \in R^n \ , \quad c, d \in R_n \ , \quad \alpha, \beta \in R \tag{15}$$

subject to

$$Ax \leq b \ , \quad x \geq 0 \text{ where } b \in R^m \ , \quad A - n \times m \text{ matrix} \tag{16}$$

It is assumed that $dx + \beta > 0$ in the whole of the admissible region.

Ranging on cost

For each cost component c^i and d^i the largest range is determined in which the component may vary without affecting the optimal solution. All other components, except that being analysed, remain fixed at their original values.

References

Dobrowolski, G., K. Hajduk, A. Korytowski and T. Rys (1984). POSTAN - A Package for Postoptimal Analysis (An Extension of MINOS). IIASA Collaborative Paper CP-84-32, Laxenburg, Austria.

Dobrowolski, G., K. Hajduk, A. Korytowski, T. Rys (1985). POSTAN 2 - An Extended Postoptimal Analysis Package for MINOS, In Theory, Software and Testing Examples for Decision Support Systems, A. Wierzbicki and A. Lewandowski Eds., International Institute for Applied Systems Analysis, Laxenburg, Austria.

Dobrowolski, G., T. Rys, K. Hajduk, A. Korytowski (1988). POSTAN 3 – Extended Postoptimal Analysis Package for MINOS. WP–88–117, International Institute for Applied Systems Analysis, Laxenburg, Austria.

Golebiowski, A. (1988). PLP - A Package for Parametric Programming. WP–88–118, International Institute for Applied Systems Analysis, Laxenburg, Austria.

Murtagh, B.A., M.A. Saunders (1977). MINOS - A Large-Scale Linear Programming System. User's Guide. Technical Report SOL 77-9, System Optimization Laboratory, Stanford University, California.

Rys, T. (1988). PC-POSTAN version 3.0. Postoptimal Analysis Package. User's Manual. WP–88–119, International Institute for Applied Systems Analysis, Laxenburg, Austria.

THE INTERNATIONAL INSTITUTE FOR APPLIED SYSTEMS ANALYSIS

is a nongovernmental research institution, bringing together scientists from around the world to work on problems of common concern. Situated in Laxenburg, Austria, IIASA was founded in October 1972 by the academies of science and equivalent organizations of twelve countries. Its founders gave IIASA a unique position outside national, disciplinary, and institutional boundaries so that it might take the broadest possible view in pursuing its objectives:

To promote international cooperation in solving problems arising from social, economic, technological, and environmental change

To create a network of institutions in the national member organization countries and elsewhere for joint scientific research

To develop and formalize systems analysis and the sciences contributing to it, and promote the use of analytical techniques needed to evaluate and address complex problems

To inform policy advisors and decision makers about the potential application of the Institute's work to such problems

The Institute now has national member organizations in the following countries:

Austria
The Austrian Academy of Sciences

Bulgaria
The National Committee for Applied Systems Analysis and Management

Canada
The Canadian Committee for IIASA

Czechoslovakia
The Committee for IIASA of the Czechoslovak Socialist Republic

Finland
The Finnish Committee for IIASA

France
The French Association for the Development of Systems Analysis

German Democratic Republic
The Academy of Sciences of the German Democratic Republic

Federal Republic of Germany
Association for the Advancement of IIASA

Hungary
The Hungarian Committee for Applied Systems Analysis

Italy
The National Research Council

Japan
The Japan Committee for IIASA

Netherlands
The Foundation IIASA–Netherlands

Poland
The Polish Academy of Sciences

Sweden
The Swedish Council for Planning and Coordination of Research

Union of Soviet Socialist Republics
The Academy of Sciences of the Union of Soviet Socialist Republics

United States of America
The American Academy of Arts and Sciences

Vol. 236: G. Gandolfo, P.C. Padoan, A Disequilibrium Model of Real and Financial Accumulation in an Open Economy. VI, 172 pages. 1984.

Vol. 237: Misspecification Analysis. Proceedings, 1983. Edited by T.K. Dijkstra. V, 129 pages. 1984.

Vol. 238: W. Domschke, A. Drexl, Location and Layout Planning. IV, 134 pages. 1985.

Vol. 239: Microeconomic Models of Housing Markets. Edited by K. Stahl. VII, 197 pages. 1985.

Vol. 240: Contributions to Operations Research. Proceedings, 1984. Edited by K. Neumann and D. Pallaschke. V, 190 pages. 1985.

Vol. 241: U. Wittmann, Das Konzept rationaler Preiserwartungen. XI, 310 Seiten. 1985.

Vol. 242: Decision Making with Multiple Objectives. Proceedings, 1984. Edited by Y.Y. Haimes and V. Chankong. XI, 571 pages. 1985.

Vol. 243: Integer Programming and Related Areas. A Classified Bibliography 1981–1984. Edited by R. von Randow. XX, 386 pages. 1985.

Vol. 244: Advances in Equilibrium Theory. Proceedings, 1984. Edited by C.D. Aliprantis, O. Burkinshaw and N.J. Rothman. II, 235 pages. 1985.

Vol. 245: J.E.M. Wilhelm, Arbitrage Theory. VII, 114 pages. 1985.

Vol. 246: P.W. Otter, Dynamic Feature Space Modelling, Filtering and Self-Tuning Control of Stochastic Systems. XIV, 177 pages. 1985.

Vol. 247: Optimization and Discrete Choice in Urban Systems. Proceedings, 1983. Edited by B.G. Hutchinson, P. Nijkamp and M. Batty. VI, 371 pages. 1985.

Vol. 248: Plural Rationality and Interactive Decision Processes. Proceedings, 1984. Edited by M. Grauer, M. Thompson and A.P. Wierzbicki. VI, 354 pages. 1985.

Vol. 249: Spatial Price Equilibrium: Advances in Theory, Computation and Application. Proceedings, 1984. Edited by P. T. Harker. VII, 277 pages. 1985.

Vol. 250: M. Roubens, Ph. Vincke, Preference Modelling. VIII, 94 pages. 1985.

Vol. 251: Input-Output Modeling. Proceedings, 1984. Edited by A. Smyshlyaev. VI, 261 pages. 1985.

Vol. 252: A. Birolini, On the Use of Stochastic Processes in Modeling Reliability Problems. VI, 105 pages. 1985.

Vol. 253: C. Withagen, Economic Theory and International Trade in Natural Exhaustible Resources. VI, 172 pages. 1985.

Vol. 254: S. Müller, Arbitrage Pricing of Contingent Claims. VIII, 151 pages. 1985.

Vol. 255: Nondifferentiable Optimization: Motivations and Applications. Proceedings, 1984. Edited by V.F. Demyanov and D. Pallaschke. VI, 350 pages. 1985.

Vol. 256: Convexity and Duality in Optimization. Proceedings, 1984. Edited by J. Ponstein. V, 142 pages. 1985.

Vol. 257: Dynamics of Macrosystems. Proceedings, 1984. Edited by J.-P. Aubin, D. Saari and K. Sigmund. VI, 280 pages. 1985.

Vol. 258: H. Funke, Eine allgemeine Theorie der Polypol- und Oligopolpreisbildung. III, 237 pages. 1985.

Vol. 259: Infinite Programming. Proceedings, 1984. Edited by E.J. Anderson and A.B. Philpott. XIV, 244 pages. 1985.

Vol. 260: H.-J. Kruse, Degeneracy Graphs and the Neighbourhood Problem. VIII, 128 pages. 1986.

Vol. 261: Th.R.Gulledge, Jr., N.K. Womer, The Economics of Made-to-Order Production. VI, 134 pages. 1986.

Vol. 262: H.U. Buhl, A Neo-Classical Theory of Distribution and Wealth. V, 146 pages. 1986.

Vol. 263: M. Schäfer, Resource Extraction and Market Structure. XI, 154 pages. 1986.

Vol. 264: Models of Economic Dynamics. Proceedings, 1983. Edited by H.F. Sonnenschein. VII, 212 pages. 1986.

Vol. 265: Dynamic Games and Applications in Economics. Edited by T. Başar. IX, 288 pages. 1986.

Vol. 266: Multi-Stage Production Planning and Inventory Control. Edited by S. Axsäter, Ch. Schneeweiss and E. Silver. V, 264 pages. 1986.

Vol. 267: R. Bemelmans, The Capacity Aspect of Inventories. IX, 165 pages. 1986.

Vol. 268: V. Firchau, Information Evaluation in Capital Markets. VII, 103 pages. 1986.

Vol. 269: A. Borglin, H. Keiding, Optimality in Infinite Horizon Economies. VI, 180 pages. 1986.

Vol. 270: Technological Change, Employment and Spatial Dynamics. Proceedings 1985. Edited by P. Nijkamp. VII, 466 pages. 1986.

Vol. 271: C. Hildreth, The Cowles Commission in Chicago, 1939–1955. V, 176 pages. 1986.

Vol. 272: G. Clemenz, Credit Markets with Asymmetric Information. VIII, 212 pages. 1986.

Vol. 273: Large-Scale Modelling and Interactive Decision Analysis. Proceedings, 1985. Edited by G. Fandel, M. Grauer, A. Kurzhanski and A.P. Wierzbicki. VII, 363 pages. 1986.

Vol. 274: W.K. Klein Haneveld, Duality in Stochastic Linear and Dynamic Programming. VII, 295 pages. 1986.

Vol. 275: Competition, Instability, and Nonlinear Cycles. Proceedings, 1985. Edited by W. Semmler. XII, 340 pages. 1986.

Vol. 276: M.R. Baye, D.A. Black, Consumer Behavior, Cost of Living Measures, and the Income Tax. VII, 119 pages. 1986.

Vol. 277: Studies in Austrian Capital Theory, Investment and Time. Edited by M. Faber. VI, 317 pages. 1986.

Vol. 278: W.E. Diewert, The Measurement of the Economic Benefits of Infrastructure Services. V, 202 pages. 1986.

Vol. 279: H.-J. Büttler, G. Frei and B. Schips, Estimation of Disequilibrium Models. VI, 114 pages. 1986.

Vol. 280: H.T. Lau, Combinatorial Heuristic Algorithms with FORTRAN. VII, 126 pages. 1986.

Vol. 281: Ch.-L. Hwang, M.-J. Lin, Group Decision Making under Multiple Criteria. XI, 400 pages. 1987.

Vol. 282: K. Schittkowski, More Test Examples for Nonlinear Programming Codes. V, 261 pages. 1987.

Vol. 283: G. Gabisch, H.-W. Lorenz, Business Cycle Theory. VII, 229 pages. 1987.

Vol. 284: H. Lütkepohl, Forecasting Aggregated Vector ARMA Processes. X, 323 pages. 1987.

Vol. 285: Toward Interactive and Intelligent Decision Support Systems. Volume 1. Proceedings, 1986. Edited by Y. Sawaragi, K. Inoue and H. Nakayama. XII, 445 pages. 1987.

Vol. 286: Toward Interactive and Intelligent Decision Support Systems. Volume 2. Proceedings, 1986. Edited by Y. Sawaragi, K. Inoue and H. Nakayama. XII, 450 pages. 1987.

Vol. 287: Dynamical Systems. Proceedings, 1985. Edited by A.B. Kurzhanski and K. Sigmund. VI, 215 pages. 1987.

Vol. 288: G.D. Rudebusch, The Estimation of Macroeconomic Disequilibrium Models with Regime Classification Information. VII, 128 pages. 1987.

Vol. 289: B.R. Meijboom, Planning in Decentralized Firms. X, 168 pages. 1987.

Vol. 290: D.A. Carlson, A. Haurie, Infinite Horizon Optimal Control. XI, 254 pages. 1987.

Vol. 291: N. Takahashi, Design of Adaptive Organizations. VI, 140 pages. 1987.

Vol. 292: I. Tchijov, L. Tomaszewicz (Eds.), Input-Output Modeling. Proceedings, 1985. VI, 195 pages. 1987.

Vol. 293: D. Batten, J. Casti, B. Johansson (Eds.), Economic Evolution and Structural Adjustment. Proceedings, 1985. VI, 382 pages. 1987.

Vol. 294: J. Jahn, W. Krabs (Eds.), Recent Advances and Historical Development of Vector Optimization. VII, 405 pages. 1987.

Vol. 295: H. Meister, The Purification Problem for Constrained Games with Incomplete Information. X, 127 pages. 1987.

Vol. 296: A. Börsch-Supan, Econometric Analysis of Discrete Choice. VIII, 211 pages. 1987.

Vol. 297: V. Fedorov, H. Läuter (Eds.), Model-Oriented Data Analysis. Proceedings, 1987. VI, 239 pages. 1988.

Vol. 298: S.H. Chew, Q. Zheng, Integral Global Optimization. VII, 179 pages. 1988.

Vol. 299: K. Marti, Descent Directions and Efficient Solutions in Discretely Distributed Stochastic Programs. XIV, 178 pages. 1988.

Vol. 300: U. Derigs, Programming in Networks and Graphs. XI, 315 pages. 1988.

Vol. 301: J. Kacprzyk, M. Roubens (Eds.), Non-Conventional Preference Relations in Decision Making. VII, 155 pages. 1988.

Vol. 302: H.A. Eiselt, G. Pederzoli (Eds.), Advances in Optimization and Control. Proceedings, 1986. VIII, 372 pages. 1988.

Vol. 303: F.X. Diebold, Empirical Modeling of Exchange Rate Dynamics. VII, 143 pages. 1988.

Vol. 304: A. Kurzhanski, K. Neumann, D. Pallaschke (Eds.), Optimization, Parallel Processing and Applications. Proceedings, 1987. VI, 292 pages. 1988.

Vol. 305: G.-J.C.Th. van Schijndel, Dynamic Firm and Investor Behaviour under Progressive Personal Taxation. X, 215 pages. 1988.

Vol. 306: Ch. Klein, A Static Microeconomic Model of Pure Competition. VIII, 139 pages. 1988.

Vol. 307: T.K. Dijkstra (Ed.), On Model Uncertainty and its Statistical Implications. VII, 138 pages. 1988.

Vol. 308: J.R. Daduna, A. Wren (Eds.), Computer-Aided Transit Scheduling. VIII, 339 pages. 1988.

Vol. 309: G. Ricci, K. Velupillai (Eds.), Growth Cycles and Multisectoral Economics: the Goodwin Tradition. III, 126 pages. 1988.

Vol. 310: J. Kacprzyk, M. Fedrizzi (Eds.), Combining Fuzzy Imprecision with Probabilistic Uncertainty in Decision Making. IX, 399 pages. 1988.

Vol. 311: R. Färe, Fundamentals of Production Theory. IX, 163 pages. 1988.

Vol. 312: J. Krishnakumar, Estimation of Simultaneous Equation Models with Error Components Structure. X, 357 pages. 1988.

Vol. 313: W. Jammernegg, Sequential Binary Investment Decisions. VI, 156 pages. 1988.

Vol. 314: R. Tietz, W. Albers, R. Selten (Eds.), Bounded Rational Behavior in Experimental Games and Markets. VI, 368 pages. 1988.

Vol. 315: I. Orishimo, G.J.D. Hewings, P. Nijkamp (Eds.), Information Technology: Social and Spatial Perspectives. Proceedings, 1986. VI, 268 pages. 1988.

Vol. 316: R.L. Basmann, D.J. Slottje, K. Hayes, J.D. Johnson, D.J. Molina, The Generalized Fechner-Thurstone Direct Utility Function and Some of its Uses. VIII, 159 pages. 1988.

Vol. 317: L. Bianco, A. La Bella (Eds.), Freight Transport Planning and Logistics. Proceedings, 1987. X, 568 pages. 1988.

Vol. 318: T. Doup, Simplicial Algorithms on the Simplotope. VIII, 262 pages. 1988.

Vol. 319: D.T. Luc, Theory of Vector Optimization. VIII, 173 pages. 1989.

Vol. 320: D. van der Wijst, Financial Structure in Small Business. VII, 181 pages. 1989.

Vol. 321: M. Di Matteo, R.M. Goodwin, A. Vercelli (Eds.), Technological and Social Factors in Long Term Fluctuations. Proceedings. IX, 442 pages. 1989.

Vol. 322: T. Kollintzas (Ed.), The Rational Expectations Equilibrium Inventory Model. XI, 269 pages. 1989.

Vol. 323: M.B.M. de Koster, Capacity Oriented Analysis and Design of Production Systems. XII, 245 pages. 1989.

Vol. 324: I.M. Bomze, B.M. Pötscher, Game Theoretical Foundations of Evolutionary Stability. VI, 145 pages. 1989.

Vol. 325: P. Ferri, E. Greenberg, The Labor Market and Business Cycle Theories. X, 183 pages. 1989.

Vol. 326: Ch. Sauer, Alternative Theories of Output, Unemployment, and Inflation in Germany: 1960–1985. XIII, 206 pages. 1989.

Vol. 327: M. Tawada, Production Structure and International Trade. V, 132 pages. 1989.

Vol. 328: W. Güth, B. Kalkofen, Unique Solutions for Strategic Games. VII, 200 pages. 1989.

Vol. 329: G. Tillmann, Equity, Incentives, and Taxation. VI, 132 pages. 1989.

Vol. 330: P.M. Kort, Optimal Dynamic Investment Policies of a Value Maximizing Firm. VII, 185 pages. 1989.

Vol. 331: A. Lewandowski, A.P. Wierzbicki (Eds.), Aspiration Based Decision Support Systems. X, 400 pages. 1989.

GPSR Compliance

The European Union's (EU) General Product Safety Regulation (GPSR) is a set of rules that requires consumer products to be safe and our obligations to ensure this.

If you have any concerns about our products, you can contact us on ProductSafety@springernature.com

In case Publisher is established outside the EU, the EU authorized representative is:

Springer Nature Customer Service Center GmbH
Europaplatz 3
69115 Heidelberg, Germany

Batch number: 10854269

Printed by Printforce, the Netherlands